For the benefit of non-American readers, we should like to point out that all dates have been written in the American style, i.e., month, day, year. Thus, January 12, 1949 appears 1/12/49.

Managing Editor: Amelia Thorpe
Executive Art Director: Leonard Wolfe
Art Director: Paul Hutt
Editorial Co-ordinator: Hilary Bunce
Caption Writer: Nancy VanArsdale
Picture Editor: Maggie Colbeck Rowe
Picture Researchers: Jackum Brown, Veneta Bullen, Diana Korchien, Laleli Lopez
Production Co-ordinator: Roger Daniels
Indexer: Chris Fayers

Special Photography by Laurie Lewis

First published in the United States by Salem House, 1985, a member of the Merrimack Publishers' Circle, 47 Pelham Road, Salem, NH 03079.

Originated by Lansdowne Press
A Division of RPLA Pty Limited
176 South Creek Road, Dee Why West, N.S.W., Australia 2099

© Copyright RPLA Pty Limited 1985

Typeset in Great Britain by Lineage Limited, Watford
Color separation by Rainbow Graphics, Hong Kong
Printed by New Interlitho s.P.a., Italy

Library of Congress Catalog Card Number: 85-50349

ISBN: 0-88162-104-8

Dear Editor:

LETTERS TO TIME MAGAZINE, 1923–1984

Dear Editor:

LETTERS TO TIME MAGAZINE, 1923–1984

Edited and Compiled by
Phil Pearman

Salem House

Salem, New Hampshire

A Letter from the Publisher

In 1923, the year TIME was born, America was still provincial. The atom was still unsplit. So were most marriages. Movies were silent, television existed only in the laboratory, and a "byte," however you spelled it, had to do with food, not information. Communication long distance was conducted via the mail. Letter writing was considered a pastime. Stamps cost 2¢, and there were no zip codes to remember. And from the beginning, TIME's editors got their share of letters. Charles Eliot, president of Harvard, wrote to say the idea of condensing news was "disgusting and disgraceful." But Franklin D. Roosevelt praised the new magazine, and so did Thomas Edison and Henry Ford.

A year after the first issue of TIME, the editors decided to publish the most interesting letters that were beginning to flood their offices. A new section called "Letters" spawned even more correspondence. Writing a letter to the editors of TIME took on all the aspects of a national fad.

In 1934, as an experiment, TIME began publication of a little magazine called LETTERS. At first it was an eight-page fortnightly supplement to TIME, accommodating the overflow of letters to the editors with, as they put it, "controversy, correction and information on TIME subjects ranging from Oklahoma's chief justice to prize lies, from Andrew Jackson's pipe-smoking wife to the Loch Ness monster." It was offered free to all who asked to be put on its mailing list. When circulation reached 25,000, readers were asked to pay a subscription price of 50¢ a year, later raised to $1. Expanded from eight to 20 pages, the magazine solicited advertising. LETTERS was always the neglected child of TIME's editorial department, "handed around," as one of its many editors observed, "from lap to lap like a baby with a wet bottom." Though at times expectations for LETTERS were inflated by the seeming ease with which it picked up subscribers, it was finally suspended in 1937.

But TIME and its readership have continued to maintain a lively dialogue within the pages of the magazine for the past six decades—what the editors have called the most amazing 60 years in history. And we thought the time had come to compile some of the best of the comment and controversy, the barbs and bouquets, many from the very newsmakers who helped to make that history. Thus this unique and, I think, fascinating volume. I hope you enjoy it.

John A. Meyers

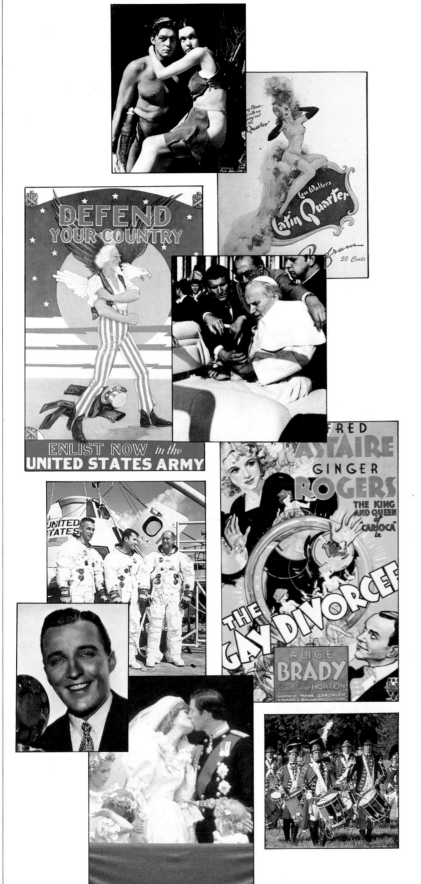

Contents

The Roaring Twenties

President Coolidge napped in the White House; Americans sported raccoon coats, danced the Charleston and tippled bathtub gin at speakeasies. Radios broadcasted the great sounds of the Jazz Age between *Amos 'n' Andy* episodes. Charles Lindbergh was everyone's hero—and TIME's first Man of the Year. In other parts of the world, Mussolini flexed Fascism's muscle, Mao Tse-tung led a peasants' revolt, Antarctic adventurers competed to discover the South Pole. Smearing her body with grease, Gertrude Ederle swam the English Channel. Bobby Jones showed everyone how to hit a golf ball. The state of Tennessee prosecuted John Scopes for teaching the theory of evolution in public schools. Black Friday brought the prosperous decade to a crashing finale.

From Pasadena

A few weeks ago you called me a Bolshevik, which I am not. Now I notice that you call the *Searchlight on Congress* a Ku Klux Klan organ, which it is not. The *Searchlight on Congress* has nothing to do with the Klan. You have, since it appears that you are supporting the Klan Kandidate Koolidge.

Upton Sinclair
11/10/24   *Pasadena, Calif.*
The charge that TIME supported Candidate Coolidge (or any other candidate) during the campaign seems to the editors to be baseless.—ED.

"Not Forgotten"

I have just read your little article, entitled *Flowerless*, in the Oct. 13 issue of TIME. I was Mr. Caruso's secretary for several years up until the time of his death, and I am in a position to give you some facts concerning the matter which this article treats rather fantastically.

Immediately upon the death of Mr. Caruso, it was the intention of his widow to build a chapel worthy of this great artist and man in which his body might rest for all time. All arrangements were made, and it was calculated that three months would elapse before the structure would finally be completed. Meantime, Mrs. Caruso preferred that her late husband's body rest somewhere else than in an exposed grave, and she made arrangements with friends of the family to keep it in a private chapel until the new one should be finished.

Labor conditions in Italy were such that great delay in the building was unavoidable; and eventually it took three years and thrice the original expense to put up the chapel. The work was carried on, nevertheless, as fast as possible, and no detail has been neglected.

The chapel is now complete except for interior decorations which are being worked on at present. I am enclosing the two pictures of the structure which were published last week in the *Musical Digest.*

I am convinced that the persons who originated this story are of that group of publicity seekers who, by associating themselves with an illustrious name, hope to attract attention to their little selves. It is a mistake to give credence to such reports. Enrico Caruso is not forgotten.

Bruno Zirato
11/17/24   *New York, N.Y.*

Insulted

Deliberately, with exactness, the editors of TIME make choice of their words, their phrases. Startled, therefore, was I to find in one and the same category these: "Trash readers, comic-strip fanatics, crossword puzzlers, gum-chewers. . . ." ["The Press," Dec. 29]. I do not read trash. Comic-strips to me are senseless. I do not chew gum. But of crosswords—I do spend considerable time fitting in the interlocking words on occasion. Others, I think, may feel as I do about your classification. Crossword puzzles and indulgence therein have met no end of favor in a variety of circles. They are worthy of better bed-fellows than literary trash, comic-strips, chewing gum.

John E. Mazuzan
1/12/25   *Northfield, Vt.*

Misled

On page 5 of the Dec. 29 issue of TIME, under the head of Prohibition, you tell how much the enforcement of prohibition costs the Government annually. You say nothing, however, about the moneys received as fines and from sale of seized cars which, I believe, are more than the amount expended.

I feel, that in fairness to the friends of prohibition, you should publish also the amount received in fines and from sale of seized cars as the mere statement as to expenditure without anything being said about returns is misleading to say the least.

Carlton J. Frazier
1/12/25   *Gouverneur, N.Y.*

TIME in its issue of Nov. 3 pointed out that the moneys received in fines totaled $12,800,000 in four years. The amount expended in this period was $50,130,000.—ED.

Drummers' Slang

As an Original Subscriber I feel privileged to call your attention to a criticism of the play *They Knew What They Wanted* [Jan. 12], in which your critic refers to San Francisco as "Frisco." Should this be quoted from the play's program, all is forgiven (as far as TIME is concerned); but should it not be, please do not allow TIME to stoop to its use!

San Franciscans have always considered it drummers' slang of the commonest familiarity.

With deepest appreciation of your high standards.

> *Mrs. C. Parker Holt*
> 1/26/25 *Stockton, Calif.*

The program contains neither "Frisco" nor San Francisco. TIME agrees that "Frisco" is a very low grade of drummers' slang.—ED.

"Fathed"

On page 16 of the Jan. 5 issue of TIME you speak of the Pope as the "Fathed". May I ask if this is a typographical error, an error in spelling or an ecclesiatical term?

> *L. N. Foy*
> 1/26/25 *Liberty, S.C.*

P.S. In spite of occasional "busts" in proofreading, TIME delivers the facts in such a way that they stick.

Typographical error. "Father" was the intended spelling.—ED.

They Pass It Around

I guess you don't know what it means to wander in a foreign land without TIME. I'd just as soon be in jail. We Americans over here pass it around until it looks like something that has been under the carpet since the Spanish-American War. It brings Home to us and drops it in our laps.

> *Homer Croy*
> 3/2/25 *Cannes, France*

The U.S.

Why use "U.S." instead of United States? Is the time of the reader and editor too short to pronounce and write the proper name of his country? Why not Gt. B. and Fr. and It. and Ger.? Surely it is not impossible to call your country by its correct name. Does it not merit as much respect as is given to foreign nations?

> *A Citizen*
> 7/13/25 *Madison, Conn.*

No disrespect is intended. For brevity's sake, TIME will continue to refer to "the U.S."—unless, of course, the majority of subscribers say No.—ED.

"Bad Taste"

Referring to your issue of July 20, containing the article on Page 14, column 1, on the subject of "Gershwin

Bros.," the writer takes exception to the nonchalance with which they have discriminated in the status of the subject of the article.

I doubt very much whether you would speak of other persons in your columns as "Young Catholics," "Young Methodists," "Young Presbyterians" or "Young Holy Rollers."

It strikes me that this continual discrimination against the Jew can do nothing but foment antagonism and aid ill-breeding, and hatred; it astonishes me greatly that a progressive sheet such as yours should have stooped to such stupid practices. Such editorial implications in your news columns is amateurish and unprofessional bad taste.

Mrs. A. M. Rheinstrom
8/3/25   New York, N.Y.
TIME *spoke of George Gershwin as a "young Jew." No offense was intended.* —ED.

"No Sportsman"

Why do you call my great countryman, the ace of all aces, Baron Manfred von Richthofen, a "sportsman"? [Nov. 30, p. 14]. That English term of praise befits him ill. He was a true German. In his person he epitomized unflinching *might*. He was no weak "sportsman." You English and American only call him one in order that as the "nations of sportsmen" you may seem to imply that he was one of you and share his glory.

Karl Busch
12/14/25   Madison, Wis.

100,000

Your publicity men have spread abroad the knowledge that TIME is "the fastest growing non-fiction magazine in the U.S." What is the present circulation of TIME? In a friendly argument I waggered $10 that it was over 100,000. Kindly advise me whether I win or lose.

George Gould
12/21/25   Pittsburgh, Pa.
Original Subscriber Gould wins $10. The circulation of TIME *crossed the 100,000 mark three weeks ago. The Circulation Manager states that the circulation of* TIME *has increased nearly 50% during 1925, thus retaining the titles of "fastest growing non-fiction magazine" and "the fastest growing $5 magazine of any sort in the U.S."*—ED.

Substantiated

In the Dec. 14 issue of TIME you have an article entitled "Friendly Enemies" in which Captain T. J. C. Martyn denies the recent report that Baron Manfred von Richthofen, celebrated German aviator, was killed by infantry after landing his machine safely in our lines.

I wish to substantiate Captain Martyn's denial of this rumor and to say he is quite right.

Von Richthofen was shot down by Captain A. Ray Browne, a Canadian attached to No. 209 Squadron, Royal Air Force, on April 21, 1918. Captain Browne was awarded the D.S.O. by the King for his gallantry.

After the fight the Baron's body and his machine were brought into the aerodrome. The machine was smashed to pieces by the fall, which disproves the report that he had made a safe landing, and the Baron had been hit in the back of the neck by a bullet which came out through his heart— it would have been almost impossible to inflict a wound like this if he had been on the ground.

I saw both the body and the machine, and I cut a small bit off one of the wings which I keep as a souvenir of a very gallant man.

I would also like to add that German aviators *were not shot* after they had effected a safe landing in our lines; they were well treated and I have never heard of a case in which a captured German airman was treated other than as a gentleman.

Von Richthofen was killed in fair fight in the air and was given a funeral with full military honors, and I can well remember seeing his grave piled high with flowers which were sent by Royal Air Force units from all over France. . . .

Carl F. Falkenberg
Ex-Flt. Cmdr. 84 Squadron, R.A.F.
1/4/26   Quebec, Canada
P.S. As a subscriber allow me to

congratulate you on your excellent paper.

"Chuff"

My commendation on your use of the word "chuff" [April 5, "In Little Rock," p. 18].

As a noun descriptive of the sound of a milk-train engine, it fits and therefore is good. Is this a new word?
John Thurston
4/26/26 *Rochester, N.Y.*
*Such onomatopoetic creations should be judged by their success rather than by the dictionaries. In this particular case credit is due to a typesetter who set "chuff" for "chug." An able proofreader, quick to sense the merit of the "new word," let it stand.—*ED.

"Dead Like Caesar"

Your publication has the unmitigated effrontery to insinuate that liberty of the press does not exist in Italy, that the people are not freely represented in parliament (witness your sneering reference to the "docile senators"), and that the Fascist government is not representative and interferes with personal freedom. All this in face of the perfectly rotten political, social and racial situation prevailing in the U.S. where an arbitrary sumptuary law has been foisted upon the nation, with which it is not in sympathy; where a single race, the Jews, has attained a degree of political control making possible a practically complete domination of the press, so that the situation cannot even be publicly exposed; where labor shares in this exploitation of the masses through the most vicious kind of class legislation; and where personal liberty is as dead as Julius Caesar.

Whatever you may have against the Fascist regime and the Mussolini dictatorship (if you like) at its very worst, it has never interfered with the personal habits of anyone, and in Italy we don't have to pay for the support of a lot of Izzy Einsteins, nor are we tied to a paternal government's apronstrings in respect of the beverages we want to drink. That may not be much, but it is something.
Edgar C. Riebe
5/17/26 *Florence, Italy*
In recent weeks, Signor Mussolini has appeared in TIME *chiefly as an orator —in his own words.—*ED.

Worth $5

I want to thank you for the excellent account of the British strike in TIME for May 17, p. 11. Being a very busy man and having only a few minutes a day to devote to trying to keep up with the world's news, I have felt myself almost wholly ignorant of the main facts in this recent strike. This evening, in a few minutes of interesting reading of TIME, I have been able to learn the essential facts in the situation. These are stated clearly, simply and effectively. I feel such a summary

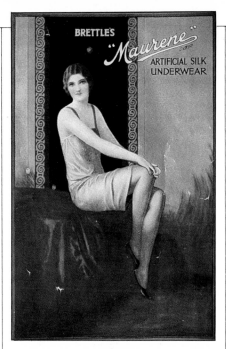

as this is worth a full year's subscription to TIME.
Robert DeC. Ward
Harvard University
5/31/26 *Cambridge, Mass.*

"Wonderful Thing"

Permit me to thank you for the very decent and extraordinarily honest treatment thus far of my newspapers and myself by your magazine. It is indeed a wonderful thing to see a magazine take such an impartial and straight viewpoint, allowing freedom and fairness to both sides of the question.
Cornelius Vanderbilt Jr.
6/7/26 *New York, N.Y.*

Heroes

A misinterpretation of the subject of dueling in Germany has crept into your extract in TIME of May 10 ["Heroes Vexed," p. 13]. The scar-bedecked men travelers see in Germany are not of the army, but university students and graduates. These, as members of rival fraternities, challenge each other to duels just as here a football team of one university plays against another. It is a test of nerve. Skill is of course also essential; the unskillful carries his mark for life. But he is proud of having gone through the ordeal, and ordeal it is.

Bismarck, on being entertained by a reception committee of students, turned to one particularly badly scarred representative and asked whether he used his face for a guard instead of a sword.

Dueling in military circles, on the other hand, is a genuine duel, fought to redress an insult, with either sword, rapier or pistol. These naturally often end fatally. Times change and therefore such duels have been relegated to the past as mentioned in your article.
Charles F. Bodecker,
D.D.S., F.A.C.D.
Columbia University
6/14/26 *New York, N.Y.*
*The new restrictions apply particularly to military men.—*ED.

Lloyd George

For some time I have been troubled by repeated occurrences in your incomparable publication. To wit: is it Mr. Lloyd George, or simply Mr. George, who has achieved fame in Britain? By those from the Island I am informed that I am correct: that it should be Lloyd George and not simply George. Kindly enlighten me. (I never had these doubts till TIME repeatedly referred to the man as Mr. George.)

TIME is excellent; may it continue its high standards. My praise is, that I have read it consistently almost, I believe, from its inception.
Wm. McK. Rutter
7/19/26 *Philadelphia, Pa.*
Mr. George's father was the late

William George, one time Master of the Hope Street Unitarian School of Liverpool. His mother, née Lloyd, a resolute Baptist, influenced him after his father's death to accept her faith and habitually to link her name (his second given name) with his surname.

Dragon's Praise

As long as TIME plays fair, it will remain a pleasure for me to receive my weekly copy. I note that some subscribers take exception to things you say about their "pet" ideas. You have rapped my Organization several times but this has not changed my opinion of TIME. In such cases I smile at your mistakes and misunderstanding and wait for the time to arrive when you will know facts. You can rest assured that TIME has a great future before it and will continue to build up a first class list of subscribers.

Arthur H. Bell
Grand Dragon, K.K.K.
Realm of New Jersey
1/3/27   *Lake Como, N.J.*

Cookie-Pusher

I read with a great deal of interest the article under LYNCHING—"In Toombs" on p. 11 of TIME, Jan. 10.

I have no doubt but that items of news in the article are substantially correct, but your reference to "*Jellybeans*" is all wrong, and especially your explanation in the note. You define a jellybean as a "Southern small town loafer." Why heap this opprobrium upon the South? We are as loyal to your publication as any portion of the country. Then again, why refer to a jellybean as a loafer? A jellybean is not necessarily a loafer, although he

may be one. A jellybean is just another name for a cookie-pusher. Members of this species may and very often do work, and could not be classed as loafers by any means. They have very exalted opinions of their ability to charm the female sex, and if you crowd them right close, they might reluctantly admit that they belong to the sheik class. As a rule they have more activity in their feet than in their heads. In fact, they are entirely too light at both ends. They exist in the South, North, East and West, and not in the South alone. . . .

Erle B. Askew
2/7/27   *St. Petersburg, Fla.*

A Roman

I collect and study everything on the subject of modern Italy, Fascism, Mussolini. Of all the long-winded articles, political, philosophical or descriptive, that exist about *Il Duce*, none present so vivid a picture of him as I find in the short, anecdotal items that you print weekly. Your system is fundamentally sound—the facts, and nothing but facts.

I think I am unprejudiced. Mussolini has achieved more power than I should like to see even in the hands of the Angel Gabriel; he has effected enough reforms to be able now to say, "*L'Etat, c'est moi.*" But it is not enough. He means to make Italy count in the world, he means to make her very great. He does not intend to keep her spiritually and intellectually enslaved as she is today. He has saved her from Communism, he must yet save her from Fascism. That is why I hope he will not die a failure.

The day will come when TIME will be

printed in Italy as well as in the U.S. *Per bacco!*

Gaitano Ricchi
4/4/27   *Pinehurst, N.C.*

Yammerings

Just to tell you that the portrait of Sinclair Lewis on the cover of TIME, March 14 gives one the best possible insight into *Elmer Gantry* and the rest of Lewis' yammerings.

But why waste printer's ink on such a shoveler of slops?

James Allen Geissinger, D.D.
Holliston Ave., M.E. Church
4/11/27   *Pasadena, Calif.*

Colossal Ignorance

I quote from TIME, May 2: " 'The Star Spangled Banner' . . . is, according to many an American, of too elaborate composition, too great a range, *to be* suitable for the national hymn."

Is it possible that in your colossal ignorance you do not know that the "Star Spangled Banner" *is* our official national anthem? You *must* know this, and therefore your expression "to be" is sneeringly malicious and *most offensive* to me, for one.

Sarah Linton Wells
5/16/27   *Springfield, Mass.*
Since the U.S. is without an official national anthem, the National Society of United States Daughters of 1812 is now disseminating propaganda with the object of persuading Congress to authorize a national anthem at its next session.—ED.

Skin Deep

. . . May I accordingly tell you something of the woman whose picture you

American Golf Champion Bobby Jones

Baseball greats Babe Ruth and Lou Gehrig

Boxer Jack Dempsey

published on p. 17 of TIME, May 2, under the caption of "Uglies"?

This unfortunate woman who sits in the sideshow of Ringling Brothers "Between Fat Lady and Armless Wonder" and "affects white lace hats, woolen mittens and high laced shoes" has a story which is far from mirth-provoking. Could it have been written up for you by O. Henry, it would have provoked tears rather than laughter. The facts are as follows:

She is, as you say, a peasant of Kent and four times a mother. The father of these four children, a truck gardener, died some years ago and left her their sole support. She, previously a vigorous and goodlooking young woman, has become the victim of a disease known as *acromegaly*. This cruel and deforming malady not only completely transforms the outward appearance of those whom it afflicts but is attended with great suffering and often with loss of vision.

One of Mr. Ringling's agents prevailed upon her to travel with the circus and to pose as "the ugliest woman in the world" as a means of livelihood. Mr. Ringling is kind to his people and she is well cared for. But she suffers from intolerable headaches, has become nearly blind, and permits herself to be laughed at and heckled by an unfeeling people in order to provide the wherewithal to educate her four children. Beauty is but skin deep. Being a physician, I do not like to feel that TIME can be frivolous over the tragedies of disease.

Harvey Cushing
Peter Bent Brighton Hospital
5/23/27 *Boston, Mass.*

Salutes

I salute you for devoting to C. A. Lindbergh a rational and fitting amount of space proper to his great but not overwhelming accomplishment, I salute you for not placing Lindbergh on your cover, and for understanding that his was a triumph of wood, aluminium, steel, oil and gasoline—whereas Gertrude Ederle, for example, swam the Channel aided by nothing but her own arms and legs.*

Who doubts that the ordinary German commercial air craft companies could not better Lindbergh's feat with a stock plane? They don't for two reasons: 1) They are too busy with profitable day-by-day passenger carrying to be interested in stunts. 2) They dare not reveal the full air power of Germany while she is still a conquered nation.

Once more, TIME, I salute you! The three columns out of a TIME issue of 40 pages [May 30] were quite adequate to "Herr Kapten Lindbergh" as his Swedish kinsmen call him. The mobpride of Americans in this blond youth is fatuous and absurd.

John Muller
6/20/27 *Milwaukee, Wis.*
TIME *readers will find a picture of*

Colonel Lindbergh not transiently printed on TIME's cover but imperishably enshrined in their own hearts.

A comparison of the issue of TIME and the New York Times in which the arrival of Colonel Lindbergh at Paris was described, reveals that, proportionately, 0.2% more space was devoted by TIME to this exploit.—ED.

**An error. Miss Ederle was materially aided by a thick coat of grease.—ED.*

Sordid, Sad

. . . But you did put my hair on end with your article about the young Prince of Wales frequenting a night club managed by a Negress and her Negro husband [June 20]. Have we sunk quite so low or was that a slumming expedition? Ah, TIME, how sordid, how dreadfully sad! In this day of fine endeavour how can such flagrantly stupid and evil things be doing? What a device of the devil is the night club! What sheer waste of human energy, moral and spiritual power and squandering of money enough to build and maintain a model city. I am sorry you printed that article. Only the lovely face, careworn but spiritually free, of dear Mrs. Pankhurst, on the opposite page helped me over the nausea of the other. I say, TIME, I am sorry *you* had to print that. . . .

(Miss) Elizabeth Fisher
7/18/27 *Cincinnati, Ohio*

Not Hysterical

You have been justly criticized [June 27] by many of your subscribers for not honoring Col. Charles A. Lindbergh, our courageous young air hero, by placing his pleasing countenance on the cover of your weekly newsmagazine, TIME (the best magazine of its kind published). Who has been more in the public mind of late years, or what picture on your cover could meet with more popular approval, not for what

he has accomplished, so much, as for what he is, and for what he stands? Your articles about him have been excellent, not hysterical, and it is a treat to read such interpretations of a character, so fine and noble, as this young American, who has forever endeared himself to the youth of our land, and to the mothers, who hail him as a perfect symbol of all that is wholesome and true. Square yourselves with the countless readers of TIME, and give us a picture of this world famous youth.

(Mrs.) Ruth Brown
7/18/27 *San Diego, Calif.*

Not Hopkins

I notice that on p. 31 of TIME, Oct. 10, you state that Babe Ruth gained his record-breaking 60th home-run of the 1927 season when he hit a ball pitched by left-handed Thomas Zachary. Press reports indicate that the Washington pitcher was Paul H. Hopkins, a young twirler who graduated from Colgate last spring. He pitched for Colgate for four years and served as captain during his senior year. Was this youngster in big league baseball the player who had the honor and misfortune to be facing Ruth when he scored his 60th homer or was it Zachary? The New York *Times* reports that it was Hopkins.

Holland L. Smith
The Colgate Maroon
10/24/27 *Hamilton, N.Y.*
Press reports naming Hopkins, were inaccurate. The unfortunate pitcher was Thomas Zachary.—ED.

Uplifting

I like TIME because in nearly every issue there is some statement, backed by irrefutable authority, which jolts me from an outworn rut of thought.

An example of what I mean is the printing in your last issue of a statement about birth control by the doctor

BRICKBATS

TIME has so much good in it, so much to recommend it that if a little better judgment were exercised, less criticism would be in order.

For instance, in your May 14 issue, 3rd column, page 18, what possible excuse have you for referring to the late Queen Victoria of England as "dumpy"; the word lacks respect when it refers to that beloved ruler of a Great Nation who during her life was described as "the most Queenly woman and the most womanly Queen of her time."

6/4/28
Charles R. Storey
Brockton, Mass.

"Dumpy" is an exact, descriptive adjective, meaning, according to Webster's New International, "short and thick, of proportionately low stature." TIME is exact.—ED.

who attends the British Royal Family. If he "can find no evidence of physical or moral harm from the practice of birth control," then I have indeed been misinformed, and I intend to seek out the facts.

I had thought that even a knowledge of this subject was in the nature of a "taint," but as a loyal citizen of the British Empire I have confidence that the example of the Royal Family is

ever uplifting, never the reverse.
Henly W. Fellows
12/12/27 *Toronto, Canada*

Seer

The cockles of my ole heart surged with joy, and I hurrahed and voiced my feelings at the top of my voice when I saw the picture of "Lindy" at last adorning TIME. . . . It must be that the Editor of TIME is a seer who looks into the future, and who believes in keeping the best to the last and making the most appropriate statements in the most logical TIME.
J. Montrose Edreht
1/16/28 *Pensacola, Fla.*

Altitude

Kindly inform me as to the maximum altitude obtained by any aviator whether in airplane or free balloon.
Dana Latham
2/20/28 *Los Angeles, Calif.*
The maximum altitude was 38,559 ft. reached by Lieut. C. C. Champion in 1927. Capt. H. C. Gray of the U.S. Air Service was credited with a balloon altitude of 44,000 in 1927, but this figure cannot be verified as Capt. Gray was killed during the flight.—ED.

Suggestion

To add to the tang and news value of your inimitable periodical, why don't you consider running a weekly best seller list? We make this suggestion, strangely enough, not as publishers but as devoted readers.
M. Lincoln Schuster
Simon and Schuster, Inc.
2/20/28 *New York City*
Simon & Schuster ideas are almost invariably happy: this one will be pondered.—ED.

Cheers Sir Robert

I have never had a journal or a magazine interest and delight me more than TIME. . . .

Under the heading Foreign News, in TIME, March 5, [appeared] " 'Lindy' v. 'Bert' " which reads in part as follows: "Last week at Canberra, the new Capital of Australia, a renowned British financier compared the feats of 'Lindy' with those of 'Bert.' The financier is Rt. Hon. Sir Robert Stevenson Horne, a director of the Suez Canal Co., of Lloyd's Bank. . . . Last week he boldly said that Airman Hinkler's flight constitutes 'the greatest single achievement in the history of aviation.' He added that Airman Hinkler has 'outclassed' Airman Lindbergh."

I admire Mr. Lindbergh but I also wish to shout "three cheers" for Sir Robert. He (Sir Robert) also completed a single-handed achievement when he openly expressed his view.

Let us have more of Airman Hinkler!
E. Keating Latta
4/16/28 *Hollywood, Calif.*

Landmark movies of the decade

What She Wanted

When I turned page 14 of TIME, April 16, and saw the smiling face of Miss Sylvia Pankhurst with her first-born in her arms, it recalled the days when this lady led the mob of wild, dissatisfied, would-be unsexed women who thought they wanted the franchise. What a different facial expression then and now, it is evident that she has got what she really desired: Motherhood; *Finis* can now be written to her political activities.

J. R. Smith
4/30/28   *Philadelphia, Pa.*

Satin Dress, Ermine Coat

TIME in its issue of April 23, printed a letter from J. F. Bassett of Boston in which he writes it would not be fitting for President Coolidge to humiliate himself by flying with Lindbergh in "those brown overalls that aviators wear."

May I inform Mr. Bassett that I have just completed a 2,285 mile hop from San Diego to Minneapolis clad in my seal and ermine coat, satin dress, white hat and corsage of roses, for I made the trip in a Ryan monoplane—brougham type, sister-ship to the one Lindbergh now owns.

Let President Coolidge don his frock coat, silk hat and cane and fly with Lindbergh.

Suggest that Correspondent Bassett obtain some back copies of *Aviation* and learn what is going on in the world outside of Boston.

Margaret Davies Yarnell
(Mrs. C. S. Yarnell)
5/7/28   *Minneapolis, Minn.*

Mercury First

In your issue of May 14 under Aeronautics we note comment regarding the North German Lloyd Air Cruise characterizing it as the first Air Cruise in history.

This is incorrect. So far as we have been able to learn,—and we have gone into it quite thoroughly—the first Air Cruise is the one scheduled by this organization, press announcements of which were made some three weeks prior to those concerning the Lloyd tour. Our Air Tour operates some two months in advance of the Lloyd trip and I cannot see how the North German Lloyd can conscientiously advertise their tour as being the first. . . .

Mercury Tours
5/28/28   *New York City*
TIME stands corrected. The Mercury Air Tour begins on July 14 when passengers sail from Manhattan on the S.S. Tuscania. At London they will take plane for Amsterdam, Brussels, Cologne, Frankfurt, Nuremberg, Munich, Zurich, Lucerne, Geneva, Paris—finally sailing for the U.S. on Aug. 25. Total cost of the tour will be $985.—ED.

Rolls-Royce

As a regular subscriber, may I get

Charles Lindbergh made the first solo nonstop flight across the Atlantic in 1927

you to settle a disputed question for me? Just write on this sheet below the name of the most expensive automobile of American make and perhaps the two leading European cars. . . .

B. E. Thom
6/4/28   *Port Arthur, Tex.*
The most expensive U.S.-made automobile is the Rolls-Royce (Lonsdale Model) $19,885. Other expensive cars are the Isotta-Fraschini (Italy) $17,800; the Hispano-Suiza (France) $20,000.—ED.

Rockefeller Caption

I very much regret the incomplete caption which you have placed under the cover-page picture of Mr. Rockefeller in TIME of May 21. This read alone gives a most unfavorable and unjust impression of what Mr. Rockefeller is alleged to have stated on the subject of money. . . . On the cover you have "I believe it is a religious duty to get all the money you can. . . ." while on page 34 Mr. Rockefeller's remark is stated:

"I believe it is a religious duty to get all the money you can, fairly and honestly; to keep all you can, and to give away all you can."

You should, I think, have made your quotation carry the words "fairly and honestly."

I have no special brief for Mr.

Rockefeller Sr., whom I have had the pleasure of meeting but once, but for whose constructive contribution to American life both through industry and philanthropy, in spite of some mistakes from a public point of view, which he may have made in the early conduct of his business, I have a great respect. Far more important is the general principle involved, namely, that of seeing that a right impression is given by every newspaper and magazine of the real purport of a public man's remarks.

Anson Phelps Stokes
6/4/28   *Washington, D.C.*
TIME's captions are often elliptical.—ED.

Hoover Drinks?

Now that you have told us just how wet Al Smith is, let us hear just how dry Herbert Hoover is. In Hoover's answer to Borah's questionnaire there seems to be a groping for vagueness. I wonder if Hoover has always held to the teachings of his Quaker fathers during all these years with the British.

J. M. Benson
7/16/28   *Jefferson, Ohio*
Following Secretary Hoover's answer to the Borah questionnaire, Lawyer Clarence Darrow said: "I don't think Hoover is any drier than I am. I ought to know. I have had a drink with him" [March 5]. Last week, questions were submitted asking Nominee Hoover to confirm or deny the Darrow statement and also to record: 1) whether Mr. Hoover has taken a drink since Prohibition; 2) whether Mr. Hoover would take a drink now if assured the liquor was legally possessed. Nominee Hoover's secretary, chubby George Akerson, refused to transmit the questions to his chief. Vexed, he cried: "A lot of foolish nonsense! Mr. Hoover is a Constitutional executive officer and as such he hasn't taken anything to drink since he's been in office. . . . I don't think Mr. Hoover ever was with Clarence Darrow."—ED.

Record by Franklin

In your Nov. 5 issue—under "Aeronautics"—in speaking of the new trans-continental flight of the "Yankee Doodle" you say, "By automobile it recently took 4 days, 8 hours, and 47 minutes."

On June 16, a stock Franklin Sedan driven by Cannon Ball Baker, completed the fastest round-trip ever made by automobile or train between Los Angeles and New York, covering 6,692 miles in 657 days. . . . On the trip east the time was 74 hours flat. . . . On the return trip, the total time was 83 hours and 23 minutes. . . .

Each was a new record. And the one-way record for automobile or train thus stands at 3 days and 2 hours. . . .

George L. Miller
United States Advertising Corp.
11/19/28   *Toledo, Ohio*

Al Jolson in *The Jazz Singer*

Enrico Caruso in *My Cousin*

Rudolph Valentino in *The Son of the Sheik*

Might, Right

The voters of this Nation
Have rizen to their might.
And dealt a blow to liquor
That cheers the friends of right.
The aim of whiskey lovers
To give us Booze again,
Has failed to meet approval
In minds of righteous men.

A. D. Hard, M.D.
12/10/28   *Long Beach, Calif.*

Not Sad

I take exception to a few words in your notice of Ethel Barrymore and her *Kingdom of God:* "the hushed, *sad* peacefulness of cloistered life." I don't know whether your writer or Miss B. is responsible for that sadness, but there isn't any such atmosphere in convents or monasteries. I ought to know, for I've been in and out of both for a good many years. Life in a convent isn't so wild and hilarious, of course, as in a night club, which must be about the saddest spot on earth. But I never yet saw a nun who wore a long face except one, and she had the cramps. Too much Christmas candy, and the dear old lady dissipated. I visited a convent recently, and I came away with a bright memory of a "lot of girls." But they are mighty aged girls for a' that. The Sister who cooks is around 80, and she told me gleefully of the monster turkey somebody had sent for Thanksgiving. How she kept dishing it up in various guises for a week. She laughed till her false teeth—if you ever beheld 'em!—fell down. Every time I think of convents, it renews my faith in human laughter.

Father Will Whalen
Old Jesuit Mission,
1/14/29   *Orrtanna, Pa.*

Father Whalen recently wrote a short story about a mediocre actress, popular in small towns. It was labeled "Twinkle", Little Star" and appeared in the New York Daily News (tabloid).—ED.

Sips

In the Jan. 14 issue of TIME, there is an article on Secretary of State Kellogg, in which the statement is made that "he sips sparingly."

Is this not an ironic comment on Prohibition? If the Secretary of State is allowed to sip, however sparingly, may we not expect a reasonable immunity from the law if we also sip? Should not Congress issue a list of those who may sip and those who will be arrested if they are caught sipping? Then you would not be troubled with letters from curious people like myself.

I enjoy TIME very much.

James Ramp
Y.M.C.A.
2/4/29   *San Francisco, Calif.*
Among the places in the U.S. where one can sip sparingly and legally are the various embassies in Washington D.C. Also, possessors of sips bought before Prohibition, or prescribed by a doctor since, may sip legally.—ED.

Flowers for Men

In your issue of Feb. 11, I noticed you referring to the Prince of Wales wearing a "red" carnation when in evening dress. You called it a "joke" but it merely showed that the Prince "knows his flowers" and you don't. A red carnation is the proper flower for evening wear.

Do you ever wear a flower in your buttonhole? Or do you think a fellow who wears one a sissy? If you do, you are wrong. The man who wants to wear one and does is more of a man than the man who wants to wear one but doesn't.

I can't see why any man wouldn't want to wear a flower!—and any man can who wishes to; that is, any man who is sure of himself. . . .

Paul T. Osterby II
("Osterby the Florist")
3/4/29   *Stamford, Conn.*

Papist

May I call your attention to an epithet "papists" that one finds only on the lips and in the writings of bigots. We Catholics resent the characterization. I am sure you do not mean to be offensive but you will submit a little more care should be exercised.

John J. Dunn, V.G.
Bishop of New York
Vicar General's Office
3/4/29   *New York City*
Webster's New International permits "papist" as the shortest synonym for Roman Catholic. Nevertheless, the word has so often been used in bitterness that TIME will no longer use it, except when quoting persons who say "papist."—ED.

Lindbergh on Banking

Thanks for recalling to the public the attitude of Charles A. Lindbergh Sr. (my father) upon banking law. He was opposed to the system which has fostered the present great concentration of wealth in the hands of a small per cent of the population. According to the figures of the Federal Trade Commission, 1% of the people own 59% of the wealth, 13% own 90% and 87% own 10%. Half the national income returns to capital.

During the last few years bank failures have become common, the number mounting into the hundreds in Minnesota alone. I am familiar with homes where after a lifetime of hard work, people are forced to live on the small allowance available from the poor fund. I know mothers who are supporting several children on a sum of $15 or $20 a month from the same fund. I know how they are housed and clothed and what rents they pay, but imagination balks when confronted with how they keep warm and what they eat.

We do need a revision of the banking laws and we also need a revision of what constitutes general prosperity.

Eva A. Lindbergh Christie
3/18/29 *Red Lake Falls, Minn.*

Dashes

I wish to enter a protest against your use of dashes in your Letters columns when you delete profanity. I approve the deletions, but I see no good reason why you should pique the curiosity of your occasionally profane readers by having all dashes of equal length.

I suggest that in future you use single, double, triple and so on dashes according to the number of letters in the words deleted. Thus if one of your correspondents referred to some person as a --- ---- --- -- - ----- it would offend no one, and at the same time members of the Ancient & Honorable Order of Occasional Swearers could figure it out and rest assured that the writer is a brother and not some rank outsider in Russian, Chinese or Sanskrit.

W. B. France
The San Diego Sun
4/8/29 *San Diego, Calif.*
Swearer France's suggestion, perhaps a ----- good one, will be taken under advisement.—ED.

Put England Right

I am an admirer and a loyal reader of TIME. It occurs to me to make a suggestion that a questionnaire having as its theme "Why Don't You Visit England?" would bring out all manner of interesting comments and criticisms which would reveal to us on this side things we ought to put right if more and more American visitors, who would greatly be welcomed, are to come to us.

I pass the suggestion on to you in this rough way. It would, I think, produce most interesting material.

*Sydney Walton**
4/22/29 *London, England*
Let readers say why they do not visit England, why they do, what they would like "put right."—ED.

*Publicity man for England's Wembley exposition of 1924.

"Putting England Right"

Re: "Putting England Right."
Tell Mr. Sydney Walton to improve the English weather, thin out London traffic, make it easier to get on a good golf course, turn out some good-looking women in the shops, streets and society, install decimal currency, teach taxi-drivers to talk so I can understand them, have the newspapers print something about America—especially business news—get some shows and nightclubs running that can compare with Broadway (and stop that annoying "club" system that makes it so hard to have a good time except in rough-neck night places). When these things are attended to (!) I *may* go again.

Lester Penniman
4/29/29 *Newark, N.J.*

What I don't like about England, since Mr. Sydney Walton of London wants to know, is the way every Englishman gets around sooner or later to saying:

"Now about these War debts. We're perfectly willing to cancel what the Italians and French owe us. Why don't you Americans join us in canceling War debts all round? Let's all forget the War!"

I have told them over and over that since France and Italy owe them and they owe us, the only result of "canceling debts all round" would be to leave the United States standing the whole loss.

They can never see it that way! Their Government and their Peer-subsidized press has got them as hypnotized on that point as a basketful of baby rabbits under the eye of an Indian snake charmer.

Let them keep quiet and pay what they owe—which is what they always pretend that they are doing.

Sitwell R. Packard
4/29/29 *Boston, Mass.*

I can tell the Johnny Bulls one thing to "fix up"—the officers on their ships! I always travel on the French or Italian lines now, even when I'm on my way to England. I suppose there is no class of men with so much concentrated snobbishness, lordy-dordy and hoity-toity as the officers on British liners. When it comes to deck games they are the poorest sports I know—and brag the loudest about their sportsmanship.

Mathew Georgin
4/29/29 *New York City.*

During an absence of more than two years in Europe, I spent 14 months in England. The reason why I have no wish to see it again is because of the insane habit the people had of saying "Beg pardon?" to every remark I made. It was not that they did not understand me, for if I refused to repeat my remark they gave me an intelligent answer, thus showing that neither deafness in them nor my American brogue had hindered them from knowing what I said. They were just as senseless when talking to one another. . . . Perhaps

Jazz was all the rage in the nightclubs of the '20s

Investors swarm into Wall Street on Black Friday

A victim of the stock market crash tries to sell his car for cash

my English cousins think their course is polite, but it is certainly not good manners to try to make persons repeat every remark they make. Life is too short for that. When an American child says "What?" to all his parents say, they reprove him until he reforms, but in England the parents were as bad as the children

Dryden Wm. Phelps
5/13/29 *San Diego, Calif.*

Early Did It

I respectfully refer you to your "Hatched, Matched, Dispatched" caption in Letters Department, TIME, May 27.

Twenty-five years or so ago, Editor Early of the Cannelton (Ind.) *Telephone* in that manner designated births, marriages, deaths respectively, in his up and doing little paper.

C. X. Henning
San Mateo, Calif.

Japan's Plan

I beg leave to call your attention to a statement in the July 8 issue of TIME, page 13, column 2 near the bottom of the page:

"Japan once planned to annex Hawaii by intensive colonization."

I challenge anyone to produce a bit of documentary evidence to prove this statement—or any evidence that would be accepted by the courts of any civilized nation.

This statement savors of international slander; it is bad etiquette and miserable ethics. To say the least, it is totally unworthy of a magazine that professes the accuracy and other quali-

ties of TIME.

Earl W. Roop
8/5/29 *Seattle, Wash.*
Reader Roop is unduly alarmed. Japan entertained the plan prior to Hawaii's annexation by the U.S.—ED.

Newscasting

Some few weeks ago we noticed an article in the New York *Sun* using the word NEWSCASTING. This appealed to us as a most appropriate expression, so that we were led to refer to our 10-Minute Radio News Service talks on Mexico under that term. We have since learned that you created that word in referring to the broadcasting of news and desire to congratulate you on your originality. We would be pleased to know if you have any objection to our use of the expression in so describing our radio news service.

H. T. Oliver
Mexican News Digest
8/12/29 *New York City*
Digester Oliver's request, both flattering and courteous, must be refused because NEWSCASTING (now given from 65 stations throughout the U.S.) is copyrighted by TIME, Inc.—ED.

Drunk Definitions

Your issue of Aug. 12, p. 50, under Medicine refers to drunkenness. I am moved by this article to give you the definition of Dean Samuel F. Mordecai, late of the Law School of Duke University:

*"Not drunk is he who from the floor
Can rise again or drink once more:
But drunk is he who prostrate lies
And cannot either drink or rise."*

I am also reminded of the definition of Dean Gulley of Wake Forest College Law School; that is to say:

"No man is drunk until he has to hold on to the grass to keep from falling off the face of the earth."

T. A. Burns
9/2/29 *Asheboro, N.C.*

Fascinating Character

In your section on Foreign News, Sept. 9 issue, you go into the Arabian-Hebrew situation in some detail. Have you, who are ordinarily more "ferrety" than the average newsmagazine, failed to wonder where one T. E. Lawrence is at this time?

It seems to me that I recall a recent issue of TIME stating that he was in North India; or thereabouts in Afghanistan, Hindustan, or Persia. A private in the Royal Flying Corps; at least so they say. It seems that he is in a very appropriate corner just now, to serve the British Empire. I wonder though, is he not a bit disappointed toward Feisal and Ibn Saud?

Can TIME really tell us where this fascinating character is, and what he is doing?

Waldo Chamberlin
9/30/29 *Seattle, Wash.*
Colonel T. E. Lawrence—now Aircraftsman A. C. Shaw with rank of private—legally changed his name, quixotically demanded and secured the demotion, suspected of having helped to topple King Amanullah of Afghanistan from his throne, was recalled from the Indo-Afghan border last January and publicly displayed in the House of Commons to prove that he was not somewhere else [Feb. 11].

The British Air Ministry declared that Private Shaw is still at Cattewater Air Station, near Southampton. There he is routed out at 6.30 a.m. daily, makes his bed, works till sundown as a mechanic on Royal Air Force planes, and at night either keeps up his Greek and archaeology or goes out for his favorite sport—a roaring moonlight ride on his special Army racing motorcycle. Hero Shaw's mother has remarked: "I never could fathom Ned. He's always led a topsy-turvy life."—ED.

Glasgow, Too

On p. 27 [Sept. 16] under "India" you say: "Proud Indians know that today only two cities in the British Commonwealth have subways: London and Sydney."

"Proud Indians" are misinformed. Glasgow has had a subway for about 30 years.

David Brown
10/7/29   Maplewood, N.J.

One-Sided Hate Party

In your issue of Sept. 30, under "Music" and "Pacific Opera," you state that ". . . San Francisco's lusty rival, Los Angeles. . . ."

To the best of my knowledge, in this year of 1929, Los Angeles is not a rival of San Francisco nor is San Francisco a rival of Los Angeles any more than the State of California is a rival of the State of Illinois.

Of course, San Francisco was for many years rather jealous of the growth of Los Angeles, and the census of 1920 caused considerable pain. It is probable that the census of 1930 will also cause San Francisco some pain because even now it is apparent that Los Angeles has at least twice the population that San Francisco possesses.

However, San Francisco has its own problems, and so has Los Angeles. Within the past two or three years, though, the jealousy of San Francisco has abated greatly, and residents of that city have undoubtedly found it more profitable to tend to their own knitting than to carry on a one-sided hate party.

Anyway, San Francisco can console herself with the fact that she isn't a nigger heaven like Los Angeles is turning out to be. . . .

I am, and have been, a staunch Republican, but I certainly deplore this *black republicanism* with which the Nation is being afflicted.

R. L. Larson
10/21/29   Los Angeles, Calif.

Whoopee

In a more or less recent article credit was given to Walter Winchell, the enterprising young "muckraker" for the coining of the word: "Whoopee." If the admirers of W.W. will pardon me mentioning the name of Rudyard Kip-ling with that of their favourite, I would point out that this word, used in the same sense, will be found in Kipling's poem *Loot.*—"Whoopee! Tear 'im, puppy! Loo! loo! Lulu! Loot! loot! loot!" *Barrack Room Ballads, I,* are dated 1889-1891. . . .

Hal. L. Campbell
11/4/29   Silverton, Ore.
But to Kipling no credit for giving "Whoopee" its current connotation, namely, hilarious sport of indefinite intimacy between two individuals of opposite sex.—ED.

Wemyss, Ruthven

Some months ago I was interested in reading a brief description—I believe it was in your "Letters" column—of the correct pronunciation of certain names and places in England.

The enclosed clipping from the London *Evening Standard*, with its "duly authenticated Explanatory Ode" may be of use to those of your readers who are contemplating a visit to these shores.

Hugh Gallaher
11/18/29   London, W1

The clipping:

Explanatory Ode
*All persons who aspire to climb
The social stair, be warned in time,
And saved from treading unaware
Upon a step that isn't there.
Each proud and unfamiliar name
May prove to be a source of shame,
If in pronouncing it you make,
From lack of knowledge, a mistake.
Great Britain absolutely teems
With men and women surnamed
  Wemyss,
And everywhere the tyro strolls
There lurks an unsuspected Knollys.*

*He's certain to be greeted glumly
Who gives four syllables to
  Cholmondeley,
Or by his ignorance disarms
The good intentions of a Glamis.
Who'd blame a self-respecting
  Tyrrwhitt,
Mis-called, for chiding in a spirit
Of gentle protest? And a Ruthven
May similarly be forgiven.
'Twere justice that my tongue should
  blister
If, having met a Mr. Bicester,
I hailed him wrongly; it would grieve a
Descendant of the clan of Belvoir
To be erroneously addressed.
It cannot be too strongly stressed:
A shock awaits the fool who wavers
Before he says, "Good-morning,
  Claverhouse."
A burden of regret and woe
Descends on those who Do Not Know,
So I've endeavoured, in their cause,
To formulate some rhyming laws,
Whereby the novice can with ease
Preserve the starch amenities.*

South Shore Jews

In your issue dated Nov. 25, p. 56, in the lower right hand corner, there is the following:
SOUTH SHORE COUNTRY CLUB
(Many a Jew)

As a subscriber to your paper and a member of the Jewish faith I am interested in knowing the significance of the statement, "Many a Jew."

Albert E. Kaye
12/16/29   Longview, Wash.
As everyone knows, Jews are discriminated against in many a leading U.S. country club. Knowing this not to be the case at the famed South Shore club, TIME mentioned it as of incidental news-interest.—ED.

Barrels of illicit beer are destroyed during Prohibition

The Threadbare Thirties

The bank system collapsed, unemployment soared—the Great Depression left its mark on Americans. F.D.R. promised a New Deal and established alphabet programs. DiMaggio ruled home plate, Astaire and Rogers conquered the dance floor: there were ways to forget the breadlines. TIME reported on the humble Gandhi and civil disobedience. After seizing Austria and part of Czechoslovakia, the less humble Hitler marched into Poland.

Capone-on-the-Cover

. . . I was . . . considerably surprised when my attention was called to the title page of your magazine of March 24. In other words, I do not understand why the title page of a magazine intended for boys and girls of high school age should be graced by the likeness of Alphonso Capone.

This note is not written in a vindictive spirit at all. It is merely an attempt on my part to express to you the honest conviction of our teachers and myself, that, in this day and generation, the likeness of the individual to whom I have referred has no place in a magazine whose business it is to set standards for American youth.

Wm. M. Stewart
Supervising Principal
Etna Public Schools
4/7/30   *Etna, Pa.*

Thanks from India

I am an Indian sojourner in the Western Hemisphere. . . .

After reading your article on our leader (Mahatma Gandhi) and his present activities in India [March 31], I have to congratulate you most heartily on the thorough grasp and clear understanding you manifest of the true spirit, morals and significance of our movement, as also on the coining, as only an American can, of the very happy and expressive term "Recpolism" to convey in a word to your readers a comprehensive idea of the movement. As an Indian I beg to express my gratitude to you, sir, for this enlightening article which is so different to the unconscious or deliberate misrepresentation of facts or the stupid jibes or fun-poking that I have seen in some English journals on the subject. . . .

T. P. Däver
5/19/30   *San Francisco, Calif.*

President & Cat

In your paper of late date you mention an alley cat being fed with milk by President Hoover from the White House [May 12]. Is this at the expense of the American people or does the President furnish his own milk?

W. W. J. Jones
6/2/30   *Batesville, Ark.*

The U.S. people furnish their President with $25,000 per annum for "official entertainment."—ED.

"St. Gandhi"

I do not consider Mr. Gandhi a saint and strongly object to your use of "St. Gandhi." If you must dignify the creature, call him "Mahatma Gandhi" or use the literal translation of *mahatma*.

Mary Pierce Newman
6/16/30   *Philadelphia, Pa.*
Atman in Hindustani means soul. With literal accuracy TIME could speak of Mahatma or "Great Soul" Gandhi. But in English such terms produce no clear cut impression. TIME, eschewing the nebulous, uses "St." for brevity and precision, as the shortest way of indicating that millions of Hindus revere the Mahatma exactly as Christians would a 1930 Saint.—ED.

Death for Communists

In TIME for June 23, p. 24, under the heading "Poland" the following news item is found:

"In Lemberg, last week one Samuel Jugend, one Naftali Propper, and one Israel Hirsch were sentenced to death. Their offense: "Belonging to the Communist Party.""

The statement has terrible implications. Not even under the Tsar was the death penalty imposed for belonging to this or the other party. There must be some mistake. How do you account for the fact that there are Communists in the Polish parliament if merely being a Communist is punishable by death? . . . If I get no response from you I shall get the cold facts somehow.

Irwine E. Gordon
7/21/30   *Cleveland, Ohio*
Membership in the Communist Party renders a Pole liable to the penalty of Death because court decisions have established a legal presumption in Poland that anyone who is a Communist is ipso facto attempting to overthrow the Government and is therefore guilty of treason.
Poland will soon adopt a new legal code upon which TIME will report, stating whether Communists will continue liable to the Death penalty after its enactment. At present the courts are somewhat lenient and the Death sentencing of Communists at Lemberg was an exception. According to despatches the accused denied that they were Communists, but the Lemberg Court held that their possession of much Communist literature established the presumption that they were Communists. Upon this presumption and its corollary that a Communist is a traitor they were sentenced to Death. Communist deputies are of course protected by their parliamentary immunity.—ED.

Texas Pun

Supporters of "Ma" Ferguson—again in the Governor's Race here in Texas—should realize the danger of electing a woman Governor. All the prisoners in the pen will be pardoned. Reason: a woman won't let a man finish a sentence.

R. P. Dryden
9/1/30   *Houston, Tex.*

Ambition

Thanks for turning up the item (in your issue of Aug. 11) about Fascist soldiers firing on a rescue party of St. Bernard monks. It did not appear in any of the dailies I read. . . .

My greatest (presumably unattainable) ambition as a modern woman with civilized tastes: to snub Mussolini.

Alice McKinstry
9/8/30   *Chicago, Ill.*

Autobiography

TIME prides itself on being brief, concise. If some of your writers become careless let the Editor give them this illustration of brevity. It appeared in the daily press several weeks ago.

Autobiography of a woman in four words: Dolls. Boys. Rings. Bridge.

Ted F. Higgins
9/15/30   *Newcastle, Pa.*

Susy's Gravestone

. . . I can't help thinking how touched Mark Twain would be with the inscription on the little pomeranian's final resting place! [Sept. 29, Oct. 13]. Over Mrs. Clemens' grave, too, stands a stone engraved with the epitaph:

    Warm summer sun,
    Shine kindly here;

Warm summer wind,
Blow softly here;
Green sod above,
Lie light, lie light;
Good night, dear one,
Goodnight, goodnight.

Eleanor Morgan Crain
10/20/30   *Mount Victoria, Md.*
*Investigation reveals that the lines are on the gravestone of Susy Clemens, daughter of Mark Twain, that they were written by Australian Poet Robert Richardson, that when Mr. Clemens learned that the lines were attributable to him he ordered Poet Richardson's name inscribed beneath them. On the gravestone the third line reads: "Warm southern wind," although in the original poem it read: "Warm northern wind." In the Antipodes the north wind is balmiest.—*ED.

Chicago's Crime Fame

Several times I have seen newspaper accounts giving statistics indicating that the murders in Chicago are less *per capita* than in several other large cities. In fact, it seems that Chicago was sixth or seventh below the leader of the list.

If this is so, to what do you attribute the nation- or world-wide publicity given to Chicago, classing it as murderers' playground and one of the greatest seats of crime?

A. R. Baldwin Jr.
11/24/30   *St. Louis, Mo.*
The Chicago Tribune's *answer to A. R. Baldwin Jr.'s question has been: "Because it is the centre of the telegraph and the telephone lines, news goes to more places from Chicago than from any other city." It is also true that: Chicago newspapers have played-up Chicago's underworld most persistently and sensationally; Chicago's murders have been most sensational intrinsically viz. the St. Valentine's Day Massacre, 1929; Chicago has had fewer policemen and more nationally-known criminals per square mile than any U.S. city; crime in Chicago is more highly organized than anywhere else in the world.—*ED.

Millionaire Hoover

. . . Is President Hoover rated as a millionaire and was he such before he entered the White House?

D. T. Muir, M.D.
1/19/31   *Alden, Kan.*
*When Herbert Hoover became President, his private income was in excess of $60,000 per year. Were his money invested at 6%, his capital would be in excess of $1,000,000. Therefore he is rated a millionaire.—*ED.

Hutton Champagne

I've sipped champagne with them that was and them that was to be; with Belgian royalty and houri French and Alsation refugees; with Red Cross girls o'er chevaux-de-frise in Coblenze and in Metz; with frauleins surreptitiously I guzzled Piper Heidsick. . . .

Aboard French cruisers I've had my fill, in the Vosges, in Nice and ocean liners; in hospital beds in Neuchateau to New York night clubs, Florida, Cuba.

I've ridden to hounds with champagne legs and cavalry mounts with hiccups. As a mouth wash, hair tonic or improvised spray I've used this precious fluid. . . .

Now, please, Miss Hutton!

"Most spectacular Manhattan func-

tion was given . . . by Mr. & Mrs. Franklyn L. Hutton for their daughter Barbara. . . . Guests: 1000. Cost: $100,000. Item: 2,000 *cases* of champagne. Setting designed by Joseph Urban: a moonlit garden with eucalyptus sprays, silver birches, potted roses, a gauze canopy speckled with stars." [Jan. 5.]

2,000 cases: 12 bottles per case equal 24,000 bottles. 1000 guests: 24 bottles per guest.

If this be true, I feel sure that Mr. Urban's stars glistened on eucalyptical roses whilst potted canopied moonlit sprays birched on every garden of gauze.

Lucullus N. D. Mitchell
1/19/31   *Philadelphia, Pa.*
*A reportorial error. But the reporter, now unable to remember whether the exact figure was 2,000 bottles or 200 cases, weakly insists, there were two of something for each.—*ED.

Son & Sire

In your issue of Feb. 9 I noticed among your British news—"Up spoke Wayward Winnie *who has long sought to wrest leadership of the Conservative Party from Baldwin. . . .*"

I am certain that a magazine of your

1937 Wolseley Super Six Saloon

The WOLSELEY SUPER SIX SALOON

1939 Packard Convertible Coupe

1935 Studebaker President

Studebaker President

high repute and obvious desire for accuracy would not publish such a statement unless it possessed some foundation in actual fact. I am always interested in my father's activities, but confess with shame that in regard to this aspect of them I am woefully ignorant. May I, therefore, inquire what is the basis of truth on which you rely for the allegation contained in the words I have italicized and in particular how long and in what way this has been going on.

Randolph S. Churchill
2/23/31 *San Francisco, Calif.*
Son Churchill well knows that Sire Churchill, ever ambitious, broke last month with Conservative Leader Stanley Baldwin on the issue of India's future status, resigned from the Conservative "shadow cabinet" on Jan. 27, 1931. He has since continued (with no appearance of success) his attempts (by loud public speechmaking) to get a wagging hold on the Conservative party through its die-hard tail, of which he is the tip.

*Son Churchill has seasoned his U.S. lecture tour with such assertions as that Prime Minister James Ramsay MacDonald is a "traitor".—*ED.

"The March of Time"

Congratulations on the best radio program I have heard over the air in—well, as a matter of fact, the best I have ever heard. We stayed up to hear it, and we almost wept over the *World-Telegram* dramatization. Whatever advertising agency is doing it for you deserves a great hurrah!

John Farrar
3/23/31 *New York City*
"The March of Time" is prepared by staff members of TIME, *Inc., directed by Arthur Pryor Jr. of Batten, Barton, Durstine & Osborne.—*ED.

Mr. Chesterton's Education

On March 3 Mr. G. K. Chesterton lectured here in San Francisco on "The Ignorance of the Educated."

Yesterday, replying to my query, Mr. Chesterton told me that he had never heard of TIME!!

W. H. Black
3/30/31 *San Francisco, Calif.*

Six or Seven Dogs

Re the item headed "Wow" in your April 20 issue. Probably the foremost dog-barker today is Tom Corwin, who takes the part of the most famous movie dog in the "Rin-tin-tin Thrillers," presented each Thursday evening over the NBC Blue Network by Chappel Bros., Rockford, Ill., dog food manufacturers.

Rin-tin-tin was a visitor in Chicago two or three weeks ago and made a personal appearance on the Thursday night broadcast. At no time was it possible to tell whether it was Rin or Corwin one was listening to.

Mr. Corwin was in our Chicago office a short time back and gave a sample of an imitation dog-fight he had perfected for use in a future "Thriller." I swear to you that half the tenants of the world's largest Merchandise Mart came running, fully intending to witness the fight. Fully six or seven dogs of various breeds, ages and sizes were closely distinguishable in his imitation.

Harry Miller
Chappel Bros. Inc.
5/11/31 *Rockford, Ill.*

Rusticated Hearst

I was in the class of '86 at Harvard. I was not expelled in '87 nor any other year. I never did anything very bad at Harvard nor anything very good either. I was rusticated in '86 for an excess of political enthusiasm and a certain deficiency in intellecual attainments. I did not return to be graduated. There did not seem to be either reason or hope. I think the less said about my college career the better. Perhaps that is so with the rest of my career. However, exercise your own judgment, only please print the facts, or perhaps I should say, please don't.

William Randolph Hearst
1/11/32 *Los Angeles, Calif.*

*Rustication: An old-fashioned academic penalty whereby delinquent or intractable undergraduates are sent away, generally to their homes to continue their studies under a supervisor designated by the college.—*ED.

Dreiser on Tacoma

In the Book Review Section of TIME for the week of Feb. 8, the following statement was quoted from the book *Tragic America* by Theodore Dreiser.

". . . in Tacoma, Wash., 'on Feb. 19, 1931, . . . 16 men were poisoned by food from the Volunteers of America soup kitchen, from which four died.' "

. . . I need hardly tell you that this statement, appearing in your magazine even as a quotation, will do untold hurt to our work. The Volunteers of America are feeding 4,000 people a day in Seattle, Wash., and at least 2,000 in Tacoma. This work is supported by public donations and those who give to it will be greatly shocked by the statement appearing in Mr. Dreiser's book.

I must ask you to publish a prominent statement in your magazine that will offset the injury done our Organization by this quotation, as we are feeding hundreds of thousands every day throughout the country.

Maud B. Booth
The Volunteers of America
3/14/32 *New York City*
TIME *gladly, swiftly prints correction of a statement for which Author Dreiser refuses to name the source.* TIME *deeply regrets any hindrance to The Volunteers of America caused by quotation of Author Dreiser's loose remark.—*ED.

"Petty Treason"

In my opinion, kidnapping is one of the worst crimes in this nation. I think Col. Lindbergh, with the help of Mrs. Lindbergh missed the opportunity to put a stop to kidnapping. Had they refused to consider the criminals, regardless of the result to their son, it is safe to say the rest of us would have followed their example. Both of them are patriotic and brave and since they yield to the demands of the Kidnapper

we assume that the rest of us would. Kidnapping is only possible on account of the payment of ransoms, and, since the public will contribute to obtain the release of the victims, such payment of ransoms must be stopped by suitable legislation. I consider kidnapping a national question and that Congress can make laws punishing kidnappers and preventing the payment of ransoms. Such laws can be designated petty treason. The law should require those who know that such a crime was committed to report to the authorities and direct that the proper authority should guard against the payment of ransoms.

I would like to known the reaction of the public on these views. . . .

August Wagner
3/21/32   *Columbus, Neb.*
*Who besides Nebraska's August Wagner considers Col. & Mrs. Lindbergh guilty of "petty treason"?—*ED.

Holmes at 91

Beside my desk on the wall there has hung since last March a clipping from TIME quoting Justice Oliver Wendell Holmes as saying upon the occasion of his 90th birthday: "Death plucks my ear and says 'Live—I am coming!'" Tonight's newspapers give an all too abbreviated report of his remarks upon his 91st birthday. I trust TIME will not cut his remarks severely, for they are usually so beautiful and mellow.

May time be kind enough to him and to us to preserve his active mind for many years. Nothing could add more to our precious heritage of literature than for him to write (or merely compile) *My Philosophy of Life and Thought*.

Frank G. Dickinson
3/28/32   *Urbana, Ill.*

"Petty Treason"

. . . That the Lindberghs are guilty of "petty treason" . . . may be a little strongly put. It does seem rather a poor commentary on the "land of the free," however, when its most representative citizen scorns the arm of the law and resorts to the help of gangsters and racketeers in getting back his child. On the other hand I wonder if August W. would mind letting us know whether or not he is a father.

A. David Bouterse
4/4/32   *Roanoke, Va.*

Believe or Not

Believe it or not, Robert L. Ripley, creator of the "Believe It or Not" Series has just reached Sydney on the luxury liner *Mariposa*.

Ripley was delighted with Sydney Harbour. He was amazed to know that the Sydney Harbour Bridge is one of the biggest of its kind in the World. He was astonished when he saw the Laughing Jackass and found not a beast, but a bird that laughed at its own jokes. . . .

He talked with Ornithologist A. H. Chisholm who told him about the Bower Bird, the bird which paints the inside of its nest. He was delighted with a luncheon which I hurriedly arranged, where he met Ministers of the State—men who were former speakers in the State House Assembly and the Federal Senate. . . .

It took some persuasion to make him believe that some of the sheep out here wear shoes to protect their feet from the burrs.

All these things interested Ripley, but the thing that grasped his interest and made his eyes sparkle, believe it or not, were two copies of TIME that I gave him—the first he had seen in Sydney.

George Fitzpatrick
Superintendent
New South Wales Community Hospital
5/16/32   *Sydney, Australia*

Rose-a-velt

Why do radio announcers, delegates, newspapermen and close friends of Franklin D. Roosevelt, the latter who should know better, mispronounce his name Rose-a-velt when it is distinctly Roos-e-velt?

I know you will tell me about the rule for proper names but the late great T.R. insisted on accenting the double O.

Spare the radio audience from this annoyance.

Reginald S. Roussel
7/25/32   *Long Beach, Calif.*
*One of the Governor's first actions as Democratic nominee was to let it be known to all the world that, whatever Theodore Roosevelt (his fifth cousin) may have called it, he calls it "Rose-a-velt".—*ED.

Pomorze

Your use of "Polish Corridor" to designate that portion of Poland which the Polish people know as Pomorze is both unTIMEly and unfair.

Polish people resent such terminology for that section of Poland. Only German propagandists relish the use of the sarcastic term, "Polish Corridor." It is a disrepectful term, and in observance of the status quo of Pomorze, and for the sake of brevity, Pomorze for all TIME please.

Stephen Bielicki
3/6/33   *Camden, N.J.*
*Since officials of the Polish Government when conversing with non-Poles, usually speak of Pomorze as the "Corridor," TIME will continue to employ, with no disrespect to Poland, this terse, descriptive TIME-worthy term.—*ED.

Gripping Events

. . . Although I heard President Roosevelt's inaugural address and have read almost countless columns of news in the press, your radio re-enactment of the gripping events of the past week held me spellbound. Furthermore, my children, who are still too young to read the newspapers, listened attentively to last Friday evening's program.

Their comments showed that they were keenly interested. No doubt the same thing occurred in millions of homes throughout the country. You rendered on that occasion, and are rendering right along, a splendid public service.

Lawrence F. Quigley
Mayor
3/27/33   *Chelsea, Mass.*

"Handsome" Adolf

I must protest!

Why in Heaven's name do you always affix the descriptive adjective "handsome" when writing about Hitler? "Handsome Adolf" indeed! That blank face with its silly little mustache gives me the "jitters" every time I see it. And as I read TIME every week I get the "jitters" every time you call Adolf "handsome."

Tessa H. Fluhr
4/3/33   *Brooklyn, N. Y.*
One of the curiosities of the Nazi movement is that, ceaselessly preaching the subservience of women, it has always gained much of its strength from women voters. Not TIME but the ladies of Bavaria, in 1923, coined the phrase Der Schöne *Adolf.—ED.*

President's Cigaret

This is not a matter of national importance but for the past three months the family has been arguing as to what brand of cigaret our President smokes. Could you give us the information? . . .

Mark Klausler
4/17/33   *Hankinson, N. Dak.*
President Roosevelt smokes Camels.—ED.

Such an Applesauce

I really do not understand how a magazine which claims to be always right and correct could have published such an applesauce about Germany as you did in your issue of March 13. I never could understand how a nation as level-headed as I consider the American nation is, could have believed all the lies this nation really has believed about us during the War. After reading your article "National Revolution," I changed my opinion. . . . I am not a Nazi but I bet if ever you Americans will have a revolution, more blood will be shed and more wrong will be done as has been at this last German one.

Max Ullrich
4/24/33   *München, Germany*

Anxious Vanderbilt

I want to compliment TIME on its splendid portrayal of the German situation in March and April.

I happened to be in Germany during this period and was eager to see how periodicals back home pictured it. TIME was in my humble estimation the only magazine which described matters accurately as they took place.

You might be interested to know also that I saw TIME on the Crown-Prince's writing table when I interviewed him at 36 Unter den Linden in mid-March and also on the magazine table of President Hindenberg, although the latter's secretary informed me your magazine was "very inaccurate."

I am now anxiously watching TIME to see what it is going to say about the Austrian situation. . . .

Cornelius Vanderbilt Jr.
6/5/33   *Salzburg, Austria*

Embellish

Shocked at first that you should run the degenerate face of Trumpet Blower Goebbels on your cover, which I regard as a place of honor, I was going to raise a bit of hell with you. But recalling that you ran Al Capone in the same space some time ago I saw the fitness of things and congratulate you. After all Germany is in the hands of gangsters right now and Goebbels is their blaring brass.

Oscar Leonard
7/24/33   *Ridgefield, Conn.*
To Subscriber Leonard, praise for able association of ideas.—ED.

Cog

TIME, usually accurate, have again slipped a cog. Suggest you either correct your estimate my earning powers or convince Mr. Hearst to meet your terms.

Elliott Roosevelt
9/18/33   *Pasadena, Calif.*
Neither Writer Roosevelt nor Employer Hearst will say how much more or less Writer Roosevelt is receiving than the reported weekly $200.—ED.

Liquor Ads

. . . I said I liked TIME but would not subscribe to it because it contains liquor ads. As a recent issue contained at least three ads of beer, vermouth and the like I am unable to understand why you could not easily see just what I meant. . . .

In plain words if you are willing to help make drinkers and drunkards of my family your paper is unworthy of a place in my home.

William R. Hutton
11/6/33   *Rosalia, Kan.*

Jew & German

In your publication of the 13th, I see a caption under an illustration, on p. 10, under National Affairs, with photo of the Hon. Samuel Untermyer, reading "Jew Untermyer."

This rather raw exhibition impels me to say to you that it is beyond comprehension in these times, in this stage of human instability, that you should display so little tact to say the least,

Hoover surrenders the Executive Office to F.D.R. at the 1933 Inauguration

as to flaunt your anti-semetic tendencies before the eyes of your readers.

. . . To all appearances, your magazine is subsidized in the main, by the fanatics who have now self-imposed themselves in Germany.

Harry C. Neuberger
11/27/33 *New York City*

Cigarettes

As an oldtime consistent reader of TIME I appeal to you for some information to satisfy my curiosity. Hearst's "Washington Chatter" column states that Mrs. Franklin Roosevelt smokes. If this be true, is Mrs. Roosevelt the first First Lady in U.S. history to do so?

H. Rolfson
1/1/34 *Oakland, Calif.*
First female resident in the White House to smoke: "Princess" Alice Roosevelt (at first surreptitiously, later in public). First First Lady to smoke: Anna Eleanor Roosevelt. But she cares little for tobacco, uses it to put her guests at ease.—ED.

"By God, Sirs . . ."

Thanks and appreciation referring to the excellent piece on James Joyce and *Ulysses* in the issue of Jan 20. TIME always has treated Mr. Joyce in a dignified manner, another proof of the intelligence of your editorship. This is a great honor for you to lay up for the future, for Joyce is the greatest writer of our time and one of the very foremost artists in the recorded history of Western civilization.

Only one detected point of question: as to the physical size of Joyce's chirography ("to scrawl his own writing hugely" . . .), where did your excellent critic get the idea that Joyce writes "hugely"? I have two specimens of his handwriting and both are small, thin, fragile. Far from being scrawling, too.

Your book critic deserves a reward for one of the best pieces of the year and one of the best short pieces ever written on Joyce and his *Ulysses*.

H. K. Croessmann
2/12/34 *Duquoin, Ill.*
Author Joyce's handwriting, normally small, varies to enormous size according to his inconstant eyesight.—ED.

Black Star

What is the significance of the small black star always in the lower left corner of the front cover of your magazine?

Arthur W. Smith
2/12/34 *New Haven, Conn.*
The star appears only on copies of TIME containing liquor advertisements, warns the Circulation Department that such copies must not be shipped to newsstands in Dry States. But copies sent direct to subscribers may now contain liquor advertisements no matter what State they enter.—ED.

Gold Medalist Jesse Owens at the 1936 Berlin Olympics

Roosevelt & Lindbergh

I desire to point out what I think is an error in your judgment. In TIME of Feb. 19 under Aeronautics you compare Roosevelt's popularity and Lindbergh's. Among all my friends I know not one who has more than a passing interest and little admiration for Colonel Lindbergh but they are all enthusiastic about our President.

You know better than I how quickly people tire of being saturated with publicity about any "fair-haired boy" type of personality.

Among ordinary people who actually bring up their own children the Lindbergh custom of going off to Asia or Europe whenever a new baby is born is not at all conducive of goodwill.

From a flying standpoint I personally believe he is not at all outstanding, even giving him credit for the hop to Paris, which was foolish when you consider that the plane he used is condemned by the Department of Commerce as unsafe. . . . .

William Corbett
3/12/34 *Brookline, Mass.*
Col. Lindbergh's N.Y.-Paris plane was never condemned by the Department of Commerce as unsafe. It was barred from commercial use only because it held an experimental license. About one hundred sister ships (Ryan Brougham monoplanes) are still in service throughout the land.—ED.

Munitions

Your comment on "Munitions Men" in the current number [March 5] is a genuine satisfaction to many of your readers.

The seriousness of the European situation is made very clear in recent books—which my own observation in Europe this last summer confirms.

The time to safeguard peace is now. Such measures as that sponsored by Senator Vandenberg to eliminate profits from the munitions business will help—but beneath all else there must be the Peace Sentiment. . . .

James W. Fifield Jr.
East Congregational Church
3/19/34 *Grand Rapids, Mich.*

Neglectful Wives

I presume that you published the letter headed "Neglectful Wives" [May 21] in the hope of receiving some spirited replies. Here's one.

The average woman, after repeating the experience of baking a cake correctly a dozen times, should be able to do it well. She needs only to wash several hundred diapers to be able to do that well. The constant repetition alone should be sufficient, if one starts out right, to have the home run smoothly, and we modern young women . . . feel that we have earned the right to see what is happening in the world and to see if we cannot do something about that, too.

To be conversant with the facts of present-day government should certainly not cause any women to neglect her home . . . My husband enjoys discussing national, international and even his professional affairs with me; he certainly does not think our twin babies

are neglected because I have read TIME and a few other journals. . . .

Does the intelligent masculine mind pride itself on the state of the world today? There is too much room for improvement and our children will in their turn ask us, as we asked of our parents: "Why did people permit such things to happen?" I at least, as a parent and a woman, do not want to feel that I can hide my head under a pile of cake batter and say: "I was too busy in the kitchen, my dears, ask Daddy." . . .

Charlotte Baron
Covington, Ky.

. . . Why should women be condemned to be ignorant ninnies all their lives while men know all the interesting things? What is there about baking a cake or scrubbing a floor or molding a child's morals that can compare with the thrill of reading about Big Business and the goings-on of Congress? The cake is eaten, the floor is dirtied and the child does as it pleases so give me my weekly Business & Finance section!

Mrs. Betty Evenson
6/4/34 *Hiland, Wyo.*

Dillinger's Place

Immediately upon receiving the July 30 copy of TIME I looked for the article concerning the capture and death of Dillinger. I wish to offer my little praise to TIME for placing the subject in its proper place in comparison to the other news of the week. . . .

R. E. Campbell
8/13/34 *Chicago, Ill.*

Pudding-Headed Brother

In your July 30 issue, p. 16, col. 1: "The porcine British Press Tycoon Lord Rothermere, pudding-headed bro-

ther of the late great Northcliffe. . . ."

Is this an unbiased TIME-worthy description of Lord Rothermere's physical and mental equipment?

How does "pudding-headed Lord Rothermere" maintain his economic and social position as No. 1 British publisher, if he is as doltish and stupid as you would have us suppose?

Paul Vonck
8/20/34 *Arlington, Mass.*
Though a ranking British press tycoon, Lord Rothermere is not demonstrably No. 1 in either economic or social status. Famed in Fleet Street for abrupt, capricious shifts and reversals of editorial policy, Tycooon Rothermere appears to have a head crammed with economic and political notions as various and assorted as the nuts and fruits in a Christmas pudding.—ED.

Ink and Air

Your article on the press-radio controversy was very welcome. . . .

. . . Just as the automobile drove the less convenient horse and buggy off the street, as the steamship out-sailed the sailing ship, as the printed book displaced the handwritten manuscript, so will radio outdo the slower, more expensive and cumbersome newspaper as a distributor of news.

. . . If newspapers are smart they will not fight radio but accept the inexorable law of survival of the fittest and find ways of improving their output—a popular defensive business move of which newspaper publishers are innocent.

B. A. Jones
11/19/34 *Cuyahoga Falls, Ohio*

Red Terror

Congratulations to TIME!
Yours was the most courageous, most interesting, and most comprehen-

sive account of Stalin's latest Red Terror campaign [Dec. 17] to appear in the American press.

Isaac Don Levine
1/7/35 *New York City*

Man of the Year

Am astounded by your picking Roosevelt as Man of the Year, he is more bitterly hated than any President since Jackson. Thousands curse him as a traitor for his rape of the Constitution. The very rich and poor may get richer but the great middle class scare their children with Roosevelt's name.

Arthur C. O'Connor Jr.
1/21/35 *Detroit, Mich.*

Peace Poll

Your note on the Peace Ballot in TIME of March 18 is highly misleading.

It is not a "straw ballot." Everyone in England and Wales is being asked to answer. Every family in Dulwich, for instance, is being visited, and worried for a reply. Percentage polls run up as high as 98% of all the people over 18—better than any election ever got. My guess is that about 55% of all English & Welsh citizens will have voted in the end, on the average of the whole country. . . .

I feel sure you will put on record this disclaimer. The Peace Ballot is *not* political. It is *not* pacifist. It is *not* a straw vote. It does *not* ask for unilateral reduction of the Empire's forces.

J. Ward Daw Jr.
Hon. Secretary & Hon. Organizer
National Peace Declaration
4/20/35 *East Dulwich, England*
Up to last week more than 6,000,000 votes had been cast in Britain's Peace Poll. Results thus far tabulated:
1) Should Great Britain remain a Member of the League of Nations? Yes—5,737,800. No—169,000.
2) Are you in favour of an all-round reduction of armaments by international agreement? Yes—5,410,790. No—431,740.
3) Are you in favour of an all-round abolition of national military and naval aircraft by international agreement? Yes—4,918,350. No—875,880.
4) Should the manufacture and sale of armaments for private profit be prohibited by international agreement? Yes—5,386,490. No—400,410.
5) Do you consider that if a nation insists on attacking another the other nations should combine to compel it to stop by
(a) economic and non-military measures? Yes—5,141,290. No—325,850.
(b) if necessary, military measures? Yes—3,472,700. No—1,213,540.—ED.

Kosher Cola

In connection with your interesting article on the celebration of Passover [April 29], you may be interested to know that, for the first time, Atlanta orthodox Jews were allowed to drink

Coca Cola during this solemn season. With the approval of Atlanta rabbis, special Coca Cola bottle caps were stamped with the Kosher symbol and signs denoting the same were displayed in soda fountains. The drink was not altered in any way.

Samuel Glick
5/13/35 *Atlanta, Ga.*

Cheating Whites

My hat comes off to Joe Louis the dark skinned fighter who ordered his mother to refund to Detroit welfare authorities $269 received during 1927-28 [Nov. 4].

For cheating while on relief and living in ease on others who work you've got to be white.

Wolfram Hill
11/25/35 *St. Paul, Minn.*
Subscriber Hill does rank injustice to Heavyweight Champion James J. Braddock and many another white whose sense of honesty prompted him to repay relief money.—Ed.

Hitler's Catholicism

On p. 21 of TIME, Dec. 2 you again refer to "Catholic Hitler."

Surely TIME's intelligent and informed Religion editor could inform the foreign department that an ex-Catholic who has not communicated for years and who has openly attacked the Church can no longer be described as a Catholic without flat inaccuracy. To be a Catholic, as TIME knows well, is to be a member of the Catholic Church, and this membership is voluntary, not racial, nor an irrevocable product of onetime membership. Hitler is a *de facto* apostate Catholic, and his status is properly describable only as that, or simply as "ex-Catholic."

One sympathizes with TIME's patience in meeting innumerable quibbles from readers, but this is one really seriously inaccurate and misleading statement. . . .

A. J. Lynd
Harvard University
12/30/35 *Cambridge, Mass.*
Asked "Is Hitler a Catholic?" the Archbishop of Munich, Michael Cardinal von Faulhaber replies: "The Archbishopric is not aware that Der Führer has ever withdrawn from the Catholic Church." Declared Herr Hitler's own Realmchancellery: "Adolf Hitler was born a Catholic, baptized a Catholic and is still a Catholic although not a practising Catholic in the ordinary churchgoing sense." The latest German Wer Ist's (Who's Who) plainly lists Der Führer as "Catholic."—Ed.

"Modern Sodom"

How fortunate that we Britishers, whether originating in the British Isles, Australia, New Zealand, South Africa, Canada or elsewhere, have so strong a sense of humor, otherwise we might permit ourselves to be annoyed at the disgustingly vitriolic attacks which your paper launches weekly against our Empire. No doubt you have accurately gauged the mentality of your people and give them what they want. But, my God, what a people! . . .

It is indeed a big laugh with us Canadians to hear and read the verbose rantings and ravings of Americans about "God's own country." Does an American ever stop to think what God has to say about it? That God sees the States as it is, in all its lecherous filth, not as the American affects to see it, but as the greatest criminal country in the world, the modern Sodom. He sees its devastating immorality, not only in its so-called society, but in its schools. (He has probably seen several startling and illuminating articles on this subject in *Liberty, Cosmopolitan* and other U.S. magazines.) The rackets, kidnappings, the graft of which the country reeks and stinks from border to border. . . .

What are His reactions to the substitution of a system of licensed prostitution for the old sacredness and sanctity of marriage? What does He think of the lynchings—and Hollywood? What a country! What a people! Having to hire and maintain armed thugs to prevent other armed thugs from tearing children from parents, holding them for ransom and finally knocking out their brains if the money is not forthcoming! Is it any wonder that Lindbergh has fled, with wife and child, from "God's own country" to England to seek the peace, protection and security that country affords all and sundry within its borders, irrespective of color, religion or race? . . . In an island which was the birthplace of parliamentary institutions which are still their greatest remaining strongholds.

As Winston Churchill said, "England, with all its faults, is still the best country in the world, whether for duke or dustman." . . . What do TIME and the Hearst atrocities hope to achieve by keeping up a continual bombardment of vulgar abuse and gratuitous insult directed at the British Empire?

James C. Barton
1/27/36 *Vancouver, B.C.*
Let annoyed Canadian Barton forget his sense of humor long enough to mind his manners hereafter.—Ed.

Splendid Manner

I would like to congratulate TIME on the splendid manner in which it handled the story of the execution of

Familiar scenes of the Depression: men search the newspapers for jobs while many people depend on soup kitchens for food

WANTED
INFORMATION AS TO THE WHEREABOUTS OF

CHAS. A. LINDBERGH, JR.
OF HOPEWELL, N. J.
SON OF COL. CHAS. A. LINDBERGH
World-Famous Aviator
This child was kidnaped from his home in Hopewell, N. J., between 8 and 10 p. m. on Tuesday, March 1, 1932.

DESCRIPTION:

Age, 20 months   Hair, blond, curly
Weight, 27 to 30 lbs.   Eyes, dark blue
Height, 29 inches   Complexion, light
Deep dimple in center of chin
Dressed in one-piece coverall night suit

ADDRESS ALL COMMUNICATIONS TO
COL. H. N. SCHWARZKOPF, TRENTON, N. J., or
COL. CHAS. A. LINDBERGH, HOPEWELL, N. J.
ALL COMMUNICATIONS WILL BE TREATED IN CONFIDENCE
COL. H. NORMAN SCHWARZKOPF
Supt. New Jersey State Police, Trenton, N. J.
March 11, 1932

1932: The Lindbergh baby was kidnapped. Above, suspect Hauptmann with inspector Lamb

Bruno Hauptman [April 13]. It was refreshing to see that at least one periodical had the good taste to give the mere facts and leave out the superfluous details which cater to the sordid imagination of a morbid public.

Russell Loftus
4/20/36   *Olivet, Mich.*

Mrs. Roosevelt's Party

Your account [May 25] of Mrs. Roosevelt's party for wayward girls is revolting to any woman, but to a Southerner, unthinkable. Surely attention could have been brought to the plight of these young women (I don't call 20-year-olds children!) in a less public manner. A visit to the White House should be preserved as a reward for more worthy groups of young people.

Emily Boothe Radway
6/18/36   *New York City*

Burghley's Run

Were it not for my extreme faith in the Cunard White Star Line, I would have been somewhat bewildered by the statement [June 8] of A. P. Herbert, *Punch's* M.P., that there is a plate on the promenade deck of the *Queen Mary* recording that Lord Burghley ran a circuit of the deck—570 yd.—in 58 seconds, "untrained and unchanged."

The world's record for 440 yd. is 46 plus seconds, and for 100 yd., 9.4 seconds. Let's assume that he ran the first 440 yd. in 46 seconds flat, and the next 100 yd. in an even nine seconds. He would then have covered 540 yd. in 55 seconds, leaving him three seconds to cover the last 30 yd.

But that's only part of the story. Lord Burghley ran in evening clothes. TIME did a sloppy bit of reporting here —neglected to mention whether 1) Tuxedo or formal, 2) stiff or soft bosom shirt, 3) high shoes or dancing pumps

Why not have the 1940 Olympics aboard the *Queen Mary*? The track must be lightning fast, thus enabling the contestants to dress like gentlemen —morning races in morning jackets, afternoon in frock coats and evening events in Tux or tails.

Julian Rice
6/29/36   *Bronxville, N.Y.*
TIME *erred in stating that the* Queen Mary's *promenade deck is 570 yd. around. Cunard White Star figures that approximately four laps around it make a mile. Length of Burghley's 58-sec. run was therefore approximately a quarter-mile, for which the world's indoor record is 49.6 sec. Not only was Lord Burghley handicapped by the sharp turns, but also by full evening dress: tails, stiff shirt, pumps.—*ED.

The Campaign

I am about fed up with all your wisecracks and criticisms of the New Deal and everything pertaining to our beloved President and his humane love of the less fortunate. . . .

What this world needs is less criticism and greed and a little more love for our brother man. . . .

Mtrs. Helen D. Harlow
8/17/36   *New Philadelphia, Ohio*

Reds & Whites

I wish to invite your attention to your inaccurate use of the terms "Red" and "White" when referring to the contestants in the war in Spain.

Those you designate "Reds" are unquestionably the forces of a legal government, as lawfully elected as was President Roosevelt. Those you designate "Whites" are a mixture of renegade officers and, mostly, foreign mercenary troops. . . .

J. R. Henderson
9/28/36   *Lynchburg, Va.*
TIME's *use of the designations "Red"*

*and "White" in the Spanish Civil War refers only to the political philosophy of the contestants, has nothing to do with the legality of each force. A government can be Red (e.g. Russia), Black (e.g. Italy) or Brown (e.g. Germany) and still be legal.—*ED.

LIFE

Received the initial issue of LIFE today. LIFE employs a new and improved style so characteristic of TIME's superb style of reporting. Long Live LIFE!

M. H. Diehl
12/14/36   *Mt. Morris, Ill.*

Family's Feet

Your reporting of political events in Germany during the last months has worked up in me a distinct feeling of animosity toward that nation. It is becoming increasingly difficult for me to maintain that objective point of view that America saw a few years ago to be the only reasonable attitude to assume toward European squabbles.

As a moulder of this country's responsible opinion I believe it is your obligation to remember in writing of the treaty scrapping of Germany, that France and England are merely reaping the rewards of their 1918 greed. After all, the Treaty of Versailles was a shameful document, one which the drafters should be ashamed of.

If the TIME family cannot keep their feet on the ground and remember that there are extenuating circumstances, who can?

J. Otis Laws
12/14/36   *Washington, D.C.*
TIME *deplores any emotional unbalance caused in its family by its reports on Germany, but must continue to make those reports full, frank and factual.—*ED.

Heil Helvetia!

I wish to correct some statements made in the issue of TIME for Dec. 21, under Foreign News regarding Switzerland and the trial of Frankfurter.

In the second to last paragraph you speak as if Switzerland were ruled by Hitler too, and that our Federal Council had to introduce that anti-Communistic bill just to please the "furious Führer" and convince him that we Swiss are "on the right side of the Nordic fence."

It may interest you to know that the same Federal Council also told Germany that they would not tolerate another *Gauleiter* (district leader) of the N.S.D.A.P. to be sent to Switzerland to replace the murdered Gustloff. . . . Furthermore, the court did not sentence Frankfurter to 18 years' imprisonment, "just to appease the Nazis," but because the law of the Canton of Grisons requires a minimum sentence of 15 years, be it for a political murder or not.

Although we speak German in the Northern part of Switzerland, we certainly are not German, but SWISS, just as the French- and Italian-speaking people of Switzerland are also SWISS, and not French or Italian respectively.

Heil Helvetia!

> *Othmar Stäubli*
> 2/8/37   *Horgen-Zürich, Switzerland*

Appalling Bastards

If you cannot refrain from joining the crowd of eternal mudslingers at Germany, you should at least keep decent and take back your statement about the "appalling number of bastards" conceived in Hitler Camps [Feb. 8]. Can you prove it? Then why the slander? If you had lived in Germany in the "Before-Hitler Time" you would look at the Führer's achievement with different eyes—but you seem to think that 66,000,000 Germans are just fools.

> *Hanna Baack*
> 3/8/37   *Sycamore, Ill.*

TIME does not think that 66,000,000 Germans are fools. However, according to the Nation, *recently the German Bureau of Vocational Guidance applied to the National Socialist People's Relief Administration to obtain support for more than 2,000 unmarried girls who had become pregnant on duty with the* Landhilfe *(farm labor brigades).—ED.*

War Guilt

TIME, Feb. 8, speaks on p. 21, third column, erroneously of "the 'war guilt' of Germany as admitted, signed and ratified in the Treaty of Versailles."

There never has been an "admittance."

The theory of the war guilt of Germany was construed by some of the Allied Governments and inserted into the draft of the final peace treaty. The German delegation to the Paris peace conference delivered a substantiated contradiction against that theory on May 29, 1919, duly received by the Allied and Associate Governments and never revoked. Therefore, when the unamended draft was signed June 28, 1919, these Governments were fully conscious of the fact that the German Government held the reverse opinion toward the so-called "war guilt." As a matter of course, no signature obtained by violence from a contracting party can pretend to mean "admittance."

> *Dr. George W. Neumeister*
> 3/22/37   *Berlin*

The clincher which proves that Germany admitted "war guilt" in signing the Treaty of Versailles is that 18 years afterward Adolf Hitler found it necessary to repudiate officially this German admission by renouncing Article 231, Section I, Part VIII of the Treaty which reads:

"The Allied and Associated Governments affirm, and Germany accepts, the responsibility of Germany and her allies for causing all the loss and damage to which the Allied and Associated Governments and their nationals have been subjected as a consequence of the war imposed upon them by the aggression of Germany and her allies."—ED.

Speed-Writers

I was very interested to read in your "Milestones" Department [Feb. 22], the paragraph dealing with the alleged speed-writing contest between the late Samuel Shipman, the Broadway playwright and my old friend the late Edgar Wallace, "ace" story teller and dramatist, whose memory we still mourn here in England.

But are your facts correct? The man who acted as Wallace's secretary for 19 years (the famous "Bob" Curtis), later worked for me. He spent hours yarning about Wallace's phenomenal feats in dictation, but he never told me anything concerning E. W.'s dictating a play in 35 hours. I know for a fact that Wallace dictated his play *The Case of the Frightened Lady* called on Broadway, I believe, *Criminal at Large*, in three bouts of 6 hours each, but *Ocean Liner* is a new one on me.

As you people appear interested in statistics, I may say that the Dictaphone used in "writing" this letter was formerly used by Wallace, who told me that he had poured no less than £80,000-worth of material down its throat. Since I have had it, another £20,000 has been added to the list—half a million dollars in all. Not a bad record, I think?

> *Sydney Horler*
> 4/5/37   *Hythe, Kent*

TIME's statement that Author Wallace dictated Ocean Liner *in 35 hours is well authenticated. Author Sydney Horler's latest published works are* The Hidden Hand, The Lessing Murder Case, The Man With Two Faces.*.—ED.*

Finest

Your story of the Hindenburg disaster, I believe, is the finest piece of work that has been done by your staff since the inception of the magazine. Will you please convey our congratulations to your staff members who did the rewrite on this horrible catastrophe.

> *J. B. Hipple*
> *Business Manager*
> The *Capital Journal*
> 6/7/37   *Pierre, S.D.*

Corking

Congratulations on your corking Hemingway article [Oct. 18]. Just as your exciting color reproductions in LIFE are furthering the cause of modern American art your TIME articles on such great writers as Dos Passos and Hemingway are waking this country to the fact that our contemporary literature is something of which every American can be intensely proud. I hate to quibble, but last time I was in Hemingway's home in Key West I definitely saw three sons. True we had taken on board a quantity of Hemingway's superb Irish whiskey, but surely not enough to render me incapable of

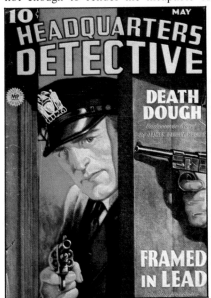

counting up to three.

Irving Stone
10/25/37   *Vannuys, Calif.*
Let Author Stone (Lust for Life) *reread* TIME, *Oct. 18, note that* TIME *gave Ernest Hemingway his full quota of children.—*ED.

"Unwarranted Hopes"

Your account of *Oxford Limited* in the issue of Nov. 15, I fear may arouse unwarranted hopes in those legions of American college playboys whose misled vision may lead them to the halls of this ancient university in search of the Bacchanalian revelry therein depicted. Although my acquaintance with Oxford began only some six weeks ago, my observations to date reveal the following facts in the categories which you have quoted from Keith Briant's book:

Sex: The Oxford undergraduate (horned-rimmed glasses and cotton stockings) has been aptly described by an English journalist as "those English women whose physical attributes are such that their only hope for social recognition is in the development of the brain." They are generally disdained by Oxonians who have to be back in college by 12:00 anyway and who, in comparison with American undergraduates, are comparatively virginal and completely innocent.

Drinking: Oxford undergraduates drink nothing stronger than beer or sherry and a "Freshmen's blind" is like a Sunday school picnic compared with a lively round of football cocktail parties, proms or houseparties in any of the American universities which I have seen. No one would even *consider* drinking at an athletic contest and what drinking occurs is discreetly confined to the privacy of college rooms.

Rowdyism: Guy Fawkes' night has completely flopped as an occasion for Oxford undergraduate rioting and I have seen nothing yet that vaguely approximates a good scrap around the goal posts or inter-class rushes—those great institutions of American college life.

Physical Education: The average of undergraduate participation in athletics is 100% higher under Oxford's college system than under any other system in vogue in the U.S.

Study: Oxford leaves the undergraduate to his own resources but his degree upon graduation is carefully marked first class, second class, etc. in contrast to the average American sheepskin which may envelope not only the sheep but also the goats under the same ambiguity of Latin phraseology.

Having thus performed the most un-American task of defending the English, I will end the day with a spot of exercise, a gobbled dinner and an evening at the movies precisely as I did for four years at Princeton.

Penn T. Kimball
Balliol College
12/20/37   *Oxford, England*

May 1937: in seconds flames destroy the Hindenburg at Lakehurst, New Jersey

TIME would like to hear further from neophyte Oxonian Kimball after he has weathered a few terms.—ED.

Name

As a comparatively new subscriber to TIME and a cover-to-cover enthusiast I am interested in how and why the name TIME was taken for your News magazine. . . .

Steve Woodson
3/28/38 *Shelby, N.C.*
Because the name is brief, pithy, sonorous; because the thing is all-inclusive, essential.—ED.

Alarmist

Thousands of Americans use salt and pepper shakers made in Japan and Germany. Because they are small and because they have a stopper in them, they are hardly ever washed before using. Could it be possible that a coating of poisoning is applied to the inside of these and other dishes made in those countries? Or perhaps disease germs? . . .

Mrs. Pat Morgan
3/28/38 *Bristol, Va.*

Fall of Schuschnigg

In the terse, blunt style that makes TIME such good reading for us who want the story without the feathers, you write the epitaph to another little institution that apparently had to fall in the achievement of the Nazi dream. "Austria is Finished," TIME, March 21, tells all that's important, and it tells it well enough to keep a chap reading.

But of all the ironical covers! A full week after Schuschnigg's fall, and the end of Austria as a sovereign independent State, along comes TIME with Schuschnigg, "The Chancellor of Austria," beaming all over your cover as though he were almost the man of the hour. . . .

John Guild Nesbitt
4/4/38 *Evanston, Ill.*

Kind and Considerate

As your magazine is a responsible publication, I was greatly surprised to find a distorted and entirely false account of my attitude towards Madame Chiang Kai-shek (nee Soong Mei-ling) in your issue of Jan 3.

I feel proud to have as my father's wife, and my stepmother, one who has shown during this national crisis the greatest courage and devotion to my country and my father.

I feel I owe to her, who has always been so kind and considerate, that you should be asked to correct the untrue statements in your article under question.

Chiang Ching-Kuo
Headquarters of the Generalissimo
4/18/38 *Wuchang, China*
To Mr. Chiang, who has a proper filial regard for his stepmother, TIME's sincere apologies for giving credence to a base report.—ED.

Ironic Reader

I have just gotten back to America from Austria in which I lived for the past eleven or twelve years. I was there when Austria was absorbed into the *Dritte Reich*, and when I got here, and read the American newspapers, I was shocked at the undertone of antagonism that seemed to pervade all of them. I want you to known that there was uncheckable enthusiasm along every street that Nazi troops marched through. Of course, it is also true that before the troops ever came across the border, thousands of German spirit-stirrer-uppers, so to speak, had permeated all the strata of Vienna, and, joined by the frenzied local Nazis began whipping the enthusiasm of the people. You can readily gather how enthusiastic the better elements of the city were, when I tell you that not less than 800 individuals committed suicide within a few days, and I don't believe that even half of them were Jews. Others were so overcome with enthusiasm that thousands of them had to go away for complete rests. . . .

E.G.V.
4/25/38 *Temple, Tex.*

Unemployed

Just a few questions regarding TIME of April 18.

Under Fiscal, you mention "after relief rolls climbed from 17,314,000 in January to 18,502,000. . . ." Can those figures be right? I thought there were only some 11,000,000 unemployed in the whole nation. . . .

Thomas B. Smother Jr.
5/2/38 *Fort Hamilton, N.Y.*
Relief rolls include not only unemployed but those who are not able to work.—ED.

"Harpers Ferry to Eagle Pass"

I'm hardly a professional Southerner, but I can't take it lying down, suh. I mean, of course, this damnable reference to Franco as "Spain's R. E. Lee." [May 2]. . . .

You may expect Southern colonels from Harpers Ferry to Eagle Pass to cancel their subscriptions. And if you do it again, I'll have to begin praying over you myself.

Virginius Dabney
Editor, Times-Dispatch
5/16/38 *Richmond, Va.*

Eire

Why do you use Eire [Jan. 31 *et seq.*] instead of Ireland as the heading in the Foreign News Department? Or has the Emerald Isle been rechristened?

Walter Korzow
6/20/38 *Newark, N.J.*
Let Reader Korzow pay attention. The Irish Free State was officially rechristened Eire last December, Northern Ireland and Eire make up Ireland. —ED.

New Deal Defined

Predict TIME will have to add to staff to handle letter deluge that will result from sly Editor's New Deal query . . . [June 20]. Eagerly I await the coming inevitable thousand different attempted definitions of the New Deal.

Ronald Jarrett
Midland, Tex.

The New Deal: Rape with consent.

E. C. Sneed
7/4/38 *Trona, Calif.*

Rooseveltiana

Among the few Rooseveltiana with a grain of truth is a story told of an occurrence at the church in Hyde Park where the President worships. The governors of the church ordered a plaque, stating that it was "The President's Church." Morning after the tablet was erected, passersby were greeted with a legend neatly chalked below it: "Formerly God's."

C. J. Murphy
9/19/38 *Winnetka, Ill.*

Anguished Voice

Generally sharp and penetrating in its analysis, TIME went askew in its appraisal of radio during the war crisis [Oct. 3].

"Touted as an instrument of international harmony," you declare, "radio has a bad record as a peace maker."

If radio did nothing else, in bringing the anguished voice of Chamberlain and the gutteral defiance of Hitler, it drove the point home that war was near, that the world was small, that what broke out in a small speck would in short envelope the entire surface of the earth. . . .

Ed Kirby
Director of Public Relations
National Association of Broadcasters
10/17/38 *Washington, D.C.*
In radio's infancy, many an idealist hoped that with man speaking to man through the air across national boundaries, international harmony might prevail. It has not done so.—ED.

Life-Saver

In his dealings with the Führer, Mr. Chamberlain seems to think that the saving of a million lives was well worth the surrender of England's honor. His conferences with Hitler at Berchtesgaden and Godesberg read like the diary of a young lady crossing the Atlantic for the first time:

Monday—I feel highly honored at being placed at the Captain's table.
Tuesday—I spent the morning on the bridge with the Captain. He seemed to like me.
Wednesday—The Captain made proposals to me unbecoming an officer and a gentleman.
Thursday—The Captain threatened to sink the ship unless I agreed to his proposals.
Friday—I save six hundred lives!

Willis H. Kingsland
11/7/38 *Bantam, Conn.*

Panic

Blame the CBS and Orson Welles for the panic that was created by the radio dramatic program [Nov. 7]? I say no! They should be commended for their realistic presentation.

People who were gullible enough to believe that it is possible for the earth to be invaded by "men from Mars" should be kicking themselves instead. They, who jump at conclusions are simple prey for war propagandists and lead others into spilling of blood.

Let Sunday night's thoughtless reactions be a lesson to all sluggish thinkers.

George Marsch
Akron, Ohio

Reference: first four lines, p. 17, TIME, Oct. 31. ["During the recent Czechoslovak crisis the British people scared worse than any other in Europe, and in the panic atmosphere of London. . . . "].
Who's scared now?

11/21/38
James M. Lee
Gatineau, Que.

stars Shirley Temple and Judy Garland
Two songs of the '30s popularized by child

Pro-Saroyan

I need a small amount of your space in which to reply to TIME's review of my collection of short stories entitled *The Trouble With Tigers* [Nov. 14].

I am a writer, not a playboy, Communist, world-saver, dilettante, or U.S. prophet. Writing is my work. I take pride in this work, and when it is good I am as pleased to say so as TIME, for instance, is pleased in its advertisements to say it is the best magazine of its kind in America. . . .

Your reviewer, whoever he is, is apparently clinging to a theory which is no longer valid for our country. Modesty, in our day, almost invariably accompanies mediocrity, and is usually an inside out variety of immodesty.

If my work does not deserve to be taken seriously, I think it would be interesting to your readers (and especially interesting to me) if TIME would name six American writers of fiction whose work *does* deserve to be taken seriously.

I would be the last person in the world to shout foul-play because TIME appears to be anti-Saroyan. That is a privilege I am delighted to insist on your right to keep. I, in turn, on the other hand, insist that I myself, at least, am privileged to be *pro*-Saroyan. One of us is certainly partly mistaken. If it is myself, time, the element or thing which goes by every day, and not the magazine, will put me in my place.

12/5/38
William Saroyan
San Francisco, Calif.

Hemingway, Faulkner, Dos Passos, Dreiser, Willa Cather, Elizabeth Madox Roberts.—ED.

Symptoms

May I suggest a method by which the American people may express their opinion of the present German Government? Why should not committees be formed in towns to make house-to-house collections of objects made in Germany, which might be destroyed in public bonfires? Almost every house contains some broken toy or picturebook, of no great value to the owner, that would serve as a symbol for this purpose. The collections could be made in a few afternoons, at small expense; and the language of bonfires seems to be the only one that Germans at present understand. If these mass-demonstrations were on a scale sufficiently large, they would suggest that democracy has something to say. The question of an embargo would soon take care of itself if the phrase "Made in Germany" became a general synonym for all that is contemptible and base.

There are millions of good Germans, as everyone knows, and no one, certainly, wishes to hurt their feelings. But some of the best Germans share one trait of the worst—they only accept the word of Germans. The rest of the human race for them consists of four or five billion Jews, who cannot be

expected to do justice to Germans. Only through the pressure of Germans will Germany be changed. This fact may teach a hard lesson, but it is one that will have to be learned. When Germans universally find that the universe detests their masters, and that precisely these masters—no one else—have made life unbearable *for them*, then we may look for a change, and not before. Let the fair play of Americans be trusted to see that the odium falls only upon Germans in high places.

Van Wyck Brooks
12/5/38
Westport, Conn.

Pogroms

There must be thousands of Americans whose free blood boils at the recent German atrocities, who wish they might make their voices heard.

Would these voices not be raised to a clamor hard to ignore if each one wrote his or her protest to Germany? I have today written my protest to Dr. Goebbels, a copy of which is attached if you wish to print it.

Why should not the people set a new precedent and protest directly to a Government? It is our business—it's the duty of anyone who has an ounce of humanity left.

Elinor Ely
London, England.

Much as we may sympathize with the Jews in Germany and deplore the fate that has befallen them, why isn't minding our own business the best thing we can do under the circumstances?

Our own record of treatment of the American Indian is none too sweet.

C. K. Kimball
12/12/38
Los Angeles, Calif.

United States of Africa

Of course I'm dumb, diplomatically and politically! Who isn't? But with all the talk about giving the African colonies back to Germany—or what not—why does no one suggest the obvious solution? *Why not give them all back to the Africans?* Not necessarily to the Negroes, though that might be proper, too; but to the *Africans?*

Because that's what will ultimately have to be done. Neither England, Germany, Italy, nor Belgium can indefinitely hold any part of Africa as colonial exploitation material. Sooner or later there will be either one United States of Africa—as the American Colonies grew to become the United States of America; or there will be several African states, all independent of Europe, as now in South America.

Grace Verne Silver
12/19/38
Los Angeles, Calif.

Man of the Year

We anticipate with dread for its effects the possible selection of Adolf

Hitler as TIME's Man of the Year. The majority of letters nominating him have been wholly condemnatory. If his picture appears on your cover only as TIME's Man of the Year, the controlled press of fascist countries and the uninformed of all nations will hail the selection as an award of merit. We ask that you confirm the trust of the people of the world's greatest democracy by refraining from conveying this title as an honor upon a man who has dominated this year's headlines with his crimes against civilization.

Dr. Bruno Frank
Melvyn Douglas
Harlan Thomson
Frank Tuttle
Groucho Marx
Donald Ogden Stewart
Gale Sondergaard
Boris Morros
1/2/39　　　　*Hollywood, Calif.*

Hitler's *Dummheit*

Herr Hitler is surely in need of a few scholarly advisers to save him from *faux pas* and *Dummheiten* [stupidities]. Unwittingly he has conferred royal titles on every last German Jew by his decree that all males must take the name Israel and all females the name Sarah.

He probably overlooked the fact that "Sarah" means "Princess" and "Israel" means "Prince of God" in Hebrew. But what else could one expect from one of his social background? . . .
James B. Thomas
2/20/39　　　　*Winter Park, Fla.*

Dangerous Campaign

Much of what we Americans in Europe have read recently from American publications about politics leads some of us to suspect that something

Gangsters Bonnie Parker, Clyde Barrow and John Dillinger became criminal legends

has gone wrong with American journalism. . . .

Only a few weeks ago it was common experience to read in American papers verbatim excerpts from specific government-controlled newspapers in Europe. These excerpts were printed without comment. . . .

In contrast with this what have we now? Examine the current January issues of Reader's Digest, TIME, New York *Herald Tribune*—Paris Edition, *The Christian Century*, publications which we believe are effective creators of public opinion at home and abroad. Taken together, do they or do they not leave the impression that American journalism—with one or two notable exceptions—has entered a dangerous campaign of hatred? . . .

Does the American journalist want America to win in a mad armaments race? Fanning to a flame the unholy passions of millions in America against the peoples of two or three other large blocks of earth is one way to bring this about. . . . Does the American journalist want peace? . . .
Benjamin Franklin Steltzfus
The American College
2/27/39　　　*Sofia, Bulgaria*
Come home and see.—ED.

Abstract Period

Your spread of Picasso deserves high praise.

The layout of the color reproductions of his various periods lends weight to a theory of mine: that artists lean to abstract painting when war is in the air. (Picasso's 1914-15 and 1935-36 periods would correspond to the beginning of the World War and to the Civil War in Spain.)

I feel a decided abstract period coming on right now.

Victor De Pauw
3/6/39　　　*New York City*

"Why?"

Why don't you ever say anything positive about Hitler? Is it not great enough a deed to have united, without bloodshed, all the Germans (since Charlemagne thousands of great Germans have fought for the idea in vain), to have saved us from another inflation, to have given work to all our workless?

Why do you kick about our censored press and only print onesided news yourself? . . .

Why do you Americans boycott German goods only because she tries to get rid of the Jews? Even if a few were killed or got put in a concentration camp last November, it is like one to a thousand compared to the killing

---

┌─────────────────────┐
│ **BOUQUETS** │
└─────────────────────┘

Orchids to you for your clear, complete and reverent handling of all the news relevant to the Vatican since the death of His Holiness, Pope Pius XI. I was surprised and pained in reading the last few issues (our last is of March 20) to find no letter commending you on those splendid articles. Where are those who gave you a severe headwashing a few months back over the nickname applied to a certain clerical radiator? Perhaps they unwisely canceled their subscriptions too soon. If not, they should be as ready with praise as they were with hysteric criticism.

TIME comes to us as the result of the kindness of a friend, and it is "the" magazine that all of us missionaries await most eagerly. No other keeps us so well informed on world affairs, and no other gets such a diligent cover-to-cover perusal. The one copy that comes to us weekly is pretty well frayed after the 18 American missionaries in our Vicariate are through.
Rev. Theodoric Kernel, O.F.M.
6/5/39　　*Catholic Mission, Chowtsun, Shantung, China*

. . . Recently I introduced TIME Magazine to the natives of the Soela Island Group Spice Islands, Dutch East Indies. It ran my false teeth a close second for popularity. Dozens of natives came and asked to see me take out my lower partial plate. After three days of this I sprung my copy of TIME on them instead. . . .

Edna Morris Devin
Missionary at large in the Moluccas
7/17/39　　　*Amboina, Ambon, N.E.I.*

Daily Mirror

IT IS PEACE
HITLER ACCEPTS NEW PLAN AND WITHDRAWS ULTIMATUM

IT IS PEACE. AT MUNICH LATE LAST NIGHT HERR HITLER ACCEPTED A SETTLEMENT OF THE CZECH CRISIS SUBSTANTIALLY ON THE BASIS OF THE ORIGINAL PLAN SUBMITTED TO HIM BY MR. CHAMBERLAIN.

The German ultimatum demanding the handing over of the Sudeten lands on October 1 has been modified as has Hitler's famous memorandum of Godesberg.

BRITAIN MUST STILL BE STRONG

U.S. VISITORS TO STAY

THE UNION JACK WAVING OVER HERR HITLER AS HE LEFT THE CONFERENCE HOUSE YESTERDAY

Following their meeting in Munich in 1938, Prime Minister Chamberlain tells the world that Hitler wants "Peace for our time."

of nuns and priests in Soviet Spain, like one to a million compared to Russia.

Why do you make fun of us because we try to step up production of eggs per hen or milk per cow? We have to, unless we want to make debts—and is it not more honorable for a poor man to work hard and to be saving, rather than borrow from his neighbors?

Why don't you try to be just?

I am disgusted at your onesided reports about underground outcroppings, rebellious laborers, etc., and never about the 98% of men and women that are *for* Hitler! He did more for us than Washington did for America and we love him for it.

E. Schöttle
Brannenburg am Inn,
3/20/39   Germany.
No one denies that Hitler has bought many fine things for Germany. But at what a price!.—ED.

Ides of March

As a most pleasant and amusing conclusion of this beautiful early spring Sunday, March 5, I happened to read your article entitled "Ides of March" [Feb. 27].

On the above dangerous date I drove to Potsdam. The sun was shining and thousands of "civil transport vehicles" (private cars, trucks and busses) were on the road, filled not with soldiers on their way to the frontier but with peaceful civilians of all ages including those between 25 and 30, enjoying themselves. The only soldiers to be seen were walking with their girls and their families on regular Sunday leave.

It is expecially interesting to read TIME in Europe, for as it arrives about twelve days after having been published, one is in an excellent position to judge how often its prophecies fail to come true. . . .

Herbert Uhl
4/3/39   Berlin Dahlem, Germany

Exasperating, Humiliating

I got into Cristóbal this morning on the 14,000 ton Hamburg-American liner *Caribia* from Curaçao by way of Puerto Colombia and Cartagena. It is one of the most exasperating and humiliating things that can happen to a human being in the world today—to travel on a German ship loaded with Jewish refugees. . . . At first, you find yourself enraged at the Germans for being so inhuman but gradually you take a deeper and more abstract view of the situation and, while you develop a sense of shame for the Germans, you come to suspect that their treatment of the refugees is just another indication of a reappearance in Germany of that peculiar quality which in the end will always bring defeat on the German nation. . . .

The *Caribia* left Hamburg three weeks ago with 400 refugees aboard—first, second and third class. All had to pay their way so the ship cleaned up on passage fare. They were shipped out with $4 apiece spending money when they reached their destination. Most of them were bound for Ecuador and Guatemala and many of them were highly educated, charming ladies and gentlemen. The lines between the Germans and the Jews and between the Germans and all other foreigners on board were drawn long before I got on in Curaçao. By the time I got on, the ship had divided into two groups with the Germans by themselves and all others on board—English, a few Americans, a few Irish, Venezuelans, Colombians, etc., all siding with the Jews. . . .

You should see what effect traveling on a German refugee ship had on the formal English. Within an hour, the English as well as the Jews were telling me about the voyage. Then I began to notice things myself. The Hitlerites did not show up at a gala dance in the saloon while the ship lay in Curaçao

—the Jews were there and the Hitlerites would not appear on the same dance floor. . . . .

The Hitlerites would not swim in the pool with the Jews. . . . The Germans ate their meals in solitary Nordic splendor—all by themselves. . . .

The Germans were angered beyond measure when we went ashore with the Jews at Cartagena and Puerto Colombia. . . .

I never was so glad as I was this morning to put foot on American soil.

Ben Caldwell
4/24/39   Cristóbal, C.Z.

Goldfish

TIME has been April-fooled. The goldfish record of 89, credited to Clark University, is spurious [April 10]. With all due modesty and measure of penitence, I still claim the championship (66 goldfish and 1 polliwog). I hereby retire from competition.

Gordon Southworth
Middlesex University
4/24/39   Waltham, Mass.
Gulper Southworth retired not a moment too soon. Last fortnight Neil Keim, of Wyomissing Polytechnic Institute (Reading, Pa.), swallowed 74 goldfish. University of Arkansas' John Goff bit of a 13-inch king snake's head, swallowed the snake. Oregon's State's Marion Salisbury downed 139 angleworms. Lafayette's Justin Stolitsky ate a copy of The New Yorker *from cover to cover in 25 minutes. Etc. ad nauseam. —ED.*

Juden Raus

In TIME, Jan 30 you described in some detail a new game that was supposed to be very popular in Germany —*Juden Raus* [Out With the Jews].

Out of curiosity, I wrote to a game and book dealer in Leipzig, asking him to send me one of these games. I have just received his reply. He says there is certainly no such game in Germany. He is of the opinion that the information must have been obtained from one of the well-known *Lügenmeldungen* (falsehood-reports) coming out of Germany.

Please advise me where TIME obtained this information, and let me know where one of these games may be procured.

Fred. N. Christensen
5/1/39   Oakland, Calif.
Let Reader Christensen write to Firma Rudolf Fabricius, Neusalza-Spremberg, Sachsen, Germany. The game is German Patent No. 1,446,399.—ED.

Draft Ages

I am certain that many thousands of your readers would be interested in knowing the range of ages which the War Department has made plans to register for draft service in the event of our becoming involved in war in Europe. . . .

It is probable that the War Department has made no official announcement as to the range of ages planned for conscription and therefore you would not be able to give this information officially. However, there must be considerable "grapevine" information on the subject among Army officers, etc. . .

A. P. Curtis
5/1/39   *Augusta, Ga.*
TIME's grapevine information on U.S. draft ages in the event of war; 1st call, 21-30; 2nd, 18-21; 3rd, 18-45 (everybody).—ED.

Deplorable Alliance

When all arguments for and against various attempts at neutrality legislation are set aside, the unobscured fact remains that our great and not-always-so-good country is supplying the Japanese military machine with well over 50% of its war materials.

A further fact is that the American citizen does not like this. . . . Is it not utterly ridiculous to consider any type of legislation whatsoever which will allow this deplorable alliance with Japan to continue? Why do not the Senate Foreign Relations Committee and the House Foreign Affairs Committe make short work of each and every proposal which does not have the mechanism TO STOP THIS COUNTRY FROM ARMING JAPAN? . . .

Despite public statements to the fact that we are no longer shipping bombing planes to Japan, informed persons know that other types of planes can be shipped, that airplane parts cross the Pacific, that the high octane gasolene which powers Japan's military planes comes exclusively from our country.

And down below Japan's fleets of bombers, American surgeons, supported by countless church missionary suppers, labor night and day removing the schrapnel which crashes into Chinese flesh almost directly from our own scrap-iron heaps. Their medical supplies diminish as Japan announces that these materials will no longer be admitted. . . .

Why do not the American people deluge such persons as Senators Nye and Borah with letters pleading that we take ourselves out of this unspeakable business? Why do we not keep our Congressmen awake nights by the continuous earnestness of our appeal?

L. R. Severinghaus
Department of English
Haverford School
5/29/39   *Haverford, Pa.*

Dead-Earnest

I feel I must write you how we, in Germany, feel about our Führer's reply to Roosevelt.

As it was done all over the Reich, the whole plant had laid down work and gathered at the radio at 12 o'clock noon.

Heavily interested, the workmen and employers and directors sat together and listened dead-earnest to the Führer's report. Then when Roosevelt was addressed, the men started smiling and finally I could not see any but grinning faces.

General impression: Roosevelt got much, but even deserves more of a stern rebuke and lesson. He had better take up more geography and history.

Comment by one janitor of the mill: "If I were Roosevelt, I'd bury myself after this right now."

As for myself, I feel ashamed for the American people to have been brought into this trouble by a too-ambitious President, and only hope that he'll mind his own business from now on. I wished your press was really "free" and not only in an anti-German way, so that the American people could read the unchanged Führer's speech, and in full, in which, I am sure, we would come to a better understanding.

Fritz Fessmann
5/29/39   *Bamberg, Germany*

German Royalties

In your issue of April 24, in which you quote German sales of *Gone With the Wind* as having reached the figure of 134,000 copies, which figure is correct, you also say "Her German publishers send Margaret Mitchell regular royalty statements but pay her no cash."

I wish to point out that the second part of this statement is erroneous and I do not know what authority you have for making this statement. Germany, together with Hungary and one or two other European Continental countries, is not able to pay royalties to her foreign authors *punctually* because of lack of foreign exchange, not for lack of good will.

I would point out that for the majority of the American authors for whose books I have received contracts from Germany in the past three years, royalties on their works are entirely paid up. In the case of *Gone With the Wind*, we have received several payments, but due to unusually large sums accrued for its sales over a short period, there are still royalties outstanding. I have no doubt that all of these royalties will be paid in due course.

Marian Saunders
Agent for Margaret Mitchell
6/12/39   *New York City*
The situation on German royalties is complicated, confused. Author Mitchell is lucky. Other U.S. authors (notably the late Thomas Wolfe) have had to go to Germany to spend their royalties. —ED.

Master Stroke

Soviet diplomacy, as demonstrated at the pact negotiations in Moscow, is today the smartest in the world. By one master stroke, Stalin became lord of Europe. Whether through mistake or necessity, Hitler entrusted the destiny of the Reich to the care of the Secretary of the Communist Party, who, with some of the neatest footwork on record, simultaneously avoided becoming a war tool of the British; usurped Hitler's dominance of Central Europe; partly destroyed his Axis (by Munich-ing the Japanese).

And now Comrade Stalin sits quietly waiting for his inning in history, content that Adolf and Germany and Fascism were Waterlooed in Moscow in A.D. 1939.

Allan Ledwith
9/11/39   *New Haven, Conn.*

Exotropic Kennedy

Before the bold Irish mug of the Ambassador to Great Britain appears again on TIME's cover [Sept. 18] or before he runs for President, I hope Kathleen or her handsome mother can do something about those horn-rimmed glasses he affects.

Some Kennedys think themselves wise as owls. Joe must want to look like one.

Richard P. Kennedy
10/2/39   *Edwardsville, Ill.*
Ambassador Kennedy's glasses are no affectation.—ED.

German infantry and tanks head to the front

World War II

World War II began when Nazi planes dropped bombs on Poland in 1939. F.D.R. hoped to keep American soldiers out of the fighting, though the U.S. became "the arsenal of democracy" through Lend-Lease. Japan's attack on Pearl Harbor precipitated American entry into the war. Heads of state, generals, battles—and finally, the Bomb—were crucial topics that concerned TIME and its readers around the world.

Hitler's War

Suggest you name this Hitler's War. Give him his due. . . .

Philip Kind
Jenkintown, Pa.
To give Hitler his due, he did not want this war—he certainly would have preferred another Munich.—ED.

. . . Why call it World War when it isn't quite a European war?

Frank C. Whitmore
9/18/39 *State College, Pa.*
Because every nation is involved economically, most nations are already involved sympathetically and, with the British Empire at war, the sun cannot set on any continent or any sea on which there are no belligerents.—ED.

"Background for War"

Your articles "Background for War" have been carefully read and enjoyed by myself, and have been passed on to men and women from many parts of the British Empire resident in this island. . . .

Marion Moore
9/18/39 *Antigua, B.W.I.*
To Reader Moore has been mailed a reprint of TIME's "Background for War" series. For any TIME subscriber, on request, a free copy is now available. Others may buy copies at newsstands, at 5¢ each.—ED.

War Head

I strenuously object to the head "World War" which TIME is using. Do you imply that you anticipate the breakdown of the present ideal of the great majority of the American people, namely, to keep our country out of this war?

Eleanor M. Hannig
9/25/39 *New York City*

Cowardly Insults

Italy neutral on the spot [Sept. 11] is the most stupid, idiotic and false statement of the Italian Strength, Italy alone is able to beat to a pulp both France and England; 8 millions of the best soldiers in the world, armed with the best and the most modern weapons ever been dreamed, guided by expert and experienced commanders, are more than a match for Marianne and John Bull. Italy is neutral because Germany alone is more than able to administer to the two thieves of Versailles the defeat of their histories. . . .

You, Mr. Editor, are a low down scoundrel, as are all the Jews, you did for years arrogate the right to offend the honor of one of the most noble nation in the world, Italy, the nation which gave the civilization to the whole world; who authorize you to do it? Because you publish a magazine you think you have the right to insulting right and left all the world which are not Jew or British.

In every words of your sheet of Sept. 11 you show your low down hatred for Italy, can you stop this cowardly insults? . . .

Antonio Funari
9/25/39 *Butte, Mont.*
Can Reader Funari?—ED.

Last Frenchman

In a broadcast . . . from Germany, the announcer stated that a fight had occurred in New York City between the crew members of the *Queen Mary* and those of the *Normandie*, because the Frenchmen said words to the effect that "England will fight this war to the last Frenchman." The fight (so the German announcer said) required the intervention of New York City police.

I have seen nothing of this trouble in our newspapers. Did it occur? Did we have a voluntary censorship in this case, or is German propaganda so unbelievably crude as to broadcast domestic items to us which are untrue and which can be easily checked up on?

J. S. Champlin
Lieut. U.S.N.
U.S. Naval Academy
9/25/39 *Annapolis, Md.*
The statement was Göring's [Sept. 18], the broadcast propaganda.—ED.

Bright Light

History repeats itself—in reverse!

It is an intriguing commentary on the Life of the Lone Eagle that the "Keep America out of War" issue which spelled death for the political career of the elder Lindbergh, marks the birth of political life for the younger.

Colonel Charles A. Lindbergh's clear call to a path of Americanism in a world of hatred marks him as the brightest light on the American political horizon. . . .

I should like to be among the first to plug Lindbergh for President in 1940; perhaps on a no-party platform of pure Americanism through this period of international stress.

Charles F. McReynolds
President
Licensed Airmen of America
10/9/39 *Los Angeles, Calif.*

Women in War

In your issue of Oct. 23 you say that TIME welcomes letters from the war zone.

The attached, received a few days ago is, to me, a good example of what

---

BOUQUETS

I am an A.A. gunner in the Royal Regiment of Artillery (Territorial Army) now serving in the west of England, and have been for several years past an enthusiastic reader of your most interesting journal. . . .

It may interest you to know how I receive your magazine. A friend of my mother's in Canada sends it to her, and I may add that every copy has come through safely since the beginning of the war, despite the efforts of the U-boats and long-range bombers. My mother, father and sister read it from cover to cover, it is then sent to me, and after I have finished with it, my friends in the Battery all devour it eagerly. It is then passed on to the Red Cross Society, so you see this copy has a particularly large circulation.

Robert A. Page
4/14/41 *Gunner, Somewhere in England*

has come to be known as the British sense of humor.

Arthur Goodfriend
New York City

11/13/39

Dear - - - -

I am so very sorry I haven't written to you sooner. You must think it very ungracious of me, but we've had a lot of war about for the time of year, which has kept us busy. . . . I leapt into my country's breach wearing a tin helmet, dungarees and a lace brassiere.

I am now an ambulance driver! In other words, I rattle round pitch dark streets in a three-ton furniture pantechnicon. God help my poor bloody patients. I bet I cause more casualties than I succour.

We haven't been bombed by any Germans yet, but are waging relentless warfare against Air Raid Wardens, who come round at all hours of the night banging on the door and shouting that they can see a crack of light through one of our windows. The dog has gallantly bitten two of them, but they have retaliated by reporting him to the police. We are thinking of resorting to stink bombs!

We have five people living with us, and are getting our family life organized on a communist basis. Daddy hates every minute of it, but mother has risen to the occasion like an old war horse. After all, she dates from the Franco-Prussian War, so this is nothing new to her. By the way, why isn't America in this scrap? It was Roosevelt who pushed us into it.

I am probably getting married in three weeks' time. With these blackouts one can't go out in the evenings, so matrimony seems the only solution. . . .

I am re-reading Jane Austen's books, which enthrall me. They seem so much more real and important than anything happening at the moment. The only other thing that is nice to remember is that we went to the last of the Beethoven concerts and came home drunk with happiness. No more concerts now. Besides, dammit sir, you can't go listening to German music these days—switch on the Gilbert & Sullivan.

Please write sometime. I need cheering. Tell me that normal life is still going on.

With best love,

L.
Kent, England

Silly Joke

. . . Your alleged wonderful news organization for the war in Europe might impress a few "Innocents" abroad and at home, whilst to those who can compare what is actually happening with what your "war-correspondents" report it is but a silly joke if you pretend to supply reliable information.

I have recently had occasion to advise you to check your turbid sources and I do so again in your interest because your readers are bound to discover sooner or later that your so-called war reports are mostly the product of complete ignorance or unhealthy imagination.

Those reports are either fabricated in your own office as a sorry mixture of stupidity and partiality or have been composed by your correspondents in a more or less intoxicated state with the assistance of European bar-keepers and their doubtful train but certainly not at the front.

It is positively disgraceful to pose as you do, as the purveyor of reliable news and to feed your readers with entirely onesided and generally false information. It is in fact a dirty trick.

If you really wish to keep what you promise, your job would be to let your readers know as well, what official Germany says and what the neutral

Less than a decade after the publication of *Mein Kampf*, Adolf Hitler assumed the title and power of *Der Führer*

June 1940: the Occupation of Paris. German troops march down the Champs Elysées

countries think about British piratical methods ruining their trade and directed as usual against women and children.

If it is compatible with American "neutrality" to supply arms to one of the belligerents only you at least should try to be impartial and strive after truth.

Otherwise you will equally be classified as a follower of purely mercenary instincts or to put it more plainly as a filthy liar.

Otto Schmidt
Adolf Hitlerstrasse 129
Stuttgart-Feuerbach,
4/1/40 *Germany*

War Sentiment

Almost overnight after the invasion of Belgium and Holland, isolationist and pacifist letters practically disappeared from TIME's incoming mail. The following letters are a cross section of recent comment about the U.S. and the war. It shows the emergence of feelings and beliefs that have evidently been long latent and inarticulate, the sharpest apparent change in reader-opinion in TIME's experience.—ED.

Two alternatives face the people of the U.S. in the event that Hitler's drive to the west produces a Nazi victory. Either his influence will invade the Western Hemisphere to such an extent that the U.S.A. will find itself actually fighting the German juggernaut in our own sphere of influence; or, in the effort to discourage his stepping into South America, we will be forced to compete with his armament production.

It would seem that, whether we like Allied policies or not, it is necessary for the U.S. to recognize their stake in an Allied victory. Perhaps if we act promptly—for instance, by supplying Allied air forces with thousands of planes—it will not come to troops. But if we do not help stop the drive now, we shall be fighting Hitler for 20 years.

Cynthia J. Willett
Lincoln, Mass.

. . . The U.S. should do something besides "holler" for peace. Each generation *must* do its share toward continued welfare. . . .

There are too many professional peace-mongers in this country.

Francis D. Chapin
Saco, Me.

. . . For the first time in many years people in this little town are no longer finding arguments for Germany's aggressions. They did it after the invasion of Austria, after Czechoslovakia, after Memel, afer Poland, even after Norway—that is, some of the people. They would say with a shrug of their shoulders: "Well, Britain and France brought it on themselves. That Treaty of Versailles. . . ."

For the first time in many years, that argument is no longer being made. . . . They are saying that if Germany can't beat France and England without raping those little nations, she ought to have the grace to take her licking. . . .

Dan Ross
6/3/40 *Clarksville, Tenn.*

Lindbergh's Foreign Policy

. . . Recently we were edified by hearing Mr. Charles Lindbergh urge us to go to sleep, forget all about danger, and pay no attention to "chatter about invasion."

Few men have ever been honored by any nation as has this man. For years he was almost idolized by the American people. Now he shows his appreciation by doing all in his power to keep this country in its present condition of helplessness. Of late practically all his public utterances have been timed and delivered to give aid and comfort to

potential enemies of this country. . . . Whether he realizes it or not, he is serving Nazi interests well in his endeavors to prevent preparedness and to lull an awakening America to sleep.

President Roosevelt gave a carefully prepared message to the American people concerning real dangers and the necessity of preparing against them. Mr. Lindbergh sees fit to deride this as "chatter." At this very time defenseless cities are being bombed; women, children, and non-combatants are being murdered; freedom, representative government and every human decency are being attacked with the utmost savaagery by the people . . . to whom he is giving the utmost encouragement in America.

Milton F. Hill
Pastor, First Methodist Church
Pecos, Tex.

. . . Since Charles A. Lindbergh's masterful radio speech on Sunday night, it must occur to thousands of people that here is the man for our next President. No one else has given public utterance to such sane and authoritative conclusions about our relation to the European conflict. . . .

Verna L. Schwanke
6/10/40 *Oak Park, Ill.*

War Sentiment

TIME's report [June 3] that isolationist and pacifist letters from readers had suddenly disappeared from its mail, promptly brought back a quota of notes from isolationists voting "Still present!" as well as more letters from anti-isolationists voting "Thumbs down!" Herewith examples of each:

The editor's remark in the current issue of the magazine that TIME's correspondents, almost to a man, favor intervention in the European war roused my determination that TIME should hear from at least one person who does not share these views. . . .

Robert W. Cope
Westtown, Pa.

. . . Youth was the first to follow Fascism in Europe; it may be the last to swallow the empty wind of those who howl for American participation in war. While there's peace, there's hope.

Ruth Firestone ('41)
Vassar College
Poughkeepsie, N.Y.

The apparent majority opinion to the contrary notwithstanding, it is a fact that an isolationist may have ideals too. However . . . in the name of Democracy, let's make the Isolationists junk them and join the loudest camp. . . .

Charles G. Sonnen
6/24/40   *Little Rock, Ark.*

Itching to Go

. . . Whether Henry Ford actually said he could produce a thousand planes a day or not, no one can doubt his ability to do so and no one can doubt that he will produce that many or more when he is called upon. I think he typifies the rugged individualists who brought this country into being in the first place. . . .

Ford is not alone in this category either. I am firmly convinced that there are thousands of big men in this country who are just as true to their ideals and just as staunch in their support of democracy and justice, and I say that the time has not yet come when their ability to produce has been, or can be, equaled.

Furthermore, there are hundreds of thousands, yes, millions, of us in lesser places who hold the same ideals and are willing to fight for them, and who are literally itching for the opportunity to demonstrate to ourselves and to the world our ability and our determination to "produce the goods." . . .

Joe Lyon Jr.
7/8/40   *Los Angeles, Calif.*

War Sentiment

. . . For some 20-odd years my generation (the cannon-fodder of 1940-41) has had preached to it day and night the brutality, the folly, the utter stupidity of war. Also presented to us—in cold, unvarnished logic—was what we got out of the last war: not the preservation of democracy in the world as we so naively hoped, but thousands of maimed bodies and saddened homes, billions in unpaid war debts. . . .

Now in six short weeks . . . we are asked to throw aside everything that for 20 years we believed was true and just and sound concerning war. . . .

If Germany defeats England and attempts to invade the Americas—God forbid—and if we have no other remaining consolation worth having, at least we will know what we are fighting for. We will also know we are not attempting to preserve a mistaken ideal, and above all, we may be spared the ignominy of making the same mistake twice.

Loren Zane Grey*
Zane Grey Inc.
7/22/40   *Altadena, Calif.*
*Son of novelist Zane Grey.—ED.

Barbarism

. . . A press dispatch from Sioux Falls, S. Dak. relates the treatment accorded Hans, an innocent little American dachshund dog by some children, because of the dog being of German descent, or rather because the breed was developed in Germany.

. . . The dachshund was popularized by the American and English people, and regardless of the country of origin of the breed, the treatment of this dog brands the malefactors as un-American, un-Christian and a disgrace to the human race. I am a dachschund owner and I might further state that my dog is a better dog than any of us are men. He has never knowlingly harmed anyone. I can't say that about any person. I trust the owners of Hans have suffi-

German Propaganda Minister Goebbels

cient money to see that he receives the care he needs. . . .

If the dog's sight cannot be restored, it might be possible to restore his faith in human nature. I can't say that about mine. . . .

Alfred J. Dehen
7/22/40   *Springfield, Ill.*

Anti-Nazi Refugees

We are deeply touched by the American offer to look after British children. . . . We have had three extremely generous offers of homes and education for our own younger children, for the period of the war. If we had been still living in London I think I should have accepted, knowing that everything would be done to make them happy; but the strain of separation on children is great, and what they may lose in formal education they will gain in the other kind of education that will come through living in a community where, at last, all must take their share in work and courage for a common end. In the meantime two are still at school in the South; one, just 14, writes from her school: "T. woke me up, shaking and calling in my ear, the beastly sirens were going full blast and they make a vile, almost tangible din. I really was very scared, you see I was half asleep and the flashing torches, the general din and semi-panic was rather horrible. And of course I couldn't find my coat or my gas mask or my shoes, and my knickers jammed in my pyjamas. Eventually we all got down and sat on benches, then everybody lay down on the stone (very cold) floor and wrapped ourselves in bathing wraps. . . . We had two more today, one very short and then a long one. We got quite blasé. . . . We giggled and talked, and it was almost dawn before we got to bed. Nobody came to breakfast before half past nine. Don't for goodness sake get rattled, the staff has been awfully decent and there has been absolutely no panic. They all look absolute screeches, especially the fat ones in tight slacks, and J. getting on her tin hat over her curlers! It has altogether been great fun."

But there are others who need a refuge almost as much as the children, and these are some of our many anti-Nazi refugees. Most of them have suffered already at the hands of the Nazis, all of them have lost their homes; some of them have broken nerves. And a great many of them have had their names down for emigration to America for months, even years. May I appeal, through TIME, to the American people to open the welcoming gates a little wider and let some more of them through? . . .

Naomi Mitchison
8/12/40   *Argyllshire, Scotland*

Foreboding

I have been reading TIME and other U.S. periodicals on the entry of Italy

Jews from the Warsaw Ghetto are rounded up and transported to Nazi death camps

into the war. . . . I confess it gave me a shudder of foreboding regarding my own beloved U.S.

Could it possibly be that she, in the world's eyes, will seem to follow an equally contemptible course?

Fascist Italy believed exactly like Nazi Germany, yet for nine months she sat on the sidelines, while Germany ran the risks, did the fighting and sacrificing, shed the blood. Italy came in so late that to the world it seemed "coming in only at the kill."

America believes exactly the same as Great Britain about Freedom, Justice, Tolerance, Democracy, and about International Gangsterdom. Yet she, too, sits on the sidelines a non-beligerent, reaping where she will not sow, safe behind the protecting British Navy.

. . . Two months have glided by since the Nazi pulverizing of Holland proved that this was no phony European war, but a world threat instead. How much longer will the U.S. bask painlessly in the western sun, while the blood, toil, tears and sweat are borne by the cousins overseas?

"With what judgment ye judge, ye shall be judged."

Marcus A. Spencer
Minister,
St. John's Presbyterian Church,
8/26/40 *Kensington, London*
(An American citizen acting as a voluntary air raid warden in London.)

Bigger Stick

Hitler said to Rauschning: "America is constantly on the verge of revolution. It will not be hard for me to foment trouble and upheavals there. I can occupy the American people sufficiently with their own internal difficulties to keep them from meddling in Europe."

Up to now Hitler has fulfilled almost to the letter everything he said he would accomplish, including "occupying the American people with their own difficulties." We are playing into his hands in a fashion even he probably never expected by our bickerings about our duty to our country. . . . For the next year or so (possibly) it might be easier for our young men to stay at home, many of them on relief, and many of them with nothing better to do than ride around in broken down jalopies to the danger of themselves and everyone on the road. But if Hitler wins this war there won't be time to ask them whether they wish to defend our way of life, and before they have a chance to wake up their days of freedom will be gone forever.

If Hitler wins this war and starts his insidious work in this hemisphere, even if he does not come with an army, he will dominate us just the same and then our young men won't be asked what they are willing to do but they will do what they are told—OR ELSE.

The only way in which we can avoid war, or worse still, loss of freedom, is to have a bigger stick than Hitler and the only way to accomplish this is to have conscription now. . . .

Betty Krause
8/26/40 *Pasadena, Calif.*

Barrier

Defense we must have, but there is no reason for TIME to go as hysterical as the rest of the mob. Someone—and why not TIME?—should point out that we are neither England nor Norway, that even if the Atlantic has been flown over it is still a barrier to conquest, that Sims said he would be happy to defend our shores with a fleet half the size of any attacker, that every single expert knows Japan neither can nor will attack the U.S.

Emil A. Erickson
8/26/40 *Berkeley, Calif.*
TIME quite agrees that there should be no hysteria, but TIME cannot point out that the Atlantic "is still a barrier to conquest." It never has been. In colonial times it was crossed by British and French Armies. In 1814-15 a British expedition took Washington, fought in Louisiana. In 1863 a French Army entered Mexico City, set up an empire. In 1917-18 a U.S. Army crossed the Atlantic in the opposite direction. The only barrier there has ever been in the Atlantic has been a fleet that could control the ocean (and nowadays an adequate air force).—ED.

True Picture

Despite TIME, despite the able work of U.S. newspaper correspondents here, the good people of the United States still do not seem to have a true picture of Britain today.

There has just arrived at my house a parcel from California containing: 2 lb. tea, ½ lb. gelatine, 8 lb. sugar, 2 lb. cocoa, 1 lb. powdered milk, 3 lb. dried fruit.

The cost of these, according to the customs declaration, was $4.88. U.S. postage was $3.32. Customs dues at this end were 4s 3d. So that the senders obviously believe that people over here are hungry. And the senders are well-read people, deeply interested in European affairs.

Here is our position: the 2 oz. per person tea ration is small for some people, and there is talk of its being increased, but we have tea left over; we have sugar to spare, in addition to the extra allowed for jam making; gelatine, cocoa, dried fruit—you can buy as much as you like; and milk—people with children won't buy as much as the Food Ministry want them to have, even at the under-cost price for children.

. . . But I do believe you will be interested in the conditions of an ordinary family.

William J. Britain
9/9/40 *Marlow, Bucks, England*

Best Wishes

Who are these so-called "neutral" military observers who frequently pontificate in your footnotes? Are they the same false prophets and professional propagandists who told the American people that the French Army was the best (sic) in the world and that the Maginot Line was impregnable? Now they tell us that the riff-R.A.F. pilots are superior to the Germans and Italians [Aug. 19]. Whence comes this sudden superiority?

With best wishes for a speedy British defeat! *Gott strafe die schmutzigen Engländer!*

Emil Adlermann
9/9/40 *New York City*
*"Neutral military observers" are soldiers of neutral countries, who sometimes make mistakes but have the benefit of professional knowledge. Is Herr Adlermann a neutral?—*Ed.

Golden Corn

I have been a resident alien in the U.S. for 17 years, and I have seen a number of letters written from England, published in various magazines.

This one from my mother seems to me to be rather more indicative.

My mother is 70 years old and has previously lost two sons in the Army. Now she lives in the Thames Valley, has two more sons in the Army and two in the Royal Navy. This is her latest letter to me.

". . . Thank you for your birthday letter which was dated July 30 and arrived on my birthday by the afternoon post. You have had a heat wave which was passed on to us. I was worried about you. I saw in the papers so many people had passed on with it. We have had a most lovely summer and everything has done so well, the vegs., plums and apples, pears, and I have never seen the corn so golden since the old days at Cuxham. We are still getting TIME but it generally comes three at a time.

"We get German planes over us every night, and we hear bombs and anti-aircraft guns in the distance. We heard this morning that Robin - - - - - is a prisoner in Germany, poor lad.

"You know of course that Government Regulations made your sister leave her editorial job. She now milks her cows and washes her dairy cans, etc. every day, and finds life very dull, I think. The boys are well—Snoops is still in Alexandria, Baba has just sailed under sealed orders. John seems to get a lot of nasty raids on the coast. Jack is having his tonsils out next week.

Irene has eleven chicks and hopes they will lay in the winter. But I believe about six are cocks.

"I hope if the war is over next year that you will come home.

"I wish someone would strangle Lindbergh.

"We are knocking the Germans down like ninepins.

"Much love,

Mother"

Does anyone question British morale?
Lady Mary Cameron
9/30/40 *New York City*

Pro-British, Anti-British

TIME is no longer impartial-free. In my opinion it is pro-Ally, pro-British, pro-war — and has done all it can to panic us into war.

Hence, I will under *no* condition renew my subscription to TIME.

Virgil Malcher
Chicago, Ill.

I have been for many years an interested reader of TIME. I am, however, becoming thoroughly disgusted with [TIME] because of the German propaganda—I can describe it as nothing less—that it is putting out under the guise of World War news.

W. L. Scott
Ottawa, Ont.

May I commend TIME for its masterly summaries of what is going on in Europe. . . . In later years, when history makes its audit your reports will be invaluable.

Daniel Bloomfield
10/14/40 *Boston, Mass.*

"Speak to Us"

I am enclosing herewith a letter which I have received from France. . . . The letter is unsigned for the obvious reason that the writer feared that it might fall into the hands of the Gestapo. . . .*
Monsieur:

This letter will reach you by one route or another, I hope. It is the letter of a woman of France, daughter of a schoolteacher, a schoolteacher herself and mother of a family of university students, students molded in one of the greatest institutions of France. Like so many others, she lives since June 17 in grief and indignation. . . .

The same men who could not or would not forestall anything, assume for themselves with loud drumbeats the honor of restoring France according to new formulas which they apply with the aid of our defeat. . . .

But let us pass on. To this shame is added that of daily hearing the voice of the radio deride the courage, loyalty and dignity of the English in the forefront of the battle, who cover themselves with glory by resisting alone, after so many betrayals. To the insults of wicked Frenchmen, the British answer with words of comfort, and

with acts which rekindle the hope of the other French people of France, of the other French people who are much more numerous than one suspects—all those who listen to the broadcasts of the BBC as if near a wide open window where pure air enters.

We need to hear all these voices so warm, so confident, so familiar. English friends, Frenchmen in England or in the United States, speak to us, keep on speaking to us; we listen with fervor, often with the greatest emotion. Our confidence, our hope in you is enormous. No, France will not die. Help her, we beg you.

It is a woman with white hair who writes to you, one of those teachers who have taught in the villages "hidden in the folds of France" as well as in the fine cities of the plain. Here as there, within these white-washed walls where the noble device of the Republic— *Liberté, Egalité, Fraternité*—imposes itself on the eyes of all as the glorious label of a regime, she teaches moral cleanliness, courage in action, respect for the given word, tolerance. . . . May those who wrought the last hours of our defeat be forever castigated in the history of our country.

Vive le Général de Gaulle, ces officiers, ces soldats qui défendent la France dans le suprême honneur!

Vive la France!

Vive les bons Français!

Merci!
10/28/40
**The signature, omitted by request is that of a distinguished scientist in a distinguished university.—*Ed.

South Belligerent

I was interested in the statement following Mrs. Marie T. Foster's intriguing letter, that "more people in the South want to go to war with Germany than in any other part of the U.S." I had suspected that this might be the case, for it seems very logical that it should be so. (I am only surprised that the percentage [24%] should be as low as it is.) I do not base this opinion on the fact that the South is still more purely Anglo-Saxon than any other part of the country, and would therefore have the strongest emotional impulse to aid Britain.

I suggest that the greater feeling of belligerency in the South springs, perhaps unconsciously, from very practical causes. It is the only part of this country that has experienced invasion within living memory, and it has had bitter proof that the war that is waged on one's own soil is the most costly of all. It is, moreover, the only part of the country that has known what it is to be under a military occupation, and the Germans have given ample proof that they have improved not only on the methods of General Sherman, but also on those of the Reconstructionists.

Marianna Jenkins
11/18/40 *Philadelphia, Pa.*

"I Ask You"

. . . The enclosed copy of a letter from Major Norris Waldron, written from England, may be of interest.

It probably illustrates what the average Canadian youth thinks of the present war and our associations with Great Britain.

H. Alexander MacLennan
11/18/40 *Hamilton, Ont.*

Dear Peter:

. . . I was talking to a London taxi driver a week or so ago. They "keep the score" and . . . they always tell you how many German planes have been brought down so far that day. . . . This particular day sixty-odd had been brought down over the Channel. Said the driver: "Coo, they are going to fill the bloody channel with their planes and the buggers will be able to walk over."

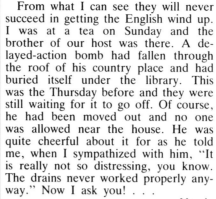

A bombed-out London householder scrambles to reach his clothes still neatly hanging

From what I can see they will never succeed in getting the English wind up. I was at a tea on Sunday and the brother of our host was there. A delayed-action bomb had fallen through the roof of his country place and had buried itself under the library. This was the Thursday before and they were still waiting for it to go off. Of course, he had been moved out and no one was allowed near the house. He was quite cheerful about it for as he told me, when I sympathized with him, "It is really not so distressing, you know. The drains never worked properly anyway." Now I ask you! . . .

Norrie

Interventionist

Should not Americans begin to ask themselves these questions: Whether England wins or not, will it have been enough for the future peace of our consciences that we only formed a safely protected cheering section? And one not quite loud enough to drown out the boos of the Communazis. Will it have been enough that we supplied England with war materials—at a nice profit and at no risk? Will it have been enough that we armed ourselves to the teeth but would not join our fighting might to the mighty fighters of Britain?

For me the answer is: No, it will not have been enough. If England goes down, there will, of course, be nothing but British graves to reproach me. But if she doesn't go down and rises, staggered and decimated, from out her bomb-craters and blood-bath, then there will be English men and women and children to face me. Shall I be able to face them? Again the answer is: No.

Even our isolationists beat their

A life is saved after the London blitz of 1940

breasts when asserting that Hitlerism is their abomination, their mortal enemy too.

If you have a mortal enemy you declare war upon him, nothing more, nothing less. And then you wage it.

Humphrey Cobb
11/25/40 *Pasadena, Calif.*
Interventionist Cobb, unlike many U.S. interventionists, knows at first hand what war is. Born in Italy of Boston parents, he enlisted with the Canadians in World War 1, was twice gassed. He is the author of Paths of Glory *[*TIME, *June 3, 1935*]*, a superb war novel, in which three brave French soldiers were executed for "mutiny" after a sadistic general had ordered a hopeless attack.—ED.*

The Peaceful Irish

Your notes on the Irish ports desired by Britain [Nov. 18] and your curious reference to Mr. de Valera's conscience are based on a misreading of the Irish situation. You say Mr. de Valera in refusing the ports is handcuffed by his Briton-hating colleagues. One could hardly accuse the *Irish Times* of being Briton-hating and yet this paper, consistently friendly to Britain, speaking specifically of the debate on the Irish ports in the British House of Commons, deprecated "the loose talk concerning Ireland which occasionally creeps into the proceedings of the British Parliament," and adds: "The people have endorsed the neutrality pursued by the Irish Government and are prepared to abide by it."

The policy of neutrality is supported by every party in the Dail, by all the people, and by every metropolitan and provincial newspaper in the country. It is based not on hatred of anyone but on a very natural love of Ireland and an equally natural desire to keep war from her shores. It is not denied that cession or lease of the ports to either side would bring war to Ireland.

The Irish didn't fight for over 700 years for their survival as a nation in order now to embark on a policy which would invite annihiliation. Consequently, Mr. de Valera's conscience is clear when he says "the Irish people will defend their rights in regard to these ports against whoever shall attack them."

Your map clearly shows that the Irish ports would be useful to Britain. Could it not also be used to show they would be useful to Germany, and will anyone contend that Germany would be justified in demanding them on the grounds of their usefulness?

Robt. Brennan
Irish Minister to U.S., Irish Legation
12/2/40 *Washington, D.C.*
To His Excellency Minister Brennan, thanks for expounding the feelings of his people. The fact that the conservative Irish Times, *long the upholder of British interests in Eire, is against the leasing of bases to England, lends his contention strong support.—ED.*

Synthetic Peat

As an American of Irish descent, I deplore the lack of logic and realism displayed in the letter of His Excellency the Irish Minister to the U.S. [Dec. 2]. That Irish ports would be useful to Germany is self-evident to average intelligence and if Mr. Brennan supposes Eire's policy of neutrality will prevent Nazis occupying it when and if possible he has quickly forgotten Denmark, Norway, Holland, Belgium. Certainly Germany would not be justified in demanding Irish ports on ground of usefulness, but when has Germany ever felt need for justfiying her grabs except with tongue in cheek? . . . She takes what she wants with no intention of returning the loot if she is victor when hostilities cease. Ireland would have nothing to fear from Britain in like circumstances, as Mr. Brennan and his government well know. . . . If as result of Ireland's stand Britain is overcome by submarine and sea bombing attacks of Nazis, Eire will see how grateful the Nazis will be. Or does the rarefied air of Eire's particular cloud cuckoo land cause her to believe otherwise? . . .

We have long lost patience with the small vociferous group of fanatics and professional Irishmen with the smell of synthetic peat about them who have worked for so long and so viciously against better understanding between this country and Great Britain.

Norman Reilly Raine
Warner Bros. Studios
12/16/40 *Burbank, Calif.*

Wrong Way?

Well, here they go again!

Now they'll be called cowards and clowns, washouts and wops, and a people who love everybody will wind up with the hate and disgust of everyone.

But before this universal razzberry is delivered, may I have my say?

An Italian will fight just as bravely and as honorably as any man who fights for justice. I know this to be true because I am of that blood. I am 22 and await eagerly my draft call to help defend America.

So, for a people who are basically warm, friendly and happy, the philosophy of coldness, hate and destruction is illogical, no matter how good the salesmen of Fascism may be.

If they quit completely in this war, I congratulate them for their intelligence.

The English are cheerful in their fight.

The French are bitter because they are unable to fight.

But those poor Italian dopes are forced to fight and to fight the wrong way.

They are fighting for Hitler and their own enslavement.

They know it, and maybe they're not running the wrong way after all.

Jon Cantelli
12/23/40 *Norristown, Pa.*

British newspapers boost the morale of a war-weary public

V.C.s

In your issue of Nov. 25, I noticed an inaccuracy in your usually precise magazine. You said Flight Lieut. James Brindly Nicolson was the first airman to win the V.C. in this war. Actually he is at least the fifth. . . .

S. M. Johnson
12/23/40 *London, Ont.*
TIME *erred. Lieut. Nicolson was the first fighter pilot, but not the first airman, to get a Victoria Cross in World War II. The first four British airmen who won V.C.s were bomber crewmen: Acting Flight Lieut. Roderick A. Learoyd (attacking a special objective on the Dortmund-Ems canal in the face of heavy point-blank fire); Sergeant Thomas Gray and Flying Officer Donald Edward Garland ("most conspicuous bravery" in wrecking the Albert Canal bridge); Sergeant John Hannah (extinguishing a roaring blaze in a bomber instead of bailing out).—*ED.

Concurrence

The Greeks claimed to have an army of fighters.

The Italians came, they saw, they concurred.

E. M. Munrab
1/6/41 *Boston, Mass.*

Joy in Europe

You may be interested in hearing how the news of President Roosevelt's re-election was received by the citizens of France.

I can best describe the reactions of the people by saying that I—an American citzen, homeward bound, had the impression of being swept along the road between Paris and Lisbon on a wave of enthusiasm and affection—all of which was meant for Mr. Roosevelt. My car bore the insignia of the American Field Service and the American Red Cross; therefore, on November 5 and 6, I became the representative of the American tradition. I took the cheers—I heard the pleas—which tried to ascend the wall of tragic and unnatural silence behind which the French people are imprisoned, which were directed toward the President of the United States—and toward the American nation. The French are enormously grateful to the American people—"for being *chic*, you know, for showing, *et si largement*, to the best man that they knew how to appreciate his merits. . . ." As the French see it, the American people have made a gesture of friendship for France in electing *their* President. their first— and last—friend.

41

Before leaving Paris on the afternoon of November 5, we—my wife and I—stopped to say goodbye to our old friend, the proprietor of the large café in the Place Marceau. We expected to find him rather sad at our departure; but no—he was all smiles: "You will be coming back before long," he said, "and to a happier France! For I have just heard good news, I have just heard a German soldier grumbling: *'Du lieber Gott*, I greatly fear that Roosevelt has been re-elected!' There is a high moral authority in question, you see, which (thank God!) is not powerless against our enemies. . . ." And we observed that the Germans sang less in Paris on that day. . . .

And people talked to us, as if—through us—they hoped to get a message through to the President of the United States. "Tell him not to forget us. . . . Tell him not to lose faith in us. If ever you have the honor of meeting *Monsieur le Président*, will you please try to make him understand that, in spite of all that has happened, France is still the same? We are not a nation of cowards and weaklings. Events are liars—we were not defeated —we were sold, betrayed. . . ."

Spain also had her message: "We are glad of the re-election of Roosevelt," the Spaniards told us. "It will mean a certain restraint on certain people! We do not want war—but we are oxen, with the yoke around our necks—dreading to be led to a second slaughter."

Portugal, too. . . . We drove over the side of a precipice in the fog—only a small rock had saved our car from rolling down the mountainside. In the pitch blackness, a crew of ten workingmen struggled to save our car from destruction, risking their necks on the slippery slope where, at any time, the car might have rolled over on them. Their work triumphantly finished, they refused to accept payment. We do not take money from Red Cross workers, from Americans," their spokesman said, "for the Americans are our friends. We look to them to save *us* from being pushed over a precipice. . . ." And we drove off to heartfelt cries of *"Viva l' America! Viva Roosevelt!"*.

Maurice Barber
American Field Service in France
American Red Cross
1/6/41 *Lisbon, Portugal*

Friday & Saturday

Below is a copy of a letter written by Flying Officer Ralph Hope of the R.A.F. to his father, Mr H. Donald Hope of Birmingham, England. Ralph Hope was flying a Hurricane Fighter during the incidents described in his letter.

It is to be regretted that Flying Officer Hope lost his life about three weeks later during flying operations over East London. Here again his plane was badly shot up but this time was partly controllable. Rather than

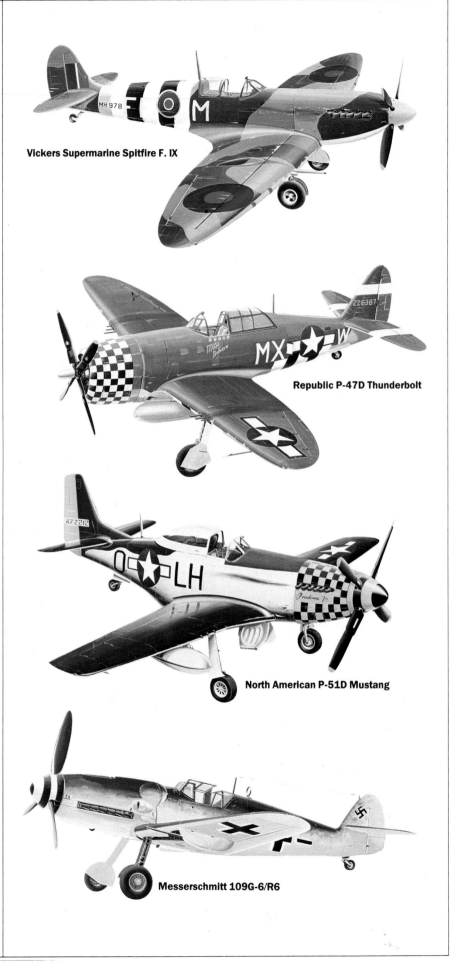

Vickers Supermarine Spitfire F. IX

Republic P-47D Thunderbolt

North American P-51D Mustang

Messerschmitt 109G-6/R6

bail out and allow the airplane to crash and kill residents . . . Hope attempted to maneuver to an open space and lost his life in this heroic undertaking.

He was an Oxford rowing Blue and . . . a nephew of Neville Chamberlain.

Frank Garratt
1/13/41 *Jamestown, N.Y.*

Dear Father:

We had a grand day on Friday with three patrols. On the first we had a glorious dogfight with about nine Messerschmitt 110s which caught a proper pasting. I must admit that they were heavily outnumbered. On the second trip we had an uneventful brush with some Messerschmitt 109s. It was the last trip which was the most fun. About twelve Junkers type 88 bombers came in and, after losing two from anti-aircraft fire, were set on by some Hurricanes. As we climbed up to them we had the pleasure of seeing one dart past us, hotly pursued, large chunks falling off it and the starboard engine on fire. When we were at last in a position to attack there were only seven left, four in front and three behind . . . We had a real field day making attack after attack—a few Me. 109s turned up but did not hinder us. The Ju. 88s went down all over the place. The scrap started at 13,000 ft. and the bombers just pushed their throttles wide open and screamed downhill in a vain attempt to get away. We bagged the lot, the last three coming down in the sea. My ammunition ran out at about 2,000 ft. so I was unable to administer a *coup de grâce*, but it had been a great day.

Saturday was not quite such a success from my point of view, as on our third patrol I lost my aircraft. We were at about 21,000 ft. when we got involved with a squadron of Me. 109s. They got me before I even saw them, which is very annoying. I first felt a kind of funny bump, and as I turned to see what was up, my controls suddenly felt funny, a lot of red sparks and black smoke appeared round my feet and a cloud of white smoke, probably glycol, began streaming back from the engine. The aircraft began going downhill fast. I slid back the hood and began to get out, my goggles were shipped off and my helmet began to lift up in the slip stream; I realized I hadn't undone my straps so I pulled out the retaining pin and stood up, standing on anything which came handy (the seat, the instrument panel or the stick, I don't know really).

The air seized hold of me, there was a wrench as my oxygen tube snapped off (I had forgotten to undo it) and I shot out into the sky. The aeroplane disappeared.

It was nice and cool falling. I was head down, of course, but found the position quite comfortable; there was no sense of speed or feeling of falling.

After a while I thought about pulling the rip cord. "What about giving the old 'brolly' a tryout? I thought. . . . The canopy streamed out, there was a hard jerk, and there I was right side up, quite comfortable and floating slowly, oh! so slowly, earthwards. I was about 9-10,000 ft. so I had fallen free for about 8 or 9,000 ft. (from 18,000 ft.) and might have fallen further with advantage. . . . A Spitfire dived down past me with a high pitched whine, but that was the only disturbance. . . .

The countryside looked pleasantly open, and after drifting quite a way I thought I saw where I should land. Two farm hands had the same idea. We were all wrong as in spite of attempts on my part to avoid it I came down in a spinney of young oak trees, pulling up short about 20 ft. from the ground, hanging in my harness. I managed to get hold of a trunk, pull myself over to it, get out of the parachute harness and climb to the ground where I remained quite still until I was found.

The army soon took charge of me, gave me a drink and some lunch and drove me back to Croydon.

The only damage I sustained was a hefty bruise on my right shoulder from hitting the tail as I jumped, and a bruise on my leg, and a torn trouser.

Now I go about with my arm in a sling, feeling particularly good as I have been given a week sick leave.

Batch of Lies

. . . Hitler, in his fondest dreams, could not hope to reach TIME's audience with his batch of lies that his own people must swallow.

I call the translation of his speech in TIME [Dec. 23] the height of foolish liberality.

Betty Sawyer
1/20/41 *Boston, Mass.*
When Baron Munchausen lies, it is literature; when Chancellor Hitler lies, it is news.—ED.

People Fooled?

This country is preparing not for the possibility of war, but for war itself within a very short time. Every statement out of Washington from official sources has two purposes: 1) to create in the minds of Americans the belief that war is inevitable, and 2) to offend a German Government which, compared to ours, has been neutral in its attitude towards the U.S.

Further, such proposals as lending Great Britain arms and half our navy, making it legal for American ships to convoy British merchantmen, and the declaration of an unlimited national emergency are timeworn steps to war.

This I cannot help but believe the Administration and "all-possible-aid-to-Britain" advocates know. But I submit that the people of the United States are being fooled into thinking these are precautions to keep us out of war. . . .

David P. Ferris
1/20/41 *Clayton, Mo.*

Sleep Killer

I was told that more than a year ago—while I was still in France—your paper published an article . . . with a special description of my anti-Hitler broadcasts over a secret transmitter. You mentioned one of my broadcasts addressed at nighttime to Hitler personally. Because of those nocturnal broadcasts they called me in France, "The man who kills Hitler's sleep. . . ."

I would very much appreciate a copy of the article in which I am mentioned.

Max Ophuels
1/26/41 *Hollywood, Calif.*
To Sleep Killer Ophuels, a cinema director in Germany before he fled that country, a clipping of TIME's June 3, 1940 story, which told how he crooned advice to Hitler on overcoming insomnia, suggested he try counting the number of his victims. "You must have a tranquil conscience," crooned Max Ophuels. "Good night, Adolf Hitler."—ED.

Man of the Year

I think your selection of Winston Churchill as Man of the Year . . . should meet with universal approval. He is, in my humble opinion, the greatest man in the world today. . . .

S. M. Casey
Batesville, Ark.

Your Jan. 6 cover is the most striking ever published by you.

On this grave face is written the sorrow of an empire but also the grim determination and courage to fight through to final victory. . . .

Charlotte Bell Ranger
Attica, N.Y.

. . . If 1940 is to be associated in history with the accomplishments of Mr. Churchill, I'm a one-legged Eskimo.

Never in world history has one man so dominated, so terrorized, so galvanized into action, or inaction, the people of the entire world. The lives and minds of men in faraway Patagonia, in Bengal, in Senegal and in Saskatchewan have been agitated by the moves of Adolf Hitler. His name hung like a pall over the U.S. political and economic scene of the year just closed and yet you say it was Churchill's year. . . .

Lyle R. Fletcher
1/27/41 *Washington, D.C.*

Punch for Punch

The man who wrote of Churchill, Man of the Year, in the Jan. 6 issue of TIME, is also a great master of words. As an Irishman, having long heard that England could fight to the last Irishman, I must now say that it can also fight to the last Englishman. A champion is never an accident—for long—said Frank Moran to me—one of the great bruisers of his era. I fully realize that there are those who say that Churchill represents a dying social system. If that is true, he still knows how to hold his hands up and to face the world throwing punch for punch. . . .

Jim Tully
2/3/41   *Canoga Park, Calif.*

Tough Wordmaster Jim Tully (Beggars of Life, Shanty Irish, Shadows of Men), ex-hobo, ex-roustabout, ex-laborer, ex-prize fighter, should know a fighter when he sees one.—ED.

Impression

I am a British girl of 13. I have been in America for about five months. Recently I was talking with some other British children. Rather naturally the conversation was about America, and Americans. About the impression we have received of the people and their country. I should like you, and all other Americans to know, and I do not think one British evacuee would contradict me. That the impression which will go back to England with us, will not be fair, nor medium, but very good indeed. It will be an impression of some of the kindest, most hospitable and generous people in the world.

Anne Day
2/3/41   *Brookline, Mass.*

Turks in the Wings

In a recent letter I received from my people in the Island of Cyprus, whose population is composed of Greeks and Turks, I am informed that the Turks are very jealous over the publicity that the Greeks are getting in Albania, and that they are dying to get into the war so that they can take the spotlight away from the Greeks.

Like a ham actor whose greatest thrill in life is to be on the stage, even if he is there just to hold a spear, the Turkish soldier is anxiously waiting for that day to act.

If you think that the Greek soldier is a fighter, wait until you see the Turk.

Paul Ralli
2/3/41   *Las Vegas, Nev.*

Back to Birmingham

German bombings may leave the good people of Birmingham, England comparatively unmoved, but if there is one thing that brings out a cold rage . . . it is having their first-class football team, Aston Villa, claimed by Liverpool, as in your issue of Jan. 13.

P. Whetham
2/10/41   *Vancouver, B.C.*

Deluged by dozens of protests in addition to Reader Whetham's, TIME hastily restores Aston Villa (soccer) to Birmingham where it belongs.—ED.

Utopia in Arkansas

Here is a letter from my recently mobilized "little" brother [Staff Sergeant Lysle I. Abbott, at Camp Joseph T. Robinson, Little Rock, Ark.]. He is 22 years old; graduated from college last year and intends to resume his education in law after his military service is completed. . . .

Mildred Findley
2/10/41   *New York City*

. . . These tents we are living in are not tents at all, but rather cabins. Canvas they do have, but the board floors, over cement blocks, plus clapboard siding, coupled with the glass doors and gas stoves, make for real convenience. However, that wasn't enough. No, the Army has to pass out spring beds, with brand-new mattresses. Still not enough; new mattress covers, great big pillows, also new pillow slips, sheets, and new blankets.

We have electric lights, thus we are fully enabled to enjoy life to radio music. Our requisition was completed today, so tomorrow we will draw our new uniforms, which include, among other things, underwear, two, both cotton and wool longies, sox, overshoes, and even wrist watches, for four of us.

Caroline should see these kitchens. Four gas ranges (all this gas for hot water and cooking and heating is natural gas), two ice-boxes that would fill our whole kitchen . . . brand-new, white-enameled.

Right across the street is the canteen, in which we can buy anything we want. Next door to that is the recreation hall, which is the nuts. Stage and movie projectors. About a half mile down the line is a swimming pool, just built, which could easily contain four Peony Parks.

When we arrived Monday, after a swell train ride, in our drawing room, workmen were still working. In fact there were 5,000 of them, who come every morning still. They are painting and plumbing as if their hearts would break. . . .

When mess call blows, we stroll into the mess hall, sit down and eat like pigs. Talk about service—we are waited on by K.P.'s Dishes of food are on the tables. We'd die if we had to wash our own mess kits. In fact we don't even have mess kits, all we have to do is eat. The plates, hotel china, are washed by cooks in the automatic dishwashers. . . . Honestly one cannot possibly exaggerate the utter comfort we have.

I can't help but feel the President has something to do about this. Really I believe it would take a man of his position to see we are getting such wonderful attention. . . .

Bombs on Düsseldorf

. . . I got in an indirect way a letter from my home town in Germany. . . . I give you the letter, which was written on Dec. 28, 1940, in my own very textual translation:

"The nights were unquiet. Up to this moment we had 160 aviation alarms here in Düsseldorf. Realize how that spoils your nerves. The two alarms at the beginning of this month were especially hideous. The industries situated on the right side of the railroad have suffered especially, likewise the Graf Adolf Strasse. Part of this street [one of the main streets in Düsseldorf] looks really devastated. In the Altstadt [old part of the city centre] too you find sad corners. A few thousand fire bombs have come down. The most terrible thing is the shooting. Often it lasts for three hours without any interruption. Soldiers who have participated in the French offensive say that it was not so bad at the front. It is difficult to learn how much industry has suffered as this is kept in great secret. . . .

"The frame of mind [*Stimmung*] was naturally sky-high during the summer. Everywhere one could hear the stereotype phrase: In three weeks the war is finished. In the meantime that has changed and the frame of mind is going downwards strongly. All people are more than nervous."

2/24/41   *Name withheld by request*

Past Performance

. . . Now that [Hitler] says straight out that he has no evil intentions or territorial ambitions on our side of the Atlantic, are we not justified, in view of past performance, in considering this a declaration of war?

Alfred Willoughby
2/24/41   *New York City*

A soldier says good-bye to his family

The U.S. and the War

. . . I hate war! And I cannot see sending the boys with whom I have grown up through a depression that in itself was one of the most defeating periods in history in which to reach maturity now giving anything they have managed to achieve to the hollow word, "Freedom." But more and more I am feeling like a lonely voice crying against something so big that the futility of struggle is totally accentuated by a maze of knitting needles for the British and pennies for the Greeks.

Mary Rohrbaugh
3/10/41   *Youngstown, Ohio*

Cripple and Lunatic

You state as rumor . . . that a large number of cripples and lunatics are being slaughtered by the German State [Feb. 3]. Be it fact or fiction, here's hoping they don't overlook Goebbels and Hitler!

Tom Hamilton
3/10/41   *Altus, Okla.*

The Thin Man

You undoubtedly receive altogether too many letters and descriptions of episodes in England to reprint in TIME, but I doubt if you have received one that can match the enclosed, which is a true description of business under difficulties, as written to me by my good friend, Philip Buck, of Woldingham, Surrey, England.

Ernest Dudley Chase
3/24/41   *Boston, Mass.*

He is a pale thin man who calls regularly each week to pick up small printing orders. He had a small plant in a basement in the City, where he had three letter-press machines for printing headings and circulars. . . . When war broke out he joined the Fire Service as a volunteer for service after business hours, for which of course he receives no remuneration. Business became very bad, and the worry of trying to make ends meet plus all-night work fighting fires made him thinner and paler than before. He managed to pick up a few jobs which enabled him to keep the plant going although he told me that his average earnings for many weeks amounted to three shillings (60c). One morning he called to tell us that he had arrived at his plant to find two feet of water there, a building near by having been set ablaze during the night. . . . For a week he cleaned up the place, salvaged what stock he could and cleaned the rust off his machines; then he was back looking for business. We were glad to be able to give him some small jobs, and off he went quite happy, although the profit from our orders would not keep his family for one week. Two weeks later, in the great City fire raid, his building disappeared and with it his machines, stock and records—and our jobs as well.

King George VI and Queen Elizabeth inspect German bomb damage at Buckingham Palace

The home of three London children is completely destroyed

He is back again looking for business; he has borrowed some money and has started up again in another basement. Round the streets he walks all day picking up what scraps of work he can. He cheerfully says, "I am now in a position to give you excellent service"—a true optimist meeting business under difficulties.

Thousands of Fellows

There are thousands of fellows like me. They left school in the early '30s. A lot of them, like myself, couldn't finish college because of the depression. We couldn't get a job at that time because there weren't any . . . and if there were, older and more experienced men got them. However, we kept looking until we got something—anything. A lot of us offered to work for nothing, like I did, to get started. . . .

Anyway, we worked hard as hell to keep our jobs . . . harder still to climb the ladder. Today a lot of us have advanced and are getting along pretty well, considering everything. A lot of us, like myself, are making between $2,000 and $4,000 a year.

Then came the draft! A lot of us were called. Frankly, we weren't enthusiastic about going, but we're patriotic Americans and we went . . . and smiled while we did it, too. Our $2,000 to $4,000 a year dwindled to $21 a month—$252 a year, but we're still not kicking.

Now the newspapers tell us that because a few of the boys working for some of the steel companies want a 5c or 10c raise, and/or A.F. of L. doesn't like C.I.O., they declare a strike, tie up production for national defense and crack a lot of heads to prove that they mean to get what they're after . . . or else.

Yep . . . there are thousands of us who have worked like hell since '31 and '32 trying to lick a depression, get experience, get established, to climb the ladder . . . yet we gladly chuck it

all to serve our country. Now, some of the boys are declaring strikes over petty arguments or small wage increases and in so doing bottleneck industry which makes possible a well-equipped Army.

We haven't got the answer. . . .

Robert F. Kemper
4/14/41 *St. Louis, Mo.*

"Oh, To Be in England"

I wonder if you have yet heard the story about the English schoolteacher who was testing the children on English poetry.

One of the questions was: Who was it who said, "Oh, to be in England? A small cockney voice piped up: " 'itler said it."

Of course TIME knows but possibly some of its readers may not recognize the quotation as the first line of Robert Browning's poem, *Home-Thoughts From Abroad*. . . .

Jennie Coe Moore
4/21/41 *St. Petersburg, Fla.*

Shipping Losses

Britain's shipping losses are becoming daily more alarming. Obviously, something must be done about it—and quickly. While we are wasting precious hours bickering about the use of American convoys for supplies to Britain, Hitler is overrunning a few more innocent democracies.

Since we have committed ourselves

to the task of aiding Britain, we must fulfill our obligation. Churchill said: "Give us the tools and we will finish the job." It is important to furnish those tools, but it is even more important to deliver them where they are needed. It now becomes apparent that the only way this can be done is by using American convoys. . . .

Marcelle Radgesky
5/5/41 *New York City*

Paradox

It is quite surprising to this reader that Germany has a contraceptive factory at all, let alone Fromm's big one mentioned under "capitalism in Germany" [April 7].

Could you give me additional information about this paradox of a big contraceptive plant in a country whose leaders preach fertility? . . .

Private William Heimer
Mitchell Field
5/19/41 *Long Island, N.Y.*
Inquiry by TIME *through a maze of German Government bureaus, divisions and departments has failed to disclose any Nazi decree against sale of contraceptives. However, contraceptive equipment used by women is not manufactured and has vanished from drugstores and doctors' cabinets. Fromm's product, a common article used by men, although doubtless much employed as a contraceptive, is considered primarily an anti-venereal prophylactic*

and so is heartily approved of by the health-conscious Nazis. This product is on sale in every drugstore, in many hotel washrooms and nightclubs. Great quantities have been shipped to France for occupation troops, among whom the demand is so heavy that French supplies have also been drawn on.

Though birth control for sound German women with sound German mates is strongly discouraged, the Reich approves of contraceptive measures for German soldiers mating with women of "inferior" (i.e., other) races.—ED.

Adolf Schickelgruber

I'm in favor of returning Adolf Hitler to his proper handle, Adolf Schickelgruber. I think it would do a great deal, psychologically, to promote his bursting a blood vessel. Mr Schickelgruber, reputedly a man whose inspirations are born of his emotions, might even be prodded to stick his neck out prematurely and thereby advance the conclusion of the current world inferno. "Heil Schickelgruber" certainly has a more deflating, if prolonged, sound than "Heil Hitler," and I venture it would mess up the little man's digestive processes no little. . . .

Harry Dutton
5/19/41 *Los Angeles, Calif.*
Alois Schickelgruber, Adolf's father, changed his name to Hitler eleven years before Adolf was born.—ED.

Fighting Formula

Can an America of cocktails, cigarettes, wisecracks and sex—so well typified by your magazine and its advertisements—stop the Hitler military machine? . . .

Howard W. Anderson
5/26/41 *Grand Rapids, Minn.*
The A.E.F., which fought very creditably in World War I, liked cocktails, cigarets, wisecracks and sex.—ED.

Wodehouse in Prison

Is there any possible way I could send a letter to Mr. P. G. Wodehouse?

Before his capture, I enjoyed a very pleasant correspondence with Mr. Wodehouse. In his last letter, written to me, which was mailed shortly before the Germans seized him, Mr. Wodehouse informed me that he was sure the Germans would not penetrate Le Touquet. . . .

E. W. Flaccus
6/9/41 *Tucson, Ariz.*
Author Wodehouse is in prison at Tost, Upper Silesia, and mail should reach him if addressed to
Gefangenennummer: 796
Lager-Bezeichnung: Offag VIII D
Deutschland (Allemagne)
Last January TIME's *Berlin correspondent, accompanied by German officials, visited Wodehouse in prison, took him pipe tobacco, a pipe, cigar-*

ettes, candy, soap, mystery books. They found him well fed ("bloated" was his word), having received Red Cross parcels and cheese, butter and jam from Denmark. He had "a sort of private room" in a house at one end of the camp where he was writing a serial for the Saturday Evening Post *which he has tentatively titled* Money in the Bank. *His main worry was that he had not paid his U.S. income taxes. When he was told that Ernest Hemingway had a new book out about the Spanish Civil War, he observed scornfully: "I can't imagine a duller subject."—ED.*

Broadcast

Extract from a broadcast by Adolf Hitler from South America, Christmas, 1943.

My beloved Sheep:

It is with the greatest pleasure that I address you today from our newly-organized countries. As you know, only the U.S.A. is so obstinate as to remain unfriendly to us, but our bloodless victory will soon be complete there, also.

You remember how my great heart was troubled in 1940-41 by their obstinacy, which might have been a menace to our world peace aims. Happily all danger is now over. They have defeated themselves by strikes, by criticism of their President, and above all, by their glorious hatred of what was once known as Great Britain.

To celebrate the end of their childish resistance I now decree that the Fourth of July, known to them as Independence Day, shall be known henceforth as "Laugh at America Day." Let 24 hours of continuous laughter at their stupidity ring through our New World on that date. I myself shall be on the air in New York to lead you in that great laugh chorus.

I also decree that, from now on, the 25th of December, formerly called Christmas, shall be celebrated as my birthday, Hitler Day: or, if you insist on the affectionate diminutive, *Dölfchen* Day. This will remove the Jewish taint, once and for all, from that holiday.

Kathleen Howard
6/30/41   *Hollywood, Calif.*

Four-Word Encyclopedia

Your heading "War of the Dinosaurs" for your June 30 story on the Commu-Nazi war was a four-word encyclopedia of rebuke for the Anne Lindbergh Wave-of-the-Future group. I don't know when I've seen four words that said so much. . . .

Nash Burger
Jackson, Miss.

The latest round-about-face of Herr Hitler is added proof that dealing with him is to be dealt with double, riding along with him is to be taken for a ride, and executing any treaties with him is merely a prelude to ultimate execution.

Max Swift
7/21/41   *Bloomfield, N.J.*

Wodehouse in the Groove

In the July 14 issue we read (under Radio) more about P. G. Wodehouse and his broadcasts from Germany. I am prompted to say that on the evening of July 1, while "fishing around" in the short-wave band, I picked up "Berlin calling—" and it was announced that Mr. Wodehouse was about to broadcast. Upon listening to the broadcast as it progressed, my wife, two guests and I were startled to hear the speaker repeat himself not once, but twice, three, four, five times—"and let us have—" "and let us have—" "and let us have—" "and let us have—." In a moment there was a telling "click" as the dissertation continued. According to the announcer, the speaker was Wodehouse in person. Was his face red when, in order to get Wodehouse "out of the groove," he had to move the needle along on the recording? I doubt it.

Perhaps his hosts do not yet consider Mr. Wodehouse sufficently trustworthy to broadcast in person, for fear of being duped by some twist of phrase or inflection. . . .

Parker F. Soule Jr.
8/11/41   *Hanover, N.H.*

Hollywood for Army

I was very interested to read the story in this week's TIME on the War Department Training Films. . . .

While the particular films shown at the recent preview in Washington happened to have been produced by the studios indicated in your story, it is of importance that *all* studios in Hollywood are producing Army Training Films for the War Department on a *non-profit basis*, under my supervision.

To quote from a booklet recently issued in Washington by the War Department:

". . . No studio is charging overhead for films produced in their stages. All equipment and facilities used in the production of these films are made available without any charge. . . . individuals in the industry are contributing . . . their time and talents to assist in the production of Training Films without cost to the Government. The only expenditures involved in the production of these films is money actually paid out for labor, film and other 'out-of-pocket' expenses."

Darryl F. Zanuck
Chairman, Research Council
Academy of Motion Picture Arts
& Sciences
10/13/41   *Hollywood, Calif.*

Posters encouraging American citizens to enlist were common sights throughout the United States

December 7, 1941: the Japanese attack Pearl Harbor; the war in the Pacific has begun

High Hitler

When war with Great Britain started, Herr Hitler made an impassioned speech. He declared he would put on his Army uniform and wear it until he won this war.

That was over two years ago and the war is still going on so he must be still wearing the same uniform. It might be for that reason he ranks so high and for the same reason his friends are leaving him.

Emily H. Rowland
11/10/41 *New York City*

No More Defense!

TIME's mail last week brought the first intense reactions of readers to the war. A few examples, not necessarily typical, are printed below:

Defense! Defense! Defense! Red-blooded Americans are fed up with the word and its implication of pusillanimity Shades of our revolutionary forefathers! . . .

Let's go! No more defense, please.
H. L. Gueydan
Barksdale Field, La.

The suddenness of this whole thing makes it almost inconceivable. . . .

This is ironically illustrated by what happened at the local Army camp on the lake front. As the radio flashed that Pearl Harbor was being attacked by the Japanese, cracked one soldier: "Orson Welles is drunk again."
Byron L. Levy
12/22/41 *New Orleans, La.*

U.S. at War

Congratulations on "U.S. at War," your issue of Dec. 15. This is the finest piece of news reporting that I have ever read.
Ralph P. Bell
Dir. Gen. of Aircraft Production
Ottawa, Ont.

Congratulations on·a magnificent job in including all news up through Monday the 8th in the issue of TIME that I received and read on the 10th.

Being familiar with what had to be done, mechanically and physically, to accomplish this, I salaam in amazement to your organization. It represents a feat I would have considered absolutely impossible.

TIME is wonderful.
L. D. Rambeau
White Marsh, Md.

Heartiest congratulations on your issue of Dec. 15, giving a fuller story of the outbreak of war than I thought possible. You had much to work with and little time to work in, but it seemed to me that the story gave as comprehensive and accurate a picture as can be found in these days. . . .
L. Bartine Sherman
Princeton Broadcasting Service
Princeton, N.J.

Congratulations on the most masterly example of precise journalism I ever have seen. . . . Breaking when it did, the war must have necessitated the rewriting of every story in most depart-

ments. As a newspaperman I can appreciate what TIME's staff was up against and how well organized your office must be to turn out such a comprehensive survey of the situation in so short a time. . . .
Carlton J. Shamo
The South Bend Tribune
12/29/41 *South Bend, Ind.*

TIME's *publisher can respond with thanks to these bouquets and others, where modesty might hobble* TIME's *Editors.* TIME's *editorial staff had about 36 hours to write its first issue about the U.S. at war.* TIME *correspondents within eight hours after war's outbreak turned in a nationwide roundup of U.S. reactions and thereafter kept it up to date hour by hour.* TIME's *printers accomplished a notable mechanical job in printing a four-colour cover of Admiral Kimmel (over a million copies) after the war broke. Only way it was possible to deliver* TIME *on schedule in the East was to charter two transport planes to ferry 300,000 copies of the cover (five tons) from Chicago to Philadelphia.—Publisher.*

Excitement

Hell broke loose over WSOY on this unusual Sunday afternoon . . . after the Kings Gospel Quartet had finished singing in our big studio.

Solid, red-faced Charlie Bruce was in the control room running a transcription of Chuck Foster and his orchestra while I sat quietly in the adjoining studio wondering how I would announce the next tune. We were in the middle of *Blue Champagne* when Bob Bruner, hat & coat on, dashed into the control room, waving a foot-long strip of teletype paper. Before I could get out of my chair, Charlie Bruce had pulled the control-room mike in front of him and had shut *Blue Champagne* off the air. Startled at such unusual action, I flung open the control-room door, just in time to hear Charlie mutter: "Japanese bombs have fallen on Hawaii."

From there on out we flashed bulletins, before, after, and in the middle of programs. The news was hot so we plastered the bulletins on the window in front of our building and hooked up a radio above the sidewalk outside. Small crowds gathered up close and read them with wondering eyes all afternoon.

But it was jovial, lazy Bob Bruner who first got wind of the story. Despite the fact that Sunday was his day off, he was at the station, doing nothing in particular. Bored, perhaps, with inactivity, he climbed the old stairway to our "newsroom," where our one stanch teletype machine pounds out the news. There, at 1:24 (C.S.T.), he noticed a simple statement, "White House Says Japs Attack Pearl Harbor." He pushed back his hat and blurted out the single word, "yippee."

From there on, pure excitement reigned. There were quick dashes upstairs for last-minute bulletins which left me so out of breath I could hardly read them. Bulletins, scratch paper littered the floor, the telephone kept ringing, most of the staff came to the station, announcers slipped cat-like into the studio with late flashes while you were on the air, and besides all this —the shows had to go on. And they did. . . .

Fear? Worry? Not a bit of fear or worry was there. It was excitement— like a big football game, or a Kentucky Derby. . . .

Jim Sanders
Announcer, WSOY
12/29/41 *Decatur, Ill.*

Propaganda Peril

TIME [Dec. 15] used the words "yellow bastards" and "Hitler's little yellow friends" in speaking of the Japanese. I suggest that none of us use the word "yellow" in speaking of the Japanese, because our Allies, the Chinese, are yellow.

In this war we must, I think, take care not to divide ourselves into color groups. The tide of feeling about color runs very high over in the Orient. Indians, Chinese, Filipinos, and others are sensitive to the danger point about their relation as colored peoples to white peoples. Many Americans do not realize this, but it is true, and we must recognize it or we may suffer for it severely. The Japanese are using our well-known race prejudice as one of their chief propaganda arguments against us. Everything must be done to educate Americans not to provide further fuel for such Japanese propaganda.

I hope that such an influential magazine as TIME will not again insult the Chinese by using a color term which classes them with the Japanese.

Pearl S. Buck
1/5/42 *Perkasie, Pa.*
TIME *emphatically agrees with Novelist Pearl Buck that raising a race issue is as unwise as it is ignoble. However, "yellow bastards" was not* TIME's *phrase but the factual report of typical angry U.S. reactions, thoroughly documented by reports from correspondents all over the U.S. It probably came to the tongues of many men in its strongest meaning—one of moral censure rather than race prejudice—for "yellow" has long been the word for cowardice and treachery. As for actual skin-color, U.S. white, pink or pale faces may well be proud to be fighting on the side of Chinese, Filipinos and other yellow or brown faces.—*ED.

Navy Defender

. . . You say "the U.S. Navy was caught with its pants down."

That is unquestionably true, but we also know that in a democracy the policy of the navy is dictated by the government, and that the U.S. Government, by its own outraged declaration, was also caught with its pants down.

. . . The Navy in peace and in war is under constant political pressure. In peace it seldom secures the funds it asks for, and what appropriations it does receive are often spent, in spite of its protests, in ways and places contrary to its best interests. . . .

So in judging the Navy's humiliation at Pearl Harbor bear in mind that the Government in Washington may be equally to blame.

Louise Cole Chapin
1/5/42 *Berkeley, Calif.*
Reader Chapin has a good point in general. Whether it has a bearing, as it may, on the defeat at Pearl Harbor remains to be seen.—ED.

"I do not doubt . . ."

. . . The talk of the day is this new phase of the war and nearly everyone condemns the treacherous way used by the Japanese to attack America. . . .

I do not doubt that millions of plain South American citizens were as deeply hurt in their feelings as I by the word-breaking of the Japanese warmongers. I do not doubt that our Governments are going to join the All-American Front against foreign aggressors. . . .

May God help us save "The Americas" and all that they stand for in the fight against the foreign forces of evil and destruction.

Walter Luiz Estevam
1/5/42 *Rio de Janeiro, Brazil*

China Relief

In the past I had always felt hesitancy in giving for China Relief. I was of the opinion that what mattered a few million more or less Chinese, that their situation was pretty hopeless anyway. I had contributed to our church (Presbyterian) mission work for schools and medical work, in the belief that

American battleships burn after the bombing of Pearl Harbor

education of the natives to work out their own salvation was the solid foundation which merited our support.

But the amazing resistance the people of China have put up in the last four years is beyond words. I can give my contribution as a token of partial realization of their superhuman struggle to survive. More than just that, the continuance of Chinese fighting strength is more apt than not to have a grim significance to us. So from a selfish standpoint too, I feel required to answer your appeal in the affirmative. . . .

It should be plain to all of us that an enslaved China would be as disastrous as a beaten England.

Hubert J. Duggan
Bradford, Pa.

I am very glad that you decided to write to TIME subscribers on behalf of United China Relief. For months I have been intending to contribute, but never seemed to get around to it. Your letter furnished the little push necessary to overcome the inertia. . . .

I served on the U.S.S. *Asheville* on the China Station from April of 1937 to April of 1940. During my three years in China I saw some of the fighting and much of the suffering and grew to like and admire the Chinese people.

L. R. Neville
Lieutenant, U.S.N.
U.S.S. Arkansas
1/5/42 *New York City*
TIME is proud to reprint this small tithe of the more than 28,000 like letters with which TIME readers responded to the appeal of Editor Luce two months ago on behalf of China Relief. Contri-

butions thus far have totaled $165,000. TIME sincerely thanks its readers for their generosity to their deserving Ally. It was a superb token of the bonds of sympathy and respect which unite the American and Chinese people.—ED.

Rules of Thumb

Your warning in TIME, Dec. 22, that the "few rules of thumb" listed for telling Chinese from Japanese are "not always reliable" is an unparalleled masterpiece of understatement. Such absurd generalities as "Japanese are nervous in conversation, laugh loudly at the wrong time," or "most Chinese avoid horn-rimmed spectacles" would have certainly made the eminent Dr Samuel Johnson apoplectic. . . . I feel the appropriateness of an admonishing Tsk! Tsk!

Martin J. Katz
Philadelphia, Pa.
Having noted that there is no infallible way of telling Chinese and Japanese apart by face, physique or mannerism, TIME felt justified in giving such general distinctions as are backed by authoritative anthropological opinion and by lay observers who have studied the Oriental races closely. If, as several TIME readers have pointed out, patriotic Japanese-Americans do not deserve to be harassed, neither do Chinese mistaken for Japanese by inflamed Americans. For trustworthy criteria having to do with names and feet, see below. —ED.

Years ago, when we were both students at Cornell, the present Chinese Ambassador gave me a simple and un-

failing rule for telling our loyal friends from Japanese: Chinese have monosyllabic, Japanese polysyllabic names. This test is far easier than calipers. . . .
J. V. DePorte
1/12/42 *New Lebanon Center, N.Y.*

Nisei in Service

I am a *Nisei*, an American citizen of Japanese parentage. Like many other *Niseis*, I am in the service of my country. This war has hit us harder, probably, than any other portion of the American society. It has caused suspicion to be cast on us, not because we have done anything of a suspicious nature, but because of our race. Let me assure you that we know and love only one country. . . .

We *Niseis* are willing to fight and to die if necessary for America and the principle for which it stands.
Harry A. Takagi
2/2/42 *Camp Grant, Ill.*

Cover Ornament

All Americans of whatsoever race abhor the tactics and the treachery of the Japanese at Pearl Harbor. . . . But I desire, for one, to register a protest against the picture on your front cover, Jan. 26, which portrays a Japanese soldier as a helmeted monkey, bayoneted gun in hand, dropping from the limb of a tree, with slanting eyes directed venomously in the direction of "Ter Poorten of the Indies. . . ."

I very seriously question the tactics of belittling any race of human beings because they are different from ourselves. . . .
Frank C. Rideout
Lieut. Colonel (Chaplain)
U.S. Army, Retired
2/16/42 *Newton Center, Mass.*
Aside from its ethical aspect there is no worse military fault than undervaluing the enemy. The little figure on the corner of TIME's cover—not a monkeyfied Jap but a Japified monkey was intended not as belittlement but as recognition of Japanese jungle agility. —ED.

Spontaneity

The Pearl Harbor Navy Chaplain [Feb. 2] who cracked, "Praise the Lord and pass the ammunition. I just got one of the so and sos," was infused with the same spirit of the Christ *(Matthew XXI:12, 13)* as He overthrew the tables of the moneychangers and the seats of them that sold doves, and also cracked. *My house shall be called the house of prayer; but ye have made it a den of thieves.*
W. A. Sunderland
2/23/42 *Las Cruces, N. Mex.*

"We Can Take It"

Some of us are getting sick and tired of the wail from Washington, echoed

in TIME that suggests that we, the people, are unaware of the war. What do you want us to do? You say we are awake. You say we are working. What do you want us to do? Shall we start ranting in the streets tearing our shirts to convince you that we are serious? Wars are not won by words but by work and sacrifice. We are working. We are willing to sacrifice.

Our sons have gone and are going gladly and we have proudly watched them go. Do you think the families of men in service are unaware that there is a war? Our way of living has been and is being curtailed and most of us have heard only cheerful acceptance of growing restrictions that affect our daily lives. In many sections, such as ours where there is little or no defense work our economic security is severely threatened but there have been mighty few complaints. I have heard scores of men whose livelihood is gone completely, say with a smile, "That's o.k., we can take it." . . .

Perhaps our critics thinking of themselves are only surprised that we make no complaints. Perhaps they are suspicious of a silence and acceptance that they cannot understand. Perhaps they do not know the infinite capacity of the people of America to quietly and without heroics give to their country. Perhaps they have lost contact with the people.

(Rev.) Russell C. Stroup
First Presbyterian Church
3/2/42 *Lynchburg, Va.*

Who is Asleep?

. . . I am constantly in touch with the class which Damon Runyon calls the "little people," and I am very sure that they are aware of the gravity of the situation and prepared to do what they can. . . . Most of them feel that they can contribute only by paying in money to the extreme limit of their ability to pay. . . . They are deeply concerned and moved and ready. . . .

D. D. Olds
Office of the Collector
Internal Revenue Service
Treasury Department
Tacoma, Wash.

. . . Who is lulling us to sleep? Our own Government through newspapers and radio keeps us ignorant of our usefulness in winning this war. . . . All we have been asked to do so far is a little more walking instead of driving our cars and, last but not least, "Buy Defense Bonds," invest our money with interest. After years of war in Europe isn't it obvious that money will not buy victory . . .

V. Andersen
3/9/42 *Chicago, Ill.*

The People

TIME's Feb. 16 account of what various commentators were saying about the U.S. people (Smug, Slothful, Asleep?)

Helldiver and Avenger bombers head off to support the invasion of Saipan

brought an outburst of letters from the people themselves. Many letters-to-TIME have reflected indignation over such issues as the Roberts report on Pearl Harbor, the retirement applications of Admiral Kimmel and General Short, the Lafayette (ex-Normandie) fire, pensions for Congressmen, Mrs. Roosevelt and OCD. But the latest batch—more than 100 of them—went much deeper. Some excerpts:

. . . What the hell do these critics want us to do—roll hoops with red, white & blue bunting wrapped around them, or turn cartwheels in the street every time a Nazi general dies of heart attack? . . .

Homer L. Kyle
Lincoln, Neb.

. . . Was a slothful "people" responsible for Pearl Harbor, General Johnson? That sounds suspiciously like a cheap bit of red herring pulling to sidestep blame for your uniformed colleagues. "Worldly-wise experts" indeed! The people of this nation are following the leadership (such as is provided for them) in the crisis as slavishly as any medieval chain gang. Thank your stars if your castigation doesn't produce the kind of sullen rancor which could one day destroy you. What this nation needs right now in these tax-ridden days is a pat on the back—not a slap on the mouth with the back of an ungrateful, irresponsible, alphabetical hand. . . .

Murray A. Cayley
First Presbyterian Church
Rochester, N.Y.

. . . We are achingly eager to help, to know, to act and we have been for a long time. . . .
Every man and woman in the nation should be drafted *at once* for war work. Those of us who can't fight can learn to make airplanes. Those of us who can't make airplanes can darn the air-

plane-makers' sox or cook their meals. Some of us can register those who are drafts. Some of us can answer telephones and lick stamps and run errands. Surely there is a place for everyone.

All of us can spare one to six hours a day on active participation in the war. We are in danger! Why aren't we asked to do, ordered to do it? . . .

Anne B. Mount
3/9/42 *Lynchburg, Va.*

Hangman Heydrich

It is impossible for any intelligent human being to have read your article on Hitler's chief hangman Heydrich without wanting to do all he possibly can do to defeat the Nazi regime. I was already shocked when I saw Heydrich's brutal face and the typical ears of that born criminal on the cover of TIME of Feb. 23. Now, on March 12, it will be exactly seven years when I had the misfortune to fall into his hands.

At that day Swiss, Dutch, French and English newspapers published the following item: "Dr. Robert M. W. Kempner, ex-legal adviser of the pre-Hitler Prussian State Police Administration was executed by a firing squad of the Nazi Secret Police (Gestapo) as an enemy of the Hitler Regime." He actually had caught me, but after three weeks of the third degree, friends succeeded in getting my release and I could escape death. Himmler's and Heydrich's police machinery is terrible but can be smashed easier than most people think!

R. M. W. Kempner
University of Pennsylvania
3/16/42 *Philadelphia, Pa.*

Nisei's Duty

Upon reading your aritcle on "The People" [Feb. 23] I was finally convinced that it was more than reasonable that we American citizens of Japanese

Airmen of the R.A.F. scurry to their planes before the Battle of Britain

parentage on the West Coast should be ordered to evacuate to the inland by the Army.

It was certainly an eye-opener for us, for until then I always thought that this demand to oust us from the sunny Southern California was nothing but a dirty scheme by some of our local politicians. But I now realize the awful necessity of us getting out of the coast as soon as possible and I do believe that it is our duty to move inland so that we may relieve the Army the burden of keeping watch over us when it must concentrate its full power on guarding the important coast. This is a fight to finish and our fate is in the balance. Then we should not be in a way of the Army when it needs every ounce of manpower to prevent more breakthrough of the enemy on far distant front lines, and we, all loyal citizens of this country, can better serve the nation by working on inland farms instead of remaining here to increase the worry and anxiety of our fellow Caucasian citizens on the coast. . . .

Whatever our fellow Japanese-Americans might have done in Hawaii at the time of Pearl Harbor attack, we *Nisei* on the California coast certainly do not wish to be looked upon as potential saboteurs or fifth columnists. Neither do we have any desire to be charged responsible if and when any single bomb is dropped here, for it is quite certain that enraged public will look for a scapegoat in us on such event. . . .

David Akira Itami
Assistant Editor
Japanese Language Section
Japan-California News
3/16/42   *Los Angeles, Calif.*

Negroes' Thanks

. . . Your article in the March 2 edition on "White Man's War?" is the most gratifying I have read. Hundreds of Negro boys have been training themselves for skilled occupations at a Federal project sponsored by the northern Negro's No. 1 college, Wilberforce University, and the much harried National Youth Administration.

Each new group of trainees comes in with an air of curiosity about these unfamiliar and denied occupations, and after completing their training and obtaining a few skills and ideas of the much-needed defense occupations they leave glorying in this revelation and bursting with ambition and pride. We who know the real answer cannot bear to tell them the bitter truth, but we still pray and hope that our boys will have the "barred gates" referred to in your article opened for them.

Henry Parks Jr.
Director, Wilberforce Resident Center
National Youth Administration for Ohio
3/23/42   *Wilberforce, Ohio*

Prophecy

TIME's account of the fall of Singapore, especially the paragraphs headed "Whose fault?" certainly makes Hendrik Willem van Loon out to be a prophet.

In his *Van Loon's Geography*, published in 1932, he closes chapter XXXVI as follows:

"It [Singapore] is as strongly fortified as Gibraltar. . . . It will play a great role when the inevitable clash between the East and the West finally takes place. In anticipation of that event, it maintains a set of barrooms, the splendor of which is famous all over the Orient. . . .

Robert French Wilson
3/30/42   *Washington, D.C.*

How to Help

I was very interested in noticing in your Letters column the many letters from persons who were asking what they could do to help win the war.

As a tangible suggestion, I would recommend that able-bodied persons in cities and towns who have experience on the farm offer their services on week ends and during vacations to farmers. This offer should be made through the United States Employment Service, local offices of which are familiar with farm labor needs. The persons should indicate the kind of farm tasks with which they are familiar, and the times when they would be available.

Agriculture is faced with the prospect of many local labor shortages which might impair the goals which the Department of Agriculture has set for greatly increased production of food, fats and oils, and fibers needed by the United States and her Allies.

M. Clifford Townsend
Director, Office of
Agricultural Defense Relations
U.S. Department of Agriculture
3/30/42   *Washington, D.C.*

Work More

. . . In TIME, March 9, Reader Donald C. Boyce asks "what do the critics except the people to do . . . about the war?" WORK MORE!

Working hours in the U.S. are just about 40 a week. If one-half of this work is spent on satisfying consumption, a maximum of 20 hours is left to serve war purposes. Let us work an additional ten hours per week and step up the flow of war goods 50%. Fifty hours a week will still be below the German or Japanese average. Five o'clock is too early to stop dam-building while the flood rises. . . .

E. G. Douglas
4/6/42   *Toronto, Ont.*

Ubiquitous Slap

Your story of the slap-on-the-bus [March 23] interested me very much.

This incident, or one notably similar, actually took place last summer in Toronto. Two girls were talking in a bus and one remarked that she was making very good money in munitions and would like to see the war go on for a long time. A middle-aged woman across the aisle hauled off and socked her. The sockee demanded that the conductor stop the bus and get a policeman. When the policeman asked the other passengers what the disturbance was, nobody on the bus had noticed a thing.

Catherine Jones
4/13/42   *Ottawa, Ont.*
P.S. The socker had two sons in the R.C.A.F.

The Lost Generation

We might as well face the facts: There are a hell of a lot of us, fairly comfortably situated, holding the usual kinds of jobs in publishing, in advertising, in sales promotion, and paper-shuffling who are not worth a tinker's damn in the war effort. We've had our jobs long enough—those comfortable berths with the clockwork pay check—to fear the alien breezes which blow just outside the office door. We started in our early and eager 20s and now we are crowding our tired 40s. We could swim and hike and dance in the old days and eat 20c lunches and look forward to the years ahead as a great adventure. We are on the paunchy side and our hair is thinner and we would rather relax with the paper or go to a movie after the day's work is done.

We know that the comfortable world we knew is on the skids. Voting the Republican ticket isn't going to save it for us. We were successively anti-labor, anti-low tariff, anti-socialistic, anti-Marxist, anti-Communist, and anti-Fascist. And now a lot of those things we were against have somehow become respectable. . . . We are only vaguely aware of the underlying reasons for which the present war is being fought. But, at least, we know that it is now our fight and, wistfully, we'd like to be doing something about it in addition to paying taxes.

We are all safely—for the time being—classified as 3-A. We have a little house in the suburbs and two children and a car and a mortgage. We cut the lawn and dig a little garden with our shortening breath and perspiring brows.

If we were called to active service, we'd feel more at home at a desk job in Washington than in a jeep in Virginia. But we hate the thought of either.

We might like to learn how to run a drill press or a lathe or a riveter in our spare time and put in two or three hours every evening helping to build war machines. But the unions wouldn't let us and there is no available machinery set in motion to make it possible. If we have been selling bonds, or insurance, or refrigerators, or cars, or real estate, or advertising, all the pep talks in the world, all the posters and all the brass bands are of no avail to urge us to roll up our sleeves, step up production and lick the Japs in the "silver months" which remain of 1942.

We are the great useless middle class. We are not Labor and we are not Capital. Our bodies are hardly good enough to be shot at and our skills for making the shooting machines is non-existent. We can only sell things—when there are no things to sell.

We are truly the Lost Generation. . . .

Laurence Wray
5/11/42 *New York City*

Pacifist Ayres

I have just read the telegram from John Huston and other Hollywood "firsts" in the April 20 issue of TIME. I feel gratified that these intelligent and courageous people have come to the defense of Lew Ayres.

I am a private in the Air Force, not by compulsion, but by desire. I am here because I want to see the new-world principles of free thought and free speech preserved. I have followed closely the furor caused by the flag-wavers who would deny Lew Ayres the right to do what so many Americans are too cowardly to do—stick by honest principles regardless of public opinion.

Most of us believe that this war is being fought so that people like Lew Ayres all over the world will be *free* to live and say what they please as long as it is not injurious to the public good. Lew Ayres, instead of being detrimental to our public good, is indicative of what the American people wrote into their Bill of Rights and what we fight our wars about—the right to freedom in a democracy.

Roughly, there are 2,500 men who do not choose to kill now in Conscientious Objectors Camps in the U.S. Doubtless, there are many more, in and out of the Armed Forces, who feel as Lew Ayres feels, but who are too *weak* to be non-conformists. Then, shouldn't we admire Lew Ayres because he is *strong* enough to face the suspicion, ridicule, and hate that is always the lot of those who do not choose to conform?

I do not agree with Lew Ayres as far as killing people is concerned. I feel that if it is necessary to kill the disciples

Women join with men as part of the war effort on this B-29 assembly line in Wichita, Kansas

Getting fit for war:

Soldiers train on an Army obstacle course

A Woman Marine jujitsu teacher blocks a knee-kick

of Herr Schickelgruber and his ruthless cohorts in order to insure freedom and democracy for the world that we must push relentlessly forward and accomplish our honorable task as soon as possible. But, when I am fighting for freedom and democracy, I want it known that I am fighting for freedom and democracy for Lew Ayres as much as for any other citizen of my country.
Private Eugene B. Crowe
5/11/42 *Lemoore, Calif.*

Broiled Cow Flesh

So the English are serving horseflesh now [April 27]. The question comes to mind why make it still worse with a name like that? . . . Me, I love a piece of good meat for dinner, but flesh . . . I'd never touch the stuff. If they ever start serving the *genus Equus* in America, let's call it Filly Mignon.
Everett Bennie
5/18/42 *St. Louis, Mo.*

Flags

Don't the Stars & Stripes on the July 6 cover break a TIME-honored precedent of devotion to personalities? . . .
Lou Baldwin
Chicago, Ill.

. . . Of some 20 covers I saw, only TIME showed a church under the flag, so I heartily congratulate Mr. Artzybasheff and you.
Rev. Charles F. Unger
6/22/42 *Readington, N.J.*

TIME broke a precedent, and gladly, to cooperate with other leading magazines in a Fourth of July Demonstration [July 6], but the precedent was not entirely one of personalities: there have previously appeared horses (March 18, 1929 and Aug. 20, 1934); dogs (March 3, 1930); and sea lions (April 18, 1932); but never any cover of inanimate things.—ED.

Two-Legged Horse Meat?

. . . May I please correct the impression given in TIME, April 27 that British housewives are eating horseflesh. . . . We do wait in a queue for it and often for a very long time, but . . . it is bought as food for our dogs, as naturally we cannot give them any of our household meat. . . .
Irene Glover
6/29/42 *London*
Many British housewives buy horse meat only for the four-legged members of their families, but in some districts (South London and Soho for example) they buy plenty of "stewing meat" and "frying meat" (horseflesh) for two-legged members. As cat-&-dog food, horse meat is price-controlled at eight pence a pound, but there is no ceiling on its price for human consumption.—ED.

Desert Dive-Bombers

TIME, July 6: "It was high time, past time that the British learned the use of dive-bombers in desert warfare. . . ."
On this July 4 morning, we all read in the newspapers and heard on the radio of the German dive-bomber attack on British ground troops in Egypt. This attack occurred July 3.
British Hurricane planes piloted by South Africans were ordered up to meet the attack. . . . There were 15 German dive-bombers, protected by a screen of Messerschmitt 109 fighters—both Germany's best. The South Africans shot down 13 out of the 15 German dive-bombers and wiped out one Messerschmitt for luck.
That is concrete evidence in support of the experience behind the British air marshals' opinions as to the value of dive-bombers in desert warfare (not in sea warfare, mind you). They are very vulnerable when opposed by fighters of an efficient design manned by efficient pilots. . . .
Harry W. Cook
6/29/42 *Regina, Sask.*
Vulnerable weapons are not necessarily useless. Example: aircraft carriers. Let not Reader Cook forget that Field Marshal Rommel might never have got beyond Libya had not dive-bombers blasted the way for the capture of Bir Hachéim and Tobruk.—ED.

Poetic Justice

Let the destruction of the Czech town of Lidice be repaid courteously yet with devastating effect.
When the war is over and won by the forces of freedom, let the city of Berlin have its name changed by the victors to Lidice, to the end that the arrogance of their leaders and the brutality of their Himmlers and Heydrichs may be forever remembered by the German people.
Let a Lidice, obliterated in Czecho-Slovakia, come to life again in the conquered Reich as the capital of a country whose pride and perfidy have become a stench in the nostrils of free men everywhere and a horror in the sight of God.
Tom Lennon
7/13/42 *Los Angeles, Calif.*
Another poetically just idea, sometimes suggested, is to offer Prussia to the Jews of Europe as their post-war homeland.—ED.

Glorified General?

. . . Your article on Rommel is full of slurs at the British—and could well have been dictated by Goebbels. How can we achieve unity within or without while you glorify the German? . . .
Trudy Lancaster
Los Angeles, Calif.

Congratulations on your story of Field Marshal Erwin Rommel. It was timely, fact-filled, and nicely written.
You no doubt will receive some criticism from people who will say you are "playing up" or "idolizing" enemy officers.
I, for one, think you are doing America a great service by providing

military men and civilians alike with a true picture of what we must be prepared to meet if we are to be successful!

Herbert H. Brown
8/10/42 *Long Beach, Calif.*

Grotesque

Thank you for printing the only articles I have seen of late which have attempted to explain and defend General Douglas MacArthur in the unhappy position in which he finds himself. . . . Like, I imagine, many others who have been deeply puzzled and chagrined by the lack of action in Australia, I read your articles with great interest. . . .

I doubt if the President wanted this state of affairs when he sent MacArthur to Australia. . . . But how grotesque that a man of such magnificent qualities and achievements, and such a wealth of world-wide experience should become the Forgotten Man while men often of lesser equipment, some of whom had served as his aides not so long ago, are given exalted posts! . . .

M. F. Macleod
8/17/42 *New York City*

Tokyo Rooting Section

Ten Americans returning home on the *Gripsholm* who witnessed the bombing of Tokyo on April 18 were interested to read TIME's and Jimmy Doolittle's accounts of the raid and are anxious to give the American public our ringside impression of it.

The raid, which came at 1:10 p.m., not only upset lunch at our internment camp on the edge of Tokyo, but kept us indoors for the next two days, extinguished the charcoal fires by which we cooked and held up mail delivery for 24 hours.

The raid was not a total surprise as reported. Early in the morning we had an "alert," and later an "urgent" warning. We first knew the show was on when an anti-aircraft battery near the Kawasaki factory district opened up on one of the two Tokyo raiders. A second plane flew within half a mile of our camp and came within an inch of destruction. A Jap battery of eight guns found the exact range at which the B-25 was flying and let go at it. The first shots were a little ahead of the plane, and the second volley would have caught it square if the pilot had not nosed down within a few feet of the ground.

A minute later a squadron of absolutely World War model biplanes took after the B-25. These machines were so decrepit that the wind from our bomber was enough to scatter them. After this the American raider flew away unchallenged and disappeared against the side of Fujiyama.

What the pilot of the plane probably does not realize is that during this phase of the show he had the most enthusiastic, if the smallest rooting section in the world. Our only regrets

Joe and Willie, two battle-grimed dogfaces, survive the war in the sardonic cartoons of G.I. Bill Mauldin, above, who sketched while serving at the Italian front

The War

"Ever notice th'funny sound these zippers make, Willie?"

"Aim between th'eyes, Joe...sometimes they charge when they're wounded."

"She must be very purty. Th'whole column is wheezin' at her."

"I'd ruther cover th'gun. I won't hafta dry myself with a oily rag."

"Now that ya mention it, it does sound like th'patter of rain on a tin roof.'

"Don't startle'im, Joe—it's almost full."

"My son. Five days old. Good-lookin' kid, ain't he?"

V-E Day. "Th'hell with it. I ain't standin'up till he does."

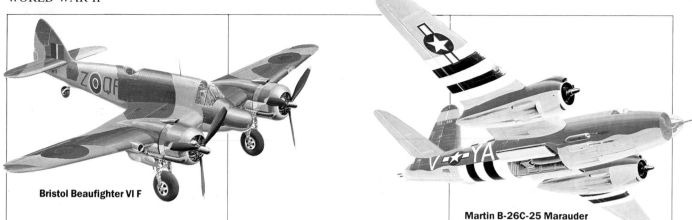

Bristol Beaufighter VI F

Martin B-26C-25 Marauder

were 1) that he did not pick us up, and 2) that he did not return with more of his friends.

Tom Crichton
9/14/42 *On board M.S.* Gripsholm

Phillogy Among the Marines

I was very interested in your article in the Oct. 5 issue of TIME on Jap. v. Marine struggle for the Solomon Islands. Only one thing puzzled me, and that is when the Japs broke into the clearing shouting *"Banzai!"* what did they mean? Three marines were discussing the situation tonight after dinner. One suggested it meant "Screeno!" and another thought it meant "Backgammon!" and the last thought the Japs might possibly have meant "Where's the head?" Do you think you could settle this dispute?

H. P. Wheeler
Lieutenant, U.S.M.C.R.
Marine Corps School
11/9/42 *Quantico, Va.*
Banzai! *Literally means "10,000 years"* (ban: *10,000;* zai: *years*). *As Japs tell it to the marines, it means "Long Live the Emperor!" or simply "Hooray!"* —ED.

On the Nose

When the news of the second front attack on North and West Africa broke last night I got out TIME of Oct. 12 with its African map on page 28. Your story hit this whole show on the nose. . . .

TIME's reasons given for such action are important enough to recapitulate: 1) cut off Rommel's forces in their rear; 2) bar the Germans' way to complete conquest of North Africa; 3) restore Allied control of the western Mediterranean; 4) assist a thrust into Germany's southern Europe.

Thomas E. Holme
11/30/42 *Bridgeport, Conn.*

"God Will Avenge"

The article "Jewish Army: Pro & Con" in the issue of Dec. 28 is a very touchy subject.

I, as an American-born Jew, feel

that the present time . . . is not the proper one to form a Jewish Army.

Let us as Jews forget the whole affair, and get behind the individual governments that we are now serving as true citizens. We have now approximately 8% of our population in the service in these United States, and every single one of us is ready to go the limit as good Americans and spill our blood for those ideals that we above all other people cherish most.

This is my country. I am part of the melting pot. I was born here, and I want to die here, and every drop of my blood will be spilt to protect those I cherish on this American soil. I am an American first, last, and always, and the American freedom shall be ours forever.

God alone will avenge our Jewish people, and history will write the curse that will befall our persecutors.

Harry Shriber
1/18/43 *Pittsburgh*

The following letter from North Africa was written to a friend by TIME's *representative in Baltimore, now in the Air Forces.*—ED.

"The Controls Are Like Iron"

. . . I wish I could describe a raid to you the way it feels. . . . You taxi out for take-off. In a few minutes you are in the air and taking your position in the formation. There is not much conversation on the way and things seem as normal as they would in a cross-country flight in the states. You know the time of arrival at the target and you watch the clock on the dashboard crawl by. Then . . . you see your destination. The speed is picked up and there is a last-minute check on the instruments. Conversation picks up briefly—"Is this the bus to Baltimore?" —"Give 'em hell, doc"—"Here we go." All this is over interphone; there is no talk between ships but you know how the others feel. And then you're in it. Black puffs of smoke begin breaking in front of the nose, off the wing, right overhead. They break suddenly in clusters and hang in the air like tiny clouds. You are twisting and turning,

diving, climbing—anything to keep those clusters from coming too close. The sky is full of them and there doesn't seem to be room to fly through. They get closer and you hear the whisper of them as they break in close. There is a gun-like report and a sharp pain in your shoulder. In the windshield a large hole through the safety glass. You think you've been hit. The co-pilot's wrist is bloody, and your shoulder feels numb. You can't go fast enough, you're crawling over that target. You've got to level off and fly straight to drop those bombs, but you'd rather do anything than give those gunners a straight shot at you. You level off and hang on. Tracer bullets stream up past the nose. You can see them coming a long way off and they come so slow, so leisurely till suddenly they whizz by like miniature meteors. The light on the instrument panel blinks rapidly as the bombs are released and you are free to begin dodging again. You have all the speed you can get and the controls are like iron. What was seconds seems hours before you are clear of the flack and can relax long enough to take stock of the damage. Your shoulder is okay, just hit by a piece of glass going two or three hundred miles an hour. Your hand looks frosted with splinters of glass sticking out. The co-pilot's all right, just cut. The bombardier crawls back. One side of his face is covered with blood but he's okay. You call back over interphone—"Everybody all right?" "Yup, all okay." The ship's been hit a number of times but it's flying and you're on your way back. You light a cigaret. The raid's over.
1/25/43 *Howard Kelly*

What Are We Doing?

Your magazine and other papers are full of "explanations" why Stalin did not turn up at Casablanca and why he did not even bother to send a delegate. None of these explanations is convincing. Why not just assume that he is utterly dissatisfied with our performance in this talking-war?

At a time when Russia has launched

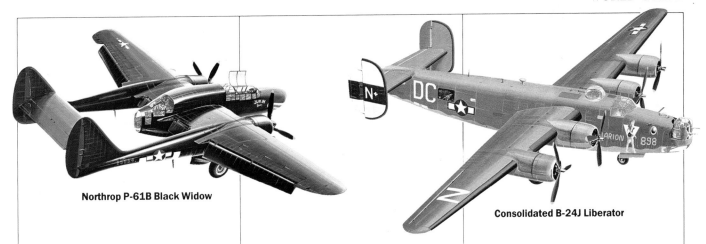

Northrop P-61B Black Widow

Consolidated B-24J Liberator

a stupendous offensive after having withstood the most terrific Nazi onslaught last summer, what are we doing? Our troops landed in French Africa on a terrain well-oiled in advance. . . . What happened? After three months, this obviously large and well-equipped army has done practically nothing. . . . We are told that it is raining terribly and continuously in Tunis and that the supply lines are enormously long. Obviously it did not rain in Libya, a few hundred miles farther to the East, and it does not snow during the Russian offensive. . . . As regards the long supply lines, one cannot imagine that the difficulties are greater than those of Montgomery in his advance of 1,300 miles, especially as Algeria and Tunis have by far the best road and rail net in Africa.

Something must be wrong in Africa. And don't you believe that Stalin thinks so too? . . . How must a man feel whose army has captured and slaughtered hundreds of thousands of Nazis in the last few weeks, when he is told that the mighty American army is not able to cope with a few thousand Nazis in three months *in its first big campaign*, for which it took so much time to get ready and which was heralded so much? . . .

Frederick H. Meyer
2/22/43 *New York City*

A List of Good Germans

. . . About 5% of the German people dared to vote against Hitler as late as 1934, were courageous enough to help the oppressed ones and to exercise humane acts under mortal danger. On these true Christian Germans, these descendants of Lessing, Goethe, Mozart and Beethoven, the inevitable new edifice of the German state must be based. They must take over the jobs of city mayors, of foremen in factories, of presidents in scientific societies. . . . But how can they be found out? I propose that a list be made up of all such Germans who committed dangerous actions to help innocent victims of Nazi persecution. . . . Let such a list come from refugees, Christian and Jewish and Russian and Polish and

French and Norwegian. Each refugee knows a few such Germans. Let these refugees know that the names procured will be kept completely secret. . . . This list will be given to the commanders of the victorious armies of the United Nations who shall put these good Germans to the job of initiating the rebirth of the true German nation.

Rudolf Schindler, M.D.
2/22/43 *Chicago*

Beyond Rifle Range

As a longtime reader of TIME, may I add a word of thanks to the many you must be receiving these days from soldiers, sailors and marines in the field on foreign service. . . .

TIME has always been important to many of us . . . but never before have we found it so essential to a comprehensive and complete picture of a world at war. Without the kind of reporting that TIME gives us, the machine gunner's vision of the world is limited to his sector of fire; the pilot's to his operating radius; and the rifleman's to the extreme limit of his own eyesight. . . .

We know, from first hand experience that your reporting is amazingly accurate.

Keep up the good work. Let those who criticize your format and style, your human shortcomings and falls from grace, take the word of American servicemen that TIME IS undoubtedly the most sought-after publication in the combat zones.

Capt. Donald L. Jackson
U.S.M.C.R.
31/1/43 *On foreign station*

Bath, Aleutian Style

(Excerpts from a letter received by J. C. Pryor, of Omaha.)

I find that I am the least sleepingest and most workingest guy in the whole army. (You would probably find about 6,000,000 other liars who said they were—but we know better). Not only am I the most workingest guy, but I am the least bathingest guy. Nothing would please me more than to see all the male population of the U.S. have themselves a Saturday bath,

Aleutian style. . . . It's so effective that it practically kills you. It's done like this.

The first thing you have to do is to wait until mess is over at night, so that you have a chance to steal two pails from the cook to carry water in. It really isn't water, it's just ice that you breathe on until it gets unstiff enough to pour. You can't light a fire, because if you do, you would probably find yourself on the singing end of a Jap bomb. Well, you take the two pails of ice water, throw a little dirt in them, to act as a counter-irritant, strip, and stand with one foot in each pail. Then you give yourself a good soaping (soap that's bear fat mixed with bacon drippings), until you are either fully lathered, or frozen, whichever comes first. Then you rinse yourself gently, by brushing away the crust of ice that has by this time formed on the top of the water, dipping it out neatly with the cup from your mess kit and pouring it slowly over your gorgeous pink (from the cold) body, being careful to cover the entire surface, so that all of you is frozen evenly. The glory of it all is that you don't have to go to the trouble of drying yourself when you have finished. The reason is that your arms are now frozen solid and rigor mortis is setting in. Of course, that really needn't concern you, because there will be a lot of men from the club, who are always willing to carry you up to your nice damp, dirty tent, and beat you back to life with the blunt side of their bayonets. I always get a great deal of pleasure out of watching them beat a man back to life after a bath—just as soon as he moves it's everybody for himself, and there is one hell of a race back to the pails to see who gets the water for his next morning's coffee. . . .

Come over sometime and have a bath with me.

Lieut. F. R. Boyles
Army Air Corps Intelligence
3/8/43 *Somewhere in the Aleutians*

Pampered Patriots

You state that many returned fighting men wonder why good news is all the news given out to American people

[March 1]. So do we! It is true that the American people are acting like a bunch of spoiled kids, but that is the way we are being treated. We are pampered patriots. We are getting a few drops of castor oil in a cup full of political honey.

The American people want the facts. . . . One's imagination is not broad enough to conjure up a true picture of the horrors of war. We must see and read about it first hand. It will take a crack on the chin to make us stand up and fight. Don't let us bask in the sunshine of victory, nibbling on chocolate-covered communiqués of military achievement, while our sons and brothers and husbands are wallowing in the mud and blood of war throughout the world.

Jess Mason
3/22/43   Sherman Oaks, Calif.

Hats Off to The Red Cross

. . . Before I came overseas I was under the impression that the Red Cross organization was simply a gathering place where middle-aged society matrons expended their ebullient ener-

Security posters warned Americans to watch their tongues

gies. I just returned to the desert from a five-day leave in Cairo where the Red Cross has taken over the Grand Hotel and converted it into a meeting place for Yanks. Why, one can get real American cooking and real honest-to-goodness "french fries" for an insignificant price. Our hats are off to them.

Staff Sgt. Edward J. Gulanica
"With the U.S.A.A.F.
3/22/43 *Somewhere in the Middle East"*

Horrible Holocausts

. . . Our forces ended the Bismarck Sea action [March 15] by wiping out barges, lifeboats and rafts from the sunken enemy vessels.

Americans were proud and delighted when they received the news of the

amazing success of MacArthur's flyers in destroying the entire enemy flotilla. They cannot have the same feeling regarding the cold-blooded slaughter of the helpless. . . .

Another matter that is being freely mentioned, even in high official quarters, [is] the destruction of "the paper cities of Japan," by aerial bombing. In plain words, this means that we propose to burn to death a countless number of women and children, the aged and the helpless. . . . But Americans want no horrible holocausts endlessly to poison the relationships between our countries. . . .

J. Howard Cliffe
3/29/43   Ivyland, Pa.

Soldiers v. John L. Lewis

The Jan. 25 issue of TIME arrived in yesterday's mail, and the main topic of conversation last night was the coal strike in Pennsylvania. We decided that we would like the following message conveyed to Oscar Servaczgo, striking Wilkes-Barre anthracite coal miner.

We can't tell how many we are, but we're a company of farmers, clerks, salesmen, miners (coal and copper), truck drivers, laborers and mechanics. . . . We're volunteers, draftees, and old army men from 17 to 37. . . .

Some of us belonged to unions and some did not; some like unionism, some do not. But one and all, we're convinced that labor dictatorship must go. Every one of us, and our Kentucky and Pennsylvania coal miners too, cheer the crumbling of John L. Lewis' domination over you coal miners.

. . . We want to come back to a free America where we can get a job without "kicking in" to some soap-box union racketeer. . . .

Incidentally, we were not so moved when Butte copper miners refused to work beside Negroes. We fight beside them over here and it's a sad day for the people of the United States when they ask the Negro to fight for them abroad and then refuse to let him work at home. . . .

Sgt. Joseph L. Heyer
"Somewhere in
4/12/43   North Africa"

Horrible Holocausts (Cont'd)

May I be permitted a word in defense of the pilots who unmercifully strafed the life rafts of the Jap survivors of the battle of the Bismarck Sea, and brought forth the horrified protests of J. Howard Cliffe [March 29]?

Coinciding exactly with the Jap ideas of the rules of war, as demonstrated in such incidents as the rape of Nanking, the strafing of Hickam, Wheeler, Iba and Clark fields, the machine-gunning of American pilots who hit the silk too soon after bailing out and the "flag of truce" incident reported from Guadalcanal, such action on our part raises our stock

A crashed R.A.F. fighter is transported to a metal dump in Germany

immeasurably in the eyes of the Japs. Had we acted otherwise, we would have lost "face." . . .

T. S. Duff
4/19/43 *El Paso, Tex.*

Housewife's Attitude

Your Background for Peace [March 22] has been in the background of my head ever since I read it. It has made me want to say something, though I have never spoken out before because somehow a person who always has to style herself "housewife" in a questionnaire does seem so insignificant. And yet there are so many of us housewives that what we want and, in the privacy of our homes, urge our men to strive for, is surely going to affect the peace. . . .

Lately we have had to give up many things we thought we couldn't "live" without. Most of us have found, to our delighted surprise that we're not only living without these services, devices and super-abundances, but liking it and being twice as alive as before. Can we get that across, first to our own men, and then out into the places where policies are made, so that our leaders will know that we care more for a sound peace than for the restoration of the exact degree of material comfort we had before?

Here is something that should scare us a bit. We are being asked to sacrifice now, but we are being told at the same time that after the war there will be more nice, convenient and delightful things than we ever had before. Perhaps, but let's forget it, let's shun the thought of it, lest we remain a collective Little Woman, who by her impatience to have again what she once had, can build up a pressure from her

small but increasing complaints, hints and suggestions, which in time will form blocs of selfishness in the nation.

I get lost easily in politics and economics. . . . But I believe absolutely that the wishes of some 60 or 70 million women will be felt at the peace table. If those wishes are selfish, there will be no real peace. But if we can persuade our men by our daily attitude, from this day forward, that we would rather have to scrimp the rest of our lives than leave any other people in need and despair anywhere in this earth, then the end result will be that those who will have the power to form the peace will go about their task free to avail themselves of that tremendous force which is rising all over the world even now, the longing for and the insistence on a world of peace and brotherhood.

Elisabeth H. Garceau
4/26/43 *South Hanover, Mass.*

Postwar Readjustment

Background for Peace has been a tonic. . . . The March 22 issue made mention of . . . "preparing the people for the orderly demobilization of 50,000,000 soldiers." . . .

What of the younger men taken directly from school and home, put through the most rigorous training program ever conceived, and as a pilot, bombardier, or paratrooper, called upon to live life so intensely that few can stand the pace? Are the people who remain home going to expect the same boy to return and to take his place in a normal existence as though nothing had ever happened? . . . Will they realize how difficult it will be for him to adjust himself to a safe and sane life again? And will they help him?

Assuming that we have a tougher job ahead in fitting these men into civilian life, I wonder if we will devote to it one-tenth of the energy and planning that we did in fitting them for war. I doubt it. In which case, can we expect them to be anything else than restless, unable to return to duller things, quick to provoke trouble (if only for the excitement), and generally unable to stabilize themselves in a peaceful society?

Private M. R. Maben
5/17/43 *Camp Young, Calif.*

Browned Off

Your recent discussion of R.A.F. expressions [March 22] was read here with much interest, especially by our friends in that organization. Americans regret, however, that you omitted reference to one RAF-ism that we take an extremely dim view of: "U.S." as an abbreviation for "unserviceable." We are browned off by it, and hope it will go for six.

Everett Fisher
Pan American Airways, Inc.
Somewhere in Africa,
5/17/43 *West Coast*

Bomb the Brains!

Japanese execution of prisoners of war [May 3] to my mind has changed the whole future policy to be followed in the war. If barbarism is indicated by the enemy, it has to be met with like cruelty. No holds barred! No silly Wilson or Roosevelt idealism. . . .

The bars are down. Our brave fighters have been assassinated for doing their duty. Why not be as realistic as the Japanese? My feeling is that the main target for bombs—or shells—should be the chancellery in Berlin, the Mikado's palace in Tokyo, Hitler's hideout at Berchtesgaden, the government buildings in Berlin and Tokyo . . . where the *brains* are! To my mind, eradicating the motivating source is more important than destroying the instruments. . . .

Leon H. Hass
5/10/43 *Davenport, Iowa*

Mayhem Wanted

Call me a cold-blooded, unAmerican monster; a soulless Frankenstein. Truss me, naked, to a whipping post. Boil me in oil, and pour hot lead in my veins, but for God's sake, spare me the overdramatized type of Hollywood corn with which TIME (May 3) and newspapers the country over treated the execution of American flyers in Tokyo.

For heaven's sake, stop preaching "cricket," and practice mayhem.

Alfred M. Merritt
5/24/43 *Herlong, Calif*

The People *v.* John Lewis

I first enlisted in the Army at the age of 16 for the hell of it. I am now in aerial gunnery for the hell of it. Like most soldiers, I think very little about the war, and let Public Relations and the politicians do my flag waving. But for the first time since Pearl Harbor I am up in the air about something—and the "something" is John L. Lewis and his strike. . . .

The men who fly over Europe through a blanket of flak would be greatly amazed if they returned to the U.S. and found that it had been forced into totalitarianism as a last resort against men of the Lewis ilk. . . .

Staff Sgt. F. M. Hillary
5/24/43 *Orlando, Fla.*

Sweet and Honeyed News

Funnyman Brown's report, in May 10 TIME, that soldiers in the South Pacific prefer BBC radio news did not surprise us Americans in Trinidad. . . .
. . . Our preference for BBC news is comparatively recent. Actually, I would say that it dates from the time the U.S. Government took over the control of short-wave news in November 1942. Meanwhile, British news broadcasting has improved and is hitting from the shoulder—the way we like to get it. Ours is being presented in a typical "American advertising agency" manner, full of optimism, sweetness and honey, seemingly addressed to morons. . . .

Robert P. Borncamp
6/7/43 *Trinidad, B.W.I.*

Hair Nets for Gentlemen

. . . German officers with hair nets appear to have aroused the curiosity

of your book reviewer [May 31].

I spent some time in Austria a few years ago and lived with an ex-Army officer who, I noticed, never retired without first putting on a hair net. As a matter of fact, our maid insisted that I wear one too. . . . On me it didn't look good.

Robert E. Clark
6/21/43 *Maywood, Ill.*

The Bombing of Cathedrals

In the July 12 issue of TIME you stated that the Very Rev. William Ralph Inge, former Dean of St. Paul's, made an unpopular point by stressing regret for the bomb-shattered cathedrals of the Continent. This may be unpopular for some, but it is not for the ones who love and appreciate beautiful and priceless art. . . .

It takes approximately two years to construct a present-day skyscraper, but it took over 600 years of patient toil and sacrifice to construct the Cathedral in Cologne.

Roy Brunkenhoefer Jr.
Yorktown, Tex.

Fight-Russia Poll

I saw in TIME, May 24 issue, Reader Galaway's sensible criticism of the soldier who awaits war with Russia. . . . Could this be general sentiment?

I went out and polled 100 men. . . . Most of these men are in the Air Corps, with I.Q. scores somewhat above those of other Army branches and of the general population. The results:

If soldiers have their way, U.S.-Russian relations are entering the most tranquil period of their history. To the broad question, "Do you think the U.S. will fight Russia?" came a definite "No" (61%), with doubtfuls or undecideds 20% and "Yeses" 19%. To the moral question, "Should it?" came an even more decisive "No" of 80%, with doubtfuls 12% and "Yeses" 8%. . . .

I believe that other branches, because of the income and allied issues, would tend to be even more "liberal," even less "anti-Russia." . . .

(Corp.) Erman W. Burger
c/o Postmaster
8/9/43 *New York City*

Conventions and Civilians

This week in San Francisco soldiers, sailors and officers are sleeping in hotel lobbies while the American Legionnaires have the hotel rooms during convention week. This summer in Denver, Army flyers slept in their bombers because the Colorado Dentists, the Colorado Mail Carriers, the Optimist Club and various other organizations held conventions in all the hotels simultaneously. Naval officers had to postpone business in a California city for several days because the Spanish-American War Veterans, the Californian Federation of Women's Clubs, the Order of the Amaranths, and several other groups filled the hotels to capacity for a week. . . . And nobody does anything about it.

Those of us in the service are wined and dined and entertained royally at

D-Day: June 6, 1944. Coast Guard barges ferry wave after wave of G.I. reinforcements across the English Channel to the shores of Normandy for the invasion

canteens and clubs, but when we try to find a place to live, we get doors slammed in our faces. I have been spending my day off each week since I reported here in April just looking for one room. . . .

I'm beginning to realize what one soldier meant when he said: "When I finish fighting the Japs, I'm going to rest a while and then I'm going to turn around and start fighting the civilians."

(Name withheld by request)
9/6/43   *San Francisco*

Pin-Ups for Morale?

Reinhold Niebuhr, according to his statements [Sept. 6], seems a bit off-beamish. . . .

When a soldier gets through drilling . . . patching up the bad gear on a tank, sitting in a foxhole or the like, he's not going to cool off by reading a nice, comfy article on the "meaning of the war and the best means of using the fruits of victory creatively." . . .

Pin-up girls? Jokes? Cartoons? The boys like them. . . . They see seriousness all day long in a heavy way. Sometimes they don't get back from that bombing mission or the reconnaissance over Hill "X" to read. But if they do—they know what they want. . . .

Relax, Mr. Niebuhr, relax—that's what the boys do when they read *Stars & Stripes.*

(Name withheld by request)
9/27/43   *Wright Field, Dayton*

Timely Eisenhower

My compliments to your great magazine on your "timely" cover of the great General Eisenhower.

On Sept. 9, Italy surrenders to this brilliant General: Sept. 10 TIME arrives with the General himself adorning the cover.

Phyllis L. Sidders
9/27/43   *New York City*

Across North Africa

To TIME from a former TIME correspondent secretary, now a Red Cross worker overseas, came the following letter:

Just a list of the cities we have visited: Rabat, Casablanca, Marrakech, Oran, Meknes, Oudjda, Algiers, Fez. We have spent a night in a Sultan's palace at Fez, we have visited the headquarters of the Foreign Legion in Sidi-bel Abbes . . . we have seen the Casbah in Algiers. . . . Three gals, two others and myself, drove all across North Africa from Casablanca to Bizerte. From Bizerte we flew over to Sicily. Bizerte was an appalling sight. . . . At night . . . the moon shines down on empty shells of white buildings with black windows.

. . . Every day has been madder than the one before and life literally never has a dull moment. . . . We never go anywhere but we get great attention. . . . They follow us in jeeps, peeps, weapon carriers. We can only date officers and it is always necessary to refuse six dates a night.

This trip across North Africa gave me a pretty good idea of what Red Cross is doing and I assure you it's a lot. They have showers, towels, soap. They have food that we try our best to make a little different from the GI stuff. Cold drinks. You have no idea what a luxury ice is. . . .
10/23/43   *Doris Riker*

Indomitable Mary

Of Mary Churchill [Aug. 30] you say: "Most of her dates are with British and U.S. officers. . . . one of

them took her to see the prize fights between British and U.S. soldiers." Since I was this particular U.S. officer I can well confirm your description of Mary's gracious charm and mature intelligence. But let me add another trait: the indomitable Churchill courage against odds. . . .

Two U.S. Army softball teams were playing on a field adjacent to the ack-ack site where Mary is stationed. Our game was suddenly broken up by some 40 highly indignant British sailors. Their near-by soccer game had been broken up by the police for lack of permit to use the field. . . . Tension was critical between all of us. . . . In the interests of international harmony we decided to withdraw. . . .

Just then I happened to run into Mary near by. Her reaction was decisive. She banged her cap on her head, her blue eyes blazed, and she strode towards the milling mob to set upon the British sailors singlehanded. But unfortunately (or perhaps fortunately) the sailors had disappeared. And a highly frustrated Mary seethed all over the place. . . .

Dave Breger
Lieutenant
11/8/43   *London*
To famed Soldier Cartoonist Breger [April 5], thanks.—ED.

High Gun

I wonder just who is the top aerial gunner of the Army Air Forces. TIME [Oct. 18] gives the No. 1 spot to Sergeant Arthur P. Benko of the Four-

General MacArthur returns to the Philippines as he vowed

teenth Air Force with 16 Jap planes shot down. I seem to recall that at least two gunners of the 19th Bombardment Group were credited with scores in excess of 16. Montana's much-decorated Sergeant Russell I. Huffman . . . was credited with 19 Jap Zeros shot down before he came home last December. . . .

J. C. Moore
11/15/43   *Butte, Mont.*
Combat returns trickle home slowly. Can fighting airforcemen update high gunners' scores?—Ed.

The Patton Case

This fuss about General Patton losing his temper [Nov. 29, Dec. 6] makes us look pretty soft. Who the hell ever heard of a war going on without some emotional excitement? If, in his excitement, he struck the wrong man, why start an uproar? . . .

R. E. Hale, M.D.
Bellamy, Ala.

. . . If Patton is off balance enough to strike a sick man, he is not fit to command troops. We would suggest examination by a civilian psychiatrist, followed by disciplinary action.

In the meantime, one of us is going to try an experiment. He is toddling down to the nearest military hospital to strike a sick colonel. If there is any protest, he will, of course, apologize.

(Servicemen's names withheld)
12/20/43   *Los Angeles*

Poor Relations

I have just read your article "Poor Relations" in the issue of Dec. 6.

Bad feelings between Allies, particularly between Britain and the U.S., are obviously very undesirable, either now or in the post-war years when close cooperation will be an even greater need. . . .

Wherever Americans are stationed, they cause ill feeling by always having more money to spend than the men who fight by their side. If the American in Britain were paid British rates of pay and had the remainder assigned to his family at home or deposited in a bank account for him, he would have a fine nest egg to come home to—at the same time would have enough money to get along on. Thus one of the chief causes of irritation would be removed. . . .

(Flt. Lieutenant's name withheld)
R.C.A.F.
1/3/44   *Trenton, Ont.*

Curious, Dead Japs

You find some strange things on Jap bodies . . . the following items were found on one deceased Nip:

One Ronson cigarette lighter; one Waltham wrist watch; one U.S.-made nail clipper; a colored picture of a tiger (possibly picked up during the Malayan campaign); a helmet with hollow pads in which was secreted a girl's photograph; a mosquito headnet full of rice. . . . One other item lying

near by turned out to be a white silk shirt, made in Sydney. Don't ask me what a Nip would be doing with a white silk shirt.

Jack M. Tucker
1st Lieutenant, C.A.C.
c/o Postmaster
1/31/44   *San Francisco*

About Medals

Your article on "Tinsel & Ribbon" [Jan. 24] struck upon a sore subject to many servicemen. The following anecdote may be cited:

A flight of two medium bombers were given the assignment of breaking apart a beached boat in Kiska Harbor the early part of 1943 by dropping 500 lb. bombs at extremely low altitude. A bomb was dropped and hit the target.

For this feat the flight leader received the Silver Star, his copilot the Distinguished Flying Cross. The pilot of the wing ship received the Air Medal, the copilot nothing. The enlisted men received no decorations. . . .

The lead plane released *no* bombs because the pilot (flight leader) neglected to check the safety switch. "The" bomb which hit the target was released by the copilot of the wing ship, the same copilot who received no decoration.

Another example:

A navigator needed some flying time to collect his flying pay for that month. His name was padded on the Form I (airplane flight log). For some reason the local Bomber Command Headquarters decided that all crew members on that particular flight should be awarded the Air Medal. He received it.

2/7/44   *(Serviceman's name withheld)*

What?

We asked . . . enlisted men at random, "What are *you* fighting for?" Their answers:

"By God, it beats me, neighbor."

"Security."

"The ultimate protection of my family."

"To preserve democracy."

"To come back home and stay there."

"For freedom; for a better world."

"Survival."

"Because I have to. I ain't mad at nobody."

"I love kids and I hate to see them just pawns."

"For the preservation of the hot dog and the ice-cream soda."

(Pvt.) Frederick Thon
Editor, First Regiment Flash
2/7/44   *Fort George G. Meade, Md.*

The Big Secret

TIME, too, missed the boat on the real inside laugh at the jet propulsion "secret" [Jan. 24].

Group Captain Frank Whittle's jet

propulsion patents were published in detail, and thoroughly analyzed, in the January and February 1939, issues of—guess what—*Flugsport*, the official publication of the German air force.

Max Karant
2/14/44   *Chicago*

Why Die for Danzig?

I have just received a letter from my son, now a lieutenant in the U.S. Army Air Forces. . . . I quote part of it:

"I wish I had more faith in the new world to come after this war is won. When I was born, Dad was in the Army. When he was born, both his father and grandfather were in the Confederate Army. When my baby boy was born, I was in the Army. When his son is born, will he also be in the Army? . . .

I hate the Army. I hate being regimented and restricted and ordered around and bawled out and ignored and insulted. I want to live and work and love in any way I please, and I want everyone else in this world to have that same privilege so long as he doesn't harm me or those I love in the process. . . . Why haven't we the intelligence and common sense to build a world order where these stupid and brutal wars would be impossible? . . . It seems that even a fool could see the necessity of a strong world organization to keep the peace. Yet we have men in our Congress who do not see it. . . ."

Those of us who have sons in this war—I have two—are thinking of the French soldier and his "Why die for Danzig?" . . .

There are no doubt honest and conscientious individuals in Congress. (I have recognized no statesmen.) One has only to study their faces, pictured at various times in your magazine, listen to their immature mouthings over the radio, to realize their heartbreaking deficiencies, their utter lack of true greatness. . . . The peace, I am afraid, is already lost.

G. S. Hurdle
3/20/44   *San Diego*

The Rest of America

I was very pleased to see the article in TIME [March 13] berating wartime Miami. . . . I think the tale of a very young soldier I met there deserves retelling.

I started talking to a rather downcast sergeant at the bar of a Miami nightclub who told me he had been a tail gunner in a B-17. He also said that two months before he had been shot down over Occupied France. For 50 days he had hidden in haystacks and had finally escaped with the help of the French underground. "You know," he said, indicating the well-tanned patrons crowding the bar for 85c drinks, the unescorted female drink-moochers, the $2-a-crack fortune

teller, "You know, if the rest of America is like this, I hope to God they send me back to England."

Leslie W. Ecklund
Ensign, U.S.N.R.
3/27/44   *Glynco, Ga.*

For All Americans

For the benefit of other civilians, I forward a message to us all from a letter written by an A.A.F. captain now flying a Liberator in the Central Pacific; he wears the Air Medal with Oak Leaf Cluster.

"I want to tell you what a group of us officers and enlisted men have been talking about tonight.

"Though we have done a good job of killing the enemy, I find no sign of an organized hate in any of our men. . . . Our men come closer to hating those at home who break faith with us at the fronts—the shirkers, the profiteers, those who bicker in Washington over our rights. If the powers that be in America deny us in the service the right to an easy, practical way of voting, they will live to regret it. And to the last man our group is not in accord with what some people in the States are trying to do with some American citizens, namely the Jap citizens. We say, if they step out of the line of faithfulness to our country, punish them severely. But don't touch one of them just because he has Japanese blood. They are American citizens. We are fighting for all American citizens, and when we die for them we don't stop to ask what kind of blood they have. We are fighting for the sacred rights of man; we don't want them toyed with behind our backs."

Donald Culross Peattie
4/10/44   *Santa Barbara, Calif.*

Mass Hara-Kiri?

My answer to Robert Sherrod's Saipan question on the possible suicide of Japanese civilians when we reach Japan [Aug. 7]:

Mass hara-kiri will be effected, in front of family and military shrines and in front of the Palace in Tokyo.

*James R. Young**
4/28/44   *Pawling, N.Y.*
*Longtime I.N.S. correspondent in Tokyo, jailed and deported by the Japs in 1940, author of *Behind the Rising Sun*.

Tokyo Rose

TIME [April 10] hit home when it spoke of Tokyo Rose. I cannot resist sending you excerpts from a letter received a few days ago. The article and the coming of this letter from "somewhere in the Pacific" so nearly coincided that you might use it to stress TIME's timeliness. The writer of the letter is at present a 1st lieutenant in the Army. He writes:

"I have just had the queerest sensation and one of the biggest thrills of my life. We received our radios today. When they turned the power on tonight, I picked up Jack Benny by rebroadcast, then I changed the set to a different wave length. What do you think I heard? A lovely, warm, cultured, female voice spoke as follows:

" 'Hello fighting men in the Pacific. Are you lonely tonight? This is Radio Tokyo bringing you your Sunday Evening Concert Hour. Tonight we feature the magnificient playing of Jesús Maria Sanroma, and the Boston Pops Orchestra conducted by Arthur Fiedler.'

"At present they are playing the second recording. Can you imagine those

"Full victory—nothing else." General Eisenhower speaks to paratroopers before D-Day

bastards hitting so near home? Reception on this station is perfect and the program must be heard by many thousands. I don't know whether to be mad at them for doing it or thank them for their beautiful music and fine recording.

". . . Now a program called *Zero Hour* . . . and the announcer: 'Soldier, how about some of that music we used to have three times a day? Imagine yourself all dressed up with that girl beside you. Listen!' Benny Goodman, at his very best, playing *Stardust*.

"It is the best music we've heard since leaving the States. I can't get over how smart those devils are. Don't you know that this must make a hell of an impression on battle-strained minds? What a smooth Yankee voice the gal has! She says that she is playing these selections because they are her favorite selections, and they seemed to give the American boys so much pleasure when she was in America that she noticed it. . . ."

That article certainly was, as this letter proves, a job well done.

Caryl Weinberg
5/1/44 *Brookline, Mass.*

Our Son Was a Marine

For those three women and the man, speaking in defense of the rights of Japanese in America [May 15], I have nothing but contempt. Let them be tolerant of fellow Americans who have given their all in this war, as my wife and I have done, before they speak of intolerance toward Japanese!

Our son was a Marine captain, flying his lonely Wildcat in the forbidding and ugly Solomons when he was shot down by Japs. He's been "missing in action" since a year ago last Jan. 2. Let those four self-righteous souls sit

at home night after night with a son missing as ours has been missing, knowing not what might have been his gruesome fate, before they condemn us who would outlaw every Jap, no matter what his nativity. . . .

H. Frederick Petersen
6/5/44 *Chicago*

D-Day, H-Hour

Everybody refers to D-Day, H-Hour. Can you please tell me what they stand for or how they originated?

(Name withheld by request)
6/12/44 *Toronto*
D for Day, H for Hour means the undetermined (or secret) day and hour for the start of a military operation. Their use permits the entire timetable for the operation to be scheduled in detail and its various steps prepared by subordinate commanders long before a definite day and time for the attack have been set.

So far as the U.S. Army can determine, the first use of D for Day, H for Hour was in Field Order No. 8, of the First Army, A.E.F., issued on Sept. 7, 1918, which read: "The First Army will attack at H-Hour on D-Day with the object of forcing the evacuation of the St. Mihiel salient."—ED.

G.I. Joe Look

I am enclosing a copy of a letter from my son, Lieut. Lester N. Fitzhugh. At the time this letter was written he had been in the line 30 days without rest (or a bath, change of clothes and haircut.) . . .

". . . In World Battlefronts [March 27], there is one of the most remarkable war pictures that I've seen. The thing which really struck me a blow was to see the caption under it and

the interpretation put on it by the editors.

"It's a picture of a bearded German soldier standing in a burning street (presumably in Russia). . . . The striking thing about the picture is the look in his face. In it, his eyes and his mouth are written the complete story of all that he had been through: eternal fatigue, loss of sleep, probably bad food, recent defeat, seeing his comrades dying countless messy deaths. There is no light left in his eyes, and probably no hope left in his heart. In short, he has what I've called the 'G.I. Joe' look. . . .

"That German is no rookie; he is very likely the last survivor of his original squad. There may be only a handful like him in his company, but he's been through the mill and has learned his business while he was being completely transformed into what you see in the picture. Look at his gear: it's worn (and obviously this isn't a posed picture), but it's all there and in good shape. . . .

"Now, for the 'demoralized' look in his face. That's not demoralization you see. It's the look we all get—Germans and Americans—when for days & days & days life is nothing but a soul-killing nightmare of death and flame and fears and fatigue. . . .

"To sum it up, as my guide said when he saw the picture before showing it to me, 'Who-ee, I hope I never meet up with that guy!' "

Lois R. Fitzhugh
6/19/644 *Lancaster, Tex.*
Civilian TIME bows to a damn sight better description than its own.—ED.

Windadge in the Schoutens

A returning veteran from the Southwest Pacific told me of the following incident:

A Warrant Officer, 2nd Class, named Wright Windadge was in charge of a landing craft delivering jeeps to our troops on Biak. Just before making the landing an unaccountable swell shook the craft and the jeeps fell into the sea. When the troops ashore demanded to know where their transportation was, Windadge replied: *"Many brave jeeps lie asleep in the deep."*

Next day this Windadge was ordered to unload on Biak a cargo of C-rations. Again, just as his craft was about to make landing, an unaccountable swell dumped the food into the sea. When the troops ashore demanded to know where their rations were, Windadge replied: *"Full fathom five thy fodder lies."*

The troops were on the verge of rioting when a Jap Zero came down to strafe them. Windadge made a quick draw with his bazooka, fired, made a direct hit on the Zero and stultified it. The rioting troops subsided forthwith, for that was shooting even in the Schoutens.

Charles G. Finney
6/26/44 *Tucson, Ariz.*
Hmm.—ED.

April 1945: several of the 20,000 or so German soldiers captured by the Seventh Army after its invasion of the Reich

TIME v. the Axis

Congratulations. Today an enemy propaganda broadcast, Jap or German, I don't know which, came on the air in a typical Axis tirade against, of all things, TIME Magazine. Here is a report, as accurately as I can remember it:

"TIME is a magazine run by Jewish influence, printing dirty, malicious stories. It uses the Winchell type of news reporting, printing lies about everything and anything."

They also attacked John Scott [TIME's Stockholm correspondent], going into detail as to his antecedents, Scotch-Irish they said, but suddenly, before you know what's happened, his real name is revealed as "Isadore Kaplan," just as surely as President Roosevelt's name is "Rosenfelt." . . .

Please keep on printing this "cheap, dirty, rotten, American propaganda." We American soldiers here in India like it.

(Cpl.) Sol Friedman
c/o Postmaster
New York City
7/10/44

"Honorable Boneheads"

After enjoying Caryl Weinberg's letter [May 1] on "Tokyo Rose" we heard "Tokyo Ann" mention it in her broadcast. It's true, their recordings are good, and they do hit close to home. But to us in the Aleutians it's a morale booster! . . .

"Our Little Enemy Ann" (as she calls herself) gets off some humor at times. We all get a kick out of the way she refers to us as "Honorable Boneheads." But . . . she always directs her broadcasts to the boys in the South Pacific, which makes us here in the Aleutians feel very much slighted. . . .

So it is a fact that "Tokyo Rose" and "Little Orphan Annie" play a good part in raising our morale here in the Aleutians. Here's hoping we can pay them a visit soon.

J. Howes, U.S.N.R.
c/o Postmaster
San Francisco
7/10/44

130,000,000 Military Experts

It seems to me that a letter I have received from a U.S. Army officer in Burma has an interest for the American people. If you agree with me, perhaps you will care to print these excerpts:

". . . I guess I have been lucky. I have had part of my pack shot off my back; I have had a mortar shell, which would have blown my head off had it exploded, fall harmlessly a foot from my foxhole; I have spent 22 hours of every day in the same foxhole for 14 days; I have had dysentery for days on end, seemingly hundreds of times. And yet, though I have lost 20-30 pounds and, in common with the rest of the men, feel like a convalescent taking his first step after a long siege, I manage to stay on the right

side of that tenuous line which separates the healthy from the sick. . . .

"Tell your civilian friends that we don't really begrudge them their luxuries. . . . What does gripe the hell out of us is that America seems suddenly to have developed 130,000,000 military experts. The Senators and press correspondents are the most vociferous and hence the most obnoxious. . . ."

Eleanor Spruance
Danville, Pa.
7/17/44

"Just Like Us"

I am just an ordinary young housewife, mother of two young children, with a husband in the Army, and like many others had heard tales of dubious behaviour by the American troops in this country.

American troops have moved into our district, and we gave them a very cool reception, but it has gradually dawned on us that it's only the minority which behaves badly, and that all along we've been judging the whole by the actions of a few.

We've found the majority are sober, quiet, homely men, with wives, children and mothers they adore, who to our astonishment *don't* boast or chew gum, are ridiculously generous.

We're all glad we've been able to judge for ourselves by having American soldiers here because now we know what a typical American is like. Perhaps the nicest way I can express what I mean without intending to appear smug is: the Yanks are just like us.

(Mrs.) Joan Hopper
Chandler's Ford, Hants.
7/31/44
England

Keats's Grave

"When the Nazis were driven from Rome three weeks ago, it is probable that few among the liberating forces realized that they had liberated, among other things, the grave of John Keats" [June 26].

In the course of one half-hour's brooding over his grave, situated in a less frequented portion of the city, I saw two American enlisted men, one American Red Cross worker, two plaid-skirted Scottish lieutenants and two Italian girls come to pay their respects.

Artillery fire had damaged several gravestones between Keats's and the pyramid of Caius Cestius, a stone's throw away. Other greats in the same cemetery: Shelley, Trelawny, John Addington Symonds. Keats's name goes unmentioned on his own gravestone ("Here lies one whose name was writ in water"), but is inscribed on that of his painter-friend Severn, buried by his side.

Their house in the Piazza di Spagna is "Off limits to Allied Troops," but the boat-shaped fountain still gushes water, and flowers in multichromed abundance still are sold at the base of the stairs ascending the Quirinal Hill.

Gilbert Goldstein
c/o Postmaster
New York City
8/7/44

Seven-Yard Beachhead

Today I received a copy of your June 12 issue . . . It gave me a picture [of the invasion]—a large-scale picture—but not the picture we saw the morning of June 6, 1944, on the

First Radio Pictures of Historic Surrender Scene

CHICAGO DAILY NEWS RED STREAK

SEIZE GOERING, HIMMLER NAZI SURRENDER TERMS

HISTORIC RADIOPHOTO OF GERMANY'S UNCONDITIONAL SURRENDER TO ALLIES

Daily Mail
FOR KING AND EMPIRE

GERMANY'S FATE: OFFICIAL
Big Three Lay Down Framework for Peace of the World

All Reich Forces to be Disbanded | General Staff to be Broken | Arms Industry to be Eliminated | Swift Punishment for War Crimes

REICH TO MAKE GOOD ALL DAMAGE IN KIND

Koniev is Swinging North Towards Berlin

The German surrender as depicted by an American and a British newspaper

---

French coast. . . .

The 1st U.S. Infantry Division spearheaded the Allied invasion from the sea. Our regiment spearheaded the division's assault. When we hit the beach we were confronted with an entire German division. . . .

The two assault battalions hit the beach at H-hour, but a great percentage never saw the beach, for their assault craft suffered direct hits. The assault troops were subjected to fire from both flanks. . . . Fields of fire for the attacker were poor. . . . Doggies* drowned. Doggies floundered in the water. Enemy fire, enemy shells, enemy mortars and the beach obstacles scored enormous casualties. Key officers, key noncoms, key scouts, key men were lost; equipment sunk.

We expected to find immense shell craters in the beach to afford us cover. Nothing—just pebbles. And then began the seven-yard beachhead. Those strong points (three to five pillboxes, 75 artillery piece in casement, etc.) had to be knocked out. The first wave was on that seven-yard beachhead when the second wave hit the beach. . . . Doggies that were hit would slip back into the water. Snipers were picking us off. H.E. and mortars kept coming on that beachhead. It still remained a seven-yard beachhead for more than three hours. Finally the strong points were knocked out, one by one. The toll was grim.

Our Commanding Officer yelled to the doggies: "There are two kinds of men on the beach: those who are dead and those who are about to die. Get off the goddam beach!"

(Serviceman's name withheld)
c/o Postmaster
8/14/44 *New York City*
*Short for dogfaces, a hoary term for U.S. infantrymen.

What About Mrs. G.I. Joe?

The G.I. Bill of Rights, while practically assuring every veteran a Chris-Craft speedboat, two cars in every garage, a home in the country, a penthouse, and an egg in his beer, has, in our opinion, failed to deal with a question which is destined to present one of the most controversial issues of the postwar world. To wit:

Will the returning G.I. be able to maintain the same balance of power in his home that he enjoyed in the halcyon days, or will the female of the species assert herself and declare the "old order" relegated to the limbo of nostalgic memories?

(Pvt.) Ed G. Lancaster
8/14/44 *Camp Claiborne, La.*

No V-Day Blowoff?

Instead of all this talk and planning about closing up shop and blowing off

steam when V-day in Europe comes, how about keeping our shirts on, sticking soberly on the job, and putting our backs into helping those one million boys in the Pacific get home the sooner?

Wm. B. Holt
9/14/44 *Laguna Beach, Calif.*

The Gripe at Home

I have a gripe. Its crux is the problem of returning servicemen.

They scream we don't understand them when they come home. We don't know what it's like to see our buddy shot down in flames or ripped to pieces with a shell burst. How in hell *could* we know? . . .

You come home from the inferno and find a placid bunch of people who don't even know there's a war on. No bombers flew over us in a storm of death, chums. No snipers lurked at the corner of 3rd and Market; no ack-ack batteries picked us off in our penthouses. But that isn't our fault. It's a tribute to you. You kept us safe and we appreciate it.

What is it you want? To know that we are sweating to back you up? When you needed a gun, you got it, didn't you? You are the best equipped fighting force in the whole world, and you didn't get that way by us sitting at home on our fat fannies. Sure, we have slackers. The Army has slackers too.

Remember why you enlisted? To keep from being drafted or because all your friends were in? Did you apply for a commission because you felt you could do more toward winning the war that way, or because you could make more money, and you liked the prestige of being an officer?

You see? We are making the best of what we have, and you are too. You are maybe not in the service from choice but it is all part of being a young man and a member of a human race whose way of life seems to include periodic wars.

You have had *esprit de corps* like a shot in the arm for so long it's like dope to you. Those now being discharged are lost without it. They feel misunderstood. They don't realize that the problem of adjustment lies within themselves, because eventually they and you, will fit back into the pattern much as we have kept it going. We at home want to help, we are desperate to help, but what is it you want? . . .

You come home from hell and find us full of lassitude and complacency and you want to kick our teeth in. We can see your point. Can you see our point? We originally were made of the same fabric. Yours is maybe now a little tattered. But it can be mended. We *can* meet on a common plane if you will understand us too. We are the reality. The scene of battle is in an obscure past. We are the future, your future. You had better accept us and our frailties and our good intentions. This is directed specifically in reply to TIME's article on morale [Sept. 11].

I might add that this is not all idle chatter, that I am looking forward with much joy and not a little trepidation to my husband's return from England where he is the navigator of a B-17 . . .

Jean P. Haydon
10/2/44 *San Francisco*

Shave for Shopkeepers?

It would seem logical and fair that, for every French prostitute so eagerly shaven and stripped by the impromptu courts held by French people, one shopkeeper and one businessman or businesswomen should also be given the same treatment. They, too, in their own way, have been doing business with the Nazis, the only difference, perhaps, being in the greater profit realized by the shopkeeper and businessman.

It seems odd that the French, whose history and literature so abound with freedom of expression as far as sex is concerned, should use sexual morality as the discriminatory basis for meting out punishment.

(T/Sgt.) Robert W. Russell
10/2/44 *Santa Ana, Calif.*

Ready for V-Day?

I have just finished reading "Ready for V-Day" [Sept. 4]. You bet *we* are ready for it, but it would seem that our definition of V-Day is not in accord with that of the patriots (?) at home. . . .

There are some of us who have been fighting the Battle of the Pacific for almost three years. It hasn't been easy and, although we are making great strides toward victory, there are still some terrible battles to be fought in which thousands of young American boys will fall. Why? So the nation can have parades and celebrations, blow whistles and get drunk after just one foe has fallen?

Let those who think this war is over with the capitulation of Germany remember this: the day they are parading and enjoying their celebration there will be men out here dying from bullets, shrapnel and disease for them; men living horrible existences in filthy, swampy, disease-infested jungles, for them. Don't get me wrong—we will be just as happy and just as proud of our brothers when they have won the great Battle of Europe. We know what sacrifices have been made and will be made to bring about this victory. *But in God's name—don't break faith with us in the Pacific!*

(Y2/C) George A. Kent,
U.S.N.R., c/o Fleet P.O.
10/16/44 *San Francisco*

Don't be Surprised

. . . If America permits the Germans to keep their heavy industry, we shall have no right to be surprised if we shall read in TIME of Sept. 14, 1964:

"The robot bombs, which through their simultaneous attack on 89 American cities have brought this national disaster, were assembled in German factories and other industrial establishments which in 1944 were considered harmless."

Let the victims of 1964 thank those who, in 1944, were too refined to be fanatical Naziphobes.

K. Kauffmann-Grinstead
10/23/44 *New York City*

Merchant Marine Casualties

Re: "U.S. War Casualties" [Oct. 2]. TIME, obviously, does not see fit to regard Merchant Marine losses as part of U.S. war casualties.

Gerald A. Cohen
Ensign, U.S.M.S.
11/27/44 *France*
For security reasons, Merchant Marine casualty figures have not been released as regularly as the armed forces'. Up to Oct. 1, the Merchant Marine losses since the beginning of the war were 5,855, of which 560 were prisoners of war.—ED.

Editorial Confession

Do TIME editors go in for New Year's stock-takings and that sort of thing? The question occurred to me when I recently read the following confession by the editor of a British magazine called *Horizon*:

"What have we lost or gained intellectually by five years of war? We have gained in seriousness, but lost in mental elasticity; the emotional strain of war has broken our curiosity, has fatigued us to the point at which we are cynical, impervious, distressed or hostile in the presence of new ideas."

I wondered: Is this only a special mood induced by the special ravages of war in Britain? Perhaps this British editor is more honest than American editors? What I especially wondered was whether this British editor's sentiment is one that TIME's editors share, secretly or otherwise.

Farley Smith
12/25/44 *New York City*
Less fatigued than Horizon's *conscientious Editor Cyril Connolly, TIME editors sanguinely observe that pessimism among editors is not infrequently a sign of editorial health. With tongue only lightly in cheek, TIME applauds the shrewd observation of Harvard's late President Eliot: "Things seem to be going fairly well, now that a spirit of pessimism prevails in all departments."—ED.*

"The Rest of My Life . . ."

Here is a letter from an ex-newspaperman in response to a letter I wrote him asking that he consider a job on our staff in days to come. I can't remember seeing a better letter of its kind:

"It's hard for me to realize that we've passed the third anniversary of Pearl Harbor. . . . I lost my time sense, I think, about the time we rounded the north turn of the training cycle in the California-Arizona desert. There have been a good many hours when, hanging between wakefulness and oblivion, I have allowed myself to consider the rest of my life. These are some of the tentative conclusions I have reached:

"1) I never intend to work as hard again as I have worked during these three years in the Army. Since I left the States in June there hasn't been an hour that I wasn't asleep or at work. I do not offer this as testimony

A Soviet soldier embraces a G.I. on German soil

to my own desperate energy; I am, in fact, gifted with a rather lethargic nature which has made the regimen peculiarly difficult. My next job will have to allow time for private, personal thinking, talking, reading and writing.

"2) I intend to live in the South again. There are the usual reasons for that decision—the ties of blood that never seem important until you've lived a long time away from home. Then, I don't think I've been really warm since I left South Carolina in 1941; in Normandy I used to sleep in a puddle and dream of the long, bright days when good Southerners sit in the shade and watch the heat waves rise off the parched red earth and feel the sweat slowly run over their ribs. I have missed the innate courtesy and good manners of Southerners. I have met too many loud S.O.B.s. I have been forced into rudeness myself too many times. . . .

"3) I want to stay in one place for a while. I'm sick of the rootless existence I led at first by choice, and later of necessity. I want to build a house, water a lawn, dig a can of beer out of my own refrigerator, get elected to a school board. I want to dig my roots into a community. . . .

"4) Some day, when the weariness has passed, I'll want to get back into the old fight, of which this war is a military phase. I've come to believe that the important things, the essential freedoms, the democratic processes, are luxuries, not inalienable rights, and the price we must pay for them is high. . . .

"5) None of the conclusions I have reached will mean much in the end. When I come home from the wars, late in all probability, my final choice of a job will be dictated not by desirable working conditions, geographic location, utilization of my special

Inmate of a concentration camp

talents, security, or the conscience of the publisher, but by the urgent need to earn a living. . . ."

J. E. Down
Editor, Charlotte News
Charlotte, N.C.
1/29/45

Girls Wanted

We are a couple of fighter pilots stationed in Assam.

Since coming overseas, we have had brought home to us, rather forcibly . . . that women aren't inclined to wait for long when a man has to take time out to fight the war. So we find ourselves the proud possessors of two big shining silver fighter planes but without any girls to name them after, as per the time-honored policy of this squadron.

We would appreciate [your printing] this in your "Letters" section in hopes that at least two girls, in whose hearts still faintly glows a spark of patriotism, will see it and send us a letter with their picture enclosed. The

picture, or a reasonable facsimile thereof, captioned by the accompanying names, will be emblazoned boldly upon the plane's nose, and we can once more soar majestically over Burma without feeling bitter towards one of the things for which we are fighting—namely *American womanhood.*

Bryant G. Newton, Lieut., U.S.A.A.F.
Leonard R. Briley, Lieut., U.S.A.A.F.
APO 629
c/o Postmaster
New York City
2/12/45

Copious Patriotism

Thanks (?) very much for printing our letter [asking two girls to volunteer to let us put their picture on our planes]. [Feb. 12]. . . . We are currently being assured by 300 feverish women a day, via air mail, that AMERICAN WOMANHOOD is not just sparked but burning up with violent, copious and passionate patriotism. . . .

The Burma Beauty Contest is fully under way, gentlemen. . . .

Bryant G. Newton,
1st Lieutenant, U.S.A.A.F.
Leonard R. Briley,
1st Lieutenant, U.S.A.A.F.
c/o Postmaster
New York City
3/26/45

Foxhole Critique

I was looking forward last night to seeing *The Enchanted Cottage* because of TIME's favorable review [April 16], and I could not understand my friend, who had already seen it, when he said, "Oh I suppose it's a good picture, but. . . ."

The moment Robert Young struck the match and revealed his war-disfigured face, I understood.

G.I. theaters are never quiet. Even during Hollywood's versions of war,

These Soviet corpses were found at Zonenburg jail in 1945

no matter how grim, constant wise-cracks can be heard. But when that match was struck the audience froze. Hollywood had touched their sore spot —the G.I.'s second most dreaded injury.

The younger generation does not need to be shielded from reality, for they are meeting and mastering it every day. But movies offer battle-tired men one of the few escape mechanisms left open to them. For them, even war pictures can be entertaining because they do not show war as they know it. But here, thrown in their faces, was something personal, something they try not to think about.

The picture ignores the daily miracles of plastic surgery and offers as the answer to the problem the enchantment of true love. From the artistic viewpoint and for the philosopher this will suffice. But G.I.s are pessimistic by profession and strict realists.

Both to those who wait and to those who daily go down into hell, I wonder if Hollywood hasn't been unintentionally cruel?

(Pvt.) Frederick E. Sontag
4/15/45   *Camp Livingston, La.*

"Lest We Forget"

Despite the slow seepage of horror from earlier reports, I was unprepared for your account [April 30] of the German concentration camps. Erla— the trapped, clawing, burning men; Buchenwald—the massive cordwood of the starved dead; Belsen—the small children "too nearly dead themselves to cry," nestled against the rotting bodies of their mothers.

Let us have an international Day of Remembrance after this war, with persistent requiem music—remembrance for those who died innocent and helpless, as well as for those who died active in combat for them.

Lest we forget, let us not pretty up these sites. Let their preservation be scrupulous in every detail. Let their numbers and distribution be sufficient so every German be acquainted with them with Teutonic thoroughness. Let them be accessible to people of all countries as one of the distinguishing monuments of our time. . . .

Hazel M. Wiggers
5/21/45   *Chicago*

The French

. . . A letter from Miss Jean Maier [May 7] certainly irked me . . . because her tirades at Gertrude Stein carried the same impression about France that I have found most people in the U.S. and Canada have. . . .

If we here in North America had half the guts and courage that the French people had through four years of occupation, this post-war peace would be assured. How many people here would risk their life and that of their entire family for a perfect stran-

May 4, 1945: the Germans surrender to Field Marshal Montgomery

Sept. 2, 1945: the Japanese surrender aboard the U.S. battleship *Missouri* in Tokyo harbor

ger from some foreign land? The people of France did. They did it for thousands upon thousands of American, British, Canadian, Australian, Polish airmen and soldiers evading capture between 1940 and 1944. I know because I was one of them. . . .

There are hundreds of American airmen alive and back home now because of these "decadent" French people. . . . They kept alive the flame of freedom under the heel of the Gestapo.

William G. Brayley
Ex-Flying Officer, R.C.A.F.
5/28/45   *Montreal*

Mt. Suribachi's Flag

In the many stories written about the famous flag-raising on Mt. Suribachi it has never been said where the flag came from. I have that story in two letters from my son, Ensign Alan S. Wood, U.S.N.R., communications officer on an LST, and I thought you might be interested in it:

"The second time we hit the beach at Iwo the marines were taking over Mt. Suribachi. When they raised a little flag on top of the mountain, the marines on the beach cheered. A little later a marine came on board asking for a large flag, so I gave him our only large flag—which is the one pictured on the first page of TIME magazine last week [March 5]. We are proud that it is our flag flying there.

"The now famous flag which I gave to the marine on the beach at Iwo was one I ran across one day at Pearl Harbor while I was rummaging around the salvage depot. It was in a duffle bag with some old signal flags—probably from a decommissioned destroyer or destroyer escort or something like that. It looked brand new and was folded neatly.

"It seems funny, now that I look back. . . . One might say that the flag was carried from a salvage heap at Pearl Harbor to the bloody heights of Iwo as a symbol of the American fighting spirit to avenge the disaster of Pearl Harbor."

(Mrs.) H. Randolph Wood
7/9/45 *Sierra Madre, Calif.*

In Defense of Patton

It seems a shame that there aren't more writers to defend General Patton. No one criticized him when he led the Third Army through Germany. Now that he has returned to his homeland, bombarding him with criticism certainly isn't very appreciative.

If he made mistakes in his speeches (and I don't think them mistakes), everyone makes mistakes. Thank God we had a man who didn't make mistakes in his strategy and leadership. . . .

If Patton makes a mistake, at least he's making an effort to impress in the strongest way upon the public that we must end wars! Goddamit, isn't there any one on your staff who has the courage to defend a great man?

Grace Dumm
7/30/45 *Garden Grove, Calif.*
Said Able Soldier Oliver Cromwell to his portrait painter: ". . . Paint my picture truly like me; but remark all these roughnesses, pimples, warts, and everything as you see me. . . ."—Ed.

Unsung Wives

In war or peace, broken marriages always make good copy. With critics shouting at women from every side, little wonder that the lonely, faithful, loving service wife remains unheard and unsung.

(Mrs.) Mary F. Porter
8/13/45 *Washington*

The Maligned Sex

Grace Moore's recent spleen on faithless wives of overseas servicemen [Aug. 6] just barely deserves the dignity of a reply. Nothing is so pitiful as

a woman maligning her own sex, and at a time when womanhood should stand together for protection from those who think in little clichés.

Who is this paragon of virtue that she should set herself up as judge and jury? And what does she know of . . . the life of a serviceman's wife?

Has she ever been a camp follower whose husband has implored her to follow him from camp to camp and who, to make it financially possible, has knocked herself out working in laundries and hash houses? Has she ever seen the light go out of a woman's eyes when something a little more glamorous comes along and all he can see is "the tired little woman?" . . .

Don't go overrating this "overseas" stuff. A uniform and a Government-sponsored boat ride won't necessarily make a good husband out of a poor one. There are bad husbands overseas as well as good ones. No, the kinds of wives the men left behind are of their own making. . . .

Mrs. Frank C. Maloof
9/3/45 *Junction City, Kan.*

The Last at Dunkirk?

The British claim that Field Marshal Alexander was "the last man off Dunkirk."

A Frenchwoman who bore a German soldier's child is publicly humiliated

The French point out proudly that Admiral Abrial, having watched the English "safely off," was the last to leave.

TIME [Aug. 6] refers to Laborite Lieut. General Mason MacFarlane as the "last man to leave the beach at Dunkirk."

Others say there was no last man, since the French divisions of General Prioux stayed back and fought their way to the main front.

Could TIME, once for good, pick out the real "last man" and tell me?

F. Arnold
9/10/45   *Montreal, P.Q.*
The Official French report says that Vice Admiral Abrial left June 4, 1940; the British official report says that Major General Alexander left June 3. But because the evacuation of Dunkirk was primarily a British show, Alexander seems most likely to receive history's accolade.—ED.

Tourists in Tokyo?

In your article on the Japanese surrender in the Sept. 3 issue of TIME, you say that the Japs were treating their invaders "as equals." I submit that they are treating them as "tourists," guests of the Emperor and of the empire. It is the same old propaganda line of prewar days. . . .

We must remember that the surrender of the Japanese served their purpose, and may in the long run prove to be only a truce. While submitting to occupation, the Japanese are keeping their sovereignty; we licked their Navy but not their Government nor their people. They meant business at Pearl Harbor and they still mean business. They saved face by a change of face; they intend to wait a while longer. . . . It will be an uneasy peace. We are dealing with a warped, suicidal and unforgiving race.

Now the Japanese will go back to their old game of imitating democracy —democracy in so far, they will make it plain, as it does not interfere with their fanatical Emperor worship. . . . The Emperor will remain a son of the Sun, instead of what our fighting men have long called him. And underneath it all the spirit of bushido will remain unbroken.

S. M. Bradley
9/24/45   *Morehead, Ky.*

A Declaration for Germany

. . . We would naturally be very grateful if you would publish this statement by former members of the German Reichstag. . . .

"Considering the impending negotiations on a peace treaty with Germany, the undersigned former members of the German Reichstag who have found refuge in this free country hereby declare:

"Even a conquered nation has the undeniable right to be represented at

Convicted Nazis Goering and Hess hear their sentences at the Nuremberg trials

the peace table. The opportunity should be given to the German people without delay to establish a central body which shall be entitled to negotiate in the name of the German people. This body should also be entitled to negotiate with the governments of the neighboring countries on all matters commonly concerning these nations and Germany. . . .

"The problems of Europe cannot be solved by shifting frontiers hither and thither as has been done for many centuries, always resulting in new wars. The tendency to create closed national states by wholesale expulsion of entire populations surrounded by insurmountable walls, will inevitably lead to general impoverishment and disturbances of international relations. On the other hand, if the peace is to be a lasting one, frontiers must cease to be impediments to the free flow of men, merchandise, ideas and news.

"In order to rebuild the destroyed area and to restore European as well as world economy, the German people must have the freedom to dispose of the treasures of their soil, and to manufacture goods for peaceful use to the full extent of their capabilities. . . . Dismantling of industries and disastrous export of vital raw materials should be stopped, the replacement of destroyed or confiscated machinery

needed for peacetime production should be permitted.

"In order to restore the rights of all men, all prisoners of war should be released immediately, and slave labor of any kind must be abolished.

"No matter at what time the state of war will be formally ended, a real peace will not begin until the last soldier of every victorious nation has left the soil of his former enemy.

"Irrespective of the question to what extent Germany has been responsible for the Nazi tyranny with its devastating consequences for mankind, the German people have been punished already to a degree unparalleled in modern history. Now the time has come to give the democratic forces of the German people. . . . a chance. The time has come to abandon vengeance and to turn to understanding and reconciliation, the only way to a durable peace."

S. Aufhauser
Dr. F. Baade
Gustave Ferl
Hugo Heimann
Marie Juchacz
Emil Kirschmann
Gerhart H. Seger
William F. Sollmann
Friedrich Stampfer
Dr. H. Staudinger
1/13/47   *New York City*

The Frightened Forties

A singer named Frank Sinatra and a musical named *Oklahoma!* entertained Americans—in spite of the war. F.D.R. was elected to a fourth term, but did not live to witness the explosions that brought World War II to a close. The United Nations was created to prevent future wars, yet a new type of war developed, a "cold" one. In the world of medicine, penicillin was discovered. At home people watched people on television for the first time.

Man of the Year

Why publicize as Man of the Year a human who has disclosed himself to be one of the most terrible of beasts?

We have been taught for generations that any descriptive term such as Man of the Year, which you use, should imply an outstanding and noble character. Whatever you may say about Ivan the Terrible inside the covers does not alter the fact that many other humans who look up to Stalin will get great aid and comfort from your giving him the cover on millions of copies of TIME, displayed prominently all over our country and other countries. As "clear, curt, concise" and cold as TIME is in giving the news, which I have read for many years from cover to cover, I cannot help but feel that you should display some grain of sympathy for the thousands of humans whose deaths are the direct results of the man you term Man of the Year.

W. S. Whittlesey
1/22/40 *New York City*

'30s

Boom (1930), Crash (1931, 32, 33, 34), Boom (1935), Slump (1936-37), Boom (1938-39), War (1930-39). . . . I suggest the *Tempestuous Thirties.*

Clarkson Hill
Burlington, Vt.

When the market crashed in 1929, it blitzkrieged me with the rest. I would call the ten years following, the Threadbare '30s.

Groucho Marx
Metro-Goldwyn-Mayer Pictures
2/5/40 *Culver City, Calif.*
To Reader Marx the threadbare distinction of pinning the aptest adjective yet on the '30s.—ED.

No Surrender

I was amazed and shocked beyond expression to find TIME this week functioning as a propaganda sheet for the Irish Republicans, and giving aid and comfort to them in their nefarious work of terrorism and assassination of innocents. . . . I strongly suspect that this article on Eire was slipped over on TIME's editors by a clever Irish Republican schemer and deceiver.

The Scotch-Irish of Northern Ireland . . . are as determined today as ever that they shall remain British and Protestant; their banner is inscribed now, as in the day of William of Orange, with this proud slogan: "NO SURRENDER." Let the Irish terrorists start a fight if they want to, then they shall see what manner of fighters these Northern Scotch-Irish are!

John Cameron
4/15/40 *Quincey, Mass.*

Unlikely Savior

. . . About your sudden "ohs" and "ahs" before the mystery of Franklin Roosevelt. . . . It is no mystery that with all his bold self-confidence, he has not solved a single major problem of his seven years' administration. . . . A man whose uninhibited wizardry has failed in peace is not likely to be the savior in war. . . .

George E. Sweazey
Tyler Place Presbyterian Church
7/1/40 *St. Louis, Mo.*

Canada's Progress

Your article in reference to Canada, July 8, p. 28, is just another illustration that still waters run deep. It is surprising that your neutral observers can only see the froth on the surface kicked up by a numerically weak but very windy opposition.

Canada was just as unprepared for modern war as the U.S. is at the present time. The progress made by a Government elected on a landslide since war was declared is simply prodigious. Canada is doing her bit in a most efficient and effective manner both at home and abroad. There'll always be an England, the champion of the liberty of subjected peoples.

J. E. Grierson
8/5/40 *Winnipeg, Manitoba*

Reason & Rhyme

Congratulations on your election extra. It was sublime, it had reason and rhyme, and it came out on time. We in

Interventionist *vs.* Isolationist: whether the U.S. should enter or stay out of World War II was hotly debated during the two years leading up to Pearl Harbor

DEFEND YOUR COUNTRY

ENLIST NOW *in the* UNITED STATES ARMY

WAR'S FIRST CASUALTY
AMERICA FIRST COMMITTEE
141 West Jackson Boulevard
CHICAGO

Canada trust and hope that the third term of F. D. R. will make a four-star final.

Sergeant Morris Goodman
12/2/40   *Ottawa, Ont.*

Roosevelt Admirer

. . . President Roosevelt was elected by a clear majority of the voters of this country on a clear-cut foreign policy, concurred in by the opposing candidate. He knows that it is impossible "to keep this country out of war" if by so doing America must abandon her place as the leader in world ideals of liberty, as the guardian of the dignity of the individual and as the champion of the right of free peoples everywhere to remain free if they so desire.

No man in Congress has Mr Roosevelt's vision, his political experience, his prestige, his patriotism and, may I add, his breeding.

Neil Martin
3/17/41   *Los Angeles, Calif.*

Man of the Year

Your selection of Mr. Roosevelt as Man of the Year deserves great praise from clear-thinking subscribers. Winston Churchill's epic words, "Never have so many owed so much to so few," can include this magnanimous figure as one of the "few." . . .

Stephen M. Walsh Jr.
1/26/42   *Lynn, Mass.*

Washboard Weepers

. . . I started this war with a morale as good as anybody's, but it started slipping after a few days of steady "washboard weepers," and by the end of a week I was ready to surrender. . . .

However, I have discovered a silver lining—an infallible technique I'd like to pass along: I leave the volume turned down so that I can't hear a word—only the tone of the voices. Then if the voice is one filled with violence and hatred, passing and pain, life and death, the show is going on. When the tone changes to one filled with lush romantic gentle coaxing and Charles Boyer's eyes—then it's the announcer. . . . But when the voice comes out cool and calm and matter-of-fact, with nothing in it but words—then I dash to the radio to turn it up and find out who's got Bengasi now.

Mrs. E. D. Perkins
2/22/42   *Lewiston, Idaho*

Objective Reporting

Congratulations upon your TIME-worthy handling of the Chinese situation in your issue of June 1. As one who has some knowledge of the Orient and of Oriental psychology, I know how much the Chinese will appreciate real help at this time, and how long and resentfully they will remember it if we give them nothing but cash and conversation.

President Roosevelt makes victory sign

Your handling of this matter was superb. Historical changes have always been brought about by significant causes so obvious that it seems incredible they weren't properly understood. Nearly always, however, they were obscured by contemporary trivia which seemed more important at the time.

Continue your objective reporting, concentrate your literary focus upon the truly significant, group-events so they are seen in their proper perspective, and you will do your country a great service, as well as re-establish the "power of the press." And we need that far more than we think we do at the moment.

Erle Stanley Gardner
6/29/42   *Temecula, Calif.*

Contrast

In your article in TIME, Sept. 28, under Education, you indicated that women were not responding to industrial training offered free by New York colleges. Our experience here in Cleveland has been entirely contrary to this.

To date we have instructed more than 300 women in courses in inspection and mechanical drawing. When these classes started, we had twice as many applications as we could take care of. Beginning Oct. 15 we plan to repeat these courses, instructing a similar number of women. Our applications to date are coming in so fast that once again we will probably be able to take care of only about one half of those interested. . . .

James W. Griswold
Field Director, E.S.M.W.T.
Fenn College
10/19/42   *Cleveland*

Liquor Question

May thanks to you for your honest reporting of the W.C.T.U. situation in this country. The spectacle of this group trying to exploit our national crisis to enforce prohibition again is to me a nauseating one.

At present there are five men in my

family in the armed services, the majority of them having enlisted. . . . There isn't one who would drink while on duty, who would drink while driving a car, or who likes to drink and roll in the gutter. But on their occasional weekends home, they have certainly earned the right to relax as they wish and they will certainly find a drink waiting for them in my home. I'll go further and state that regardless of the success achieved by the W.C.T.U., these men will *always* find a drink waiting for them in my home. . . .

Let's clamp down on the dirty dives; let's crack down harder on drunken drivers; let's ration our remaining supply of drinkables. And let's quit arguing over prohibition till the war is won and the boys are home to discuss it, too.

Edith L. Thornton
11/9/42   *Philadephia, Pa.*

The Nine Others

On page 59 of TIME, Oct. 25: "*La Prensa* . . . is one of the world's ten greatest papers." What, in your opinion, are the other nine? . . .

R. M. Markham
St. Petersburg, Fla.
11/23/42

As a proposal: the London Times, Manchester Guardian, *New York* Times, *New York* Herald Tribune, Baltimore Sun, St. Louis *Post-Dispatch,* Washington *Post,* Kansas City *Star, and one more to be named by the reader.*—ED.

Man of the Year

In choosing Joseph Stalin Man of the Year, TIME not only hit the nail on the head, but sunk a spike in one blow. Stalin stands for the Russian people, for what they are and for all they have done, the way they've done it, their guts, patriotism and downright loyalty to him as a leader in a country at war. The Germans fight like devils, but the Russian people, all of them, are fighting like all hell and their fight is in the name of Stalin. In him has the impossible been attained—for a second time. Whether or not we agree with his form of government, let us in 1943 look toward this giant, take heed of his meaning and fight like hell.

Michael James
Seaman 2nd Class, U.S.N.
1/25/43   *Cape May, N.J.*

Anzac Tide

In your issue [Nov. 2] you referred to Air Vice Marshall Coningham, R.A.F., as an Australian. The reason his nickname is "Mary" (a corruption of "Maori," the name of the New Zealand native, TIME, Nov. 9) is because he is a New Zealander, born and bred.

. . . We are very touchy about the confusion between Australians and New Zealanders, even though your splendid Marines ask, "Where do you go when the tide comes in?"

William M. E. Tweed
3/22/43   *Heretaunga, New Zealand*

Abortion

TIME's story on abortions [March 6] ended sadly in mid-air. After shocking its readers quite justifiably . . . then pointing out that police raids are no cure . . . TIME sighs and says that no one has yet figured out the answers to such questions.

If TIME had leafed a few more pages in the late great Dr. Frederick J. Taussig's standard text on abortion . . . it would have found this statement: "Of all the measures suggested for the control of abortion none equals in importance the widespread establishment of clinics for contraceptive advice and provision for the free distribution of contraceptive materials among the poor. . . . By the prevention of the undesired or undesirable pregnancy we can reduce the number of cases requiring abortion to a relatively small number. . . ."

D. Kenneth Rose
National Director, Planned Parenthood
Federation of America, Inc.
3/27/44 *New York City*

Ford's Food

Henry Ford, observing his 81st birthday, is quoted as saying, "The time is coming when man will be able to determine the length of his life span by controlling his diet. I think he will find everything he needs in wheat; wheat is the divine food."

On other occasions he has referred to the soybean as an indispensable food. . . .

I am sure it would be of great interest to your readers to print Mr. Ford's diet. . . .

Golding Fairfield
8/28/44 *Denver*
Henry Ford's two basic ideas on eating are 1) never to satisfy his hunger completely at any one meal; 2) never to eat sugar (because he believes sugar crystals get in people's blood streams and cause infections). He takes a healthy, if restrained, interest in such substantial items as roast beef, lamb and pork chops, baked potatoes, butter, cream. His present enthusiasm for wheat is more industrial than dietary, like his onetime predictions that roads would some day be paved with coffee beans, and automobiles be made, in part at least, from cantaloupes.—ED.

Inter-Faith Committee

I am a Catholic. Please see that the enclosed check for $50 reaches the young Presbyterian minister whom you quoted in TIME, Aug 7—"I am determined to be known in my community as a minister of God first, a Protestant second and a Presbyterian third. . . ."

More such spirit will draw us nearer to Christ and peace.

Elizabeth Norris Lynch
9/18/44 *Merion, Pa.*
TIME forwarded Reader Lynch's $50 check to ex-Army Air Forces Chaplain Ayers, now a Presbyterian pastor in Wilkes-Barre, who says he will use the money to develop an inter-faith committee on "religion and returning service personnel."—ED.

Lend-Lease Cigarettes

There is a rumor snowballing up on this coast that the reason the market has been exhausted of popular-brand cigarettes is because they are being shipped to civilian populaces of European countries. Is it true?

Diana Dunning
10/9/44 *Culver City, Calif.*

Who threw that snowball? In the last tweve months Lend-Lease exported six million pounds of cigarets. Typical pre-war-year (1934) exports: eight million pounds. Prime reason for the home shortage: increased smoking by both U.S. servicemen and civilians.—ED.

"Oh, Brother!"

Senator Claude Pepper is, politically, completely impossible to me, but I must now, I confess, "give the devil his due." His idea of putting Congress on the air [Oct. 9] is a classic. It could not fail to have a salutary effect. It would result in a new awareness by most people of the gigantic problems of running the nation, and the difficulty in finding methods for solution. It would create a beneficial change of thinking of national scope.

And, oh brother! It would certainly expose the absentees, logrollers, floorhoggers, etc., in our legislative houses!

Henry Lee, Jr.
11/6/44 *Chicago*

The Election

The people of the U.S. have elected Franklin D. Roosevelt to be their President during the next four years, and history will record that the voters of America made a wise choice. Mr. Dewey started off with fine prospects but proceeded to talk himself out of any chance of winning. Mr. Roosevelt's success in winning elections is no mystery. He just sits back and lets the Republican candidate defeat himself.

Isidore L. Caron
12/4/44 *Sandwich, Mass.*

F.D.R. Tribute

. . . So that we and all the peoples of the days and years to come may

dutifully and lovingly honor Franklin Delano Roosevelt's great beneficence and vision, let us, the people of America, suggest to all the leaders and common folk of the world that the Franklin Delano Roosevelt Court of Nations be erected to house the conferences and meetings that are to come in the days of peace. It would indeed be suitable for the leaders of the world to congregate at such a place, built perhaps at Hyde Park or Warm Springs, rather than some faraway land from the country which produced the man, the prosecution of whose fundamentals are still necessary for a successful peace. If his spirit pervades its halls, we Americans as well as all freedom-loving peoples of the world will be well represented.

Sidney Weger
Washington

4/30/45

Adam & the Archbishop

So Archbishop Cushing of Boston blames the women for the "course and vulgar" modern world [May 14]? So did Adam: "The women Thou gavest to be with me, she gave me of the tree, and I did eat."

Shame on both of them. Very ungallant, to say the least.

Scott F. Aitken
Hood River, Ore.

6/4/45

Churchill's Cigars

The pipe-smoking Earl of Halifax has overrated Cigar Consumer Winston Churchill [May 21]. Winnie may be the British Empire's No. 1 cigar smoker, but he cannot smoke 54 extra-large, especially made cigars in 18 hours out of every 24. It takes most cigar smokers approximately 30 minutes to smoke enjoyably a normal-sized, popular-brand cigar.

(Cpl.) William R. Gibbon
Quantico, Va.
6/11/45
But not Winston Churchill, who chews as he smokes.—ED.

Canadian Japanese

I am writing to you as an individual about an article which appeared in TIME [April 2]. It was an unfortunate article entitled "Who Wants Japs?" Actually the facts on Canada are as follows:

Racism in Canada is even more virulent and vigorous than in the U.S. We have had pitiful pleas from Japanese-Canadians and Caucasian-Canadian friends of the Canadian Nisei asking if some pressure might not be brought to bear by America on the Canadian Government to ease the situation. . . . Just as in California, they have been forcibly evacuated even though not one of them has committed any acts of treason or sabotage.

Second, their property has been actually seized and forcibly held by the Government at whatever price the market brought—and much suspicion

July 23, 1945: Prime Minister Churchill greets President Truman in England

of collaborated underbidding exists. . . .

Thirdly, Canadian and British citizens of Japanese ancestry cannot attend—for all practical purposes—any college or university. Thus, McGill bars them on the frank contention that serfs of inferior race deserve no education. Fourth, they cannot practice any profession or engage in business. . . . Fifth, they have no franchise rights now, except a few "honorary Aryans" who were already residents of Ontario before the war. Sixth, I understand that even outside of British Columbia they cannot reside in the communities where any one objects. . . .

It would mean so much if a magazine like yours, so influential, so widely read, would be careful of how it spreads this evil doctrine, against which we have just concluded a war in Europe.

Pearl Buck
Perkasie, Pa.
6/18/45
Reader Buck has overstated her case. For instance: McGill is the only Canadian university which bans Canadian Japanese, and indications are that the ban will be lifted; Toronto recently licensed a Nisei beauty-parlor operator; all Ontario cities but Toronto are at present open to Canadian Japanese. —ED.

Army Behavior

. . . People who read your article [Aug. 13] will condemn the Russians for being savages and rapists but will not stop to consider the fact that our own Army and the British Army along with ours have done their share of looting and raping. . . . Germany has been picked so clean by our troops . . .

that just about the only stores . . . left with anything to sell are the hardware stores. . . .

It is also common knowledge that American soldiers are *persona non grata* in the homes of decent girls in many of the liberated countries because of their attitude that any foreign girl is automatically a prostitute. Pick up almost any daily copy of *Stars & Stripes* and you will find letters to the editor complaining that the girls over here are closing their doors to our troops. This offensive attitude among our troops is not at all general, but we too are considered an army of rapists.

This letter is in no way intended to be an apology for misbehavior among the Soviet troops. It is merely an attempt to show that the Soviet Army is no different from the American or British Army when it comes to looting and behavior among women. . . .

(Army Sergeant's name withheld)
c/o Postmaster
9/17/45
New York City

Not I, Sir

I would like to send you a word of thanks to be passed on to the reviewer of my book, *Prater Violet*, in the Nov. 5 issue of TIME. I think he did a marvelous job, and he certainly helped to start the book off in the biggest way.

I have only one mild word of protest. I am not, as you have twice stated in your columns, the original, or part-original, of Larry in Maugham's *The Razor's Edge*. I can stand a good deal of kidding from my friends, but this rumor has poisoned my life for the past six months, and I wish it would die as quickly as possible.

Christopher Isherwood
12/17/45   *Santa Monica, Calif.*

Bad Word for Britain

It is time that blunt attention be called to a state of mind prevalent among a shockingly large percentage of American servicemen with regard to Great Britain, our principal ally in the war just ended. Nobody who has had an opportunity to talk to representative numbers and cross-sections of men in various theatres of war can escape the conclusion that never have more violent anti-British feelings been uttered by more young Americans than at the present time. . . .

I am not referring to half-jocular sportsmanlike expressions of rivalry, nor to informed criticism of British institutions, but to open antagonism based on superficial stray bits of information and on hackneyed slogans picked up at random, all interwoven in a net of prejudice which would brighten the last hours of the German war criminals if they were aware of its extent. . . .

Henry H. Remak
Warrant Officer, U.S.M.S.
c/o Fleet Post Office
12/17/45   *San Francisco*

Man of the Year

In one breath, you name and apolo-gize for Truman—the Man of the Year. . . . One might as well say the flea is king of beasts because he rides in the lion's mane.

TIME elevated him and time will relegate him to "plain food, whiskey-&-water and lodge meetings."

Frederick H. Levis
1/28/46   *Philadelphia*

Unweary, Unbeaming Londoners

Having read your articles on Great Britain [March 4], we cannot avoid feeling that it is necessary to correct your apparent misinformation. . . .

We are not weary—except when it is time to go to bed, and not always then. . . . We no more "beam" at the Royal Family than you at the President. None of us has heard of squirrel pie—and as for eating it!

British courtesy has not cracked. London's "cheerful cockney" still exists and always will, as long as London stands.

As if anyone would make such a fuss about a banana! We should probably be ill if we did eat one!

Pauline Federoff
(and 24 other 16-year-olds)
4/8/46   *London*

Who Is Ed.?

The perspicacity of the character disguised as Ed.—[Letters column]—is . . . obvious.

U.S. Marines raise Old Glory atop Mount Suribachi on Iwo Jima

What I would like to know is, who is this Titan of titillation, this wizard of caustic wit, or would divulging his name release a deluge of voodoo curses, symbolic hexes, and homicidal fan mail upon his sainted head?

G. A. Swankie
4/22/46   *Sharon, Pa.*
He is a footnote on the sands of TIME. *—ED.*

Hangman Pierrepoint

I find it a bit difficult to understand how the passage of so short a time could have mellowed Captain L. E. Davidson's recollection of Pierrepoint, the British hangman [April 8].

I too was attached to the 6833rd Guardhouse Overhead Detachment, the Army's execution plant at Shepton Mallet, England, and as I remember Mr. Pierrepoint, he fell far short of Captain Davidson's picture of "a farmer who had come to the village to sell his produce." As far as I'm concerned, he was straight out of *The Hound of the Baskervilles*, and would have been right at home with *Inner Sanctum*.

C. J. Anzulewicz
5/6/46   *Shamokin, Pa.*

Dyed or Blowed?

Have I been kidding myself or have you been deluding me for the past two decades? . . . I know a Republican who thinks you are dyed-in-the-wool New Dealers and a Democrat who states you are blowed-in-the-glass Republicans; a Protestant who claims you are too pro-Catholic and a devout Catholic who wouldn't give your publication houseroom because he swears you're anti-Catholic. . . .

Eamon Antony
5/13/46   *Bridgeport, Conn.*
If Reader Antony's circle of informants were complete, he would also have heard that TIME *is 1) backed by Moscow gold; 2) owned by Wall Street.—ED.*

Mae West's Play Clothes

The person who described Miss Mae West as wearing two "slinky" negligees [June 3] obviously doesn't spend much time in bedrooms. For your information she wears two evening gowns and one negligee. I know that to be an absolute fact, as I am the person who designed the clothes Miss West wears in her play. . . .

Peter Johnson
7/1/46   *Los Angeles*
Mae West has a way of modifying the absolute.—ED.

Forecast for China

. . . In my experience, even conservative bankers and businessmen, if not themselves involved in the official rape of the people, will bitterly admit that the Communists are more efficent and

Mae West

Jack Benny, George Murphy, Joan Crawford and Reginald Gardiner perform in Guild broadcast

less corrupt, that they take less from the rice bowl of the common man.

Should our policy in China continue to give the National diehards the comfortable feeling [that] we will support them come what may—a feeling they have been entitled to ever since the removal of General Stilwell—we may well be a principal agent in the promotion of a full-scale and tragically bloody civil war. . . . This will mean in all likelihood that the Communists will dominate China, that Russia will become China's big brother. . . .

If we are unable through diplomacy to put our weight behind realization of a coalition government, democratic in spirit and action, it would seem better for us and for China that we fold our tents and quietly depart.

Preston Schoyer
7/8/46 *Pittsburgh, Pa.*

Don't Be Ashamed

When Dorothy T. Pearse [Letters, July 1] expresses sympathy for the hungry of Europe and grows impatient with delays on the British loan and on food relief, I agree with her. But when she says she feels "a sense of shame at being American . . ." then I get mad.

Is she ashamed that her country, through progressive, intelligent industry has become the richest in the world? Is she ashamed of America because the nations of Europe, in contrast, have impoverished themselves through ignorance, intolerance, greed and hatred? . . .

That's why they're hungry today. That's why they'll be hungry tomorrow, too. . . .

Don't let's be ashamed. Miss Pearse —tell them to be be.

Morris Cohen
1st Lieutenant, A.U.S., Ret.
7/22/46 *Los Angeles*

War Risk

I hate war. . . . I hated combat. . . . I hate the prospect of another war, but I have learned something since 1941.

Haven't we all learned from letting Hitler march into the Ruhr, from Munich, from many another failure that the best way to get into a big war is to go too far in trying to avoid a smaller one?

Russia is so obviously insincere, so plainly not playing the game with U.N. that I want to see her forced to back down, even at risk of war in the near future. I should like to see our military establishment rebuilt at once to show that there is a limit to what we will take and that that limit is not much beyond where we are right now.

For my part, I'll take the risk of being called to active duty, perhaps to combat. Are there not thousands and thousands like me?

Paul C. Hawkins
1st Lieutenant, O.R.C. Air Corps
7/29/46 *Eustis, Fla.*

In concert with many other Americans, allow me to utter a hearty "aye" to the sentiments expressed by Lieut. Paul C. Hawkins in his letter published in the July 29 issue.

The laxness of our State Department and its individually indolent members has led to one Russian *fait accompli* after another . . . from Berlin and Vienna to Seoul and Peiping, and the jelly-spined attitude of America's "diplomats" (sic) allows Russia to dare to plot still other grabs and double-faced deals. . . . Now, in 1946, is the time to give Stalin, Molotov & Co. to understand that this nation will tolerate no ambitions of world conquest.

Let me assure Lieut. Hawkins that I, and thousands like me, agree with him and stand ready to return to active duty in order to stop dead and hurl back, by force of arms should it be necessary, the Iron Curtain that Moscow seeks to forge around the world.

Ex-T/Sgt. Stanley H. Firstenberg
8/19/46 *New York City*

The Gush & the Dribble

Accompanying an illustration of his new China, Russel Wright is quoted [July 29] as saying: "[I] want to do something practical for the housewife. The 18th Century is kept alive by Emily Post. I have no sympathy with the idea of keeping traditional design alive."

In reply to Mr. Wright, I would like

BOUQUETS

. . . I was impressed . . . by the manner in which details of my career were gleaned from all parts of the country in a few weeks' time and then so effectively pressed into a capsule of four pages [Oct. 20]. The next time I want to cut a show, I'll call you all in. . . .

11/10/47 *Oscar Hammerstein 2nd*
New York City

to suggest that he himself test the "practicability" of the 18th Century cup whose fine and slightly flaring rim was skillfully designed to check the escape of any drop of liquid down its side. A thick edge—especially one curving inward—defies every effort of human lips to hold back the gush of liquid which dribbles down the sides and even makes a ring in the saucer!

After all, the continued appreciation of "traditional design" must have a reason—other than my opinion!

Emily Post
8/19/46   *Edgartown, Mass.*

Mrs. Post is quite right . . . in that the "18th Century cup [with] fine and slightly flaring rim" does not drool, but her fine teacup requires tender care—more time in dish washing.

Mrs. Post's point illustrates my statement that she attempts to keep the 18th Century traditions alive in these times which can hardly be called similar. She stands for drinking tea gracefully—I suppose with the pinky raised. Tell Emily I stand for more drooling, less fancy "etiquette," and less housework.

Russel Wright
9/9/46   *New York City*

Bee in Boot

You state in your Oct. 7 issue that Sam Rayburn got four bee stings on one foot from a bee.

I live down here in Texas and our bees are so big we use 'em for primary trainers at Randolph Field. But sting a man four times? Don't let Sam feed

you that! They only sting once, in the orthodox manner, and then quietly die.

Lee E. Echols
11/4/46   *Laredo, Tex.*
TIME promises not to get stung there again.—ED.

Dictatorship of Mediocrity

Please extend my congratulations to Miss Elliott, the British schoolteacher who told us [Jan. 6] what she thinks of U.S. schools. I absolutely agree with her. After five years of high-school teaching, I gave it up for a less well paying job where the strain was less and where I could lead a normal adult life.

Our American idea that "youth is always right," or "don't be too hard on them, they'll outgrow it," are responsible, along with lack of home discipline, for the unnecessarily loud and crude behavior of high-school youth today.

Much as I liked teaching children who behaved like human beings, there were too many who didn't, and too many principals who were afraid of both parents and children. I am sure that one reason for the failure of young people to enter the teaching profession is that less and less teaching is possible because of the students' misbehavior.

Mrs. Kathryn Connell
1/27/47   *Fort Devens, Mass.*

There'll Always Be . . .

We are as resilient as we were in 1941, when we were sentenced to death

by many in the U.S.A. "There'll always be an England!"

W. G. Priest
London

. . . The Empire is today more alive than ever in its history, because we are in the actual process of that experiment never before tried—the evolution of colonies towards self-government.

Try and understand this, and then perhaps even you too can help us as a creative force in the 20th Century.

M. A. Morrison
3/3/47   *London*

Yes, She Had No Bandanas

You say: "The dusky St. Louis song-&-dance woman (Josephine Baker) had ruled the jungle of the *Folies Bergère* clad only in several bananas" [June 16]. This is a wonderful typographical error (bandanas), priceless!

Mrs. Lula P. Rossmassler
7/7/47   *New York City*
But the word is bananas; Josephine Baker did not hide her jungle charms behind bandanas.—ED.

The Inheritors

"Neither war, rationing, nor the advent of the atomic age had altered U.S. teen-agers' preoccupation with malted milk, two-hour telephone calls and jukebox music" [March 31].

As one of those teen-agers, I resent this attitude. TIME's article described only a small portion of the high-school students, and left out the vast majority who are sane, earnest, and hard-working. . . . More than ever before, today's students are aware of world problems.

If people would worry a little less about how the "younger generation" is going wild, and a little more about the kind of world that generation is going to inherit, maybe things wouldn't be in such a mess now.

Carrol Cox Jr. (16)
4/21/47   *Benton Harbor, Mich.*

Competition for Communism

What democracy is not was expressed by Secretary of State Marshall in Moscow [March 24] when he said: "To us a society is not democratic if men . . . are not free to express their beliefs and convictions without fear that they may be snatched away from their home and family," and without fear "of being deprived of the right to work or deprived of life, liberty and the pursuit of happiness."

The question now arises whether or not we can function as a democracy if the legislation to outlaw the Communist Party is passed. If men can be deprived of the "right to work" because of political beliefs, if men are in "fear" that they may be fired from their jobs because of the illegality of holding certain political beliefs, if under the dubious standard of democracy, men are persecuted for radical opinions,

Satin evening dresses, photographed by Cecil Beaton, featured in *Vogue*, 1948

then where is the freedom outlined in the Bill of Rights, the Atlantic Charter, the basic tenets on which our country was founded? . . .

If our way of life cannot compete with Communism in the open, then perhaps there is a deficiency on our part. Are we as truly democratic as we have professed to the world at large?

A. Hamilton Mencher
4/21/47 *Albuquerque, N. Mex.*

Gross Understatement

Your comment that Connecticut's Blue Law is widely disregarded [April 21] is a gross understatement. In both Massachussetts and Connecticut it is illegal for doctors to give contraceptive advice to married women, and the Roman Catholic citizens are told that "Birth Control is against God's Law." Yet the birth rates in these two states are among the lowest in the country, and before the war were lower than those of France—about one-third of the physiological maximum. Obviously the majority of the people in both states practice birth control regardless of legal restrictions and religious taboos.

Karl Sax
5/12/47 *Jamaica Plain, Mass.*

Stays & Armor

Our modern women are demanding equality with men in almost every field of activity these days, but they will never be respected as intellectual equals as long as they allow money-seeking style-mongers to dictate a complete change in wardrobe every few years. This style lobby seems to be much stronger and better organized than the ones we have here in Washington; and it has almost no opposition. Of the women I have talked to, none like the new long dresses at all, but all said that they would have to. wear

them if the dresses were pushed by the style setters. . . . When our women stop letting the fashion people push them around, they will have taken another big step toward sexual equality.

C. C. Moore Jr
9/8/47 *Washington, D.C.*

Ace in the Hole?

It seems to me that the TIME articles on Japan have been the first to call attention to the fact that the Japanese people have been the first, and only, of the war ravaged nations, to pitch into the ruins and start rebuilding.

While other nations have given in to self-pity and threats to go all-out for Communism, the Japanese are proving that hard work and plain guts are the only methods which will enable a beaten nation to revive itself. Japan may be America's "ace in the hole" in a future war. General MacArthur knows it, but does Congress?

Edward J. Doyle
9/22/47 *New York City*

Anger on Loans

. . . We object to being taxed to furnish loans for Britain . . . so that the British can compete with us in our markets and raise the already soaring prices still higher.

Let Britain get its loans by popular subscription from those in this country who for some reason think that such loans are a good investment.

Harlan Houpt
9/29/47 *Terre Haute, Ind.*

The New Look

The answer to the question on TIME's [Sept. 15] cover—"Who wants the New Look?"—is appropriately contained in the word printed immediately beneath: "Business."

Those least desirous of it: men.

(Rev.) Tom Fuhr
New York City

. . . The New Look is expensive, uncomfortable, impractical, and unshapely and I DON'T LIKE IT!

Laurel Weber
10/6/47 *Seattle*

Chromium-Plated Madness

I am a regular reader of your magazine. Each week I am amazed by your overbearing conceit. Your country has inherited all the idiotic pomp of 19th Century Britain. You are beyond doubt the greatest country in the world, but it is the "Bomb" and your material power that gives you this claim. Your material power has far outstripped your intellectual ability, and you are bereft of moral and spiritual values. . . .

You wish to remove the Veto because it is the stumbling block in the way of your American Century crusade. . . .

That the fate of Palestine, and the starving peoples of Europe, hangs on the 1948 presidential election is proof of your egocentric, chromium-plated madness.

Leon G. Hindle
Warrington, Lancs., England

If I know Americans, I suspect that your correspondent Jim Chambers [Sept. 29] writes with such sorrowing regard for the British and urges a ten-billion loan just for the pleasure of seeing the words "Britain is broke" in print.

It's time someone told you that the average Briton, if he had any say in the matter, would much prefer to starve quietly than see our loathsome, contemptible politicians conniving with you to tie us up for generations with the dollar loans (and attached conditions) you hurl in our faces with such howls of sneering derision.

Don't think, too, that we aren't well

79

BRICKBATS

I must protest your article about me [Jan. 26]. You quote me as severely criticizing radio reporting as superficial and radio reporters as unthorough. . . . Out of a two-hour conversation with your reporter in which I tried to give an honest estimate of what is fine and what is bad about radio journalism, you have chosen to print four sentences. These . . . have rather cruelly misrepresented my views and have done injury to my position vis-à-vis my profession and my colleagues in radio for most of whom I feel the greatest respect.

2/9/48
Eric Sevareid
Washington, D.C.

TIME regrets that its snapshot of Newscaster Sevareid caught him in an expression that failed to do justice to his fine features.—ED.

aware that the chief reason you lend us money is because you hope to hold us in front of you (as before) in your coming war with Russia. Another million British dead while you make leisurely preparations to rush in, when everyone else is exhausted, and save civilization.

Funny how America, while professing (eyes turned heavenward) to bear the heat and burden of these wars, always ends up with less casualties than anyone else and richer in direct proportion to the degree in which everyone else is poorer.

11/3/47
Robert Yates
London, England

Loan Bitterness

. . . I am fully in accord with Mr. Yates' statement that: "The average Briton . . . would much prefer to starve quietly than see our loathsome, contemptible politicians conniving with you to tie us up for generations with the dollar loans. . . ." I only wish there were more average Britons.

W. C. Metz
Sioux City, Iowa

. . . We Anglo-Saxon Americans still retain a warm regard for what we knew as England. But that was a fighting and not a whining England. We think that it is England's tragedy when Englishmen accuse us of wanting to use England as our shield in war with Russia.

What kind of a shield would England make? Unless she gets off her spiritual fanny, she will be a minor province of the Russian Empire—and soon.

E. P. Wilson
St. Joseph, Mo.

. . . No one likes to be a debtor—that is natural enough in any walk of life, but don't think we are not grateful for the American loan. Our bitterness over it is because we consider it has been misspent by incompetence.

However, when it comes to a fellow countryman criticizing the amount of blood shed by Americans, that is going far beyond the borders of decency . . . In the name of all your countrymen and mine who died for a cause they rightly believed in, I can only abhor such a contemptuous statement. . . .

I believe that I speak for all Englishmen who still retain a common heritage in their honor.

11/24/47
Victor Silvester Jr.
London

H.C.L. in Minutes

The comparative table showing what the Soviet and U.S. worker must give in working time in order to obtain the same quantities of food and other items [Dec. 29] was most interesting. Is it possible to publish a similar comparison between the British and U.S. worker?

2/9/48
Alex I. G. Farquharson
Glasgow, Scotland

A British Board of Trade economist figured out a table for British workers:

	G.B.	U.S.	USSR
	(Minutes)		
Wheat bread, lb.	5	7½	70
Veal, lb.	37½	34½	315
Butter, lb.	30	48½	642
Beer (1 pint draught mild)	22½	6¼	171
Cotton dress	450	142	1,911
Woolen suit (man's)	2,700	1,684	34,815

The economist added: "The only item missing is rye bread; I am afraid we have to make do mainly with the National Loaf. We see very little veal nowadays, so my figure is in fact based on the cost of home-produced first quality beef."—ED.

Royal wedding souvenir

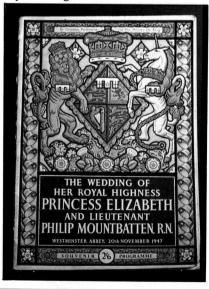

THE WEDDING OF HER ROYAL HIGHNESS PRINCESS ELIZABETH AND LIEUTENANT PHILIP MOUNTBATTEN, R.N. WESTMINSTER ABBEY, 20th NOVEMBER 1947

A New Era?

. . . The film, *Human Growth*, will prove a godsend to this country and its children. Not too long after the other 47 states adopt this program, I predict a new era, heralded by a decline in sex crimes and divorce. Take the mystery out of sex, bring it before the eyes, and indecency flies out of the window. Let's all endeavour to see that our own states follow it.

4/12/48
Robert A. Cossaboom
Bridgewater, Mass

Moderate's Dilemma

While I appreciate the growing seriousness of the "cold war" between Russia and the U.S., I also deplore the serious dilemma which faces many moderates, like myself, who favor a compromise between the extremes of American free enterprise and Russian Marxism.

Unfortunately, in the present political temper, compromise is not appreciated in either country—people must be all or nothing, black or white, for or against. I am thus forced to accept elements I dislike in the Greek political setup and condemn many excellent measures for improving the lot of the peoples of Eastern Europe. I must whole-heartedly accept the corruption of the Kuomintang and refuse to admit that the Chinese Communists have done good as well as bad.

I naturally support America in the present political struggle—as do all freedom-loving people in Europe—but, like them, I hope the struggle will not mean an end to liberal aspirations throughout the world, and the revival of those reactionary forces against which we all fought so recently.

5/3/48
Russell Spurr
Essex, England

Pragmatic Colossus

Your article on Canada's reaction to the idea of customs union with the U.S. [April 26] misrepresented the depth of Canadian feeling. . . . Canada is more unanimously and fervently opposed to economic union than you intimated. . . .

Canada's role in world affairs is not the same as that of the U.S., nor is it based on the same premises. We take a somewhat more objective view of world affairs, and feel ourselves more directly concerned in the welfare of the whole rather than the exposition of a single foreign policy. . . .

We like Americans, and cherish our close association with the U.S.; but there are many things in American culture which we resent, many aspects of our own life that we regard as superior. Finally, we are not prepared to sacrifice Canadian ideals, desires or culture to the colossus of a pragmatic system, which destroys ends for the sake of means.

Peter B. Waite
University of British Columbia
5/17/48 *Vancouver, B.C.*

State of Israel

Amazed that the cover of TIME, May 24, did not honor Dr. Chaim Weizmann, the first President of Israel, rather than Britain's "stooge" King Abdullah of Transjordan. . . .

Leroy L. Landau
Wilkes-Barre, Pa.

. . . Is TIME . . . unaware of the historic and spiritual significance of the establishment of the state of Israel?

H. G. Loeb
Richmond, Calif.

. . . Considering the autocratic nature of the Arab states ruled by Abdullah and his partners in perfidy, the obvious democratic nature of Israel, the still-standing decision of the United Nations in favor of partition, the undisguised aggression of the Arab states into Palestine, and TIME's espousal of democratic causes and hatred of aggressors, don't you think a cover featuring the President of the new democratic state of Israel, Chaim Weizmann, would have been more fitting?

Frank Ehrlich
6/14/48 *Brooklyn, N.Y.*
No. TIME considered Abdullah the key figure to the unlocking of the British mandate. The rise of the state of Israel is another story, now beginning to unfold.—ED.

Wholesome New York

. . . TIME's New York is one which dwells pointedly on its noise, crowding, aggressiveness, hellish glare at night, marijuana, cockroach-infested kitchens, tigerish and provocative women, obsession with the present, propensity to sneer at Philadelphia and jeer at Boston, and coolness to visitors. . . .

There is no visible place in TIME's picture of New York for wholesome American living or normal American people. . . . The article passes over New York's true importance in the national scene, allowing only an incidental word for the city as a port, a marketplace, a tourist center, as a "fountain spout" of culture, finding time for no mention at all of its place as a national center of music, higher education, medical research, managerial leadership, publishing, or the American tradition of human rights.

As a native New Yorker, I find TIME's article profoundly offensive as well as inaccurate as a portrait. . . .

Edward G. Bernard
6/28/48 *New York City*

More Hickory, Less Twaddle

. . . Dr. Grace Fernald's clinic school at U.C.L.A. [July 12] unwittingly puts a finger on the fundamental fault of present-day grade school education. Why was a boy who was unable to read or write promoted year after year until he reached the fifth grade? And how much further would he have been promoted if he hadn't gone to the clinic school?

Spencer Tracy

Ingrid Bergman

Susan Hayward

Glenn Ford

For many years I have dealt with the products of our elementary and high school education mills. No longer do I gag over weird English, amateurish spelling, fuzzy thinking and inability to add and multiply. . . . But I do feel an intense disgust when it is necessary to explain to juniors and seniors in the university such things as . . . the mysteries of decimals; why one multiplies by 100 when calculating percent; that . . . benzene should not be boiled over, an open flame. . . .

I say: More of the good old days of the three Rs and a little hickory rod or harness strap, and less of the twaddle that infests our [educational system].

William V. Sessions
Associate Professor of Chemistry
Wayne University
8/2/48 *Detroit, Mich.*

Pipeline for Democracy

. . . I have to confess that despite all the trouble they caused us, the onetime National Socialists had my sympathy, after the war even more than before; perhaps it was a captured paratrooper's obstinacy. But after returning home from captivity in the fall of 1946 my opinion began to change. . . .

During these days and nights of increasing Soviet pressure, when the Communists are trying to suppress every democratic thought and every opinion diverging from theirs, during these days and nights of the unceasing roar of U.S. Skymasters supplying Berlin with food, the very last remainder of sympathy for Fascism has died in me. . . .

Many friends have expressed the same thoughts. . . . The air bridge may be expensive, but it's the pipeline through which democracy is flowing into Berlin. . . .

Wolfgang Haeussler
8/23/45 *Berlin*

Israel—to the End of Time

Thanks for the sympathetic article on Israel and Ben-Gurion [Aug. 16].

Allow me, however, to correct one statement: "It costs between $1,800 and $5,400 to join the bus drivers' union." The fact is that the drivers own all the vehicles, garages, repair shops, etc., in the form of a cooperative. . . . One cannot simply "join" the union; [he must be] willing to work for the cooperative and be financially capable of buying a share of the physical property of the transportation cooperative.

M. Albrecht
Charleston, W. Va.

No Israelophile, and never guilty of distinguished sympathy for Jewish problems, TIME remains true to tradition in [its] treatment of Israel's Premier, David Ben-Gurion:

By its subtle suggestion that Israel will be an irreligious state. . . .

By its intelligence-insulting simplification of British treachery in the Middle East as being a mere desire for "stability". . . .

The State of Israel—founded on ideals and aspirations as old as time—will flourish as a living symbol of humanitarian civilization at least until the end of TIME.

Irving Waldman
9/6/48 *St. Paul, Minn.*

Ghosts

Your [Aug. 30] contributor from Evansville, Ill. is incensed about the decision of the Archbishop of Canterbury's commission concerning artificial insemination, which deems it at least a "Breach of Marriage" [Aug. 9]. . . .

The best analogy that occurs to me is that of "ghost" writing. Many a political leader who can't write good

speeches . . . lets his advisers . . . write speeches for him. Then he delivers them, as if they really were his own, and the crowd applauds. That . . . is a "breach of personality," I think. It makes a man what he is not.

"Ghost" siring of children by artificial human insemination (except when the husband is the donor) is of the same character. It . . . turns a Christian marriage into what it is not. "Ghost" siring of children makes eventually for "ghost" marriages. That is why a lot of intelligent Christians are against it. . . .

(Rev.) Louis L. Perkins
St. John's Episcopal Church
9/20/48 *Auburn, N.Y.*

Caldwell's Millions

In your review of Erskine Caldwell's *This Very Earth* . . . it was stated that sales of Mr. Caldwell's books were "above 9,000,000 copies" [Aug. 30]. This properly represents the sales of one reprint publisher. The number of copies of Mr. Caldwell's books in print, at home and abroad, including not only quarter books but dollar books and 75c books as well, is at present slightly more than 14 million.

June Caldwell
9/27/48 *Tucson, Ariz.*
Wow!—ED.

The Heart of the Problem

Your brilliant reporting of the plight of the British middle class [Nov. 1] goes to the very heart of Britain's

great social problem.

A Gallup poll earlier this year showed [that] over 50% of the young middle-class people would like to leave the country. My wife and I, who came to live in the States one year ago, found it impossible to maintain old standards [in England]. . . . We totaled $45 weekly between us, of which $20 went in apartment rent and income tax. We dipped steadily into savings. . . . Emigration was our best course.

John N. Rogers
11/22/48 *Portland, Ore.*

Patton and Prayer

I have just sent your article, "Patton Talking," to a friend in Uppsala, Sweden, asking him to show it to the clergy there. . . . The sacrilegious story . . . was pure fiction. . . .

After what my husband did for America, I am amazed and deeply hurt that you should publish such an article about an honorable Christian gentleman who can no longer speak for himself . . .

Beatrice Ayer Patton
1/3/49 *South Hamilton, Mass.*
TIME intended no disrespect to General Patton. It assumes that the Swedish Life Guard Grenadiers' regimental journal, from which it quoted, also intended no hurt to the memory of a great soldier. General Patton's own book, War As I Knew It, *edited by Mrs. Patton, quotes him as saying, when the weather cleared after he had ordered Chaplain O'Neill to pray: "God damn! Look at the weather. That O'Neill sure did some potent praying."* —ED.

On Eton's Black Block

The Jan. 3 article about Headmaster C. A. Elliott of Eton is excellent, but the term "cane" is technically incorrect. Caning at Eton is only carried out by certain privileged boys of the upper school, and is essentially a punishment for delinquencies connected with the discipline of the boarding houses and on the playing fields. It has nothing to do with academic offences.

When these academic offences are sufficiently serious, the headmaster intervenes and *flogs* the culprit. He does this with a birch rod [and] the procedure is attended by time-honored ceremony and ritual.

The victim is informed, through the intermediary of the prepositor of the week, that "The headmaster wishes to see him after twelve." If it is merely for the purpose of being reprimanded, the boy will be shown straight into the sixth form room. If it is for the more painful reward for his misdemeanour, he will be met by the school messenger (usually an ex-soldier of the regular army), who leads him up to the ancient, oak-paneled room where stands the famous block.

The block is centuries old, black with age . . . and looks like the first two steps of a staircase.

American Gussie Moran beats her British opponent at Wimbledon, 1949

The school messenger, having loosened the offender's braces and lowered his trousers, causes him to kneel on the block. Two prepositors then step forward and place their hands on the victim's shoulders. This is called "holding down," and is supposed to prevent the flogged one from rising to defend himself from the headmaster's assault. The school messenger now opens the door of the sixth form room, and the headmaster rustles in in his robes of office. A third prepositor goes to a cupboard, from which he takes the birch rod and ceremoniously hands it to the headmaster. The headmaster approaches the kneeling boy and, holding the handle of the birch with both hands, smites the bare behind of the boy six times. He then hands the birch back to the prepositor and rustles out of the room again. No word has been spoken . . .

Outside in the School Yard, friends of the victim are waiting eagerly to hear a first-hand account of what occurred . . . For a few days, he will be a hero. The slight pain which the flogging caused will be highly compensated by the interest it has created. The punishment is greatly preferred to copying out lines which take up hours which could be spent at leisure.

The only possible unpleasantness can come from the boy's parents . . . While there may be no official report to the home circle from those who rule the destinies of Eton, among the school bills will be one which reads: "To one birch rod, 7/6." The price may be higher now, but in my day at Eton it cost the equivalent of $2 to be flogged!

Colonel R. V. C. Bodley
Washington, Conn.
1/24/49

Out of China

. . . On the verge of leaving China

with the Marines, I cannot help but write this note of praise to you.

Very often the public views a news magazine on variations between two extremes: either believing every word, or doubting every report. China is indeed a perplexing problem. Even living here for the past two years has not lifted the screen of mystery. Nevertheless I must let you know . . . that your coverage of the situation has fitted the actual situation to the last dotted "i."

Chaplain Calvin H. Elliott
Tsingtao, China
2/14/49

Mindszenty Trial

I appreciate the unbiased [article] on Cardinal Mindszenty in TIME, Feb. 14, and think that you should be commended highly for the masterful way in which you portray his background, education, ideals, and plight. So seldom does one read a fair exposé of a rather complicated ecclesiastical situation such as this in which the cardinal was placed. . . .

Rev. J. Schmeier
St. Joseph's Rectory
Waukegan, Ill.
3/7/49

Gigantic Revolution

As a short-term resident of Britain, I heartily endorse your sympathetic evaluation of Aneurin Bevan and his part in the socialization of Britain [March 21]. Thank you for your help in enabling Americans . . . to understand the comparatively quiet but nonetheless gigantic revolution in one of the world's greatest nations.

Last year I lived in Edinburgh, where I studied at the University and benefited directly from British Socialism (orange juice, cod-liver oil and special rations for my 2½-year-old daughter, and cheaper food prices through gov-

ernment subsidies) . . . It was evident that in spite of austerity the people on the whole were faring better than ever before in food and health, with the more equitable distribution derived from a planned economy and socialized medicine.

(Rev.) James R. Woodruff
Orangeburg, N.Y.

TIME has written an excellent article on Bevan as Britain's medicine man, but fails to give an actual picture of the problems that confront the actual implementation of Britain's socialized medicine . . .

Doctors simply cannot see, give diagnosis to and treat patients in a process in which they are overwhelmed by trivial complaints. If a doctor tried to see 40 patients a day, he gives all of them less than what medicine requires. If he tries to see 100 patients a day, with a view to developing an income, he is reverting to the kind of diagnosis and treatment that prevailed in a previous century . . .

Hyman Geller, M.D.
Hempstead, N.Y.
4/11/49

Poland's Share in the Finest Hour

A small "but" to your fine review of Mr. Churchill's *Their Finest Hour* [April 25]. According to Mr. Churchill's statement, Sept. 15, 1940 was the crux of the Battle of Britain. He describes it in fascinating words on five pages, and underlines that on this day every available fighter was in the air and no reserves were left on the ground. A great gamble—as he said—because when the fighters landed for refueling, there was no air cover. But not a single word was said that on this crucial day two Polish fighter squadrons were in action . . . The claims of Polish fighters on this day (after verification by the Air Ministry) represent 14% of the total "bag" of the R.A.F.

A whole chapter is devoted by Mr. Churchill to the Battle of Britain, but again not a single word about Polish and other Allied pilots. The Polish score in the Battle of Britain was 7½% of the total . . . Among all British and Allied fighter squadrons who took part in the Battle of Britain, the top scorer was the Polish Fighter Squadron 303.

Exactness and impartiality is *conditio sine qua non* for every historian, even among the great history makers, where Mr. Churchill has undoubtedly a prominent place.

A. Jaworski
5/30/49 *Ottawa, Ont.*

Japan Says Thanks

I thank you very much for your thorough view of occupied Japan . . . I want to tell you that we are steadily recovering from moral chaos . . . Small kind behaviorisms are seen in the street very much oftener now than just after the war. If we are able to go through the economic hardships of this year and the next, we should be one of the peaceful and honest nations of the world.

Hiroshi Yamaji
5/30/49 *Tokyo, Japan*

Sweet Debauchery

Thank you for an accurate description of the candy-gorging scenes in Britain when "sweets" came off the ration [May 2]. I would like you to record, however, that such debauchery was short-lived. All available supplies of chocolate soon disappeared into stomachs craving for extra sustenance, and now queues are everywhere for such

Sinatra and Kelly in *On the Town*, 1949

sparse and less glamorous confectionery as licorice sticks, peppermints and barley sugar.

Trevor Henley
6/13/49 *South Croydon, Surrey, England*

Back to Normal

Recently in TIME . . . and other publications I have seen increasing use of "recession," "slump" and "depression" regarding our present business situation. It seems to me that by using these terms we are talking ourselves into a good, all-out depression. This sort of talk scares customers . . . They tighten up their purse strings and wait for more price cuts. Businessmen begin to worry and slash payrolls needlessly. Pretty soon the scare builds up like a snowball going downhill.

Would it not be better to refer to our "recession" as a "return to normal" after the unusual postwar highs, which we all realize were due to pent-up savings, unsatisfied demand during the war years, and the inflated dollar? Many businessmen, wishfully thinking, seem to have taken these "unusual highs" for their normal business and are now crying because the balloon has burst as we all knew it would.

George A. Retelle
6/20/49 *Detroit, Mich.*

Warning: No Smoking

Novelist Charles Yale Harrison may flaunt his return to heavy cigarette smoking after a serious coronary attack at the age of 49—if he wishes—in his book *Thank God for My Heart Attack* . . . However, great harm may come from TIME's blithe presentation [May 23] of Harrison's stand to millions of readers, without inserting some hint of the possible dangers involved.

Harrison and your readers should be told that there are very few men dying of coronary attacks below the age of 60 who are not tobacco smokers; that all men below 41 (on whom information could be obtained) dying from this cause during 1946 and 1947 in Cincinnati were cigarette smokers; that abnormal addiction to tobacco smoking is present to a highly significant degree

in male coronary victims of all ages; that these facts and similar ones for peptic ulcer are most likely based on the well-known toxicity of nicotine for nerve cells of the automatic (involuntary) nervous system controlling these organs.

Clarence A. Mills, M.D.
Professor of Experimental Medicine
College of Medicine
University of Cincinnati
6/20/49 *Cincinnati, Ohio*

The Good Life

I would like to give a word of hope to college graduates of '49 [June 6].

We have been married less than ten years, have three healthy, intelligent children, a city home furnished and paid for, a car, and have just bought a country place with 15 acres of land—fishing and swimming available—which should be paid for within five years; and we have done this on less than $5,000 a year (we could have made more but we want time to enjoy the good life, and don't believe in working that hard anyway).

Of course I don't own a pair of stockings to my name, my husband has sometimes had only one pair of threadbare trousers, but we have always had meat every day, plenty of eggs, milk, and real butter to eat, and TIME to read.

Mrs. A. Peter Emig
6/27/49 *Houston, Texas*

Light Up and Relax

. . . Dr. Clarence A. Mill's finger-shaking warning on the evils and dangers of smoking after an attack of coronary thrombosis [June 20] will frighten no one acquainted with the more recent scientific literature on the subject . . .

Dr. Robert L. Levy of the College of Physicians and Surgeons, Columbia University, conducted extensive tests . . . on the effects of cigarette smoking on the heart. At the 69th Annual Session of the American Medical Association on June 12, 1947, he said: "It has been our experience, over a period of years, that most patients with a cardiac disorder, including those with disease of the coronary arteries, can smoke moderately without apparent harm. In fact, for many, smoking not only affords pleasure but aids in promoting emotional stability . . . There are many unknown variables, of which one of the more important is the constitutional factor. Heavy smokers may well be of the type susceptible to arterial degeneration."

As for myself, with the permission of my doctor, I smoke about 30 Pall Malls a day, more than half of which smolder away in the ashtray as I work at my typewriter . . . Never felt better in the past 20 years.

Charles Yale Harrison
7/4/49 *New York City*

Favorites

I was glad to see your balanced comments on Wimbledon [July 4] . . . There has never been a grander set of Americans than those who came over this year—good sportsmen, good players and good lookers, and all great favorites of the crowd. Ted Schroeder won our hearts in one short fortnight, and Louise Brough's courage and Gussie's panties kept the female flag flying high.

Yet a section of the press in both countries chose to fasten on the only exception, Bob Falkenburg. They magnified the regrettable incident in which he was booed by a small section of the crowd and printed his statement that the Wimbledon crowd is anti-American. It is enough to make a confirmed fan gnaw the net. The Wimbledon crowd is not anti-anybody. They queue for hours to study tennis and personalities, in that order. And they ask not if you won or lost, but how you played the game.

A. Steward
8/1/49 *London, England*

Giveaways

The recent to-do about the ban on give-away shows [Aug. 29] is of particular interest to the average good old American.

I don't think I am qualified to judge whether or not these radio programs are good or bad, but it does seem to me that they are typically American and . . . have done some good. Take myself for instance:

Last December my wife and I had finally found a suitable apartment in a nice neighbourhood to raise our children in. But we still had to buy furniture for the apartment . . . We went to a broadcast one night—*Winner Take All.* I was chosen as one of the contestants. I answered the questions first and right, and I won the one thing we needed to get us started on the road to furnishing our new home, a seven-piece bedroom suite.

At a time when things looked pretty dark this wonderful thing happened . . . So I say, let the FCC ask the radio

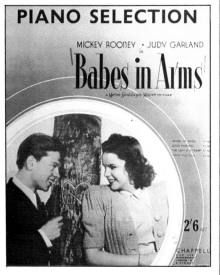

audience what they think, and I'll bet there won't be any doubt but that "Giveaways" are here to stay.

G. J. Nelson
Chief Yeoman, U.S. Navy
9/19/49 *New York City*

Yank at Oxford

. . . The oceanic calm of Oxford remains undisturbed by my article in *Isis* magazine [Oct. 24]. Americans write me, however, and urge me to "give the Limey's another smack." They are determined to picture me as a wholesome American youth pointing the finger of shame at drunken, decadent Oxford. Nothing could be further from the truth. I am no youth, and Oxford is not decadent.

Like most Rhodes scholars I like it here, enjoy my work, find the English hospitable and kind. The Rhodes scholarships, to my mind, are the best use to which diamonds have ever been put.

I do believe that England is going through a collapse which is one of the most subtle tragedies of our time, but the courage of the English, sensing full well the shape and extent of the collapse, is awe-inspiring. My article was not designed to offend a worried and overworked host, but to entertain.

Eugene Burdick
11/14/49 *Oxford, England*

Push-Button Popcorn

"In Portland, Ore., Mrs. Elizabeth Slaney called attention to a special feature planned for her new drive-in theater: a button system for every car to bring a vendor on the run with a fresh supply of popcorn" [Nov. 14].

May I call Mrs. Slaney's attention to Dallas. Our drive-in theaters have been so equipped for some time . . .

Jim Evans
12/5/49 *Dallas, Texas*

Good Germans?

Very disgusting to find a German (Konrad Adenauer) on my Dec. 5 cover of TIME . . .

Please don't tell me that there are also good Germans . . .

In Holland in 1918, the Dutch people fed and helped starving German children, but the same children came back in 1940 with tanks and hand grenades to kill their well-doers—and history will repeat itself . . .

A. M. De Mol
12/26/49 *The Hague, Holland*

BOUQUETS

What perfect Time-ing! Have TIME [Aug. 22] in my hands with the nice remarks about me as I am celebrating my birthday. By the way, I am not 26, I am 24 (the studio told me to say). Time marches on, but not for me. Thank you.

9/5/49

Shelley Winters
Universal City, Calif.

The Fabulous Fifties

TIME readers had quite a bit to say about the Korean War. Voters twice preferred war hero Ike to egghead Adlai. The blast that launched Sputnik announced the beginning of the space race. Senator McCarthy warned of internal enemies and fanatically pointed his finger in every direction. From the summit of Mount Everest, men gazed down on a world where the highest aspiration of some kids was to be the local Hula-Hoop champ.

Man of the Half-Century

Your choice of Churchill as Man of the Half-Century [Jan. 2] is preposterous.

Fred Rice
Saranac Lake, N.Y.

Winston Churchill best choice. His courage and wisdom led us through the dark days. One of the great leaders of all time.

George F. Greve
Cleveland, Ohio
1/23/50

Thanks for the Candy

Some months ago you published a letter from me describing the shortage of candy after "sweet rationing" was temporarily discontinued in this country [June 13]. As a result of that letter, a number of people in the U.S. wrote me asking for addresses to which they could send candies for needy kiddies, and many a young face has since smiled delightedly at the sight of the gifts.

Though all these people have been answered personally, I should like . . . to express my thanks to, and admiration of the U.S. people for their never-failing generosity where those less fortunate than themselves are concerned.

Trevor Henley
South Croydon, Surrey
England
2/27/50

Homespun Humor

Re your portrait of Arthur Godfrey [Feb. 27]: for once I am at odds with Fred Allen. Godfrey is not mediocre, in my opinion, any more than this is "an age of mediocrity." It is a vital and disturbing world; tense and watchful, it finds strength in home-spun humor and casual friendliness . . .

Stanley R. Sinclair
Oakland, Calif.
3/20/50

Test Run

In your Feb. 27 issue, under "Test Run," you quote the contest's sponsor: "These mileages give the general public something to shoot at. They prove what a properly driven and properly maintained car will do."

Comedian Milton Berle amuses TV audiences with his slapstick routines

How about giving us the results in average miles per gallon for each car?

R. P. Walbridge
Boothbay Harbor, Me.
3/27/50

Willys Jeepster 26.10; Chevrolet Fleetline 21.07; Plymouth P-18 21.25, Ford DeLuxe "6" 23.33; Studebaker Champion 26.55, Nash Statesman 25.52, Dodge Coronet 21.39, Kaiser Special 23.95; Studebaker Commander 23.79, Mercury 26.52, Hudson Pacemaker 22.60, Nash Ambassador 26.42, De Soto Custom 18.78, Oldsmobile "88" 20.19; Packard "8" 18.92, Chrysler Windsor 19.85, Oldsmobile "98" 19.45, Studebaker Land Cruiser 24.89; Lincoln 18.15, Frazer Manhattan 23.91, Chrysler New Yorker 17.11, Packard Super 16.00, Hudson Commodore 21.39; Kaiser Virginian 23.97, Cadillac "61" 22.97; Cadillac "62" 22.53, Lincoln Cosmopolitan 17.56; Cadillac "60" Special 22.08; Cadillac "75" 17.24. —ED.

For the Record

In your issue of July 10 you credit me with "the first successful removal of an entire lung, in 1933." Out of fairness to others this statement requires some explanation.

Although my operation was the first successful one in which a whole lung was cut out at one stage, two other pioneers in this field deserve much praise for their courage and success. Rudolph Nissen, then of Berlin but now of New York, in 1931 caused the lung of a child to slough out by operating on her in two stages in such a way as deliberately to shut off the blood to the lung. In 1932 Cameron Haight of the University of Michigan . . . performed a similar operation on another child, but a report of his case did not appear until 1934. Both patients recovered . . . In each case the reason for the operation was a severe chronic infection of the lung which probably would have caused the death of the patient without the surgical intervention. The reason for the operation in my case was a cancer of the lung. The patient is living and well . . . This case, therefore, was the first successful removal of a whole lung for cancer.

Evarts A. Graham, M.D.
Washington University
7/24/50 *St. Louis, Mo.*

Shades of Dec. 7

. . . [Some] politicians in Washington seem to think that the Korean campaign will be a trivial one, in which a few of our forces will get some combat experience for a month or two, and it will then be polished off.

Shades of Dec. 7, when we thought we'd lick the Japanese in six weeks!

Kemp Catlett Christian
7/24/50 *Chicago, Ill.*

Time & the War

Three years ago I subscribed to Time. For the past several weeks, I have been receiving a warlike, manifesto-styled communication replete with war maps and pictures of warriors on the cover. I would not mind receiving this new publication if I could continue to receive my regular copy of Time as well.

Lee Rosen
The Bronx, N.Y.

Let Reader Rosen complain to Stalin & Co.—Ed.

Please, please, please stop Armageddoning the hell out of us.

John F. Nihen
8/21/50 *Squantum, Mass.*

Hangman's Hope

In an Aug. 7 article, "Hangman's End," reference is made to Master Sergeant John C. Woods "of San Antonio" . . .

Sergeant Woods was born in Wichita, Kans. . . . After he was assigned [as official U.S. hangman in postwar Germany], he was afraid his wife might worry about his safety. As a result, he listed his address as San Antonio in the hope that . . . she would not identify him as an executioner. [And] Mrs.

EARLY TELEVISION

TOAST OF THE TOWN

THE HONEYMOONERS

FATHER KNOWS BEST

I LOVE LUCY

Woods did not learn of her husband's activities until after the hangings at Nürnberg prison . . .

Sergeant Woods always said that when he hanged the top-ranking Nazis, he did not think of them as human beings, but as rats who deserved the punishment they got . . .

He always liked to needle someone into asking him what was the biggest disappointment he ever had in his life. Then, with a wide grin, he would reply: "When Hermann Göring committed suicide. He's the one I wanted to hang most of all . . ."

Ernest A. Warden
Wichita, Kans.
8/28/50

The Ugly War

John Osborne did a fine piece of reporting in "The Ugly War" . . . by giving us a sympathetic report on our young fighters in a rough country, among "people whom they don't like" —and, let us admit it, whose people do not have any great love for us . . .

And let us be frank about it; all Orientals are alike in their contempt for human life and dignity. They are cruel where we have pity; they are brutal where we show compassion; they are ingratiating to those they fear or think superior, but merciless with the weak or inferior who fall into their hands. Osborne commends the South Korean army for bravery and effectiveness, and exempts its soldiers from the accusation of cruelty heaped upon the police . . . It may perhaps, in a measure, be due to the three years' training of the South Korean soldier under capable and understanding American officers and noncommissioned officers. Possibly some faint idea of—I will not say democracy —human fellowship may have seeped in.

Under the subheading "War & Politics," Osborne touches on a weak point in our armor. Americans, great globetrotters that they are, have never shown any great capacity for trying to understand the people among whom they traveled or worked in foreign countries. . . . For three years, and even up to the time of the North Korean invasion, we had a "considerable staff" of military and civilian officials in Korea. But it is dollars to doughnuts that only a pitifully small number of them learned even the rudiments of the language, to say nothing of the country's history and culture . . .

It takes more than just words to teach anything, it takes examples and repeated demonstrations of right methods, even the correct use of a shovel or wheelbarrow, tools which many Koreans have never seen.

During this Korean war we have repeatedly heard of the morale-stiffening effect of high-ranking officers exposing themselves to front-line dangers in company with their soldiers. The same course on the peaceful industrial front is just as necessary and effective . . .

C. S. Anderson
New York City
9/11/50

BOUQUETS

A salute to TIME and its correspondent Frank Shea and LIFE photographer Leonard McCombe for continuing the battle against Juan and Eva Peron's Fascist state.

A few months ago I delivered two former U.S. Navy LSMs to an Argentine firm . . . Peron's Mussolini-patterned police force had a wonderful time collecting all the TIME magazines I had aboard. . . .

3/26/51

Walter H. Seiferle
Miami

I bow low in admiration to your writer who pulled: "Tradition is that chorus girls get mink coats the same way minks do" [March 19]. One of the greatest opening lines ever put to paper . . .

4/9/51

Stephen G. Freeman
Balboa, Calif.

Brink of Illiteracy

What has this scheme of education done for us? It has produced millions who border on the illiterate in reading, writing, and arithmetic . . . Public school education has been taken over by a coterie of spurious experts who have erected it into an esoteric "science" with a jargon which is cloudy, innocuous and meaningless.

During the war the armed services uncovered an appalling degree of rank illiteracy among school graduates. For this we can thank the modern "educators" who flourish in the teachers' colleges. Their emphasis is on methodology, you know . . . You don't have to know anything to teach it, they say. You just have to know how! *Mirabile dictu!*

If we do not go back quickly to the days of readin', writin' and 'rithmetic, to classrooms where substantial knowledge is transmitted, where discipline prevails and where the thinking process is incited, we will lose our heritage. We are on the brink of it now.

Julius Sumner Miller
Professor of Physics and Mathematics
Dillard University
11/6/50
New Orleans

MacArthur's Sacking

Let me commend your magazine for trying to focus our attention on Asia. Truman has relieved MacArthur of all his posts. The general purposely sacrificed himself, to focus attention on the desperate need out there. I hope many millions more will join me in a fervent prayer that at the next election, the commander in chief be relieved of all his duties. Two years more may be too late, however.

Tibbs Maxey
Louisville

. . . It seems that the sword of righteousness so handily wielded by Mr. Truman at the outset of the Korean conflict has become an umbrella.

Ruth E. Hankinson
Basking Ridge, N.J.

. . . The only thing that I see wrong . . . is that President Truman tolerated MacArthur's insubordination as long as he did . . .

Edith Smith
Muskegon, Mich.

It is high time that Congress does something to curb the Mad Man from Missouri—the petty politician who puts politics before honor—before he makes a complete shambles of everything . . .

Francis R. Soike
4/30/51
Fond du Lac, Wis.

Letters received, as TIME went to press, were 8 to 1 in favor of General MacArthur.—ED.

More Collective Nouns

Re the dither in the London *Times* over collective nouns for animals [June 4]: Sir Arthur Conan Doyle's 14th-Century romance *Sir Nigel* speaks of a cete of badgers, a singular of boars, a sounder of swine (when hunted), a nye of pheasants, a badling of ducks, a fall of woodcock, a wisp of snipe.

Modern prose might use new collectives for professional people and others. I suggest an ibid of historians, a ponder of scientists, a scathe of bureaucrats.

W. W. Woodside
6/25/51
Pittsburgh

Advice from Abroad

I read with no little amusement the fuss stirred up in Newmarket (England) by Mrs. Stocker [Sept. 3]. Mrs. Stocker is still young—by all standards. You Americans are sometimes perturbed by the growing "anti-Americanism" now to be seen throughout the world . . . What is the cause of all this? It's all so very simple . . .

Until 1939, we were a world power, almost THE world power, and it was always good politics to twist the lion's tail. It raised a laugh all the way from Capitol Hill to Cairo and Teheran. We, in England, could never understand the ingratitude of other people whom we had helped (for their own benefit of course—and our profit), but we were rich enough to shrug our shoulders and let the matter pass. Now there is little fun in twisting the poor lion's tail. Instead, a new game has been invented. Uncle Sam has a nose. If that nose gets twigged, it's owner lets out a yell. What fun. That is a sign of greatness, power and wealth.

Long may this last, for our benefit, for the benefit of the fellow round the corner and for your benefit and to the discomfort of the fellows in the Kremlin. You have got just one more lesson to learn from this old country of ours. Take the nose-twigging gracefully. It's a sign of envy, and when we cease to be so-called "anti-American" it will be a sign that you have lost your vigorous health and ability to lead and be great.

Ernest J. Bourne
9/24/51
London, England

Apartheid Monster

From my father I derived a sympathetic interest in the Boers of South Africa and a reverence for their great commander, Jan Christian Smuts . . .

It seems to me that Afrikaners have created the terror for themselves, as men so often create the monsters which

eventually devour them. It was a sad day for South Africa when Malan and his program of *apartheid* took over her destinies . . . South Africa lost her soul when she lost Smuts.

Frank Van Oosbree
Korea
10/1/51

Intelligent?

The Intelligent Man's Guide to Women sounds as dull as two virgins discussing sex.

Marcia Matthews
McAllen, Texas
12/3/51

Of Mice & Women

The new drug which stops pregnancy in mice by "resorbing" the fetus may be called a contraceptive by some. If this plan is to be used on humans, I call it murder . . . Let Dr. Goldsmith take heed of the countless thousands of murders he will be responsible for if he puts his new "contraceptive" [Oct. 29] in the hands of the people. Why must our scientists use their brilliant minds . . . as tools of the devil? . . .

Mrs. A. G. Kramer
Parker Dam, Calif.

Re the possibility of an oral contraceptive: discriminating women since Eve have employed one very effectively, *viz.* NO!

Frederick W. Sanders
Marblehead. Mass.
12/3/51

The Ploy's the Thing

Your Dec. 17 account of the non-playing captainship of Mr. Frank Shields during the recent lawn tennis matches in Australia gave me much pleasure. I have long been accustomed to expect the more brilliant gambits from the younger people, and the junior nations.

In retirement, my function now is to keep Gamesmanship from wandering from its basic principles, and may I therefore remind your Sport Editor that the suggestion that "the final score is the proof of the gambit" is a deviation from the Gamesmanship line?

It is the final *state of one-upness* which counts; and Losemanship shows how this can be achieved . . . Savitt was beaten by Sedgeman. Mr. Shields should have drawn attention to the inexplicable speed of this phenomenon (58 minutes) . . . Surely the only explanation of the collapse of the one living exponent of the Tilden backhand must have been due (Shields should have said) to the "unfortunate atmosphere" and the "definite tension." These of course were fostered by the typical non-playing criticism, from the stands, of non-playing Captain Shields, who complained of the non-giving of a foot-fault against Seixas . . . To make sure that the point was rammed home, Savitt could have made a special statement to the press that he had been "fairly and squarely beaten."

Stephen Potter
London, England
1/28/52

To Author Potter, discoverer of Gamesmanship,* TIME's thanks for his authoritative analysis of Davis Cupmanship. —ED.

* The Theory and Practice of Gamesmanship, or The Art of Winning Games Without Actually Cheating— TIME, Sept. 6, 1948.

Wherefore Art Thou Roger?

It was with deep regret that I read the new phonetic pronouncing alphabet [set by the International Civil Aviation Organization—March 3].

All of the words have been changed except V for Victor. What is of most concern is imagining how the television "space cadet" will sound. Instead of saying, "Roger and out," it will be "Romeo and out." What a mouthful for the youngsters, and a slur on love.

I. William Oberfelder
Detroit

The spectacle of grown men fiddling with new, multi-syllabled names for the Navy alphabet flags, at a time when we are told we are in dire peril, overwhelms me. And I shudder to think of the response from a group of sailors when an unfortunate signalman is required to sing out, in the course of his duties, "Foxtrot, Juliett."

Robert S. Seese
Detroit
3/24/52
Or Tango, Oscar?—ED.

Sheen on TV

. . . You've done a wonderful job of introducing and explaining Bishop Sheen to those who may wonder what a Roman Catholic clergyman is doing on television. Too many people (Roman Catholics included) have the feeling that priests should be as inconspicuous as possible, lest someone think that Rome is running the U.S. . . .

Patricia M. Madden
New York City

I am truly amazed. I had no idea our nation was blessed with a theologian of such stature that he influenced the popularity rating of Milton Berle to the extent of a ten point drop . . .

John Meehan
Boston
4/28/52

All's Fair

By God, finally someone (General Sir Gerald Templer) has had the foresight, common sense and guts to fight Communists in the manner to which they should become accustomed. Templer's action in Malaya [April 21] will be effective, will raise horrified outcries from the intellectual do-gooders, and give hope to frustrated and baffled Red-haters like me.

Anti-Communist tactics based on Christian principles have failed universally. The argument that Temler-type combat is too reminiscent of Commun-

---

BOUQUETS

The picture of me on the cover of TIME has changed my entire life. Where formerly my hours were spent playing golf and chasing girls, I now while away the days loitering around Beverly Hills' largest newsstand, selling copies of the Dec. 31 issue of TIME at premium prices . . . yesterday, despite the fact that it was raining, I made $13. This is all tax free, for I steal the copies of TIME while the owner of the newsstand is out eating lunch . . .

Groucho Marx
Los Angeles
1/21/52

ist tactics is both specious and suicidal. In hand-to-hand street fighting, no man ever won by appealing to the spectators that he was being fouled. The victor must concentrate on winning, and if it takes a rabbit-punch or kidney blow—he uses it, and quickly . . .

Dan H. Rowan
5/12/52 *North Hollywood, Calif.*

Storm over South Africa

. . . We do not tell you how to handle the Negro. Well, do not criticize us, Dr. Malan knew perfectly well what he did when he started his *apartheid* policy. It is the only way to save South Africa.

H. De Blij
Johannesburg

. . . I went to South Africa to settle, saw the storm coming, and wishing to have no part in it, left job, future and friends. And I have never regretted it. Yours was a fine description, penetrating, comprehensive and so brutally true.

Mark F. Levesley
Montreal

I am, by birth, a British South African, and take the stump on behalf of the much-maligned Prime Minister. . . . I have recently returned from an air trip to South Africa after an absence of 24 years . . .

In all, I saw nothing but good being done by the fanatical Daniel François Malan's down-the-middle government. They are trying to make South Africa not a "Boer Republic" but a homeland for all white South Africans and a homeland for all non-Europeans in South Africa—even the definitely foreign Indians. All power to heroic Dr. Malan, a fanatic with his head screwed on so rightly that even the Communists cannot gain a foothold . . .

Arthur Trevenning Harris
5/26/52 *North Hollywood, Calif.*

The Myth of Munich

In your review of the fourth volume of the *History of the Times* in your issue of May 19, you refer to "Britain's ally, Czechoslovakia." The myth that Britain was the ally of Czechoslovakia at the time of Munich has long been fostered in the United States, and it is regrettable that it should gain new currency in your own authoritative columns. Though some of us thought at the time of Munich that it was in Britain's interest to fight in defence of Czechoslovakia's freedom, our country had no more moral or legal obligation to do so than had the United States. The "holier than thou" attitude adopted by some Americans in regard to Munich is wholly unwarranted, the more so since—a fact seldom adverted to in the United States—President Roosevelt was among those who sent a telegram to Signor Mussolini congratulating him on the calling of the Munich Conference.

Randolph S. Churchill
6/9/52 *London*

British Prime Minister Winston Churchill

Kennedy v. Churchill

In your June 9 Letters Column, Randolph S. Churchill says TIME was wrong in referring to Czechoslovakia as "Britain's ally" and denounces the "holier than thou" attitude adopted by some Americans towards the English in regard to Munich, and states that England had no more moral or legal obligation to defend Czechoslovakia than had the U.S. Mr. Churchill implies that the respective positions of Great Britain and the U.S. towards Czechoslovakia were on a par . . .

Britain's military alliance with France under the Locarno Pact of 1925 . . . although it did not guarantee Czechoslovakia against aggression as it did Belgium, made it inevitable that if France went to war to fulfill its own direct obligation under the Franco-Czech Treaty of 1924, England would be drawn in . . . England was deeply committed, by her treaty with France and by her official actions . . . The illustrious father of Mr. Churchill has admitted that Great Britain was deeply involved and that "it must be recorded

with regret that the British Government not only acquiesced but encouraged the French Government in a fatal course" (Churchill, *The Gathering Storm*).

The U.S. had no political involvement in Europe in 1938 . . . President Roosevelt never sent congratulations to Mussolini for arranging the Munich Conference, as alleged by Randolph Churchill . . . The President's telegram to Mussolini on Sept. 27 was a final appeal asking Mussolini to intervene with Hitler . . .

John F. Kennedy
House of Representatives
7/28/52 *Washington, D.C.*

Snay, Snah, Snyfoo

Re your July 14 report of reactions in the House of Commons to Mr. Churchill's quotation of Mr Acheson's reference to "snafu" on the vexed question of the Yalu River bombings: Churchill "rolled the unfamiliar word around for a while and it came out snayfooo"; . . .

The vulgar snafu derivatives may have been American in origin . . . but acceptance and widespread dissemination of their useful addition to Anglo-Saxon idiom was peculiarly British and essentially Eighth Armyish. Your correct if prudish definition of snafu as "situation normal, all fouled up" is a reminder that there were exclusively British ascending and descending degrees of snafu. There was the "self-adjusting snafu" and the "non-self-adjusting snafu." And there was the climactic "cummfu," which, roughly translated, meant "complete utter monumental military foul up."

. . . The correct pronunciation, incidentally, was "snahfoo" . . . Had Churchill's astonishingly forgetful mispronunciation been correct, all Australian personnel in the Eighth Army, including myself, would naturally have pronounced it "snyfoo."

Richard Hughes
8/4/52 *Tokyo, Japan*

Suggestion No. 44,201

Advise Jack O'Leary ["Marathon Hiccupper"—Aug. 25]: Try ten drops vinegar on teaspoon sugar.

Mrs. E. R. Mann
9/8/52 *Oakridge, Tenn.*
*After receiving 44,200 suggestions, none of which has worked, Four-Year-Hiccup Victim O'Leary now takes all recipes with a grain of salt.—*ED.

Postage Paid

I wish to relate an experience I have had in connection with Senator Nixon. . . . I have the hobby of collecting autographed pictures of the persons who appear on the front covers of TIME . . . My method is to cut the picture from the magazine, mail it to the person concerned, ask for their autograph, and ask that they return the picture to me . . . Of 17 returns of pictures which I have mailed to U.S.

Senators and Representatives, Senator Nixon's envelope was the only one on which postage had been paid—the other 16 Congressmen preferring to return my picture in a franked, postage-free envelope . . .

Peter J. Kuyper
Bremerton, Wash.
10/13/52

Unsuspected Cancer

Many women will sadly misunderstand your Oct. 20 article, "Unsuspected Cancer." The figures quoted from my paper—90% chance of survival for five years, and 65% chance of living ten years"—do not refer to the very early cancers usually discovered by vaginal smear, but refer instead to localized invasive cancer (Stage I) of many months or years growth. Stage I cancer used to be considered early cancer; but with the vaginal smear we are now detecting cancer long before Stage I is reached. These very early malignant lesions (Stage 0) have not yet invaded the tissues, and are curable in almost 100% of cases . . . Periodic vaginal smear examination of "well" women is about the only way of finding these very early lesions. Women should realize that this earliest type of cancer is entirely curable.

Maurice Fremont-Smith, M.D.
Boston
11/10/52

The Election

. . . , Congrats and plaudits on your choice (and mine) for President. A great general—an even greater President.

Stan Tigerman
Norfolk, Va.

Your precise comments on the election, "The Will of the People." Well put, elegantly stated. Would that Ike tear it out, tack it up, keep it in mind —always.

Bill Fisher
Milton, Pa.

Now that Daddy Warbucks has been elected President, everything is going to be just dandy. . . .

D. C. Brown
West Newton, Mass.

I am wondering if the Republicans (I'm one), who are happy about the results, are giving sufficient credit to President Truman.

It occurs to me that the way Harry conducted his office in general and his campaign speeches in particular had more to do with the landslide than all other factors put together.

H. Corwin
Huntington, N.Y.
11/24/52

A Greater Destiny?

And now has come the time when General Eisenhower must leave his European command . . . It may be said truthfully that many of us, be we Italian or British, sometimes resent the feeling of playing second fiddle to the U.S.A., but never have we resented General Eisenhower, for the man he is or for what he stands for . . . He leaves, we hope, for a greater destiny.

The foreign policy of President Tru-

man and Dean Acheson has marked a new era. But let not those who follow this Administration underestimate or belittle the potential power and influence of this Continent. In all likelihood, the fight with Communism will be decided here.

Derek Whiting
Beckenham, Kent, England
12/5/52

The Frightfully Smug?

Every week I read your "Letters-to-the-Editor" column. No matter who they are, or for whom they are, or whom they are against, the writers of these letters have one thing in common; all of them are frightfully smug.

Malcolm L. Storm
Toronto, Ont.
1/5/53

Of Flies & Men in China

Re our visit to China, noted in your Dec. 8 issue: we would like to add that we made no false statements and violated no law in obtaining and using our passports. We wish every American could see what we saw. In three years the new China has eliminated inflation, famine, floods, and flies—yes flies! The standard of living is rising 15% each year. For the first time in history, half a billion people are bursting with confidence and hope. They are eager for peace, eager for friendship and trade with our country. Should not all American citizens be encouraged to witness these phenomena?

Henry Willcox
New York City
1/5/53

China's Three Fs

I have just arrived here after 25 years in China (the past year being spent in a Communist jail), to find the Jan. 5 issue of TIME with its astonishing letter of Henry Willcox. I have wit-

Watched through special viewers, 3-D movies were one of the new crazes of the '50s

nessed the flight of the Nationalist armies, the arrival of the Red Army, the process of Sovietization since the autumn of 1949, but not the phenomena of which Mr. Willcox writes . . .

It is true the people are bursting with hope—hope that their Communist masters will be quickly driven out forever. The people are eager, desperately eager for freedom from the despots who harshly rule them.

If space permitted I might mention mass arrests, crushing taxation, the omnipresent gun with red tassels, the three Fs: Fraud, Fear and Force. I can verify all of these facts because I was an eyewitness to the subjugation of a free people to virtual slavery.

(The Rev.) Jos. P. McGinn, M.M.
Maryknoll House, Stanley
2/9/53 *Hong Kong*

BOUQUETS

Many thanks for your [section on] "Death in the Kremlin" in the March 16 issue. It was truly a masterpiece of information. As usual, TIME gives its readers what they are asking for.

William Lindley
4/6/53 *Chamberlain, S. Dak.*

Fearless Fighters

Your article on Israel paints a black picture for the future of that country. Israel's position wasn't improved when they had to open their doors to every Jew in Europe that Hitler didn't murder. But never forget that the kids who witnessed these horrors are now a fearless fighting group of men and women . . . They haven't "got their backs to the wall"—there are no walls.

George Barkin
4/27/53 *Brookline, Mass.*

London Taxis

With some of your criticisms of London taxis any Londoner must agree. . . . The basic design of the London taxi has changed little with the years, yet . . . the "rubber bulb horn and the

wheezy engine" have now been superseded by a large and growing fleet of "radio cabs," conforming . . . to a design intended to make turning and parking easy in narrow streets, yet clean, up-to-date and as comfortable as most cabs in most cities. We still have a few Georgian relics . . . but they are vanishing fast. Some, no doubt, have gone to California where, for the next few years, they may serve to perpetuate a legend (fog, a barrel-organ and a 1921 Unic taxi honking its way through the murk). The remainder are finding their way, rather quickly, to the junkyard.

Ewan Butler
Deputy Editor, Time & Tide
5/11/53 *London*

Keeping Score for Ike

I have been reading President Eisenhower's golf scores in your columns without being too disturbed at their being given as much space and coverage as the budget, but, alas. Now it's bridge scores, yet [May 11] . . .

Henry L. Kirchner
6/8/53 *Bellevue, Texas*

End of the Line?

I read with interest your June 8 article, "Memories Before Birth?" With psychiatry entering into all phases of human life, psychological gobbledygook has finally reached the end of the line. *Et tu, fetus?*

Sidney Merlis, M.D.
6/29/53 *Central Islip, N.Y.*

Giddy Denims

Re the June 29 article on the cotton industry: Have the gals of the fashion world been able to figure out what we suburb-dwellers do with our new-spangled, giddy denims once they've hit the clothesline? . . .

(Mrs.) Sheila Schmidt
7/20/53 *Los Angeles*
The word: don't mangle that spangle; it's a case for the drycleaner.—ED.

Senator McCarthy's witch-hunt of those he accused of being "too soft on Communism" gave rise to much controversy in the early '50s

Intellecual Immunity

We see that Joe McCarthy thinks that Albert Einstein is "an enemy of America" [June 22]. There are quite a few of us over here doing some fighting in the real sense of fighting Communism while the Senator is "fighting" it with his mouth.

It is our opinion that Einstein will assume a place among the ten greatest men of this century. Where McCarthy's name will be if it is remembered we aren't certain, but very likely in the same obscure corner of history occupied by the late Theodore Bilbo.

(Cpl.) John Moran
(Cpl.) Frank Cronin
(Sgt.) D. M. Moore
(Sfc.) Mervyn Miller
40th Infantry Division
7/27/53 *Somewhere in Korea*

On the Roof of the World

"Conquest of Everest" [July 6] is strikingly written. Part of it sounds Biblical . . . Beautiful prose!

Louise Dyer Harris
Newtonville, Mass.

Historians of the future will record this striking commentary on the spiritual decline of Western civilization:

Time: 11:30 a.m., Friday, May 29th, 1953.

Scene: Two men, roped together, stand on the roof of the world and gaze at the scene before them. One is Hillary, representing the spiritual heritage of Europe. The other is Tenzing, representing the spiritual heritage of Asia.

Hillary: "Damn good."

Tenzing: "I thought of God and the greatness of His work."

(Rev.) James I. Cook
7/27/53 *Blawenburg, N.J.*

Truce in Korea

. . . Not a few of us were astonished at the manner the Administration has adopted to bring an end to the Korean war [July 6], a method that literally shouts for "peace" at any price. Since returning from the Korean war last year (I served with Okalahoma's 45th Infantry Division), I have persistently worked to do something about a condition which permits Americans to be sent into combat and then have victory denied them, not by the enemy but by the very Government we were fighting to preserve . . . Have the words of MacArthur, Van Fleet, and the thousands upon thousands of Korean veterans been of no avail? Have over 24,000 American men, killed by steel from the sanctuary of Manchuria, died in vain? . . .

Jimmy Lyons
7/27/53 *Searcy, Ark.*

Dressed to Kill

Legend has it that Mata Hari . . . wore a beautiful fur cloak on the . . .

1952: Eisenhower and Nixon, Republican running mates, at a VFW gathering

morning of her execution. As the command rang out and the muskets were leveled, she unfolded and tossed back her cloak—her sole and only garment. Unshaken, the French marksmen never wavered—which may be attributed either to their splendid discipline or many evenings at the *Folies.*

Malcolm R. Wilkey
8/24/53 *Houston, Texas*
*Contrary to the lively legend, Mata Hari died wearing a neat, tailored suit especially made for the occasion, plus a pair of new white gloves.—*Ed.

Adenauer's Germany

Being myself a half-German . . . I was deeply moved when I read your

1953: Hillary and Tenzing conquer Everest

superb story. It is interesting to notice that Germany, as a defeated country, is much more powerful and advanced today than some of its conquerors. Let us hope that this nation which is capable of accomplishing great things, will not fall into the hands of maniacs similar to the ones who came into power in 1933.

George Kovacs
9/21/53 *Montreal, Que.*

P.S.: Report Card

Your article on New York schools [Oct. 19] was excellent . . . I thought I knew something about education, having taught at each level from kindergarten through post-doctoral research (I'd been in private schools, public colleges and large universities). But a New York woman schoolteacher stopped me dead. When I asked her to give a map demonstration, she stood in a most awkward position, and I told her to move over to the other side. "I wouldn't dare to work myself into a corner so far away from the door," she said seriously . . . "First thing a woman teacher learns in our school is never to get too far away from the door. Otherwise the big boys might trap her in a corner and beat hell out of her."

Later, when I visited this teacher in New York, I found that her students had chopped down all the classroom doors on the first floor. I concluded there was a lot about education that I didn't know.

James A. Michener
11/9/53 *Tinicum, Pa.*

Eisenhower Disappoints

That a President of the U.S. should lend himself to an accusation that his predecessor, Mr. Truman—who declared war on Communist aggression in Korea—actively preferred a man he knew to be a Communist is an action both foolish and unjust. Whatever Mr. Truman's faults, few will deny he was a patriotic American with the best interests of his country at heart. For many Englishmen, such as I, who so tremendously admired General Eisenhower, President Eisenhower is a disappointment.

David Piper
Cambridge University
12/7/53 *England*

Smoking Too Many?

All doctors will applaud your courageous and pertinent article on cigarette smoking. This should effectively confound the "unnamed specialists" . . . who report via TV and radio that there are no harmful effects to the cigarette smoker . . . Cancer is but one of many possible results under present investigation by groups throughout the country . . . While it is probably true that suburban or city dwellers are in general heavier smokers than those in rural areas, no true conclusion can be reached until a frank appraisal of the grave problem of air pollution can be made.

Robt. B. Marin, M.D.
Montclair, N.J.

. . . The American Cancer Society through its volunteers is undertaking the most extensive survey ever envisaged in this field. The complete smoking histories of more than 200,000 males throughout the U.S. between the ages of 50 and 69 will be recorded in detail . . . The health histories of each of them will be followed for at least five years. At the end of that time, or possibly before, we should be able to correlate the relationship between their smoking histories and the extent of lung cancer among the smokers and non-smokers . . .

Charles S. Cameron, M.D.
American Cancer Society, Inc.
12/21/53 *New York City*

Magic Formula

Re Northern Ireland's general election [Nov. 2]: Many of your readers must have wondered what magic formula the Northern Ireland pro-British Unionist Party has, to enable it to remain in power since Ireland was partitioned 33 years ago. Significantly, this European record is beaten only by Russia. Wholesale gerrymandering (splitting up of areas and voting lists so that a minority of Unionists can win seats in areas with Nationalist antipartition majorities) is part of the formula. Add intimidation, arrests, and Unionist British-backed skullduggery,

and presto! magic formula . . .

Frank J. Curran
1/4/54 *Galway, Ireland*

Faith Justified

On the night of Sept. 23, 1952, I was one of the many Americans who listened to Richard Nixon's "Checkers" speech. I was so impressed by his sincere manner that I immediately wired the Republican National Committee to retain Mr. Nixon as vice-presidential candidate. I believe my faith in this young man has been fully justified. Your article has echoed my sentiments wholly.

Mrs. Gloria Chiariello
Vestal, N.Y.

It will take a lot more than a TIME build-up to create a great man out of Richard Nixon. TIME can quickly gloss over this little politician's drive for power and his incredibly dirty and ruthless campaigns in California, but those campaigns still remain a shameful memory in California . . .

Richard N. Mason
2/8/54 *Beaumont, Texas*

Trickie Dickie

Richard Nixon has been getting a pretty good press lately, topped off by TIME's cover story [Jan. 18]. But now that he is the Vice President, is he any less the cheap political huckster who insulted the intelligence of his country-

May 1954: Roger Bannister becomes the first man to run a mile in under 4 minutes

men a year ago last fall? Some of us are not forgetting that this is the same "Trickie Dickie" of the fighting Irish wife, the cloth coat and Checkers. Remembering that irresponsible tearjerker he gave on television, could we ever have faith in anything he tells us? Long Live Ike!

James F. Considine
2/8/54 *Stamford, Conn.*

O Brave New World!

First we justified abortion in order to spare the mother's life. Now Geneva's Dr. Flournoy justifies it [Feb. 22] in order to spare the mother social disgrace and psychological traumata. The next step—which already has been taken in some places—will be to justify abortion in order to spare the mother the inconvenience of completing a pregnancy and rearing a child she hadn't counted on. And all this . . . will be done in the name of reason and human dignity. O brave new world!

Frank Patrick
3/8/54 *Durham, N.C.*

Ray & Pete

Re TIME, May 17: A guy runs the mile in less than four and you put Ray Jenkins on the cover. Honest to Pete!

H. M. Mosher
5/31/54 *Oakland, Calif.*

Liberace

Your June 7 article on Liberace was a bit too critical . . . It would seem, in this age of cowboys, comics and Gmen, that a nice, pleasant soul with a few dimples and an appeal for the older generation need not be so condemned . . .

Yvonne S. Burpee
Jeffersonville, Pa.

. . . Any artist who can hold the attention and thrill 15,000 people in one evening with a piano and a smile should be asked for advice on how he does it—not criticized . . .

Mrs. Helene Janecko
6/28/54 *Chicago*

Kith & Skin

Your otherwise excellent article [June 7] on General Sir Gerald Templer was spoiled for me by the usual reference to "diehard British . . . made to open their posh clubs to men of all races . . ." Apart from General Templer not having done this, there was no necessity for him to do so. They are and have been for many years "open to men of all races." The fact is that people in their leisure hours generally enjoy the company of their own kith and kin, and tend to flock together . . . One never hears references to the exclusive Chinese clubs in Malaya, which are not open to Europeans . . . How many Negroes belong to the "posh"

American clubs? Whatever our faults may be, we make a point of never stoning or assaulting the Asian families who move in next to us, which appears to be one of America's less attractive habits. I read with great distaste of youths stoning a pregnant Negro woman who had the temerity to live in the same neighbourhood as some of your white Americans. This "die-hard British" angle is a bit outmoded, and should be abandoned for some other angle of attack.

Geoffrey Trubshaw
7/12/54 *Bangkok, Thailand*

Tombbusters

Re the recent Egyptian archaeological discoveries [June 7 *et seq.*]: Are the archaeologists in Egypt now playing a new game of Cheops and robbers?

Gustave von Groschwitz
7/19/54 *Cincinnati*

Anxious Addict

The conclusion of Drs. Hammond and Horn that "regular cigarette smoking causes an increase in death rates from heart disease and cancer" [July 5] seems to me to overlook, at least as far as heart disease is concerned, the real cause. The majority of cigarette smokers belong to the "nervous" type, and heart disease is to a considerable extent of psychosomatic origin. The fact that cigar smokers are much less affected and that the death rates of pipe smokers are not at all different from those of nonsmokers points in the same direction . . . It is quite possible that in many instances of premature death it is not the cigarette that kills, but rather that those who are susceptible to heart disease because of their emotional makeup smoke cigarettes.

J. Choron
8/2/54 *London*

The Shoulder Trade

Thoroughly enjoyed the "Do-It-Yourself" cover [Aug. 2] story. I had my wife read it to me.

Philip Minoff
Oceanside, N.Y.

. . . I noticed one gap in your reporting. How do members of the professional trades—plumbers, carpenters, painters, etc.—feel toward the loss in business when prospective customers compete with them? . . . Could it be that our society is moving toward a more self-sufficient home-centeredness such as existed during our pioneer era?

Joseph V. Thomas
8/23/54 *Clarksville, Tenn.*

How to Grow Old

Re your Aug. 2 story, "How to Live to 100": Please be informed of the remark made to the press last April 6 by Mrs. Athalia Neuville of Angouleme, France, who, on her 101st birth-

day, declared: "I've always preferred cognac to doctors."

William Kaduson
8/23/54 *New York City*

The Battle of Detroit

With automobile fatalities running at an annual rate of [almost] 40,000 General Motors comes up with a 260-h.p. motor in its 1955 models. For what purpose?—so the pinheaded, slap-happy . . . drivers can have bigger and gorier smashups? The U.S. needs high-powered automobiles like it needs a hole in the head . . .

Gordon Smith
11/22/54 *New York City*

Great Scots

In your excellent review of Scotland's contribution to Britain's prosperity, it might not have been out of place to record a truly remarkable fact concerning three men of outstanding achievement in 20th-century science. John Logie Baird in television, Sir Robert Watson-Watt in radar, and Sir Alexander Fleming, who discovered penicillin. All were born and bred north of the Tweed. This makes them British, but never English . . .

Robert B. Myles
1/17/55 *Aberdeen, Scotland*

Cha Cha Cha

In your April 4 issue I noted . . . that possibly the Dominican dance, the merengue, would succeed the mambo craze in the U.S . . . At the present time, a new dance-music craze is sweeping Mexico . . . it is called the Cha Cha Cha, and I would venture a guess that within a year it will have a strong hold on the cool cats of the U.S. . . .

Madeline Tourtelot
5/2/55 *Cuernavaca, Mexico*

French Ills

Congratulations to TIME's correspondent in Paris on his article, "France: the Younger Generation"; he has hit all his nails squarely on the head, and seldom have I read an article so deeply comprehensive — and sympathetic — of all the ills that plague France at the present time as reflected by French youth and interpreted through American eyes. Even after years of close and happy association with my French friends, I still never fail to be appalled by the very typically Gallic shrug of the shoulders accompanied by the time-worn and threadbare excuses which reach back to the War of 1870 and the Prussian occupation of Paris.

As long as France remains hopelessly divided by its innumerable political parties, all pulling in different directions, and its general population remains totally indifferent to the various crises through which the country regularly passes, then the younger generation can little hope to be sparked with the inspiration or incentive necessary

Fans struggle to get close to their idol, Elvis Presley

to lift them out of their dolesome lethargy, which has been so notably lacking in the older and past generations.

Carl B. Humphrey
6/27/55 *Casablanca, French Morocco*

Down on the Farm

We farmers appreciate your fine July 4 article, "Automation on the Farm." However, lest the urban public think that farming has become a soft, push-button operation, let me emphasize that today's farmers work as hard as their forebears, and under much more ten-

sion, to keep the expensive machinery and larger herds producing.

The cost of modern farm machinery reminds me of the oldtimer who figured he could use the time his machinery saved him to run to town to make his payments on it.

Brad Benedict
8/1/55 *Lynden, Wash.*

Mr. K. in his Cups

. . . I am moved to some brief comment with regard to the statement that Khrushchev "seems not to have suf-

fered for making a drunken spectacle of himself in Belgrade." . . . The choice of Mr. Khrushchev as an "ambassador of good will" is downright Machiavellian on the part of the Politburo. Mr. K. . . . in his cups or otherwise, talks and sounds remarkably like a human being. He invites everybody home with him; he cavorts like a Legionnaire at a department convention (but never really forgets the business at hand); he lowers his voice discreetly when he fears his remark may be a little off-color for the ladies present. For the first time in memory, the Politburo has presented a living, breathing character to our gaze and, from what has so far been revealed to us, one could lose him any day anywhere between the Atlantic and Pacific at a businessman's lunch-eon, a political rally or a baseball game . . . The best way to disarm an American is to make him laugh . . .

N. C. Guerra
8/15/55 *San Antonio*

East Side, West Side

As mayor, and on behalf of the citizens of New York City, I wish to register my exception to the statement printed in the Aug. 22 issue of TIME, that "New York is still far behind many other cities in its municipal services . . . with filthy potholed streets and clumsy police." Today we have the largest police force in our city history, and a report issued by Police Commissioner Francis W. H. Adams just prior to his resignation showed a drop of 13% in major crimes during the past six months, which is evidence of the ability and service of our police . . .

I agree that an apathetic citizenry contributed to littered streets, but a current and continuing campaign of public education and strict enforcement of municipal ordinances have

Another big craze of the '50s was Hula-Hoops: competitors get ready to spin in the great hoop contest

paid off with a great improvement and a most cooperative public. In trying to keep our city clean, we have more than doubled the number of curb miles of streets swept mechanically at least three times per week . . . Refuse collections cover 51% of the city's entire area daily, and the remaining areas have collections three times a week, a peak of service which is unparalleled in any city in our nation . . . It might also interest you to know that a recent survey by scientists shows that the air in New York City is adjudged the second cleanest of the cities of our nation. . . .

Rober F. Wagner
Mayor
9/19/55
New York City

Ike's Illness

It was with grief for all the countries of the world, as well as for the United States, that I heard of President Eisenhower's heart attack . . . How appalling must be the weight of the responsibility of the decisions we put upon our President, no matter how much advice and assistance we give him, when so many of those decisions are, in the long run, his alone to make . . .

Julia M. Pryke
10/17/55
Detroit

Better Deal for Lions

The Nov. 21 article on Ecologist Lee Talbot's Survival Service travels through South-east Asia was extremely interesting; the fauna and flora of this continent need a rigid protection if they are to survive. TIME readers may be pleased to learn that the rigid protection afforded the Asiatic lion by the government of India has resulted in not only their survival but in an increase of their numbers. Their destruction was not so much at the hands of the Indian maharajas but rather at the hands of officers of the old British Indian army during the latter half of the last century. These gentlemen, hell-bent on showing their superiority in shikar, vied with each other in butchery, and though some of them showed extreme courage in tackling lions and tigers with sabers, several of them notched

THE Power of Positive Thinking

NORMAN VINCENT PEALE

AUTHOR OF THE GREAT INSPIRATIONAL BEST SE...
A GUIDE TO CONFIDENT LIV...

KON-TIKI
BY THOR HEYERDAHL

Bestsellers of the '50s

up records of more than 300 lions each to their credit.

K. M. Kirkpatrick
Gudur, Nellore District
1/9/56
South India

Godspeed to Ike

Anyone in his right mind should not even consider letting Ike decide who should be Vice President. I sincerely believe Mr. Nixon should be running the Government.

W. J. Hall
Mobile, Ala.

Practicing the virtues of a true Christian, together with the duties of a perfect gentleman and patriot, President Eisenhower's tested leadership inspires confidence and trust. All those who toil for a peaceful world will wish him Godspeed in a second term of office.

Baronne De Furstenberg
3/26/56
Brussels

The British Dream

The British Empire and the British Commonwealth and the British dream are not rotten or dying or disintegrating. Perhaps TIME [March 12] can

think only in terms of guns, dollar balances, wealth, but in the terms of history the British Commonwealth is writing a page in History's book of a greatness never conceived by man before . . . Let the frustrations of foreign ingratitude . . . not blind TIME in honoring its true friends and loyal allies. The mighty British Commonwealth and Empire has experienced these things for centuries.

John Haig
4/2/56
Belleville, Ont.

Subways didn't bother Marilyn

BOUQUETS

Congratulations on TIME's Feb. 27 astute and keenly observant article on Bill Holden. But he is still an enigma, isn't he?

Deborah Kerr
3/12/56
Hollywood

I think that for an American magazine you handled the question of U and non-U speech splendidly [May 21]. But there is one aspect of this enthralling subject which seems to me to have been generally overlooked: the U-attitude, around which a whole school of humor has grown up. The classic story of this school is, I believe, the following: A young officer who had lived through the Battle of Dunkerque was being urged by his hostess at a dinner party to describe his experiences. With a shudder he replied: "The noise, my dear! And the people!"

Mary Strickland
6/11/56
New York City

S. for Something

TIME, May 28, says "Harry S. (for Swinomish) Truman." Is that a bit of humor lost on me? My biographical material says that "S" alone is used because the Truman family was unable to agree upon whether it really stood for Shippe or Solomon.

Mrs. L. A. Stoddart
6/18/56   *Logan, Utah*
The Truman middle initial originally stood for nothing. Recently an honorary one was provided by Washington State's Swinomish Indian tribe and formally accepted by the former President [Dec. 19].—ED.

Tugging at the Iron Curtain

God be praised! How many Americans, who did not believe us D.P.s when we told them what a madman Stalin was, can now read what his close friend Khrushchev is saying about his former master [June 11]. But what a scoundrel Lenin was during his short reign.

R. Chudlarian
7/2/56   *Philadelphia*

My Fair Lady: the British musical of the decade

How to Handle an Actor

Your July 23 article on the fascinating Rex makes me long to be among the lucky ones who have been and will be enchanted by *My Fair Lady*. But why not mention the unforgettable performance by the late Leslie Howard as Professor Higgins?

Mrs. Philip G. Terrie
8/6/56   *Charleston, West Va.*

Canal Crisis

Thank you for your long, detailed Aug. 27 description of Nasser. He is banking on the theory that the West is too busy with the Communists to bother with him right now and that the Communists will help him along just to make trouble for the West. Perhaps he thought he would be appeased as was Hitler. I hope hindsight has taught us to the contrary.

Ralph M. Freydberg Jr.
New York City

Reading your report one has the impression of reading a propaganda leaflet from the British government. As long as Egyptians pay for nationalized property and keep the Suez Canal open for traffic, there is no reason for TIME to jump on the Egyptian neck.

Mitchell Stachea
9/10/56   *Beverly Hills, Calif.*

Revolt in Hungary

We stand aghast at the failure of U.N. to act immediately to save the Hungarian people from Soviet reprisals. The events in Hungary have shattered all Communist influence in Europe. Firm initiative by the U.S. can strengthen democratic forces everywhere. We have cabled President Eisenhowever a message urging him to speak

out, to use this moral authority to obtain immediate U.N. action, to broadcast in his voice a warning against reprisals. The influential U.S. press must urge similar actions by Eisenhower. The Hungarian students, workers and writers have given the world a lesson in simple courage that shames all inaction. We hailed their first triumph; we must act to halt the shedding of their blood.

Ignazio Silone
Michael Polanyi
David Rousset
Denis De Rougemont
Raymond Aron
Stephen Spender
Carlo Schmid
Nicolas Nabokov
11/26/56   *Paris*

Hot Under the Color

The TIME staffer who wrote the Oct. 22 color TV article should be sentenced to black and white for the rest of his misinformed life.

Alan Steinert
Cambridge, Mass.

I for one am not a bit surprised that color TV's a "resounding flop." G.E. President Cordiner is right, and the trouble is that the system now in use is much too complex, too fussy as to its internal adjustments. In effect, it is a magnificent laboratory toy, utterly out of place in an ordinary home.

Kerry Gaulder
11/12/56   *Burlington, Ont.*

Five Free Days

I was not shocked by the Russian Communists' brutality in Hungary. Those of us who have had contact with them and their victims in Europe know full well the demonic barbarism that characterizes their actions. The thing that shocks and shames me is the inaction of the free world during Hungary's five free days. As soon as it was clear that it was a popular uprising against tyranny, and that travel was possible in the areas under the control of "the rebels" (actually Hungarian patriots), the U.N. should have sent in neutral teams (perhaps Swiss) with U.N. flags and banners declaring every city, town and countryside neutral and free territory under the jurisdiction and protection of the U.N. at the request of the Nagy government. The defeat of Hungary is not only a defeat of a brave people but a defeat for the free world.

Gene Madeira
12/10/56   *Guayaquil, Ecuador*

Eden & Suez

You should be ashamed of your Nov. 19 issue on Sir Anthony Eden. It only shows once more that the U.S.A. is congenitally incapable of understanding world problems, and thus for its attempt at world leadership, being intellectually immature. It has not yet occurred to the State Department—called Misstate Department—that Egypt under Nasser is nothing but a satellite of Soviet Russia.

Charles I. Margry
12/10/56 *Paris*

It ill behooves TIME to criticize Sir Anthony Eden. Regardless of what Ottawa says, the majority of Canadian citizens were heartily in agreement with the British and French stand. The U.S.A., as usual, won't wake up until it is almost too late.

G. Rae
12/17/56 *Vancouver, B.C.*

If there is such a thing as universal justice, Sir Anthony Eden would be tried under the same statutes of international law applied to Hitler and Goering, as a war criminal.

Millicent Sewell Coleman
Van Nuys, Calif.

You Americans criticized Neville Chamberlain for talking and not acting; you criticize Anthony Eden for acting and not talking. Do you know what in hell you do want?

John E. Raven
Managua, Nicaragua

In any English pub the vast majority of people will quite openly say that the sooner we British get out of the alliance with the Americans the better. The view here is largely that you are out entirely for your own interests, especially where oil is concerned, that you have not the power or "guts" to come out into the open with a firm policy on one side or the other.

L. Thompson
12/24/56 *Beckenham, Eng.*

If Eden has resigned in the interests of Anglo-American unity, then presumably we can expect a similar gesture from the U.S. Whatever he may believe himself, Dulles is a pontifical pain-in-the-neck to most Englishmen. Let's have a new man on your side too—fair's fair, y'know.

Peter Stevens
2/4/57 *London*

Eden is gone. David is vanquished at last, his Goliaths forgotten and replaced by others who call themselves friends, and who then proceed to preach him to death. Eden's world is going with him—the world in which courage and intelligence used to be of some account. These qualities are slowly being smothered by the grey horror—mediocrity.

Cedric Rogers
2/11/57 *Hellertown, Pa.*

Man of the Year

Congratulations on naming the Hungarian Freedom Fighter. Since the embattled American farmers stood at Concord in 1775, there has been no greater and finer and braver blow

Popular musicals of the '50s

struck for human liberty and freedom than that by these modern sons of Thaddeus Kosciusko.

Cyril Clemens
1/21/57 *St. Louis*

Foreign Policy

Our old foreign policy was like the house policy of the gambling casino: cover all bets, wager everybody he is wrong and depend on the constant and modest profit of the house odds inherent in the dice or deck or wheel. Our new one seems to be the house manager's asking his syndicate to let the bouncer carry a pistol.

William Faulkner
2/11/57 *Oxford, Miss.*

A Fair Bottler

Mates:
I dips me lid: that caper about *Smiley* was a fair bottler. Who drummed you on our yabber?

Phil Rubinstein
3/18/57 *Sydney, Australia*
*Three dingoes have we.—*ED.

Hell Defined

After reading the Letters to the Editor concerning the Billy Graham crusade, I have concluded that hell is a place where Catholics are forced to listen to Billy Graham and Protestants to Fulton Sheen.

Jack Wright
7/15/57 *Shreveport, La.*

Pressure at the Faucet

Dr. Louis Dublin's report [July 22] is another step proving the value of the recommended amount of fluoride content in the drinking water as a safe, effective health measure to reduce tooth

decay. Educating the masses to the benefits and acceptance of health measures is a job that requires much outside assistance, such as your publication gives.

Wm. A. Jordan, D.D.S.
Department of Health
Minneapolis

City fathers have no right to force citizens to drink water which any expert opinion considers dangerous. People who want to drink fluoridated water are free to buy it.

Barbara Betteridge
8/12/57 *Glendale, Calif.*

Moonlight & Wages

Re your July 22 article on "Moonlighting," [holding two jobs at once]: instead of doubling husbands' wages, fire all working wives. Result: happier husbands, wives and homes. Lower divorce rate.

John Brady
Detroit

A recent survey by this organization shows more than 50% of our 115,000 postal clerk members are indeed "moonlighters"—not by choice, but by dire necessity. And there's a darn good reason for it: one small pay raise in six years just isn't enough to live on!

E. C. Hallbeck
National Federation of Post
Office Clerks
8/12/57 *Washington, D.C.*

Rock 'n' Shockers

Producer Cohen's teen-age werewolves [Sept. 9] are doing a thorough job of degenerating America's youth.

Ellen M. Edmunds
Kenbridge, Va.

As for this young chick, I think they're the greatest. After all, no one put you down for braving the sawmill with Pearl White—and King Kong wasn't born yesterday, you know. I saw *Teenage Werewolf* three times, and as yet I haven't had any trouble with fangs or unsightly facial hair.

Lori R. Koff
10/7/57 *San Francisco*

Sputnik Launched

I say thanks to Russia. May their little moon shock this country right off its arrogant pedestal.

Emily E. Schofield
10/28/57 *Gladstone, Mich.*

Moon Glow

Let us congratulate Russia on finally getting a first.

M. L. Vincent Jr.
Lake Charles, La.

Congratulations on your color spread of the mighty Atlas fizzle at three miles. The Russians also had a scoop at the same time—which beat us by 557 miles. When will the U.S. awaken —or will high-level bickering and indifference, strikes at atomic weapon plants, and official stupidity prevail?

Joseph J. Gabry
Albuquerque

The U.S. doesn't need an artificial satellite to circle the globe every couple of hours. We've got John Foster Dulles.

Maurice Murphy
10/28/57 *Los Angeles*

Booming Bulwark

Cheers for a nation which, ruined in 1945, can now double our annual gross national product increase rate. Erhard and Adenauer certainly should be applauded for making West Germany's *Marktwirtschaft* stand today as the strongest European bulwark against socialist pressures.

Jim Kilgore
Wooster, Ohio

Probably many people have already told you that your article was an extremely fair and penetrating judgment of Professor Erhard's achievements. It gives a complete answer to the one question Americans have most regularly asked me on my various market research trips all over the U.S.: "What happened to all our taxpayers' money in Germany?" Your story is the best possible confirmation that the Marshall Plan was an investment, not an expenditure, in West Germany. The U.S. furnished the seed, Erhard tilled the soil and planted it; the cold war provided the hothouse atmosphere; the German people, you might say, manured it and are bringing in the harvest.

H. E. Reisner
Publisher, Made in Europe
11/18/57 *Frankfurt, W. Germany*

How many students can pack a phone booth?

Ups & Downs

The way things are going these days, it's the optimist who thinks bread will cost $2 a loaf within five years. The pessimist says it will cost 2 rubles.

Cabal Amador
11/25/57 *San Francisco*

Reds Riding High

The Russians have messed up their life on earth, their treatment of their fellowmen has shut them out of heaven —so there is no place for them to go but outer space.

V. P. Stuterman
Mendham, N.J.

I am convinced that some people are more concerned over the welfare of a dog in Sputnik II than they were over human beings during Hungary I.

Darvia E. Schroeder
11/25/57 *Ames, Iowa*

You Beautniks!

May I congratulate the American scientists who built the American satellite under the guidance of Wernher von Braun. Of course we know that Von Braun was educated in Germany and built V-2 rockets for the Nazis, thus killing thousands of innocents.

Hank K. Van Poollen
Duncan, Okla.

Re the Explorer: You beautniks!
Ray Smith
Melbourne, Australia

What'll you bet *Pravda* renames our Explorer satellite Spitenik?

Rip Reilly
2/24/58 *Cleveland*

Out of this World

In this scientist-starved country of ours, one wonders what salary Wernher von Braun draws for his missile-expert job to shoot Alpha 1958 into orbit. Would he make more if he grew sideburns and played the guitar?

Hans W. Schwark
3/3/58 *Milwaukee*
His salary is $16,000 a year. No doubt he would make more if he could send cats out of this world.—Ed.

Losing Battle

The lesson of Indonesia (not yet ended) should teach the U.S. and its inhabitants that one must be very careful to whom and at what moment independence is given. The Americans are fighting a losing battle against Communism, especially in the non-white world.

G. Van Reede
Blaricum, The Netherlands

The Commie bastards are certainly getting nearer and nearer to us.

J. Morison
3/31/58 *Melbourne, Australia*

Freedom & Bigots

I hope that TIME never discontinues its Letters column. Freedom-loving Protestants who preach tolerance and then open their mouths—proving what bigoted people they really are—always give me a chuckle.

D. F. Hinds
4/14/58 *St. Louis*

Hideous Garment

One of the factors that has contributed to the recession is the effort by dress manufacturers to sell American women on the sack dress. There must be millions of middle-aged women who feel as reluctant to buy this hideous garment as I do.

Mrs. E. Williamson
5/5/58 *Clayton, Mo.*

Fins & Finish

About "Those '58 Cars" [May 12]: Why don't they just dip the damn things in chrome? Think of all the labor saved.

John S. Parilli
New York City

An ever-increasing number of motorists are becoming thoroughly fed up with the overweighted, undersprung, swerving, swaying, tire-screeching, chrome-splashed, trinket-laden, gaseating monsters that Detroit has been forcing upon the American public.

Edward Fisher Jr.
5/26/58 *Groton, Mass*

Crybaby Generation

Only one with a heart of stone could stand unmoved by the trials and tribulations of the American Beats and the English Angries [June 9]. Nor

BOUQUETS

It has just been my pleasure to read the review of Masters of Deceit, *which appears in the March 31 issue of* TIME, *and I want you to know how much I appreciate this frank appraisal of my book. It is my earnest hope that it will assist in alerting some complacent Americans to the real threat posed by the atheistic Communist movement.*

J. Edgar Hoover
Federal Bureau of Investigation, U.S. Department of Justice,
Washington, D.C.

4/21/58

Nash Metropolitan

is history likely to forget them either. As long as man stands just a little straighter, his head a little higher, in the presence of whines and howls and poor-folks writing, there will always be a place in his memory for the Crybaby Generation.

Nunnally Johnson
Beverly Hills, Calif.

6/30/58

The 49th State

With regard to your picture captioned "Drinks on the House in Fairbanks": there have been and are many who, during and after the celebrations, went to their churches to offer prayers for guidance, that this land may also become a great state. Martini glasses may ring, but church bells ring louder.

(The Rev.) Philip E. Jerauld
Episcopal Church
Valdez, Alaska

8/4/58

The Middle East

Isn't it ironic to note that today's Middle East crisis revolves around the area of the Garden of Eden—the Biblical birthplace of mankind? As present situations indicate, this very same spot could be the beginning of the end of mankind.

Joel D. Altman
North Attleboro, Mass.

8/11/58

Raising Hell with Nasser

Thank you for your thought-provoking stories on the Middle East. We should have a Nasser around this black man's hell and white man's paradise to kick out the color-conscious white men, whose only interests seem to be getting good salaries out of this so-called democratic British colony.

Mohammed Torah
Nadi, Fiji

9/22/58

Leotights & Leotards

The outrageous new fad known as leotards, leotights and legotards [Sept. 1], is known as lollitards in this town. However, lunatards would be a more appropriate label since they make the wearer look like something from outer space.

Kathryn Smith
Jackson, Miss.

9/22/58

Try Beer

Why continue to pour billions of dollars of aid into Communist countries when it has failed to make them cooperative or even happy? Let's try beer.

Mrs. F. S. Kaczmarek
Milwaukee

9/29/58

Hollywood movie star weds her Prince Charming: the marriage of Grace Kelly to Prince Rainier of Monaco

The Blasted Americans

Concerning your Oct. 13 story on Franco's anniversary: We are one of the "poorest" countries in Europe because we are still recovering from the money we gave Christopher Columbus to discover you blasted Americans. Keep your money and your awful manners. You are still Indians.

Presentacion Martinez
11/3/58   *Madrid*

Chinese Poised

Last month my husband and I visited Red China as tourists. Not for a minute would we underestimate the value of their primitive blast furnaces or their national scrap-metal drives.

China's entire population is organized to lift this country into the 20th century, and when you refer to her 500 million peasants as "ants" it is worth remembering that quotation from *Proverbs:* "Go to the ant, thou sluggard; consider her ways, and be wise; etc."

Prudence Myer
11/10/58   *Melbourne, Australia*

Other Voices, Other Rooms

Why, oh why with its scientists and engineers designing Sputniks, mooniks and misseleniks, hasn't the world been able to produce one simple toilet tank that will not run, leak, stick, snort, rattle or roar, dribble, burble and gurgle?

Frank Klock
11/10/58   *Pasadena, Calif.*

Golf Idiot

After reading your whitewashing of Ike, I want to cancel my subscription. When I subscribe to a magazine, I want news—not love notes about that golf-playing idiot in Washington.

Gordon H. Martin
11/10/58   *San Francisco*

Zhivago Damned

I was amazed that *Doctor Zhivago* was damned by Russia's so-called intellectuals, who obviously have not been able to read the book. Even in Boston we always read a book before we ban it.

James J. Nolan Jr.
12/1/58   *Boston*

And Serve Instead of Turkey

Penguins make very good eating indeed and not strictly as a last resort of hunger as you suggest in your Nov. 24 issue. During three years spent in the southern regions, I have prepared and served this dish frequently. Do not try to pluck the penguin's feathers, skin it as you would a rabbit. Cut the breast meat into slices and roll in seasoned flour. Fry in deep fat. If available, serve with red currant jelly, but any other piquant jelly will do as well.

T. G. Owen
12/22/58   *Hong Kong*

Sunny Side Up

Re TIME'S Dec. 1 article on Australia's election: I disagree with you that our Prime Minister Bob Menzies is "stolid, unimaginative and not popular." His campaign speeches have always been witty, clever and a joy to listen to, and he does not "angrily shout at hecklers" but ridicules them —a much more effective weapon. Of course, he does not drive around in open cars with colored slogans fluttering around as some of your "popular" politicians do. As for the egg-throwing incident, why not? We throw eggs, you throw ticker tape. It all depends on the country's economy. But no hard feelings. I love your magazine.

Emma Roesch
12/29/58   *Manly, N.S.W., Australia*

Missiles: Theirs & Ours

The success of the Russian moon rocket should teach you Americans a lesson. Concentrate more on science and less on jazz, hula hoops and the almighty dollar.

B. R. Chibber
2/2/59   *Nairobi, Kenya*

A Half-Nelson

Some wag remarked that it took only a few short weeks for Rockefeller to get a half-Nelson on every taxpayer in New York.

Paul W. Bachman
3/9/59   *Pittsford, N.Y.*

Kiss of Death?

Your April 13 photograph of Boston's Cardinal Cushing taking the political stump for Senator John Kennedy's henchman implants the kiss of death on the Boston Boy Wonder's presidential hopes.

E. G. Talbott
5/4/59   *New York City*

Castro Forecast

Let us hope that our administrators are fully aware that Fidel Castro is going to cause the American hemisphere more trouble than it has seen since World War II.

Larry Hamilton
5/18/59   *Oklahoma City*

Kennedy & Catholicism

Re your May 18 story on whether a Roman Catholic can win: if only 47% of all voters are aware that Kennedy is a Catholic, it should be the patriotic duty of every newsmagazine to see they are made aware of it! I believe a Catholic President would appoint fellow Catholics to high places in our

Dick Clark's popular TV show featured contemporary musicians

Government just as the Catholic voters frankly admit they would jump the party line to vote for a Catholic.

Mrs. M. W. Anderson
Oxon Hill, Md.

How can we be sure that a law—such as the law in Connecticut banning the sale of contraceptive devices and publication of birth control literature—won't be passed throughout the U.S. if a Catholic becomes President? It frightens me to think that even one state can be dictated to by a Roman Catholic majority.

Betty Thompson
Pittsburgh

6/8/59

Touring with Intourist

I liked your June 22 story "Rubber-necking in Russia," since I returned on June 10 from 15 days on the first American bus tour in Russia. I thoroughly enjoyed my stay, and I take exception to "the food is heavy and generally dull." At all times, I liked the Russian food; it was always different, and rather exciting as you never knew what, when or how long it took to be served. We had eggs, fish, cheese, etc. for breakfast.

Ruth G. Brown
Wellsville, N.Y.

My husband and I recently returned from Moscow. We were de luxe $30-a-day-apiece customers. But though Intourist here assured us "a private guide, all transportation in Russia, room and bath, four meals a day and use of a private limousine," this is what Intourist gave us: a bedroom with sagging springs and thin pallets at the Metropole Hotel; pillows that might have been stuffed with scrap iron—so lumpy, so hard, so heavy were they; a big bathroom with a proportionately large drain smell; a face towel and a thin, worn, stiff bath towel apiece (unchanged during our five-day stay).

Eleanor Howard
Malibu, Calif.

7/20/59

Sick, Sick, Sick

Re your July 13th article concerning the "sickniks": one essential of humour is that there be something real to rebel against. Let's face it, when the sickniks strike out at home, mother, religion, they're beating a dead horse. For society (yea, even the prunes-and-prisms middle class of suburbia) no longer has the sincere belief in these things that it had 50 years ago. Rebelling against old-hat philosophies is a poor basis for humor.

Joan Guerin
Wyncote, Pa.

The sickniks might be sick, but people who pay money to see them are even sicker.

Mrs. Roy Schroeder
Chicago

8/3/59

Hit albums of the '50s

Symbol of America?

The great strike between the forces of management and labor of the steel industry is more than a present threat to the welfare of the U.S. It is a vivid symbol of what America has come to treasure most and fight for the hardest: material security and monetary wealth.

Lynn W. Foell
Milwaukee

During the Depression, management bled labor white until labor had no other choice than to organize against the arrogant bosses. Gradually during the 1950s, many union leaders are becoming just as arrogant as their bosses used to be.

Roy Wolfe
San Francisco

11/16/59

Rare Experience

Is it now considered bad taste to have such wholesome entertainment as *The Sound of Music*?

Is it mandatory that the stench of the gutter must permeate most of today's viewable entertainment?

H. Remillard
Linwood, Mass.

Have we really reached a time when it is not fashionable to enjoy music, children, nature, or the lovely, lovable, admirable and talented Mary Martin?

The answer to that, thank heaven, is no—except from a few tired, disillusioned intellectuals. I know, because a group of us saw Mary Martin in *The Sound of Music*, and we can't wait to see it again and again. We left the theater walking on air, our spirits soaring—a rare experience in the Broadway theater these days.

Jessie Wolf
New York City

12/21/59

Not the Answer

Man has thus far survived the challenges of nature by adapting to and overcoming them. Has the human race lost its self-confidence? The only progress the race has made has been through expansion and growth.

Birth control can't possibly be the answer to any of our problems. A society that stops breeding stops living, both intellectually and, eventually, physically. The human race cannot grow by limiting itself.

Henry E. Chaput Jr.
Cumberland, R.I.

12/21/59

The Swinging Sixties

J.F.K. appealed to voters in the great TV debates; he backed down a greater foe in the Cuban missile crisis. Americans savored every move of the young, almost royal, White House family. Assassins' bullets caused the tragic deaths of three leaders. The Viet Nam War was protested, yet escalated. Hippies were In. The beginning of the decade saw men blast into space; before it was over, Astronaut Armstrong walked on the moon.

On Altruism

I read "objectivist" Ayn Rand's anti-altruistic philosophy [Feb. 29] with a shudder of horror. Her whole idea of life is incredibly wrong. She seems an embittered, unfortunate woman who has never learned the joys of giving to other people, liking other people and being liked by them.

AraBelle M. Parmet
3/21/60 *Bryn Mawr, Pa.*

Thunder from Down Under

The new "maturity" which your April 4 cover story credits to Australia also applies to TIME's coverage of that vigorous country. Congratulations for writing five meaningful pages of American prose on Australia without once using the words "kangaroo" or "boomerang," or evoking the usual images that these terms have contributed to a now outdated view of Down Under.

Robert Menzies may eloquently summarize the new Australian vigor, but the national motivation of which you speak comes directly from those dinkum "blokes, coves and coots" who see a job to be done and are quietly going about doing it, fortified by a slightly irreverent bush spirit and the best bloody beer in the world.

Henry Heikkinen
4/25/60 *Minneapolis*

To Have or Have Not

Your report on pregnancy control, and especially the boxed-in column on contraception, in the April 11 TIME issue shows how far Americans have come in considering the problem of birth control and family planning.

When I first heard Margaret Sanger in Portland, Ore. in 1925, she was arrested after her lecture on the great human need for birth control. Americans have moved far in half a century.

Mrs. G. J. Watumull
5/2/60 *Honolulu*

The U-2 Over the Summit

As one citizen of the U.S., I will sleep a little better each night now knowing that this Government has been for some time securing my future by sending reconnaissance expeditions to spy on clever, clandestine and cunning Russia.

Margaret Morton
New York City

No amount of sugar-coating by your reporting of the U-2 incident or any amount of fast footwork by soothing politicians can gloss over the cold, hard and terrifying fact that this nation is provoking war. How many Russian observation planes have been shot down over the States lately? After this incident, Khrushchev smells like a rose, and America just smells.

L. R. Nicholl
5/30/60 *Colorado Springs, Colo.*

Breath of Fresh Air

The Malayan Premier, Tengku Abdul Rahman, has shown the Asian feeling over racial discrimination [by walking out of the Commonwealth Conference in objection to the policies of South Africa's External Affairs Minister Eric Louw—May 16].

Mr. Nehru once said that the inactivity of the Commonwealth Conference had its weakness and virtue. It was this inactivity that created the atmosphere for a solution of such problems. However, Tengku Abdul Rahman, with his straight-from-the-shoulder criticisms of the South African stand, has been blowing lately quite a volume of fresh air into the musty atmosphere.

S. Nadaraja
6/13/60 *Temerloh, Pahang, Malaya*

Justice & the Beast

Let me congratulate you for the excellent coverage of Nazi Eichmann's kidnapping [June 6]. It is beyond my limitations to realize how strongly the Jewish people must feel against such an aberration of human being.

But what right has the State of Israel to violate Argentine sovereignty and capture one of its citizens? What right has the State of Israel to put on trial and condemn a subject of another state for crimes committed outside its territory?

I am not condoning the man Eichmann in any respect, but trying to point out that international relations must be above individual passions and hates in all instances.

J. R. Whitaker Penteado Jr.
New York City

This should be a lesson for the thousands of Eichmanns still at large; the hand of justice has patience, but it will catch up with them.

Jack Greenspan
Concentration Camp Inmate No 80459
6/27/60 *Monterey Park, Calif.*

Election Fear

As we approach the 1960 presidential election, I become more and more disturbed as I think of what may happen to the man who will be elected President this year. What disturbs me is the fact that every President elected in a year divisible by 20 beginning in 1840 has died in office:

1840	W. H. Harrison	Died in office
1860	Abraham Lincoln	Assassinated
1880	James A. Garfield	Assassinated
1900	William McKinley	Assassinated
1920	Warren G. Harding	Died in office
1940	F. D. Roosevelt	Died in office

J. C. House
7/25/60 *Princeton, N.J.*

Catholics & Contraceptives

Msgr. De Blanc and others of the Roman hierarchy have placed themselves in an untenable position. He is indeed correct when he assumes that Catholics are using contraceptives and even requesting surgical procedures for sterilization. Many of my Catholic patients tell me that they think the Church is wrong in its teachings on birth control.

R. G. Allen, M.D.
Bartlesville, Okla.

Having been a so-called "good Catholic" all my life, I find that the majority of happy marriages among Catholics are those in which the couples either practice birth control (in one form or another) or find it very difficult to conceive anyway. Most of the avid advocates of the church's viewpoint are in the latter category, and I'm sick of it. There are many people—Catholic, Protestant, Jewish and what have you—who want a great many children, and for them that's fine, but my very happy marriage to a fine non-Catholic could easily be ruined by the church's viewpoint and my fertility.

Mrs. Charles T. Holroyd
7/25/60 *Rumford, R.I.*

Problem Solved

As an independent voter, I had yet to understand what Senator Kennedy's qualifications are for President. But I find there is one qualification, and it also solves the problem of the Vice Presidency. We wouldn't need one. If anything happened to Jack, Brother Bobby would fill in, and if Bobby died, Teddy would take over for him. Ah—but what if Teddy went too? Well then we could fall back on that granddaddy of all shrewd operators, Joe Sr.

Mrs. L. Simon
8/1/60 *Van Nuys, Calif.*

A Royal Family

The blithe spirits of the Kennedy clan can give this country just what it needs: a royal family with a pipeline to Frank Sinatra.

Kenneth S. Hodge
8/8/60 *Chehalis, Wash.*

Congo Chaos

Belgium messed up her attempt at Empire. After systematically looting that unhappy land for 80 years was she honestly surprised at the outburst of hatred against her? To commit the indecency of shamelessly abandoning the Congo to chaos only to return a week later in the guise of cop appears to me typical of the hypocrisy that now seems the accepted hallmark of international diplomacy. I am not impressed.

Peter C. Obi
8/27/60 *Ikeja, Nigeria*

The Candidates

With Sputniks, Luniks, beatniks, surely the G.O.P. will start plugging their hopeful as Dicknik.

David McLennan
Schagen, Eastern Transvaal
10/10/60 *South Africa*

The Great Debate

The "great debate" on TV showed that Kennedy has looks, charm, and the gift of eloquent speaking. I only wish Nixon could express his views with Kennedy's finesse.

Barry Lyerly
10/17/60 *Boulder, Colo.*

Battle of the Sexes

Please allow me to congratulate Reader B. F. Bayruns on his outright, earnest, objective summing up of our modern women.

Today what we have is a constant striving for superiority between male and female. Man is no longer considered the stalwart breadwinner of old; he is now brought down to the level of a junior partner in a family enterprise. The modern wife is judged not for her qualities as a mother and homemaker but for her qualifications and potential in the business world.

I predict that if this situation continues, within the next 20 years the basic roles of man and woman will be completely reversed.

Noel G. Johnson
10/17/60 *Kingston, Jamaica*

The Right Man

What I am afraid of is the American public that rejects a candidate only because he has a 5 o'clock shadow, something only a stereotyped American screen-crook is supposed to have. Nixon is the right man at the right hour. He is not the people's hero like Eisenhower, but he has decidedly more executive qualities. If I were an American and had a thousand votes, Nixon would get all of them.

Hilding Borgholm
10/31/60 *Malmo, Sweden*

Proof Positive

I am glad Mr. Kennedy won—if for no other reason than to give proof positive that we are a tolerant people. This should lay low, once and for all, the hue and cry that Protestants are a bigoted and intolerant lot of people.

Cornelius Nicholas Bakker
Minister, The Manasseh Cutler
Church (Congregational)
11/28/60 *Hamilton, Mass.*

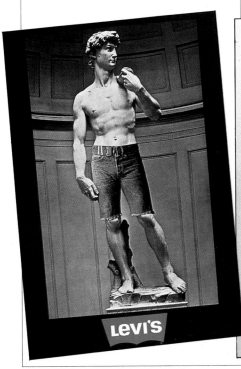

Make way for the all-new

DODGE DART

A complete new line of economy cars in the low-price field!

things go better with Coke

Adolf Eichmann, on trial in Jerusalem in 1962 for the murder of millions of Jews during World War II, hears his death sentence pronounced with perfect composure

Debt Forgiven

How nice it was of Uncle Sam to forgive Germany the $3.2 billion debt [Nov. 14]. I bet Adenauer and Erhard have the big laugh at Uncle Sam, their benefactor. It's about time we started telling the Germans to take some of the burden off our shoulders.

John S. Anisko
12/26/60 *Easthampton, Mass.*

Norman Mailer

TIME's assurance that the critical reputation of Norman Mailer has declined since *The Naked and the Dead* [Dec. 5] needs correction. Many critics and fellow writers feel that Mailer's work is of continuing significance and brilliance and that he is one of the few young writers who have not "fallen hard."

James Baldwin
Jason Epstein
Lillian Hellman
Alfred Kazin
Robert Lowell
Norman Podhoretz
Lionel Trilling
William Phillips
12/26/60 *New York City*

The New Germany

I find your story on West Germany's Franz Josef Strauss most interesting. The rapid German recovery from World War II does not come as any great surprise to me.

During that war, at the ripe old age of 19, I had, as did many other young American G.I.s, the expense-paid tour of Britain, France and Germany. The one thing that has always stuck in my memory is the way the industrious Germans began to rebuild their homes and

factories while the dust of their destruction was not yet settled. Let's give the Germans and Minister Strauss the nuclear warheads and the choice of when to use them. The Russians would not be so foolish as to provoke a conflict with a strong alliance of the U.S. and Germany.

Emmett Bailey
1/6/61 *Durham, N.C.*

New Frontier

Israel's Prime Minister Ben-Gurion has again made the statement that Jews, especially young Western Jews, should emigrate to Israel and do their share in its buildup. Money is not enough. He needs bodies.

If Prime Minister Ben-Gurion is looking for American Jewish pioneers he will have a long wait. The only pioneering of a New Frontier that American Jews will be interested in will be the New Frontier of President John F. Kennedy.

(Mrs.) Marilyn K. Murray
2/3/61 *Rome, N.Y.*

First Lady

It was surprising, to say the least, to find an inaccuracy in a TIME article.

I am referring to the remark made in your article on my niece, Jacqueline Kennedy: "But other Bouviers were not so enthusiastic" (*i.e.* about Jackie's engagement to John F. Kennedy). The statement is wholly untrue.

If I may presume to be the spokesman for the "disunited" (another untruth) Bouvier clan, let me say that *all* of us were proud and delighted about Jackie's engagement at the time, and that we are united in wishing her and her husband splendid years of ser-

vice to our country.

Maude Bouvier Davis
New York City

That baby carriage on the White House porch was a touch of Chaliapinesque genius.

I'm just a little tired of watching the royal darlings of European crowned heads grow up. It will be much more fun looking in at the nursery at 1600 Pennsylvania Avenue.

H. Hartman
Mount Vernon, N.Y.

Every time one of the Kennedy offspring has a leaky nose, will we be subjected to a detailed, blow-by-blow account of the catastrophe?

G. A. Sherbert
2/3/61 *Wausau, Wis.*

Bread into Stone

The back of me hand to C. H. Dodd [who heads the group working on a new translation of the Bible]. The "archaic phrases" are one of the features that make the Bible the jewel that it is. If the "moderns" want seduction, incest, etc., it's all there for them, only in poetic form. What modern novel cuts a prostitute in twelve pieces, one to be sent to each tribe of Israel?

B. J. Williams
2/3/61 *Evanston, Ill.*

The Glass Womb

The article "The Glass Womb" [which described the fertilization of a human egg on glass slides outside the womb] made me wince at the way some men can tamper with the laws of nature and morality as they please, and appear justified in doing so. I think there is a point that Dr. Petrucci has failed to realize: if Dr. Petrucci is actually growing human life, he will be committing murder each time he kills one of the specimens.

Paul Gunther
2/10/61 *St Louis*

What Jackie Did

Please don't keep me in suspense. What did Jackie do for the 40 unexpected luncheon guests?

Doyle L. McCuller
2/10/61 *Houston*
She bought a casserole course from a neighborhood Greek restaurant, served it with a salad and raspberries for dessert.—ED.

The Unemployed

With all the foofaraw about our "over 6%" rate of unemployment, too many people have forgotten that during the first two terms of Franklin Roosevelt's Administration unemployment remained above 14%, and in 1938, his sixth year in office, it was 19%.

Today, by contrast, with a far larger labor force, we're worrying because it's above 6%.

Have our years of unprecedented prosperity warped our perspective?

C. L. Sibley
3/3/61 *Wallingford, Conn.*
Reader Sibley's figures are correct. The recorded peak of unemployment was 24.9%, in 1933; the postwar low was 2.9%, in 1953.—ED.

Chinese Resentment

Cheers for Britain's Foreign Minister, Lord Home! Even an average housewife, with an average husband, average children, and living in an average neighborhood, cannot help but recog-

nize that one cannot banish evil by refusing to know it's there. Keeping Red China out of the U.N. only tends to increase their resentment and stall any progress toward disarmament.

Dorothy A. Nilsen
3/10/61 *Carlsbad, Calif.*

The Birch Society

Thank God for the "lunatic fringe!" I was beginning to think our patriotic heroes of the past had spilled their blood in vain—heroes who died to preserve America only to have today's soft, confused population surrender, compromise, conform and wishful-think it all away! Your article, "The Americanists," has restored my faith in the American people once more. How do I go about joining the John Birch Society?

Mrs. Peter M. Thompson
3/24/61 *Houston*

Peace

I suppose one should be tolerant of sincere efforts to achieve peace, however futile and misguided. But not since Henry Ford's ill-starred Peace Ship of World War I has there been such a visionary and utopian proposal as that embodied in the Kennedy Peace Corps.

Heaven help the Laotians, the Congolese and other unfortunate peoples as our starry-eyed young zealots march forth under the banner of the Peace Corps to escape the draft and save the world!

Howard J. Murfin
3/24/61 *New York City*

Apartheid Explained

Re your account of South Africa's agony at the Commonwealth conference: allow me to comment on the *apartheid* which caused our virtual expulsion. At least 90% of the whites in this land—both English and Afrikaans-speaking—believe in *apartheid*. We are not all ogres; indeed, we are no worse and no better than white people elsewhere. We hold the view that it is not possible for large numbers of black and white to live amicably together in one house.

At present we dwell uneasily together and the whites rule. This is unjust and humiliating to the blacks. Were the position to be reversed, the whites would be in the same sorry plight.

The solution is not to grant voting and other privileges to the blacks. This would merely be the first step toward signing our death warrant, and we and our children's children would like to live here, unmolested.

The alternative is to divide our country between black and white. This is *apartheid*. When there is a black

minority within the white areas, then we will have nothing to fear and can grant full privileges to all citizens.

In the meantime, none can deny that there is oppression, injustice and racial discrimination, but this is only because white and black live together instead of apart.

J. Ross
4/14/61 *Johannesburg*

The Fluoridation Issue

TIME is to be commended for its forthright reporting on fluoridation.

It is unfortunate that the unfounded charges made by a "vocally organized minority" should penalize and deprive children, who have no voice in the decision, of the benefits of today's most effective means of reducing tooth decay.

After twelve years of fluoridation, 12-to-14-year-old children in Evanston, Ill., show an average reduction in caries of 51% as compared to children of comparable ages in the base period prior to fluoridation. The greatest benefit has been obtained by twelve-year-olds who have now had a "lifetime" of exposure to fluoride—nearly 13 times as many children were free of caries as their base-line controls were in 1946.

Joseph B. Weeden, D.D.S.
President
California Dental Association
4/14/61 *San Francisco*

Man in Space

In regard to Russia's astronaut shot: it seems sobering to realize that we Americans, who used to feel that we were first and best in everything, have reached the point where we not only calmly accept the Soviet "firsts", we *expect* them.

Mrs. Gerald Durbin
4/28/61 *Cresskill, N.J.*

John F. Kennedy met Richard Nixon in the first televised presidential debates, 1960

Hero's welcome: Cosmonaut Yuri Gagarin, the world's first space pilot, is greeted in Moscow by Soviet Leader Khrushchev

So the Russians have done it again! What a tragic waste of talent has gone into the duplication of effort in the U.S. and the British Commonwealth. With British genius for original research and U.S. genius for application and production, we could be way out in front.

The blame for our failure must lie fairly and squarely on the U.S. The Truman Administration, by its refusal to share atomic secrets, abruptly ended the Churchill-Roosevelt understanding about the full exchange of information. All too tragically the rift between us is widening. There seems to be a sneaking satisfaction in this country that the Russians have again licked the U.S., and more than a sneaking satisfaction in the U.S. about the continuing decline of the British Empire.

It is not too late for the U.S. to dismount from its lofty pedestal and renew the Churchill-Roosevelt understanding on a basis of full equality, with no strings (or royalties) attached.

K. D. Barritt
5/5/61 *Ashtead, Surrey, England*

No Columbus, He

Gagarin was named hero. But Gagarin was only an experimental object whom the scientists placed into a cabin for a flight around the world, not unlike what they did to dogs and monkeys. What a shame to compare him to Columbus. Columbus was the leader and explorer who sailed on his own with full responsibility for himself and for his men.

O. Tarnawsky
Philadelphia

Gaga has guts and so does TIME to have given such an unbiased and gracious salute to the world's first man in space. This earthling, in turn, salutes you.

Mrs. D. C. Jones
5/12/61 *Melbourne, Australia*

Spaceman

May I nominate as Man of the Year Commander Alan Shepard, the first man in space. As an anti-Communist Maltese, I do not believe that the Communists have yet sent a man into space.

Vic Carabott
Albion, Australia

My warm congratulations to Commander Alan Shepard on joining the exclusive Spacemen Club. This heroic feat is a glowing tribute to the freedom-loving people of America. This timely success of the U.S. has given a good kick to the depressed free world. No more shame, no more fury. There is no time to lose—tell Shepard to get ready, because it is the turn of America to fling some surprises at the Kremlin.

Kanwal B. Singh
5/26/61 *New Delhi, India*

Space Heroes

Well done, U.S.! Congratulations on Commander Shepard's successful flight into space from Cape Canaveral. It's all the more pleasing, now that he has joined the select few, the coterie of eminent explorers. May he live long!

Major Gagarin and Commander Shepard have now paved the way for man's flight into space. In the history of human endeavor, there has been no other exploit excelling the significance of their epoch-making flights. How I wish Galileo were alive today! He would have been the happiest man to greet and meet Gagarin and Shepard.

The U.S. and U.S.S.R. should, under the aegis of the U.N., cooperate and issue a stamp, in commemoration of their astounding achievements, bearing the portraits of the two famous spacemen above the inscription "Gagarin-Shepard 1961." The cold war should not be a bar to this joint venture.

Tet Khaung
6/2/61 *Bassein, Burma*

"Nehru of America"

The latest trend of American citizens is to criticize their President for no fault of his—such as the fizzling of Cuban affairs, the lagging behind in the space race, and the lowering of prestige in Laos. As an Asian, I can view it only as self-condemnation. President Kennedy's personal stature in the eyes of Indians has grown larger and greater than anybody else's. He is a Nehru of America.

S. Yadav Reddy
6/16/61 *Hyderabad, India*

Ponder This

Scheduled for conferences within a few hours with Tough Customer de Gaulle (friendly rival) and Khrushchev (rival), Kennedy still remembered to notice the new hairdo and provide an object lesson for American husbands.

"Well," he gushed. "I'm dazzled."

Ponder that, youse guys.

Anthony Sant Ambrogio
6/16/61 *Bloomfield, N.J.*

No End to Acronyms

Why omit Boston from your "Acronymous Society?" [July 28]. Have you not heard of the agency dedicated to the reshaping of Dame Boston into a new, more uplifting community? I refer to BRA—the Boston Redevelopment Authority.

Robert A. Olson
8/11/61 *Arlington, Mass.*

Berlin

The soul-baring, grim message of our young, brilliant President has given life again to the famed declaration of a World War I French marshal: "They shall not pass."

Joseph M. McLaughlin
Fort Richardson, Alaska

It's the same old story: speak strongly, but give them what they want.

Mrs. Norman G. Shanahan
8/11/61   *Los Angeles*

Aura of Fear

Your grim story of life under Socialism-Communism in East Germany [Aug. 25] should be reprinted weekly and distributed to every American to read. Nonsubscribers have missed a strong reminder of what the free world faces.

Better our own system of individual private initiative, even with occasional inequities, than life as a "dreary procession of rules and slogans that dragoon mind as well as body," pictures of dictators looking from walls, and the "ever present aura of fear."

O. O. Wiswell, M.D.
9/8/61   *Hollywood, Fla.*

Cry for Help

One reads of the horrible, indifferent, heinous crimes of U.S. teen-agers today—appalling! But, then, one goes on to read the rest of your magazine about their glorious elders, and the teen-agers are absolved of guilt. Their so-called "crimes" are the most harmless pranks compared to those who would wield tanks, water cannons, H-bombs, and death for millions. Please, please, somebody right the world . . . and above all don't blame the young whom we have created in our own image.

John D. Sepesi
9/29/61   *San Francisco*

Mary's Beads

I do not want another day to pass without writing to you my heartfelt

thanks for the extraordinary article entitled "Mary's Beads" [Oct. 13]. Over the phone, friends of mine read it to me from New York to San Francisco. As I heard the words and sentences with that wonderful exposition of the essence of the Rosary and its power, my heart went back to you in tribute, in praise and in gratitude.

(The Rev.) Patrick Peyton, C.S.C.
Family Rosary Crusade
Sacramento, Calif.

Our 500 Sioux children at Holy Rosary Mission say the rosary every day, praying for peace. We wish that the rest of the world would join us. Then we could have "peace on earth and good will to men."

Silas Left Hand Bull
10/27/61   *Pine Ridge, S. Dak.*

Liturgical Renaissance

Bravo to TIME and to my brethren in the Lutheran, Presbyterian and other evangelical churches! Liturgical reformation involves 20th century participation in both the church's Eucharist and the world's need for service and social action by contemporary disciples of Jesus.

The most powerful discovery for all of us can and will be that Catholics and Protestants are vitally experiencing each other's life and worship because

of this liturgical movement While Protestants are rediscovering the centrality of Holy Communion, Episcopalians and Roman Catholics are re-discovering preaching and the fuller participation of the congregation in the liturgy celebrated from free-standing altars and communion tables. Both Catholics and Protestants are being led to a deeper concern for the church's primary mission to the secular world as a result of awakening to each other's worship. The liturgical movement is one of the brightest stars in a very dark world.

(The Rev.) Carl Sayers
St. Stephen's Episcopal Church
1/5/62   *Birmingham, Mich.*

Automatic Sinner Converters?

That's for me, automation!

Please order for this parish the following automatic machines: One sermon writer and preacher, one acolyte trainer, one paper-work machine with built-in duplicator, one parish caller, one sinner converter, one confession hearer and consultant. Both my curate and I are fed up with being human beings in a 70-hour week.

(The Rev.) Albert Olson
Rector, All Souls Parish (Episcopal)
1/12/62   *Berkeley, Calif.*

Sniffing Glue

As a teacher in a New York City high school, I wish to protest an article about a new teen-age kick—glue sniffing [Feb. 16]. To go into the exact techniques for enjoying the effects of glue vapors is just short of criminal.

My own students often use model-airplane glue in construction work in my art class. We have always been aware of the pungent smell of the stuff—and found it distasteful. Now I am afraid that your article has planted

the seed of something that we may be unable to control.

William M. Spilka
2/23/62 *New York City*

Impressed

The successful launching of the first American astronaut Lieut. Colonel John Glenn deeply impressed me and also the people of the free world.

Soe Thein
Mandalay, Burma

My youngest son's imagination was captured by Glenn's flight over our part of the world. During the night, Roger's alarm clock woke all the household. Then he went outside scanning the heavens, hoping for a glimpse of his hero.

Of course, the fact that the capsule passed over Woomera and Perth (hundreds and hundreds of miles away from our place) didn't deter Roger.

Jean Oliver
3/9/62 *Kew, Victoria, Australia*

Obscure Destiny

Despite a commendable effort to brush and polish his fading image, it now seems clear that L.B.J. is destined to occupy the obscure niche reserved for U.S. Vice Presidents during the past 173 years.

Donald B. Leverett
3/9/62 *Overton, Texas*

Help Abroad

I am now back at school. During my holidays, I lived on corn and dried milk that Americans sent us as a famine relief. Please, TIME, convey my hearty thanks to all Americans. I hope I may come to the U.S. and learn how to be kind.

Martan Hgalomba
St. Andrew's College, Minaki
4/6/62 *Dar es Salaam, Tanganyika*

From Blades to Needles

Reading your comment on the gentleness off the battlefield of Nepal's deadly Gurkha troops [June 1], I recall a 1947 stop at a British base near Hiroshima, Japan. Saturday, as busloads of Gurkhas unloaded after field maneuvers, the depot seemed alight with the gleam of curved daggers shining from belts. Sunday morning I saw a

President Schärf of Austria was host of the Kennedy-Khrushchev meeting in Vienna, June 1961

group relaxed, laughing and chatting, not a dagger in sight—but every one of those "most fearsome fighters" was knitting.

Verna I. Crofts
6/22/62 *Chicago*

Dessert Dance

Your June 15 report of Dr. Raper's theory—that desserts should start the meal—has excited my husband more than the twist. Arthur has been eating dessert first for years, and now, finally, someone agrees with him.

"Ex-ulcerite Arthur regards a foodless stomach as a puddle of acid. This, he says, must first be neutralized by something bland. He has cheesecake at Sardi's while others order martinis. He starts with custard at Le Pavillon as guests pepper their soup.

A long time ago, I once complained: "How can you order mocha cream cake for a first course!" Arthur said: "Whom do I have to impress—the headwaiter?" Dr. Raper can try that on his wife.

Mrs. Arthur Murray
6/29/62 *New York City*

Mass Appeal

Attending mass at the Basilica of Our Lady of Guadalupe was the biggest thing that President Kennedy did to win Catholic Mexico's heart. The saying here is that you can tell a Mexican there is no God and there are no saints, and he will just shrug his shoulders. But tell him that there is no Lady of Guadalupe—look out!

Kennedy's popularity now is almost unbelievable. I went to a movie last night and when the filmstrips of Kennedy's visit were shown, everyone stood up yelling and cheering so loud and long that I didn't hear the sound track.

Frank Cox
7/20/62 *Mexico City*

Satellite TV

I fear that the recent launching of the Telstar satellite, permitting American television programs to be directly broadcast to Europe, will be viewed by future generations as being almost of as much benefit to European culture as was the sacking of Rome by the Goths.

Allen J. Potkins
7/27/62 *New Hyde Park, N.Y.*

Term of Trial

Let me commend you on your article about oral contraceptives [July 20]. We are all anxious to solve the population problem, and most of us believe it can best be done with reliable contraceptives. There seems to be no doubt but that these pills, taken by mouth, will suspend ovulation in the female, but it is inconceivable to me, an embryologist, that any chemical of sufficient specific potency as to suspend the normal

maturation of eggs in the ovary can be free from adverse side effects. The absence of side effects for the short period of five years is an insufficient trial period. Some cancers have a latent period of 17-35 years following the irritating cause. It would be much safer to prevent the union of sperm and egg by the more conventional methods of contraception than to embark upon a widespread use of a pill, the full effects of which cannot yet be known.

Robert Rugh
8/3/62 *New York City*

Marilyn's Judgment

Within hours after her death, Marilyn Monroe faced her Last Judgment at the hands of TIME magazine. In quick, merciless thrusts your writer depicted early guilt, perverted dreams, and a "kittenish romance." It advanced a "death long in coming," "self-doubt," and just plain "body."

Who asked this writer to play God? And such a God—who sees only the public image, only the sensational, only the body? Who dares to judge a human being, the person Marilyn? "Judge not that ye be not judged." The real Last Judgment may reveal a much wider responsibility for this death—it may even reveal you and me.

(The Rev.) Martin L. Deppe
Mandell Methodist Church
8/17/62 *Chicago*

The Army's Choice

We the soldiers of the United States of America, think that it's about time someone put the "critics" in their places when it comes to judging Jacqueline Kennedy.

To say the least, she is a very beautifully proportioned woman, and we are very proud to have her as our First Lady and representative to the world.

The critics condemn her for waterskiing and wearing a bathing suit in public. If their wives looked like her, they would be very proud to have their wives in bathing suits.

Jackie is a young and beautiful woman, yet they want her to sit around like an old bag who can't move for fear of breaking a leg or something. We don't think they realize what a hit she is making with the world by being herself and not acting as if she were some sort of semideity.

We hope she continues to do as she has done and the critics mind their own damn business.

Pvt. Stephen Meigs
Pvt. Jesse Estlock
9/7/62 *Fort Dix, N.J.*

The Wall

The Berlin Wall was conceived from fear and forged out of hate. A monument to slavery and suppression, the ominous wall divides a great city. The Berliners call out for the destruction of this senseless structure. But Robert

Frost, in his "Mending Wall," has said it best of all:
Before I built a wall I'd ask to know
What I was walling in or walling out.
And to whom I was like to give offense.
Lieut. Thomas D. Walters
9/14/62 *Fort Bragg, N.C.*
Poet Frost himself read this poem to a Russian audience in Moscow last week, was greeted with uncomprehending silence.—ED.

Blockade

At last, with the Cuban blockade, we are standing up to Communism. And I shall let nothing spoil my satisfaction and relief.

True, we have known about Castro's offensive missiles for several months, and most Republicans have been clamoring for action. But I refuse to believe that political considerations had any bearing on the fact that President Kennedy waited until two weeks before the national election.

Granted too that the Administration had a two-year history of appeasement and retreat before Cuba became an unavoidable issue. But I can't believe that our no-win foreign policy will seep back, once the polls have closed.

I don't believe it. I don't believe it. I don't believe it . . .

Donald C. Bates
11/2/62 *South Windsor, Conn.*

Khrush

Who says nobody is qualified to receive the Nobel Prize for Peace for this year? After his retreat from Cuba, Khrushchev certainly deserves it, and if given to him, he might even start living up to his new reputation.

H. Nazer
Purdue University
11/23/62 *Lafayette, Ind.*

Pope John's Example

John XXIII is a marvelous example of how the immensities of theological disagreement can be transcended by simple human warmth and love. He has, above all, obeyed his Master's command to love thy neighbor.

Robert L. Capizzi
1/11/63 *Philadelphia*

Catholics on Show

The Vatican Council of 1962 may be the window that has been needed for Protestants and non-Christians to look into the Roman Catholic Church as it really is, as well as the means whereby the Roman Catholic Church can see the real world in which it finds itself.

TIME is to be commended for allowing the world to see a branch of the church on its best behavior. It is an example of what the church should constantly be doing in order that it really meet the needs of the world which it is committed to serve.

(The Rev.) Carlton Bauer
Evangelical United Brethren Church
1/18/63   *Grey Eagle, Minn.*

Cry-Baby Attitude

Though I hold no brief for General de Gaulle, and wish he'd retire tomorrow, I don't hold him entirely responsible for the mess we are in today.

Britain had the opportunity to join the Common Market when it was first formed, and probably would have, had it not been for the cry-baby attitude of such countries as Australia, New Zealand, and my own Canada, who by now should surely be old enough to stand on their own feet, rather than continue to cling to Mamma's skirts.

Britain is no longer the great nation she was, and it is time she started thinking of herself, rather than of her children.

C. P. Howell
2/15/63   *Vancouver, B.C.*

A Dog's Life

Last night I dropped Woody Allen [Feb. 15] into a bowl of water and my chihuahua drank him. Please advise.

Jack Douglas
2/22/63   *New York City*

Einstein on Taxes

I was interested in the article on taxes [Feb. 1] in which it was pointed out that "the late great Albert Einstein once admitted that figuring out his U.S. income tax was beyond him—he had to go to a tax consultant. 'This is too difficult for a mathematician,' said Einstein. 'It takes a philosopher.'"

From the time Professor Einstein came to this country until his death, I prepared his income tax returns and advised him on his tax problems. However, contrary to the statement that you quote, at no time did he allude to me as a philosopher.

One year while I was at his Princeton home preparing his return, Mrs. Einstein, who was then still living, asked me to stay for lunch. During the course of the meal, the professor turned to me and with his inimitable chuckle said: "The hardest thing in the world to understand is income taxes." I replied: "There is one thing more difficult, and that is your theory of relativity." "Oh, no," he replied, "that is easy." To which Mrs. Einstein commented, "Yes, for you."

Leo Mattersdorf
2/22/63   *New York City*

Seat Belts

What? No crash helmets? I agree seat belts are a truly fine safety measure—if you can get the public to use them. But shoulder straps AND seat belts on a two-block trip to the grocery store? After all, I'm not plan-

ning on going into orbit!

Mrs. Max A. Crothers
3/22/63   *Twin Falls, Idaho*

Young Cassius

What a refreshing change! Cassius, a young Negro, but not an angry young man; a fighter, but a colorful addition to the otherwise colorless and, of late, bloody fight game.

I've never been a fight fan, but I'll watch Cassius and enjoy every prediction and nervy remark he makes.

I am not a Negro, but if I were, I'd be really proud of this young man!

(Mrs.) Maryann Genova
4/5/63   *Kenilworth, N.J.*

Malaysian Federation

Your excellent cover story on Malaysia [April 12] again illustrates the dis-

Christine Keeler, key figure in the 1963 Profumo scandal

mal economic failure of Communism, as compared with the more prosperous economy of the free world. In this hemisphere, we have the thriving nations of Central America's "little Common Market" versus Castro's poverty-stricken Cuba. In Europe, there is booming West Germany located across the barbed wire from destitute East Germany. And now: Rahman's Malaysian Federation lining up against Communist-leaning Sukarno's Indonesia, a most impoverished nation. The West should ensure that no Communist interference will be tolerated in the forming of Malaysia.

R. D. Christensen
4/19/63   *Marion, Iowa*

African Unity

The recent heads of state conference held here in Addis Ababa [May 31], a conference that has possibly laid the foundation for a united Africa, may well be remembered in history as a significant event in world, not just African affairs.

The fact that 30 African heads of state agreed to gather together is a major accomplishment in itself. That they were able to draft a charter for the Organization of African Unity; contribute for the liberation of Africans still under colonial rule; that the finance ministers of the 32 African governments will soon meet in Khartoum to discuss setting up an African development bank are indications that the Africans are serious about African unity, however different their ideas about this may be at the present.

Thomas A. Grange
Peace Corps Teacher
Prince Makonnen School
6/14/63   *Addis Ababa, Ethiopia*

Outdoors Type

Barry Goldwater is the type of man one might expect to find in a Marlboro ad. And speakin' for myself, I'm a Marlboro man.

Jack V. Sexton
6/21/63   *Tulare, Calif.*

Distinguished Service

With all your excellent coverage of the Keeler-Profumo extravaganza [June 14], how could your reporters possibly have missed getting her vital statistics? Deplorable.

Leonard Butcher
6/21/63   *Seattle*
No so deplorable: 36-24-36, tidily arranged at 5 ft. 6 in.—ED.

Sex in Britain

Re Christine Keeler, Ltd. [June 21] —worst mistake in years? This gal is as *unlimited* as anybody could get.

Paul E. Reed
7/5/63   *Tucson, Ariz.*

The Kennedys

I gasped when I read in the July 5

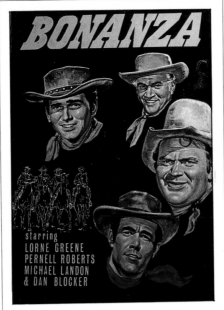

issue of TIME a quotation allegedly coming from me that my family is nicer than the Kennedys. That quotation not only misrepresents me, but it does great harm to a distinguished family and to my son, whom I admire and love. I don't think that way. It is contrary to my life and to my convictions. My sincere appreciation of each of them is of the highest quality. They are intelligent, with sound convictions, a great desire to help their fellow man, and they are way ahead of most American families I know or know about. Certainly they have many admirable qualities that most of us lack.

Hilda Shriver
7/12/63 *New York City*
TIME's reporter understood Mrs. Shriver, the justifiably proud mother of Robert Sargent Shriver Jr., to say: "We're nicer than the Kennedys. We've been here since the 1600s. We're rooted in the land in Maryland. The Kennedys like to be around people who are in the news. They are flamboyant."—ED.

Lord Astor's Help

I should like to put on record some facts about Lord Astor that are relevant to the suggestion that he "was never really intellectually attuned to his sophisticated circle" [July 5].

I first met Lord Astor at a dinner party in London a good many years ago, when I was little known in my own country and not at all outside it. He showed the most sensitive and delicate appreciation of my books, which he knew intimately. It was not patronage that he offered me, but the kind of support, steady and discriminating, that a writer most appreciates when he is feeling discouraged. Since that meeting we have been friends, and, at least on my side, will remain so.

It is for others to speak for themselves, but I know that he has given generous and selfless help, financial

and otherwise, to a good many writers and artists who were in need.

C. P. Snow
8/9/63 *London*

Pennies to Heaven

With the money the space department has spent rushing to be first to the moon [July 19], it could already have made five stacks of pennies that would reach it.

Rick Ayers
8/9/63 *Glen Ellyn, Ill.*
That's exactly $12,107,183,616.—ED.

Oh ZIP!

ZIP, schmip.
I'm so mad I can't find the numbers to express myself.

J. Paul Hunter
208-24-6254 (Social Security)
413-4583560 (Telephone)
319 (College)
01267 (ZIP)
Williams College
8/9/63 *Williamstown, Mass.*
Reader Hunter is also 038-516292 to his bank. 7K-3598 to the New York Public Library, 26-HT-5556 to the Diners' Club, while TIME fondly thinks of him as 00000J71T342014.—ED.

Of Tarts & Men

That typically male remark by Prime Minister Macmillan [July 19], "I was determined that no British government should be brought down by the action of two tarts," annoyed me exceedingly. That male arrogance of Unflappable Mac's is annoying and can't be allowed to pass unchallenged. Men were involved in the scandal, as I recall, but Mac blames *all* on the women.

(Mrs.) Esther Wilbur
8/9/63 *East Stroudsburg, Pa.*

Elephants Are Very Big

Why do elephants have trunks?
Because they don't have any pockets.

Colin Cahill
Sydney, Australia

How can you tell if there's an elephant in the bathtub with you?
You can't get the shower curtain closed.

Dennis Dudley
Cincinnati

Why do elephants have short tails?
So they don't trip themselves when they pole-vault.

John S. Sorenson FTG3
U.S.S. Boxer LPH4
c/o Fleet Post Office
New York City

How can you tell if an elephant is standing on your back in a hurricane?
You can hear his ears flapping in the high wind.

Dan Hide
Portales, New Mex.

Why do elephants wear sunglasses?
Because with all this publicity they don't want to be recognized.

Patty Roth
8/16/63 *West Hartford, Conn.*

Why did the elephant lie across the middle of the road?
To trip the ants.

Judy Schwartzstein
New York City

Why do elephants clip their tiny toenails?
So that their ballet slippers will fit.

Ron Hamilton
Jasper National Park, Alberta

Mass Participation

I have attended Mass in Manhattan, Mantua and Manila; while I am hard of hearing, I nevertheless can follow the celebrant throughout the Mass, because I made it my business to learn cathedral Latin. I would rather attend a High Mass, chanted in Latin, than be a spectator at the finest opera. And a pontifical Mass simply sends me into ecstasy. The secret of the appeal to people of the celebration of the Mass is just all this pomp and ceremony in Latin, a universal language. If the "litniks" [Aug. 30] succeed in reforming the liturgy to the vernacular, then the Roman Catholic Church will have ceased to be a universal church, and the entire liturgy will have lost its meaning to me.

Tony Rieber
9/13/63 *St. Louis*

The Quick & the Dead

Since American funeral directors, funeral services and Christian funerals are not on trial, and while the Christian funeral directors of America are minding their affairs, WHY don't you mind yours [Sept. 20]?

Show me the way in which a nation cares for its deceased and I will measure with mathematical exactness, the tender sympathies of its people, their respect for the laws of the land and

November 1963: Johnson becomes President. Kennedy's assassin is shot.

their loyalty to high ideals.

May God bless the American way.

Richard L. Studebaker
Universal Institute of Mortuary
Directors
10/4/63 *Las Cruces, N. Mex.*

Shah Admired

I was moved by the picture of the Shah of Iran giving a land deed to a landless peasant. The Shah is not trying to save his throne. There are a hundred and one ways to save a throne. The Shah is merely fulfilling his people's hopes for a better life in a changing world. It is this inclination of his that makes him the most admired leader in the Middle East, excelling even Nasser himself.

A. Neguse
10/18/63 *Addis Ababa, Ethiopia*

Hats on to Motherhood

You state [Nov. 1] that there are ten or eleven children in the average Bolivian family. Could it be the bowlers?

About 80 years ago, the story goes, a salesman took bowler hats to La Paz but could not sell them. Playfully, he placed one on the head of an Indian woman and told her that if she wore it she would have many children. Agreeable, she soon gave birth to twins. That did it. Today every Indian woman in Bolivia wears a bowler or derby hat.

James B. Stewart
American Ambassador, Retired
11/15/63 *Denver*

Kennedy Shock

Like everyone else, I was deeply shocked at the cruel murder of President Kennedy. However, that is no excuse for the political chicanery of President Johnson in asking Congress to put over the Kennedy legislative program *in toto*, regardless of its merits, or lack thereof, as a "living memorial" to the dead President. Johnson, in effect, asks Congressmen

who have opposed certain measures to set aside both conscience and Constitutional oath so that the Democratic Party can make capital of the assassination.

Certainly the program's virtue or shortcomings are not altered by the untimely death of President Kennedy.

William A. Cook
12/13/69 *West Palm Beach, Fla.*

The Bodyguard

I believe Rufus Youngblood, who was guarding then Vice President Johnson at the time of the assassination, is the same man with whom I served in World War II. I would like these additional facts to be known if he is the same man.

On his 14th or 15th birthday, he was flying combat missions over Europe. At 18, he was commissioned a second lieutenant in the Army Air Corps. Rufus Youngblood was already willing to lay down his life for his country even before he was a man.

Robert S. Picha
formerly Captain, U.S.A.F.
12/13/62 *Alexandria, Minn.*
Rufus Wayne Youngblood was not quite as young as Reader Picha remembers, but almost. He enlisted in the

Army Air Corps at the age of 17 in 1941, telling the Air Corps that he was 18. As an aerial engineer he flew combat missions in B-17s over Brest, Romilly and Saint-Nazaire, earning a Purple Heart and an Air Medal. He was discharged as a second lieutenant in 1945 at the—finally admitted—age of 20.—Ed.

Kennedyana

I hold that many of the tributes to J.F.K. are fitting. One of his pet projects, the Peace Corps, for example, could be rightly rechristened the Kennedy Corps. The Kennedy Memorial Library fund in Boston is also a fair gesture. However, Kennedyana, the Kennedy International Airport, Cape Kennedy, etc. are all exceeding the bounds of respect and entertaining the absurd.

The nation is gripped with a falsely intensified grief that is causing a disgusting outbreak of irrationality. People are acting on impulse. John F. Kennedy was not a modern Paul Bunyan.

It would be a far more patriotic and respectful act for a U.S. citizen to stop the bandwagon of pseudo-grief before they rename New York's

Seventh Avenue "Avenue of the Kennedys."

Walter J. Pfeil
Schenectady, N.Y.

I was very disappointed in my fellow Americans when I read that the city council of Cape Canaveral, Fla., is objecting to changing the name of the cape to "Cape Kennedy."

All over the world people are changing the names of schools, streets and towns to honor our late President. Shouldn't Americans join this tribute? And what place in the U.S. is so closely associated with the century— the very decades—that produced John Kennedy as the site of our space triumphs? I find the protestations of "a disruption of the history of Florida" very petty.

John Kennedy gave his life for his country. Cannot the people of a small town give up sentimental attachment to a name of obscure meaning in order to honor him?

Marjorie Smith
Aguana, Guam.

12/20/63

High-Walled Subcontinent

Your article on Australia's immigration policies [Dec. 20] is grossly misleading in tone.

I particularly deplore your use of the phrase "immigration *apartheid*." The whole objective of Australia's immigration policy and, in fact, the very nature and organization of the Australian society, are the complete antithesis of *apartheid*, which, as generally understood, means the segregation of racial groups within a country.

We seek to ensure that our society is so composed that, regardless of their race, *all* citizens of Australia—not to mention the thousands of Asian students and other visitors—are fully accepted and have equal rights without encountering any of the barriers which *apartheid* creates.

Howard Beale
Ambassador to the U.S.
Embassy of Australia
Washington

1/10/64

Strange Justice

A sense of justice that demands the death penalty for the slayer of an assassin is strange and bewildering. It must appear to the world that we had little regard for our late President when we demand the supreme penalty from the man who desired to avenge him, however mad and ill-advised the act was.

Mrs. F. H. Cronawert
Colville, Wash.

While Ruby's guilt for his insane and violent act should not be minimized, it is the police department of Dallas that should have been on trial for conspicuous lack of precaution

The Kennedy and Johnson families mourn a murdered President

resulting in the deaths of both the President and Oswald.

George Topas
3/27/64 *Lakewood, N.J.*

Disconcerting

Your account of President Johnson's cavorting across the hills of Texas at speeds up to 90 m.p.h. while sipping a cup of Pearl beer, was, to say the least, disconcerting at a time when the nation is still adjusting to the tragic loss of President Kennedy.

I appeal to our President to exercise the greatest amount of care in protecting his life and limb, without, of course, curbing his zeal for life.

Frank G. Barnett
4/17/64 *East Lansing, Mich.*

If Lenin Rot . . .

When you explained the procedure that the Russians go through to preserve the body of Lenin, I was reminded of those wonderful lines from Robert Service in his *The Ballad of Lenin's Tomb:*

And there was Lenin, stiff and still,
a symbol and a sign,
And rancid races come to thrill and
wonder at his Shrine;
And hold the thought: if Lenin rot
the Soviets will decay.

Perhaps this explains why Khrushchev & Co. go to the expense that they do to keep the old goat on display.

Charles A. Petersen
5/8/64 *Powell, Wyo.*

The Talkingest

Whenever we turn on TV, President Johnson is on the screen. He drones on with Pollyanna prunes and prisms and a string of soppy platitudes. He is the talkingest President we've ever had. It would be better for the country if he did less talking and more thinking.

Margaret A. Mann
Charlottesville, Va.

I've been a straight-ticket Democrat for 50 years but if Lyndon Johnson picks them beagles up by the ears one more time, he's a dead duck in my book.

J. S. White
5/8/64 *West Palm Beach, Fla.*

Gentleman's Totem

You misuse the term "aristocrat" in relation to Faulkner [July 17]. Faulkner was by birth a gentleman, but he let down the totem by appearing tieless and unshaven before his audience. There is a certain *noblesse oblige* that prompts a gentleman to keep up appearances, even though he may be a week's march through the jungle from the nearest outpost.

Adrian Conan Doyle
8/14/64 *St. Paule de Vence, France*

Doggie Bags

Having had occasion to take my meals in U.S. restaurants, my entire sympathy is on the side of the dogs [Sept. 4].

Petter C. Omtvedt
9/18/64 *Oslow, Norway*

Tokyo's Charm

The charm, intelligence and serenity of Tokyo's people, their constant efforts to please visitors, and their appreciation of beautiful things are the real Tokyo. I saw those "orange-helmeted" streetworkers, after finishing their hard tasks, standing in front of store windows, enchanted by the beauty of a pearl, a piece of sculpture or a painting.

I have seen the capitals of many a country on several continents—Tokyo alone has a soul in its cement body.

Alice A. Leeds, M.D.
9/25/64 *Bethesda, Md.*

A Great American

In 1943, when he received the Mark Twain Gold Medal, Sir Winston Churchill wrote me: "It will serve to keep fresh my memory of a great American, who showed me much kindness when I visited New York as a young man by taking the chair at my first public lecture and by autographing copies of his works, which still form a valued part of my library."

Cyril Clemens
Mark Twain Journal
2/5/65 *Kirkwood, Ill.*

Bottoms Up, Weight Down

I've been on that "Drinking Man's Diet" [March 5] for a while now, and I've losht lotsh of weight.

Frank Nosoff
3/19/65 *New York City*

Tools or Tyrants

TIME's cover story on computers [April 2] helped tear away the shroud of fear that envelopes the greatest tool our society has ever produced. Computers are not spectres of doom; they are friends of man.

Arnold E. Keller
Honeywell Electronic
Data Processing Division
Wellesley, Mass.

Oh, there's really nothing cuter than a shiny, bright computer.
  It blinks,
  it thinks,
  it calculates.
  It pilots planes,
  it chooses mates.
  It gobbles cards
  and spews out facts.
  It's capable
  of endless acts.
Oh, brave new world and future bold
—will it also cure the common cold?

Rita Boscia
Tuckahoe, N.Y.

The most tragic aspect of the future of man is that computers will be masters, not slaves. Either laws must be passed to prevent displacement of men by machines or men must destroy the

1960s sloganeering was enlivened by the new lapel buttons

machines. The only thing machines can produce is a total welfare state. To employ machines to do the work men did is to display contempt for men. Most of the men behind automation have never known what it is like to be displaced by a machine, and have never undergone the humiliation of "retraining." The dream world they have created is a nightmare to everyone else.

Robert P. Fitzgerald
4/9/65 *Havertown, Pa.*

Power of Peanuts

We have learned never to underestimate the power of *Peanuts*. *The Gospel According to Peanuts* has soared in popularity. Its seventh printing brings the total number of copies in print to 210,000. The book's success has backfired on Author Robert Short. While he has been conveniently putting himself through school on *Peanuts* by giving color-slide lectures on the theological implications in that comic strip, he now finds himself in danger of lecturing himself right out of his Ph.D. program. Receiving so many requests now to "unshell *Peanuts*," he hasn't cracked a book since Christmas!

Tadashi Akaishi
Associate Book Editor
John Knox Press
4/16/65 *Richmond*

Sihanouk Replies

As an anti-American, I thank you for your rotten article devoted to my person in your issue of May 7. Your insult to a head of state and your odious lies dishonor not only your magazine but also your nation . . .

I assure you that I would much prefer to die from the blows of the Communists (who are certainly hostile to royalty, but who have no contempt for us) than capitulate before you, who symbolize the worst in humanity, *i.e.*, racism, discrimination, injustice, death and lies.

Norodom Sihanouk
Chief of State
5/21/65 *Pnompenh, Cambodia*

Artificial Hearts

The cover story on artificial hearts and Dr. DeBakey was both interesting and informative. In it you make brief reference to the possibility of using a nuclear source to power these devices. The possibility is not so remote as your brief reference would make it seem: the National Heart Institute of the National Institutes of Health will be giving serious consideration to the feasibility of using nuclear power for the complete artificial heart it hopes to have developed by 1970.

Robert J. McCluskey
News Editor, Nuclear Industry
6/4/65 *New York City*

Feat of Clay

Even a cursory examination of the

Allen Ginsberg, poet of the hippies

Clay-Liston bout [June 4] should convince the severest skeptic that vaudeville is not dead.

Richard Swerdlin
Cincinnati

Hell, my wife and I could put on a better fight than that.

W. R. Jones
Great Falls, Mont.

Is it true that both fighters were Olympic champions, Cassius in the butterfly stroke and Sonny in the high dive?

J. Paul Hunter
6/11/65 *Riverside, Calif.*

Overfulfillment

Your report on German prostitution [July 23] says that the Dusseldorf brothel with 228 tenants handles nearly 8,000 customers per day. If the Dusseldorf gals are typical, then the enthusiastic reports we have read on the industrious nature of the German worker are, in fact, greatly understated.

James M. Pollak
8/6/65 *Los Angeles*

Author's Fear

The people who write the books that may henceforth be made available by electronic networks wonder how they will live if the entire return to them is the royalty on one copy. Authors do not want to keep the "information explosion" from reaching those who need knowledge. What they urge is recognition of the fact that photocopying, search and retrieval, and elec-

tronic networks between libraries add up to a publishing revolution just as much as did the introduction of printing by movable type. Let us all work to find some way of seeing that writers are not automated out of existence.

Rex Stout (President)
Abe Burrows
Elizabeth Janeway
Herbert Mitgang
Leo Rosten
Jerome Weidman
Theodore H. White
Herman Wouk
The Authors League of America Inc.
9/17/65 *New York City*

Is God Dead?

What is being testified to by the God-is-dead group [Oct. 22] is the difficulty of faith today, rather than the death of God. The difficulty of having faith means that the doubter's resources are so meager that he can conceive only of a God whose existence can be denied.

(The Rev.) C. E. Stollings
First Methodist Church
Derry, Pa.

To a dead man, everything is dead, even God. Clearly, these modern theologians have been choked to death by their own philosophy.

(The Rev.) Stefan Gulyas
11/5/65 *Torrington, Conn.*

Christian Atheism

The God-is-Dead theologians [Oct. 22] are spinning the rope with which

I PRESSED THE FIRE CONTROL... AND AHEAD OF ME ROCKETS BLAZED THROUGH THE SKY...

WHAAM!

Pop art by Roy Lichtenstein

to hang themselves. If, as they claim, man's intelligence was used to create a God who does not exist, it could then be argued that man's intelligence is now being used to murder a God who does. Saying God is dead is about as intelligent as saying that a city's electrical power is dead when your own reading light doesn't work.

Ray F. Purdy Jr.
11/12/65 *Buenos Aires, Argentina*

The Blackout

If you look at certain pictures of blacked-out New York City, you can see very plainly, hovering over the city, a flying saucer. Obviously the power failure [Nov. 19] was only a preliminary to a massive invasion by alien forces bent on destroying the human race. You must be relieved to know it wasn't Russian sabotage at all.

Harold F. Whitney
Boston

Your story, which struck me as un-unusually superficial, omitted mention of the fact that the telephones were working. No doubt you are aware that telephones are powered by electricity—and Mother Bell was prepared. Similar efforts were made successfully by the radio stations. Other public utilities were found sadly wanting, including the bus system and the fraternity of New York taxi drivers, who were either unwilling to take fares or over-charged them; they deserve contempt.

Eric Holzer
New York

The "brown-robed Franciscan friar" who was directing traffic was no amateur. Before joining the order, Brother Patrick O'Leary, O.F.M. was for seven years one of "New York's finest."

Fr. Patrick Adams, O.F.M.
St. Francis Monastery
11/26/65 *New York City*

Blackout Humor

History does indeed repeat itself. In your account of how a rescue-team

member called out to some people trapped in an elevator in the Empire State Building: "Are there any pregnant women aboard?" and received the well-timed answer: "Why, we've hardly even met!"

In Britain, during the blitz, special air-raid shelters were created for pregnant women and invalids. One night, an air-raid warden called down into the depths of the Piccadilly Circus tube station: "I say, are there any pregnant women there?" Instantly came back your answer: "Gor-blimey, guv'nor, give us a chawnce—we've only been here seven minutes!"

T. A. Jarvis
12/3/65 *Regina, Sask.*

India's Indira

The choice of Indira Gandhi as Prime Minister of India [Jan. 28] is not only a tribute to the lady herself and her dedicated nation-building family, but also to all the women of India.

Frances S. Bond
Former President, Calcutta Y.W.C.A.
2/4/66 *East Dover, Vt.*

Classic Tricks

Your mention of classic tricks designed to disqualify the draftee brings to mind the story that was circulating in Britain at the time of the Suez crisis. A Teddy boy, having received his draft notice, showed up for the pre-induction physical wearing a truss borrowed from a friend. The doctor looked him over, asked how long he'd been using the truss. "About two years," came the confident reply. Whereupon the medic stamped the inductee's papers NEAR EAST, explaining, "If you can wear a double truss upside down for two years you can sure as hell ride a camel!"

Clifford E. Landers
2/18/66 *Rio de Janeiro*

Huxley's Prophecy

One wonders if TIME is trying to prove Aldous Huxley right when he said, "In a few years, no doubt, marriage licenses will be sold like dog licenses, good for a period of twelve months, with no law against changing dogs or keeping more than one animal at a time."

Peter P. Zuk
2/25/66 *Bakersfield, Calif.*

In the Year 2000

Your Essay "The Futurists" [Feb. 25] leaves me with just one happy thought: that I shall not be alive in the year 2000.

(Mrs.) Ruth Chase
Ferrisburg, Vt.
3/11/66

Humor

About your Essay on humor [March 4]: You were right to include among the alltime big ones Jack Benny's reply to the robber who demanded his money or life. When I mentioned this old radio classic to Benny recently, he said: "That was our longest laugh. But the one I like best was on our TV show. My trousers were draped on a rack, and when a delivery boy came in, Rochester got a quarter out of my pocket and tipped the boy. Then I came in, hefted my trousers once, and said, 'Rochester, who took a quarter out of my pants?' Now THAT'S damn funny, if I do say so myself!"

Elston Brooks
Amusements Editor
Fort Worth Star-Telegram
3/18/66 *Fort Worth*

The Only Way

The way kids dress today, maybe naked parties are the only way to tell the boys from the girls.

C. D. McCarroll
3/25/66 *Pittsburg*

Word on God

Let us hope that the cogent arguments brought forth in the "God is dead" movement will encourage many people to lay aside their superstitious crutches and learn to walk like men.

Jon L. Mikesell, '66
Massachusetts Institute of Technology
4/15/66 *Cambridge, Mass.*

London Bridge

Many thanks for your simply wizard London cover story [April 15]. As a native Londoner, I assure you that London has always been a wonderful town. But it needed a shrewd Yorkshireman and TIME to turn the spotlight on the old girl.

Dorothy M. Wilson
Wichita Falls, Texas

That's a hell of a test by which to measure a city's greatness: its ability to appeal to the moronic fringe, the smart alecks and the social climbers. The attractions you emphasize aren't those that brought me halfway round the world to earn my living in London. London is also the mist along the river, the cries of the street markets and the smell of old books. "Everyone parties with everyone" indeed! Nuts to you.

T. H. Sadler
Tonbridge, England

You aver that London is in the midst of a renaissance, that its theater is "in a second Elizabethan era." Nonsense. While it may be the world's pleasure capital, London smacks more of Las Vegas desperation than of Renaissance gusto. Compare the solitary John Osborne with Marlowe, Shakespeare, Jonson and Webster. The contrast is humbling.

Richard S. Reid
Robert College
Istanbul

Thousands of young people with the same haircut, the same facial expression, rush out every Saturday to buy what everyone else is wearing so they can look different. One can no longer have his own opinion: he must wait until he is told whether a movie is In before he can like it. He can't buy a suit unless it comes from Carnaby Street. He must listen to mass-produced, discordant noise sung by rude, pseudo-intellectual malcontents because it is the sound of his generation. He must be atheistic, anarchistic, hedonistic. Hooray for liberated British youth! I can hardly wait for the brainwashing machine to come to America so I can be liberated too.

Sara Oswald
4/29/66 *Montclair, N.J.*

Those Who Sleep

In announcing the expulsion of American installations and personnel from France [April 22], De Gaulle did not specify whether or not the expulsion order included the service personnel who lie sleeping in the French

soil that, in two wars, they gave their lives to save.

Judson M. Smith
5/6/66 *Lincoln, Neb.*

Question of Ethics

The heart surgery performed by Dr. DeBakey [April 29] was interesting and exciting. However, I believe the play-by-play news releases went beyond the limits of medical ethics, violating the physician's obligation to keep his patient's problems and therapy to himself. Experimental medical procedures, though necessary to medical advancement, should not be displayed to the public like a baseball game; the dignity of the patient and his family is too important for that.

Michael Treister
Washington University School
of Medicine
5/13/66 *St. Louis*

Tempering the Wind

TIME's thoughtful Essay on Red China [May 20] should do much to temper the rantings of the bomb-'em-now crowd. It brings hope that China might yet, given another generation, become a world neighbor again.

Milton S. Katz
6/3/66 *Sherman Oaks, Calif.*

Bumper Crop

Add to your bumper sticker collection [June 17]: *Trouble Parking? Support Planned Parenthood.*

Walter N. Forges
White Plains, N.Y.

The most profound sticker I have seen reads: *Make Love, Not War.*

Diane McCurdy
7/1/66 *Santa Rosa, Calif.*

Now You Know

"When does middle age begin?" When the phone rings on Saturday night, and you hope it's a wrong number.

Dave Breger
8/5/66 *S. Nyack, N.Y.*

The Laager

In view of the assassination of Prime Minister Hendrik Verwoerd, it is remarkable that TIME, in the cover story on South Africa [Aug. 26], could have "pre-scooped" all other news media with such an interesting and educational article relating to "The Great White Laager."

Norman Silversmith
New York City

As a matter of curiosity, was your Verwoerd cover story allowed to circulate in South Africa?

E. Morison
9/16/66 *Melbourne*
Though TIME has been banned on previous occasions, this issue was allowed to circulate after a delay of five days, during which Verwoerd read and personally passed the story through censorship.—ED.

Giant Steps

My compliments on the informative, accurate, and very readable article explaining those Lilliputian giants—integrated circuits [Sept. 2]. As an electronics engineer working toward a doctorate in the field, I feel a very keen anticipation for the Dick Tracy wrist TV communicator and the domestic computerized control center in each home—both well within economic possibility because of those highly processed wafers of sand (silicon). You have removed part of the mystery that

Hot pants: a late '60s swinging fashion

the general public feels surrounding the operation and fabrication of such unfathomably tiny circuits.

Howard E. Abraham
General Dynamics
9/23/66
San Diego

Muddling Through

Most would agree with your diagnosis of Britain's current crisis and fondness for muddling through. Not all Britons are Alfies lolling on the production lines or Algernons dozing in the boardrooms! There are still many decent folk who are only waiting for proper incentives—and some leadership. In the past two years there has been precious little of either, in spite of all Harold Wilson's boasts that he would get Britain moving again.

J. H. K. Lockhart
9/30/66
London

Reagan Despair

After I watched Ronald Reagan in a television interview program, it became obvious that the people of California should realize that Mr. Reagan is indeed maturing—he is beginning to look more and more like Edward Everett Horton.

James Wallace
10/14/66
Toledo

Acting the Part

Ronald Reagan [Oct. 7] is destined for greatness. He is articulate, intelligent, and above all he has imagination, which this country lacks today. I am sure the California electorate will elect a creative Governor.

Fulvio S. Amodeo
10/27/66
Boston

With Intelligent Reservations

The stand that the Roman Catholic Church has continued to uphold on the subject of birth control [Nov. 18] is narrow-minded, archaic, and oftentimes psychologically and economically cruel. We feel that the church should condone the use of birth control, with some intelligent reservations. For instance, birth control should not be used outside of marriage or to completely prevent parenthood. The use of birth control to produce a family that you are psychologically and economically able to have, can only be termed wise and not "sinful." With modern science the world has progressed in many ways. Why shouldn't it also progress in this humanitarian matter of helping build a durable family unit?

George E. Engdahl Jr. ('70)
Robert M. Conway ('70)
College of the Holy Cross
12/2/66
Worcester, Mass.

Write to Dissent

As a graduate of a Jesuit institution (University of Santa Clara) like the College of Holy Cross, I should be in-

Black nationalist Malcolm X

terested to learn how the two young men (Mr. George E. Engdahl Jr. and Mr. Robert M. Conway) have fared since they dared to write—and have published—a letter [Dec. 2] correctly stating that the stand of the Roman Catholic Church is "narrow-minded, archaic," etc. *re* birth control.

Their correct appraisal is equaled only by their outright courage—for I can recall the day when to voice, much less to publish, a critique of the church, by a student within one of its institutions, was to have culminated in immediate expulsion—preceded by a dictated letter of recantation. Either the church has indeed changed, or these individuals are now seeking academic pursuits elsewhere.

Thomas M. Edwards
12/16/66
San Francisco
They are still at Holy Cross and doing very nicely, without a word from anyone in authority.

The Now & Future Kings

My husband, who teaches at Brown University, and I, who teach at the Rhode Island School of Design, are filled with enthusiasm and optimism for your young men and women of the year [Jan. 6].

Long hair and short skirts are only variations on the crew cuts and dirty saddle shoes of our generation, but the compassion, honesty, earnestness and lack of hypocrisy of today's student (and his utter contempt for anything

akin to hypocrisy) are far beyond anything that seemed possible to us.

Meg Licht
1/20/67
Providence

To Bring the Spring

As a 30-year-old American in my ninth year of religious life, may I express another viewpoint on "The Restive Nuns" [Jan 13]?

The members of religious communities are the only ones who can change them. To stay within the community and help renew it according to today's insights is, I think, very worthwhile. A seminarian friend of mind put it in a nutshell: "We are not in the real 'light of Vatican II' as yet; we are only at the dawn of a stormy day. But we have the opportunity to determine the weather. We can't go south for the winter; we have to stay and bring about the spring."

Sister Bernadette Marie
SCMM
Medical Mission Sisters
1/27/67
Philadelphia

Of Gallantry & Patriotism

The entire world will mourn the loss of the three astronauts at Cape Kennedy [Feb. 3]. It is certain that the last thing the three gallant men concerned would wish for would be for the space program to be abandoned. The benefits already given to mankind as a result of the space program are indeed tremendous, thanks to the devotion to duty of all concerned. Thank you, U.S.A.

G. O. Priestly
2/10/67
Yorkshire, England

Never Say Die

Planning to be a freezee some day just as Dr. Bedford is, I must voice some objections to "Never Say Die" [Feb. 3]. You call the process of freezing "strange rites," but, as Jessica Mitford has ably pointed out, interment is the method that is eerie. Cryobiology is a young science but the mass of individuals now planning on being frozen should give it a stimulating boost. Last year predictions ran that it would be 50 years before a mammalian brain would be successfully frozen but one was successfully frozen and thawed that very year (*Nature*, Oct. 15, 1966). Now *you* are saying that success with a human organ lies in the distant future. How distant?

Judie Walton
2/17/67
Spartanburg, S.C.

Under the Big Sky

This morning I awakened to another windy Montana morning. I grumbled a little as I dressed; I've never liked wind, and we get a lot of it in this prairie country.

Something happened this morning, though, that made me change my mind forever: I read your cover story on air pollution [Jan. 27]. Then I went to the door and opened it. The turbulent air was clean and bracing, and the snow that had fallen a week ago was still white and clean.

I will never complain about the wind again. I will thank God every day of my life that I am privileged to live in this Big Sky country. But what is more to the point, I will support every effort to alleviate air pollution elsewhere and to prevent it in Montana.

Jean Billings Hartman
2/17/67 *Great Falls, Mont.*

The CIA

Until the recent publicity, I had no idea the CIA was doing such an efficient job around the world. It is reassuring.

Fay Stross
3/10/67 *Seattle*

Soul of the Navigator

Before I met Sir Francis Chichester [March 31] in Sydney, Australia about Christmastime, 1966, I thought his ambition beset with madness, his folly shrouded with hope. But when I had a visit with him, brief as it was, I knew he would make it.

In a jiffy, I felt the soul of this wonderful man, for he displayed a quiet strength, utter conviction, a competence unassailable. He told me, "I am a navigator." Hearing his voice recently from his radio as he rounded the Horn, I wept. It is wonderful.

Julius Sumner Miller
Professor of Physics
El Camino College
4/14/67 *Via Torrance, Calif.*

War of Words

I read with consternation your piece "Sound and Fury" on the explosive situation in the Middle East [May 26].

The statement that the state of Israel has never seriously tried to make peace with the Arabs is absurd in light of the repeated appeals by Prime Minister Levi Ashkol and by his predecessor, David Ben-Gurion, for a peace meeting between Israel and the Arab states, a meeting repeatedly rejected by Nasser and other Arab leaders.

You describe Israeli tanks as having "whipped" into Jordan, one of Israel's "least aggressive neighbors." I was not aware that there were degrees of aggression, some worthy of condemnation, others to be countenanced due to their mildness. Even if this were true, Jordan, jumping-off place for the terrorist Palestine Liberation Front, is far from being a mild aggressor.

Israel is an island of Western culture, freedom and law in a morass of premedieval hate. The land "carved from the land of the Arabs" was under Arab rule a desert; it is now a rose garden in a wasteland of thorns. Israel is the only democracy in the Middle East,

Militant black spokesman LeRoi Jones

and the only nation in that area openly siding with the U.S. in the international power struggle.

Henry M. Hocherman
6/9/67 *Baltimore*

Hail to Israel

While in the Middle East last winter, I fell in love with the Jordanians most of all. But today my hat's off to Israel. What a tableau: There it stood, tiny and alone, cursed and menaced on every border by 14 scowling enemies. Yet today—"how are the mighty fallen!" But beginning with Abraham himself, Jewish history is replete with amazing exploits like this. Guts and stamina—the Israelis have them. Hail!

David M. Campbell
6/23/67 *San Diego*

The Hippies

Write what you will about the hippies. They are a repugnant, repulsive, nauseating, filthy, immoral, and utterly useless glob of humanity serving absolutely no purpose.

William C. Heller
San Francisco

You're kidding yourselves, just like all straight people who say: "This is the creed of every hippie; they all think the same, talk the same, look the same, are the same." All hippies have a different purpose. Of course, we all love and want to be loved. We see beauty

in things other people take for granted. We love flowers because they symbolize freedom. We want to live as flowers do, sway with the wind, belong to the world in a lovely sort of way. Stop writing articles on us, please. We are not to be studied. We are human beings, even though we have different ideas than you do.

I was a straight person until a year ago. I was so miserable that I decided there must be a better life. I found it, and now I am living with people of my own kind. We are happy and we enjoy ourselves. You should try it some time. I do not take drugs, and I don't smoke pot or marijuana because I don't enjoy it. Some people have pleasant trips and others have baddies. I had a baddie. I do take part in love-ins and demonstrations, though. I am happy, and I wish the world could be the same.

Mary
(I have no last name)
7/21/67 *Chicago*

Source of Embarrassment

TIME owes it to its readers to name the anonymous Governor whom I allegedly told that "Dick Nixon is a loser" [July 7]. It will be especially interesting, since I have never said it or thought it. I am sorry that at a time when Republican leaders are working hard for party unity, TIME would stoop to quoting nameless sources in an effort to destroy that unity.

Ronald Reagan
Governor
7/21/67 *Sacramento, Calif.*
TIME's source is not at all "nameless," but we are bound to honor his request that he not be identified—a request with which Governor Reagan, as a political figure, can surely sympathize.

Miniskirt Swindle

Hooray for the miniskirt! But only if it is worn by gals with gams like Cyd Charisse and the 1940-model Grable. The current crop of knobby-kneed kuties just ain't got what it takes to look attractive in that sort of stern-type wrap-around.

James Lowry
8/12/67 *Los Angeles*

The Free & the Fettered

Your Essay on Singles [Sept. 15] was an accurate portrayal. I should know. I run a singles club. Many months ago, when I started this club, I felt that the single life was exciting and that my members were really getting a full measure of life out of it. I am a little older now—and a lot wiser. The single looks for lasting friendships or relationships—but these do not seem to materialize. There is no one who really cares, who is really concerned about him. This kind of realization is almost unendurable for some; the singles in my club who seem to survive the emptiness and void are the ones who have close family ties. The rest are constantly casting about. They are very bored, very depressed. No, the single life is not all that exciting or fun or fulfilling. If it were, the singles would not be joining my club—and hundreds of clubs like mine —in an almost desperate attempt to get out of the single life.

Nona M. Aguilar
9/29/67 *Los Angeles*

Liberalized Abortion

The very idea that abortion should present a dilemma [Oct. 13] infuriates me. The morality of satisfied, waist-coated male legislators complacently discussing the academics of ending a prenatal life while terrified women are desperately inserting pointed objects into their wombs is, to my mind, infinitely more questionable than the subject of abortion itself. What is the theory behind keeping abortions from those who need them most, wives who already have too many children and unwed pregnant girls? I assume it is a Puritan hangover of a need to punish them for enjoying sex, in which case denying them the operation is as logical as castrating their husbands and lovers. The objection that an abortion prevents a human from entering the world is purely intellectual, since a major problem today is precisely the fact that there are already too many people to be adequately fed, cared for, and loved. As for the Catholics, abortion legislation is none of their business; nobody wants to force abortions upon them, only to make the operation available to women who want it.

Jacquelyn S. Lanman
10/20/67 *Poughkeepsie, N.Y.*

Hair Today

In your Essay on longer hair [Oct. 27], you fail to emphasize that long hair on a man is not feminine. The current difficulty of differentiating a male from a female is not due to long hair—or to clothing—but to the feminizing effect of shaving. Men were intended to have beards and women to have smooth cheeks. Men have chosen to violate our Creator's dictum—and we pay for it in blood every morning.

Donald A. Windsor
11/10/67 *Norwich, N.Y.*

Agonized Figure

TIME'S "Election Extra" in 1964 featured a smiling, victorious Lyndon Baines Johnson in his hour of triumph after amassing the greatest popular vote in U.S. history; that, in awesome contrast to the agonized figure we recently viewed on TV. If ever we need to illustrate an example of America's ingratitude to an elected President (*i.e.*, his achievements on behalf of civil rights, aid to education, the elderly and handicapped, Medicare, urban renewal, social security, conservation, etc.), this

should certainly be unparalleled in its savagery.

Caroline Settles
Lexington, Ky.

It is with almost unbearable pain that we have witnessed the end of the chase, a lion brought down by a yelping mongrel pack.

Robert Paul Alberts
4/12/68 *Dallas*

Towards New Highs

It has taken cigarette smoking a little over 30 years to become the generally accepted and prosperous habit that it is today. It has taken science about 20 years to correlate, effectively, lung cancer with cigarette smoking. Alcoholic beverages, however, have had a rougher time, with Prohibition and Carry Nation standing in the road of progress. The offspring of its success have been thousands of suffering alcoholics and the A.A. If marijuana is legalized, it will be interesting to see what vicious effects it will have on our already precarious society by the year 2000. Perhaps everyone will be so high that they won't care to come down and find out.

Anne N. McGinn '68
Vernon Court Junior College
5/3/68 *Newport, R.I.*

It's in the P.S.

Picturing Mr. Dubcek with Jan Hus on your cover [April 5] is as inspiring as the reformation taking place in Czechoslovakia today. Mr. Dubček, unlike Jan Hus, has succeeded, without violence, in freeing the bonds of the Czechoslovak people. For the first time in 20 years, basic freedoms can now be enjoyed by all Czechoslovaks, in an atmosphere of free will and self-expression, without fear of persecution. Bravo! to Mr. Dubček, his ministers, and aides for succeeding in placing the foundation stones for the New Republic. And hats off to TIME for a concise account of events.

P.S. Please feel free to print this letter, as it would present no threat to the security of myself or my family.

Joseph A. Basso
5/3/68 *Prague, Czechoslovakia*

Sexties or Sicksties?

It will be interesting to note whether future historians refer to this decade as the Sexties or the Sicksties.

C. M. Williams
5/10/68 *Jacksonville*

No Tears Left

Only because I wept so for John Kennedy, I have not enough tears to weep for Bobby Kennedy, for Martin Luther King, for the young men in Viet Nam, for the poor, for President Johnson and those others who today

bear such heavy burdens and who, while still living, suffer character assassination. Or to weep for those of us who mistake anarchy for dissent and free speech or violence for justice.

Michael A. Shell
Columbia, S.C.

Bonnie and Clyde are glorified in an "artistically creative" movie, civil disobedience is condoned by churchmen, children are allowed to do whatever they please so as not to injure their development as total persons, and American youths are justified when they seek freedom without responsibility as a way of life; yet the nation expresses shock at one man taking another's life. Come now, if a disease is allowed to spread, why such surprise when it kills?

James L. Telfer
Public Relations Director
Vanderbilt University
6/21/68 *Nashville, Tenn.*

On Assassination

In your Essay "Politics and Assassination" [June 14], you make the statement: "No French President has been murdered since 1932." De Gaulle has survived some six or eight murder attempts. The French are not law abiding, merely lousy shots.

Harvey L. Sobel
6/28/68 *Mexico City*

Gun Laws

The right of an honest American to own a firearm for self-defense, oldest of all human rights, is more important than the life of any leader who ever lived.

C. H. Hauser
6/28/68 *Oklahoma City*

Just Wait

If we think we're a violent nation now, just wait until our children grow up. My childhood was neuter dolls, chutes and ladders, and Little Lulu. Today's childhood is erotic dolls, authentic replicas of war guns (complete with sounds) and a Saturday morning TV listing with enough sadism and murder to give even the most hardened criminal ideas.

Mrs. Norman L. Jacobson
6/28/68 *San Antonio*

Death of ERA

The death of ERA was caused by its radical advocates who sought not so much to equate as to castrate.

Thomas M. Edwards
8/2/68 *San Francisco*

The Papal Encyclical

Pope Paul's latest encyclical vetoing birth control [Aug. 2] is offered as a reaffirmation of the sacredness of human life as based on truths of divine and natural law. Though very reasonable in tone, there are moments in the document when a faint note of hysteria can be detected. The pill, writes the Pope, might lead to infidelity, loss of respect for women, and could even precipitate political anarchy. However real this social danger may be in the modern world, it is a mistake to make discussion of it depend on teachings of divine and natural law about the *sacredness* of life. How the holiness of human life can in anyway be abrogated by a mere technology (the pill) is very unclear in the encyclical. Is fear for the stability of a social structure, the family, in a way the same as fear for one's salvation? The latter is a true religious question, while the former is not.

Judson J. Emerick
Philadelphia

The reconfirmation of the age-old Catholic stand that no one has the authority to deny the continuance of life is refreshing in the days made easy for everything else in America. And in the areas of our world where population increase is an alarming concern to science it is reassuring to know that God alone gives the test of faith. Pope Paul, mindful of the unfortunate the world over, stands with every Pope be-

fore him to remind the world that to live, no matter what the circumstances, brings honor and glory to the Creator.

Perhaps if all Catholics were really Catholic, there would be less of a problem with population scare, for in conscience they would be directed to wait until they were capable of caring for offspring before they enter into holy matrimony: a simple solution for a lot of problems in any church.

A decision other than that pro-

nounced by Paul would have severely shaken my faith.

James J. Kunz
Cape Coral, Fla.
8/9/68

The Pope & the Pill

Despite Pope Paul [Aug. 9], many of us will continue to do as we have done in the past: take the Pill, go to Mass and receive the sacraments, because we live by our consciences, which tell us that the law of charity, affecting our relations with our husbands, children and society as a whole, is more binding than an encyclical filled with unrealistic opinions.

Mrs. R. Lambert
Arlington Heights, Ill.

As a Catholic mother, wife, lover, therapist, chauffeur, social worker, comforter, healer, organizer, charity worker, cook, gardener, laundress, carpenter, secretary, messenger, nurse, artist, interior decorator, landscaper and homemaker, rhythm has wrought me babies, frustration, anger, frigidity, sorrow, incompatibility, bitchery, unhappiness, disillusionment, dissatisfaction, discontent, bitterness, instability and more babies.

To the Pill I can accredit harmony,

War: wounded Americans in Viet Nam, above

Peace: Flower Power on the home front, below

123

June 1968: Senator Robert Kennedy is assassinated in Los Angeles

communication, fulfillment, satisfaction, happiness, stability, understanding, acceptance, relaxation, achievement, compatibility, courage, love, peace and Christ.

Rosemary E. Dalton
Livonia, Mich.

On Aug. 22 the Pope will come to Colombia. Of course we will show him the best of this city, but we *should* take him to the horrid places where people try to survive, like animals, in an incredible misery, full of sickness, without any education and without any hope for a better tomorrow. We should introduce him to family fathers who earn $1 daily with which to provide the needs of a family of twelve. The government, not the church, makes an effort to solve this situation; but every day it is bigger, and it grows in a proportion that prevents solution.

The Pope says there's a way for birth control. Yes, let's tell the Pope to talk about fertile periods with an illiterate woman and talk about abstinence, with a drunken and brutal man who keeps his woman like a slave.

Catholics are no longer sheep who can be taken by their shepherd through any gate, without question, terrified by the menace of being burned as heretics. There are people who think like the Pope, and nobody stops them from having as many children as they want, or making of their love something like a medicine, given by doses in a certain amount and at a certain time.

Ana De Vargas
Bogota

Paul VI's reasoning goes deeper than the surface problems of sexuality and birth control. He bespeaks man as a spiritual as well as a material being. He upholds continence as a possible virtue whereas his every critic (including, sadly, many Catholic priests) at least implicitly regards continence as an impossible virtue to modern man.

To deny the possibility of continence (in any human field) is to profess the democratically fatal doctrine that man is a determined being, not a free one—a doctrine at the base of too many political, social and economic practices already eating away at the foundations of human liberty.

Douglas J. Murphey
8/16/68 *Roslyn Estates, N.Y.*

So Depressed

Nixon stood by his party in its hour of need, and now the party stands by Nixon. It's so simple. I don't understand why I'm so depressed.

Darene H. Lennon
8/23/68 *Evanston, Ill.*

Tragedy in Biafra

Your article on the plight of Biafra [Aug. 23] was timely. There have been far too many Nigerian propaganda articles, and far too few truthful ones on the subject. I find a ghastly parallel between the murder of 6,000,000 Jews by Germany, and the attempt by Nigeria to destroy Biafra, which will ultimately result in the death of 8,000,000 Ibos if nothing is done. In World War II, a stunned world finally

intervened. It remains to be seen whether the world will eventually wake up and stop what may turn out to be one of the worst examples of genocide and savagery in history.

Llewelyn Gryffyth
8/30/68 *Washington, D.C.*

Brutality and Hysteria

The invasion of Czechoslovakia [Aug. 30] further demonstrates the brutality and treachery of which the Soviet leaders are capable. We've been painfully aware of these traits for some time. What I had not realized was the state of mind of these men. They have sacrificed improved Soviet-U.S. relations, dealt the antiwar faction in the U.S. a severe blow, lessened the chances for a peaceful end to the Viet Nam war, and even blackened themselves in the eyes of other Communists, all to smash a growth of freedom that was in no way a threat to Russia's security.

The invasion was obviously conceived in panic and carried out in hysteria. The hope for peaceful coexistence rested in the good sense and rationality of the Soviet leaders, but men controlled by fear have neither.

Nikki Patrick
9/6/68 *Pittsburg, Kans.*

Call for Trudeau

Re Prime Minister Trudeau [Sept. 20]: Americans should all join together, face north, and shout "come on down!"

Wayne M. Masterman
University of Pittsburgh
10/4/68 *Pittsburgh*

dust." In the '30s they sat on flagpoles, danced marathons, leaned on WPA shovels and attended Pink meetings. In the '40s they ate live goldfish and carried books to avoid carrying rifles. In the '50s they staged panty raids, crowded 18 into five-passenger cars, burned rubber and played chicken. In the '60s they let their hair grow, smoked pot, read poetry in the rain, went nude. In the '70s, to top their forebears and get attention, they could only throw bombs.

Grady Johnson
11/23/70   *Santa Eulalia, Ibiza, Spain*

Family Crisis

We may survive the ecological crisis. We may survive the economic crisis. And we may survive the ecclesiastical crisis. But we may not survive the present family crisis. Unless the American family is soon restored to its place of respect and honor, our entire fabric of life in this country will come apart. For the stability of America is dependent on the stability of its family life.

Danny Schwab
1/18/71   *Santa Barbara, Calif.*

Role Reversal

I cannot swallow the socialistic pap that welfare recipients have a "right" to raid my wallet. Their presumed privilege cannot become my enforced

---

BRICKBATS

Your attempts to put down the 1950s generation [June 29] as a bunch of selfish, unfeeling nonsensitives stuck in my craw.

I don't know what part of that generation you were in, but my group was in college, desperately trying to get good grades, and all the time wondering whether we would go to Korea (remember Korea?) or the Berlin Wall. We kept our mouths shut and worked, not because we were mindless robots but because we were not stupidly arrogant enough to think that we knew better than persons with 20 years more experience in the world.

But the ultimate insult is to state that we are envious of the present generation. Of a generation so incredibly naive that it equates fornication with love, liberty with license, freedom with selfishness; a generation so irrationally hypocritical that it gets stoned on pot while decrying air pollution, screams "Get out of Viet Nam" while advocating arms for Israel, and expresses disgust with the profit-making Establishment while greedily wasting its parents' money on luxury items made by this Establishment; a generation so arrogantly self-centered that it has no belief in anything but what it sees, no respect for anything but what it wants, no responsibility toward anything but what it feels is "relevant" today, this minute, now.

Envious? Come on!

Richard F. Oles
7/27/70   *Baltimore*

---

obligation just because they like it better that way. In effect, it is a form of indentured slavery in which the traditional roles are reversed in the cynical name of "dignity."

Robert Tropea
3/1/71   *Philadelphia*

Brilliant Necklace

Naturally, in our homes we have TV, which we often watch; and when

the American astronauts were making their first unprecedented moon trip, we were looking on the screens most eagerly. And now we have learned from the press about Apollo 14 [Feb. 22] and its tremendous success. We are proud of our Soviet motherland's own great achievements in space research, but equally we are delighted by this brilliant necklace of heroic moon trips of the American astronauts. It is my desire that others should join with our

---

"Have a care with that helmet, mate!" Streaking comes to England

Scenes of violence have become everyday sights in Northern Ireland

two great countries in peaceful co-operation in space research to the good of man!

Igor Mikhailusenko
3/8/71 *Moscow*

Chinese Thaw

Much gratitude is owed to the members of the U.S. Ping Pong team. Because of their friendly reception in Red China, we will hopefully be able to ease the tensions of more than two decades. Thanks is also due President Nixon, who acted swiftly to thaw relations with Red China. Premier Chou En-Lai has stated that he would like to visit the U.S. Let's hope that if he does come, he will receive the same friendly greeting that the Ping Pong team recieved.

J. Edward Lovell III
5/10/71 *Odessa, Fla.*

Graduates and Jobs

Your graduate [May 24] has the bewildered look typical of the class of '71. He thinks he can't find a job be-because the big bad Establishment won't let him. The truth is he has nothing to offer. He has occupied space—educated he is not!

He has busied himself with "relevant" courses like group interaction, and meaningful activities such as sit-ins. He cannot write a correct English sentence, has no idea how capitalism really works, but having bought the myth fostered by the media that his is the "best-educated generation," he expects a good job from the system he has learned to denigrate.

E. V. Manthey
6/14/71 *Rocky River, Ohio*

No Benefits

Your article on the Common Market [June 28] listed various grounds on which people here oppose entry, but ignores the most important. This is that a large selection of "informed thinking people" believe that it will not bring economic benefits. One of the main reasons for this is the annual cost of £500 million (after the transition period) to the balance of payments. Recent experience here has shown the immense difficulty of achieving such a "surplus," and economists are totally justified in opposing the terms arranged at Brussels.

Jim Bourlet
7/26/71 *London*

Aquarius and China

President Nixon is to be sincerely congratulated on a brilliant stroke of diplomacy in arranging a trip to Communist China [July 26]. After so many years of pretending that 800 million Chinese do not exist, play no role in world politics and are our bitter enemies, it is very heartening finally to see a courageous and imaginative President take a step toward a more realistic China policy. Perhaps the Age of Aquarius is still alive.

Gary Jankowski
8/9/71 *Toledo*

England's Viet Nam

While in Northern Ireland this summer, I saw the Orange parade on July 12. The only comparison I can conjure up to describe such an event would be to ask you to imagine the following: a Ku Klux Klan parade through Harlem under the protection of the Alabama National Guard—which certainly would be explosive and provocative.

No matter which way they try to throw the blame, the war in Northern Ireland is England's Viet Nam, a war it has been waging for 500 years.

Sean P. O'Neill
9/13/71 *Rheydt, West Germany*

No Irish Mist

As I write this letter in Belfast, bombs are exploding in different parts of the city, and ordinary people are suffering. I have not had an easy day, visiting homes that are heartbroken with grief, and this afternoon seeing one of my church 17-year-olds, a leg amputee, the victim of I.R.A. gunshot wounds. It is against this background that I listened with shock at the statement of Senator Kennedy [Nov. 1].

I am not a follower of the Rev. Ian Paisley; I am one of the hundreds of clergy in this province striving for objectivity in a situation that is as explosive as it is strewn with adjectives to describe it.

It is easy for the Senator to pontificate and even rationalize for doing so, but this is not the dream of a dewy Irish mist on an American St. Patrick's Day that he is talking about.

There are many things in Northern Ireland politics and policies that must and will change, but the removal of the border tomorrow would unleash a force that would engage the United Nations for the next 20 years. It might surprise the Senator to know that in Northern Ireland the majority, the big two-third majority are Irish, but proud to be British.

I would like to say that people of all churches here thank God for the presence of 15,000 of our soldiers, for we know only two well what the alternatives would be for both Catholic and Protestant.

(The Rev.) John Stewart
Woodvale Methodist Church
11/15/71 *Belfast*

U.N. Decline

The decline of the League of Nations began with the League's refusal to extend its support to Ethiopia against Italy. History will record that the decline of the United Nations began on Oct. 25, 1971, when the U.N. expelled Nationalist China.

Gert P. Arnstein
11/22/71 *Los Angeles*

J.C. Superstar

Something more than God died in Broadway's Daliesque pastiche, *Jesus Christ Superstar* [Oct. 25]. With the last days of Christ acted with flashy vulgarity onstage, and the last days of Sodom and Gomorrah lived with frightening reality at the opening-night party, *JCS* writes the R.I.P on the tombstone of Western civilization. Like *Superstar's* hero, civilization has given up the ghost without any assurance of a resurrection on the third day.

Douglas Schoenherr
New Haven, Conn.

The theater having sunk into the depths of filth and obscenity both in sound and sight, is the church to do likewise? Is there no Christianity left, no morals, no standards, no faith? Now are we back to the heathens and barbarians again? We certainly have crucified Our Lord a second time.

Dame Gladys Cooper, D.B.E.
Henley-on-Thames, England

A black Judas! I think I am beginning to learn now that it's really a hell to be black.

Yusuf Yakub
11/15/71 *Mombasa, Kenya*

The King is Naked

Now that he is 90, let's stop over-rating Picasso. I for one have found most of the Picasso exhibitions that I have visited dreary and uninteresting. I have stood for half an hour in front of *Guernica* and it was still only cheap bombast.

My advice to all the millionaires who have invested so heavily in his pictures is to sell, and sell quickly, before more people join me in saying "The king is naked."

Nathan Schur
11/22/71 *Zahala, Israel*

Russian Catastrophe

For the Russians to lose the race to the moon was disappointing, but to lose the World Chess Championship will be a catastrophe, especially if the winner is American Bobby Fischer [Nov 8]. It is akin to the Russians sending us football, basketball and baseball teams and then beating the Colts, the Celtics and the Orioles, all on the same day!

J. C. De La Torre, M.D.
11/29/71 *Chicago*

Kent State Mothers Speak

May we the mothers of the four killed at Kent State, express our horror at your conclusion that the dropping of 20 indictments by the State of Ohio heralds the passing of this tragedy "into history."

We believe that this is a nation of laws, wherein violators, whoever they may be, are accountable to the people through our courts and juries of their peers. The dropping of indictments against students and others for offenses allegedly committed during the disturbances at Kent State does not in any way alter the fact that our children were killed by what Attorney General Mitchell called an "unnecessary, unwarranted, and inexcusable" use of force by the state.

It has become all too painfully clear to us that the lives of our sons and daughters are to be sacrificed on the altar of political expediency in a country posturing to the world as the citadel of equal justice for all. We can think of nothing more brutal than this cruel rejection of our children's Constitutional rights to due process of law from any kind of judicial accounting.

Doris Krause
Sarah Scheuer
Florence Schroeder
1/10/72 *Elaine Miller*

Man of the Year

I commend you for naming Richard Milhous Nixon as Man of the Year [Jan. 3]. At the time of his inauguration, he was faced with troubles at home and many more abroad. Yet he has taken his stand and made for himself a well-deserved place in history. This country isn't perfect and neither is Mr. Nixon, but his undying concern and his faithful help have led me to believe that someone finally turned on the lights. Things do look brighter. This man has filled American minds with hope, replacing the despair that lived there for so long.

Glenda M. Goodrich
1/17/72 *Washington, D.C.*

Machine-Mad

Now that a machine has said it, perhaps this machine-mad society will believe what we human ecology nuts have been saying for years. The human race is breeding itself into extinction, and, in an all-too-human way, bringing about the destruction of all other forms of life on this planet as well. What a shame, too—we had a great potential!

(Ms.) Ann S. Patrick
Portland, Me.

How ironic that the data for your article "The Worst is Yet to Be?" in which you deplore growth and progress, was obtained from a computer, practically a synonym for growth and progress.

William R. Taylor
2/14/72 *Old Lyme, Conn.*

Times Have Changed

Being a woman is more fun than it was ten years ago. Times have changed and I with them. Only now do I realize the source of my past discontent and I relish my new-found freedom. At times speaking my mind may make others uncomfortable, but oh what it does for me.

Pamela Lucarelli
Kirkland, Wash.

I'm a Peace Corps volunteer nurse, 24 years old and married. I do health teaching and counseling in a poor *bairro* clinic. And boy, have my attitudes changed!

I don't think I can ever be content only with home and hearth to look after. I too have something to contribute besides domestic and maternal skills. After our Peace Corps service is over, I plan to continue my education in public health and to develop in my profession. My husband and I will have children when we're *both* ready and willing to give that much more of ourselves.

Don't get me wrong. I do glory in my womanliness, as long as it does not

Artifacts of the fast food era

Two faces of terrorism:
Above, funeral after the murders of the 1972
Munich Olympics; right, masked gunman

entail categorization as a childish, sub-
missive, madonna-ish, delicate, mindless, very limited type of person.

Dione S. Mahoney, R.N.
3/20/72   *Itu, Brazil*

Emerging

As a member of the "do nothing"
generation (college class of '59) I'd
always accepted the role of wife and
mother. Pantie raids came before my
time and rioting, hippies and pot came
after. Thirty-three years of condition-
ing told me that achievement really
wasn't expected of me because I was
female. My parents were noticeably relieved when I married.

Becoming involved in the abortion
reform issue during the past year has
opened up a whole new world to me.
Women are at last emerging from their
cocoon and saying "why?" Maybe we
do have a workable brain after all.
I'm having a wonderful time using
mine at last.

(Mrs.) Virginia Hanson
3/20/72   *Jackson, Mich.*

Disfigured Treasure

The horrors of war and assassination
are sadly becoming old news these
days. Even as things appear grim
enough, a maniac has wilfully des-
figured one of humanity's most treasured works of art, namely the beloved
Pietà [June 5] in Rome. For the love
of God and the sake of art, when does
this lunacy cease?

Eleanor M. Roesing
6/19/72   *Armonk, N.Y.*

Against All

How could the Egyptian government
hail a massacre? Could it really express
pleasure at the bloodshed in the airport
at Tel Aviv [June 12]?

That assault was not against Israel,
or against the Jews. The murderers did
not fight, but killed defenseless, powerless pilgrims and innocent tourists.
That crime was against all the people
of this world; the victims could be
any one of us, they could be you and
me, your sister, my father.

In my opinion every government
that did not condemn that ugly act extended indirect encouragement to the
killers and their leaders.

George M. Hye
6/26/72   *Ramatgan, Israel*

Good News, Bad News

"Good News, Bad News" jokes
[June 5] did not originate, as you suggest, a few years ago "probably as
spoofs on in-flight announcements by
airline pilots." They date back far
enough to have been contemporary
with my grandfather. The best prac-
titioners were Smith & Dale, their routines built around a dream one of them
had, with the other analyzing it: "I
dreamed my wife ran away." "That's
bad." "No, that's good. But she left
the children with me." "That's good."
"No, that's bad; they're not my kids,"
etc.

Alan Shean
7/3/72   *Hollywood*

The Consequences

The dates 2035 and 2300, when fuel
supplies are expected to run out, are
unreal to the people now in a position
to do something about conserving the
world's energy sources for future generations. I believe they simply cannot
envision a world in which they personally will not be alive. But now, at 24, I
may well be around to see the oil and
gas run out—and my as-yet-unborn
children will certainly be alive in 2035.
They and the rest of the world will
have to cope with the consequences of
our "good life" today.

Sheila L. Claydon
7/3/72   *Honolulu*

Idiot-Proof Photography

I do not question that Edwin Land
[June 26] is a genius and that his new
SX-70 will yield tremendous profits for
both Polaroid and its stockholders. Unfortunately, however, this entire concept of rendering picture taking "idiot
proof" desecrates the art of photography. Idiot-proof photography elimin-
ates virtually all the challenge and the
opportunity for creativity.

John E. Turner
7/17/72   *New York City*

Agnew Fear

The realization that Spiro Agnew
will once again be running for the
office that is a heartbeat away from the
presidency makes my heart beat with
fear.

Jonathan Hunt
8/21/72   *Riverside, Conn.*

After the Nonokini?

I presume that in the wake of the
bikini and the monokini, as described
in your article "The Naked and the
Med" [Aug. 28], we shall soon be
regaled on our public beaches by the
"nonokini."

And after that, what?

Jack Conrad
9/25/72   *London*

Events in Munich

The introduction of barbarism into
the Olympic Games by the so-called
"Black September" organization is the
most unwelcome achievement of modern civilization. It ranks with that most
cowardly attack at Lod airport and
the use of Japanese mercenaries. The
world must agree with me that this
notorious organization has lost all
claims to the title commandos.

I now appeal to the civilized world
to adopt the use of the word "cowar-
dos" to refer to the Arab guerrilla organizations and any other bodies that
may in the future elect to perpetrate
such cowardly, barbaric and uncivilized
acts.

Jerry Oscar
Lagos, Nigeria

Once again, the legitimate interests of Arab people have been betrayed—by Arabs.

John Brotherhood
Farmington, Conn.

Clearly, the Olympics should have been forgone this year in favor of the Barbaric Games. Suitable sites would have ranged from Death Valley to a moon crater. Contesting teams would have made up in color what they lacked in numbers: the Arabian Assassins, the Belfast Bombers, the Pakistan Predators, and an unattached club representing almost every nation—the Skyjackers.

Consider the appeal of the events. The grenade thrown. The chop, rip and thump. The high dive (out of a 727). The .32-cal. ambush. The hostage relay. The knife in the backstroke. The decapithlon. The duel meet. The cemetery vault.

Traditional ritual could have been observed—if modified—had the official torch bearer put the torch to the entire Barbaric Village before it was vacated.

The Barbaric Games '72 might have provided an orgy of violence sufficient to satiate the bloodthirsty tastes of mankind for a century or two.

W. F. Taylor
10/2/72 *Pittsburgh*

American Symbol

It was amusing to read of the corruption and deterioration in the quality of the great American hot dog [Oct. 2], yet it occurs to me to point out that in the eyes of many around the world, the hot dog in its present state sadly qualifies still as "an American symbol."

Richard Trevor
10/20/72 *Melbourne, Australia*

Daylight Saving

I take issue with your article "Seize the Day" [Nov. 13] advocating year-round Daylight Saving Time. Far more people than TIME realizes start work at 8 a.m. or earlier. D.S.T. would have these people awakening and commuting in the dark six months of the year. Those interested in year-round D.S.T. should start their day one hour earlier.

G. Robert Cooley
Chicago

Bravo on your article "Seize the Day." As one who lives on the extreme Eastern Seaboard (Cape Cod), I find myself driving home from work in the dark at 4.30 p.m. And the winter solstice is still weeks away.

John J. Dingess
12/4/72 *Pocasset, Mass.*

Happiness Is . . .

Why do I love Jonathan Livingston Seagull? I am a teen-ager growing up in a world of hate and intolerance. Jonathan Seagull simply makes me happy.

Sherron Moore
12/4/72 *Wexfood, Pa.*

Gloom in Sweden

After watching the dismal election returns, I will wait at least four years before I pack my bags and move home.

Augusta Jane Palm
12/4/72 *Bromma, Sweden*

Too Fast Moving

It is not necessarily the foods we eat and our lack of exercise that are causing us to have so many health problems. We are living in times that are too fast moving, with too many pressures. No amount of vitamins or organic foods will alleviate the pressures of living in our nonstop society.

Christina A. Norden
1/8/73 *Woodbury, N.Y.*

Goodbye to LIFE

In a strange town I heard the sad news and on a borrowed typewriter I send my condolences.

LIFE played a significant role in my maturing. I read those exciting early issues with real delight. In my classes I taught from it. And I have had few pleasures in my professional career to match the one that occurred when LIFE devoted an entire issue to one of my short novels.

Most important to me were the color pages on American art. I treasured them and in years that were to come made my own collection of such art, guided in the early days by the magazine's good judgment.

I know that things must change. I only hope that what takes LIFE's place will be half as good as it was.

James A. Michener
1/8/73 *Denver*

Senseless Destruction

I weep for the hundreds of thousands of innocent lives to be destroyed as a result of the Supreme Court decision on abortion [Jan. 29], for the tremendous waste of human resources, and I weep for my children who will live in a society where property is protected by law but human life is denied such protection.

The Viet Nam atrocities end but not the senseless destruction of human life.

(Mrs.) Anna Faust
3/19/73 *Norristown, Pa.*

Decision in Darkness

I most sincerely appreciate TIME's Essay [July 16], "Deciding When Death Is Better Than Life."

American opinion is divided on the question of legalized abortion

Homerun king Hank Aaron

John McEnroe rises to stardom at Wimbledon

The great soccer star Pelé

As a doctor, I have faced this decision and, in the darkness of night, with hope for the patient lost, have been at the hospital with sorrow in my heart. Speaking meager words of comfort to an anxious family, I have put my arm around a mother, wife or husband as they sobbed on my shoulder and then "pulled the plug."

Afterwards I have come home and in bed turned my back to my wife and her comforting arms and tried to find sleep. It is not easy.

It also is not easy to awaken in the morning to find the newspapers rasping away at heartless, moneygrubbing doctors.

Jonathan M. Williams, M.D.
8/6/73 *Silver Spring, Md.*

Hope with Kissinger

Your cover story on Henry Kissinger [Sept. 3] sounds very promising for future foreign relations.

I have great hope that at last there will be a Secretary of State who will not only give to Latin America the attention these countries deserve, but will also understand their people and cultivate their friendship, so much neglected in the past.

Carl Heumann
10/1/73 *Lima*

Worthy Candidate

I support and applaud the nomination of Academician Andrei Sakharov for the Nobel Prize for Peace, as proposed by my friend Alexander Solzhenitsyn [Sept 24].

Solzhenitsyn and Sakharov are the conscience of that part of mankind that is in slavery. They ceaselessly call upon the Soviet government to end its persecutions, and to democratize the regime. Each in his own way addresses himself to the world, and their words resound with concern for the future of humanity. Thus, they are attempting to halt the infernal cycle of mutual hatred and military adventures. Sakharov, who is leading this heroic battle, is supremely worthy of the Nobel Prize.

Dimitri Panin
10/8/73 *Sèvres, France*

The author of this letter is "Dimitri Sologdin," one of the heroes of The First Circle *by Solzhenitsyn, who served in the same Soviet camps and prisons with him from 1947 to 1952.* —ED.

Tolkien Memory

Though your words were of course well intended, the lamented J.R.R. Tolkien would not have been pleased with being called a "creative mythologer." Barely a month before his death, he told me with emphasis how much he disliked the overused word creative, saying, "There is only one Creator." When I remarked that for many years I had told students in my fiction-writing course that there was only one forbidden word in my classroom, to wit "creative," he left his station by the fireplace, darted to my chair, and wrung my hand in approval. It is a memory to be cherished.

Richard L. Greene
10/8/73 *New Haven, Conn.*

Over the Wall

I was one of those fortunate enough to gain my freedom from the "socialist paradise" beyond the wall. In 1969 I left behind a life full of fear, oppression and shades of gray, convinced that freedom was worth any price. Your article on East Germany [Oct. 1] served to strengthen my deep gratitude and appreciation for freedom, man's most cherished possession. Thank God I am free at last.

Helfried Flacke
10/29/73 *Wiesbaden, West Germany*

Shrine of Fantasy

In our mundane, functional age, Utzon has provided Australia and the world with a symbol of grandeur and a shrine of fantasy. The Sydney Opera is both myth and monument.

Wallace Van Zyl
10/29/73 *Muncie, Ind.*

Death of Democracy

All Americans have good reason to be embarrassed by the military coup in Chile; we helped bring it on. Are we not on the wrong side? Have we not assumed the role of oppressor rather than liberator? After defeating Nazism in Europe, do we now sponsor fascism in Latin America?

As an American citizen living in South America, I am sickened by the "death of democracy" and Salvador Allende in Chile.

(The Rev.) Robert L. Armistead
10/29/73 *Quito, Ecuador*

The Lightning Strikes

When we heard of the resignation of Vice President Agnew, we could not have been any more shocked if a streak of lightning had hit us. We were guilty of criticizing TIME and other news media for their factual reporting and must now eat crow.

Now what? I often said, if we cannot trust Mr. Agnew, whom can we trust in Government? It would be frightening if all political officeholders were thoroughly investigated—for we might not have a Government at all.

Edward J. Johnson
11/5/73 *Palm Desert, Calif.*

Henry's Prize

The awarding of the Nobel Peace Prize to Henry Kissinger and Le Duc Tho is like granting Xaviera Hollander (the Happy Hooker) an award for extreme virtue.

Lorne L. Eliosoff
11/19/73 *Toronto, Ont.*

Grandpa Was Right

As a young boy, I had always viewed my grandfather, who constantly scurried about the house turning off unused lights, water faucets, and the like, as a man of the past unwilling to face the bountiful future.

But after reading Stefan Kanfer's Essay "The (Possible) Blessings of Doing Without" [Dec. 3] and my latest electric bill, I now know that I was disgracefully shortsighted. Indeed, who would have ever guessed that Grandfather was, in reality, a harbinger of things to come?

Paul Cavallo
Poway, Calif.

I am miserable when I am cold; I just don't function. But if the President can turn his thermostat back, then I can turn my thermostat back.

If it's good for the President, then it's good for me.

However, if the President or any of his family should go to a warm climate this winter, then I will be forced to turn my thermostat up and go for a Sunday drive. If it's good for the President, it's also good for me.

Mary Lamb
12/24/73 *Ann Arbor, Mich.*

Victim or Criminal

The increase in world crime—hijacking, murder, general corruption, vice of every sort—owes entirely to treating criminals as victims and victims as criminals. If all hijackers were shot as soon as they were caught, hijacking would soon come to an end. If hanging and the electric chair came into fashion again, you would find hardly anyone murdering old people for "kicks", beating children to death because they were feeling frustrated, robbing banks because they were too lazy to work,

etc., and after their crime offering excuses. Nowadays you can commit any crime, and the courts will bring in some chicken-brained doctor to get you off.

Mrs. Y. T. Dempster Adams
1/21/74 *Nairobi, Kenya*

The Extra Day

I have one question concerning the British three-day work week [Dec. 24]. How is Mr. Heath going to get them to work the extra day?

C. Randolph Williams
Bryanston, South Africa

Britain's problems provide a nostalgic reminder to expatriate Britons of why we would all love to go back—but only to visit. Even the royal wedding took on the air of a rather tired public relations stunt to draw attention from the nation's ills.

Unfortunately, there is one area where British exports are booming: British migrants have brought their attitude toward work with them to Australia, and the easy life in a warm climate is just one step closer to the British worker's idea of heaven on earth.

The result is the chaotic state of Australia's industrial relations.

S. F. A. Pask
1/28/74 *Cremorne, Australia*

She led two lives: Tanya, the Symbionese Liberation Army revolutionary; Patti Hearst, the bride

Lost Love

I am sure that I speak for many others when I say that the "romance" with the big car [Dec. 31] was a beautiful thing. What is the old saying—"It's better to have loved and lost than never to have loved at all"? It surely was nice while it lasted.

Sue Friloux
1/28/74 *New Sarpy, La.*

Martinis and Role Reversal

Being laid off after working 20 years and reduced (raised?) to househusband status [Feb. 18] certainly creates new habits. I empty the garbage even if the bag is empty, check the mail several times before the mailman arrives, and raid the refrigerator when I'm not hungry. Just ridiculous, but as the attitude improves, so do the habits. I pushed the study habit. I have already earned a B.S. degree, and I expect to receive an M.S. this summer.

It appears that two crucial factors are required to accept this role reversal: a good attitude and an understanding wife. But an occasional double martini doesn't seem to hurt either.

Marlon D. Dykas
3/11/74 *Milwaukee*

Is There an Offer?

We have experienced a devastating rash of tornadoes [April 15]—more

135

than 300 dead and hundreds of millions of dollars in damage. Is there one country on this planet that rushed to our aid?

Marilyn Engel Link
4/29/74 *Tulsa, Okla.*

Compulsory Seat-Belting

You can lead a man to slaughter, but you can't make him think.

Jim Charlton
Honolulu

The most irritating aspect of compulsory seat-belting is not so much the bother of it all as the violation of basic principles of individual freedom. By "protecting" individuals from the hazards of cigarette smoking, by banning cigarette commercials on TV, by requiring that autos carry seat belts that must be fastened in order to start the car, or (heaven forbid!) fining people for not fastening belts in the privacy of their own vehicles, we violate long-standing tenets of liberty.

Independence and self-reliance are rather old American principles which should not be forgotten as we approach our bi-centennial.

Albert L. Weeks
5/20/74 *New York City*

Only Women?

We resent the unsupported insinuation in your story about the Patricia Hearst kidnapping [April 29] that *women*, as opposed to men or children "can fall under the spell of their captors . . ."

Karen Hanna Witten
Maria Lewis Minick
Thun, Switzerland

Looking at the photograph of Patricia Hearst posing with gun in hand before the S.L.A. emblem, I noticed that she is clearly still wearing her engagement ring. I find it hard to believe that a girl who denounced her family and fiancé to join the Symbionese Liberation Army would continue to wear such an obvious symbol of her former status. Could this be evidence that she has been brainwashed?

Madeleine Huck
5/27/74 *Edmonton, Alta.*

Lifelong Economizing

I am sick, fed up, had it, with all the guides to economizing [April 8] that are appearing in magazines now during the current inflationary period. Lots of us have lived this frugal way all our lives.

(Mrs.) Mary Jean Bey
5/6/74 *Portland, Ore.*

Bombs Before Butter

It is very depressing to read that while 50% of its 600 million people are suffering chronic food deficiencies, India is testing atomic bombs with the

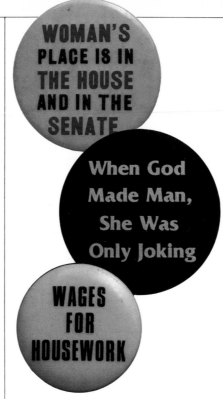

excuse that atomic power will be used to improve the life of future generations.

Bahman Azizian
Milan

Twelve years ago, in the foothills of the Himalayas I saw a man on his hands and knees eating grass. And I have never forgotten.

Now that India has the expertise to produce a nuclear blast, she should demonstrate the ability to feed her hungry millions and drastically curb her population growth. The World Bank estimates that India requires $12 billion aid over the next five years; yet India plans to spend some $316 million on atomic energy development over the same period. What do the homeless, jobless and foodless think of this?

Duncan Kinnaird
6/24/74 *Bangkok*

Jesuit Spirit

Your article "The Presidential Priest" [June 3] missed the spirit that has governed the Society of Jesus for centuries.

This spirit can be illustrated by an old Florentine joke. It goes like this: The light went off suddenly in a chapel where three religious were praying. The Capuchin immediately started a prayer to God to send back the light. The Carmelite engaged himself in a theological explanation of the might of God upon this earthly misery. When the Jesuit rose to walk out, the other two asked him, "Brother, aren't you going to join us to pray to God?" "In a moment," said the Jesuit. "Let me first go to change the fuse."

G. S. Mazzanti
7/8/74 *Utrecht, The Netherlands*

Nixon in Egypt

The Egyptian people have recognized President Nixon for what he is: the greatest peacemaker in the history of the world [June 24].

James Storrs
Deer Park, Texas

In view of the very warm Egyptian reception afforded Nixon, dare we hope he will seek asylum?

Ed Wachsman
7/8/74 *Columbus*

In Favor of the '50s

Count me among the admirers of Stefan Kanfer's Essays. But in "Back to the Unfabulous '50s," he has gone too far! When he says that "it was rather like taking a walk in a fog," he misses the point entirely.

The 1950s in the U.S. were as close as this nation is likely to come to happiness. There was a tranquillity (at least in my small Appalachian home town) that has not been matched, and won't be. There was a trust (unlocked doors, nighttime walks, gentle camaraderie) that has disappeared. And there was a social movement (the 1954 *Brown* v. *Board of Education* decision, public schools desegregation) that was challenge enough for an entire nation.

The Silent Generation was as dopey a myth as any foisted on us. Adlai Stevenson, Paul Douglas, Harry Truman . . . they may not have talked in gusts of 350 words a minute, but they were able to speak intelligently. I ask that you record at least one vote in favor of the '50s.

Reg Murphy
Editor, The Atlanta Constitution
9/9/74 *Atlanta*

Pardon of Nixon

America's great President was a man of compassion. A century later we have a new President who is also a man of compassion. Long after the vultures and biodegradables have departed, the pardon of Richard Nixon by President Ford will go down in history as the mark of a man who is both courageous and decisive.

A. E. Alexander, M.D.
9/23/74 *New York City*

Inflation's Saving Grace

Thank you for making me realize by your story "Hidden Side of Inflation" [Nov. 4] that sky-high prices are not hurting me as much as I thought. Now all I have to do to make ends meet is what every other average American is doing—give up my European vacation, my summer home, my houseboat.

I also realize that because of inflation, I have an extra bonus. Now that I can no longer afford all those materialistic items (like food), I am finally free to appreciate "older, nonmaterialistic American values." Thanks, inflation, for saving my marriage.

John Alvey
11/18/74 *Joliet, Ill.*

Ford: Palms Up

President Ford's words comprise the most uncomforting assessment of the State of the Union that the American people have had to hear. Even during the Civil War, President Lincoln each year offered gratitude for the excellent health of the people and for abundant harvests. Even in 1814, when British troops had recently set fire to the city of Washington, President Madison felt that he could anticipate the expulsion of the invaders. Even in 1931, with economic disaster everywhere, Herbert Hoover promised that the value of traditional American virtues would soon prove itself again.

Ford's willingness to come to the people palms up is admirable. Still, he is in no position to offer soothing syrup. The spreading economic distress now reaches into every home daily, in living color, in living reality, or both. He cannot blink the fact that foreigners now hold significant strings, pulling on the nation's destiny.

In having to lay down a timetable that takes the U.S. well into the 1980s, he is seeking to undrape ready resignation in a notoriously impatient people. And he is the first President to report that America's beacon light to the world has dimmed. Above all, Ford could not help conveying what

his countrymen also sense—that the way out of the maze is technological as well as political. That is a burden on presidential leadership no other Chief Executive has had to bear.

Henry F. Graff
1/27/75 *New York City*
The writer is a Professor of History at Columbia University who has written extensively on the presidency.—ED.

Jobless Solution

With 6 million unemployed we are bound to reduce demand for the supply we can so readily produce. So what do we do? Well, I suggest, first, that we put our workers on a 30-hour week. We are coming to that sooner or later. Why not begin now?

Then make it illegal to employ anyone to work overtime while unemployment exceeds 2 million. If we can black out a football game because all seats have not been sold, surely we can black out overtime when 6 million people are unemployed.

Next, we should restrict households to one job each until unemployment sinks below 2 million once again.

(The Rev.) W. Hamilton Aulenbach
1/27/75 *Claremont, Calif.*

Death Companions

Your article on "Companions to the Dying" [Feb. 17] caused an uproar at our party last night.

The Threshold concept of paid friendship to those who are dying seemed to some ghoulish. Others at first saw it as unethical, crassly com-

mercial and the ultimate indictment of a decadent society.

After hours of controversy, the consensus was that the Threshold concept is neither immoral nor unduly commercial. Rather, the ethical problem lies with the medical profession, which for years has been taking money for not doing the things Threshold companions intend to do.

Linda and Joe Cox
Encinitas, Calif.

I find it hard to believe that paying $7.50 an hour for a companion would help me die more comfortably.

Personally, I'd rather go alone than with a gigolo!

(The Rev.) Robert J. Dexter
3/3/75 *Lafayette, Ind.*

We Could Use You Here

For the first time in my life as an American, I envy something Britain has: Tory Margaret Thatcher [Feb. 24]. Her defense of "middle-class interests," espousal of rewards for skill and hard work, and resistance to the excessive power of the state strike a tiny bell of recognition, reminding us (however dimly) that we used to have representatives who spoke in this fashion. May I say, "We could use you here, Margaret"?

William P. Earley
3/10/75 *Worcester, Mass.*

Tennis Excitement

Tennis matches like the one between Jimmy Connors and John Newcombe will always have an appeal. There is an excitement about the game when two fine players are contending.

I am pleased to see the increased interest in tennis, which started in 1968 when professionals were first allowed to play at Wimbledon. It is healthy for the game that more good players can make a comfortable living from it. I do have reservations about some of the directions that tennis is taking. I do not enjoy watching one-set matches. Even the best player can lose a set. Also, I do not like what they are calling audience participation. The language sometimes used between players and spectators is embarrassing and tends to bring the game down to a mediocre level. Tennis is not wrestling.

Still, tennis today is superior, and I am sure that the problems can be worked out.

Donald Budge
5/19/75 *Acapulco, Mexico*
Grand Slammer Budge was the first player to win the Australian, French, Wimbledon and U.S. championships in the same year (1938).

Writing Britain Off

Do not write the British off [May 26]. Read your history books. We have been around a long time now, and we are still the most civilized country in

President Gerald Ford signs the pardon of Richard Nixon

Europe. You can feel safe here as no-where else, and that is why so many Americans make their homes with us. We are still your best ally, and we won't rat on you if it comes to a showdown. We don't talk much these days about the "special relationship," but everyone knows that it still exists. We share more than just a common language—our men have died side by side in two wars. As for our being "ungovernable," Eric Sevareid has been listening to too much saloon-bar talk.

William J. Selleck
Pulborough, England
6/16/75

Betty's Boudoir

Any assumption that Mrs. Ford eagerly volunteered to tell me all about her boudoir life [Sept. 1] is unfair to her.

I brought up the previously published quote, "They've asked me everything but how often I sleep with my husband, and if they'd asked me that, I would have told them," and asked for a response. Rather than duck the question, she answered with humor, "As often as possible." At no time have I heard Mrs. Ford volunteer any smart quips on any of the subjects the press is currently chastising her for.

Sleeping with one's husband is, presumably, one of the accepted joys of wedlock. The way you tsk-tsked, one would think her refreshing admission was endangering national security. Only last year TIME did a cover story that in part took political wives to task for their dreary role playing. Now that we have a First Lady who speaks her mind, she is branded as tasteless. No wonder so many political wives hide behind frozen smiles and innocuous comments.

Myra MacPherson
Washington Post
Washington, D.C.
9/22/75

A President's Life

The attempts on President Ford's life [Sept. 29] underscore our ridiculous way of campaigning. Why must we use methods that were necessary 150 years ago, when the only way to reach people was to travel across the country and stop at every town?

Anne Munson
Rochelle Park, N.J.
10/13/75

Gun Rights

If Squeaky Fromme or Sally Moore had tried to run the President down with a car, would the people who are so vehemently determined to ban all private ownership of guns be equally insistent on elimination of privately owned automobiles?

Long live the National Rifle Association. It will be a sad day for America when the brownshirts are able to knock down my door because I am the suspected owner of a firearm.

William E. Pings
Clear, Alaska
10/27/75

Idi Amin, tyrant dictator of Uganda

A Better Dictator

I wish to express my indignation at your continued filthy reports and attacks on Field Marshal Amin. It is my notion that he is a better dictator than some quiet and innocent-looking Presidents. And by the way, which is better, dictatorship or corruption?

Shadrack Nzige
Lusaka, Zambia
11/3/75

Afraid to Look

As a student of history, I watch with great interest the emerging of new African states. I see Uganda's Amin, Angola's bloody civil war, and now Malawi's brutal persecution of Jehovah's Witness [Dec. 1]. I am afraid to look for what will emerge next!

Arthur V. Johnson II
Nashua, N.H.
12/22/75

New York Broke

For decades, the rest of America and the world expected the Big Apple to be the prime source of sustenance for the poor, homeless, huddled masses. Now, because it's gone broke trying to fulfill the American dream for so many, we turn our backs.

The blame isn't just New York's. It's also America's.

(Mrs.) Susan L. McVey
Walkersville, Md.
12/72/75

Gloomy Outlook

Despite all predictions of economic recovery there remains a gloomy outlook: 5 million or more unemployed in Europe for many years. How long will we have to wait until politicians, unions, employers and employees realize there is only one way out: cutting working time for all employees, enabling us to give back jobs to our unemployed.

Helmut Matthias
Heidelberg, W. Germany
1/12/76

Was It Camelot?

Re J.F.K. and recent revelations [Dec. 29]: I had thought he was King Arthur in the Camelot analogy. It appears that he was Sir Lancelot all along.

Bruce E. Ingmire
New York City

J.F.K. had a little fun while in the White House. So what? What man with his charm, wit and charisma would not have enjoyed the likes of Monroe, Mansfield, *et al.*, if given the chance? Apparently it did little harm to the country.

Ronald A. Sanders
Washington, D.C.
1/19/76

Two Hoovers

I know it is a modern journalistic trend to set about denigrating famous men after they are dead, but I must deplore the bundle of inferences of a discreditable nature drawn in your story about J. Edgar Hoover [Dec. 22].

I am aware of Hoover's sometimes irksome quirks and foibles. Every one of us has his faults, but that man built the FBI into the most incorruptible and efficient police organization the U.S. has ever seen. To British policemen, who have always sympathized with their U.S. counterparts whose appointments so often depend on political influence, that was a colossal achievement; as a nation you should be immensely proud of it.

Ranulph Bacon
London
1/19/76
Sir Ranulph is a former deputy commissioner of the Metropolitan Police (Scotland Yard).

Helping Hand

Have you seen the "Jerry Ford doll"? You don't wind it up—you help it up!

John J. Lyons
Chicago
1/26/76

It's Too Serious

I am startled at your TIME Essay by Michael Demarest on "Smoking: Fighting Fire With Ire" [Jan. 12].

As the Surgeon General who issued the Advisory Committee Report on Smoking and Health on Jan. 11, 1964,

I am proud that the report has stood the test of time in that the conclusions have been reconfirmed and extended.

It is scientifically established that many persons can be made ill by exposure to smoke from others. In addition, a vast majority of the nonsmokers find such exposure uncomfortable. It is too serious a problem to have fun poked by a tongue-in-cheek essay.

Luther L. Terry
Surgeon General, Ret.
U.S. Public Health Service
2/9/76 *Washington, D.C.*

Reality, Soviet Style

Your article "Hard Times for Ivan" [March 8] is unworthy of the magazine's readers.

Some of the U.S. news media, including TIME magazine, have long cultivated distorted ideas about the Soviet Union. No wonder that many Americans have lots of "surprises" when the American press cannot conceal the most eloquent Soviet achievements (as was the case, for instance, when the first Soviet Sputnik was launched), or when they personally acquaint themselves with Soviet reality: the patriotism of the Soviet people, their devotion to the socialist way of life, real equality for all, an inflation-free economy, not a trace of unemployment, free education and medical care, not to mention significant cultural, scientific and technical advances in a short historical period.

I am sorry that TIME still publishes stories filled with distortions and hostile emotions. They will not hurt the Soviet Union. But they do a disservice to the American people.

Valentin Kamanev
Press Counselor of the
U.S.S.R. Embassy
3/22/76 *Washington, D.C.*

Carter's Success

Political experts seem baffled by Jimmy Carter's phenomenal success in the primaries [May 10]. I think the answer is quite simple. The other candidates are trying to reach into the minds of men; Carter reaches into their hearts.

Jean Maggio
5/31/76 *New York City*

Soweto Uprising

The Soweto uprising demonstrates that shooting blacks and clubbing whites only help to polarize South Africa. The leaders on both sides should take a long hard look at America in the 1960s in order to see how killing, rioting and looting polarized the U.S.

Thomas Ward
Collegeville, Pa.

Much of what you say is true, yet blacks in South Africa enjoy far greater income, more protection from violence, greater justice, even freedom, than those blacks in countries they govern themselves, including Haiti and Jamaica.

Frank Valerius
7/19/76 *Guatemala City*

Congratulations

Congratulations to big beautiful America on your 200th birthday. May you continue to prosper and lead the world for the next 200 years!

J. Frank McCaffrey
7/26/76 *Strathfield, Australia*

Shackles of Lust

Re Jimmy Carter's confessions [Oct. 4]: there was another person with lust in heart, and his name was Mahatma Gandhi. He wrote in *My Experiment with Truth:* "I have always regarded myself as a lustful, though faithful husband. It took me long to get free from the shackles of lust, and I had to pass through many ordeals before I could overcome it."

T. V. Krishnan
11/15/76 *Singapore*

Votes for a Vision

Jerry Ford ran his campaign primarily on his record. Unfortunately for him, Jimmy Carter ran on what he will do, and the American people have decided they want to pin their hopes on a man with a vision to get America moving again [Nov. 15].

President Ford has nothing to be ashamed about. Morally, he gave us what we needed at the time he assumed office. But what America now needs is change—an energetic, thoughtful man—and America has chosen Jimmy Carter.

John Hill
Columbus

Happy Birthday, America: the Bicentennial celebration

Carter and Mondale win the 1976 election.

Carter's wife, daughter and mother also receive media attention

I voted for Carter. My team won and I should be rejoicing. But suddenly I have this funny feeling in the pit of my stomach.

Mrs. James P. Dunn
Summit, N.J.

Maybe this is the end of the Civil War.

Clancy W. Pollock
Hagerstown, Md.

The South's revenge: Carter.

Margie Thompson
11/29/76 *Rockford, Ill.*

Hughes' Irony

Re your story on Howard Hughes [Dec. 13]: it is ironic that a man capable of building and directing a billion-dollar conglomerate was the architect of such a pathetic paranoid prison for himself. However, his Christian aides resemble piranhas more than Christians.

Those of us who drink and smoke couldn't be any worse off than that wretched soul surrounded by Kleenex boxes and paper toweling.

Donna W. Blue
1/3/77 *Birmingham, Mich.*

Thank You Note

TIME has kindly lent me this space so I can thank the many thousands of you who were so kind to write to me after the Olympic Games in Montreal [Aug. 2]. Since it is really very difficult to answer personally so many letters, let me tell you here how grateful I am to you all for your friendship.

I wish you all good health, happiness and peace in the coming new year.

Nadia Comăneci
1/24/77 *Bucharest, Rumania*

Credit Rating

The credit card is the greatest invention since the wheel. It instantly converts thrift into greed and makes it possible for all of us to buy things we don't need, with money we don't have, to impress people we don't like.

Peter Simmel
3/21/77 *Culver City, Calif.*

God's Little Hectare

Enough! While TIME's effort to get us all used to metric measurement is probably commendable, "The Battle of Alaska" [May 9] assaulted me with no fewer than 13 different parenthetical metric conversions.

Go easy on us oldsters for a while, eh? May your Environment editors be exiled to God's Little .405 Hectare for a time.

Robert G. Campbell
5/30/77 *Indianapolis*

Jogging

It's true: jogging is a tonic, a vitamin pill and an alternate to Valium all rolled into one long mile.

Lois Gaines
6/20/77 *San Luis Obispo, Calif.*

I see that jogging is now a full-blown fad. Good! If we are to judge from other fads, that means it will blow over in a few months, or at most a year or so. Like, for instance, Hula Hoops.

As an old Army man, I can tell you what jogging really is. Jogging is double time. And I say, the hell with it!

John S. Carroll
6/27/77 *Emlenton, Pa.*

Soccer Craze

Pelé's mission was also the soccer enthusiast's dream: having soccer spread across the U.S. [Sept. 12]. Now millions of people are into soccer, and it is evident by the record crowds that soccer is here to stay.

I got into soccer when Pelé joined the Cosmos in 1975, and from then on it's been the only sport I enjoy playing. I soon found out that more and more people were getting into soccer, and it made me feel great to think that soccer was becoming a big thing in America. And I owe it all to one man: the Black Pearl.

Richard Pawlak
10/10/77 *Berwyn, Ill.*

To Your Health

Re Indian Prime Minister Morarji Desai's practice of drinking his own urine each morning [Oct. 24]: I too began this custom while living in India and have faithfully maintained it for the past twelve years, gaining a sense of vigor that few of my contemporaries (I am 74) can match.

Fellow Indians who also partake of this "cistern of life" must certainly

140

fare better than those who drink from the hopelessly polluted Ganges River.

Harish Jirmoun
11/14/77 *New Bern, N.C.*

Baring Breasts

Rykiel, Kenzo, *et al.* design clothing that makes women appear as if they doubt their sexual identity and therefore must bare their breasts in order to prove to the world that they are indeed women. Either this or it is once again apparent that the designers do not like women and do whatever is necessary to make them look garish and foolish.

(The Rev.) G. B. Baumgardner
Princeton, Ill.

Weren't the see-throughs enough? Now Sonia Rykiel wants us to let it all hang out. Outrageous.

Kathryn W. Barnard
11/28/77 *Tacoma, Wash.*

Risk for Peace

I've watched numerous world leaders take risks that might lead their countries to war. Now Egypt's President Sadat seems willing to assume equal risks for peace [Nov. 28]. His act of courage is a deeply moving moment in history. .

Karen R. Brown
12/19/77 *New Concord, Ohio*

Cooking Craze

Your article on the recent cooking craze in your country seems very ironic. You are the inventors of the fast-food chains (McDonald's) and the frozen food section of the local supermarket. Coming from Montreal, I'm amazed at all the junk that is eaten every time I go on business trips to the States.

It's about time you started enjoying *pâté de foie en croûte* and *homard à la Provençale* with a nice Bordeaux, instead of hot dogs and a Budweiser. *Bon appétit.*

Pierre Belisle
1/9/78 *Montreal*

If Quebec Goes

Since the election of the *Parti Québécois*, a number of writers have assumed that Canada would inevitably be absorbed into the U.S. if Quebec votes to go it alone [Dec. 26].

If Quebec leaves, I do not see why the extinction of my nationality should follow. We, like other peoples of the world, are willing to sacrifice for our survival, and we would find a way to survive.

Dale Overall
1/23/78 *Ottawa*

The Greatest

There will always be debate as to whether Muhammad Ali [Feb. 27] is the best boxer ever, but there can be

no doubt that this boxer, poet and philosopher truly is, as he claims, "the Greatest."

Alfred Nicolosi
Pompton Lakes, N.J.

No champion had a more colorful history, and no one has every stood taller in defeat.

Michael Clark
3/20/78 *Kalamazoo, Mich.*

The West Bank

Dispossessed, deprived, desperate and daring Palestinians, living outside Palestine, are more of a danger to the security of Israel than 3 million independent Palestinians settled in a homeland on the West Bank under the observation of the U.N., the U.S. and Israel.

The Israelis have two choices to eliminate Palestinian terrorism. The first is to kill every Palestinian refugee in Lebanon, Syria, Jordan and in other Arab countries as well as anywhere else in the world. The second is to return the West Bank and other occupied lands to their rightful owners and let the Palestinians have their independence under the eyes of the Israelis, who can watch them.

George Haig
4/10/78 *Washington, D.C.*

True Beauty

Re "In Praise of Older Women" [April 24]: grace, wit, style and charm. At last we are beginning to realize what true beauty is.

Christopher Miller
5/15/78 *Strasbourg, France*

Deep Sorrow

I am writing to express the feelings of a young Italian man who was a student of Professor Aldo Moro [May 22].

Italy, my country, the country of bureaucracy, of superficiality, of inefficiency, is not easy for a young person to live in and love. During these terrible moments I feel both deep sorrow and great discouragement for the murder of Aldo Moro, a brilliant example of a university don and a teacher of life, and because I am pessimistic about the possibility of our weak democracy being able to deal with terrorism.

Gianfranco Celani
6/12/78 *Rome*

The Best Man

Both the brevity of the papal conclave and the selection of a dark horse as the new Pope defied the predictions of worldly analysts. The inescapable conclusion is that the Holy Spirit intervened.

Richard Y. Norrish
9/25/78 *Edwardsville, Ill.*

One Small Step

What an ineffable thrill it was to watch Sadat, Begin and Carter shaking hands [Sept. 25]. It was as singularly breathtaking as the feeling I had when Neil Armstrong murmured through the heavens, "One small step for man, one giant step for mankind."

Edward S. Yoste
Germantown, Tenn.

President Carter's triumph: President Sadat and Prime Minister Begin celebrate the signing of the Camp David agreements

BOUQUETS

Never has a magazine cover had such an impact upon me. That single photograph of the dead in Guyana [Dec. 4] brought the entire Boschian horror into focus. The scene will be forever engraved in my memory.

12/25/78

Michael Swartz
Alexandria, Va.

No matter what happens or does not happen as a result of the Camp David agreements, the next Nobel Peace Prize should be awarded jointly to Sadat, Begin and Carter.

10/16/78

David A. Lane
Ossining, N.Y.

Pope's Death

The time has come to elect a Pope physically capable of the office. The election should not be a death sentence.

Donald E. Lawton
Burghausen, West Germany

Why not a vice Pope?

10/30/78

Jane Keckeissen
North Caldwell, N.J.

The Polish Pope

Pope John Paul II [Oct. 30] is going to be a sensational Pope. He seems to be sure of himself. The Cardinals made an excellent choice. He's just like the man next door, except he just happens to be a Pope.

11/20/78

Terri Freedman
Camarillo, Calif.

Jonestown

Your picture of a Jonestown family huddled in death is probably the most touching one I have ever seen. What right had anyone to deprive this profoundly innocent child of life?

1/1/79

Bal Ram
Suva, Fiji

Carter and China

I applaud President Carter's historic decision finally to recognize the People's Republic of China [Dec. 25]. It is about time we joined the rest of the world in the acceptance of what has become a political fact.

1/15/79

Neil H. Butterklee
Stony Brook, N.Y.

The High Cost of Dreaming

Re "Inflation: Who Is Hurt Worst?" [Jan. 15]: boo, hiss to the American Dream! My husband and I now find that even though we have obtained that hallowed ground called "the upper middle class" we are hard put to have meat on the table three times a week. We put off doctor visits. A family vacation is a joke. Most depressing is watching Congress continue to set up programs that we finance but cannot use because we "make too much money." So tell us: What is the American Dream?

How long do you think the ever giving middle class will continue to support this country?

2/12/79

Joy Ross
Brookfield, Wis.

Children and the Future

Even thinking about the question of whether children are necessary [March 5] angers this ten-year-old. Children are the future. No children—no future.

William M. Sanders
Manchester, Md.

The real reason why many people today do not want children is their fear that they would produce children as awful as they are.

3/26/79

Charles L. McGehee
Ellensburg, Wash.

Jonestown, Guyana, Nov. 1978: more than 900 members of the People's Temple sect, led by Jim Jones, commit suicide by drinking cyanide

Carter's Coup

Sound the trumpets, beat the drums in honor of and with profound gratitude to that peanut farmer from Plains, who has accomplished, by his own initiative, what no other President has [March 19].

When the peace treaty is signed, a holiday should be declared by Israel, Egypt and the U.S. so that people can pay homage to three courageous leaders.

Elsie Kendis
Philadelphia
4/9/79

Amen to Amin

The overthrow of Idi Amin [April 23] will be welcomed by all decent, freedom loving peoples of the world, but I, as an African, can only sit and wonder how long it will take the Organization of African Unity (OAU) to realize that human rights also mean advocating the elimination of despotism, autocracy and carnage being practiced on black Africans by black Africans. God bless Nyerere of Tanzania.

Bah Tanwi
Houston
5/14/79

Thatcher Wins

It is about time a major nation has realized the potential of a woman. Congratulations, Margaret Thatcher [May 14]!

Now, will the American Margaret Thatcher please stand up for 1980?

John H. Ferguson V
Mount Airy, Md.

With Thatcher & Co. in office in Britain, may God have mercy upon her victims, Irish, Indians, Pakistanis and blacks.

Kenneth Tierney
Yonkers, N.Y.

Margaret Thatcher is more beautiful than either Cheryl Tiegs or Cher, and furthermore, she has brains. She has carved for herself a place in history in which she will rest long after sagging breasts and graying hair have felled those sex symbols.

Carolyn Foust
Memphis
6/4/79

Carter's Crisis

President Carter [July 23] has tried being Moses, Isaiah and Jesus Christ all at once, when what we need is a Caesar.

John R. Warren
San Antonio

In time of crisis we must be extremely careful in accepting the leadership of those who claim to have all the answers.

Jacob Weitzer
North Miami Beach, Fla.
8/13/79

It must have been a stunt double who wrote that item about me and *The Legend of Walks Far Woman* [Sept. 3]. The truth is that I have done most of my own stunt work, much more than the insurance company would have liked, suffering numerous injuries in the process.

By the way, the Indians do not refer to their women as "squaws"—this is a demeaning term used only by the whites—and though I have often been the object of sexism it wounds me deeply that TIME would stoop to racism in an attempt to make a joke. The Indian I portray in this film is no joke to me.

Raquel Welch
Los Angeles
9/24/79

Followers of Ayatullah Khomeini bring Islamic revolution to Iran

British Races

You, as you show in your story on Britain's multiracial society [Aug. 20], like Hitler, have not understood the solid British character. All of us, browns, pinks, blacks, whites and any other color that is relevant to you, will give proof of our love and loyalty to our country when the time comes.

Britain has already passed the most difficult test in race relations. In contrast, see the executions, persecutions taking place elsewhere on this planet. A million articles like yours cannot succeed in spoiling even an iota Britain's standing in the world in this respect. As a proud British Sikh, I say hands off our country.

Rajinder Singh
Meinerzhgen, West Germany
9/10/79

Mountbatten's Murder

Assassination by political terrorists is a reprehensible and morally unjustifiable act. But it is perhaps because of centuries of barbarous oppression and injustice under British rule that some Irish have yet to learn the laws of civilized warfare.

Norma McCormack
Rockville, Md.

The dastardly murder of Lord Mountbatten [Sep. 10], his 15-year-old grandson and an 80-year-old woman has shocked the civilized world. This kind of act only serves to set back any real solution of Ireland's problems.

Stewart J. McClenahan
Hazel Crest, Ill.
10/1/79

Running Low

So our pension funds are running low, eh? I had better not plan on retiring until the day I die.

John P. McGrath
West Seneca, N.Y.
10/15/79

The Iran Crisis

Let us hope that the U.S. will never bow to Khomeini's blackmail. If the Carter Administration agrees to Iranian demands, it will be a blow and a very bad example to those who love democracy.

H. Sarhan Salem
Sharjah, United Arab Emirates
12/24/79

The ? Eighties

By mid-decade, Americans thought of Ronald Reagan as the Great Communicator, although the Soviets might not agree. White males were no longer the only candidates seriously considered as presidential hopefuls.

Education came under new scrutiny while youngsters spent hours in front of video and computer terminals. Boycotts were widely covered facets of the Olympic Games; at home Americans competed at Trivial Pursuit.

Cool America

"The Cooling of America" [Dec. 24] chilled me so much that I put on an undershirt and a sweater and resolved to dig out my flannel pajamas and get a blanket for the bed. If you send any more issues like that to Hawaii, I may have to close the windows.

John F. Mulholland
1/14/80   *Honolulu*

Tired of Carter

Soviets in Afghanistan. Soviets in Cuba. Hostages in Iran. I'm tired of Carter's patience and idle threats. I

think it's time we quit talking and kicked somebody.

Mike Stroud
1/28/80   *St. Louis*

Indira's Return

The Indians have ousted the biggest nongovernment of the century. Indira Gandhi's spectacular return to power is appropriately a nonviolent revolution in the land of the Mahatma.

Shyam B. Wadhwani
2/4/80   *Bombay*

Invasion Costs

I cannot judge whether the U.S. should boycott the Olympic Games, but I do wonder about the comparative costs of the movement of Soviet troops into Afghanistan and of the TV networks' right to televise the Games. Is it possible that the invasion was funded by NBC?

Allen Dale Olson
2/4/80   *Karlsruhe, West Germany*

Draft Call

The only thing the U.S. should draft is beer.

Tim Pickl
2/25/80   *Duluth*

Mugabe's Victory

By leading his party to an honorable victory, Robert Mugabe [March 17] has liberated 7 million blacks of Zimbabwe Rhodesia from tyranny and oppression. This liberation is like the freeing of the Jews by Moses from the Pharaoh's power.

Sudhangshu B. Karmakar
4/7/80   *New York City*

The Great Inflation

I've spent a lifetime listening to another generation tell us all how tough it was during the Great Depression. Sadly, I must have found my "Top that!" in the Great Inflation of the '70s and '80s. The things that saw families through the Great Depression were hope and the promise of a better tomorrow. What have we to use as tools

to see us through the Great Inflation of today? I can only promise my children they will have less.

D. Kent Lloyd
4/14/80   *Gladstone, Ore.*

Election Blues

Having through negligence or providence reached the age of 38 without ever having seen a Ronald Reagan movie, my dearest wish at the present moment is to reach the age of 39 without seeing a Reagan presidency.

David Helsdon
4/14/80   *Doha, Qatar*

Failed Rescue

Finally an effort to free the hostages [May 5]! The fact that it ended in failure is secondary; what is important is that the Iranians know that we have the will and determination to free our people.

Peter J. Plourd II
Prince George, Va.

The raid seems so childishly conceived that one must assume it was not intended to succeed. Was it Carter's Watergate, an attempt to self-destruct?

Robert Brundin
Torrance, Calif.

It's so easy to blame President Carter. But if the rescue had succeeded, all of us would be cheering in the streets and taking credit for American strength.

Barbara B. Willis
5/26/80   *Middletown, Ohio*

The Shock from Eton

Those of us who had the privilege of education at an English public school must be shocked by your news that fagging is to be banned at Eton next term [May 26]. For the men who built the British Empire knew that character is the most important product of education, and discipline must be learned when young. It is a rule of life that a man cannot control others until he has learned to control himself.

We shall be hearing next that all rank has been abolished from the

The faces of the '80s: British punk rockers favor spiked hairdos and metal-studded garb

armed forces on the ground that rank is cruel and discriminatory.

Brian Aherne
7/7/80 *Vevey, Switzerland*

Exodus from Israel

If 400,000 Israelis prefer living in the U.S. to Israel [June 30] and more are emigrating every month, is it time to rethink the Promised Land? Is what Zionist Jews wanted in 1948 necessarily what they want or need in 1980? Since so many are now happier elsewhere, how about returning the land to the people who really want it—the Palestinians?

Helen Livingston
7/28/80 *Olympia, Wash.*

Suicidal Thoughts

Many will await the publication of the guidebook on how to commit suicide [July 7] and many will use its information gratefully. As a volunteer in nursing homes, I hear prayers nightly pleading to die before morning.

LaVere Hoskins
7/28/80 *Topeka, Kans.*

Remedies for the Back

When I had a serious bout of back trouble [July 14], my Indian doctor gave me one valuable piece of advice. He said that Indians living in the villages hardly every suffer from back trouble because they spend hours each day squatting on their haunches. He therefore suggested squatting for five minutes each day.

J. B. Madan
8/18/80 *Calcutta*

Reagan's Sincerity

I am an actor of some years' experience and I assure you that Reagan was completely sincere in his acceptance

speech. He was not acting, and even as a Democrat I was most moved.

Keenan Wynn
8/25/80 *Los Angeles*

A Hostage's Thank You

I am writing this letter to your magazine so that it can be read by the largest number of people possible. My fellow Americans and I have for the past eight months been held hostage here in Tehran, and as a result of this our morale becomes quite low at times. One of the reasons for an uplift of that morale is mail sent to us by family and friends. But what continuously amazes me is the mail sent to us not only from my country but from people all over the world, whom I've never met, wishing us good luck and a speedy return to our family and friends. It is to these very kind and generous people I direct this letter. From myself and my fellow hostages, please accept our deepest thanks for taking the time to show your concern for us in this most trying situation. I hope that you will all continue to write in the future.

Donald R. Hohman
9/1/80 *American Embassy, Tehran*

Land of Hope and Glory?

Margaret Thatcher's Conservatives and those old-school-tie traditionalists dedicated to preserving Britain's Establishment should reconsider the lyrics of their rallying hymn, *Land of Hope and Glory* [Aug. 11]. What glory can be gained in a land of continual industrial recession, rising prices, and where is there hope in a postwar record of 2.5 million unemployed?

Michael W. D. Jeffs
9/1/80 *Luton, England*

How Cake Adds Life

After the uproar over the new wave

of Cuban refugees, it is refreshing that a Cuban who arrived in this country at age 32 would 16 years later become president of Coca-Cola [Aug. 18]. Coke adds life to the American dream!

Rene L. Colina
9/8/80 *Detroit*

Contraception and the Church

The statement in Rome by Archbishop John R. Quinn that the Vatican line on birth control is being ignored by many U.S. Catholics [Oct. 13] reflects the misconception that the doctrines of faith and morals proclaimed by the Church are changeable. Yet there has never been an about-face on any of those doctrines. The great secular breakthrough allowed by the promotion and acceptance of contraception has curiously brought us the age of state-countenanced abortion, community-standardized pornography and a more than embryonic euthanasia movement. This pro-pleasure, anti-child mind-set won't intimidate Archbishop Quinn's church or the Church of Peter ever to modify the doctrine that sees more to sex than orgasm and more to aging than diminished utilitarianism.

Kevin A. Joyce
Grosse Pointe, Mich.

Having grown up with the idealistic teachings of the Roman Catholic Church, I found myself ill-prepared for the harsh, realistic world that exists beyond it. In a world where overpopulation breeds starvation and unwanted children are subject to abuse and neglect, I'd say it's about time the church's archaic stance on contraception was rightfully challenged by its own rank and file.

Susan M. Balczuk
Essex Junction, Vt.

Pope John Paul II may call Roman Catholics who practice artificial birth

145

The first space shuttle, Columbia

control immoral. Archbishop Quinn may not be sure what to call them. But the fact remains that most Catholics who use the rhythm method exclusively are generally known as parents.

John G. Patronik
11/10/80 *Hagerstown, Md.*

A Little Bitter

If I could I surely would make apologies for all the disrespect and indignities President Jimmy Carter has been made to suffer by many dim-witted ingrates. But I can only say, never was a decent, dedicated man so cruelly maligned. The low-down littleness of it all makes me bitter also, Rosalynn.

Lorena B. Poole
12/8/80 *Horatio, Ark.*

Unmanly Bible

The King James version of the Bible is good enough for me without any desexing [Dec. 8], but it looks as though feminist nitpickers are going to keep sending Moses back up the mountain for those tablets until he finally gets it right! God must be shaking his head wondering if Eve was such a good idea.

Eleanor M. Cockerline
Warren, Mich.

Last night I prayed to "God the Parent, God the Offspring and God the Holy Ghost." I hope it heard me.
Paul B. Horton
12/29/80 *Sun City, Ariz.*

Age of Robots

"The Robot Revolution" [Dec. 8] graphically illustrates a couple of phe-nomenal achievements—microcomputers and computer imaging—that came out of the space program. Americans who have been grumbling for years that the only thing we got out of the space program was a bunch of rocks should have their calculators repossessed.

Jim Wood
Lumberton, N.C.

The ultimate insult to the blue-collar workers standing in long lines at the unemployment office will be a Civil Service robot electronically reporting, "Your claim has run out, run out, run out . . ."

James M. Kahn
Portland, Ore.

I can see it now—TIME's cover story for the year 1999, written by a robot, informing us that the magazine is planning to experiment once again with human reporters.

Norm Eklund
12/29/80 *Sumner, Wash.*

Man of the Year

Congratulations on your choice for Man of the Year [Jan. 5]. Ronald Reagan brings a new philosophy, pride and confidence to our country, and will sweep away the gloom and doom of the '70s.

Cecil Betz
1/26/81 *Flintridge, Calif.*

Space Shuttle

With the launching of the space shuttle this year [Jan. 12], Americans will once again be migrating to a new frontier. As in California more than a century ago, the colonization of space offers the same hope for new resources, new industry and a renewed sense of national spirit.

William N. Ellis
2/2/81 *Huron, Ohio*

Hostages' Release

Watching TV coverage of the hostages' release with my neighbors, we sat with tears streaming down our faces, hearts bursting with pride for America and a yellow ribbon tied around an old plant pot. What's so unusual about that? We are all Europeans.

Vera Symm
Cramlington, England

One gets the feeling that America is exploding with emotion. There is love for the mistreated hostages and a renewed love for the country. There is hate for Iran, but there is also guilt for not taking aggressive action in the first place. A dangerous mix.

Mark H. Burnett
2/23/81 *Lancaster, England*

Who Will Fight?

The advice given to the populace is: Carry money to appease the attacker, don't cry out, don't fight back, submit to the rapist. Someone has to put up resistance. If the victims won't, who will?

Marjorie Dishron
4/13/81 *Fort Worth*

Not Again!

I felt just as frustrated and saddened as everyone else by the attack on President Reagan [April 13]. Only this time the shock waves weren't there. That is how I realized the real horror of this mess. I am adjusting to violence.

Carolynn Loughridge
Denver

Ronald Reagan stood taller in this real-life drama than in any of his celluloid screen efforts. Perhaps now we can stop associating him with Bonzo, train robbers, cattle rustlers and pretty girls.

Ward Kendall
5/4/81 *Montreal*

Rome, 1981: an assassin's bullet nearly kills Pope John Paul II

The Pope

Shooting a world leader who is also a man of God has got to be the greatest shame for mankind [May 25]. All the Pope did was condemn violence and hate among us.

Misael C. Balayan
Cheyenne, Wyo.

How ironic it is that Pope John Paul II was able to survive the brutality of both World War II and a Communist regime, only to be nearly silenced by an assassin's bullet.

Mary Sue Timar
Toledo

Whom do they shoot next? If God were riding in a motorcade, some nut would take a pot shot at him.

Randy Johnson
6/15/81 *Santa Clara, Calif.*

British Riots

Your story on Britain's summer of discontent fails to mention a key triggering element. Britain's frustrated lower classes have had a bellyful of exposure to overweening privilege, particularly during this time of a spectacle wedding.

Thomas J. Bush
Pasadena, Calif.

As a lifelong Anglophile, I felt deeply the horrors of the English riots. Yet a certain part of me recalls clearly my 1977 visit, when New York's blackout and looting occurred. My English acquaintances all seemed shocked and proclaimed, "It can't happen here." Can they really have been so blind?

Elizabeth Knajdl
8/10/81 *New York City*

Australian Films

It was good to see Australia's film industry [Sept. 28] finally getting some well-deserved praise and acceptance in the rest of the world. The film industry, however, is just the tip of the creative iceberg. Australia abounds with young talent, emerging from the heart of an up-and-coming country.

Likita Marley
10/19/81 *Paris*

On Swearing

The growing use of swearing, like the increased use of the phrase "you know," illustrates how impoverished our language has become.

Bill Feddersen
President, Napa College
1/4/82 *Napa, Calif.*

Poland's Plight

The suffering! The sorrow! The face of Lech Walesa is the face of Poland.

Thomas C. Moran
1/25/82 *Longboat Key, Fla.*

As the Falklands war begins, the British garrison surrenders to invading Argentine troops

Video Games

Legislators who want to shut down arcades featuring video games [Jan. 18] should close the race tracks instead. If adults can waste their pay on the horses, then kids should be permitted to spend their allowance the way they want to.

Heidi J. Jamison
2/8/82 *Pine Grove, Pa.*

Labor Blues

Even though I was a child of the Depression, I know that joblessness is much more than an economic disaster. My father was haunted all his life by the doubts and fears he developed during those terrible years about himself and his ability to provide for his family.

Roberta Van Winkle
3/1/82 *Saratoga Springs, N.Y.*

El Salvador's Anguish

Americans are dismayed to see our Government back the wrong party in El Salvador [Feb. 15]. Sadly, the Reagan Administration has not learned a lesson from our experiences in Viet Nam and Iran. As long as we support repressive regimes in the Third World, the people of these nations will hate us.

The U.S. is now pinning its hopes on the coming election, but to consider the voting in El Salvador as free is a terrible joke. The people will not be heard, only guns will be audible. If the leftists win, so be it. America is going to have to get used to dealing with Communist governments.

Charles Wyman
3/8/82 *Longmont, Colo.*

Salt Menace

So now we add salt to the list of prohibited comestibles. Eventually we will all starve to death, but boy will we be healthy.

David A. Huber
Drexel Hill, Pa.

The Falklands War

The seizure of the Falkland Islands by Argentina is an act that cannot be justified by any reasoning. Nevertheless, where was Britain's concern for self-determination when it took the Falklands from Argentina almost 150 years ago? Great Britain's current reaction is more a case of sour grapes and wounded pride than any genuine desire to right a terrible wrong. The sun set on the British Empire a long time ago. History has long recognized that fact. The British should also.

Philip Naff
Fort Sheridan, Ill.

It has been the Falkland Islands good fortune to have lived under British rule for 150 years. It is a pity that all South America has not had the same fate. In spite of being a Latin American, I recognize what the British have contributed to the world: freedom, life under law and respect for the individual. These rights must be defended even if it takes warships to do it.

Vicente Echerri
5/10/82 *New York City*

No Other Choice

After 149 years of patiently asking Britain to return the islands, we Argentines had no other choice.

Carlos I. Salgado
5/17/82 *Buenos Aires*

Marine's Offer

Many of us Marines who served in the Pacific in World War II would willingly take out our mothballed uniforms to defend our English friends with whom we served.

Bernie Watts
5/24/82 *Silver Lake, Ohio*

Doublecross

Latin Americans are stunned by the American doublecross. The U.S. has forfeited its right to be a member of the Organization of American States. Reconciliation with Latin America will take an eternity. Neutrality would have been wiser.

Michael Oliver
6/7/82 *Lima*

Social Security

The Social Security program [May 24], which now has millionaires picking up Social Security checks, has strayed far from F.D.R.'s intent to "ward off destitution" for the elderly. The system makes a mockery of what started out as a humane social program.

Mary J. Hill
6/14/82 *Lakewood, Ohio*

Life in the Red

"The American Way of Debt" [May 31] would be amusing if not so tragic. It is stupefying that educated young people making $40,000 a year can wind up in a financial mess. Despite their college degrees, they have no values, no priorities, no common sense.

Henry Goldstein
6/21/82 *Vineland, N.J.*

Falklands and Peace

Now that the war in the Falklands is over, the State Department is wondering whether the Argentines and the rest of Latin America are going to love us or not, [June 28]. Nobody really likes a rich uncle. U.S. support of the British in the Falklands needs no apology. We were on the side of justice in opposing aggression.

Edgar W. Riebe
Edison, N.J.

What do you call it when a country with 130% inflation illegally "takes control" of territory it does not own, prepares to fight to the finish for that desolate territory, leads its citizens to believe they are winning and when it loses blames the U.S.? I call it the most common occurrence of our times.

Scott E. Grant
7/19/82 *Bakersfield, Calif.*

Lebanese Rampage

Ironically, it is the American taxpayer who is indirectly financing the destruction in Lebanon and the killing of thousands of people there, with the more than $6 million a day in aid the U.S. gives to Israel. If we are to be thought of as a humane, just people, money should instead be channeled to the victims of this brutal rampage.

Andy Vulez
7/19/82 *Phoenix*

Hinckley Furor

We the people find the jury guilty of temporary insanity for its verdict in the trial of John Hinckley [July 5].

Sastry K. Ganti
Wheeling, Ill.

Hinckley's acquital should stir our national pride, not our anger. The compassion to pardon a lunatic's offenses reflects our society's determination that justice triumph over blind vengeance. Public safety requires benign isolation of those who suffer a dangerous mental defect, but no man deserves condemnation for actions beyond his control.

Harry Lerner
Los Angeles

John Hinckley Jr. tried to deny us our electoral choice, and for that he should spend the rest of his days in jail.

Michael G. Blee
Boston

Does Hinckley get the gun back too?

Richard A. Lumpkin
7/26/82 *Mattoon, Ill.*

Israeli Attacks

I cannot understand why world sentiment is against Israel. The nation is finally responding to continuous attacks against its border towns. And the P.L.O.? They hide behind innocent civilians. The blame for these casualties lies solely with Arafat, who sets up shop in urban ghettos.

Jeff Stober
Toronto

When Britain fought a war 8,000 miles from home, it was deemed justified. When the U.S. struggled in Viet Nam, it was judged to be a warranted invasion. But when Israel battles across its border for self-preservation against those who are bent on annihilating it, the action is roundly denounced as improper.

Anne Winter
8/9/82 *Willowdale, Ont.*

Hong Kong's Future

Although there are still 15 years to go before the British lease on Hong Kong runs out, panic is spreading through the colony. More than one-third of the people have sought asylum from Communist suffering. They cannot bear the thought of once again losing their freedom. The Chinese in Hong Kong have the right to decide their future: to be either autonomous or independent.

Ray Dahtong
11/1/82 *University Park, Pa.*

Jimmy's Offer

Considering his record, former President Jimmy Carter's offering advice to President Reagan on the Middle East is like Liz Taylor's authoring a book on *The Secret of a Successful Marriage!*

Breck M. Swanquist
11/1/82 *Sugar Grove, Ill.*

Outlawing Solidarity

I was dismayed at your pessimism over the future of Solidarity [Oct. 25]. Although the Polish parliament has officially destroyed the independent trade union, the Polish people have undergone too much anguish in their tragic past to abandon their cries for freedom. Even if General Wojciech Jaruzelski has been successful in banning Solidarity from the Polish socialist system, the dream of independence will reshape itself and continue.

Alexander J. Opalinski
11/15/82 *Toronto*

Continuing tragedy in the Middle East: war rages in Lebanon

Canada's Pocketbook

Canada's economic situation [Nov. 1] has been exacerbated by Prime Minister Trudeau's socialist and nationalist policies. It is ironic that this country, which is among the most naturally rich in the world, has suffered such an unnecessarily severe decline. Up to his neck in debt, his financial cupboard bare, Trudeau is reduced to begging from the same American businessmen he spurned but twelve months ago.

Richard Sanderson
11/29/82 *Montreal*

Lethal Rain

Congratulations on your acid-rain cover [Nov. 8]. It is time that the Canadian and American governments begin working together to pass legislation to combat this threat. The natural environment is a precious gift. No price tag should be put on its existence.

David Waddell
11/29/82 *Calgary, Alta.*

A Vote for Paul

If we have to have an actor for President, I'd rather it were Paul Newman.

Judy Tunkle
11/29/82 *New York City*

Older Experience

With the passing of Soviet leadership from Brezhnev to Andropov, the chance of a major war breaking out is minimal. Although we may deplore one elderly leader's replacing another, older men become involved in military engagements only when their losses can be held to a tolerable level. Former President Gerald Ford has related that Brezhnev told him they must do everything possible to prevent war. Brezhnev had seen too many Soviets slaughtered during World War II. The next generation of leaders, who have never experienced a major war, may be the most dangerous.

James J. McDonald
12/20/82 *San Antonio*

Kennedys Dropout

Senator Kennedy may not run in 1984 [Dec. 13], but don't count him out. He'll be back. As he said just two years ago. "The hope still lives, and the dream shall never die."

Monica Friedlander
Berkeley, Calif.

Four more years of Ronald Reagan, or possibly Fritz Mondale or John Glenn? We will need Ted Kennedy in 1988 to save this country.

Greg W. Prindle
1/3/83 *Toledo*

Too Much Me

It is not Abraham Maslow or self-fulfillment that destroyed America's traditional values and institutions. It is

Polish Solidarity leader Lech Walesa

the many changes that occurred in our society after World War II, including materialism, hedonism, sexual licentiousness, reckless behaviour and overindulgence. Together these traits have prevented people from maturing. This situation is graver than the Soviet threat and our economic crisis combined.

Stanley B. Stefan
1/10/83 *Monterey, Calif.*

Ulster's Troubles

The people of the Republic of Ireland who desire peace and reconciliation with their neighbors in Northern Ireland would be grateful if the misguided Irish Americans would cease sending money to the mindless terrorists on this island.

Francis Farrelly
1/10/83 *Dublin*

Man of the Year

I was shocked that TIME chose the computer as its Man of the Year [Jan. 3]. But I failed to come up with someone or something better. Nothing else has so permanently affected the world in 1982. A wise choice.

John M. Scott
Edna, Texas

It is appropriate that a machine should replace the Man of the Year in 1982, especially when one considers the colossal absurdity of the times in which we live.

Ned Gross Jr.
Sarasota, Fla.

Your cover picture shows a man who resembles one of those people glued to the TV playing video games. In the future, folks will come to look like that: plastic-covered, dull and witless.

Helen K. Ruth
1/17/83 *Lansdale, Pa.*

Australian Intrigue

I write as the former Governor-General of Australia who in November 1975 terminated the commission of Gough Whitlam as Prime Minister of Australia and thereby dismissed his government. You discussed that event in your issue of Dec. 13. Your article stated that since the dismissal, allegations have surfaced that "the CIA had a hand in Whitlam's fall." You referred to a recent piece in *Foreign Policy* magazine in which a Professor James A. Nathan stated that "a plausible case is being developed that CIA officials may have also done in Australia what they managed to achieve in Iran, Guatemala and Chile: destroy an elected government." I do not know what the CIA did or did not do in those other countries, but it is totally false to say that it did this in Australia.

Before publishing your story you gave me an opportunity to comment, but I decided to continue my longstanding policy of not speaking to the press about these events. However, Nathan's article presents much rumor, gossip and allegation as fact. As a result of being mentioned in TIME, his piece has received widespread circulation in the U.S. and the world. Thus I have come to the conclusion that my denial of CIA participation in any act of mine should be equally widely published.

My decision to dismiss Mr. Whitlam was exclusively my own, made upon my sole and full responsibility as Governor-General. No one else produced it. The CIA had no part in it.

The Rt. Hon. Sir John Kerr
2/14/83 *London*

Suicide Know-How

The rise of suicide manuals [March 21] has occurred as a reaction to the medical profession's insistence on prolonging life through technology. For those of us who do not want to spend our final days manipulated by machines, it is helpful to know that there is an alternative.

John Stillman
New York City

No one would deny the right of people in agony to end their life. In most cases, however, pain is controllable, and not all cancer patients suffer with severe pain. If the pain is bearable, life continues to have meaning until the end. Suicide is not the only option.

Robert W. Buckingham
4/18/83 *Tucson*

Nuclear Energy

Re TIME's story on the troubled nuclear industry [April 11]: it is a rare business that has not faced problems resulting from the economic recession and inflation of the past decade. While nuclear pioneers may have been overoptimistic, the record is nonetheless remarkable. This technology will soon provide close to one-fifth of the U.S.'s and the world's electricity with small environmental impact. The price of the electricity produced has been a bargain and for most plants will remain competitive for the foreseeable future. As for the industry's problems, all of them appear solvable. What more can we ask?

Marilyn Lloyd
Chairman, Congressional Subcommittee
on Energy Research and Production
5/16/83 *Washington, D.C.*

Forged Diaries

Hitler's odious power to spellbind an audience has wreaked havoc once again in the furor over the fake diaries [May 16]. Even in death, Hitler has destroyed the reputation and credibility of gullible historians and editors, most notably those at the magazine *Stern*. All it took was a forger for the Führer to bask in the limelight yet another time. Had the diaries proved authentic, then collectors would have been at one another's throats to own the journals of a man who caused such worldwide suffering.

Christina Marion Rieger
6/6/83 *North Little Rock, Ark.*

Shunning the Sun

After a very rainy spring, a bright warm day finally appeared. I rushed pool-side with a sugar-free soda, a salt-free snack and TIME. To my dismay, I read about the harmful effects of the sun [May 30]. One more pleasure in life to do without! On second thought, I decided just to give up reading.

Joan McIntosh
6/20/83 *Norman, Okla.*

Maggie Mops Up

Margaret Thatcher should serve as an example to America [June 20]. She represents many of the virtues that have faded in our nation. She is hard-working, thrifty, self-reliant and not afraid to believe in herself and her ideals. Britain's Iron Lady is as classically American as Superman.

Peter M. Eicher
7/11/83 *New York City*

Abortion Decision

I am not a member of NOW, Planned Parenthood, the National Abortion Federation or any other pro-choice group. I am the mother of three children and the guardian of my 50-year-old retarded sister. Until faced with an abortion [June 27], few women can say

with certainty what they would do. For those of us who subscribe to God's will, so be it. For those of us who simply cannot handle it, so be it. But let the decision be ours.

Joan Graham
Bloomfield Hills, Mich.

With the decision that it is a woman's right to choose whether she wants an abortion, the Supreme Court has given women permission to continue to kill the unborn within their wombs.

Philomena Haas
7/18/83 *Denver*

Sally's Sacrifice?

As a woman, I felt a special pride when I watched Sally Ride aboard *Challenger* [July 4]. But why couldn't she accept the flowers? Why didn't she carry lipstick or makeup? Now that women can do anything men can do, must they sacrifice being women?

Lynn Hall
7/25/83 *Anderson, Ind.*

Sally Ride, first American woman astronaut

AIDS Crisis

Your article on disease control was fascinating, and your depiction of the AIDS crisis sensitively written. More frightening than the disease are the attitudes of some people in the mainstream of society. Comments like those of the Rev. Greg Dixon, who warns that America will be destroyed if homosexuals are not stopped, present a much greater threat to our tradition than the infection caused by any virus or organism.

Martin J. McGlynn
7/25/83 *Dedham, Mass.*

Ladies' Day

I assume that the Essay "Women Are Getting Out of Hand" [July 18] was written in jest. However, I must

respond to your closing comments: "Clearly the future belongs to women." With the ERA not passed, with women being paid only 59¢ for every dollar that men earn, and with reproductive freedom still threatened, it is hardly assured that "the future belongs to women."

Catherine Oliver
Pittsford, N.Y.

One does not have to be a sociologist or a psychologist to realize that men have made a shambles of this world. So why not give the ladies a chance, despite Anne Burford and Indira Gandhi?

Robert G. Arthur
8/8/83 *Kings Park, N.Y.*

Japan Today

As an American who has lived in Japan for four years, I have observed that the reason Japan functions so well is that the Japanese try very hard to make it work. They are extremely honest and have an insatiable curiosity about the world. Although America was built on the dream of a hard-working, free-enterprise system, most Americans today would rather work less, blame others more, and pack a gun to protect what they have left. It is time that Americans went back to making products with the kind of spirit and concern for quality that America used to stand for.

Garry Bassin
Tokyo

I have often wondered how Japan rose to world-power status after it was leveled in World War II. Your issue makes it clear: people make a country. Unfortunately, we in the Philippines lack that feeling of nationhood with which the Japanese are blessed.

Wilfredo G. Villanueva
8/22/83 *Manila*

Black Power

Congratulations on your coverage of Jessie Jackson and his attempt to mobilize black voters for the presidential election of 1984 [Aug. 22]. Jackson represents a rallying point for all voters disillusioned with the status quo of American politics. His dedication to fulfilling the dreams of Martin Luther King Jr. should remind Americans of their obligation to ensure equality of representation for everyone, regardless of color or station in life.

Bill Graves
9/12/83 *Brady, Texas*

Murder in Manila

I am sickened by the assassination of Benigno Aquino [Sept. 5]. In all the furor over human rights in Afghanistan, Iran, El Salvador and Soviet-bloc countries, the U.S. has consistently overlooked the atrocities committed in the Philippines. Now is the time to

Cast members of *Dynasty*, a steamy prime-time serial

Stars from *The A-Team*, an adventure-comedy show

take a close look at what is happening there and with whom we are allying ourselves.

Joann Cole
9/26/83 *Newport Beach, Calif.*

Death Flight

Even bearing in mind the extenuating factors that directed the judgment of the Soviet pilot to down the Korean passenger plane, one must still be appalled by the conscienceless response and by the inhuman and dehumanizing brutality of the system that conditioned him.

Violet S. Tartell
Durham, N.C.

What killed 269 innocent people was hatred. Hatred between two political superpowers who, I fear, will never understand each other.

David Francis
10/3/83 *Greenbrae, Calif.*

Winning the Cup

With its stunning victory in the America's Cup races [Oct. 3], Australia has again surfaced in the sports world. I was getting worried about the Aussies after not seeing them mentioned in the coverage of tennis playoffs and auto racing

Rohan Campbell Goodsir
10/24/83 *Charleston, S.C.*

60th Anniversary

For some of us, your special anniversary issue could be called "This Is Your Life." The magazine will become a grand textbook of contemporary history.

J. Calvin Koonts
Professor, Erskine College
10/24/83 *Due West, S.C.*

Reaching 60

Your entire 60th anniversary issue is a masterpiece of condensation and analysis, but the Essay "What Really Mattered" is especially poignant and thought-provoking. One sentence, in particular, tells it all: "In the realm of politics, had the world been inspired by the idea of justice rather than freedom, it might look a good deal healthier."

Indeed, freedom, for all its preciousness and sublime connotations, is often a dubious blessing, if not an outright curse. The Bible celebrates freedom with the liberation of the Israelite slaves. But it also emphatically teaches that for man to survive, law and the administration of justice must be placed above freedom.

Elijah J. Schochet
Rabbi, Congregation Beth Kodesh
10/31/83 *Canoga Park, Calif.*

Unbiased Bible

I have just read your article "O God Our [Mother and] Father" [Oct. 24]. I am a liberated woman, yet I have never been offended by the sexism in the Bible or in any other literature from an earlier period. I question the rewriting of religious books to suit the ideas put forth by contemporary society. Future generations may find something just as distasteful in the new National Council of Churches edition and further revise it. Somewhere down the road the Bible may cease to be recognizable.

Karen A. Cole
11/14/83 *Chattanooga, Tenn.*

Hungry and Homeless

The 2 million homeless Americans [Dec. 19] are the public's responsibility. The problem cannot be solved simply with free food and shelter. We need a federal program that will offer the homeless work, thus giving them hope for the future and respect for themselves.

Joetta Keene
1/9/84 *Fort Worth*

Men of the Year

TIME's Men of the Year [Jan. 2] choices are appropriate. Ronald Reagan and Yuri Andropov have not only profoundly affected the news of this year but will undoubtedly have an impact on the news of next year and probably for many years to come. Depicting them back to back implies a continuity for catastrophe. Face to face would imply communication, which could reap a harvest of home for peace on earth to men of good will.

Charles T. Sweeny
Quincy, Mass.

In the most crucial time in the world's history, when our hopes for the future of mankind are at stake, TIME's choices for Men of the Year are the men most responsible for proliferation of arms and increased global tensions.

Bill Godin
Yale Norwick
1/16/84 *Minneapolis*

Children's Cholesterol

As an editor, I have seldom seen a more knowledgeable or valuable handling of an important theme than your article on cholesterol [March 26]. This is public service as one might always wish it. A recent study of schoolchildren in New York and Los Angeles shows that their cholesterol levels are about 35% higher than they ought to be. This is when the time bomb begins to click.

Norman Cousins
U.C.L.A. School of Medicine
5/7/84 *Los Angeles*

Reagan in China

President Reagan's visit to the People's Republic of China [May 7] proves once again that we need not see eye to eye in order to walk hand in hand.

(The Rev.) Larry N. Lorenzoni
5/28/84 *San Francisco*

Movies

From the silent antics of Chaplin's little tramp to the amazing technological universe of *Star Wars*, TIME has watched and commented on movies, Hollywood, the stars. Any subject—an overgrown gorilla, a belle named Scarlett O'Hara, a lost extraterrestrial—can mean gold for the moviemaker. The reviewer considers what shade of gray best describes the motion picture. But when the issue is entertainment, everyone has an opinion.

Surprised

I am surprised that your paper deems it necessary to mention the engagement and marriage of Fatty Arbuckle. You should leave that for your Gum Chewers' Sheets that you refer to so often.

Oliver Kecthtson
Washington, D.C.
3/9/25

From the Virgin Islands

Does your correspondent, Oliver Kecthtson, know anything about Fatty Arbuckle that causes him, in your issue of Mar. 9, P. 27, to sneer at the mention of his marriage as a news item? If he feels that all mention of that unfortunate victim of a series of circumstances over which he had absolutely no control, should damn a man who, previously to his persecution in San Francisco, made the cleanest pictures the screen ever displayed, he should have had my privilege, that of having him, as I did, as a guest of the hotel (The Plaza in San Francisco) of which I was one of the associated managers during his three trials, and the gentleman would not be so ready with his slurs.

I not only enjoyed his friendship but followed his trials day by day, and not one scintilla of evidence was introduced to show him guilty, a fact agreed upon by both District Attorney Brady and the judges before which he appeared.

Joseph Reynolds
St. Thomas
4/20/25 *Virgin Islands*

Makes a Suggestion

May I make a suggestion for your cinema department? I would appreciate it very much if you would indicate when a cinema production had been made from a novel. For example, some time ago you ran a review of a film entitled *I Want My Man*. You never suggested where it came from and, had I not met Mr. Struthers Burt personally and learned the facts from him, I should never have known that it was taken from his novel *The Interpreter's House*. In the issue of June 15, Page 13, you review the film *I'll Show You the Town*. I presume that that had been made from Elmer Davis' book by the same name, but you do not suggest that it was.

When one has read a certain novel, he may be interested in seeing a film made from that particular tale; but, as the title is often changed, how is he going to learn the facts unless you give them? I depend upon your column for all the information I have of the cinema world . . .

I am living abroad, and depend on TIME for my knowledge of American events. TIME and green celluloid eye shades are the only things I have to import from America.

Dale Carnegie
Paris, France
7/27/25

Subscriber Carnegie speaks well. Wherever possible TIME will follow out his suggestion. But it is not always possible: A) often the program fails to indicate from what novel the movie came, B) often the cinematized plot has little-or-nothing in common with the novel.—ED.

Hard on Managers

Why have such a crepe-hanger review your CINEMA? Or if this must be, why not change the heading to VINEGA(R)? The two words have letters only in common, and the result is not at all in keeping with your usual attitude. I have seen many of the "New Pictures" written up in your issue of Dec. 26, and from the reactions of the audiences on those occasions who, after all, are the ones to be pleased, it would seem that your reviewer is entirely out of line with public opinion. Don't you think it rather hard on the theatre managers, who book their plays far in

Former U.S. marshal turned cowboy, Tom Mix starred in more than 400 westerns. Right, 1939 movie starring Betty Grable, soon to become World War II soldiers' sweetheart

Singer Al Jolson starred in this first-ever "talkie" in 1927

advance, to give the pictures negative advertising, which no doubt influences many to stay away from an evening's enjoyment for them. . . .

Don't bother to look for my name on your list of subscribers as it isn't there, for I am continually on the move and find it much easier to pick one up somewhere each week, than to bother trying to have one trail me, but I haven't missed reading one in ages, and don't intend to.

Robert Wilmer
1/9/28   *Warrington, Fla.*
*Newsstand buyer Wilmer's criticism is sound, will be heeded.—*ED.

Mr. Menjou

In a recent issue of TIME in your Cinema column you print, "Those who knew Adolphe Menjou when he was a waiter in a Cleveland chop house. . . ." If facts are of any interest to your valuable publication I shall be very happy to furnish a complete history of my life. Although I have followed a number of professions, I have up to the present never been a waiter in real life.

Also, further your writer continues, "Two years ago, his entertainment was impeccable. Since then his expression has taken on a tired, wooden, what-does-it-matter manner." I wonder if the writer has seen *Service for Ladies, Gentleman of Paris, Serenade,* all made within the past year.

Adolphe Menjou
7/9/28   *Los Angeles, Calif.*
P.S. I am an original subscriber to TIME.
Time erred. The father of Original Subscriber Menjou was the owner of a Cleveland chop house on Prospect Street, famed for its beer; young Adolphe, home from Cornell University, helped in the management, greeted customers, but donned no waiter's costume Yet, Adolphe Menjou, by his cinema roles, has done more than any man alive to glorify the profession of waiters, both plain and head. . . . With the exception of two brilliant scenes, Mr. Menjou's recent films have not been up to the high standards of his earlier ones (such as A Woman of Paris). *Let Mr. Menjou return to those standards, as easily as he sets the standards of a cosmopolitan gentleman who is at home in three languages (English, French, German).—*ED.

Gum Chewers

I have noticed in recent issues of TIME that moving picture followers are referred to as "the gum-chewing public" and "gum-chewers."

This may be a very witty expression and evidently is intended to convey that those who patronize picture shows are an uncouth or blatant lot. It has been my observation that all classes attend the "movies" and that many of these theaters provide an entertainment which can well be enjoyed by a person of at least the average intelligence. It may be that even your wise-cracking

Made in 1936, *Stowaway* was eight-year-old Shirley Temple's 20th film

This 1934 version of *Don Juan* starred Douglas Fairbanks Sr. as the legendary lover

theatrical writer is not so *much* above the average.

R. L. Lyons
8/27/28   *Omaha, Neb.*
Never did TIME *say that all cinemaddicts are gum chewers.—*ED.

Ear v. Eye

It has occurred to me that the following astonishing statement by Professor Walter B. Pitkin of the Columbia School of Journalism, who is co-author of *A Million and One Nights,* a history of motion pictures, deserves editorial comment:

"We hereby file our official forecast on the moral effect of the talkies. We assert that the ear is more moral than the eye. And we predict that the talkies will uplift the movies more than all reformers ever can."

This is quoted from the April issue of *Children, The Parents' Magazine.*

George J. Hecht
Publisher
The Parents' Magazine
4/15/29   *New York City*
*One year from now, let Publisher Hecht report such evidence as may have been discovered to prove Forecaster Pitkin right or wrong.—*ED.

Mix

In reading your magazine of April 29, I note on page 20 under the caption "*Life,* Tom Mix last week agreed to quit cinema and work for the 101 Ranch Wild West Show for the rest of his career. Alleged inducement: $15,000 per week."

Mr. Tom Mix has a signed contract with the Sells Floto Circus Company

for his services starting on May 26 and lasting—I hope forever. . . .

Zack Terrell
General Manager
Sells Floto Circus
5/20/29   *Pittsburg, Pa.*
*Mr. Mix was last week indicted by the Federal grand jury in Los Angeles charged with trying to defraud the U.S. of $175,967.65 in income taxes. He, performing in Minneapolis, said time would prove him innocent.—*ED.

"Simply ———"

I beg to advise that your cinema reviews are simply ———.* Two cases in point appear in TIME. Aug. 12. The one having to do with *Street Girl* would have kept me away from that picture. The one about *The Single Standard* would have fortified me in my hour of waiting to get into the Capitol to see it. The two pictures merited just the opposite treatment. *Street Girl* was splendid entertainment, the acting capable and mature. The other could fix the attention only of one who had never been places, who was attracted by the liquefaction of Garbo's garments. I felt like a chump for standing as aforesaid.

Robert Emmet Connelly
8/26/29   *New York City*
*Do other readers agree? Disagree?—*ED.

*Unpleasant word deleted.

How Hell's Angels

Please tell an interested subscriber the technical device used in *Hell's*

Angels in the scene in which the airplane cut into the Zeppelin [June 29]. I understand no models were used. Is this correct? If so how did the pilot of the plane get out in time?

Your reply would help settle one of those irksome controversies that for principle's sake men are loth to leave unsettled.

M. Kosofsky
3/11/30　　　*New York City*
Caddo Co., the producers, insist no models were used. The Zeppelin was a dirigible one-half the size of the Los Angeles, *constructed in Hollywood under the direction of Dr. Karl Arnheim formerly of the German Zeppelin works. The pilot of the airplane diving into the Zeppelin, jumped, parachuted, escaped with his life.—Ed.*

Fairbanks Classics

We note with regret the announcement of the retirement from the screen of one of the best exponents of fine clean sportsmanship before the public in the last ten years.

Douglas Fairbanks in his work has always been not only delightfully entertaining, but we fear the consummate grace and artistry of the man has not been fully acknowledged by the Press.

Let others destroy their screen efforts if they will, we would like the Fairbanks Classics preserved.

T. E. Creigh
8/17/31　　　*Scarborough, Me.*
Letters from readers who feel as Reader Creigh will be forwarded to Cinemactor Fairbanks.—Ed.

Pickler, Assassin

May I take this occasion to come to TIME's defense and to differ with Janet Lindsay Pollock in her letter concerning Fredric (Bickel) March that is published in the Feb. 20 issue of TIME. TIME states in its Nov. 28 issue, "Fredric March would have been vastly surprised a dozen years ago had anyone predicted that he would ever receive . . . the Academy's Approval."

I knew Fredric Bickel at the University of Wisconsin. I was in some of the same college shows with him. In particular do I recall his appearance with Charles Carpenter in a Union Vodvil sketch in 1920 called, "Carpenter & Bickel, the gloom Picklers" and in 1919 in an act with "Chuck" Carpenter in which they termed themselves, "Assassins of Sorrow." From the titles you can guess that they were comedians.

Through all of these performances the thing that I remember distinctly is the extreme nervousness and stage fright of Fredric Bickel. Back stage before, during, and after each performance Fredric drank copious draughts of ice water and during dress rehearsal required considerable prompting from his partner. Fredric Bickel was always a modest and sensible sort of person; hence, I am led to agree with TIME that twelve years ago he would have been vastly surprised. . . .

Howard ("Sparks") Dodge
3/6/33　　　*Chicago, Ill.*

Kay Francis' "Tomorrow"

Having received from five separate sources the following clipping from TIME of Jan. 23, with the query "Is this true?" I write my comments to you for whatever correction the statement may need. The statement:

"In Hollywood, Calif., cinema sound engineers listed ten words barred from cinemas: Cohesion, distilling, aluminum, catastrophe, seething, felicitations, nemesis, procrastination, hippopotamus, and rural. Reason: most film actors hiss or swallow them."

This is a rather fantastic list, and they may be barred from the scripts of some studios. Most of them I have heard in one or another of our recent pictures with a fair accuracy of reproduction. Sound apparatus nowadays records just what is spoken in the way it is spoken with a high average of measured accuracy, and individual words are no difficulty. However, often adjustments of various kinds have to be made to counteract individual peculiarities of voice or inflection. On our own lot: George Arliss' sibilants are especially strong. Richard Barthelmess' vowels have a tubby-throaty effect. When Kay Francis says tomowow, wobber, twouble, however, we must record it that way.

Frederic MacAlpin
Recording Dept.
Warner-First National Studios
5/8/33　　　*North Hollywood, Calif.*

Sniveling Barrymore

We wish to protest most vigorously against the sentence in your Feb. 19 review of the cinema *Carolina*, wherein you say: ". . . Lionel Barrymore plays a sniveling old Confederate veteran."

For your information, sir, we would have you know that there were no "sniveling" Confederate veterans. With more perspicacity you might have said, "The sniveling Lionel Barrymore played a Confederate veteran."

Nash Burger Jr.
W. B. Hamilton Jr.
3/12/34　　　*Jackson, Miss., C.S.A.*

Slipping Barrymore

Reference made to Columbia's row of hits needs some correction [Nov. 12].

You included *Twentieth Century* as one of the trio. I think Columbia would rather substitute *Lady for a Day* for the John Barrymore picture.

Twentieth Century was not even a good grosser. Even Columbia's luck for

Lionel Barrymore played the title role in *Rasputin and the Empress* **, 1932, with Brother John and Sister Ethel in other lead roles**

Shanghai **, made in 1935 with an international cast of movie actors**

taking slipping stars and rebuilding them couldn't affect Barrymore's box office ability. Barrymore may remain a starring figure, but as far as the box office is concerned, he has never proved the sensation most people think they believe he is.

Herbert M. Miller
Managing Editor
Jay Emanuel Publications
12/3/34   *Philadelphia, Pa.*

$30,000 Drop

In your review of *The Lives of a Bengal Lancer* [Jan. 21] you report that most of the picture was filmed on location within 50 miles of Hollywood.

True, some shots were taken at Chatsworth within the radius given. But for two weeks this mountain town [200 mi. from Hollywood] was overrun with synthetic Bengalese, an increase of 33⅓% in population. Paramount dropped $30,000 of the million and a half here, gave most their first glimpse of an elephant, almost succeeded in driving a few of our topers into taking the pledge. My congregation upped one, a gloriously illuminated grip-man, one of eight rewarded with a gallon-of-whiskey bonus by the director for working all Saturday night.

. . . If your readers will look up the company street they will glimpse the top of the U.S., Mt. Whitney. Despite your account, Whitney is not yet within the Los Angeles city limits, nor has it gone Hollywood.

(Rev.) John J. Crowley
Santa Rosa Church
2/18/35   *Lone Pine, Calif.*
P.S. *Oil for the Lamps of China* is on location here today with four camels. I may get my convivial sheep into dry pastures yet.

"It Must Continue"

While exhilarated from the world première of *The March of Time* on the screen, I want to commend you for the finest historical drama I have seen depicted in movies.

It had all the verve, compactness and stimulus of your printed page and radio broadcasts, and above both it had the thrilling appeal of seeing history march on. The Japanese section was superb.

Showing here with *David Copperfield* in its second week, I was glad to again see that great movie in order to see *The March of Time*. It must continue.

Charles Edward Thomas
2/18/35   *Indianapolis, Ind.*

Permission to Gloat

Many thanks for your splendid reviews of our pictures *Les Miserables* and *Cardinal Richelieu* [April 29]. However, I must call to your attention one incorrect observation: Producer Zanuck came to New York to gloat over the success of *Les Miserables* and *Richelieu*. Facts are as follows: Producer Zanuck came to New York before either picture had opened to quiver and tremble and hope that the public and press would permit him to gloat. Strangely enough public and press were unanimous, thank Heaven. Otherwise this telegram would not have been sent, at least not from this magnificent, restful, awe-inspiring address.

Darryl Zanuck
5/20/35   *Ketchikan, Alaska*

Garbo's Feet

Why is there such a to-do about the size of Greta Garbo's feet [June 17]?

Almost every woman I know wears a shoe size between six and eight. I could name 10 personable young women, average height and slender, whose feet couldn't be fitted in less than a six and a half. Even a 5-ft., 90-pounder wears size five.

I'd like to know what size feet the rest of the movie queens totter around on if "7AA" is considered so unusual.

Elizabeth F. Gearheart
7/8/35   *Shaker Heights, Ohio*
*At least one film actress, Binnie Barnes, is credited with a larger shoe than Greta Garbo's—7½AA. A cursory survey of other foot sizes produces the following: Claire Dodd 7AAA, Helen Vinson 7AA, Joan Blondell 6C, Marion Davies 6B, Carole Lombard 5½A, Norma Shearer 5½A, Jean Harlow 3½C.—*Ed.

Harlow

What a shock it was to receive TIME, Aug. 19, and find Jean Harlow's picture (dis)gracing the front cover. I thought TIME was a bit selective in choosing subjects for their cover but this instance proves me wrong. From the vast numbers of Hollywood stars from which to choose, surely you could have done better than this. . . .

Verna L. Freeman
9/2/35   *Rahway, N.J.*

Astaire's Discoverer

Your excellent cinema columnist trod on a sensitive spot and misled the public in the article on Fred Astaire [Sept. 9]. Mr. Astaire was established on the screen in *Flying Down to Rio,* for which picture I brought him to Hollywood and teamed him with Ginger Rogers.

Owing to a slight delay in getting the picture started, he was farmed out to MGM, purely for economical reasons and not because of any lack of esteem on our part for him. The few feet accorded his two feet in *Dancing Lady* went practically unnoticed, whereas in *Flying Down to Rio* he was acclaimed by public and reviewers alike all over the world.

I grabbed him as a "sleeper" the minute I saw his first test from New York and practically used the megaphone to tell everyone in Hollywood that here was the next big male draw in pictures. . . .

Mr. Merian C. Cooper, then executive producer on the lot, also saw Astaire's possibilities. Mr. Astaire will be

glad to tell you that I accurately predicted to him in New York, before he ever came out here, what his future in pictures would be.

Louis Brock
Author and producer of
Flying Down to Rio
9/30/35   *Beverly Hills, Calif.*

Miss MacDonald's Teeth

. . . I am quite put out by your review of MGM's *San Francisco* [July 6].

[*Said* TIME: "*San Francisco (Metro-Goldwyn-Mayer) offers cinemaddicts views of two unusual phenomena: the San Francisco earthquake and Jeanette MacDonald acting with her teeth. . . . The picture is a shrewd compendium of romance and catastrophe. . . ."—*Ed.]

That you make much of Jeanette MacDonald's acting with her teeth is unjust. . . . What strikes me as peculiarly outstanding is that you have failed to remark on Miss MacDonald's acting with her eyes. That love scene in Blackie Norton's office is one of the most genuine I have ever seen on the screen. . . .

Harry Farnham Meadow
7/27/36   *New Haven, Conn.*

Not with Mirrors

TIME has made history right in broad daylight by erring in its otherwise excellent review of my new picture *History is Made at Night* [March 29]. What you term the best shot in the picture was not made with glass on a split screen, but was actually an iceberg constructed on one of our largest sets and then combined by a special technical process with the view of men on the bridge of a full-sized ship which was also built especially for the picture. Would appreciate publication of this

155

correction since the current tell-all-the-technical-secrets trend in motion picture reporting tends to convince the public that every unique, unusual scene is done with miniatures or mirrors, when, as a matter of fact, the studios are expending huge sums of money to create authentic scenes whenever possible.

Walter Wanger
4/12/37 *Los Angeles, Calif.*
United Artists' Manhattan office, whence came TIME's information, should synchronize with its Hollywood office when explaining U.A.'s cinematographic wonders.—ED.

"Current & Choice"

We like your new feature, "Current & Choice." We have so often in the past not been sure whether you thought a picture worth going to or not. We hope that this feature will be continued. We keep the Cinema section for reference and like your comment, but we will appreciate it if you continue the rating of the best pictures.

Earl D. Irick
6/21/37 *Lancaster, Ohio*

Program Credit

Tst, tst. Broderick Crawford's shoes in *Of Mice and Men* [Dec. 6] have a 4½-in. build-up, not 4 in., as reported. I ought to know—I made them. In street shoes Crawford stands 6 ft. 1½ in., in my shoes (Trademark "Staturaid" patent pending) he's a 6½ footer.

Incidentally, this was only the second theatrical order I executed and with that build-up you can't expect inconspicuousness. My regular customers, business and professional people (average sales 200 pairs a month), generally need only 1½ to 2 inches, and I think you'd need a slide rule to tell it wasn't the usual shoe. From 75% to 80% of my business is done by mail; a good proportion of these deliveries go to small cities and towns, in plain addressed wrappers and general delivery.

Doesn't a fellow get program credit anymore?

Joseph Burger
1/3/38 *New York City*
Shoe-Builder Burger received over a column program credit in the Oct. 23 issue of the New Yorker.—ED.

Index

TIME's news is so far-reaching that I have been rather astonished to find you have omitted to state the sad fact that our benighted, bigoted—and therefore backward—province of Quebec has banned the picture *Zola*.

B. Taylor
1/17/38 *Quebec, Canada*
Warner Brothers' The Life of Emile Zola, which was voted best film of the year by U.S. critics, is forbidden in Catholic Quebec because all of Emile Zola's works are on the famed Catholic Index of Banned Books.—ED.

Olivia de Havilland and Errol Flynn

Ginger Rogers and Fred Astaire

Johnny Weissmuller and Maureen O'Sullivan

Temple & Life

While your comments on Shirley Temple may perhaps be fair from your point of view, may I mention that if your almost savage criticisms should have any effect on her career, you would be robbing all the little girls of the one character they can really enjoy. There are pictures for adults and boys galore—but for little girls there are practically none, save Shirley Temple's and Walt Disney's. . . .

Little girls from the time they are conscious of their own personalities want to be "glamorous." . . . As boys identify themselves with daring heroes, girls identify themselves with the rescued heroine. Life as portrayed by Shirley Temple is life as it is known by most little girls. . . .

So please realize that while sophisticates go to the movies and should have their tastes catered to, there are also many nice little girls, and many women who can see in Shirley Temple's portrayal of life, a life you know nothing of—but life as they know it. . . .

Mrs. Ralph E. Glayd
5/9/38 *Plainfield, Mass.*

First Love

The statistical critic who reported on the cinema *Love Finds Andy Hardy* [Aug. 8] must have been an insurance agent, surely is a sourpuss.

Was TIME's critic never in love a first time? Actor Rooney didn't overemphasize a youth's first love one bit. Take it from me, I know.

D. F. B. II
8/22/38 *Dayton, Ohio*

Favorite Actor

Is Walter Huston the President's favorite actor—or have more vital matters prevented his attendance at the theatre—or does he care little for the theatre?

For a good tonic, I respectfully suggest that President Roosevelt go to see "quick-silvered," electric Tallulah Bankhead when he wants complete relaxation. Miss Bankhead has the faculty to make you forget *everything*, except what is transpiring on the stage

Calder B. Vaughan
A Roosevelt Admirer
11/14/38 *Chicago, Ill.*
No ardent theatre-goer, Franklin Roosevelt prefers to watch movies at the White House. He has never said that Walter Huston is his favorite actor; he has never seen Actress Tallulah Bankhead, the daughter of his Speaker of the House, on the stage, but has met her at a White House reception.—ED.

Jesse James's Horse

We are grateful that TIME has seen fit to publicize the cruelty inflicted on animals in making the picture *Jesse James* [Feb. 6]. So many pictures are being shown in which horses are thrown violently to the ground; animals are made to fight furious battles, which they would never do in the wilds, and other cruel acts are depicted that it is time the motion picture industry was made to understand that such acts are contrary to public opinion. . . .

Marie Rosato
Secretary
Louisiana State Society for the Prevention of Cruelty to Animals
2/20/39 *New Orleans, La.*

Shouting Sex

After all—dear sophisticated TIME—Mr. Errol Flynn is one of those rare souls, who does not have to act, to have the feminine population positively swooning at his feet! All he has to do is—be Errol Flynn—he simply shouts masculine appeal so shame on your severe criticism of *The Private Lives of Elizabeth & Essex* [Nov. 13]. Accent on sex—Errol Flynn.

Olivia Hathaway
12/11/39   *Dayton, Ohio*
TIME's Cinema Editor is in some ways hard of hearing.—ED.

Boyer's Pate

Under picture of Charles Boyer and wife, TIME says: "Mrs. Boyer is quite adequate." Is Mr. Boyer's hair adequate? Did he leave it "somewhere in France," or has trick Hollywood photography been used on us poor fans all these years?

Mrs. Levis Hall Jr.
Sherman, Tex.

Might as well beat the ladies to this one. Is Charles Boyer as bald as your cut on p. 60, TIME, Dec. 4, would have us movie fans believe?

Kerwin Hoover
12/25/39   *International Falls, Minn.*
Actor Boyer is bald halfway back on top. He wears a toupee (hairpiece or divot in Hollywood) for cinema and most public appearances.—ED.

Dodge City Showdown

In the last issue of your magazine in that part dealing wih the première of *Gone With the Wind* at Atlanta, Ga. recently you report the mayor of Atlanta as cautioning the people of the city not to tear the clothing off of the movie stars as was done at the première of *Dodge City*. A letter has been dispatched to the mayor requesting him to prove his statement or publicly retract and apologize; in other words, "to put up or shut up."

Since reading that extraordinary disclosure this organization has made inquiries of newspapermen, business men, and others associated with the première here last spring, and not a single person can recall a single incident of the sort reported by the mayor. Of course, the stars may have been pushed around some. . . .

This great city needs no defending.

James A. Williams
The Dodge City
Junior Chamber of Commerce
1/15/40   *Dodge City, Kansas*

Wrath

Do TIME's editors consider their cinema critic an accredited judge of books as well? And does TIME's book reviewer agree with his associate's opinion of John Steinbeck's *Grapes of Wrath* as a "so-so book" of "phony pathos"? I don't.

Guild Copeland
3/4/40   *Boston, Mass.*

Of John Steinbeck's The Grapes of Wrath, TIME's book reviewer said: "It is Steinbeck's best novel . . . one of the most impassioned and exciting books of the year . . . Steinbeck is a writer, still, of great promise."—ED.

Pistillate West

Your review of *My Little Chicadee* [Feb. 26] reads: "highly staminate Flower Belle, Mae West. . . ."

. . . Dull as the sex-life of flowers may be, they still distinguish between stamens and pistils, and the stamens are indubitably masculine.

Laura B. Alexander
3/18/40   *Portland, Me.*

Plus Fours

I take violent exception to a sentence in a letter published in your Jan. 20 issue, signed A. G. Ellis, M.D.: "First, how could anyone be elegant in a pair of those inelegant, nondescript outmoded golf trousers?" Nondescript, inelegant, outmoded indeed!!! Where has Dr. Ellis been all his life? I know a few who look elegant in them, H.R.H. the Duke of Windsor, Jimmy McLarnin, MacDonald Smith, Gene Markey, and several million English golfers and hikers. I personally possess 15 suits with golf trousers and wear them in Hollywood, at every appropriate occasion.

Adolphe Menjou
2/17/41   *Palm Springs, Calif.*

Menjou's Dither

Civilization totters perilously on the brink of destruction while men of valor and conscience are giving their "sweat, blood and tears" to sustain it!

Adolphe Menjou, basking in the radiant sunshine at Palm Springs, Calif., is in a dither [Feb. 17]! Some gentlemen dared to say plus fours were inelegant! Menjou has 15 suits! Therefore he takes not simple but "violent exception" to the statement!

Isn't his unhappy plight a shocking pity? . . .

Elvira Dunn
3/10/41   *Los Angeles, Calif.*
Everybody can't fight the war all the time.—ED.

Un-Hollywood

Your excellent Gary Cooper story in the March 3 issue seems marred by one statement, slightly inconsistent with the unaffected picture otherwise created, that he lives in "an elaborate white Georgian mansion." This statement . . . is exactly 75% wrong. The house is white.

Mr. Cooper's requirements when he first came to me were that the house be unpretentious, Bermudian and un-Hollywood. Lest liberal-minded fans be alienated by visions of Blenheim or Buckingham Palace, I enclose a photograph.

Harvey Stevenson
Architect
3/24/41   *New York City*
TIME bows to Architect Stevenson, who designed Gary Cooper's house.—ED.

"Away He Went"

You may be interested in a discrepancy in your story of Gary Cooper's life [March 3].

You say he took a job in Los Angeles selling electric signs and got fired for not selling any. This is not true. I know because Gary worked for me. He did not get fired . . . He was selling ads on theatre curtains which simulated electric signs.

Clark Gable and Vivien Leigh star in *Gone with the Wind*, 1939

The last time I saw Gary was on the old studio steps. It was Saturday afternoon. He wanted to know how he could get $10. I told him to go down to Santa Monica and collect the customary $10 deposit on an ad he had sold to a washing machine company. This $10 was his commission. Away he went. I have never seen him since except on the screen. I don't believe I have ever missed one of his pictures.

John Slattery
3/31/41 *Los Angeles, Calif.*

Shindig Defended

Scallions and resounding boos to TIME's reporter who covered the Academy Awards Dinner [March 10]. Perhaps he didn't get enough free drinks. Perhaps he wasn't introduced to Dorothy Lamour. Perhaps he wasn't there.

I attended the dinner. I would like to correct a few of the misstatements on behalf of the motion-picture group which for years has been unjustly maligned, criticized, misunderstood. . . .

1) Cinewigs did *not* "alcoholically splurge for a couple of hours . . ." There was far less alcoholic consumption per capita on that occasion than at any other representative American gathering.

2) David Selznick did *not* "pant." He was sincerely thrilled at his award.

3) Ginger Rogers did *not* "scream." She was so affected, her voice was scarcely audible.

4) There was no "dog-show din." What TIME's misguided reporter heard was a genuinely enthusiastic acclaim of the year's best actress.

5) Ginger Rogers did *not* "gush a tribute to her mother." She gave a heartwarmingly real and simple word of appreciation and homage to her nearest and dearest, which moistened the eyes of the toughest audience in the world. . . .

Dorothy Howell
3/31/41 *Beverly Hills, Calif.*
TIME's reporter was there, he already knew Dorothy Lamour, and he claims

he had no drinks. Far from being the "toughest audience" in the world, Hollywood's cinema people are among the tenderest. Living and working in a medium copiously suffused with sentimental hokum, it would be strange if they weren't.—ED.

That Hayworth-Petty Cover

Shame on TIME for distinguishing Petty's indecent vulgar distortions of female form by cover publication. Miss Hayworth's photograph surely sufficient. Let such crudeness stay in advertising world where sane people can ignore it. . . .

Professor Thomas E. Cassidy
St. Johns University
11/24/41 *Collegeville, Minn.*

Right Guy Rooney

I noticed in the Cinema section of TIME for Jan. 19 a story concerning the marriage of Mickey Rooney. Mickey was here in this hospital ward twice to see a personal friend. Both times he went through the ward with his wife, trying to cheer the fellows up. . . .

I must say that morale was sadly lacking in that ward, since it is a fracture ward. Mickey and Ava both gave unselfishly of their time and energy to cheer us up. I have a broken ankle. Mickey and his wife sat on my bed and talked to me and autographed my cast. . . . He let the fellows who could walk take pictures of him and drive his car. I think that . . . Mickey should be given proper credit for a very noble deed. . . . He is a right guy in Army talk. So please give him credit for coming here.

Phillip White
Private, Company G.
1st Medical Regiment
2/16/42 *Fort Ord, Calif.*
Take it away, Mickey.—ED.

King Leer?

Considering Ernest Baker's admirably characteristic portrait of Come-

dian Bob Hope [Sept. 20], I am disappointed in the apparent waning of your subcaptioning potency.

A TIMElier subcaption: King Leer.

Lawrence Defoy
10/11/43 *Rochester, N.Y.*

For Ten-Year-Olds

Your article concerning the movies for men overseas [March 6] hit the nail right on the head. The pictures we've had here, for the most part, would suit the taste of a ten-year-old, or would fit in beautifully in some home for the aged.

What we want out here are musicals, preferably in prewar settings, because it gripes us no end to see some dashing young bum in an Army uniform surrounded by beauteous blondes, fighting the battle of "Celluloid."

The first question heard in our quarters after we knock off work is, "What's the movie tonight?" and usually, the reply is: "It stinks." If we don't go to the movies, we just sit around and go "hut-crazy," so we really appreciated TIME giving us a swell plug. . . .

(Sk2/c) Paul E. King
c/o Postmaster
4/10/44 *San Francisco*

G.I.'s *v.* Hollywood

Exploiting the present world tragedy, Hollywood has manufactured a series of war pictures that makes soldiers overseas practically retch, and causes even entertainment-hungry troops to file out of movies before a picture ends, expressing their disgust and scorn with jeers and boos and very much-to-the-point one-word descriptions. They have just "seen themselves" portrayed on the screen à la Hollywood's idiotic hoopla. Some marcelled hero with rouged lips and a do-or-die voice has just charged a Jap battalion with six grenades clenched between his Pepsodent-perfect molars, a Tommy gun in each hand and enough knives and bay-

onets stucks in his belt to start a hardware store; he has not only wiped out the battalion singlehanded, and held the bridge that saved his division from annihilation, but he killed the last 180 Japanese with his well-manicured bare hands, and has stopped twice in battle to make a five-minute oration on the Four Freedoms.

Two recent "war pictures" dealing with soldiers in training camps, at home and in U.S.O. clubs have portrayed the average American soldier in such a ridiculous manner as to arouse the derision of other Allied soldiers present and cause Americans acute embarrassment.

(Serviceman's name withheld)
c/o Postmaster
9/11/44 *New York City*

Largesse in Hollywood

In its Jan. 15 issue, TIME printed a statement by a professional campaign director for charity and other funds, reflecting on Hollywood's generosity. We in Hollywood's organized charity effort do not know of any contact he has had with this industry in any fund-raising effort.

Truth is that the 25,000 employees of the motion-picture industry in Hollywood give more per capita in approved charity campaigns—and more closely approach 100% participation—than does any comparable group or community anywhere. In the recent War Chest drive an alltime high of $1,170,407 was contributed by a record number of 24,741 donors.

Because of the traditional generosity of people in show business, Hollywood has been a target for more than its share of charity appeals. To be sure that its money goes where it will do the most good, the motion-picture industry five years ago set up a Permanent Charities Committee composed of representatives of all guilds, unions and other industry groups. . . . Hollywood's record for giving [was] termed by P. G. Winnett, campaign chairman, Los Angeles area War Chest, "an ex-

ceptional one" and "a convincing example for less civic-minded groups."

Edward Arnold
Exec. Vice President
Permanent Charities Committee
2/19/45 *Hollywood*

Most fund raisers agree that Hollywood is a soft touch (for officially approved charities). Among its highest known gifts in World War II: $137,500 from Cary Grant for British war relief (in 1940); $100,000 from Edward G. Robinson to the U.S.O.—ED.

Who's Burning?

You had better keep a fire extinguisher handy because this is going to burn you up. You had a lot of nerve writing what you did about Errol Flynn [Feb. 12]. Personally, the only reason I take TIME magazine is because our teacher makes us. I wasn't the only kid that got mad over that article. I'm writing as a spokesman for the others and are we mad! . . . You had no right to say something about his "rape trial. . . ."

I'm in a classroom now so I'd better sign off.

Helene Biederman
3/12/45 *Cincinnati, Ohio*

Memo to Hollywood

No matter how hard I find it to digest parts of your magazine, I confess to getting the biggest kick out of your pickle-pussed Cinema editor. He, or she, can sure fling a wicked but clever review. The review of *Uncle Harry* [Aug. 27] is typical. I find myself going to the movies more often just to see if they are as bad as TIME says they are. They are.

William L. Hart
9/24/45 *Austin, Tex.*
It's he.—ED.

Flat Betrayal

I am pained by TIME's flat betrayal of a lovely girl [April 8]. As author of Paulette Goddard's first screen test and as the fortunate producer of

several of her pictures since, I am in a position to assure you that we have never felt it necessary to call in the Blimp Section of the Make-up Department.

Arthur Hornblow Jr.
5/27/46 *Hollywood, Calif.*

TIME bows to the swelling blast from various quarters (including costumers, make-up artists and union officials), cheerfully admits that it would be supererogatory for anybody to add anything to the lady's charms. TIME's apologies to Miss Goddard.—ED.

Mr. Sherwood Saw *Henry*

You ask [April 29]: "Has anybody here seen *Henry*?" (Meaning Laurence Olivier's motion picture production of *Henry V*.)

Well, I have—and I wish to testify that TIME was right.

In acting and direction and production, Laurence Olivier has done one of the greatest jobs in the history of the screen or the stage. The script is good, too.

I say all credit to TIME for having given credit where credit is so amply due.

Robert E. Sherwood
5/27/46 *New York City*

Inept Outlaw

Why so much emphasis on the sex angle of *The Outlaw*? The torrid effect of certain scenes is no more pornographic than some of the remarks heard in the Hope-Crosby picture *Road to Utopia*—to cite one example, for comparison. . . . The various "blue nose" organization [which] so generously provided box-office fodder for *The Outlaw* by their hysteria over certain scenes [should have] publicized *The Outlaw* in its correct perspective: a film containing the acme of inept acting, with a puerile story stupidly directed, and interwoven with obtuse editing and cutting. . . .

Gilbert G. W. Steed
7/8/46 *Los Angeles*

The Well-Bred Strain

I was greatly interested by your article [Feb. 10] about Mrs. Anthony C. Bartley (Deborah Kerr) because of the fact that I knew R.A.F. Squadron Leader Bartley when he was stationed at the Orlando, Fla. Army Air Base. I do not doubt that Miss Kerr is all that the many adjectives claim, but have wondered why the great L.B. [Louis B. Mayer] doesn't make his find a double-header and make a movie star out of Tony.

He not only has a background to convince anyone of "the well-bred strain," but his good looks and personality, plus a superb vocabulary, would do a great deal to influence our American "bobby-soxers" towards the charm of a polished young man, instead of our variety of glamor boys.

(Mrs.) Irene M. Price
3/3/47 *Palm Beach, Fla.*

Garbo & the Waiting World

Will you please inform a waiting world what else, besides wearing the hat and traveling in silence [Oct. 20], Greta Garbo is doing now. . . .

(Mrs.) Lillian P. Davis
11/17/47 *Nashville, Tenn.*
Since her last picture, The Two-Faced Woman *(1941), Garbo has kept busy ignoring rumors. In Washington last week, she was back on the screen—thanks to the Thomas Committee's anti-Communist inquiry. At the hearings M-G-M had been criticized for making* Song of Russia *(1944), a wartime boost for America's Red ally. M-G-M's comeback was a reissue of Garbo in* Ninotchka *(1939), a picture that kids the pants off Bolshevik commissars. As soon as prints are ready,* Ninotchka *will be re-released in most of the nation's larger cities.*—ED.

Wrong Guess

The article in TIME, Dec. 22, concerning me in connection with *Forever Amber* and the Legion of Decency, cannot possibly be classed as factual reporting. You gave the mischievous impression that I slyly maneuvered the Legion into placing that film in the "C" or condemned classification for the sake of box-office stimulation, when you said that I "guessed, correctly, that Legion disapproval would whet public pruriency and boost attendance." Your guess as to my guess was completely wrong as to the facts. Let me state these facts:

From the time the Legion formally notified me, Oct. 16, that the picture had been given a condemned rating, until it announced, Dec. 8, the change in classification, arduous and painstaking negotiations were in progress every day. The day after I received a letter from Father Masterson, Assistant Director of the Legion, informing me of the classification, I met with him for an extended discussion, during which I told him that we were prepared to do anything possible to eliminate those features of the film which the Legion found objectionable. From that day on, officials of the Legion and executives of our company met almost daily in an effort to agree on changes. Two days after the picture opened, I proposed that a prologue be added to the film, and gave notice to Father Masterson that the way would be open for other changes.

Throughout the unbroken series of discussions, the Legion itself indicated no concern that its own action might add to the box-office appeal of the picture, and at no time complained that matters were being delayed. At my request, Judge Stephen Jackson, who is assistant to Joseph Breen, director of the Motion Picture Code Authority, came on from Hollywood to act as an impartial negotiator. I also had Otto Preminger, director of the picture, fly on from California as soon as I received word of the Legion's action, and he participated in discussions on possible changes.

When agreement was finally reached and rough changes had been made, it was then necessary to make the actual finished emendations and additions in this Technicolor picture via all the technical processes at the studio. Thereafter it was also necessary to review 475

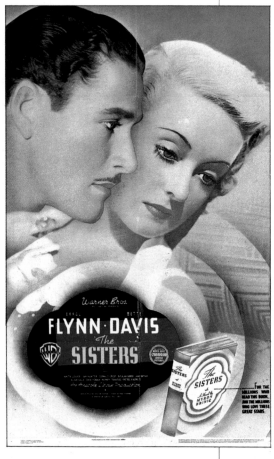

prints scattered in exchanges throughout the U.S. I made a statement Dec. 5, announcing the changes, and Dec. 8 the Legion of Decency followed up by announcing that the picture had been put in the "B" (objectionable in part") classification.

Spyros P. Skouras
President
20th Century-Fox Film Corp.
1/19/48 *New York City*
TIME indeed guessed wrong as to Cinemogul Skouras' intentions, thank him for setting the record straight on Forever Amber's "clean-up."—ED.

Time Flies

Yes, Time does fly but not that quickly. . . .

Nice to learn [Jan. 12] that Dale Evans, who married Roy Rogers, is only 29 years old, although she has a 20-year-old son. . . .

Edythe Bell
2/2/48 *Montreal, Canada*
Dale Evans married her first husband at 14, and is now 35 (chronological age). But her "professional age" is still 29.—ED.

Screen Censors

The letter of Spyros P. Skouras, president, 20th Century-Fox Film Corp., is most amazing [Jan. 19]. He has seen fit to publish the fact that his company will meet with self-appointed censors, who without any vestige of constitutional authority, shall determine what you and I shall view on the screen. . . .

Do the studios that knuckle under to the slighest pressure from any of many varied religious, political, business, or other groups, thus selling freedom of expression down the river, deserve the patronage and support of the, as yet, free people of the United States?

Stanley Erle Brown
2/9/48 *Berkeley, Calif.*

Absorbing Bogart

. . . *Treasure of Sierre Madre* should have been released before the Jan. 1 deadline to qualify for the Academy Awards—which it would have won hands down in at least three departments: Best Picture, Best Director, Best Supporting Actor (W. Huston).

Treasure is the sort of picture most intelligent filmgoers have been hungry for, a hunger which has been sated only by the foreign markets of late. . . . I have never been a Bogart fan, but it is tremendously gratifying to realize that Hollywood's evil star system can sometimes be defeated and that an erstwhile painfully stylized tough-guy hero can play an unsympathetic weakling and make him an absorbing character study. . . .

Alice Hartmann
2/23/48 *Los Angeles, Calif.*

Hartford Accent

. . . In its caustic review of *State of the Union*, TIME [May 3] said that Katharine Hepburn's God-given Hartford accent was an "affectation" sounding like a "woman trying . . . to steady a loose dental brace" which "limits her range of expression." This affected "bridgework" voice did not seem to limit her range of expression in *Woman of the Year*, in which your reviewer said she was "just right" [Feb. 16, 1942], nor in *The Philadelphia Story*, in which he praised her to the skies [Jan. 20, 1941] . . .

Miss Hepburn's beautiful voice has, thank God, never changed, although sometimes I wish TIME's critic would.

Thomas Ashworth
5/24/48 *Watertown, Conn.*
Unlike Miss Hepburn's voice, TIME's critic does.—ED.

Anti-Semitic *Twist*?

With reference to the article "Anti-Semitic *Twist*?" [Oct. 4], am I to believe that minority groups are now attempting to censor and to prohibit the presentation of certain [cinema] classics, particularly English classics? If this be the case, it seems as though they have met with some success.

Some individuals could go so far as to accuse a jealous Hollywood. This, too, is food for thought, because J. Arthur Rank has produced some truly great cinemas which to date have not been equaled by Hollywood.

It is my honest opinion that the Toronto [Jewish Congress] handled this "ersatz" problem in a most dignified and rational manner. All persons involved should be congratulated.

I trust that we in the U.S. shall soon

be able to see *Oliver Twist* at our local movie theaters.

David A. Sherwood
10/18/48 *Washington, D.C.*

Dead End

While TIME's ho-hum reviewer of M-G-M's *The Three Musketeers* was enjoying the Technicolor "enough to deserve a special mention" [Nov. 1], he might have stolen a glance at the plot.

"In the end," he writes, "D'Artagnan gives up skewering his enemies to settle down in the country with a seamstress at the court (June Allyson)" . . .

"In the end" Miss Allyson has been dead for reels, and Mr. Kelly (D'Artagnan) accepts Richelieu's invitation to stay on in Paris, presumably for further skewering.

John T. Kelley
11/28/48 *Chicago, Ill.*
A skewering to TIME's Cinema Editor for violating the first rule of picture previewing: Keep Awake.—ED.

Rainy Night Stars

Despite the charms of Elizabeth Taylor, the only stars I would go out on a rainy night to see are Joan Crawford, Bette Davis and Clarke Gable.

Elizabeth Boulon
9/5/49 *Hampton, Va.*

Joan Crawford's Shape

May I take exception to your editorial comment that the public is not "clamoring" to buy Joan Crawford? Having had the privilege of producing her last four pictures and starting on her fifth. I can assure you that the only people in America who like Miss Crawford are the moviegoers . . . Since when is "sophisticated fortyishness" not attractive? I firmly believe that this country is growing up, and in so doing can have other tastes than dewy-eyed youngsters on their screens. . . . Miss Crawford's legions of followers are larger today than at any previous time, while her career has never been in better shape. Neither has her shape.

Jerry Wald
9/5/49   *Beverly Hills, Calif.*

That Gardner Girl

Glamor, sex, Ava Gardner, et al.! Oh, boy! Just what Hollywood needs! . . . Half the world in slavery; U.S. morals in a questionable and precarious position, amply aided by Hollywood; and TIME [Sept. 3] says what Hollywood needs is GLAMOR! Where, oh, where, is your sense of values.

Rita Holachek
9/24/51   *Milwaukee*

KING KONG

FAY WRAY
ROBT ARMSTRONG
BRUCE CABOT

Praise for Wayne

I enjoyed your March 3 John Wayne cover story . . . Wayne's tolerant reaction to Actor Larry Parks's confession of having been a Communist was much more admirable than Hedda Hopper's Old Testament cry for vengeance. Instead of Wayne being "a little dumb about these things," I'd say Hedda is the one who's in need of instruction . . .

Ridgely Cummings
Hollywood, Calif.

. . . John Wayne may be no Alec Guinness or John Gielgud (just imag-

ine them intoning "Let's get charging! Saddle up!"), but he is a damn fine actor.

Charlie Stanton
3/24/52   *New York City*

Groans for a Groaner

I am writing for a group of "aging" college girls—19 to 22 years old.

When Bing Crosby played an exhibition golf match [here] for charity, we were on the Junior Committee.

If only some of our brash young entertainers would take a leaf out of his book! He is the most enchanting, modest, literate, charming, patient, lovable gentleman in show business today, and he wasn't wearing his toupee, either!

If you ever dare to call him an aging [48] groaner [June 30] again, we'll cancel our subscriptions!

Helene Stratford
7/21/52   *Roanoke, Va.*

King Kong Cuts

. . . Each time *King Kong* is revived [July 14], more of the picture is cut. Not since 1933 have audiences seen the scene on the cliff in which Kong sits to examine his prize (Fay Wray) and tears off part of her dress . . . Is this scene in the 1952 revival or does blue-nose prudery win another round?

Edward Connor
7/28/52   *New York City*
RKO happily reports that Kong continues to triumph over prudery.—ED.

Home-Town Boy Makes Good

. . . Whatever success the revival of *King Kong* is now enjoying in the U.S., it must be trifling compared to its appeal in West Africa . . . Hardly a week has gone by, since the film was first distributed in this area, that in some town it hasn't delighted huge audiences of fascinated natives who go again and again to see the great ape which they think is enormously funny . . . In the Gold Coast, one movie owner possesses only two features, *King Kong* and *The Mark of Zorro* . . . On Mondays, Tuesdays and Fridays he has packed them in for years with the former; on Tuesdays, Thursdays and Saturdays with the latter. On Sunday there is always a sure-fire double feature—*King Kong* and *The Mark of Zorro.*

Sam Olden Jr.
8/18/52   *Lagos, Nigeria, B.W.A.*

Knocking Is No Bother

It appears that the Hollywood producers have really slipped in offering the public (including teen-agers) such a degenerate movie as *Don't Bother to Knock* [Aug. 11]. Even from the producer's point of view, the movie can have a bad effect—it may make patrons think twice before hiring a baby-sitter while they go to the movies . . .

Mrs. William Toultant
9/1/52   *Annapolis, Md.*

Historic Precedent

Marilyn Monroe's purr "I had the radio on" when she posed for her now historic nude calendar picture was after a historic precedent. When Pauline Bonaparte, Princess Borghese and sister of Napoleon, was chided for having posed in the nude for Canova's famous statue of her as *Venus Victrix*, she calmly stated: "I wasn't cold with a fire in the room."

E. L. McColgin
9/1/52   *Detroit*

How Long, O Bogie?

In your issue of Sept. 22, I read with pleasure that Lauren Bacall has switched from Ike to Adlai and that she is working on Bogie.

The great issue of the campaign has now been made. All red-blooded American men await the decision! How long can Bogie hold out!

Thomas B. Sawyer
10/6/52   *San Pedro, Calif.*

Lemon Squash

I'm convinced that Zsa Zsa Gabor is the most conceited female on this universe, and is concerned about no one except Zsa Zsa. My sympathy goes to George Sanders, for I'm sure he's worse off than just a "squeezed lemon."

Verna Hill
11/10/52   *Detroit*

Bosomy Babes

In glancing through the Nov. 17 issue of TIME I was shocked and horrified when I glimpsed the full-page color photos of Marilyn Monroe and Zsa Zsa Gabor . . . Certainly you have never printed anything quite so disgustingly sensational before.

Nancy Hynes
College of St. Benedict
12/8/52   *Saint Joseph, Minn.*

The Women

We are average . . . American college girls who want to go through life with the belief that sex is a beautiful thing. Marilyn Monroe has done more to lower the standards of womanhood in the eyes of both men and women than any one person in history.

Janet Egelston
Rebecca Church
Edith Lyday
3/16/53   *Mars Hill, N.C.*

Starlit Disaster

TIME's April 27 review of the 20th Century-Fox picture *Titanic* states that the ship went down [April 15, 1912] in a moonlit sea. There was no moonlight that night. Starlight, yes, but no moonlight. I happen to be one of the survivors.

August J. Abrahamson
5/25/53   *Brooklyn*

Marilyn Monroe

Elizabeth Taylor

Katharine Hepburn

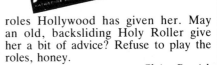

TIME'S Cinema section, taken in by Hollywood lighting effects, thanks Reader Abrahamson, one of the 512 survivors (1,513) were lost), who was traveling steerage at the time as a 19-year-old Finnish immigrant.—ED.

3-D Gimmicks

. . . The only shots in the arm our movie industry needs are better material and a few actors who look like people—3-D and kindred gimmicks are no substitute . . .

Susan D. Fannon
Alexandria, Va.
6/22/53

CinemaScope

. . . You can well imagine my dismay in seeing not only myself described as a "pitchman," but the whole subject of the motion picture industry's new dimensional developments presented with an air of erudite derision . . . The motion picture industry is in a critical phase, and it is true that there is a certain amount of groping at this stage of its progress. Uncertainty is characteristic of any institution, art or industry at a time of upheaval or radical change. On the other hand, 20th Century-Fox has completed two pictures, *The Robe* and *How to Marry a Millionaire,* in the new CinemaScope medium, and moreover we have shown scenes from both pictures to . . . thousands of . . . persons, both here and in Europe, who are versed in the technical aspects of . . . motion pictures. In not a single instance was there an expression of opinion that was lacking in respect for CinemaScope as a technical advancement . . . We are [also] completing the production of two other CinemaScope films [and] will soon commence production on nine more . . . This represents an expenditure of approximately $30 million . . .

When TIME electrified the publishing world by coming out with a new type of journalism . . . it was compelled to take an enormous moral and financial gamble. It took great courage . . . to . . . give the public something new and enlightening. With Cinema-Scope we faced a similar problem . . .

Your story deliberately dismissed the subject with glib levity and disparagement . . . Such a treatment is not only calculated to do great harm to the motion picture industry, but it tends to prejudice millions of motion picture fans in advance against an important development long before it reaches the theaters where the public can judge for itself . . .

Darryl F. Zanuck
Beverly Hills, Calif.
6/29/53

Pretty Antidote

My sincere congratulations for your article on Miss Audrey Hepburn [Sept. 7]. Such a stimulating antidote to all the recent publicity, relating to a sad analysis of the deterioration of values among a fraction of our womanhood . . .

Dr. L. F. V. P. Vanderhorst
Sunmount, N.Y.

. . . You quote some fellow [Producer William Wyler] who asserts that "that girl is going to be the biggest star in Hollywood" . . . When you come to think that Jean Simmons was only 18 when she gave her brilliant performance in Sir Laurence Olivier's *Hamlet,* you start wondering whether [24-year-old] Miss Hepburn hasn't started too late . . . Her soulful looks will take her far. She's pretty . . . But I'd like to see her future work way over par before taking my hat off to her . . .

Elmer Jackson
Madison, Wis.
9/28/53

Hollywood Notes

You say in your April 12 issue that Miss Jane Russell deplores the sexy

roles Hollywood has given her. May an old, backsliding Holy Roller give her a bit of advice? Refuse to play the roles, honey.

Claire Parrish
Hollywood, Calif.
5/10/54

Hats off to Bogie

That Humphrey Bogart is also a pretty rugged individual off the screen is borne out by the manner in which he recently sailed his ocean-racing yawl *Santana* to victory in the rough, three-day, 265-mile Channel Islands' race. Out of 15 boats to start, only seven finished. During 14 soaking, wet, day & night hours, the *Santana* beat into gale seas and winds up to 50 m.p.h. Most of this time the "old man" was either at the wheel or on deck. As members of his crew, our hats are off to him.

Larry Dudley
Bob Dorris
John Freiburg
Jeff Richards
John Swope
Los Angeles
6/28/54

The Bogeyman

Re Humphrey Bogart and your June 7 story: Add unprintable quotes—when someone tells Bogart . . . he made the same issue of TIME as Liberace.

Jules M. Lieberthal
New York City

I have never been a particular fan of H. Bogart. I warmed a little when I heard he was going to be Queeg in *The Caine Mutiny*—but now . . . I am a hard Bogart fan. He is the only Hollywood bum that ever told the naked truth: it is an absolute fact that everyone is drunk at 4 a.m.

Keith Tye
Floydada, Texas
6/28/54

U.H.F.

You said in the Aug. 2 Cinema review of *Rear Window* that Grace Kelly has "a sort of U.H.F. sex that not everybody will be able to hear." What does the abbreviation stand for . . . Upper High Falutin?

A. Benjamin
9/6/54 *New Britain, Conn.*

Ultra-High-Frequency.—ED.

Branding Brando

. . . Your Oct. 11 article on Marlon Brando reveals a person who is finally worthy of the teen-age adulation that frequently erupts in our midsts, usually for the most foolish reasons . . . What we are to hope for is that Mr. Brando does not go the way of all the finer talent Hollywood has collected—dissipating his talent in the meaningless assembly-line production of films . . .

C. V. Foster
11/1/54 *New York City*

Hollywood Caliph

Re the Nov. 1 review *The Adventures of Hajji Baba:* In the name of Allah the Compassionate, the Merciful, O Great and all-Seeing Splendid TIME, I will agree to send you forthwith a dancing girl from Ispahan if you can prove one set used in *Hajji Baba* was not designed and built especially for the luscious Persian CinemaScope.

Walter Wanger
11/15/54 *Hollywood*

O.K. Can she type?—ED.

Fantasia Too Much

TIME's review of Walt Disney is one of the best bits of Americana that has ever graced your pages. After going along with Walt since the birth of Mickey Mouse, today I like him better than ever. But . . . I walked out on *Fantasia*. As a lover of Bach, and especially the Miltonic grandeur of the *D Minor Toccata and Fugue,* the paraphrasing of this musical earthquake with a series of silly moving-color patterns was too much . . .

Marguerite M. Crolly
1/17/55 *Jacksonville*

Okaying Miss K

Congratulations on the fine article [Jan. 31] on Grace Kelly. I am very glad to know she has a mind of her own as far as her career and the publicity involved are concerned. Hollywood has miscast and ruined Greer Garson . . . Deborah Kerr will probably be in the same boat soon . . . and Audrey Hepburn will probably be playing in something called *The Eleanor Roosevelt Story* before long. But it looks as if Miss K can take care of herself . . .

Elida Debevoise
2/14/55 *Northampton, Mass.*

Haul of Fame

Your March 7 Cinema review of *Jupiter's Darling* has another gem:

"Esther Williams' pictures are generally just so much water over the dame." It deserves to go in the haul of fame together with an early TIME comment on a Clifford Odets picture after Odets had first gone to Hollywood: "Odets, where is thy sting?"

Harry Lantry
3/28/55 *Harden Lake, Idaho*

The Big Front

Thanks and appreciation for the things I found in TIME's Oct. 24 com-

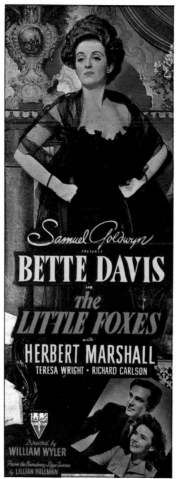

ment on *The Big Knife*. It might interest you to know that one of my children, commenting on the picture you ran, remarked that the cameraman took it on my bad side. When asked which side was bad, the child replied, "the front." But, like me, they are really very proud of it.

Robert Aldrich
The Associates & Aldrich Co., Inc.
11/14/55 *Hollywood*

Burning Questions

With the increasing costs of paper, how can you afford to fill your pages with such boring topics as the President's State of the Union message and the Middle East crisis when the burning question on the lips of every red-blooded American is: Can a poor little rich girl from the banks of the Schuyl-

kill River find happiness as the wife of a wealthy and titled Monégasque?

Harold J. Newman
Brookline, Mass.

". . . Grace nibbled at Rainier's ear and danced with him until 4 a.m." I fear this will cause an international ear-nibbling craze, and ears are delicate things. Think of a whole generation of earless males. However, Gracie can nibble on my ears any time.

Holcombe McDaniel
2/6/56 *Baton Rouge*

Marilyn at Elsinore

Sir Laurence and Cheesecake Marilyn! [Feb. 20]. The world is now crumbling on all sides of us! Britain's leading thespian has sold his cinematic soul. Surely this knight errant is jousting when he refers to Miss Monroe's hip-flipping talents as "ethereal." Perhaps a remake of *Hamlet* is proposed? If so, the event would truly be an occasion to make the Danes melancholy, for the dramatic climax would, no doubt, be Marilyn as Ophelia frisking about the lily pads clad in a bikini for a real razzle-dazzle death scene. At this point, the profit-sharing prince would no doubt be moved to make his quietus with a bare bodkin.

Robert L. Morrison
3/19/56 *Brooklyn*

How did Boris Chaliapin, in his cover picture of Marilyn, capture that wistful appeal for something higher than physical attraction? And how could you give us the full story of her life with much utter frankness without degrading her, but making those who have made profit out of her, and all the rest of us, accord her the respect for which she now yearns as the lines of maturity begin to show around eyes and neck? May the girl on the calendar raise our sights to higher ideals for our country's women.

(The Rev.) Allen H. Gates
First Congregational Church
Chesterfield, Mass.

I was prejudiced against Miss Monroe, but after reading your excellent article I now have a deep respect for her capacity and survival. With such a childhood and such a family background, it must have taken some of the best human qualities to have emerged spiritually whole—and smiling.

Walt Montez
5/28/56 *Forest Hills, N.Y.*

Ferber's Giant

Your Oct. 22 review of the motion picture *Giant* was a lengthy review, a fine one, and most gratifying to the producers of the picture. Certain statements having to do with the actual business foundation of the picture should be corrected. It was the eventual business producer, Henry Ginsberg, who read the novel and who first presented the partnership plan. Other offers were presented and considered but George Stevens and Ginsberg had the courage to follow the intent of the book. In this I felt repaid for the four years of travel, research and writing.

Edna Ferber
11/12/56   *New York City*

Pride of Place

Your film reviewer recently dismissed [Oct. 1] as "H Opera" and "bad bouillabaisse" Jacques-Yves Cousteau's *The Silent World,* surely one of the finest things ever put on film. I am delighted that your reviewer placed my film *Friendly Persuasion* [Nov. 1] in a similar category.

William Wyler
11/19/56   *Beverly Hills, Calif.*

Seductive Baby Doll

TIME's Dec. 24 review of *Baby Doll* is sickening. When you say an admitted stream of carnal suggestiveness is fit for your readers' attention because it is expertly served up, you insult your reader's moral integrity by implying that he has none. Elia Kazan may have had puritanic motives, but look at the lewd billboard and newspaper ballyhoo that sings the seductive praises of *Baby Doll.* Who's kidding whom?

Harry Plate
1/14/57   *San Francisco*

Hollywood's Hearts of Gold

I enjoyed your warm and moving review [Dec. 9] of *Paths of Glory.* It is gratifying to learn that Hollywood can again make films that portray war as something other than glorious and that do not have to show that under every officer's tunic there beats a heart of gold. If this movie leaves the spectator "confused," it may be because it has started him thinking of truths he would rather not face.

Edwin Krauser
12/30/57   *West Lafayette, Ind.*

Billy the Kidder

As a reader of your Cinema section, I find myself increasingly nauseated by the 21-pun salute which greets each new picture (except, of course, the ones from Italy). In the May 26 Cinema review of John O'Hara's *Ten North Fredrick,* your critic finds it necessary to hedgehop from Pennsylvania, where the picture plays, to Japan, which has nothing whatsoever to do with the picture. By way of samurai and *Bushido,* he ultimately arrives at that peak of comicality. "O'Hara-kiri." Obviously, we in Hollywood are no match for such devastating wit. Why doesn't he take on somebody his own size? Bennett Cerf, for instance, I suggest a sunrise duel in the old offices of *College Humor*—with puns at 20 paces. And may the best man wince.

Billy Wilder
6/16/58   *Hollywood*

Norman Krasna

TIME, being a written medium, surely realizes the importance of a writer. In reviewing *Indiscreet* [July 21] you toss kudos, deserved I'm sure, to Stanley Donen, the director; you do nip-ups

over the magnificent performances of Ingrid Bergman and Cary Grant; but for some curious reason you neglect to mention the name of the author. It is Norman Krasna. I repeat his name is Norman Krasna. I only mention it twice because you failed to mention it once.

Groucho Marx
8/11/58   *Old Saybrook, Conn.*

'Ell's Hangels

Having seen the British film *Dunkirk,* I was surprised to see your criticism in TIME, Sept. 15. Was the attempt at cockney a protest at the British daring to make a war film without Errol Flynn's wiping out Panzer Divisions as he sang "God Bless America"?

P. A. Ryan
10/6/58   *London*

Here to Stray

Re your Sept 22. story on the Eddie and Debbie Fisher-Liz Taylor triangle, Liz's beauty will bring her no good unless money and phony fame give it. I am also disgusted with Eddie Fisher. They both mistake glands for love.

Esther H. Nyberg
Bellingham, Wash.

At the ripe old age of 26, Elizabeth Taylor has been married three times. divorced twice, widowed, a mother of three, a stepmother and a homebreaker. Isn't it about time she took one of the final steps of life—retirement—so that her close friends and acquaintances can live a normal life?

Susan Poe
10/13/58   *Laurel, Md.*

Hot Mix-Up

Re a Nov. 17 Show Business item on Marilyn Monroe in M-G-M's *Some Like It Hot:* M-G-M does not stand for Metro's Got Monroe. Billy Wilder's *Some Like It Hot,* starring Marilyn Monroe, Tony Curtis, Jack Lemmon, is a Mirisch-Ashton production for United Artists' release.

Harold Mirisch
12/1/58   *Hollywood*
T-G-M-U stands for TIME *got mixed up.—*ED.

The Old Man & the Sulk

In your Oct. 27 review of *The Old Man and the Sea,* a picture I directed, you said that Spencer Tracy "sulked at the director and hardly bothered to act at all." It is certainly the privilege of your reviewer to either like or not like Mr. Tracy's performance, but I assure you this statement is untrue. Mr. Tracy worked on this picture with the same drive, enthusiasm and integrity which has always made him the great actor he is.

John Sturges
12/8/58   *Hollywood*
*And he sulked and sulked at the first director, Fred Zinnemann, until Zinnemann quit. That's when Reader Sturges took over.—*ED.

Bang!

TIME's Cinema review of *The Inn of the Sixth Happiness* [Dec. 22] was more jejune than usual. The sophomore-with-typewriter who pecked out this tirade quite evidently cannot distinguish between sentiment and sentimentality. The movie has more "treacle [than] the Great Boston Molasses Flood." Why not park your lad next to his cliché factory and pray for a small explosion?

(Rev.) Anthony S. Woods S.J.
Church of St. Francis Xavier
1/19/59 *New York City*

Youth Has Its Say

I thank you for your complimentary words on my performance in the picture *The Perfect Furlough* [Feb. 9]. However, my wife is 26 years old, and she took umbrage at your line, "Even bored old Keenan Wynn is back at his best."

I can understand you, as movie critic, using the word "bored" because of the number of pictures in which I have played the same part, *i.e.* the friend of the hero. However, my "child bride" does not understand what you mean by "old." Despite five years of marriage and two beautiful daughters she still fails to consider me old. She may be a considerably old 26, but I prefer to think of myself as a rather youthful 45.

Keenan Wynn
3/2/59 *Los Angeles*

Eddie & Liz

In reference to your April 13 picture of Eddie Fisher and Liz Taylor, it's too bad that while Mr. Fisher can afford to give Miss Taylor a 50-diamond bracelet, for an engagement present, he can't afford to keep her dressed! For a minute I thought I was reading the *National Geographic*, and looking at a picture of one of the natives.

Frances Kelly
5/4/59 *Detroit*

Frankie & Ava Down Under

Nothing I have read in recent months has given me so much satisfaction as did the account in your April 20 issue of how Ava Gardner and Frank Sinatra dealt with the "gentleman of the press!" It happened in Australia, but it should happen here—and more often.

It is heartening then to see two people such as Ava and Frankie with the courage and ability to stand up to the arrogant reporters and photographers. When they tell them off, and instruct them as to where they can and should go, these two of my favorite people are, I am sure, speaking for millions.

S. W. Burnett
Chicago

Speaking for myself, wish you would go a step further and inform the public about the attendance at his shows. This, I think you will admit, would give a truer picture of Sinatra in Australia.

Eddie Cantor
5/11/59 *Beverly Hills, Calif.*
West Melbourne Stadium (seating capacity: 10,000) averaged two-thirds full for each of the four Sinatra concerts.—ED.

Broken Spell

For years I let myself cheer and sneer right on cue from your movie editor. But now the spell is forever broken, and I think for myself. *A Hole in the Head* was the best picture of the year. Your Aug. 3 review was the worst.

Rudy Ertis
8/24/59 *Toledo*

Movie Morals

If TIME and Miss Shirley MacLaine sought to present American movie morals and manners in a light calculated to encourage an alarming decadence of American values, both achieved that end with effectiveness.

William W. Tomlinson
Vice President
Temple University
10/12/59 *Philadelphia*

Happy Equation

I am not at all unhappy about being a "compensation," and I suppose I don't mind being a "sort of Ivy League Dracula" [in the Oct. 19 review of *Pillow Talk*]. I can smell a compliment better than anyone I have ever met. No, all I really have to complain about is that I think you underrate Clark Gable [in the Oct. 12 review of *But Not for Me*]; he's really a deceptively good artist. That's all—but if overrating me goes with underrating him, then God praise the equation.

Tony Randall
11/2/59 *Los Angeles*

Pique over Peyton Place

Re Grace Metalious' blast at me over *Return to Peyton Place* reported in the Dec. 21 TIME: it is to laugh. I am no Svengali and she's no Trilby. I did not guide her hands across her golden typewriter. And when it comes to riding the gravy train, I'm in the caboose. I have yet to make the picture. which will cost several million dollars. It is a gamble as to if it makes money or no as are all pictures these days. She has her gravy and can eat it already. The paperback rights of *Return to Peyton Place* were worth $265,000 in the hand to her, plus the not inconsiderable amount 20th Century-Fox and I have paid her for the film rights. Grace says that we did her "a foul and rotten trick"—this is the kind of trick I wish someone would do to me.

Jerry Wald
1/4/60 *Los Angeles*

Off the Beach

In the light of the review in your Dec. 28 issue of the motion picture *On the Beach*, I feel that your readers should be advised that this review is not typical of the reception which the picture has enjoyed in all of the principal capitals of the world. I can safely say that no motion picture in history has been treated with more respect or importance. So many people around the world rely on TIME to keep them *au courant* on international affairs that I felt TIME owed them a word of caution to the effect that, with the exception of your review, this has not been considered as just another "boy does not get girl" motion picture.

Arthur Krimm
President, United Artists Corp.
1/18/60 *New York City*

Dig the Galahs

Fair dinkum, you galahs make a bloke do his block! The codger who reviewed *The Sundowners* is off his rocker. I've lived in Australia 30 years and never come across the word borak. (Sure, it's in the slang dictionary, but it ain't in the vernacular.) Most of us down under speak normalish English.

Sid Fassler
Melbourne

I feel crook about bringing this up, but your movie crit bloke in his bloody good review of *The Sundowners* described the film as being "square dinkum." He probably means "fair dinkum," which means a bit of all right.

Pat Robb
1/6/61 *San Francisco*
'*orl right.*—ED.

His Geisha

Your statement that *My Geisha* is a "by product of one of Hollywood's oddest marriages" is obviously a byproduct (by which I mean illegitimate offspring) of odd reporting and tasteless editing. Two years of time, effort, near heartbreak and $2,000,000 devoted to *My Geisha* does not add up to a byproduct.

If all marriages in Hollywood—or on Park Avenue or Main Street, U.S.A.—were as soundly based on honesty, hard work and understanding as Shirley MacLaine's and mine, there would be far fewer divorces for you to record.

Steve Parker
2/17/61 *Tokyo*

Poochlitzer Prize

As far as we're concerned, your publication deserves the Poochlitzer Prize for your movie review of *101 Dalmations*.

Jordan Berliner
Tomlin Stevens
3/10/61 *Chicago*

Tarnished Oscars

All I know about motion pictures is what I read in your reviews and see advertised. (I'm a missionary.) But I wonder if anyone else had the same impression I did concerning the Academy Award presentations. The "best" of the American motion picture industry: a comedy concerning the adulterous use of an apartment; best actor—the portrayal not of an honest evangelist but of a sin-ridden imitation; best actress—in the role of a woman of no virtue. God help us! Doesn't this add up to an awful moral degeneracy in our midst? Aren't the folks in Hollywood, who are responsible, disturbed?

(Mrs.) Louise Prinsell
5/5/61 *Ventnor, N.J.*

Same Shade of Scarlett

If you can't write a clever review without taking a negative approach, couldn't you just for once be a little less condescending in your evaluation and exhibit a little more forthright enthusiasm?

I'd be interested to see what TIME had to say about *G.W.T.W.* 22 years ago.

Joyce Gunter
5/25/61 *Lafayette, Calif.*
The judgment was about the same as 22 years later, but the blade was not so sharp. Said the cover story on Vivien Leigh, Dec. 25, 1939:
"Gone With the Wind was a U.S. legend. Producer David Selznick sensed that the first rule in retelling a legend is exactly the same as retelling a fairy tale to children—no essential part of the story must ever be changed. So long as they swore by the book, producers of Gone With the Wind *were free to make as great a picture as they could, and the film has almost everything the book has in the way of spectacle, drama, practically endless story and the means to make them bigger and better."—ED.*

Useful Giggle

I agree about most everything you said in your review of *Francis of Assisi*

[July 28], except the line about giggling. With all sincerity, I believe that a good giggle would have improved my performance greatly. I think I giggled more at your review than I did in the picture; and your review was nothing to giggle about.

Dolores Hart
8/11/61 *London*

Sunday School Rubbish

Thank you for your honest review of the blasphemous *King of Kings* [Oct. 27]. Casting blue-eyed Jeffrey Hunter as Christ is like casting a certain French *femme fatale* as the innocent Snow White . . . UGH!

Johnathon Todd
11/3/61 *Baltimore*

Arise & Dissent

I have as good a sense of humor as the next man, but when you quote me directly as saying that I was not interested in how many Senators came to the preview of *Advise and Consent* [March 30], I must respectfully request a correction. I arranged the private showing in Washington and was particularly honored by the great number of Senators and their wives present.

Otto Preminger
4/6/62 *New York City*
Producer Preminger's under-the-marquee quote, "Never mind how many Senators, I'm only interested in the Robert Kennedy's," had ear-witness corroboration.—ED.

Joe, You Made the Asp Too Short

Re your report on Cleopatra's death scene [June 8]: the Egyptian asp is a cobra, attaining a length of about 5 ft.

when grown. Newly hatched asps would probably be at least 9 or 10 in. long. The 6-in. Egyptian asp—in training for two months—used by 20th Century-Fox in its forthcoming film *Cleopatra* evidently is a retarded baby, poor thing.

Does Joe Mankiewicz seriously expect people to believe that a creature like that would be capable of dispatching so formidable an object as Elizabeth Taylor?

Hilda Simon
6/22/62
New York City

Tomato Surprise

What a difference a few pages can make. In the Show Business section of your April 19 issue, you credited me with helping Joan Crawford become the most photographed star at the Oscar presentations. My cup of pride ran over until I turned to Cinema, where your movie reviewer put me in the tomato-stuffing business as the result of a red chiffon dress Judy Garland wore in *I Could Go on Singing.*

Of course, since I was credited as costume designer, your critic would have now way of knowing this, but please, just for the record, I designed all of Judy's costumes for the picture with the exception of one. Uh-huh. You're right. I don't know how that red number slipped in. I plead innocent. Hollywood gremlins, I imagine.

It's always a pleasure to appear in TIME, but please, not as a tomato specialist.

Edith Head
4/26/63
Los Angeles

Enough

I sometimes think that your cinema reviewer (one can't call him a critic) is desperately afraid that his ineptness at his job may escape the reader. The fact that he hates *The Ugly American* [April 19] and I love it is not what prompts me to take pen in hand. His snide, destructive diatribes couldn't provoke me to write in the past, and it isn't that this last piece of his has struck a new low. He has delivered himself of this caliber of filth before. It's just that I've had enough.

This retort can only be feeble, compared with what I feel. I wish I had the talent to adequately convey how revolted I am by this kind of hooliganism. Consider this letter a panicky gasp, on my part, for some clean air.

Is it me? Aren't others, as well, alarmed at his public debauch, at his joyous wallowing in the insensitive, at his brazen certainty that we all will join him, slapping our thighs as we screamingly laugh at his vulgar barbs? And for this poison to be lent an aura of legitimacy simply by its appearance in your pages!

I'm not writing out of personal pique. I've had no connection with the film in question, and this is not the occasion for me to discuss the many virtues of the picture or the unique talent and towering stature of Brando

as an artist. Besides, it would be a thankless task to attempt a discussion on this level with an unfeeling, culturally murderous fool. I repeat: I've had enough of him.

Lee J. Cobb
5/3/63
Woodland Hills, Calif.

Look Forward in Hope

Having seen Mr. Burton several years ago in the notable movie *Look Back in Anger,* I sincerely hope that he will forsake his tempestuous tempt-

ress and again pursue the great feats of which he is so capable.

Mrs. Marvin N. Nelson
5/3/63
Iowa, Utah

9-0-1-T-P

I was relieved to read that TIME, too, remains puzzled about *Last Year at Marienbad!* I'm sure the U.S. film industry could create the same sensation by running *PT 109* backward in slow motion.

Hulon W. Myers
10/4/63
San Francisco

Quite Right

Ah, that write-up on Actor Laurence Harvey [Dec. 6] had an old TIME flavor. I thought perhaps the anonymous chap with the curare-dipped stiletto had been put to pasture and was perhaps pursuing some hobby, like milking rattlesnakes. It would appear instead that he merely paused to sharpen his fangs. While it is difficult to work up much sympathy for the victim, who is probably tapping his glass slipper in protest, any poor bastard blitzed with such deft and delicate razor strokes is deserving of pity. Wait until he tries to turn the other cheek.

Earl Smith
Van Nuys, Calif.

Perhaps the reason that Mr. Harvey called me "that ghastly woman" is that I protested indignantly when I learned he was going to play my lover in the movie *Walk on the Wild Side,* I had seen Mr. Harvey make love on the screen, whch he does aloofly, as if he were a playing card—the jack of clubs. He lifts one knee defensively so that the heroine, whom he is supposed to adore, has to make a sudden flanking movement if she wishes to embrace him.

Capucine
Lausanne, Switzerland

Thanks for spelling my name right.
Laurence Harvey
12/20/63
Hollywood

CRERTHWTFB

As president of the Committee for the Reputation of Elizabeth Taylor, I would like to officially protest your mention of her in your March 27 article as "Elizabeth Rosamond Taylor Hilton Wilding Todd Fisher." This is an obvious attack on the reputation of Mrs. Burton, and CRET takes exception to this type of smart-aleck reporting.

Napoleon Jones
President, CRET
4/3/64
New York City

Harlow the Actress

So Jean Harlow [July 3] "could not act," eh? I wonder if your book reviewer ever saw *Bombshell* or *Red-headed Woman* or *Dinner at Eight* or *The Girl from Missouri* or *Red Dust* or *Beast of the City* or *China Seas* or *The Public Enemy* or even *Hell's Angels?* I wonder, in fact, if your reviewer has ever seen any Hollywood films made in the '20s and early '30s; if he had, he would not have singled out Jean Harlow for "refusal to wear a brassiere." That was standard practice. Nor is he up on his clinical psychology. Nymphomania is not something girls have "bouts" of. You either got it, or you ain't. The details of Jean Harlow's short, unhappy life may not be savory, but that is no cause to sully her image as it remains to us on the screen: that of a vibrant and beautiful woman with more temperament and talent than a carload of today's pneumatic wonders.

Dan M. Morgenstern
New York City
7/17/64

Send a Male!

I think your readers might be interested to know that your story about me [Sept. 18] was researched by a woman. The next time you want to inquire into my sexuality, would you please send a male reporter? Ho-hum, your "Housewife in Houriland" must stop now, take off her transparent gown and diamonds, and get back to those dirty caviar dishes! Love and kisses.

Carroll Baker
Hollywood
9/25/64

Critic's Respect

I appreciate the fairness of your report on my movie-reviewing career [May 14]. I should like to clarify one point: my description of the "cowlike creature" in *The Pumpkin Eater* applied to the character and not to Anne Bancroft, an actress I respect.

(Mrs.) Judith Crist
New York City
5/21/65

Sam Spiegel Speaks

Re your article on *Doctor Zhivago* [Dec. 24], I did not say, "I hear they've made it into a soap opera." I said, "The danger is that it might be turned into a soap opera." At no time in the course of a long interview with your London correspondent did I "snort." I have developed an abiding admiration and deep regard for Mr. Lean and his enormous talents.

Sam Spiegel
New York City
1/7/66

Scout's Honor

Must a motion picture depict wife-trading, homosexuality, crime, violence, or other perversity to receive a favorable review by TIME? Clean, wholesome pictures that emphasize the better values in life are consistently spoofed by your Cinema department. A recent case in point is the cynical and smart-alecky review of the late Walt Disney's *Follow Me, Boys!* [Dec. 16].

Your review of this fine picture is positively nauseating, and an insult to the hundreds of thousands of scouters who devote their time, talents and energies to the youth of this nation.

They do this, just as did "Scoutmaster MacMurray," because they believe adherence to the scout oath, or promise, by the youth of today will make better citizens tomorrow.

Alton A. McDonald
Judge, Court of Common Pleas
Cambria County
Ebensburg, Pa.
1/6/67
TIME feels that the movie—not the review—insulted the Boy Scouts.—ED.

Friends of the Family

Your piece on Britain's justly noted Redgrave sisters [March 17] was excellent, not so much for what it had to say on the sisters themselves but for its comments on the modern moviegoer. An increasingly educated and intelligent American public cannot accept the glittering bedroom farces and unreal gods and goddesses that Hollywood is, unfortunately, famous for. Let the American film industry take a cue from the realistic poignance of Julie Christie's *Darling* or Lynn Redgrave's *Georgy Girl*.

Alvin Cordeaux
Baton Rouge, La.
3/31/67

Dear Little Buttercup

Psychiatrists Schaefer and Hatterer are slightly off in their explanation of why the cult of Judy Garland [Aug. 18] has so many homosexual members. It is not that they "gravitate towards superstars" or else they would surely flock to the Beatles' concerts; and it is certainly not that Judy Garland has "become masculine and powerful." The answer is simply that they identify poor little unattractive, unwanted Dorothy who eventually had all her dreams come true in the magical Emerald City. You will notice that the majority of Garland fans in her audiences are just about her age, give or take a few years. This is an Ugly Duckling syndrome embodying wish fulfillment—identifying with someone who has succeeded time and time again in spite of being blacklisted, shunned, laughed at and teased. Luckily for Judy Garland, she succeeds even though

these would-be Cinderellas almost ruin her concerts with their fanatic screaming.

J. C. Glerum Jr.
San Francisco
9/1/67

Good Deal Sicker

The thought of Shirley Temple Black in Congress makes me a good deal sicker than *Night Games* ever did.

Dale M. Hellegers
Manhattan
9/22/62

More Than He Can Chew

After reading your review of *Bonnie and Clyde* [Aug. 25], I had to write

to you. I can't remember being as upset with anything you've written about films as I am with this unjust, unfair and just plain unkind rap at one of the finest films ever projected on the American screen. The production. technique, the performances and the direction, the whole attitude of what a film should be is there to see and understand. Why don't you people stick to writing about politics and I might add, try reviewing some of the politicians' performances? You'd really have something to bite into.

Jerry Lewis
Jerry Lewis Films, Inc.
Hollywood
10/13/67

When There's Hope, There's Life

Reading your cover story on Bob Hope [Dec. 22] was like opening the very best Christmas gift. In a world torn by war and famine and racial tensions, it's gratifying to know that we can still have hope—and Hope.

John William Dowler
San Francisco

Your excellent story on Bob Hope, one of the world's greatest humanitarians, did not mention that for the past nine years he has served as honorary national chairman of the National Parkinson Foundation. He has been a staunch supporter in our continuing quest for the cause of, and cure of, Parkinson's disease.

Not content with giving up his valuable time and talent, Bob has for a number of years given us an annual personal check for $10,000. When the big break-through comes through research on Parkinson's disease, as surely it will in the not too distant future, much of the credit for financing that research must go to our friend Bob Hope.

(Mrs.) Jeanne Levey
National Chairman
National Parkinson Foundation
1/8/68
Miami

Graven Idol

I was overcome with a fit of nostalgia to read that John Wayne was back winning the wars as a Green Beret [July 19]. Marvelous. I was never happy with him in all those westerns. Those shared hours at Wake Island-Guadalcanal-Bataan had created a vision of sweat-stained jungle kit, tin hat at a rakish angle and clenched teeth never to be forgotten. I must own to a secret wish as a teen-ager that we British had been left inslightly direr straits so that Mr. Wayne would have perforce crept up our beaches and liberated our hamlets; what ecstacy the idea gave me! I shall see the film with all speed.

(Mrs.) M. Sullivan
8/9/68
London

Character Actor

You describe Robert Mitchum well indeed [Aug. 16]! One day in the late '40s, he came alongside as I was getting the car out and asked for a lift. He asked if I would mind driving down to the RKO studio and waiting for a minute. I did, and in about ten minutes he came out with two suits over his shoulder. "Something you forgot?" I asked him. "No," he said matter-of-factly. "RKO gets a fat fee for loaning me to Warners, and doesn't share it; so I needed a couple of suits, went in, and snitched these." He cast me as driver of the getaway car in a robbery—and he enjoyed it.

Barney Oldfield
Vice President
Litton International Development Corp.
8/30/68
Beverly Hills

Buster Crabbe and Johnny Weissmuller, well-known Tarzans of the '30s

Look, No Puns

Congratulations on having no goddam puns in the Cinema section this week [Nov. 15].

John Huston
11/29/68
Berlin

Happiness is Mia

In a period wallowing in the grotesque and fawning in voyeuristic escapism, it follows that Mia Farrow would succeed as a flower-nibbling, pseudo-mystical boy-girl and that Hoffman would see a psychoanalyst five days a week, no doubt to discuss his anxieties about the impending tax deadline.

The sight of Farrow and Dustin salting down the scratch, the former looking like a sand-kicked 97-lb. weakling in *Rosemary's Baby* and the latter as a watered-down Holden Caulfield in *The Graduate,* is enough to confirm to this aging mind that when eccentricity and grotesquerie become the prime movers of modern society and grace the cover of society's most powerful conscience, the Flat Earth Society might have something.

James B. Allen
Ann Arbor, Mich.

Mr. Sinatra's loss is our gain. I am so glad I am living during this Mia Farrow era. She not only has talent beyond words, but also personality. beauty, intellect, enchantment and charm. Happiness is Mia.

Nancy Powers
2/21/69
Detroit

Hail to the Duke

"Now listen, and listen tight . . ." I can't tell you what a pleasure it was to open my mailbox this week and find John Wayne mounted on his faithful steed [Aug. 8] staring at me.

As usual, your reporter did an excellent job. His portrait of one of the last of the rugged individualists was as good as mom's apple pie and as carefully woven as granny's old shawl.

Many, many thanks from one who grew up with Sergeant Striker, Big Jim McLain, John T. Chance, *et al.*

William N. Woodworth
8/29/69
Ashtabula, Ohio

Original Cast

Re the 20th Century-Fox epic, *Tora! Tora! Tora!* [Oct. 5]: I'll make you a little bet that the original cast pulled off the attack for a lot less than $25 million. Oh well, you can't win them all.

William F. Krivohlavek
10/26/70
Fresno, Calif.

Parched Tear Ducts

The question of whether or not *Love Story* [Jan. 11] represents a "return to romanticism" is not in itself that important. I think more significant is the fact that people have found something to cry about.

Hearts hardened by the nightly showing of killing and destruction are now affected by the tragic death of a young girl. The real tragedy is that we have not cried for a long while. Parched tear ducts are now filling up; and where there is compassion, there is hope.

Dan Caldwell
12/8/71 *Cambridge, Mass.*

What's So Funny?

Woody Allen should be named "Wooden" Allen, for his brand of humor is worm-eaten. What, for example, is funny in "I don't believe in an afterlife, although I am bringing a change of underwear"? All his quips seen corny to me. The question arises, "Is American humor *sui generis* and incomprehensible to foreigners?"

(The Rev.) Wynne Jones
2/24/72 *Co. Limerick, Eire*

Tarzan's Yell

Buster Crabbe may have relied on a recorded hog caller for his Tarzan yell [Nov. 13], but I have heard Johnny Weissmuller give the call.

In Mexico, I assisted in the production of *Tarzan and the Mermaids*, featuring Johnny Weissmuller. One holiday evening an incredible banshee wail burst into the courtyard of our hotel, culminating in a shrieking, howling scream. Jet planes were not in use then, so this jetlike roar was unearthly. Windows flew open and heads popped out in curiosity and fear.

All the guests at the hotel that night —perhaps much of Mexico City—will confirm that the yell is the genuine voice of Weissmuller, who had serenaded us that night on a dare.

Julian Lesser
12/11/72 *Hollywood*
According to Johnny Weissmuller, the Tarzan calls are his own. His yells were recorded and used in some of his later movies in order to save his voice.—ED.

Girls on Main Street

Why a cover story on Liv Ullmann [Dec. 4]? I see dozens of girls every day on Main Street with more of everything she has. For one thing, her mouth is too "loose." Is this all that Hollywood can find?

Gladys E. Talbott
12/25/72 *Richmond*

Jane Testifies

Whose voice gave Tarzan's call [Dec. 11]? I ought to know: I was there. Johnny Weissmuller can—and did— do his own Tarzan call. End of discussion?

Maureen O'Sullivan ("Jane")
1/1/73 *New York City*

Thinking Man's Sex Goddess

I was delighted to see you give overdue recognition to British Actress Diana Rigg [Dec. 18].

The famous chariot race in the 1959 version of *Ben Hur* for which Charlton Heston won an Oscar

In an age accustomed to the dumb blondes of Hollywood and the Barbie-doll types who are crowned annually in Atlantic City and elsewhere as the supposed epitome of femininity, it is indeed refreshing to know there is such a thing as a thinking man's sex goddess.

She may well do more to change the image of modern woman than all the Gloria Steinems put together.

John J. Pierce
1/22/73 *Dover, N.J.*

Generosity

You report *Variety's* report of the gross of *Ben-Hur* at $40,750,000 [Jan. 15]. My participant statement from Metro-Goldwyn-Mayer Inc., dated July 29, 1972, reports a gross of $78,821,678, almost double your figure.

Since both TIME and *Variety* are regarded as Holy Writ, I can only conclude that MGM is padding my statement in order to be generous and pay me more than I'm entitled to receive.

William Wyler
2/12/73 *Beverly Hills, Calif.*

Honest Sexuality

Congratulations on your courageous and objective reporting in the cover story on Marlon Brando and his new movie.

There are those who will support the proliferation of visual reporting of blood, gore, murder and destruction while hypocritically desiring to censor honest portrayal of human sexuality.

Your straightforward discussion of Brando's strikingly controversial movie allows your readers to make an educated judgment as to whether or not they would want to place this offering on their entertainment schedules.

Jay H. Lehr
2/19/73 *Columbus*

The Serious Mr. Schickel

Did I read right? Is Mr. Schickel reading social commentary into a James Bond film [July 9]? James Bond the Great White Hope? *Live and Let Die* is fantasy! Mr. Schickel is taking somebody far too seriously.

K. M. Drennan
Portland, Ore.

Agent 007 a racist pig? Oh, come on!

Wendy Hogan
7/30/73 *New York City*

A Hex for a Whammy

You really wowed me with the whammy you whacked on *The Exorcist* [Jan. 14]. What the devil got into you?

For those of us who appreciated the film as a brutal but nonetheless brilliant portrayal of the power of faith in God, I say a hex on you, Jay Cocks!

Susan Tietz
2/4/74 *Park Forest South, Ill.*

Gatsby in Hollywood

Your coverage of *The Great Gatsby* [March 18] omitted a great irony in the production of the movie. In his novel F. S. Fitzgerald removes the façade of wealth by portraying how it can corrupt morals, foster waste and breed human carelessness. Absurd how his admonishment to "beware the American dream" is so carelessly discarded by the makers of this monetary extravaganza, I question if they did indeed read the book.

(Mrs.) Marie M. Collins
4/8/74 *Colts Neck, N.J.*

Shake, Bake and Bite

After *Poseidon Adventure*, I fear cruising on an ocean liner. After *Airport* and its follow-up, I cringe at the thought of flight. *Towering Inferno* gives me indigestion before I arrive for dinner at my favorite restaurant on the 62nd floor of the U.S. Steel Building. *Jaws* [June 23] now forces me to abandon my vacation spot on Cape Hatteras in favor of the safety of the Allegheny River.

Ah, the brilliance of Hollywood! In one short year it has transformed Americans into cowering paranoids whose only security is found in the tenth row of a darkened cinema.

Tom Steiner
7/21/75 *Pittsburgh*

To The Rescue

Thank God Stanley Kubrick has come back to rescue all us tired victims drowning in the current movie trend. It will be a joy to see art instead of dollar signs in the eyes of a film maker once more. I promise to treat myself to *Barry Lyndon* five times. That's what it will take to wash away my sorrows for having wasted $3.50 on *Jaws*.

Malia P. Lunday
1/5/76 *Huntingdon Beach, Calif.*

A Credit for Kesey

I think it is rather sad that with all the Oscars won by *One Flew Over the Cuckoo's Nest* [April 12], and all the thank-yous for the golden idols, not one of the recipients mentioned Ken Kesey, the author of the novel, "without whom none of it would have been possible."

Todd Norlander
4/26/76 *Williamsburg, Va.*

Message in a Medium?

If Brando [May 24] can only sit around on an island and bitch about the world, I don't respect him. With his talents, money and supposed intellectual vision, it seems to me he could create a message (not a spectacle) in the movie medium similar to that of Chaplin. So far—zero .

John Helfer
6/21/76 *Valladolid, Spain*

Remakes and Remakes

It seems to me that with all these "creative geniuses" involved with the movie business, someone could come up with a plot just slightly new or different.

For the past few years, the movies have been remakes and remakes. Are you telling us all the real moviemakers lived in the '30s? I'm beginning to believe it.

Bill Wilson
11/15/76 *Catonsville, Md.*

Star Wars

Let the record state that I am a science fiction junkie. If *Star Wars* [May 30] is at least half the movie your article claims it to be, I will be found in the local moviehouse for the next three months straight.

Kenneth Cerveny
6/20/77 *De Kalb, Ill.*

British Foul-Ups

Just how nasty can your Richard Schickel get? In his review of the film *A Bridge Too Far* [June 13] he writes that Operation Market-Garden was "in

the great tradition of British military foul-ups."

He should really read his history, and then he would learn that British military foul-ups were, percentage-wise, usually less than the enemy's. Had this not been so, an empire that eventually straddled the world could not have been built.

Norman Partington
7/11/77 *Durban North, S. Africa*

Worth the Wait

Waiting for my generation to produce a comedienne with half the class of Hepburn or her contemporaries, I had given up hope. Diane Keaton [Sept. 26] is here, and it was worth the wait.

Stephen Erwin
10/17/77 *Bowie, Md.*

Clint is Fun

I'm one of the legion of moviegoers (and a lot of us are *not* culturally disfranchised) who like Clint Eastwood movies [Jan. 9]. Why? Because after a tough day of lecturing and sitting through a department meeting on course changes for the 83rd time, I find it fun to watch, in *Gauntlet*, a bus get the hell shot out of it.

Sure, it's silly, but so is *Star Wars.* Maybe that's why both movies are fun!

Paul J. Nahin
1/30/78 *Durham, N.H.*

Travolta Fever

I can't think of a more delightful way to usher in spring than that of your story on John Travolta [April 3]. He is an electrifying, sumptuous boy-man, who exudes a magical aura on-screen that could cause volcanic eruptions. In our part of the world, he *has* caused disco-dance-contest crazes, polyester-chrome-hair crazes, neon *Saturday Night Fever* T shirts, etc.

Patricia Cahill
4/24/78 *Montreal*

Beatty, Wow!

Warren Beatty [July 3] is what Hollywood is all about: good looking, successful, but a bit mixed up. Yet, the public loves him—as it loves Hollywood—anyway. Travolta's O.K. but Beatty, wow!

Lisa A. Forte
7/24/78 *New York City*

Woody a Genius?

Woody Allen a genius? Well, if he is, he is a sick one. He and his characters are so trapped in themselves and their hang-ups, sex and masochism that they don't know the world out here is beautiful and that most people aren't like that.

Katherine Hoyer
St. Louis

Nine to Five:
Lily Tomlin, Dolly Parton and Jane Fonda starred in this 1980 comedy

John Travolta was nominated for an Academy Award in the 1978 hit *Saturday Night Fever*

Not many humans can be funny and serious and be remembered forever as I predict Woody will be.

Ed Aronson
5/21/79 *Pittsburgh*

Coppola's *Apocalypse*

Maybe Director Francis Coppola should not have bragged to everyone that he was making the definitive film of the Viet Nam War with *Apocalypse Now* [Aug. 27]. Maybe he was his own worst p.r. man. But what he did do was create one helluva cinema experience that stunned me into silence. The film, like the war, is overpowering, brutal, unrelenting, spectacular. Who cares if Coppola had second thoughts about the ending? Did the war itself end as we planned it?

David St. Clair
9/17/79 *Westport, Conn.*

Sellers' Selves

Year after year, Peter Sellers [March 3], "real" or otherwise, has made a rare contribution to the world by expressing another self, each of whom has entertained and enchanted all.

Maxine Lundberg
3/24/80 *Newport Beach, Calif.*

That's Entertainment

I was amused at the review of *Private Benjamin* by Richard Schickel, who couldn't, it seems to me, give the movie any credit for being just entertainment. The film is an amusing way to face the fact that it is—has been, and always will be—"a man's world." Hawn was great.

Patricia O'Brien
12/15/80 *Detroit*

Winning Streep

Meryl Streep is an artist, not a celebrity [Sept. 7]. She doesn't play a part—she is the part. That's magic.

Corey A. Zimmerman
Lutz, Fla.

Ever since reading John Fowles' *The French Lieutenant's Woman* years ago I've been mentally casting a film version. Try as I might, a "right" Sarah never came into focus until the first time I saw Meryl Streep. She is the only actress capable of playing that demanding, elusive role.

Patricia Johnson
9/28/81 *Sonoma, Calif.*

Ma's Temper

Mr. Schickel's review of *Mommie Dearest* [Sept. 21] stands as tragic testimony to one of the most serious obstacles to recognizing the extent of child abuse in our country, namely, that it's really no big deal for parents to haul off at their children now and then.

John E. Imhof
12/7/81 *Port Washington, N.J.*

Forever Gold

Katharine Hepburn and Henry Fonda are not just "golden oldies" [Nov. 16]; they are pure gold, and they always have been.

Cynthia Evans
12/7/81 *La Selva Beach, Calif.*

Spielberg's Creations

We are blessed that Steven Spielberg [May 31] has the means to share his incredible imagination with us. He has done much to stimulate thoughts of adventure, love and wonder in many who have forgotten these aspects of living.

Thomas M. Loushine
Lawrence, Kans.

Time has made E.T. and me very happy. However, a comment slipped in that is unfair to Tobe Hooper, the director of *Poltergeist*. I am quoted as indicating that I took over the project. While I was creatively involved in the entire production, Tobe Hooper alone was the director.

Steven Spielberg
6/21/82 *Los Angeles*

Rocky's a Big Hit

Thank you for your story on Syl-vester Stallone. He has made three excellent films portraying that lovable character, Rocky Balboa. I never thought I would enjoy watching two grown men beat each other up, but the *Rocky* movies have brought me to like the sport.

Connie Crowley
7/5/82 *Vienna, Va.*

Academy Rewards

I loved Columnist Joe Morgenstern's quip about the Oscars that "*Gandhi* was everything the voting members of the academy would like to be: moral, tan and thin" [April 25]. We all need heroes, and apparently the committee preferred that the heroes be noble and real rather than unbelievable and extraterrestrial.

Doris Sullivan
5/16/83 *Grosse Pointe, Mich.*

Star Wars Magic

No one save Walt Disney matches the creativeness of George Lucas [May 23], the originator of the Star Wars universe. If anything is retained from Lucas' magical movies, it should be the concept that peace and good will always triumph.

Jeff M.P. McFarland
6/13/83 *San Francisco*

Music

From the Jazz Age to the era of rock video, TIME has listened to the music and revealed the personalities behind the sounds. An operatic tenor, swing trumpeter and rock guitarist, as diverse as their styles are, have all become legends. But where there's music, there's often controversy. The "bedroom" songs of Sinatra and gyrations of Presley, like the androgynous poses of contemporary stars, have aroused criticism as well as applause.

"Pah!"

We have been hearing opera singers at the Metropolitan for a number of years. Also we have heard a great deal of petty gossip about them: back when Amato was greeted with favor, tongues were no kinder than they are today. Jean de Reszke had his enemies! So we are most interested to hear what you say about Caruso's "large paid claque" [April 6]. Who, we ask, ever accused Caruso of a claque? We agree that in his youth, Caruso loved Bronx Park, he was no moral stickler, he was fond of his spaghetti, his jokes may have been coarse, his "abdomen large." But Caruso had a voice, whoever gave it to him, God, Lucifer, or Nature—it was there as natural as morning, as awe-inspiring as the elements. A super-voice needs no claque, sirs, and what's more, this voice had none. Ask the box office of the Metropolitan Opera House who was the only tenor they had that could draw a capacity house or an over-flowing one! Ask the standees who was their God! Ask anyone who had anything to do with the Metropolitan Opera House—chorus, orchestra, scene shifters, soupers, who it was they adored?

Does Helen of Troy need Pond's Cold Cream or Mars Nuxated Iron? A claque—Pah!

Emilie Bushnell
New York, N.Y.
4/13/25

TIME did not say that Caruso had a paid claque, but reported a rumor from reputable musical quarters to that effect. If the alleged fact be true, it is neither extraordinary nor particularly reprehensible. Many, if not most, Italian singers have paid claques, regardless of how successful they may be. A claque is a sort of musical insurance against an occasional unresponsive audience. Not infrequently it is more a parasite upon an artist than his tool. If there had been Pond's Cold Cream on sale in Troy or Nuxated Iron on Olympus, what is more likely than that Helen and Mars respectively would have availed themselves of these things? Queen Marie of Rumania uses Pond's Cream (according to advertisements) and Jack Dempsey takes Nuxated Iron [July 16, 1923].—ED.

At Nigger Mike's

As a lover of good music and a lover of fair play, I protest against the sneer at Irving Berlin in TIME of May 10, p. 18. I fail to see why the cafe in which the little boy earned his living should be dragged out again and again for the sole purpose of insulting one of our real musical geniuses . . .

Do you suppose a little newborn baby would choose a slum to be born in? . . .

Why should democratic Americans put on airs?

Why shoudn't Berlin use his own love affairs to bring out the sweet and lovely music of his soul? Isn't he doing what the great poets have done all through time?

"Always" floats into our homes over the radio every evening. We hear bits of it as we stop for gasoline at a filling station. We waltz to it and we love it. What does this country stand for if not to give each man his chance? We can do with a lot more good music.

Great American jazz musicians: left, Louis Armstrong; above, Duke Ellington

All honor to Berlin and the lady of his heart!

L. E. Jewett
5/31/26 *Los Angeles, Calif.*
TIME *gave no sneer at Mr. Berlin. Let Mr. Jewett read the item again.* TIME *merely said: "Irving Berlin once worked as a waiter in Nigger Mike's, an East Manhattan saloon. His talent was schooled by the clink and shuffle of a nickelodeon."—ED.*

Tunes

Why are you so highbrow? Or is your record reviewer asleep half the time? Two of the season's best tunes are *Ten Cents a Dance* and *Sing, You Sinners* but I have seen no mention of them listed in TIME's music. Perhaps you are not aware that Frank Harling wrote the second and that he has composed a grand opera, *The Light from St. Agnes*, for several years in the Chicago Company's repertoire. Doesn't that make his jazz worthy of mention? . . .

Fred Wismer
11/3/30 *Chicago, Ill.*

In Musical Circles

More power to May Breen for her stand (as reported in your issue of Dec. 21) in demanding recognition by American Federation of Musicians for ukuleles; and I trust that I will not be out of tune in suggesting that in spite of our half-pint size there is just as much music in us as there is in a lot of brass horns, piccolos, saxophones and other instruments I have known.

As a matter of fact, I am taking up this matter with the Musicians Union in Honolulu, and the American Federation of Musicians will hear more from this little uke, you bet.

As we say in musical circles, *aloha oe!*

*A Honolulu Ukulele
Words and music by
Harold Coffin*
2/22/32 *Honolulu, T.H.*

Berlin's Key

I was interested in your write-up on p. 27 of your issue of April 25 in connection with Mr. Berlin's playing of the piano. I was familiar of course with the fact that he was unfamiliar with the instrument but I am wondering why he picked out as the only key he could manage that of F sharp. As you know this key is in six sharps, one of which is not even a black note, and I am surprised that someone merely picking out melodies by ear would select such a difficult key to play.

Most amateurs would unquestionably pick out either the key of C with no sharps or flats—or G with one sharp, or F with one flat.

I am also interested to know something about the sliding keyboard and what is meant by the effect of playing

Irving Berlin, popular songwriter, with his wife Ellen McKay

another key. The piano as you know is an instrument on which, due to its construction and temperament, there is no difference between the effect of keys other than that of pitch.

Laurence McKinley
5/23/32 *Albany, N.Y.*
F sharp and G flat called the "nigger keys" because they use all the black notes, come easily to many a person who plays the piano by ear. Like Composer Berlin, Negroes who pounded out ragtime in old-time honkey-tonks were partial to F sharp. Composer Berlin plays his songs over first in F sharp. Then aided by the sliding keyboard, an old invention operated by a crank on the side and a supplementary pedal, he transposes them to fall within the easiest singable range.—ED.

Buried Musicians

Plaudits for giving space to *Aux Frontières du Jazz* [Jan. 2], a much-needed book in America and one which we hope will let in the light about true jazz. The "musicians' " jazz band, as opposed to the public's, has never before had a champion. As jazz music auditors become educated they invariably rely on the concoctions and artistry of such as Frank Trumbauer, the Dorsey brothers, the late Bix, Red Nichols, Jack Teagarden and Louis (The Great) Armstrong for satisfaction.

Because great musicians, like great authors, lack the now necessary gift of self-exploitation, the genius of those mentioned above today lies buried beneath the sugar-&-water slop of Vallée, *et al.*

*Edward J. Fitzpatrick Jr.
Robert Fender*
2/13/33 *Del Monte, Calif.*
When colored Bandmaster Louis Armstrong read TIME's *review of Robert Goffin's authoritative book, he remarked: "I don't know where those cats get all they know about me, but they certainly get it right."—ED.*

Brainy Crosby

Your word picture of Actor-Singer Crosby is the best "actual publigraph" of the star this writer has had the pleasure of reading [Jan. 1]. . . .

Good as was your critique on Crosby, it contained some holes. May I offer correction?

Crosby never attempted to "imitate Rudy Vallée's low register waves," was never hired by CBS or Cremo for that purpose. Paley did not discover Crosby for CBS. Talent-Scout, Burt MacMurtrie, associated with Crosby and the writer on the old Old Gold-Paul Whiteman program, brought Crosby into the Columbia fold, MacMurtrie spent many months trying to sell CBS on Crosby!

Prediction: Crosby's popularity will grow. He has brains, a growing wisdom, a recently acquired balance. He's good for America.

Jackson M. Leichter
1/22/34 *Los Angeles, Calif.*

Cohan's Gift Song

I was severely shocked to see in TIME Sept. 24, a naive and entirely unnecessary attack upon George M. Cohan for the song of "Night of Stars" which he wrote as his contribution to the show which was staged at Yankee Stadium to raise funds for German-Jewish refugees.

There was no thought in the mind of the United Jewish Appeal, and certainly none in that of George M. Cohan, to present a musical masterpiece. The words and music were the sincere expression of the emotions of a fine personality moved by the situation in Germany.

It seems to me that TIME has displayed an unforgivable lack of good taste and sense of proportion in undertaking to evaluate this free-will offering to a philanthropic cause on the background of his long and successful professional record as a song composer.

*Nathan Burkan
Chairman, United Jewish Appeal*
10/15/34 *New York City*

Count Basie

Muddy Waters

Fats Waller

TIME made no "attack" on Songwriter Cohan. In reporting his "Night of Stars" as Music news, TIME viewed it squarely for its newsworth as the latest and least meritorious product of an eminent composer, a view unaffected by the fact that he wrote it for a cause and asked no pay.—ED.

Maestri's Wages

The American public as a whole labors under the delusion that entertainers and show folk are wealthy groups. This is far from true and it is about time that someone with first hand information rectified this impression.

As an example let us take the case of the radio maestri. When a top-notch orchestra leader is engaged for a series of commercial broadcasts he may receive a salary in the neighborhood of $2,000 per broadcast. The newspaper radio columns and gossip columns immediately exaggerate this and say that he has been signed for $4,000 or $5,000. However, of the actual $2,000 at least $1,000 goes as commissions, and a good part of the residue goes for arrangements and orchestrations. Next, money must be deducted for office expenses, photograph and pubicity service, entertaining, electrical transcription and recordings of all programs, unions dues and fees. Federal, State and municipal taxes.

If the average band leader retains 20% of his salary he's doing very well. With other entertainers the figures may vary slightly, but none of them makes nearly as much money as he's supposed to.

Loring "Red" Nichols
9/23/35 *New York City*
Trumpet-playing, band-leading "Red" Nichols should know the wages of maestri. One of the great white jazzmen of the middle 1920's, he recorded with his bands variously under the names of The Ramblers, The Little Ramblers, Red Nichols & His Five Hot Pennies, the Louisiana Rhythm Kings and Goofus Five. Great Nicholsnumbers: Riverboat Shuffle, Plenty Off Centre, Get With, Eccentric.—ED.

Swing to Swing

Congratulations to TIME on what, to my knowledge, was the most intelligently written article on swing music to appear in a lay publication.

. . . Greater stress might have been attached to the emotional appeal of swing music. Swing fans, when listening to real swing music, work up a sort of satisfied glow that in especially meaningful passages reaches a climax of nerve stimulation—a "kick." . . .

Charlie Emge
Editor, Tempo
2/10/36 *Los Angeles, Calif.*

Deft Language

Referring to the Theatre column in TIME, April 26, your review of *Babes in Arms* does not opine but states authoritatively—"Lyricist Hart—never topped since he observed in 1925, 'beans could get no keener reception in a beanery: bless our mountain greenery home!'—still maintains the lightest touch in the business."

Is it possible your reviewer has been a victim of amnesia since 1925? Otherwise, how could he have failed to consider Mr. Ira Gershwin?

In Mr. Gershwin's own deft language, "I'm seeking phrases to sing his praises." But, better—let him speak for himself to show your reviewer Mr. Gershwin has not only the lightest touch in the business but also the most penetrating wit.

Here are a few of his inimitable rhymes repeated from memory:
Girl Crazy—
   "I'm bidin' my time
   For that's the kinda guy I'm"
Also
   "I'd make a Mother like no other,
   If you could bother to be the Father."
Of Thee I Sing—
   "If a girl is sexy,
   She may be Mrs. Prexy." . . .
Also
   "She's the illegitimate daughter of
      an illegitimate son
   Of an illegitimate nephew of
      Napoleon." . . .

This letter is not meant to be uncomplimentary to Mr. Hart. He is delightfully talented and deserves his "Orchid," but Mr. Ira Gershwin rates a streamlined everlasting "Oscar. . . ."

Fran Pallay
5/10/37 *Hollywood, Calif.*

TIME bows to Lyricist Gershwin, but still maintains that for grace of rhyme and cleverness of sentiment, Lyricist Lorenz Hart has no peer, nominates two more old snatches of Hart, whose present works speak for themselves, to bolster its case:

> From *Bye And Bye:*
>   ... scheme a while
> When lonely, dream a while
> Twill only seem a while
> And love will do the rest ...
> Ev'ry cloud just flies on,
> Love is on the far horizon.
> You'll be my sweetheart
> Bye and Bye

> From *Manhattan:*
>   ... we'll go to Greenwich
> Where modern men itch
> To be free;
> And Bowling Green you'll see
> With me;
> We'll bathe at Brighton
> The fish you'll frighten
> When you're in;

—ED.

Disca Data

Not three, but *five* rousing cheers to TIME. At last, one of the better weeklies devotes a page to the one thing that this country has long needed —first-rate "disca data" [June 6, p. 22].

Let's hope the excellent standard of the first week's reviews is kept up.

George S. Spelt
6/20/38   *Jamaica, L.I.*
TIME's list of outstanding new records is published in its first issue of each month. For the next list, let Reader Spelt and other music lovers see TIME for July 4.—ED.

Floy Floy

... I know I am asking a great deal of you but your position will warrant it. In deciding this, lay aside position and loyalty to you party and tell me from the fullness of your heart: What' the deuce is a floy-floy?

Paul E. Lamalé
8/22/38   *Wabash, Ind.*
Authors of The Flat Foot Floogie *with the Floy Floy, Slim Gaillard and Slam Stewart, do not know themselves what the words mean. Said Slim: "We were sort of talking a new language." The dance they had vaguely in mind was to be done flat-foot. "When we put the floy floy on it, that was extra business. You got the whole dance right there; you're swinging. See what I mean?" —ED.*

Father's Fan

It is hard to believe that TIME [Oct. 2] the national magazine that has given hot jazz music the most recognition, is guilty of such an error of judgment regarding the review of the *Earl Hines Album*. ...

Earl Hines is to the hot piano what Louis Armstrong is to the jazz trumpet. The Father's influence is felt by many of today's greatest pianists. ...

Let TIME's reviewers listen to *Just Too Soon* or *A Monday Date* again before they say "Hines on these sides does not do so well for himself."

Grover Sales
10/16/39   *Allston, Mass.*
TIME's reviewer listened before he wrote, well aware that his appraisal of the Hines album would not find unanimous consent in the jazz cult.—ED.

Juke Box

Perhaps I am getting blind in my knowledge of slang, but where did you get the name "juke box" for nickel phonographs in your article about Glenn Miller? [Nov. 27]. In Michigan, Indiana and Ohio, everyone calls them "Groan Boxes" and the expression, "Flip a nickel in the groan," is generally understood.

Have you any other nicknames on file?

G. Carlton Burandt
12/25/39   *Bakersfield, Calif.*

Sage or Joy-Killer?

... I highly respect the work of Editor William Allen White, but after reading about his opinion on swing music and jitterbugging I must admit that he now takes his place among the group known as fogies and joy-killers.

... I don't know how the kids in the North and West feel about this thing but I'm sure they will agree with me when I say that there isn't a damn thing wrong with the modern dance music.

Editor White may have felt important with a "buxom armful" or enjoyed the "pressure of a warm, sticky hand," but that was 55 years ago and this is 1940. The way we dance today is doing no more than keeping pace with the times. ...

And another thing: since when is our dance music not tuneful, and not whistleable? ...

Ask Editor White to listen to the music of some of the other dance bands such as popular Glenn Miller, Eddie Duchin, Artie Shaw, T. Dorsey, Paul Whiteman, Dick Jurgens, Orrin Tucker, and many more. Then may he tell us what he thinks of the music that is "squawked and shrieked and roared and bellowed."

Bob McGuire
6/17/40   *St. Augustine, Fla.*

No Reaction

In TIME, Sept. 8, you report that "*Variety* last week showed that there is no U.S. reaction whatever against German music."

Can you or *Variety* inform me as to what has caused the music of Richard Wagner to almost entirely disappear from the air lanes? If our people have no "reaction" against it, who then is denying radio audiences the greatest dramatic music ever written? ...

Lieut. Martin Hunley
9/29/41   *Fort Knox, Ky.*
The big symphony orchestras are mostly silent in summer and little Wagner is played then (except on high-class recorded programs like WQXR). This autumn and winter, there is every

Benny Goodman

Glenn Miller

likelihood that Reader Hunley will again get his fill of "the greatest dramatic music."—ED.

That Sinatra Look

In your article titled "Symphonic Sinatra" [Aug. 23], you have left a very distasteful impression of Mr. Sinatra's appearance at the Bowl. Now, I am not one of the Sinatra Swooners, but . . . I attended the concert . . . I was curious to see this so-called "bedroom" singer who had strangely become the idol of American girlhood.

I was amazed. . . .

From his opening number, *Dancing in the Dark*, to his last encore, *All or Nothing at All*, Sinatra had the greater majority of his audience in the palm of his hand. . . .

I think that the main reason most of the men say they do not care for Sinatra's voice is that they are jealous of him. . . . When my girl looks at me with that "if you could only sing like Sinatra" look in her eyes, I know that I am. . . . Secretly, I've got to admit I think his voice is terrific, and I hand it to the guy. . . .

Charles Pearson
Los Angeles

Sinatra may come and go; but Crosby goes on forever—thank God!

Jean McLaughlin
9/13/43   *New York City*

Sousa Swung

I have just read with complete disgust . . . that Captain Glenn Miller has begun to "swing" the age-old, magnificent marches of John Philip Sousa [Sept. 6]. . . .

When Sousa wrote them he left no room for improvement.

- - - - - - - - - - - -
Portland, Me.

Captain Glenn Miller has the right idea swinging those Sousa marches. The tunes are marvelous but the way Army bands have played them in the past has made them sound like an old-fashioned victrola which needed to be wound up. . . .

Lee Tyler
9/29/43   *Newton, Mass.*

Bebop

Do not dismiss "bebop" so lightly [May 17]. After all, jazz is the only genuine contribution to contemporary music that America can boast of. Our jazz masters are the world's finest, which is more than I can say for our "serious" composers. Bebop is a tremendous thing—it must be heard with the brain and felt with the soul; it packs as much emotional intensity as any symphony. . . .

If you can discover no element of beauty or genius, I fear that you are missing one of the most exciting things that has happened in the music world in many, many years.

Carleton Ryding
Detroit, Mich.

Dizzy Gillespie*—how great can you possibly get?

M. J. Swartz
6/14/46   *Omaha, Neb.*

*Highflown trumpeter and highfalutin high priest of beboppers.

Symbolic Recognition

I have waited many years for Louis Armstrong to achieve symbolic general recognition with an appearance on TIME's cover. This happy recognition is sobered only by the haunting memory of the obscure and impoverished deaths of such musical giants as Jelly Roll Morton, Johnny Dodds, King Oliver and Bessie Smith.

Richard E. Madtes
3/14/49   *Ithaca, N.Y.*

Rudy Vallee, crooner and dance-band leader

Flipping Recap

What a gas it was to pick up a copy of your crazy mag and glim Dave Brubeck on the cover [Nov. 8]. At last those of us who dig the modernists won't receive gleepin' stares when we mention Brubeck or Rogers . . . These cats are the wailin'est! Thanks for your flipping recap of the '54 jazz scene . . .

Adrienne Griffin
Indianapolis

I needed that dictionary of "cat" jargon—if only to help me understand what my children are talking about. I deplore the senselessness of it all, sigh resignedly, and wish that today's bopsters would be more specific and less prolific . . .

Paula Maran
11/29/54   *Detroit*

Frankie Boy

Your vivid Aug. 29 story on my favorite American, Frank Sinatra, was

as colorful and exciting as the man himself . . .

Trudie Morris
London

. . . A pretty picture, indeed, of a nasty little boy and later of a bigoted show-off of a man . . .

Carrie Krieger
Hollywood, Calif.

Says Sinatra: "I don't need anybody in the world. I did it all myself." He is forgetting a kind fate which provided him with a "public," large in numbers but very low in IQ . . .

John K. MacKenzie
9/19/55   *Golden Valley, Minn.*

Running Into the Gutter

Better watch what you say about this Elvis Presley cat [April 2], or you'll have all of young America, TIME-readers or not, down on your neck. This boy is the new god of the beanie brigade and the kiss-me-quick clique, and he's not to be spoken of lightly. Johnnie Ray was never like this; above the background of screams and the thud of falling female bodies, you're hearing another Frankie Sinatra with both pop and hillbilly appeal.

Alan C. Elms
LaCenter, Ky.

In your pop record reviews, you ran into the gutter a recording by Elvis Presley. If you think the teen-agers of this country are taking the slander you printed about our man Elvis you are sadly mistaken, Man! Elvis is the most in all us cats' books.

43 Elvis Presley Fans
4/23/56   *Waterbury, Conn.*

Teeners' Hero

For heaven's sake, leave Elvis Presley and Marilyn Monroe to the pulp magazines. They are both utterly nauseating. Why don't we marry them off to each other and send them to a South Sea isle?

Mrs. Francis McGuire
Arlington, Va.

There must be some error, since in your May 14 issue I find Elvis Presley in the Music section. What does that idiotic howling have to do with music —except the fact that it is on records? Seems to me, the attitude to take would be one of ignoring the whole noise, hoping it will go away.

Arvydas Barzdukas
Cleveland

That "Hi lul-huh-huh-huuv yew-hew" article: Are you sure that fellow's real name isn't Pelvis Presley?

Robert E. Jordan
6/4/56   *Seattle*

Making the Welkin Ring

As one of the 30 million who tunes in on Lawrence Welk's "Champagne

Music" program each week, I resent your May 21 implication that it is only morons who do so. His musicians are all good in their respective fields and it is my opinion that what you call Welk's "oleaginous manner" is true humility. I don't wonder you don't recognize it: it is so rare in today's world.

Rosalie M. Brickett
6/11/56 *Akron*

Rock 'n' Sock

I think your June 18 article on rock-'n' roll music is utterly ridiculous. This type of music is for young people to enjoy while they can, not for crusading adult hypocrites and pessimists like you to criticize and discriminate. The rock-'n'-roll fad is equivalent to the Charleston and its music of the '20s that you yourself probably danced to and enjoyed. There were people like you then to condemn this fad.

Skippy Broussard
Lafayette, La.

How did you fuddyduddies feel about Dixieland when you were young? How many of you wore bell-bottom trousers and danced the Charleston? How many of you were juvenile delinquents? I wear blue jeans and dig rock 'n' roll. I am not a juvenile delinquent.

Rosemary Caldwell
9/3/56 *Flora, Miss.*

Cornball Disk Jockey

In your Aug. 13 mag you call me a "rock 'n' roll" disk jockey. Now it's a well-known fact that I have been actively fighting the stuff for years, and am known far and wide as the fearless champion of genuine cornball music. This way-out rock 'n' roll is strictly for the squares.

Red Blanchard
9/3/56 *Hollywood*

The Most

I am a teen-ager, and I think Elvis Presley is disgusting. Why should he be making $7,500 a week when schoolteachers who are educating us only make a small sum of $60 a week. We'd have an awful time with a Government run by people like Elvis Presley.

Pat Hansford
Hollywood

Why does TIME keep running Elvis Presley down? People who dislike him are mostly hangovers from the Gay Nineties.
We really think he's the most, to say the least.

Tenley Jones (aged 14)
10/15/56 *Washington, D.C.*

That Man (Ugh) Again

We were shocked and disgusted by your extensive coverage of Elvis Pres-

ley in the Nov. 4 issue. It is disillusioning when a magazine of high caliber stoops to a low level.

Helen Schoembucker
Al Gourevitch
Oberlin, Ohio

Why don't you conduct some research on why Elvis Presley appeals to some normal people? There must be something good about him.

Carla Schultz
11/25/57 *Chicago*

Counterpoint

Your June 9 reporting on rock-'n'-roller Jerry Lee Lewis and *The Beat Generation and the Angry Young Men*, leaves me generously nauseated. After returning from two years duty in the Far East, I am seriously concerned over the very evident change in our country's cultural and amusement pursuits. When a supposedly enlightened people commence raising such types to positions of wealth and influence, then we as a nation have taken a long step toward fulfilling Karl Marx's prophecy

for capitalism. It is quite obvious that our churches, schools and parents have a monumental job of youth education ahead.

D. H. Callahan
Captain, U.S.A.
6/30/58 *Fort Riley, Kans.*

What Is It?

Exactly what does your magazine (the finest in its field) have against Frank Sinatra (the finest in his field)?

Al Azose
9/15/58 *Seattle*

Disk Jockey's Lament

Lest the picture of egocentric, overblown disk jockeys sketched in TIME [June 8] be thought typical by sponsors, neighbors and the Internal Revenue bureau, it should be categorically stated that most of us are (relatively) sober, mildly hard-working types, quite outside the pale of the play-for-payola crowd.

Al Covaia
KJBS
6/29/59 *San Francisco*

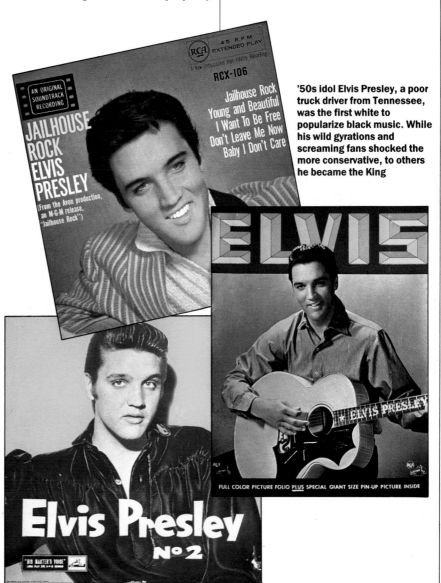

'50s idol Elvis Presley, a poor truck driver from Tennessee, was the first white to popularize black music. While his wild gyrations and screaming fans shocked the more conservative, to others he became the King

White House Guests?

Will someone please tell Mr. Sinatra, and his ring-a-ding-a-ding-a-ding, ding ding middle-aged cheatniks to keep their pizza-pickin' paws out of the White House? If American prestige is as low as Mr. Kennedy claims, Mr. Sinatra and his friends will certainly not improve the situation at home or abroad.

Mrs. Warren Kenefick
Chamblee, Ga.
12/26/60

Elvis Blues

I happen to be a fan of Elvis Presley's, even though I don't particularly like his contortive wiggles when he sings, and I consider it damn common of you to ridicule him the way you did in your review of *G.I. Blues*

Bruce Smith
Charlottesville, Va.
12/26/60

Background Music

It was disheartening to see TIME [Aug. 30] devoting two columns to that insipid "tranquilizer," Muzak. It might have its therapeutic value, like television, for those who enjoy being entertained without having to think; but TV has a finite advantage—you can turn it off. It is Muzak's complete blandness and lack of character, which its makers try so hard to achieve, that I find so annoying. God save the day when its "innocent murmurs" pour forth from every lamppost in its at-tempt to create a euphoria for millions of unsuspecting Americans.

Jonathan Laitin
New York City
9/13/63

Singing as an Englishman . . .

As an Englishman who has been removed from his fatherland for scarcely two months, I feel I must contest one of the key statements made in your article on the Beatles and "Beatlemania" [Nov. 15]. In it you state: "Americans might find the Beatles achingly familiar. . . ." This I think is a radical misjudgment, for it will become plain to anyone who cares to listen to some Beatles' music that nothing could be farther removed from the syrupy banalities that seem to be the order of the day on the American *Hit Parade*.

Timothy Fleming
Pomfret School
Pomfret, Conn.
11/29/63

Hurrah for the Beatles

Please don't joke about the Beatles. Encourage them! As a music teacher and composer of children's music, I like to see anyone become successful in the music field whether he's a Beethoven or a Presley. We need musical expression! So I say hurrah for the Beatles.

Alfa Kent
Austin, Texas

I think the Beatles are one of the best things to come to America since jazz. Their music is different, but not if you understand the feel. The way they look and the way they sing is so parallel to our own life. We teenagers love the Beatles, shag-mopped,

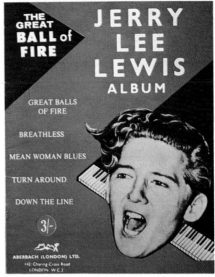

Jerry Lee Lewis, '50s rock 'n' roll star

screaming and pop-wailers that they are.

Kristine Fontes
Lancaster, Pa.
2/28/64

Streisand, The Greatest

Thank you, thank you. It is about time the world knew that Barbra Streisand is the greatest [April 10]. I now find great pleasure in flashing your fine cover and excellent article in the faces of my previously unenthusiastic and preoccupied friends, saying "Ha, did the Beatles make the cover of TIME?" I have been a fan since her first album. That girl is a spook.

Jim Winker
University of Wisconsin
Madison, Wis.
4/17/64

Still the Greatest

Pale, sick, exhausted Judy Garland should never have been forced to undergo the ordeal of the Melbourne concert [May 29]. Superb in Sydney, sick in Melbourne—in any shape, size or condition she is still the greatest entertainer alive.

Rodney Fisher
Melbourne
6/5/64

Elvis Beats the Beatles

Please allow us to clarify a statement in your story "The Beatle Business" [Oct. 2], which implied that more records by the Beatles have been sold than by Elvis Presley. You undoubtedly refer to the certified awards by the Record Industry Association, which date back only to 1958. Some of Mr. Presley's biggest hits on singles were produced in prior years.

Henry Brief
Executive Secretary
Record Industry Association of America
New York City
10/16/64

Rock 'n' Roll Escape

The article on rock 'n' roll [May 21] was both forceful and revealing. Primitive, noisy, anti-intellectual, coarse,

Clockwise:
Jimi Hendrix, Janis Joplin, Bruce Springsteen

unlyrical, and provocative as it is, rock 'n' roll provides an active means of honest, uninhibited expression, and an escape from the pressing realities of a 20th century world that is all too often the burial ground of lighthearted amusement.

John Winebrenner
Washington, D.C.

News, it may be. Timely, it is. But music, it is not.

Mrs. Joseph L. De Groot
Plainfield, Ill.

I am 30, and, as often happens to oldsters in their senility, impressions of the long ago are much more lasting than those of the recent past. Thank goodness for Artie Shaw, Glenn Miller, Wayne King and the Dorseys.

Mrs. D. H. Winship
Milwaukee

I have a feeling of disgust for middle-age people doing dances like the frug or jerk. We have not as yet invaded their "adults only" world, so please, if you can't give us anything to grow into, kindly leave us something to grow out of.

Joel Rosenberg
5/28/65   *Highland Park, Ill.*

What's Buggin' You?

O.K., what's buggin' you guys? Is everyone anti-us? Yea, we dig the Beatles, go ape for causes, and cut out to discothèques, but man, weren't you ever a teen-ager? Sonny and Cher, Bob Dylan, the Beatles, and the Rolling Stones are like us. They're part of our era. Everyone used to say we didn't care. Well, now we do, and what do you do? You make fun of us.

A. T. Nager
10/1/65   *New Haven, Conn.*

Rocks in the Wind

Anyone who can interpret the lucid lyrics of Ray Charles's *Let's Go Get Stoned* as "a call to take part in a freedom march" [July 1] has scrambled eggs in the head. Are *double-entendres* in music new? Such old songs as *All or Nothing at All, All The Way* and *Come Fly With Me* could never pass a purity test. Was Jerome Kern a dirty old man when he wrote *Easy to Love?* Was Oscar Hammerstein thinking lewd thoughts as he penned *I'm Just a Girl Who Can't Say No?*

Carol Coviello
New York City

Cleans and Dirties be damned. The Rolling Stones didn't *invent* the bawdy song; it's been around for some time. As for LSD and pot, they are what's happening, and it would be surprising if pop songs didn't take account of them. Rock 'n' roll didn't write the script, it only made the scene. But the main thing is that rock 'n' roll is the first original development in popular music since jazz. Groups like The Beatles and The Stones display a phenomenal melodic inventiveness and a harmonic and contrapuntal imagination that even us squares can dig.

(Prof.) Louis H. Mackey
Rice University
7/15/66   *Houston*

Odd Part

So the DJs are all in a dither because Beatle John Lennon [Aug. 12, Aug. 19] has been mouthing off again. You'd think people'd be used to his snickery, sneery philosophy by now. And anyhow, in this country we're supposed to have a traditional respect for people voicing their considered opinions. But that respect, like Christianity, is something we see little of. The

Mick Jagger

odd part of the story is that what the guy said is true. Of course the Beatles are more popular than Jesus. So are Volkswagens, golfing, blondes, politics, football, pop art, Batman, drag racing and money.

Ann Brent
8/26/66   *Royal Oak, Mich.*

Playing By The Rules

Though the Stones' personal lives are hardly exemplary, you have neglected to point out several less sensational but just as important facts about them.

Mick Jagger is recognized as one of the most authentic "white blues" singers. Consequently, it is unfair to condemn him because he "bumps, grinds and jiggles" onstage—anyone who has seen James Brown work up himself and his audience into an orgasmic frenzy will realize that Jagger is merely playing by the rules of the game.

Some Stones' songs may be suggestive, but not any more so than, for example, Mississippi John Hurt's classics *Salty Dog* and *Candy Man*, with their blatant phallic references.

The Stones' talents are not exclusively "leeric" oriented. They can also write such songs as the tender *As Tears Go By*, the haunting *Play with Fire*, and the baroque *Ruby Tuesday*.

Dean Niles, '69
University of Chicago
5/12/67   *Chicago*

Like Wow!

An excellent article on the Beatles [Sept. 22]. We knew that sooner or later the older generation would be forced to admit that the Beatles are brilliantly talented, just as we've always said. What took you so long?

Dona Woldow
Haverford, Pa.

With every album since *Rubber Soul*, the Beatles have been approaching an all-encompassing pop-music nirvana. Pray that they make it before old age and the Establishment catch up with them.

H. Franklin Johnson Jr.
Blauvelt, N.Y.

You did the Beatles proud with your magnificent cover story on them, but you also did yourself proud in an indirect sort of way by printing the article when you did. Most national magazines rushed out hastily written copy on them when the Beatles burst on the music scene, but you waited until the Beatles reached the zenith of their genius before undertaking to do a write-up. I am glad you did.

Gail Lynn Larsen
9/29/67   *Lombard, Ill.*

From the Soul

If finally people have learned to understand the Negro's music [June 28] why the hell can't they understand the man or woman who's singing it? Soul music is not something that just came on the scene, it has been here since the black man came to America; it started way back in those cotton field in Mississippi, Georgia, etc. That was all we had, when we were out in the hot sun picking cotton; finally a nice cool breeze came and you just had to let someone know that you had the feeling, so you started singing.

Even though we didn't have any music to sing by, we still had soul.

Vickie Murphy Brown
Washington, D.C.

In referring to Aretha, you stated that "she leans her head back, forehead gleaming with perspiration." Aretha does not perspire, she sweats. Sweat has soul. Perspire is a word invented by blue-veined little ladies who spoke of limbs instead of arms and legs, boy cows instead of bulls.

Richard Wilson
Aspen, Colo.

Soul is acting and being yourself—doing your thing, naturally. Like I eat chitlins, yams, greens and corn bread because I dig them, not because I am black or have any false illusions that these "soul foods" will make me soulful. Soul is being, not trying to be.

Robert L. Teal
7/12/68 *Berkeley, Calif.*

The Saddest Words

To me, the saddest words that Janis Joplin [Oct. 19] ever sang are from *Turtle Blues:* "I'm gonna take good care of Janis—Yeah. 'Cause there ain't no one gonna dog me down."

God rest her troubled soul.

Barbara Cordes
Bakersfield, Calif.

Like Jimi Hendrix, Miss Joplin made one meaningful contribution in her life: the manner of her death. Hopefully, the younger generation will get the message.

Harry Preston
11/9/70 *Hollywood. Calif.*

Amazing Mick Jagger

As a longtime fan of the Rolling Stones, I read Robert Hughes' TIME Essay with great interest, only to find that Hughes' awareness of Jagger's personality is about the same as was a dinosaur's awareness of it own existence. Surely anybody who has seen Jagger perform live knows that his audience control is amazing—he can turn it on or off with a flick of his hair.

Certainly I as a political hopeful only wish that I could generate half as much excitement in an audience and still keep it under my thumb.

Alan D. Moore
8/7/72 *Nairobi, Kenya*

The Duke's Stature

TIME's story of Duke Ellington [June 3] dwelt mainly on items of gossip, and gave little clue to his real stature as a composer.

By 1933 Ellington had established himself as a creator of an original

music. It was jazz-based, but as TIME recognized, it transcended the limitations of jazz. However, no mention was made of his two most important larger-scale works. *Black, Brown and Beige* (1943) and *Harlem* (1950).

His music reached people in all parts of the world, from Africa to Russia and the Far East. He ranks as one of *the* 20th century composers.

Alan Martin
7/1/74 *Melbourne, Australia*

Schizophrenic

Despite the expected overstatement, your story on the various species of rock audiences did contain its modicum of truth. One thing your reviewer failed to note, however: some groups display a nearly schizophrenic change between concert and album. The recent LPs of Hot Tuna and the Grateful Dead, for instance, have been finely wrought blends of virtuosity and lyricism, not rowdyism.

Carl F. Hoffman
7/15/74 *Franksville, Wis.*

Incredible Paul

Paul Anka is as incredible as your article says. As president of the Song Writers Hall of Fame, I am qualified to tell you of his great talents. As his old and personal friend, I can testify to his great humanity.

Sammy Cahn
12/29/75 *New York City*

Mediocre Paul

First it was Springsteen, now it's McCartney. Your magazine has about as much musical taste as a smelly old warthog. McCartney may be a commercial success, but he is a mediocre, washed-up musician.

Reedy Jay
6/21/76 *Berkely, Calif.*

The Ultimate

It's about time somebody put Linda Ronstadt [Feb. 28] where she belongs: out in front, spotlighted and highlighted. Linda is not just a superstar, she is the ultimate: she is song, she is now, she is forever. Music is alive and well in Linda.

Joseph M. Wall Jr
3/21/77 *Washington, D.C.*

Rape of the Beatles

Beatlemania [Aug. 8] is a rape of the Beatles. The show is a disgusting moneymaking perversion of what the Beatles have meant to me. I would never see such trash. The Beatles can only be remembered and cherished by listening to their music, watching their films and retaining memories of having lived under their influence.

James N. Thompson
8/29/77 *Hamden, Conn.*

The Beatles in a psychedelic rendering

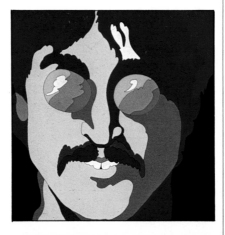

Modern Mozarts

I cannot believe Robin Gibb has the audacity to compare the Bee Gees to the Beatles. The Bee Gees' music consists only of pre-teen whining, while the Beatles are thought of as modern-day Mozarts.

Dennis Fischer
4/29/78 Pittsburgh

Cheers for The Who

The review Jay Cocks did on The Who at Madison Square Garden [Oct. 1] was one of the nicest and most honest reviews of the group I have read in a while. I went to New York City for the second of those concerts, and Cocks described it like it was. The Who have proved themselves to be the best rock 'n' roll band ever. I was so touched, excited and happy for The Who and all their fans that words couldn't express my emotions, I'm glad Cocks feels the way I do.

Ellen Campbell
10/22/79 Bloomington, Ind.

Rock Defined

The Who [Dec. 17] is pure energy. After a concert, the band is drained and the audience is drained. Rock is as important and effective an outlet for energy as is sports. To paraphrase Pete Townshend, rock is the only thing that can verbalize the frustrations of youth and at the same time give you the vehicle to dance the trouble away.

Glenn S. Hall
1/7/80 Camillus, N.Y.

Lennon's Legacy

John Lennon and his music [Dec. 22] were like a great parade—gaudy yet sweet, outrageous yet poignant, raunchy yet delicate. And, like all parades, it passed by too quickly.

Mary A. Sarno
Philadelphia

"All you need is love"—but a gun for your protection is also useful. Shame on you, America, shame on you!

G. Morison
1/12/81 Paisley, Scotland

Roll On Rolling Stones

Have you lost your mind? What you said about the Rolling Stones was absolutely terrible [Oct. 26]. I'm only 16 so I wasn't in diapers or even around when the Stones started. I first heard their music when I was twelve, and since then have thought they were grand.

Lee Ann Hill
Grand Marais, Minn.

I am 17 years old. When the Rolling Stones played Seattle recently, I got up early and waited in line 24 hours for a ticket. I did this not because I wanted to "ease into the slipstream of

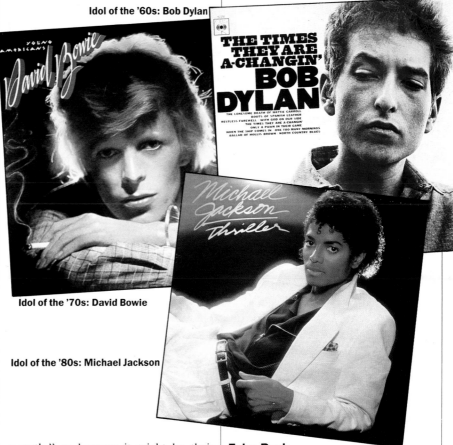

Idol of the '60s: Bob Dylan

Idol of the '70s: David Bowie

Idol of the '80s: Michael Jackson

a myth," or because it might be their last tour, but because I love their music, wanted to see the band, and have a good time.

Rebecca Gates
12/14/81 Portland, Ore.

Dead Rock

Your article "Rock Hits the Hard Place" [Feb. 15] is saying exactly what the 1960s "older generation" bemoaned: they don't make music like they used to.

Michele DeVita
3/8/82 New York City

Simple Melody

The term minimalism for the new music [Sept. 20] is a misnomer. Far from being a look at sound through a microscope, it is more like a Xerox machine run amock. Steve Reich's *Four Organs* is not deceptively simple, it's just simple.

Michael Ingham
10/11/82 Santa Barbara, Calif.

Rock Star Bowie

David Bowie [July 18] in any role is exciting and frightening.

Gaye A. Muilenburg
Hartley, Iowa

Bowie is timeless. He is not a fad; he is not a "rock idol." He is a musician who clearly stands above the rest.

Eleanor Jones
8/8/83 Kingsport, Tenn.

Tube Rock

As a rock deejay, I wonder how many of the letter writers who put down rock video [Jan. 16] are aware of how much they sound like their parents. Perhaps these naysayers will remember how their mothers and fathers complained when they stood on the corner singing do-wop, grew long hair and went crazy over the Beatles. Change is the essence of life. Those who refuse to change and grow are doomed to decay and middle age.

Bob ("Bob-a-Loo") Lewis
2/13/84 New York City

Michael's World

Michael Jackson is to the 1980s what Sinatra was to the '40s, Elvis was to the '50s, the Beatles were to the '60s and Elton John was to the '70s.

Daniel Guder
4/7/84 Dayton

Rural Lingo

Country expressions, as Steve Allen observed [*Letters*, April 2], are the most colorful in our language. My wife, who is from Oklahoma, has given me many that I have used in my work as a motion-picture songwriter. She told me of one student who, when asked by the teacher if he was finished with his exam paper, answered: "Purt nigh but not plumb." This became the title of a song for Dinah Shore in *Aaron Slick from Punkin Crick*.

Jay Livingston
4/23/84 Los Angeles

Television

When commercial television was launched in 1946, 7,000 sets were sold. By 1949, 60,000 sets were sold—per week. Within a decade, the average American family was spending 42 hours a week in front of the tube. Its shows created a new 20th century folklore: a witch named Samantha, a villain named J.R., a jester named Johnny. Is it a wasteland? The debate continues while viewers zap from cable channel to network, and back again.

"Logie Baird"

I suppose you can now return the photo of J. L. Baird* that I sent you last June (and you published in TIME, Sept. 19, page 24), as you promised in your letter of July 6.

By the way, it may interest you to know that Mr. Baird's middle name is LOGIE—John Logie Baird. This I learned in a letter I received from him the other day. Someday when he comes into his own, has his hair cut and is placed on a pedestal—by reason of his discoveries in NOCTOVISION—he may be known as Logie Baird, after the manner of Rudyard Kipling, Woodrow Wilson and many other notables who had the good sense, after getting firmly fixed in the limelight, to discard their first Christian names. Somehow I never think I know a fellow intimately until I ascertain what the second initial in his name stands for—mine is Cunninghame. It so often explains so much about who he is—his mother's side of the house, which usually (if he amounts to anything) is the better one.

Speaking of NOCTOVISION, in his letter of Sept. 29, Logie says: "I quite agree that NOCTOVISION has greater potentialities than TELEVISION, both in peace and war." So hereafter I shall hook up J. L. B. with NOCTOVISION rather than TELEVISION, which latter others appear to be as busily working out as this bushy-headed Scotsman.

The Experimenter Publishing Company, 230 Fifth Avenue, New York, has issued "ALL ABOUT TELEVISION," an illustrated 110-page pamphlet by H. Winfield Secor and Joseph H. Kraus, the second chapter of which is devoted to Baird's discoveries. Someday I hope to see John Logie Baird's picture on the front page of TIME—when he does something deserving such fame.

James C. Moffet
12/5/27 *Louisville, Ky.*

*Scottish inventor, after traditional hardships, of television and noctovision.—ED.

Accurate, Succinct

I wish . . . to congratulate you on the accurate and succinct description of my television landing system.

John Hays Hammond, Jr.
4/8/30 *Gloucester, Mass.*

Travesty

LIFE, in its issue of May 16, carries an advertisement of TIME, which tells of the editors, writers, researchers and correspondents of the new Radio Department, who have for three months been exploring the field. They are described as having gathered news "from London, where television has failed dismally."

Some member of your team has surely betrayed you here. Any of the many thousands of people, who watched on the television screen Bois Roussel make his winning dash in the Derby, or Eddie Phillips knocking out Ben Foord in the ninth round, or Donald Budge playing at Wimbledon, could have told him better. Television in England has its own difficulties to overcome; but it is now providing a daily service of excellent quality to many thousands of viewers. It is a travesty of the facts to describe it as a dismal failure; and as a regular, if transatlantic, reader of TIME, I am jealous for its reputation for accuracy.

Stephen Tallents
British Broadcasting Corp.
7/18/38 *London*
Sir Stephen is quite right. TIME's advertising copywriter was off base. However, TIME's Radio section has pointed out several times in recent weeks the technical excellence of British television.—ED.

A Monster in Our Midst

Startling to me was your article on television [May 24]. Any sensitive reader is awakened to a realization that an infant monster is in our midst —a monster with tremendous potentialities for good or evil.

Return of The Honeymooners, 1978

"Mr. Television,"
Comedian
Milton Berle

Our haunting fear is that the gentlemen of advertising will grasp this marvelous instrument and flood our homes with the moral mediocrity of the soap companies and the sensualism of Hollywood . . . The people of America must voice their conviction that television programs be an enlightenment to the home and not the saloonkeeper's prop.

Robert Kreider
University of Basel
Basel, Switzerland
6/21/48

Video Verbiage

. . . I, like H. L. Mencken, am unimpressed by the suggested name for TV fans [Dec. 20]. But I would like to submit "televice" as a term to describe the condition which is demoralizing erstwhile model housekeepers, and which is paralyzing the boys at the corner bar . . .

Johnsie M. Fiock Fildes
Olney, Ill.

Concurring with . . . the deplorable lack of an expressive name for TV

fans, may I venture: teleadict and telemaniac.

John D. Nichols
Toledo, Ohio
1/10/49

The Shape of Things

By far the most terrifying glimpse of the future to date is a picture of the living room devoted to television and other forms of escapism [Feb. 7]. To the many people who still love books, good conversation, and the sense of well-being that comes from a bit of Spartan living, this business of sitting in spineless comfort, allowing vicarious emotions to take over, then tottering feebly to a still more softly cushioned car seems too horrible for words. Are we drifting rapidly back to the jelly-like, shell-less and boneless creatures of the azoic period?

J. Hilton Legh
Yarmouth, Nova Scotia
7/3/49

TV Taste

. . . We do want TV to become a

medium of education for our children, but our teen-agers are embarrassed and younger offspring wide-eyed at the poor taste shown by the Barbours of *One Man's Family* [May 14].

We want our children to know the facts of life—not see them enacted. And we certainly don't want them to have the idea that all homes discuss sex at the breakfast or dinner tables. I greatly disagree that "the strength of the U.S. lies" in such a family as the Barbours.

Dorothea Sommer
Massillon, Ohio
6/4/51

Pure Slurvian

TIME, May 24, reports that the BBC is concerned with the enunciation of some of its announcers. They needn't be. Our own *Toast of the Town*, Ed Sullivan, has used nothing but pure Slurvian for years. As our leading exponent of Slurvian, Sullivan surpasses anything ever dreamed of by the BBC. To wit:

Edward Byrnes, the "Kookie" of *77 Sunset Strip*

George Burns and Gracie Allen

The Lone Ranger and Tonto

Edward R. Murrow

The Andy Griffith Show

The Waltons

Red Skelton

MERKRIES and LINKS—two cars advertised on his program.

AWYENCE—the people who attend his show.

LAZENJELM—complimentary greeting to the awyence.

YERP—the continent east of us.

NITESTAYS OF MERKA—our country.

6/21/54

J. K. Shallenberger
Long Beach, Calif.

Household Gods

It is indeed a pathetic situation when a TV set's proximity to the dining area is the big selling point of a house; how the visiting Russian housing administrators must have laughed at the spectacle of American parents hurrying to satisfy the slightest whims of their "progressive children" [Oct. 17]. "Howdy Doody" is no substitute for a harmonious family whose members enjoy food and congenial conversation equally well.

11/7/55

Mrs. John Chiariello
Elba, N.Y.

Assa Maddera Fack

Clifton Fadiman should have given some credit for the growth of Televenglish [March 11] to Ed Murrow's *Person to Person* program. Most of the "persons" on his show never fail to begin a statement without "Assa maddera fack."

Alice E. Christgau
Minneapolis

I agreed to give my 13-year-old son a .22-cal. rifle for Christmas—provided that his first target would be our TV set. The bargain was duly carried out. His grades have improved; he spends more time in our workshop; and none of us miss the delights of television in the slightest degree. Want to borrow our rifle, anyone?

C. E. Tripp
Hudson, Ohio

Your article was awright, but in twenny years Televenglish will definitely sound natchral.

4/1/57

Richard Corliss
Philadelphia

Whom TV Hath Joined

Your Aug. 19 article on the *Bride and Groom* show convinces me that my own original idea for a TV funeral show can garner a large and enthusiastic audience. Awards to the dying participants will include a solid silver casket, a tasteful marble tombstone and the privilege of being tootled into heaven by the NBC staff orchestra playing *Swing Low, Sweet Chariot*. After all, if the profanation of the sacrament of marriage can enrapture 3,000,000 housewives, my show ought to knock 'em dead.

9/9/57

Elisabeth R. Lewis
Hollywood

The Man Behind the Cigarette

Don't you think you may have been even too generous in rating Murrow's current performance [Sept. 30]? As Britain's Boswell in her crisis some years ago, he was indeed great. Now we seem to have a slightly frustrated anachronism (including cigarette) solemnly orating poorly digested everyday news and personal political prejudices. Avast there, Murrow! Why not follow up that inspiration of taking a protracted vacation and give all of us a rest? Besides, we may need you for later!

10/21/57

Ed Jones
Langley, Wash.

The Shock-Up Generation

When psychiatry became the vogue several years ago, we were told to handle the teen-ager with kid gloves—"he's a sensitive adolescent"—*ad nauseam*. It's now grown to a frightening overemphasis via the movies and TV, which cater to the teen-age audi-

The Brady Bunch

Charlie's Angels

Johnny Carson

ence, and too often justify violence and sadism.

Marian L. Gilbert
4/28/58 *Three Rivers, Mich.*

View Though the Tube

Your article on the sad state of television was excellent. I have thought for several years that the industry would go through a shakedown period and would level off with some measure of quality. The situation has become progressively worse, and from the looks of next year's programs, it will not improve. Apparently, the networks have forgotten that the airwaves belong to the American people and not the sponsors.

William A. McDonald
Durham, N.C.

In personal defiance of this passing season, I have returned to reading.

Mrs. Gloria Weller
Brookline, Mass.

Whoever writes the reviews on television doesn't know what he is talking about. In the first place, I watch television to be entertained and to relax my mind from the everyday grind, and as such I do not like, and will not watch, any program that tries to delve into racial or religious or any other turmoil of the day. And it just makes me boil when some joker implies that people are jerks because they don't demand symphonies or opera or some other kind of high-toned programs.

Clarence N. Cooper
4/21/61 *Port Huron, Mich.*

The Big Eye

In regard to whether or not public hearings should be televised [*see* Press], I offer my authoritative opinion: there

should be no such intimacy going on. In campaigns America has already been drugged into measuring only what the candidate looks and sounds like, not the importance of what he puts on paper. It frightens me to think what would have happened if TV had been as influential in the time of Socrates, who was not very pretty; or of Moses, who had a great impediment of speech; or of Jesus, whose Hebrew had a strong Galilean accent; or of Lincoln, whose wart, beard and shrill voice would have made Madison Avenue get rid of him immediately. It was what Mr. Lincoln said at Gettysburg that will be remembered, not how he looked or sounded on television.

George Jessel
12/18/64 *Los Angeles*

Douglas Salutes Schaefer

An apology and a salute—to George Schaefer, director of the *Hallmark Hall of Fame*. TIME [Nov. 26] correctly quotes me as finding fault with Schaefer because he did not fight for a scene in *Inherit the Wind* with some mild profanity in it that the agency wanted to cut. I spoke after I had viewed the first studio screening of the tape, from which the scene had been cut. I was indignant. It was a good scene—an important one. Cutting it was one more example of the puerility that dominates and emasculates too much of our television fare. But I had underestimated George Schaefer's integrity and stamina. In the final version, the scene was restored. So—three unre-

Happy Days

All in the Family

Dallas

served cheers for George. He is, as you say, an oasis in the desert.

Melvyn Douglas
12/18/65 *New York City*

The Way It Is

As a regular listener to CBS news, I heartily agree with you on the authoritative, relevant and objective newscasting by Walter Cronkite [Oct. 14]. When Walter concludes his daily assortment of often unpleasant news with "That's the way it is, October . . .," somehow I feel his silent remark, "and I can't do a thing about it."

Masato Takahashi, M.D.
Los Angeles

Who can forget Walter's tremendous coverage of the Kennedy assassination? I can still hear his emotion-laden voice as he tried to keep control. It was an insight into his character for him to reveal himself as a warm human being; to let the world know that he felt the same as the rest of us during those black hours.

(Mrs.) Vivien Beirlein
10/21/66 *Northville, N.Y.*

Bright Blue Eyes

I am very closely acquainted with Walter Cronkite, and TIME's cover portrait infuriated me. Walter Cronkite

does *not* have mud-brown eyes. He has the most beautiful, clear, bright blue eyes I have ever seen. Also the *bluest* blue eyes.

Kathy Cronkite
10/28/66 *New York City*
Now the mud's in our eye.—ED.

The Big Brother Tube

British television's candor is refreshing, even as a substitute for content. But BBC doesn't quite warrant your sugar-coating endeavor [March 10].

BBC Director Green's "assured source of income, which we can spend as we think right," as "it may be better to give intense pleasure to a small number of people than mild pleasure to a greater number," smacks of a bureaucrat's lofty disregard of the interests of those who assure that income.

The $14 license fee is mandatory for all radio-TV-set owners, irrespective of their videosyncrasies. License dodgers (of whom there are about 2,000,000) are flushed out by government post-office detection vans that patrol the streets nightly, homing in on addresses where unlicensed sets are operating. A current government proposal would raise the fine for first-offense "pirate-viewers" from $28 to $140, and would require TV dealers to inform the post office of set purchasers or renters. While BBC's program directors may not be "state controlled," the viewers certainly are.

Endure the commercials, fellow

Americans, and think twice, or more, before letting Big Brother tend to your watching.

Fred Bruner
Hampton Hill,
3/24/67 *Middlesex, England*

Johnny-on-the-Spot

"Midnight Idol," your cover story on the Johnny Carson phenomenon and on television in general [May 19] was excellent.

Carson is a refreshing breeze in what is a wasteland, with the exception of an occasional documentary or sports event. The average television series is created for an adult with the mentality of a twelve-year-old. This is an egregious affront to the American populace. When will program planners realize that the "average" viewer does not identify with the antics of *Petticoat Junction* or *Gomer Pyle*?

Sally Sax
6/2/67 *Malibu, Calif.*

Here's to Life

Just as important as its educational value is the fact that *Sesame Street* shows the diversity of life: companionship, laughter, frustration, wonder, beauty. For once we get away from too simplistic and shallow programming. Watching *Sesame Street*, a child may realize that life, after all, can be interesting, challenging and worthwhile.

(Mrs.) Alie Jansen
12/14/70 *Tarrytown, N.Y.*

Gooseberry Tie-In

So the *Upstairs, Downstairs* television series has spawned some treacly tie-in books [April 28]. I regret to report that your reviewer's worst fears have been realized—*Mrs. Bridge's Upstairs, Downstairs Cookery Book* is already available here. Gooseberry Fool, anyone?

Cedric Pulford
5/26/75 *Cardiff, Wales*

Nothing But Sex

Re your cover story on *Charlie's Angels* [Nov. 22]: Forget the intellectual analysis. The show is nothing but raw sex. I love it.

Jock K. Chung
12/13/76 *New Haven, Conn.*

Learning from Roots

Ever since I was old enough to see movies about "Africans," I felt ashamed about my ancestry. *Roots* showed me that my ancestors weren't stupid, ignorant savages just a little higher than monkeys. It helped me understand that my ancestors were not always slaves.

Yvonne Tyson
3/7/77 *Jersey City*

Queen Lucille

Call Lily Tomlin the Crown Princess or whatever nice title you might want to bestow upon her, but "Long live the Queen!"—Lucille Ball.

Eugene Tatom
5/2/77
Fairfield, Conn.

Muppet Mania

John Skow's article on the Muppets [Dec. 25] was the most delightful, touching and refreshing story I've read in years. You missed a golden opportunity, however. A centrefold of Miss Piggy would have made the issue a collectors' item.

Frank Bachenheimer
1/15/79
Glenview, Ill.

Low Ratings

Isn't it curious that there's such universal agreement on the poor quality of many of today's TV shows [March 12], yet these very same programs are the ones that garner the highest ratings? Someone must be watching. Who, and why?

Jay T. Lindell
4/2/79
Bayside, N.Y.

Dallas Mania

After coping with a brutal heat wave, Billygate, Iran and other insanities, there is nothing so refreshing as a little tad of honest lust, greed, incest and vicious moneygrubbing à la *Dallas* [Aug. 11]. J.R. has restored my faith in escapist TV.

Julie Taylor
Webster Groves, Mo.

That millions can be mesmerized by such trivia as *Dallas* only proves the average American seeks excitement by means of the tube rather than by making an effort to raise his life out of the rut of bland mediocrity.

Tom Hart
9/1/80
Port Monmouth, N.J.

TV Boycott

Why should the Rev. John Hurt [Dec. 15] force on me his opinion of what television America should watch? I enjoy *Dallas*, *Soap* and the other "immoral" programs, and I don't feel I have been adversely affected by them. Mr. Hurt does not have to watch these programs if he feels they are immoral, or have he and his fellow believers forgotten that there is an Off switch?

Kevin Lee Sutter
1/5/81
Blacksburg, Va.

Campaign to Clean Up TV

I agree that there is too much sex and violence on TV [July 6]. But to return to the Ricardos and the Cramdens of *I Love Lucy* and *The Honeymooners*, as the Moral Majority's Dan Fore suggests, would be ridiculous.

Lucy Ricardo was a scheming, deceitful, bubble-headed idiot. Ralph Cramden was a pompous, irrational, loudmouthed, overbearing jerk. Are these the examples Mr. Fore would set before his children as good marriage partners and role models?

Judy Ruths
7/27/81
Minneapolis

Winds of War

First there was *Roots*, then *Shogun*, and now *The Winds of War* [Feb. 7]. It is great to see a major network willing to risk $40 million to produce quality programming. My hat goes off to ABC for bringing seven nights of history into our living rooms.

Stewart S. Dixon Jr.
2/28/83
Lake Forest, Ill.

Farewell, *M*A*S*H*

Most of the programs on TV are populated by voluptuous females, lonely police officers and superhuman doctors. *M*A*S*H* [Feb. 28] dared to break stereotypes and tradition. It was an intelligent, enlightening and enchanting show that brought an unusual touch of class into our living rooms.

Vinnie Senatore Pratt
3/21/83
Totowa, N.J.

I am sad to see *M*A*S*H* end. I feel as though a family member has died.

Barbara Blamble
3/21/83
Baltimore

M*A*S*H*

The Muppett Show

Viet Nam

The French left, and the U.S. stepped in to support the fight against Ho Chi Minh and the Viet Cong guerrillas. *Alice's Restaurant* was one choral response to the escalation of American involvement in Viet Nam. Young men burned their draft cards; thousands marched in demonstrations for peace. Others fervently defended the fight against Communism. War victims fell not only on the Vietnamese battlefield but at My Lai and Kent State. Seated in their living rooms, Americans watched a war on television for the first time. There was no victory band when the last troops came home in 1972.

In Viet Nam

Those of us living in Saigon's Metropole Hotel when it was bombed by the Viet Cong in 1957 knew that, militarily, the handwriting was on the wall. From that day, U.S. military strength in South Viet Nam should have been bolstered without consideration for the inevitable howls that would emanate from Hanoi, Peking and Moscow.

If we had taken rapid, positive action the Viet Cong today would consist of only so many bones scattered though the quiet jungle.

(S/Sgt.) John R. King
Bitburg Air Base
5/25/62 *Germany*

The General's Diplomacy

I appreciate your excellent coverage [June 7] of the support U.S. forces are giving the republic of Viet Nam in its struggle against the Viet Cong insurgents. However, despite my high regard for the capability of the UH-1B helicopters and the crews who fly them, I have never stated that they are the most essential unit in my command. This is a team effort, and every component of that team is considered equally essential. Our advisory personnel include members of the Army, Navy, Air Force and Marines, all of whom are doing an outstanding job and deserve equal praise for such efforts.

I am also concerned about your statement that fixed-wing fighter bombers sometimes drop napalm on innocent civilians. These aircraft are flown by pilots of the Vietnamese air force being trained and advised by U.S. Air Force personnel. Both are just as concerned about safety of noncombatants as our U.S. Huey pilots. Investigations have failed to substantiate such reports, although obviously the Communist Viet Cong would like to perpetuate this canard.

Paul D. Harkins
General, U.S.A.
Military Assistance Command
6/28/63 *Viet Nam*
Time appreciates General Harkins' diplomatic problems, applauds his confidence in his team, also has confidence in its own team of correspondents.—Ed.

American troops following a village firefight

The Governor's General

May I join you in your tribute to an outstanding soldier and great American, Lieut. General William C. Westmoreland [May 8]. Having served for more than two years as "Westy's" executive officer with the 34th Field Artillery, 9th Infantry Division, both at Fort Bragg and in North Africa and Sicily, I can testify to the fact that he is a leader who brings to our Viet Nam campaign soldiering that inspires the men who serve with him, and a wisdom in war which in my opinion is unsurpassed. In World War II, his officers and men called him "Superman." It was a title that he earned by his deeds and capacity for deeds.

Otto Kerner
Governor of Illinois
5/22/64 *Springfield*

Reverses in Viet Nam

It appears that the U.S. is considering either a negotiated settlement or a withdrawal in South Viet Nam [Jan. 8]. Any solution short of victory, which is possible, will nullify all the efforts of those who have given so much. They will have died in vain. Unfortunately it is the Vietnamese people who will suffer the most. Our involvement in Viet Nam is rapidly becoming the greatest political and military debacle in our history. If we were incapable, there would be an excuse. There is no excuse.

James Russell
1/15/65 *Saigon*

The High Price

I cannot understand our present situation in Viet Nam. It seems that our military force over there is like the mythical Sisyphus, fated forever to push a boulder up the mountain only to have it slip away and roll to the bottom. The 35,000 Americans over there are too many to make peace and not enough to make war. It has been a pleasant interlude since the Korean War ended, but has the time come to pay the price? The price, I think, is a hell of a lot of dead Americans.

Phillip Harney
Danielson, Conn.

You described how "Rangers, backed by air support that sowed the field with some 288,000 bullets, 4,000 20-mm. cannon shells, 1,552 rockets and 37,000 lbs. of bombs, scattered the Red nest. At least 87 [out of 1,500] Viet Cong were killed." At the above rate, to kill one of the enemy took 3,310 bullets, 46 20-mm. cannon shells, 18 rockets and 425 lbs. of bombs.

Let's quit!

Thomas C. Moran
1/22/65 *Pittsburgh*

The U.S. Role in Viet Nam

Would the U.S. sit back and watch the Communist Chinese wage war in Mexico and foist Communism on the people there? Similarly, you cannot expect the Chinese to idly watch the U.S. wage war in Viet Nam and foist an American-style administration there. The ugliest thing in all of Asia is the American image. The West should leave the East alone to sort out its own affairs, live the way it likes, and have governments that suit it.

S. Jawad
4/2/65 *Karachi*

War & Peace

I have a suggestion for the State Department: Give those students who took up a collection [June 25] for the Viet Cong a one-way ticket to Hanoi.

Andrew L. Fauci
Las Vegas, Nev.

Who says "most Americans" don't swallow the idea of U.S. "combat support" in Viet Nam? Has any major pollster tapped grass-roots opinion lately?

Ronald H. Limbaugh
7/9/65 *Boise, Idaho*
The Gallup poll last week reported that, of those expressing opinions, 23.6% would continue present policy in Viet Nam, 35.4% would increase military action, while 38.4% would stop it.

Vietniks *et al.*

TIME's analysis of the Viet Nam protests [Oct. 22] is distorted and untruthful. Most of us who participated in this demonstration have no love for the Viet Cong or Hanoi, but we do believe that their defeat is not worth the price of adopting the values that seem to make their defeat so necessary. The leaders of this nation, like those of Nazi Germany, no longer seem capable of tolerating dissent. The great consensus has become a patriotic duty, and some have gone so far as to suggest that those who cannot accept it ought to be pulled up by the roots and thrown aside like worthless weeds.

Leo A. Despres
Associate Professor of Anthropology
Western Reserve University
10/29/65 *Cleveland*

Pacifists, Vietniks *et al.*

About TIME's story on my burning

U.S. soldiers with a suspected collaborator

my draft card [Nov. 5]: I am quoted as saying "Destruction of a draft card poses no greater threat to national security than the destruction of a bubble-gum card." Those are not my words: they are from an American Civil Liberties Union news release. Moreover, you are wrong to consider draft-card burning "a post-adolescent craze" like panty raids and telephone-booth packing. I can't deny that there is shallowness in some dissent, but it is wrong to believe that most dissenters are merely exhibitionistic. There is no threat to peace from me or from other protesters; the danger lies in blindness to the fact that we have something to say.

David Miller
Onondaga County Penitentiary
Jamesville, N.Y.

I have never written a letter to an editor in all my 40-odd years, but your Nov. 5 issue drove me to it. Seeing the photographs of our soldiers in Viet Nam and on the facing page the picture of the yellow-bellied draft-card burner is more than a mother with a 19-year-old son waiting his turn to serve his country can take.

Mrs. B. Mader
11/26/65 *Troy, N.Y.*

Viet Nam

It is inappropriate to view the burning of Norman Morrison and the Immolation of Roger LaPorte [Nov. 19]

fundamentally as suicides. These men sought to convince us of their sincere rejection of militarism and violence in Viet Nam. How else could they penetrate the cultural screen of advertising, propaganda, image making, and superficial public-opinion polling that separates us from 20th century human realities? The courageous self-sacrifice of these two men deserves the utmost public respect.

David S. Tillson
Professor of Anthropology
State University College
12/10/65 *Brockport, N.Y.*

Fighting Myth

Your story saddened me, because it bolsters the myth of fighting efficiency in Viet Nam. Australian troops, speaking to our correspondents, describe the Americans as poorly led and poorly trained in jungle warfare. Our men will not go on patrol with Americans, because it is too dangerous. These examples of dangerous practices are cited: marines yelling to one another on patrol, unburied mess tins and cigarette butts, transistor radios blaring, lighted cigars at night, an appalling lack of observation of danger signs.

Alan MacDonald
12/31/65 *Hamilton, N.Z.*

An Answer for Alan MacDonald

Letter Writer Alan MacDonald says Australian troops have a low regard for the fighting efficiency of G.I.s in Viet Nam [Dec. 31]. What Australian troops? Does he refer to the corporal's guard of Aussies sent when we asked our allies to stand with us there? If we had dispatched 500 men, instead of millions, to the South Pacific when the Australian government begged for help in World War II, Australia would now be a slave outpost of Japan.

J.A. McFadden
1/14/66 *Upper Darby, Pa.*

Carrying the Mail

You report [May 27] that "80% of all the U.S. bombing of North Viet Nam" originates from four airfields. Permit me to offer a correction.

Since the beginning of air strikes against North Viet Nam, more than 50% of such strikes have been flown from U.S. Navy aircraft carriers off the coast of Viet Nam. With only two attack carriers continually on Yankee station launching these strikes, that figure may seem incredible. It is, nonetheless, accurate, and a tribute to the skill and determination of the officers and men of these ships to whom a 16-hour day of hard physical labor, tension and danger has become their expected routine.

(Rear Admiral) H. L. Miller
Chief of Information
U.S. Navy
6/17/66 *Washington, D.C.*

Voices from the Foxholes

As I finished reading about the frustrations and inconveniences visited upon the poor students facing the draft [June 3], I received the news of the death in Viet Nam of my nephew, Lance Corporal Philip Dorn of the Marines. No one had to twist his arm to get him to go and help out in the job he knew had to be done. He and the thousands like him who have enlisted have made possible the deferment of many students who are using someone else's future to educate themselves. I wouldn't trade one of the memories I have of my nephew for the whole, smug, overeducated carcass of one of these bearded, unbathed louts who are infesting our colleges and using them as a haven for their cowardice or as a sounding board for Red propaganda.

Victory Dorn
6/24/66 *Shrewsbury, N.J.*

The Meaning of Patriotism

We are Hospital Corpsmen in the Navy, serving with the 3rd Marine Division. We sympathize with students facing the draft [June 3]. But what they do not seem to realize is that we, too, have plans for the future. Some of us plan to get married, to finish our education, to try to live our lives in peace. Some of us have died to keep our nation free, and many more will give their lives in the future. It is not our wish that there be a war in Viet Nam, but there is.

A student describes Viet Nam as "foreign and remote." To those of us who are here, it is very near and a great threat to our loved ones at home. We are witnesses to things we would not want to happen in our country. As for personal freedoms, we all believe in them. But what freedoms would we have if we let the "not-so-big," Communist-inspired wars go unchallenged?

Jack E. Hasty
Edward Savage
William D. Pickett
Thomas L. Boggs
Ralph M. Smith
7/1/66 *Viet Nam*

Show Our Teeth

The bombing of Hanoi-Haiphong POL areas was long overdue. Had we done this months ago, or even two years ago, many lives would undoubtedly have been spared. The time has come for the U.S. to stop playing a cat-and-mouse game with the North Vietnamese; we must show our teeth, since this seems to be the only language they understand.

Paul S. Schueller
7/22/66 *Brooklyn*

Seconding the Notion

I add a strong second to Military Historian S. L. A. Marshall's view of "The Basic Flaw in Viet Nam" [Oct. 21]. I spent a year there as an intelligence officer with the 1st Air Cavalry Division. In the three months I have been back in the U.S. I have been struck by the incredible lack of substantive news on military operations. While the infrequent and unavoidable accidents of war claim headlines, major Allied operations are usually dismissed in two or three sentences, or are wedged somewhere between *Anne Landers* and *Peanuts*. All too often these reports, when they do appear, are nothing more than repetitions of the canned Saigon daily news briefing, not the actual observances of reporters in the field.

Part of the problem lies with the generally low caliber of reporters in Viet Nam, and having dealt with many of them in the past year, I strongly concur in General Marshall's statements. However, not all the Viet Nam correspondents are that bad. Fact stories that are not bloody or sensational just don't sell. A major portion of the Viet Nam news failure lies with editors at home. A comparison of the extent and depth of news coverage of Luci Johnson's wedding or Senator Robert Kennedy's every move with that afforded the war effort really makes me wonder.

Patrick G. Colloton
11/4/66 *Madison, Wis.*

What Chances?

With Robert Kennedy wanting to give his blood to the Viet Cong, a group of Quakers who want to send gift packages to the North Vietnamese, and Administration leaders who do not want to bomb certain targets in North Viet Nam because the bombing would cause suffering among the enemy, what are the chances of the American soldier in Viet Nam?

James Eliopolo
12/30/66 *Atlanta*

Demonstrators

From TIME's article and photographs, one would think that the demonstrators were almost exclusively New Leftists, acidheads, pacifists, young, and not to be taken seriously.

TIME neglected to mention the veterans, many wearing their campaign ribbons and decorations, who participated. TIME neglected to mention the many groups of professional people who marched; teachers and medical groups were well represented. My impression of the crowd was one of middle-class respectability. The turned-on, tuned-in, dropped-out set was a minority. Yes, Stokely Carmichael shot off his mouth, but he was more than counterbalanced by the reasoned arguments of the other speakers. Yes, there were some radicals and fanatics and Viet Cong flags. They were more than counterbalanced by the overwhelming majority: normal, everyday people who believe that patriotism demands more than unquestioning support of one's government who remember that the standard defense at Nürnberg was "I only followed orders."

Peter Vanadia
4/28/67 *Manhattan*

Pride & Prejudice

Thank you for "Democracy in the Foxhole," that wonderful cover story on the Negro in Viet Nam [May 26]. As a Negro living here in America, I have never felt such a deep sense of

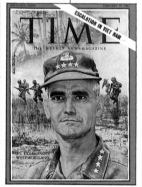

pride for my people. I believe that your story has accomplished almost as much, if not more, than many of the civil rights demonstrations that have taken place recently.

Betty McCrary
The Bronx, N.Y.
6/2/67

Not When, But What

"What Negotiations in Viet Nam Might Mean" [Dec. 22], is one of the most realistic and constructive analyses of the present situation in Viet Nam that I have read.

For too long we have been overly preoccupied with the question as to *when*, *whether* and *how* we can get to a negotiating table. All of this discussion tends to persuade the enemy that our position is weaker than it is and creates suspicions as to our motives, as he feels he received the worst of the bargain struck in Geneva in 1954.

Looking beyond *when* we will negotiate to what is negotiable, and talking in specific terms about the kind of points that can and should be resolved, might even help bring about discussions and cause both sides, the South Vietnamese government and the V.C. to see that some gains can be made as against the terrible price being paid by endlessly continuing a conflict that cannot bring total military or political victory to either side.

Charles H. Percy
United States Senate
Tel Aviv
1/8/68

The TV War

Like most other Americans, I have become steeled to the "television war" watched on the early news across the dinner table. Television coverage of the attacks on the U.S. embassy, therefore, caused only a momentary pause in the trajectory of my peas from plate to mouth.

In the security of my office, I leafed through the Giap cover story while eating lunch. On the first page of your color spread covering the embassy attack my eating came to an abrupt end. No one, certainly, would applaud your printing of such photos, but maybe such gruesome sights are what we need to be brought back to the grim reality that the news on TV is not just reruns of *Combat*, where the guy killed this week will return to co-star next.

Ronald T. Menet
San Pablo, Calif.

I look at your pictures of our boys' bodies dumped on a truck in a country that no longer matters, and I weep. I am tired, tired, tired of this war. Why can't we get it over with or get out?

(Mrs.) Jane Battey
Media, Pa.
2/23/68

The Shock of Chicago

As a young historian born during World War II, I had never really been

Riot squads arrest student demonstrator in an anti-Viet Nam protest at Berkeley, 1969

able to form a mental picture of the way the Nazi storm troopers came to power in Hitler's Germany. After watching the scenes of the brutal and savage attacks by the Chicago police on the peace demonstrators. I think I now know what that tyranny must have been like. Mayor Daley's inhuman repression was a blot on the fabric of human dignity. Daley for Anti-Man of the Year.

Hugh B. Hammett
Charlottesville, Va.

My husband and I were among the onlookers who were tear-gassed on Michigan Avenue. We thought it a minor discomfort to endure while the police attempted to control that frenzied, filthy, foul-mouthed mob of cretins. We watched these "innocents," as you called them, doing their "thing," i.e., overturning police motorcycles, setting fires on the sidewalks, rocking a van containing policemen in an attempt to overturn it, foisting signs in our faces reading "F - - - the draft," waving the Cong flag as they chanted "Ho-Ho-Ho Chi Minh."

Spare me the bleeding heart's ac-

count of how they were brutalized. They were a danger to every one of us in Chicago that night and, unless stopped as they were here, constitute an even greater danger to our nation tomorrow.

Mrs. Richard J. Waterbury
Glen Ellyn, Ill.
9/20/68

War is Lost

I wholeheartedly agree with those who demand an immediate, 100% withdrawal of our troops from Viet Nam. The war has been lost. Lyndon Johnson's capitulation in March 1968 merely served to punctuate the defeat. From that day forward, the future of the people of South Viet Nam was no longer at issue.

The Communist victory was not won at Chu Lai, Danang or Bien Hoa, or at any of those now not so strange sounding places. The victory was won exactly where Ho Chi Minh had known and said it would be won, in the hearts and minds of the American people: "The people of the United States do not have the determination to persevere in the struggle in Southeast Asia. When they grow tired of fighting, we will still

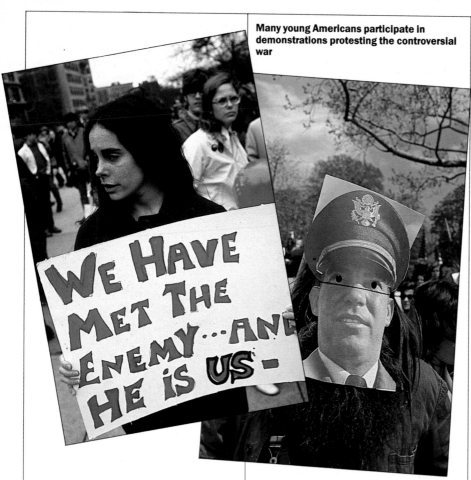

be here."

Yes, I join in the protest. I protest in the name of those who have given their lives in vain, in the name of those who believe *all* men have the right to self-determination, in the name of those who believe that no man is free until all men are free.

Charles M. Freeland
10/24/69   *Dyer, Ind.*

God Help Us

I opened TIME and saw the young battle-weary trooper, and I wept openly. Why must this young man be in such a position? He did not ask for Viet Nam. Why must some be called upon for such a sacrifice? Do we care enough? Some of these fine men are not even old enough to vote, yet they are asked to give their lives for a war that seems endless. God help us to care, and most of all, to end this senseless mess in Viet Nam.

Evelyn B. Martin
10/31/69   *Colorado Springs, Cola.*

The My Lai Masscre

Perhaps the horror-filled memory of My Lai will awaken more of us to the belated knowledge that no nation has a monopoly on goodness, truth, honor and mercy—all the virtues habitually ascribed to Americans, and particularly the American soldier.

Bernice Balfour
12/12/69   *Anaheim, Calif.*

Co-Defendants?

O.K. So Lieut. Calley stands indicted as the heinous mastermind of the whole My Lai incident. In the interest of judicial equity, however, shouldn't Nixon, Johnson, *et al.* be co-defendants?

Paula Katz
12/19/69   *Woodmere, N.Y.*

Ghastly Event

I wish to congratulate you on your Essay on the tragic massacre at My Lai. It is the most penetrating piece of writing that I have come across on this ghastly event.

Jane Wyatt
1/5/70   *Los Angeles*

Widening the War

Richard Nixon's incredibly assured decision to escalate the war [May 11] is beyond comprehension. In search of that illusory turning point, that single decisive confrontation that for years has confounded American military strategists in Southeast Asia, Mr. Nixon has consciously chosen to disregard the lessons of recent history and threatens to involve this country in a still wider war. In the context of existing concern, his failure to consult congressional leaders is indefensible.

Why Viet Cong sanctuaries in Cambodia suddenly became an intolerable threat to a reduced American presence in Viet Nam remains a mystery. How the destruction of antiaircraft installa-

tions in North Viet Nam will ensure the safety of departing U.S. troops is clearly open to critical debate. What is to be gained from a six-to-eight-week "defensive" probe across the Cambodian border is at best fuzzy speculation, and miserably incapable of justifying the immediate cost in American lives and the potential costs of an Indochina war.

Ned Freed
5/25/70   *Pacific Grove, Calif.*

Again the Spotlight

I find the suggestion that President Nixon is considering more raids on North Viet Nam's prison camps [Dec. 7] quiet disturbing. Faced with Green Berets on the outside and hostile but unarmed prisoners on the inside, it is only logical to assume that the guards will attack their enemy at his weakest point by eliminating the prisoners. Such a horrible denouement would only serve to spotlight once again the combined brutality and stupidity which is the Viet Nam War. Would the epitaphs of the prisoners read, "We had to destroy them to save them"?

Brian F. Wood
12/28/70   *Eggertsville, N.Y.*

Only a Shred?

Hedley Donovan's Essay "Coming to Terms with Viet Nam" [June 14] is a thinly disguised attempt to absolve the increasingly guilt-ridden conscience of America.

The U.S. role in Viet Nam over the past ten years has probably been the most misguided and evil in our country's violent history. The only shred of honor left, and it is a small one, is in apologizing to the world for our terrible mistake and in setting about to see that it is never repeated.

Gary Forrester
7/12/71   *New Amsterdam, Guyana*

Draft Evaders

There are at least two young men from this town who, because of the Viet Nam War, are exiled from their homes and families.

One of these unwilling exiles is my husband, who has been a prisoner of war for more than four years. The other young man chose to desert the Army rather than serve in Viet Nam. It is apparent that this war has hurt our country terribly. I am still enough of a patriot, even a chauvinist, to feel that when we begin the restructuring of our society, America will need all her sons.

I will actively support amnesty for the American refugees.

(Mrs.) Valerie M. Kushner
Danville, Va.

I served four years in the military, a year of it in Viet Nam, and I would very much like to see these men granted amnesty. They did exactly what many of the people I knew in the service wished they had done, but didn't quite have the convictions or were afraid of living as black sheep in a country where the Government determines what is morally right or wrong.

Rob Martin
Fort Worth

The essence of freedom being the right of choice the resisters and deserters have followed their consciences and should now be prepared to accept the consequences of their actions, as have the 55,000 men who have died in the quagmire of Southeast Asia.

F. James Cummings
1/31/72 *Frontenac, Kans.*

What War Has Meant

You suggest [Nov. 6] that "this is the moment to look back on what the war meant, and to look ahead to . . . what peace will mean."

My friends and I were about twelve years old in 1959 when the first Americans were killed in Viet Nam, a place no one had ever heard of. We know too well what the war meant; it has become a part of us. We are not able, however, to look ahead to what peace will mean. It will be an entirely new experience.

Steven L. Stern
New York City

If the peace in Viet Nam comes true, it is the duty of all nations of the world to organize a war-crimes court as was held in Nürnberg after the second World War. The accused should include many of the American political and military leaders, such as Richard M. Nixon, Lyndon B. Johnson, Robert McNamara and William Westmoreland. Besides these, the deceased Presidents Dwight D. Eisenhower and John F. Kennedy must also be accused formally.

Matti Kyrö
11/27/72 *Helsinki*

Tremendous Relief

I had trouble understanding the emotions I felt on hearing that the Viet Nam conflict was nearing an end [Feb. 5]. I did not feel like breaking out the champagne, but I did feel a tremendous relief. I echo the commentator who said it is not that something wonderful has happened; it is more a feeling that something terrible has finally ended.

Karen P. Olsen
2/19/73 *Bellingham, Mass.*

The Deserters

As a commissioned infantry veteran of Viet Nam, I have never held a strong opinion on the amnesty issue. However, after re-entering the job market, I find that the four years spent in the service were of no value whatsoever in securing a means of supporting my family. My contemporaries who did not serve are four years ahead of me.

I do not particularly regret having served. However, don't ask me to accept

the deserters back with open arms. They voted with their feet.

Jack Selecky
4/15/74 *Sterling Heights, Mich.*

Foolish Waste

I served as a Marine infantryman in Viet Nam, where I saw one of my best friends killed and where I was severely wounded. I now realize how purposeless that war was, and I believe that the U.S. was wrong to get involved. All those who resisted serving in Viet Nam should get unconditional amnesty. They should not be punished or forced to do public service work just because they recognized the foolishness of our involvement sooner than most.

Michael Burton
9/30/74 *Grand Rapids*

Flowers are Better

It has been five years since Allison, Sandy, Bill and Jeff were killed by Ohio Guardsmen. They were killed because they, along with others, were protesting our incursion into Cambodia. What do we have to show for these five years except thousands of American soldiers killed, 1 million Cambodians killed or wounded, hundreds of thousands of refugees, rampant inflation in our land, unemployment and destroyed dominoes?

Allison was right when she stated,

"Flowers are better than bullets."

Arthur and Doris Krause
5/12/75 *Pittsburgh*
The writers are the parents of Allison Krause, who was shot at Kent State University on May 4, 1970.

A Simple Fact

I cannot understand why no one has commented on the simple fact that the U.S. would have been spared more than $200 billion, more than 50,000 lives, and all the present tragic and so stupid horror of evacuation of Americans, and these poor wretches to whom we owe nothing in any way, shape or form, had our allied air power been permitted to proceed with all-out pinpoint bombing of the Viet Cong's power and supply depots, thus bringing them to their knees and terminating the action long before the year 1967!

Rudy Vallée
5/19/75 *Hollywood*

Out at Last

Out at last, out at last. Thank God we're out at last.

Phil Hummell
West Branch, Mich.

It is very sad to realize that the "light at the end of the tunnel" was a red one.

Peter Collinson
5/26/75 *Mount Pleasant, Mich.*

May 4, 1970: demonstrations at Kent State end in tragedy

Civil Rights

TIME was created in the '20s, a decade when K.K.K. membership swelled past four million. The N.A.A.C.P. tallied statistics on lynchings around the country. "Separate but equal" was challenged; in 1954 the Supreme Court ruled racial segregation in public schools unconstitutional. A year later, Dr. Martin Luther King Jr. organized the bus boycott in Montgomery. *We Shall Overcome* became the anthem of the national revolution he led. The black power fist was raised. Though riots and assassinations tarnished Dr. King's dream of a nonviolent battle, the fight for civil rights changed America.

Affront

Is the glorification of the Negro now an accepted policy of your magazine? I had hoped that after the protest of one Southerner you might show some consideration for the sensibilities of our people by the discontinuance of your practice of referring to the colored man as "mister." I was deeply grieved, therefore, to find two new instances of this kind in your Sept. 7 issue. I refer to your entitlement of Robert Taylor on Page 6 and Walter Cohen on Page 8.

This practice, it seems to me, is wholly unnecessary, from your standpoint, and from that of the Southerner, assumes almost nauseating proportions. Furthermore, its protraction, in the face of previous protest, impresses me as a flagrant affront to the feelings of our people. If it be, as it appears, your desire to alienate and force from your ranks such readers of TIME as hail from the South, you are pursuing a most effectual course.

Barlow Henderson
9/28/25 *Aiken, S.C.*
It is not TIME's desire to lose the good will of its Southern friends. TIME will, however, continue to employ the "Mr." in referring to men who lack other titles. Would Mr. Henderson himself care to be styled plain "Henderson"? —ED.

"Courage, Decency"

Do not worry about losing Mr. Henderson's subscription. You will gain more readers by your courage and decency than you will lose. Certainly I will do everything in my power to induce more intelligent readers to subscribe to TIME because of your reply to Mr. Henderson.

Walter White
Assistant Sec. of the N.A.A.C.P.*
10/19/25 *New York, N.Y.*

*National Association for the Advancement of Colored People.

Ready to Die

I received my first copy of TIME in the morning mail.

I was enjoying the news as portrayed until I came to p. 10, your article on the Ku Klux Klan—which I read and reread.

I have been a member of the much abused Klan for years, and I expect to be a member as long as I live and the need for such an organization in these United States exists. I have never received any financial benefit from my membership, on the contrary it has cost me a considerable sum to attend the various meetings, etc. The only benefit received by myself has been the strengthening of my patriotism, my love of Country and God.

I do not know your religious affiliations, nor do I care about them. But, I do know that you are grossly mistaken in the article above referred to. The name of the organization has not been changed, and I never expect to see it changed. The Klan is simply following the course originally planned for it—but you and the likes of you, through ignorance or prejudice are trying to kill an undying organization of American born white citizens, who are as much entitled to organize as any other block of people in the Country, and certainly more so than a lot of them.

Every knock is a boost—keep it up, but you can discontinue my subscription to TIME.

James L. Milstead
3/17/28 *Dahlgren, Va.*
Born in and ready to die for the United States of America.
Publish if you dare.

"Bad Niggers"

TIME, June 11, under "Races" p. 15,

Detroit police made little attempt to protect this black man from a white mob in the early '40s

you say Lee and Dave Blackman, Negroes, killed en route to Shreveport jail, "had done nothing but be born their brother's brother" and that, "the Parish people wanted more blood." You don't know what you are talking about and you are what decent Southern people call "nigger lovers." The Blackmans were bad niggers, bullies, bootleggers, makers of moonshine and thieves. Last year their father shot out the eyes of a little white boy. We live in harmony with our good niggers—strange ties of affection exist between the white gentry and the darkies. There had not been a lynching in Rapides Parish in twenty-five years, yet you call this "the customary thing." Be ashamed of your slander.

(Mrs.) Annette Armand Stolle
7/2/28 *Alexandra, La.*

Judge Lynch

I have just read Negro White's "Judge Lynch." What a dirty lot of lies. I have read a number of articles by both white and black, but never has my blood boiled before.

I think if anyone ever needed a coat of tar and feathers it's the author of "Judge Lynch."

Yes, we do lynch the Negro in the South. Some day the North will be sorry they didn't try the same cure for certain things that the Negro knows will cost him his life—the white man is subject to the same law.

I would love to meet the author of this article and show him that Southern people are not "crackers," but a Negro is a nigger and always will be one regardless of the Hoovers. No doubt the present President will have more to do with the killing of Negroes in the South, who are trying to climb the social ladder, than all the crimes that the Negro has committed for years past.

Robert E. Lee
Greenville, N.C.

Congratulations are due you for a TIME-worthy report headed Judge Lynch, page 43, TIME, June 24 issue. You print a picture of "Negro White," the author. It might have well been "white Negro" because you say he safely passes for white. . . .

The well-balanced Southerner hopes that lynchings of Negroes will increase rather than decrease, that Cracker fiendishness and cruelty (N.A.A.C.P. terms) will never diminish, that persecution, prosecution of and fury against the Negro will prevail until their numbers are eliminated or substantially reduced, and preferably exterminated.

With a congress of men of the type of Senator W. F. George of Georgia, the Constitution will be amended so as to cure the 65-year-old wrong done the Southern people. The way should be opened to State legislation against the Negro. There is no longer excuse for evasion.

Down here we don't care if all the

"Colored Only" were permitted in this shack at Belle Glade, Florida in 1945

Negroes are lynched, or even burned or slit open with knives. The outrageous, damnable, unbearable spectacle of lawlessness of the Negro is infinitely greater than would be the entire extermination of the cursed race by the white man. The Northern "nigger-lovers" are going to be forced to see our position some day."

Eldon O. Haldane
7/8/29 *Atlanta, Ga.*

Smith & Wesson Line

TIME has brought two delightful experiences to me within recent weeks for which I am grateful. One of these was caused by the excellent, impartial review of my book on lynching, *Rope and Faggot*, which appeared in the issue of June 24; the other by TIME's printing in the July 8 issue of letters from below the Smith and Wesson line threatening me with lynching, tarring and feathering and other courtesies. Such solicitude and statements as Mr. Eldon O. Haldane's that "the well balanced Southerner hopes that lynchings of Negroes will increase rather than decrease" amply prove, it seems to me, some of the main contentions of *Rope and Faggot*—the inherent lawlessness of certain parts of the United States and trigger-quick propensities to defend positions which are morally, ethically and practically indefensible.

Such correspondents of yours as Messrs. Robert E. Lee and Eldon O. Haldane reassure me. The reviews of *Rope and Faggot* have dwelt almost without exception upon the judicial, impartial tone of the book. . . . Messrs. Lee and Haldane by their denunciation of me will help mightily in bringing the whole matter of lynch law to the attention of Americans who need to know the facts. Their brazen defense of murder, however, must not be attributed to all Southerners for some of the finest comments upon the book have

come from Southern white newspapers and correspondents. . . .

Walter White
7/22/29 *New York City*
No more letters on the whites v. White controversy will be published.—ED.

North Carolina's Debit

In a paragraph on page 14 of your issue of December 2 you debit North Carolina with one lynching in the year 1929. This is an error. There has been no lynching in this State this year. Fact is, there has been no lynching in North Carolina since 1921.

The people of this State will appreciate your making the correction.

Dennis Brummitt
Attorney General
12/23/29 *Raleigh, N.C.*
TIME's source for lynching information was the National Association for the Advancement of Colored People, which set down as a "lynching" the shooting of Ella Wiggins, white, in Gastonia last September. She was killed when a mob sprayed bullets in a truckful of men and women going to a Communist mass meeting [Sept. 23].—ED.

Lynching Enumeration

I note in TIME for Oct. 6 that you list the lynching of Willie Kirkland, on Sept. 25 at Thomasville, Ga., as the sixteenth lynching of 1930.

According to our records, copy of which is enclosed, this lynching was the twenty-first of the year. Since Kirkland was lynched there have been two additional ones—Lacy Mitchell, on Sept. 27, also at Thomasville, Ga., shot to death by a masked and robed band for testifying against two white men who were charged with rape upon a colored woman; and on Oct. 1, John Willie Clark was lynched at Cartersville, Ga., charged with the murder of the Chief of Police.

The Cartersville, Ga., lynching makes the twenty-third authenticated lynching of the year. There are five additional cases of which investigation has not yet been completed. . . .

This recrudescence in lynching, which has taken eleven victims more than were killed during all of 1929, is, we are certain you will agree, an appalling one. We trust that TIME, with its usual careful attention to details, will make such inquiry as it wishes into the facts. . . .

Walter White
Acting Secretary
National Association for the
Advancement of Colored People
10/27/30 *New York City*

California Minds

It would be useless to question the intent of the following sentences from TIME of March 28, p. 19:

"No Negro can legally marry a white woman in any Southern State. But Wisconsin does not mind, nor California."

The effect on the uninformed is to give the impression that marriage between a white and a Negro is legal in California. You are referred to Sec. 60, *Civil Code* of California: "All marriages of white persons with Negroes, Mongolians, or Mulattoes, are illegal and void."

Vincent Whelan
4/18/32 *San Diego, Calif.*

Sectional Preacher

Your Cinema review, issue of July 3, of *Hold Your Man* says that Eddie and Ruby were married by an elderly colored clergyman. The picture shows the marriage performed by a white minister.

By the way, Negroes do not relish the use of the word "colored." It rather is a slur—as indicating a mixture of white and Negro blood, and therefore not to be desired, either way. In our town, county and State, there is no race problem. The lines are clearly and unmistakably defined, and there is no attempt, nor I believe desire, to cross that line. The Negroes regard our white people as their real friend.

Isaac S. London
Editor, Post-Dispatch
7/31/33 *Rockingham, N.C.*
In the South, Eddie (Clark Gable) & Ruby (Jean Harlow) are married by a white preacher, MGM having shot separate sequences for sectional exhibition.—ED.

Old Southern Woman

I listened to your dramatization of the lynching of that Negro in Maryland. Now then, why not dramatize the scene of the crime? Let the world hear the piteous cries and pleadings of that poor old woman when that burly black brute attacked her and why not turn back the "March of Time" a few years and dramatize the scene of the brutal attack and murder of a young woman —the mother of little children—that occurred near Durant, Okla. That little woman was a kinswoman of mine. That was one of the most fiendish crimes I have ever heard of. I can't say that I approve of the methods that are sometimes used in these lynchings, but they *should* be handled rough and they *should* be lynched. The law would only give them prison terms, and sooner or later they are pardoned or paroled, and do the same thing over. Just *suppose* that old lady had been *your* Mother. If you have read this, I thank you, for it comes straight from the heart of an old Southern woman.

Mrs. G. M. Rutledge
11/20/33 *Ste. Genevieve, Mo.*

Only Decent Manner

In TIME, March 6 there appeared an article dealing with the refusal of the Daughters of the American Revolution to permit the Negress Anderson to sing in Constitution Hall in Washington. In this article, Washington was referred to as "provincial." This was spiteful and entirely unjustified. Remarks of that nature show that all small people do not live in small towns.

You mention a "mass" meeting of 1,500 (probably all Northerners) who protested the D. A. R.'s action, but no mention is made of the four hundred-odd thousands of white citizens of Washington who do not want the theatres which they patronize contaminated by colored entertainers. . . .

I am not sympathetic toward the D. A. R. in most matters, but I feel that in this case they have acted in the only decent manner possible. After all, it is better to pique Mrs. Roosevelt than to insult the entire white population of a big city.

Alvin R. Schwab
3/20/39 *Washington, D.C.*
P.S. As a matter of fact, there is a colored theatre, the Howard, which could have been used without arousing any protest as it is a fit place for a Negress to sing.

Blatt to Schwab

May I have the pleasure of replying to the letter from a person named Schwab in the March 20 issue? Perhaps he is justified in his objection to Washington being typed "provincial." My only reaction as a one-time visitor was: "disappointing." His letter proves that all bigots do not live in small towns.

I could say "thank God I am a Northerner." Instead, I merely state that it is indeed fortunate the educated Southern-American is not as narrow and intolerant as one Schwab. Apparently Washington has not buried all its intellectually dead—it lets them write letters!

C. R. Berry
Rochester, N.Y.

Any one as allergic to Negro entertainment as Alvin R. Schwab [March 20] should move from Washington to the North Bay country. He must break out in hives when he hears Al Jolson sing *Mammy*. . . .

Morton F. McKinney
Clarion, Pa.

Because the Daughters of the American Revolution recently denied the

Police officers arrest Dr. Martin Luther King Jr.

use of their Washington hall to Negro Singer Marian Anderson, and because of their consistently illiberal stand on political, economic and constitutional questions, we recommend that their name be changed to the Defenders of the American Reaction.

Bill Slayton
John Miller
University of Omaha,
4/3/39 *Omaha, Neb.*

Marian Anderson still hopes to present a concert in Washington, D.C. If Central High School auditorium, only other suitable hall, remains unavailable, plans are to hold a free open-air concert on Easter Sunday in front of the Lincoln Memorial.—ED.

Zoot-Suit Riots

With regard to zoot-suit disorders in Log Angeles, I think you have exaggerated the race angle out of all proportion. It is true that Mexican and Negro boys wear zoot suits out on the coast perhaps more than others. But to a soldier who has been taken from his home and put in the Army, the sight of young loafers of any race, color, creed, religion or color of hair loafing around in ridiculous clothes that cost $75 to $85 per suit is enough to make them see red.

You know they are loafers because no business house would allow them to work in such fantastic outfits. If you are a serviceman with a few dollars in your pocket, you also know that some of them are ready to hoist you into an alley and roll you. . . .

If the Mexicans and Negroes and all the rest of the zoot-suit fraternity want to avoid trouble, there is a very simple way. Just get out of a zoot suit and into a uniform or a pair of overalls.

(Pvt.) Kenneth King
7/12/43 *Kearney, Neb.*

Racial Disunity in America

The reprehensible race riots of the past couple of weeks [June 28] may serve to good purpose in throwing a spotlight . . . upon the menacing growth of racial consciousness in America. Undoubtedly many have listened in recent months to a strangely swelling chorus of ominous predictions having to do with prospective internal conflict after the world war is settled. One hears of "real trouble coming up"; of "somebody" (unidentified) who is "going after" this or that "minority group." . . .

Yes, the propaganda seeds of viciousness have been well planted—already their poisonous, ugly little heads shoot up. . . .

But listen—listen closely! Do you hear it—that sour note in the background that helps create the discordant theme for a copyrighted tune called *New Order?* Remember when it was composed? . . . One verse had some-

thing to do with the Sudetenlanders—that ravaged, long-enduring little band of people huddled away in Czecho-Slovakia. Through the anguished hoarse-voiced howls and sobs of one Mr. A. Hitler, the world audience was introduced to a curious new circumstance—namely that some of the people born in a country weren't necessarily a part of that country at all. . . .

It was this same Mr. Hitler (or one of his crew) who said that "taking America would be an inside job"—easily engineered by working upon the strains and stresses of racial disunity.

Frank Lebell
Hollywood

. . . We work and drill pretty damn hard here at Camp Wheeler, preparing for the time in the near future when we are going across to fight the enemies of democracy. . . . your article on Detroit's little race riot makes us begin to wonder whether we should be shipped to Africa or Detroit. . . .

I for one would just as soon run my bayonet through the foremost young man in your race riot photo as I would through any other enemy of democracy. And I think there are plenty of other bayonets down here to back me up.

(Pvt.) Richard Russell
7/19/43 *Camp Wheeler, Ga.*

Negro Recognition

I want to congratulate the editors of TIME upon the recognition which your magazine has given to the achievements of individual Negroes. In many of your recent issues, I have found articles dealing with the success of Negroes such as Mary Lou Williams, Lieut. Colonel B. O. Davis, and many others. . . .

You are bringing to the attention of your readers the fact that Negroes are able, both in groups and singly, to achieve success in terms comparable to the best efforts of our "superior white race. . . ."

Another value in your efforts to portray . . . Negro achievements is the encouragement which it must bring to many of them. . . . The Negro, seeing himself and his race presented fairly and honestly in your magazine, cannot help but take new heart in his struggles to better himself and his race.

Mrs. S. Sollberger Jr.
9/6/43 *Norman, Okla.*

Owens Analogy

You are undoubtedly correct in suggesting that Negro pilots are unlikely to develop their full potentialities in a segregated setup. A good analogy is the case of the Negro athlete. Jesse Owens, Brud Holland, etc. were products of unsegrated playing fields and more or less open competition. . . .

Anne Bontemps
10/18/43 *Nashville*

Birmingham fire-
fighters turn
hoses on black
demonstrators

100% Yes

The poll by the "poll-minded" Army officer in the Southwest Pacific [Feb. 7], as it pertains to the Negro, certainly does not reflect a clear picture of the attitude or thoughts of Negro troops in the Pacific or European theaters. There can be no doubt as to what the results would be if such a poll should be taken among those who suffer as a result of discrimination. The result would show 100% "YES" to the question, "Do you think there is too much discrimination shown against the Negro. . . ."

This happens to be the second World War for the preservation of Democracy in which I have volunteered my services. . . . During the first World War, for one reason or another, awards and decorations were given to me. . . . The Distinguished Service Cross, Purple Heart and Croix de Guerre medals are lovely souvenirs and reminders, but without sufficient merit to enable me to purchase a first-class railroad ticket from Washington to a point south. . . . It is indeed strange that it should have been necessary upon two occasions for me to don the uniform of my native land and be transported to foreign soil to enjoy the privileges of everyday normal living without the bogie of discrimination rearing its head.

The Negro soldier of this war . . . will no longer be satisfied with disenfranchisement, Jim-Crowism and the denial of the rights and privileges granted by the Constitution of the United States. He will expect the United States to set the example for the world as being a true Democracy where all men regardless of race, creed, or colour will enjoy the benefits of those principles for which men are giving their lives. He will recall that the bullets, shell fragments and bombs of this war were indiscriminate in their

toll of lives sacrificed upon the altar of Democracy.

(M/Sgt.) William A. Johnson
c/o Postmaster
4/3/44 *New York City*

Negro Forecast

I am a Negro soldier stationed deep in the heart of Texas. . . . We Negro soldiers have been told in plain English that we have no right to ask for the same privileges as the white soldiers. Yet why are we given the same right to fight . . . and die?

I believe that the Negro 20 years hence will be far more powerful and will get far more respect from the white man. There will be a change made. With the help of God and the liberal-minded Americans, the problem of "Jim Crow" will be banished. . . .

[Serviceman's Name Withheld]
7/31/44 *Camp Barkeley, Tex.*

The Negro

Congratulations on your article on Negroes in the service [July 10]. It gave a very clear picture of what kind of a problem we face. We Southerners must look about us and see that we are headed for that point where the Negro will fight for his just rights. May God grant we wake up before then.

(Serviceman's Name Withheld)
7/31/44 *Chapel Hill, N.C.*

Return to the Dark Ages?

It is strange how we of the occupation forces over here on the other side of the world sometimes find ourselves feeling as though we are now watching our country somewhat as we watched a football game or a school play back home—from a spectator's viewpoint.

I would like to try to present a brief picture of how it looks to an

American on this side. . . . It is disturbing to see examples of that same ideology against which the war was fought rearing their ugly heads again. Are we now to re-establish the class-consciousness which the war tempered so much—discrimination by color, nationality, religion, wealth, or even bars on the shoulders and stripes on the sleeve? Now that the fighting is over, is the Negro our inferior because his skin is dark, or is the Jew to be condemned for reasons unknown to me? . . . Can we pretend to have a "democracy," with organizations such as the Ku Klux Klan operating unrestricted? . . .

If this nation, with our allies, could thwart the greatest plot against world liberty and equality in history, why then can't we direct our unparalleled efforts for our cause to within our own borders, and purge the remaining domestic elements of dark-ages intolerance, ignorance, and disunity? . . .

Robert V. Willis
5/20/46 *Korea*

Processional

. . . In selecting a Negro to teach music . . . [Antioch College (May 20) is] really following a procession. I am told on good authority that within the past five years 40 colleges and universities, which previously had all-white faculties, have added Negro instructors.

. . . We did not choose Mr. Anderson merely because he is a Negro. He seemed to us to possess the best qualifications among some 60 candidates for the position.

A. D. Henderson
President, Antioch College
6/10/46 *Yellow Springs, Ohio*

Home-Grown Swastika

Before the war criminals have been tried, and while America preaches its doctrines of democracy to a war-weary world . . . the Ku Klux Klan in Atlanta, Ga. can advertise publicly, attract a crowd of 2,000, and gain 500 new initiates [May 20]. How can the fiery cross be considered in any other light than as a home-grown swastika, when it stands for the promotion of racial supremacy? . . .

Now, before our dead are in their final resting places, the beer hall in Munich has moved to Stone Mountain in Georgia.

I am a veteran from the Asiatic-Pacific theater, and I'm tired of war; but not too tired, now or ever to fight for freedom for myself and all other peoples, at home or abroad. Out there I used a gun; back here I use a pen. Let's dig out our local fascists before we all have to trade our pens in on our guns again!

Welton I. Taylor
6/10/46   *Urbana, Ill.*

Justice for All

I hope that I may be able to lay aside my bitterness and express in a temperate manner my deep convictions regarding the murder of Negro Robert Mallard in Toombs County, Ga. [Dec. 6].

With pride and satisfaction I became a citizen of the U.S. in 1936. I believed, then, that these states were united, and that there was liberty and justice for all. Had I been told that the word "all" was to be used rather loosely, it is doubtful whether I would have sought American citizenship . . . Life is not worth living without justice—justice for all—even for "biggety niggers" . . .

TIME would doubtless be surprised to learn that of twelve people I interviewed for their reactions on the appalling Mallard story, only two evinced unqualified moral indignation. All the others hedged with the usual dishonesty: "It's a matter for the South to handle . . . He was an uppity nigger . . . Probably a Communist wrote the article . . . TIME is just getting people stirred up." All, of course, offered the noble sentiment that the murderer "shouldn'ta done it," but it was unthinkable that he should be hanged for such a minor offense . . . We have maudlin sentiment by the carload; justice we mete out with eyedroppers.

Rev. David W. Ewart
12/20/48   *Los Angeles, Calif.*

The U.S. Negro

Thank you for your splendid survey of the Negro in America [May 11]. As a Negress, still in my 20s, I am old enough to remember prejudice here in New York. Now, as one of three stenographers in a firm in the Wall Street area, I am accepted as "one of the gang." I still encounter certain prejudices—people move to other seats at some lunch counters, I can't buy a girdle at one store near my office, and occasionally I hear the

word "nigger . . ." However, I must leave my position in three weeks since I am pregnant—and I have been refused admission to four hospitals in Manhattan. Yet, one of these hospitals admitted a friend at the identical time I will be due.

Yes, prejudice still exists, even in New York, but we have come a long way . . .

(Mrs.) Dorothy Phyllis Johnson
5/25/53   *New York City*

Equality Defined

. . . Too often, I believe, we are confused by the term "equality," which the American Negro seeks, and which, whenever applied to a minority group, seems to stir up a controversy. To me, a Negro, equality does not mean forcing my way into the home of my Caucasian brother . . . I simply want the right of competing for any job for which I am qualified; of moving into and living in the neighborhood of my choice because it suits both my temperament and my purse; to enter, with dignity, the theater, restaurant or lunch-counter in whatever vicinity because it suits my immediate needs; to become, eventually, accepted by my fellowmen, black or white, on the basis of my contribution to society regardless of race, creed or color . . .

William R. Givens Jr.
502nd Repl. Co.
2/8/54   *Bad Kreuznach, Germany*

White Pledge

. . . We the white people of the South, like the whites of South Africa, are determined to keep our land a

white man's country. We Southern whites, unlike the majority in the North, have not been bemused and misled and culturally destroyed by a multiplicity of meaningless noble-sounding words and phrases . . . I feel certain that my views are those of the great majority of Southern whites under 35 years of age. Segregation is going to last in the South, even though we have no Dr. Malan to inspire us in our determination to save white culture in America.

Charles D. Hendon
3/15/54   *Newton, Miss.*

Racial Flare-Up

It was to be expected that the desegregation decision of the Supreme Court would bring out whatever beastly intolerance exists in what we flatteringly speak of as "Christian America."

But the actions of those intolerant yokels in Delaware [Oct. 11] pinpoint the problem and show that while we have gone a long way in decency as interpreted by our high court there is a great segment of our population that is still essentially a backwoods mob without the slightest comprehension of democracy or of Christianity . . .

Lewis A. Lincoln
10/25/54   *Kansas City, Mo.*

Racial Flare-Up (Contd.)

The articles [Oct. 11 *et seq.*] on the anti-segregation disturbances . . . certainly must be edifying to non-American readers the world over, especially here in the Middle East, where the inhabitants' skin color is usually a shade or two darker than those lofty-browed

Police and the National Guard patrol outside a clothing store wrecked during riots in Los Angeles, 1965

Anglo-Saxon types in the photographs accompanying your [Oct. 11] article. . . . What a profound impression this must make—these Americans, always broadcasting about freedom and equality and the "American way of life" and what a great little country we are . . . As an American living abroad, I find myself wondering about my countrymen, especially that superior breed of bigots south of the Mason-Dixon line.

R. N. White
11/8/54   *Rafha, Saudi Arabia*

Interracial Marriages

TIME, June 27 listed North Dakota among those states in which marriages between whites and Negroes are prohibited. If this statement had appeared in the next issue, TIME would have been in error because by Chapter 126, Laws of North Dakota, 9155, this prohibition was repealed, effective July 1, 1955.

Manley G. Paisley
8/1/55   *St. Paul*

Southern Faith

You have a great deal to say about segregation these days, and apparently consider yourselves the only champion of the cause . . . The shocking instances of sadism and violent prejudice are just as sickening for a Southerner to read as it is for any other citizen—regardless of his geographical location . . . Desegregation will soon become a fact—not one to ponder over or argue about—but one to live with and adjust to. And when it happens, we will go about our business as usual and I rather doubt if many Southern gentlemen will brandish their weapons or many Southern ladies will collapse with the vapors. Quit creating the impression that the average Southerner is two steps away from starting another Civil War. All we want is to face the days ahead and the changes we must adjust to with Christian faith . . . and handle these changes with wisdom and diligence.

Jane Williams Hiers
2/27/56   *Nashville*

Southern Hospitality

I was shocked to read in your Aug. 13 issue that segregation in the Southern states had reached the point where the picture of a Negro is not permitted in a Southern newspaper.

Neil Buchanan
9/3/56   *Winnipeg, Man.*

Whose Ism?

Your Sept. 17 News in Pictures reminds me of Hitler's concentration camps, where innocent victims of racial prejudice had to live behind barbed wire guarded by the SS. Now our own children in some states cannot go to school unless protected by tanks and machine guns.

O. Branchesi
10/15/56   *Cincinnati*

Race & Education

I know I speak for my more experienced colleagues when I assure the congressional investigators [Jan. 7] that we who teach genuinely integrated classes simply see no sense in segregation. A Negro face does not tell us a thing about what sort of mind is behind it, any more than a white face does. I have Negro pupils who are problems; I have lily-white children who are problems. It just happens this semester that the only truly sensitive intellect studying under me belongs to a Negro.

Race and education are mutually irrelevant concepts, and nobody is going to get anywhere thinking about education in terms of race. I know this not because it was taught to me as an article of piety, which it was, but because unlike most of my early articles of piety, this one turns out to be true on testing.

Winifred Scott
New York City

The truth is that at this stage of their development Negroes get along faster and better in ther own schools. When you get a sufficient number of them in a white school, both whites and coloured suffer. It was all tried out in our Reconstruction days after the Civil War, and both sides reached the conclusion that it would not work.

R. B. Herbert
1/28/57   *Columbia, S.C.*

Change Comes Hard

Believe it or not, the South is a part of the U.S., and is entitled to majority

The Rev. Ralph Abernathy, Ralph Bunche and the Kings lead the 1965 march from Selma to Montgomery

Black America 1970

Jesse Jackson

MIDDLE-CLASS BLACKS
Making It in America

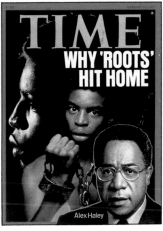

WHY 'ROOTS' HIT HOME

Alex Haley

rule. If the majority of the people of a state want segregated schools, they should have them. The minority have the right to demand equal facilities, and a state which fails to provide them should be penalized. But to integrate the schools against the will of the vast majority is a crime against democracy.

Terrell W. Ecker
Laredo, Texas

Florida's Governor Collins says: "Negroes must contribute by changes in their own attitudes." Are the whites in Montgomery, Ala. contributing to their change of attitudes by bombing the Mt. Olive Baptist Church?

Albert E. Hutchins
2/18/57 *Bradford, Pa.*

The Strong Man

Your brilliant Feb. 18 story of the Rev. Martin Luther King is a picture of early Christianity. It left me ashamed of my own ministry as I realized how cowardly I have been in the struggle for justice, mercy and equality. Thank you for opening my eyes, and congratulations on a thought-provoking piece of journalism.

Frank A. Kostyu
Pastor, Immanuel Evangelical and Reformed Church
Alliance, Ohio

Thank you for a heartening story. May King's words live in history: "The strong man is the man who can stand up for his rights and not hit back."

James H. S. Moynahan
Milton, Mass.

Have just read your nauseating article on the Rev. Martin Luther King. Cancel my subscription at once.

George Harris
Dallas

What a fitting article for you to publish on the day following Lincoln's birthday. As history has revealed Lincoln to be the Negroes' Moses, I doubt not that Martin Luther King Jr. will be their Joshua.

Victor Sharp
3/4/57 *Lorain, Ohio*

Crime & Color

Your Feb. 11 article on Negro crime is a timely one, as have been others within the past year. However, it should be made clear that this is one of the self-sown seeds of American destruction. Negro crime will diminish in proportion to the amount of participation afforded the Negro in American affairs. This Negro crime is the price America pays for her racial double-talk and social hypocrisy.

Al Calhoun
Montgomery, Ala.

The average Yankee just cannot know and will not believe what the average Negro in his own environment will do to himself and his neighbors when he feels like going on a tear—nor how often he goes. The average Negro is treated as a second-class citizen because he is a second-class citizen.

Charles C. Laughlin
Colonel (ret.), U.S. Army
3/4/57 *Rocky Mount, N.C.*

The actions of Governor Faubus are a disgrace to America. Even more upsetting, however, is the statement by Mr. Sam Rayburn: "I'm not making any comment about segregation at all, my friend, one way or another. It's not my problem." It is bad enough that the Speaker of the U.S. House of Representatives makes no comment on segregation, but to say that it is not his problem is worse. Dictatorships have been established in the world just because of the "It's not my problem" attitude of the people.

Gisela Barbatschi
Brooklyn

I am quite sure that you Americans have the faith and brains to solve the colored problem in a way that we all can be proud of you—not like that Faubus.

Guy Baumann
10/7/57 *Olten, Switzerland*

Thanks, Orval

Let us all thank Orval Faubus for

reminding us of a forgotten privilege —states' rights!

J. G. Thornburg
Wheeling, W. Va.

Might it not be prudent to withdraw statehood from Arkansas and give it to Hawaii?

Janet W. Billings
10/14/57 *San Francisco*

Successful Integration

Results from the Olympic Games at Rome suggest that the integration of Negroes into U.S.A. sport is a howling success. Could you inform readers how your crop of medals was shared between black and white?

W. B. Edwards
10/10/60 *Melbourne*
American athletes took home a total of 112 medals for all competition, including team sports such as basketball. Of these, 27 were won by 24 Negroes and 85 were won by 76 Caucasians.—ED.

Played Down

The most frightening aspect of the recent race riot in Washington is the manner in which it was so obviously played down or ignored by the news media of this country. If those were white students performing those acts, it would have resulted in pictures on the front pages of the papers, television coverage, and wrathful indignation by political, religious and business leaders.

Mrs. James Heath
12/21/62 *Chicago*

Crumbling Wall

Your conclusion that the Negro can crumble the walls of segregation only by earning acceptance [June 7] is a good, idealistic approach. But don't stop there. Many Negroes of intelligence, prominence and respectability have been led to believe that they are acceptable; but time and again, with despair and humiliation, they have found the barriers to be still solidly in place. After a hundred years of frustration, it appears quite evident that the walls will be crumbled at last, either by increasing pressure at all points, or with the helping hands of the people on the other side.

Walter Clark
Philadelphia

You apparently intended to deliver a little sermon to the American Negro militants of the spring 1963 revolution, on the need not only to "take" but to "deserve" their place in this society. You mention that Southern and Northern whites have pointed to the high rate of crime and illegitimacy among Negroes, and seem to imply that the Negro has not wholly justified "acceptance" into the mainstream of American life because of his questionable morality. As a thinking person, I take exception to this vicious and dangerous insinuation. As a Negro, I take offense at it.

No one would deny that there is wide demoralization among American Negroes, who are generally frustrated from cradle to grave in their attempts to find a "place in the sun." If, indeed, the crime rate among my people is high, it is because the Negro, in his rage, is striking back at a society that denies him the chance to be a man and to make an honorable life for himself.

Norman E. Hodges
6/21/63 *New York City*

Land of the Free?

Perhaps you can appreciate the resulting confusion in the minds of many Africans upon their consideration of a nation of people that will allow such violations of human dignity and conscience as Birmingham and at the same time enthusiastically support such a program as the Peace Corps, which has sent thousands like myself throughout the world in the name of freedom, justice, and a deep respect for human rights. An African said to me this week in all sincerity, "What is all this nonsense about your country being the land of the free and home of the brave? America acts as if it were a land free only to whites, and the Negro must be brave to live there." I am inclined to agree with him. It certainly appears that way from this side of the world.

Jo Ann Cannon
Peace Corps Volunteer
6/28/63 *Mlanje, Nyasaland*

Powerful Sermon

The cover portraying Governor Wallace and a bomb-mutilated "Good Shepherd" window in a Birmingham church is a powerful sermon.

Thanks to TIME millions of Americans both north and south of the Mason-Dixon line are beginning to realize the utter stupidity and unChristian and antiquated thinking of those who for the past 100 years have done all in their power to keep the Negro in an invisible cage.

Harold Detlefsen
Editor, RFD News
10/4/63 *Bellevue, Ohio*

Man of the Year

Fifteen of us were arrested at a restaurant on the outskirts of this "progressive" little North Carolina town. Our crime was attempting to order Sunday dinner—or, in local parlance, "trespassing" in a "public" restaurant. Twelve of us are black, three white.

A young lady who had refused bail and been imprisoned here for 16 days, refusing to eat the food sent in to us by a segregated restaurant, went out on bond. She returned an hour later as a "visitor," her arms laden with hamburgers and coffee, her steps somewhat wavering from her fast and her eyes shining. Tucked among her gifts to us was the latest issue of TIME, with the painting of Rev. King under the banner: Man of the Year.

Thank you.

Kathryn J. Noyes
Chapel Hill Jail
Chapel Hill, N.C.

It is my opinion that if King had not flitted from one city to another stirring up trouble, there would not have been the deaths and trouble in the country today due to the integration.

He should have been jailed as soon as he arrived in the different Southern cities, for he was there only to incite violence.

John A. Laird
1/10/64 *San Mateo, Calif.*

Lynchings

In spite of the consideration due the circumstances under which it was written, I must protest Martin Luther King's statement, "but when you have seen vicious mobs lynch your mothers and fathers at will and drown your sisters and brothers at whim . . ."

For the information of those inter-

ested in accuracy, lynchings are now largely a thing of the past. (There is no intention to defend even one lynching.) Very few Negroes of King's age have ever witnessed a lynching.

Furthermore, during the past 25 years, there has been a revolution in the way Negroes are "treated" in the South.

I believe that time will show that "the Negro revolution of 1963" (due largely to the type of leadership involved) retarded rather than speeded Negro progress.

Frank Wallace
Editor and Publisher
Mississippi Journal
1/17/64 *Clinton, Miss.*
Since 1900, nearly 1,800 Negroes have been lynched, the last one in 1959.— ED.

Civil Rights Bill

With God's help, I hope Americans will accept their moral responsibility by doing what they can to make life, liberty and the pursuit of happiness a reality for Negro people as well as white.

David W. Mandyck
Afton, N.Y.

The civil rights bill is not "the product of national demand." You should have said "the product of noisy minorities who terrify politicians."

Darrell C. Steers
7/3/64 *Chevy Chase, Md.*

The Face of King

It is not Martin Luther King but the spirit of the Negro movement that TIME has captured on its cover. Expediency has made a demagogue of the Reverend, but that is the only way a battle against overwhelming odds can be won.

Daryush A. Irani
4/2/65 *Bombay*

Why Watts?

I must express my embarrassment and humiliation as a result of the terrible violence in Watts [Aug. 20]. We in Los Angeles had felt proud of the way the racial situation had been handled; we must have been blind not to see the melting pot of hate bubbling in the Negro sectors of this great city. I feel a great sense of sorrow for the Negro and his plight.

Robert J. Tobias
Los Angeles

I am a Negro, but I am an American first, and I am ashamed of the rioting and murder and looting that occurred in Los Angeles. The causes of this tragic event must be corrected. How can police say they do not practice brutality when millions of people watching TV saw a white policeman kicking a suspect? If we are to respect law and order, let the officers of the law set a proper example.

Dorothy M. Davis
El Paso

There is growing revulsion against the civil rights movement and the so-called "downtrodden" American Negro. I have talked to several Midwesterners who were very sympathetic with the movement. Now, because of the inhuman and barbaric riots, they have become disgusted.

9/2/65

Donald Forcum
Poynette, Wis.

Defining Power

As a Negro, I regret that the term "black power" [July 22] has been introduced into the civil rights movement, because it has a detrimental and misleading connotation. The Negro wants power only in the sense of being represented, heard and accepted. Because of his lack of power, he has been stripped of human dignity. Even steel wears out: many Negroes are tired of being subservient. I have been taught to turn the other cheek, and I definitely believe in this philosophy. However, many Negroes are adhering to the natural instinct of man to retaliate before being mutilated.

8/5/66

Archie W. Bates
Norfolk

Between Aspirations & Reality

That was an interesting and perceptive Essay on Negro achievements and aspirations [Oct. 28].

You correctly identify Negro violence and cries of "black power" as potentially the most destructive phenomena on the civil rights scene. What must be added, however, is that, in the civil rights movement, as in other revolutionary movements, the narrower the gap between aspirations and reality becomes, the greater the frustration and anger over the remaining obstacles tend to be. We would be expecting something more than human from the Negro were we to demand that he stifle these emotions. The problem, rather, is to channel Negro anger and dissatisfaction into constructive avenues, such as self-help. That is what this commission and its federal and state sister agencies are about.

George G. Lorinczi
Chairman, Governor's Commission on Human Rights
Milwaukee

11/4/66

Reliving the Riots

Because I am a mere 17 years of age and am one person in a country of millions, what I say doesn't make much difference to anyone else. But what I have witnessed in the past week makes me feel somewhat sorry that I am even the small part of it that I am. I have seen my city, the fifth largest in the U.S., reduced by one-sixth its original size. Not by a tornado or flood, or any other act of nature or God, but because of people who somehow seemed to lose every bit of their sanity and proceeded to loot, burn and murder innocent citizens. Why? I don't know, maybe someone does, but all we who do not know see is smoldering rubble, homeless people, and the corpses of those who were the sniper's prey. There is nothing more frightening than seeing what appeared to be a sane world turn into a grotesque horror picture. I am sad; I cannot even begin to describe how sad I am to see what has happened to my people. I will be proud to tell my children that I was alive when the first astronaut went up into space, and how I saw science and medicine advance at an unbelievable speed, but it will be nearly impossible for me to look at them and say that I was here when my city went mad, when the people arose, took all the good and peace in my city, and destroyed it.

Elizabeth Hoffman
Detroit

I am a widow woman, am a Negro, and I have to say the truth is I don't have anything to fear from white folks, but the colored boy hoodlums in my neighborhood scare me to death. You might as well be living in the Congo. The white folks in neighborhood stores where you get a little credit have moved and are moving away and property is not kept up and is ruined. I have to say we Negroes did it all. We destroyed a fine neighborhood that others built. We got to quit blaming others and depending on the Government and expecting miracles overnight and now we got to work ourselves up. It's up to us and it's going to take time.

Winnie May Boston
St. Louis

Want my advice? Establish a Negro-stan. Set aside one or two of your Southern states where Negroes can enjoy privileged status. The rest of America can be their diaspora. A people must have a home.

J. Ross
Johannesburg, South Africa

8/11/67

March On

Martin Luther King was murdered because he was our uncomfortable conscience. I am filled with shame and loathing for my race. My heart grieves for his family and friends who must abruptly substitute memories for his warm reality. My mind cries out to know how I, one single me, insulated in my white suburb, can redress the ancient wrongs.

Joyce K. Laird
Lafayette, Calif.

4/19/68

King's Death

As a Negro, I, too, must bear my share of the shame and horror of Martin Luther King Jr.'s untimely death. Whether I burn or kill (by God's grace, I hope to do neither), I am associated with those who do. And we dare to point indiscriminate accusing fingers at whites. The answer to whether Dr. King labored in vain will not be determined alone by the success or failure of civil rights legislation or by improvement of housing and economic opportunities for minorities, but also by the degree to which all of us, blacks and whites, are committed to the pursuit and practice of nonviolence and love. Any commitment short of total is a farce.

(The Rev.) Lewis P. Bohler Jr.
Episcopal Church of the Advent
Los Angeles

4/26/68

Widow Replies

The children and I have always understood the significance of my husband's work and would have preferred personally to ignore Mr. Hoover's ungentlemanly attacks on my husband, but my husband is dead and cannot reply for himself. Moreover, his memory is too precious to us and to tens of millions of Americans, black and white, to permit unfounded slurs to remain unanswered. J. Edgar Hoover, in alleging that he called my husband a liar during their meeting in 1964, has exposed himself. There were witnesses present, three distinguished clergymen, who explicitly denied that Mr. Hoover made such a statement or any other attack on my husband's veracity to his face.

It is unfortunate for our country that a person of such moral and mental capacity holds a position of such importance. It is equally unfortunate for race relations in these troubled times that a person revealed in this interview to be so arrogantly prejudiced against Puerto Ricans, Mexicans and blacks is a high Government official.

Mrs. Martin Luther King Jr.
Atlanta

1/4/71

Watergate

Five men were caught breaking into the Democratic offices at Watergate. Richard Nixon's second term was soon bogged down in scandal. Spiro Agnew resigned; the President's men were under indictment. John Mitchell spoke bitterly, John Dean extensively. Judge John Sirica, Congress, the public listened. TIME took a stand by publishing "The President Should Resign." President Ford took another when he issued the pardon.

Scared

Incredible! First we have massive evidence that the Committee for the Re-Election of the President has been engaged in unprecedented political espionage, then we discover [Nov. 6] that the once respected FBI is also on Mr. Nixon's payroll.

Whether the President in fact meant for the FBI to become involved in political studies relating to his bid for re-election is not important to me.

The problem is that I believe that he might have. Color me scared.

Eric L. Wheater
11/27/72   *Lyons Falls, N.Y.*

Resurrecting Common Sense

The Essay on common sense [June 11] was delightful, and I was especially pleased that you resurrected the wit and wisdom of Kin Hubbard.

There is so much of his material that is relevant today. Watergate buffs might enjoy the following, first published in 1912:

"It pays t' be honest, but it don't pay enough t' suit some fellers."

Mike Kraft
7/2/73   *Washington, D.C.*

Accomplishments of Watergate

As a former university student who saw action in Washington during the demonstrations and riots of '69 and '70, it strikes me as enormously ironic that a handful of conservative Republican lawyers and officials have accomplished what thousands of long-haired, rhetoric-spewing radicals could not—*i.e.*, the destruction of the American people's faith in Nixon, the Cabinet and the Republican Party.

The President's last memo will read: "We have met the enemy and they are us."

John Feiten
7/2/73   *Malibu, Calif.*

The Truth

John Dean said, "My dad once told me that when you're cornered, there's only one thing to do—tell the truth."

On the other hand, my dear old dad raised me with this thought: "If you always tell the truth, you'll never have to worry about being cornered."

Diane S. Soder
7/16/73   *Lafayette, Calif.*

Excuses

Mr. Dean is the only person I have heard who can surpass my teen-agers with excuses about why it wasn't their fault and why they shouldn't be blamed and how they really didn't mean to be there, and after all I said "Good evening" to them when they came home, so I must have known what was going on and agreed to it.

M. S. Whitehead
7/30/73   *Beltsville, Md.*

Basic Distrust

Naturally Nixon feels at home with Brezhnev and Mao: he shares their basic distrust of Americans.

A. M. Navid
7/30/73   *Durban, South Africa*

Puzzled

As a foreign observer who had some experience of the Viet Nam situation at the time when President Diem was still alive, I am puzzled by one of the

A Nixon supporter

accusations in the Watergate case. Why would Hunt find it necessary to "fake" a State Department cable linking the Kennedy Administration to the 1963 assassination of Diem? Isn't this rather like "faking" evidence that Senator Edward Kennedy was somehow concerned in a girl's drowning at Chappaquiddick?

Graham Greene
8/6/73   *Paris*

Nixon's Nose

According to the Pinocchio principle, Nixon's nose should be somewhere just west of the Mississippi at this point in time.

Catherine Arthur Smith
Nashville, N.C.

The results of President Nixon's meetings with Russia and China are far more important than the whole Watergate affair.

Jake Phillips
8/6/73   *Charleston, W. Va.*

Impeachment

If the majority of Americans believe the President culpable but oppose impeachment [July 23], that is a sad commentary on the complexity of modern life.

If Nixon is guilty and refuses to resign, then he is a threat to the liberty of every American. In such a case, impeachment is the only recourse the Constitution provides. The process is fraught with uncertainty, and it is reasonable that people should fear it. But it seems strange that a nation quick to war against imagined enemies abroad should be afraid to protect its freedoms against subversion by its own leaders.

Don B. Wittenberger
Seattle

On the matter of impeachment: this country has survived a Civil War, two World Wars, a Depression, and a dozen or so assassinations. I think it could survive an impeachment. Such action could in fact strengthen the country by demonstrating that no one is above its laws.

Richard Rynen
8/13/73   *Madison, Wis.*

Kangaroo Court

Watergate—from boredom to tedium to nausea to outrage! If the President himself had tapped every phone in Washington, he could not have done one-tenth the disservice and injury to the country that the Ervin investigating committee, aided and abetted by the anti-Nixon news media, has done, in what can only be called self-serving political maneuvers. While they conduct their kangaroo court, ignoring the real problems that face the nation (inflation, the energy crisis, pollution, drugs, balance of trade, the devaluation of the dollar), what kind of image of the U.S. are they transmitting to the world by their condemnation of political enemies without a fair trial? And which of their victims can anywhere receive a fair trial after this massive brain-washing of the whole country? And has anyone stopped to wonder why the Democrats were so upset by the tapping of a few phones if they had nothing to hide?

Inez H. Coryell
8/27/73 *Bella Vista, Ark.*

Nixon's Thanks

Why is it that you Americans are bent on making Watergate Nixon's Waterloo? Are you sure this is what you want to do to the man who got you out of Viet Nam, made friends with the Chinese, lifted the Iron Curtain a bit—all within the past few years? Is this your way of saying thank you to a great leader who has done a lot for peace?

Alberto M. Soriano
9/3/73 *Davao City, Philippines*

Beleaguered

After the interminable drone of the Watergate hearings, the picture that lingers in the mind is of a beleaguered President gathering the dignity of his presidential robes about him and responding with an almost superhuman patience and courtesy to a group of reporters, all with their knives out and all visibly thirsting for his blood. It reminded me of the howling savages dancing around the suffering Uncas tied to the stake in *The Last of the Mohicans*.

Anne Hughes
New York City

If Nixon were seen walking on water, hand in hand with Jesus Christ, the press of this country (TIME included) would say that he was trying to drown the Lord.

John C. Rowden
9/17/73 *Fresno, Calif.*

Bored with Watergate

Your article "Who's Bored with Watergate?" [Oct. 8] accurately expresses my feelings. After hearing such

An anti-Nixon demonstrator makes his point

a recital of dirty tricks, I certainly sense a powerful pressure being exerted on the press and TV to make Watergate "out of fashion." If the people of our country are really bored by Watergate. I feel they deserve Watergate and will get more of the same in the future.

(Mrs.) Dorothy B. Kennedy
10/29/73 *Portola Valley, Calif.*

Why Agnew?

Why is Agnew resigning when we all know that Nixon's the one?
Maggie McComas
Brussels

I'll never go to the races with Nixon. All he does is pick the losers.

Susan Baum
11/5/73 *Washington, D.C.*

207

Media Mafia

In 1972 we elected Richard Nixon to another four-year term as President of the U.S. We would like to see him complete that term without harassment from the media Mafia! Please exhibit the restraint you would if he were a Democrat.

(Mrs.) Jaqueline W. Hillenbrand
11/26/73   *St. Petersburg, Fla.*

Time's Stand

TIME is to be congratulated for finally taking an editorial stand that is vitally necessary to the well-being of this nation. Only one other President has divided this nation as badly as Nixon: Lincoln. His reasons for doing so were motivated by a sense of human justice; Nixon was and is being motivated by purely selfish political considerations and an exaggerated sense of self-importance. The present crisis in leadership was caused largely by Nixon and those he surrounded himself with, and the people no longer have faith in his ability to effectively govern the nation. If he does not step down on his own, then Congress should remove him.

Bruce W. Nusbaum
San Francisco

If there was ever a time when the political adage "Don't change horses in the middle of the stream" was true, it is now.

While confidence on the domestic front may be low, the international stakes have never been greater. No President, bar none, has been able to achieve what President Nixon and his able associates have accomplished regarding world peace and the easing of tensions.

Suggesting that he resign, when it is doubtful that sufficient evidence exists for impeachment (to say nothing about the odds of finding him guilty), is just about as silly as firing the captain and crew of a damaged jetliner while they are fighting for a successful landing in a pea-soup fog. Who would take over?

Vinton K. Ulrich
Waltham, Mass.

You are hereby directed to stop publishing. You are under citizen's arrest for sedition, treason, subversive activities and other high crimes. You were not elected leader of this nation. That function was given to Nixon in 1972 to be carried out for four years. Just close down and conserve needed energy.

Mr. and Mrs. David Moylan
Roanoke, Va.

By adding your voice to the baying of the hounds, you are contributing to the forces that are tearing this country apart.

C. W. Dutton
11/26/73   *Riverside, Calif.*

At the Heart

I wish to commend you for your editorial "The President Should Resign." Your observation that the President must be held accountable for one of the most corrupt Administrations in U.S. history is the heart of the matter.

Jack McRae
Mesquite, Texas

The process of dismissing a President of the U.S. should begin in the chambers of Congress, not in the editorial offices of the nation's news media.

John A. Faylor
12/3/73   *Heidelberg, Germany*

Last Year's Echo

Does anyone else in the U.S. find it somewhat ironic that Judge John Sirica is this year's Man of the Year for having the courage to investigate what last year's Man of the Year and his hand-picked advisers did all year?

Diane L. Muehl
2/4/74   *Schenevus, N.Y.*

Anticlimatic

By the time those chickens get around to impeaching the President, it will be so anticlimatic that I expect we'll hear about it in between sports and the weather.

Joan Margalith
2/18/74   *Poland Spring, Me.*

Sleeping Cure

Recent events have caused me to ponder these times at night. If I can't sleep, I don't bother counting sheep. Instead I count the guys who have gone from Nixon's herd in Washington.

Allen R. Derr
4/1/74   *Boise, Idaho*

The Press and Nixon

Harry Reasoner recently took TIME to task on ABC-TV for certain instances of its obsessional and below-the-belt reporting on Watergate, which he said had betrayed the canons of both objective and ethical journalism.

It was predictable that sooner or later TIME would begin to pay the price for its editorial overinvestment in the destruction of the President. That price as Reasoner noted, is the loss of journalistic prestige and credibility. How ironic, and how fitting, that a distinguished media colleague and certified Nixon critic like Reasoner should blow the whistle on TIME for its phobic Watergate reporting!

No President of the U.S. except Lincoln (in retrospect, now to be considered another impeachable character) has ever been more savaged by the press than Nixon. For one solid year the press has been beating on him mercilessly. And he has shown that he can take it and take it and take it, with cool and courage. But few journalists—none on TIME—have had even the sportsmanship, no less the journalistic objectivity, to report that whatever Nixon is or is not, he is one helluva gutsy fighter. To be sure, the capacity to take punishment as well as dish it out is not widely associated with journalists, which is no doubt why they do not recognize it as a virtue in Nixon.

Pity. Because when, or if, the New York and Washington press succeeds in knocking out Nixon, the country is going to need an even tougher President, for America's economy and world prestige are bound to take the count along with him.

Clare Boothe Luce
Honolulu
4/8/74

Dishing It Out

Cheers for Clare Boothe Luce [April 8], the widow of TIME's founder, for speaking out against TIME's egregious posturing and phobic Watergate reporting.

Count me among those Americans sick and tired of the incapacity of journalists to take punishment as well as dish it out; Americans proud we have "one helluva gutsy fighter" in the White House; Americans sick and tired of Nixon baiting who say it's high time to get off his back.

Edward C. Ames
Toledo

Thank God for Clare Boothe Luce, who so eloquently expressed the sentiments of so many millions of Americans. I hope the day will come when all the press will rue its editorial over-investment in the destruction of the President.

L. Wilfrid Coleman Jr.
Bryn Mawr, Pa.

It is astonishing that Mrs. Luce berates the press for reporting the facts of Richard Nixon's dismal career. Her sour-grapes ukase harks back to the Byzantine protocol that required the beheading of the messenger who bore evil tidings.

J. C. Clifton
New York City

Mrs Luce tells us in elegant prose that Nixon is "one helluva gutsy fighter." So is a cornered rat.

Finis Farr
Wyckoff, N.J.
4/29/74

Total Hypocrisy

It looks like a "swearing-in" at the White House doesn't necessarily mean a new Cabinet member is being appointed.

Jennie Larson
Spokane, Wash.

It's not the profanity that is so disturbing. Many people today use four-letter words. It's not even the obvious lack of moral indigation. That seems to be the temper of our times.

It's the total hypocrisy of the whole affair. This is the man who ran on a platform of "law-and-order." This is the man who criticized the language of Harry Truman. This is the man who vetoed the child-care bill because it would take mothers away from home. This is the man who set himself up as the guardian of home and family, morality and apple pie.

He has now proved what some of us

have suspected all along—that he's really no better than the rest of us.
Nancy Alpert Mower
Honolulu

You quote the Rev. Billy Graham as stating, "The Lord has got his tape recorder going from the time you're born until you die."

Looking over my own sinful life, I surely hope that he will give me a break by having my tape, or edited transcription, punctuated by hundreds of $18\frac{1}{2}$ minute gaps. On second thought, I hope that he lengthens the gaps to 127 minutes. Some of my transgressions were lengthy.

Don Olix
Fairport Harbor, Ohio

Impeach Nixon?
Let's wash out his mouth with soap.
Donald A. Windsor
Norwich, N.Y.
6/10/74

The Solution

I say keep the expletive, delete the executive.

Alexander King
Berkeley, Calif.
6/17/74

On the Verge

Our President, who finally brought our men back from Viet Nam and has desperately tried to bring about peace in the world, is on the verge of being impeached. Watergate was no worse than country boys upsetting outhouses on Halloween. The threat of Communism is another matter.

Francis Whitcraft
Bel Air, Md.
8/19/74

On the Side of Mercy

President Ford would be wise to announce that Mr. Nixon will be given a

August 9, 1974: President Nixon leaves for California after resigning

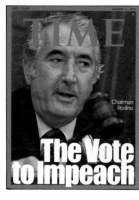

general grant of amnesty because, as a noted jurist once said, there are times when "forgiveness is deemed more expedient for the public welfare than prosecution and punishment." To make such a move palatable to those who believe that justice should be even-handed, President Ford should couple amnesty for Mr. Nixon with amnesty for the thousands of Viet Nam-era draft evaders still at large. Let us err on the side of mercy. Unless this quarrel between the past and the present is quelled, we shall lose the future.

Bill Simons
8/26/74 *Swampscott, Mass.*

A Gross Insult to Justice

That our country has had to go through the agonies of the recent months is depressing, and yet how fortunate that the very circumstances once again bring to the forefront the basic rights our Constitution guarantees. There comes a time when the only way an unwholesome situation can be treated is by facing it and proceeding through the appropriate legal system if we want to retain our individual rights as well as law and order. Now that President Nixon has resigned rather than subject this country to the trauma of a trial in the Senate, to want to go even further and offer amnesty or "off the record" equivalents would be a gross insult to our system of justice.

To make a "deal" with the former President would be a breach of faith with the future. The American people have had enough secret deals and plea bargaining. There must be no more deals. Now I think we have to go back to Harry Truman's statement, "The buck stops here," and apply it to the

prosecutors and the courts. If any deals are made with the ex-President, I fear that much of our agony has been in vain.
Norton Simon
8/26/74 *Los Angeles*

The Pardon

The Supreme Court was widely praised in the "tapes" case for its holding that no man was above the law. President Ford, with all good intentions and even with personal magnanimity, has dealt this principle a serious blow. What are we now to do about John Mitchell, who may have already suffered as much as Richard Nixon and is still being prosecuted, or with the other underlings who, as far as anyone can tell, really executed orders from above? This effort to heal the wounds of Watergate has inflamed the existing and far more serious wounds in the principle of equality before the law. Even if one decided to achieve some equality by pardoning all of those who are accused of doing the President's bidding, there stand thousands of others accused of criminality. They have also suffered, but they may differ from Richard Nixon primarily in more forthrightly acknowledging their guilt, as do most embezzlers, or in having acted out of conscience, as have many of our draft evaders. Presumably they, too, would be content with being judged by history if they were not prosecuted.

This affront to the sense of justice —and that is essentially what it is—is not, to be sure, fatal to our criminal-justice system. But this action certainly does add to the all too popular view that our criminal law is a mass of hypocrisies. It is interesting to note that California's Governor Ronald

Reagan, who applauded the refusal to allow prosecution of Richard Nixon on the ground that "he has suffered as much as any man should," had two days earlier announced his intention to veto a bill lowering the possible penalty for possession of small amounts of marijuana from ten years' to six months' imprisonment. Is it any wonder that the poor, the ethnic minorities and the young, who are the real consumers of the criminal law, regard it as stacked in favor of the rich and powerful?

John Kaplan
Professor of Law
Stanford University, Palo Alto, Calif.

President Ford has insulted every law-abiding citizen of this country.
Muriel Swango
Quincy, Ill.

President Ford, by his unexpected action, has destroyed his own credibility.

In 1960, while I was Governor of California, I had a similar situation, which hurt me all the days of my governorship. I am referring to the case of Caryl Chessman.

Mr. Chessman had been convicted of raping two girls on two separate occasions at the point of a gun. As attorney general I had fought hard for affirmance of the conviction and the execution of Mr. Chessman. I then became Governor and was faced with a difficult problem—not of justice but of clemency (mercy). I felt Mr. Chessman was guilty, but that the death penalty was too severe because it had been so long delayed. On the very eve of his execution I granted a 60-day reprieve. This was attacked by almost every newspaper in the state of California. You would have thought I was guilty of the offenses rather than the person to whom I gave the reprieve. Wherever I went I was booed. I was in somewhat the same position in which President Ford now finds himself. My first year had been a great success and I enjoyed a high popularity rating in the polls. After this act of mercy, I never really recovered. I did defeat Richard Nixon in 1962, but if I had not commuted Mr. Chessman's sentence, I don't think Richard Nixon would ever have been a candidate against me.

Jerry Ford has unquestionably hurt himself with the American people. A great many think there might have been a deal, or if not a deal then his timing was so stupid and unintelligent that he hasn't got what it takes to be President. Whatever the situation, Ford has crossed the Rubicon as I did, and he will pay the heavy penalties of never regaining the popularity he had during the first weeks of his presidency.
Edmund G. Brown
Beverly Hills, Calif.

The final cover-up.
W. Ward Fearnside
9/3/74 *Wellesley Hills, Mass.*

The Bomb

The mushroom clouds over Japan ended the Second World War, but the competition for advanced nuclear power never ceased. Scientists worked on the H-bomb while others studied the deadly effects of radiation. Edward Teller told Americans to build fallout shelters; skeptics scoffed at the pretense of nuclear survival. The sense or folly of the nuclear age continues to be debated while the superpower arsenals expand.

"Ye Fools and Blind"

The atomic bomb [Aug. 13] remains the principal topic of conversation. It is of course too soon to try to evaluate its infinite possibilities for good and evil. . . . my initial reaction is a feeling of deep regret that science has apparently learned how to utilize atomic energy. I hold with Churchill that the secret of atomic power has been "long mercifully withheld from man."

It looks as if humanity is moving inexorably toward Armageddon and into the limbo of forgotten things, an oblivion of its own making. Only the remnant now left of what Mr. Wilson called the "enlightened conscience of mankind" can save the situation. Unless prompt action is taken it will again be "too little and too late," and *this* time destiny plays for keeps.

"Ye fools and blind" are words as applicable to our civilization *(sic)* as they were more than 1900 years ago.
W. G. Martin
Kerrville, Tex.

The United States of America has this day become the new master of brutality, infamy, atrocity. Bataan, Buchenwald, Dachau, Coventry, Lidice were tea parties compared with the horror which we, the people of the United States of America, have dumped on the world in the form of atomic energy bombs. No peacetime applications of this Frankenstein monster can ever erase the crime we have committed. We have paved the way for the obliteration of our globe. It is no democracy where such an outrage can be committed without our consent!
Walter G. Taylor
8/27/45   *New York City*

The Atomic Bomb

. . . In any case, the split atom is here to stay. Let us accept it with some fear and trembling, but let us also accept it with all the faith we can muster in man's intelligent capacity and desire to harness it beneficiently, as he has electricity. . . .
Theodore E. Merritt
Salem, Ore.

TIME's discussion of the atomic bomb and its implications deserves serious consideration. . . .

Fortunately, the atomic bomb, in one fell swoop, struck down three enemies of human progress. It destroyed the hopes of the Jap fascists and their followers; it shattered the illusions of the isolationists; and it all but demolished the silly argument that governmental planning is ineffective and incompatible

Beyond Bikini Lagoon, the mushroom cloud rises above the site of an atomic bomb explosion in 1946

Exploded by the U.S. in a 1956 test, the hydrogen bomb produces a fireball that measures 3½ miles across

with democracy. It was public investment and government planning—the kind of planning that we rejected in peacetime—that enabled us to discover the instrument which finally smashed the last hopes of those who still think in terms of superior and inferior peoples, predatory individualism, and unrestrained aggressiveness.

Irving H. Flamm
9/10/45 *Chicago*

"This Blessed Bomb"

The remarks of Walter G. Taylor [Letters, Aug. 27], vigorously denouncing our use of the atom bomb, should point out clearly what type of thinking we have to fear in the future.

We know that the Germans came stunningly close to perfecting this fearful weapon . . . It was simply a race to see which of us could complete it first, and the Jap trail of bestiality gives us to understand that they would certainly not have hesitated to use this force, had they won the race.

If those who share Mr. Taylor's opinions will look under the ashes of those dead Japs, they will probably see that our strict control of this menace can turn it into the most powerful deterrent to future wars of aggression which has or is likely to come to light.

Carter Holmes
Dallas

. . . Mr. Taylor has the colossal gall to decry democracy, and to compare us to the recreants who planned the mass murder at Dachau. To this I can only say that thousands of us owe our lives to the "brutes" who devised this bomb, and the "monsters" who had the courage to use it.

(RdM2/c) R. E. Cody
c/o Fleet Post Office
9/17/45 *San Francisco*

"Secret"

If we intend to keep the "secret" of the bomb, in the face of almost universal opposition from scientists, then we must expect distrust and eventual aggression from nations claiming to be fearful for their own safety. . . . If, however, we give the "secret" to an international control commission, we 1) show the Russians (against whom, after all, this secrecy is being directed) that we are ready to trust them, 2) give a strong impetus for success of the United Nations Organization, 3) furnish a strong moral persuader to other nations to follow our example in cosmopolitan behavior, and 4) lose nothing which we won't lose shortly in any event, if we haven't already done so. . . .

This all seems so clear and logical

to us. Does it sound "idealistic" to you?

R. C. Cogswell
Captain, A.U.S.
C. R. Henderson
Captain, A.U.S.
C. W. Denko
1st Lieutenant, A.U.S.
(S/Sgt.) W. E. Grundy
11/19/45 *Chicago*

Fermi Says Scientists Are Sane

In your issue of Dec. 3 under Science, you imply that U.S. scientists are a group of madmen who are itching to exterminate life on earth in order to prove their theories. The possibility of an uncontrollable, disastrous chain reaction has been carefully considered, and there is no known or foreseeable way of starting one. Furthermore, your statement that Dr. Fermi bet that the New Mexico test would end in worldwide disaster is completely false.

We need only point out that in a development so new and so dangerous, in which many thousands of people were involved, only one fatal casualty occurred, aside from ordinary industrial accidents. As a matter of record, it has been stated officially that every possible consideration was given to all conceivable dangers of every step in the development and use of nuclear bombs and other chain reactions. This is true in any potentially hazardous research undertaking. Where calculated risks were taken, the extent of the worst conceivable damage that could occur was considered.

The purpose of science is to extend our knowledge and thereby our control of the forces of nature. The whole history of civilization is witness to the compelling necessity of this process. Any danger to mankind lies in the destructive use of discoveries which could have been used for its benefit. It does not lie in the discoveries themselves, least of all in the possibility that they may get physically out of control as you suggest in your article.

Enrico Fermi
and The Executive Committee
Association of Los Alamos Scientists
12/24/45   *Santa Fe, N. Mex.*
TIME, which wondered why there were no takers for such a bet (what could they lose?), is glad to be reassured that U.S. scientists are not really mad—just very, very inquisitive.—ED.

Complacent Talk

Is there anyone in this world who really wants another war—who truthfully believes that an atomic war could be won satisfactorily by one nation or a group of nations? Then why are we complacently talking about the next war as a foregone conclusion? . . .

(Pfc.) Robert W. Poindexter
U.S.M.C., c/o Fleet Post Office
4/1/46   *San Francisco*

Hero of Los Alamos

The full story of the death of Dr. Louis Slotin as told by a visiting scientist adds an ironic twist to TIME's story [June 10]. Slotin, whose field was originally biology, became so expert at handling sub-critical masses for bomb assembly that he was put in charge of testing the materials for Operation Crossroads. He was working on his last assembly on his last day in the lab before taking off for the Pacific.

Apparently for no better reason than the pressure to get the stuff together and on its way, he was working only 18½ inches from the sub-critical masses without any protective guards. Admittedly going too fast for safety, he let his screwdriver slip. In less than a flash he received a fatal dose of radiation. Fully aware that death was certain, and not wanting any knowledge to die with him, Slotin returned the next day to the laboratory and explained everything to the staff which he had been instructing in assembly. Not until the end of the day did he go to the hospital to await the end.

Frances Henderson
7/1/46   *Washington*

The People Are Afraid

I was rather surprised by the inference TIME drew [March 18] from the fact that people no longer talk about the atomic bomb. TIME seemed to believe that people had accepted and forgotten it, and had gone their merry ways, changing neither their modes nor philosophies of life. . . .

In the first few months after the news of the existence of the [atomic] bomb, I broached the subject to several people. My cousin said, "You'll never know what hit you," and changed the subject. My closest friend said, "What difference does it make?" and changed the subject. . . .

How can we expect a better world when the people of a democracy just sit back and try to repress their anxiety? The classic joys and sorrows are puny today; the laments of the poets are ridiculous. Men cannot be concerned with the age-old struggle for personal improvement when whole nations of men are face to face with destruction. . . .

No, the people do not talk about the bomb. They do not, because they are still afraid.

D. Purcell
7/15/46   *Los Angeles*

Path to Victory

. . . Utter astonishment could not describe my feelings when I read the tirade let loose by a Washington minister at two men who contributed such a large part in the defeat of our enemies. He would "damn to hell" these men; he would call down the wrath of God on these men were he a medieval priest; he would put in torment their souls for their base, utter disregard of all the principles of humanity. . . . Who is he? This minister might just as well damn every Air Corps officer, every bombardier, every flame-throwing private, every machine gunner and every rifleman to everlasting hell for using a weapon as destructive as the one he carried in defense of his country. . . .

Personally, it is my belief, and I am sure the belief of the majority of servicemen, that the atomic bomb accomplished at the proper moment a complete demoralization of the Japanese and led to ultimate surrender, thus saving the lives of hundreds of thousands of American men who would otherwise have been lost. . . .

J. N. Talbott
Lieutenant Commander, U.S.N.R.
12/9/46   *Philadelphia*

Lingering Radiation

". . .Two years and three months after Bikini, all four [ships] were still radioactive . . . the carrier *Independence* is still afloat . . . but is so 'hot' that it can be used only as a laboratory for decontamination training . . ." [Oct. 18].

In an advertisement elsewhere in this issue, entitled "The truth about atomic hazards," sponsored by the U.S. Army and U.S. Air Force, it is stated that radiation is the least important aftermath of an atom bomb explosion, as regards danger to humans, and that "only 15% of the deaths at Hiroshima and Nagasaki were caused by radiation . . . No significant amount of radiation appeared to linger after the explosions."

Explain, please.   *Paul Van Auken*
11/8/48   *Indianapolis, Ind.*
The advertisement was right about above-ground explosions like those at Hiroshima and Nagasaki. There radiation was the third hazard, since most of the radiation went upward and was absorbed into the atmosphere. But the Army failed to say that with underwater explosions like the Bikini bomb blast (as TIME reported), radiation is the No. 1 hazard.—ED.

Papaya & Poppycock

TIME deplores atomic "spine-chilling" but manages to give it a fling. Two years ago a scientific expedition heard the rumour of "radioactive coconuts" on Bikini, and not one was found. Despite your statement that "it may be years before the food products of Bikini are safe" [Oct. 3], dozens of us have partaken daily of Bikini's coconuts and papaya, with full clearance from both radio-chemist and radio-medical officer. For six weeks we swam daily in the "poisoned lagoon" and walked hip-deep by the hour in the "radioactive water." Poppycock! Over two years ago the scientists reported that a man living for months on twice-A-bombed Bikini would be exposed to radioactivity roughly equivalent to one chest X-ray.

W. A. Gortner
10/24/49   *Honolulu, T.H.*
Says the University of Washington's Dr. Lauren Donaldson, director of the AEC-sponsored investigation at Bikini and Eniwetok: "What we have found, up to 1949, is that radioactivity still contaminates Bikini after three years. The quantities of radioactivity are

minute, it is true. But we know that the activity is being circulated about the lagoon and is being retained and concentrated in the tissues of fish, animals and plants. We also know that these concentrations can produce radiation of sufficient intensity to form a hazard to health and life. The point is not that men soon will sicken and die if they touch Bikini's foods. But all radiation must be regarded as potentially 'dangerous,' and the more complex the life form the greater the chance of 'dangerous' effects.—Ed.

"We Must Fight to Win"

Time, July 31: "Said Dwight D. Eisenhower, who thought the [atom] bomb might be considered for material targets in Korea, but not against human beings: 'We're trying to stand before the world as decent, just, fair people not as judges to exterminate those who oppose us.' "

No ordinary stay-at-home citizen knows whether the use of the atomic bomb against the enemy is good military strategy now. But if the strategists decide that a telling blow with the bomb might be struck, we would be foolish indeed to hamstring ourselves for fear of being considered indecent.

Is it more indecent to kill many human being at once with one bomb than to kill the same number over a period of months of bombing, as we did in Europe during World War II? War is indecent, but we are involved in war, and we must fight to win.

It is considered by many moralists more immoral to kill women and children than to kill able-bodied men . . . In Russia, as much as anywhere in the world, women have been striving to achieve equality. Let us be prepared to meet the price of equality . . .

Eleanor N. Henry
8/21/50 *Long Island City, N.Y.*

Bomb Preparations

It was with considerable surprise that I read your article on the preparations that are being made for an atom-bomb attack on New York City. To say the least, and with due respect to the integrity and intelligence of men like Governor Dewey and General Lucius Clay, the preparations, based on what Clay and his staff call "thinking of the worst," defined in terms of their horrendous hypothesis, are fatuously out of relation to reality. The scope of the preparations, although five years late, are sound, rational and laudable, but if the Civilian Defense Commission cannot lift its imagination higher than its tepid, horrendous hypothesis of one paltry, now almost obsolete fission-type bomb being exploded . . . it may as well confine its activities . . . to teaching junior to "fall instantly, face down, elbow out, forehead on elbow, eyes shut . . ."

What could be more dangerously ridiculous than the hypothesis that only

Antinuclear protesters in Bonn, Germany

one bomb would be dropped, only one city or industrial area attacked? . . . Billions have been spent on the manufacture of the atom bomb, and many more billions will be spent on further production and improvements. It is both idle and dangerous to think that these bombs will not be used by either the U.S.S.R. or the U.S. should open conflict break out between them.

Stanley R. Hockman
Royal Arsenal
10/23/50 *Woolwich, London*

The Bomb at Nagasaki

In the March 9 article, "Don't Look Now," Time quotes [two scientists]: "In the case of a 'nominal' (Nagasaki-type) atomic bomb, the heat cooks the skin up to two miles away. But if a person happens to be looking at the detonation, he will certainly be blinded permanently at more than four miles away, and even at a greater distance his eyesight will be seriously damaged."

I saw the Nagasaki bomb fall at about a distance of three miles away . . . I was a civilian internee at a camp in a suburb of Nagasaki, and on the morning of Aug. 9, 1945, was out on a hill-

side . . . cutting grass for two cows which we had to keep for our Japanese guards . . . A plane swooped over my head . . . I watched it as it was about to disappear over a low ridge which lay between me and the center of the city. . . . Suddenly, there was a tremendous flash, far brighter than the sun . . . The next thing I knew, I was lying on the ground. As I scrambled to my feet, I saw the great mushroom of smoke rising into the sky . . . The skin of my bare arms seemed as if it had been held before a hot fire and was tingling . . . I was wearing dark-tinted spectacles at the time . . . I thought this fact might be of interest to Ophthalmologist Rose and Biophysicist Buettner . . .

Laurence D. M. Wedderburn
4/20/53 *Crieff, Perthshire, Scotland*

Atomic Boss

. . . I sincerely believe we are all extremely fortunate to have such a man as the boss of our atomic weapons program [Sept. 21] . . . Our so-called security and civil defense systems . . . are still "a big joke" . . . We must be "educated" to realize we're on the verge of complete destruction, the atomic clock is running out of time, and it's now or never! . . . My personal recommendation is that we . . . arm to the teeth with super-bombs and attack the Russians first . . .

Van B. Russell Jr.
Civilian Personnel Division
Air Force Flight Test Center
Edwards Air Force Base
10/12/53 *Edwards, Calif.*

H-Bomb & Consequences

Your cover story on the H-bomb [April 12] was superb, not only for the style in which it was written, but especially for the analysis of the moral problems involved (or not involved) . . .

Joan O. Falconer
Rome

Time's article . . . reads like a scene from an Orwellian nightmare. More and more, responsible people are coming to realize that the U.S. is becoming just as great a threat to civilization as the Soviet Union when men like Dr. Edward Teller and Lewis Strauss are allowed to play God with the H-bomb.

One wonders why the people of the free world . . . weren't consulted on a decision which so imperils our survival. At least they . . . might have had the chance to vote for or against their annihilation . . .

William James Hall
Cobden, Ont.

In your article on the hydrogen bomb . . . you describe the reaction to the explosions in terms of public alarm and hand-wringing. Here in the Pacific proving ground, you would find people from two laboratories working together effectively and in friendship. Of these two laboratories, Los Alamos scientific laboratory is senior in every respect. You mention only the junior partner, the Livermore branch of the University of California Radiation Laboratory, with which I am connected, and which works under the direction of Dr. Herbert York. You gave to our laboratory the kind of publicity which is most welcome to a new organization; but you did not mention the great accomplishments with which Los Alamos is starting its second decade of existence. I should like to convey to you that the spirit on this island is a spirit of cooperation, modesty and awe in face of the forces of nature, which we are trying to explore for the defense of our country to the best of our ability.

Edward Teller
5/3/54 *Eniwetok*

British Fears

No one here supposes that if America fights Russia, Britain will be spared hydrogen-bombing just by staying neutral. We would be liquidated as a precautionary measure . . . What frightens us about U.S. policy is that nonrecognition of China implies the intention to fight . . .

R. Apsion
7/26/54 *London*

Maidens from Japan

The Hiroshima maidens who journeyed to Manhatten for plastic surgery have asked us to write you and tell you that they have seen the Oct. 24 story of their progress. They feel you should tell the American people of the other devoted members of the project whose time, labor and efforts have been as important to their return to life as even the surgery itself. The three men who have made their trip possible and who have been saintly in their care for them have been Mr. Norman Cousins, Dr. Arthur Barsky and Dr.

William M. Hitzig. Dr. Hitzig, who brought to fruition Mr. Cousins' inspiration to bring the maidens to America, has been the medical director and has been a dear father, bringing smiles of happiness to their faces and keeping them warm and well day and night. Plastic surgery is repairing their bodies. But the great love of these people, we feel, is just as significant and should be recorded.

Helen Yokayama
Counselor to the Hiroshima Maidens
Tomin Harada
Director, Hiroshima Atomic Bomb
Treatment Council
11/14/55 *New York City*

Railways & the Atom

Physicist Edward Teller is to be commended for his timely warning that this nation must take urgent and far-reaching steps to prepare itself for survival in a nuclear war [Jan. 21]. However, Dr. Teller's suggestion for placing principal reliance on highway transportation on the unsupported assumption that "our system of railroads is likely to be completely knocked out, at least for the moment," deserves further examination. From experience as a combat commander in Europe during World War II and more recently in Korea, it is my firm conviction that our system of railroads is not likely to be completely knocked out by a nuclear attack, even for a moment. It is a matter of record that at Hiroshima and Nagasaki railroad-type structures stood up among the best, while at Hiroshima regular railroad service was resumed within 18 hours after the first atomic bomb was dropped.

James A. Van Fleet
General, U.S. Army (ret.)
4/8/57 *Auberndale, Fla.*

Fallout

More and more of us are getting the fallout blues as we become increasingly aware of the dangers:
Ashes to ashes;
Dust to dust.
If the Bomb doesn't get you,
Radiation must.

P. H. Baez
6/24/57 *Sausalito, Calif.*

Reactor Progress

Under the heading "A Baby Is Born," there is an excellent description of the Shippingport reactor in which, however, the following expression occurs: "The nation's sluggish atomic energy program will show its first practical results." Four atomic power plants have been completed this year and are delivering civilian power; the Shippingport plant will be No. 5. One of these plants has been financed entirely by private capital, and seven other full-scale plants likewise are scheduled to be built by private capital without any direct Government financial contribution. Fifteen other atomic power plants, for civilian use, are under construction.

Lewis L. Strauss
U.S. Atomic Energy Commission
12/16/57 *Washington, D.C.*

Fallout Fallout

Your article on the nuclear test debate was excellent, especially in view of the publicity given to the "Ban the Bomb Boys." For the layman, there appears to be only one choice: Should he put his faith in Edward Teller, the "father of the H-bomb," or in Linus Pauling or Edward Condon, two scientists who have so long leaned toward the left (politically) that they are no

Rain does not deter this Campaign for Nuclear Disarmament demonstration in London, 1982

longer able to discern what is right (militarily or morally)? I prefer to trust my nuclear future to Dr. Teller.

Edwin McDowell
Philadelphia

Should we end nuclear tests? No. If we have a weapon equal to that of our enemies, they will be afraid to use it, as Hitler was afraid to use gas in the last war.

Alec M. Earle
Charleston, W. Va.

Surely the U.S. would be committing diplomatic suicide if it were to continue with plans for H-bomb tests in the Marshall Islands this spring, now that the Soviet Union has made a unilateral (if conditional) promise to quit.

Marianna Prichard
4/28/58 *Hannibal, Ohio*

Hiroshima Recalled

Like most Americans, I am very sorry for the deaths caused by the A-bomb at Hiroshima, but not more sorry for those than for the tremendous number of deaths caused by the government that Hiroshima eagerly supported. Perhaps someone ought to remind the bitter mayor of Hiroshima just who and whose friends started the bitter war. The Japanese are an odd bunch to be talking about ethics. Who can forget their concentration camps and the death marches?

Jerry W. Yarbrough
9/8/58 *Danforth, Me.*

The Bomb

It's not that Americans have their heads in the sand in regard to civil defense [Aug. 25]. Rather, the terror and horror of thermo-nuclear attack is comprehensible to even the dullest imagination. When the first siren blows, no shelter for me; I want to be right on target.

Elizabeth Hitz
9/15/58 *Madison, Wis.*

Dead to the World

I am opposed to fallout shelters, as a form of militarism that increases the probability of nuclear war. I write to object to the following statement in TIME's article about fallout shelters [Aug. 4]: "In a full-scale nuclear attack, as many as 50 million [Americans] might die."

It is true that in the 1959 hearings before the Joint Congressional Committee on Atomic Energy the estimate was made that about 50 million Americans would be killed if there were to be a nuclear attack involving 1,446 megatons.

A full-scale nuclear attack on the U.S. would without doubt be many times the size of the 1,446-megaton attack that is estimated to kill 50 million Americans. A full-scale nuclear attack would probably kill everybody, whether

or not fallout shelters had been built.

Linus Pauling
8/18/61 *Pasadena, Calif.*

Russell Protest

There is at least one (undersigned) American who is very eager to protest the prosecution of Bertrand Russell for planning an anti-nuclear demonstration in London [Sept. 15]. He is the king of the intellectual world, and tampering with him invites comparison with society's past disrespect toward its best products—Socrates, Bruno, Galileo, to name the obvious.

Suellen Hess
9/29/61 *Washington, D.C.*

"Better Ready Than Dead"

A national campaign to build fallout shelters should start immediately. Communist rocket rattling might cease if our whole country could shout "Better Ready Than Dead."

June Ornsteen
Gladwynne, Pa.

My family and I plan to spend our last radiated hours in the woods or on a beach. Let the more foresighted and morally secure have it out with submachine guns at their shelter doors.

Peter G. Earle
10/27/61 *Middletown, Conn.*

Atomic Toll

I agree with the narrative part of your article on Nagasaki. I dispute your statements concerning atomic casualities. The figures stated by you are 38,000 killed and 21,000 wounded. For a comparison estimate, I submit the statistics listed in the Peace Park as 78,889 killed and 79,600 wounded.

Harold J. Berger, M.D.
6/8/62 *Itazuke, Japan*
TIME's figures for the number of dead and wounded are based on the latest AEC figures.—ED.

Starting the Debate

The test ban treaty that was negotiated in Moscow is a rare achievement in human history. Although limited in scope, when compared with the unlimited dangers of uncontrolled nuclear explosions and nuclear war it is an important step toward peace.

Thomas Tsakanikas Jr.
8/9/63 *Yonkers, N.Y.*

Chinese Firecracker

Neither of the presidential candidates has offered any solution to the increasing danger posed by Red China's belligerence. Now that Red China has exploded an atomic device and will soon be capable of delivering it, hadn't we better start a program of preventive medicine? Or do we just wait for the bomb to drop on us, smug in the know-

ledge that it will probably be smaller than ours?

Richard E. Eddy
10/30/64 *Atlanta*

Armageddon

If it is true that "the superpowers between them have ten tons of nuclear destruction for every being on earth," then we are much closer to Armageddon than many of us realize.

Quentin O. Nolte
7/30/65 *Chicago*

A-Bomb Warning

Your Essay on Hiroshima implies that the Japanese were not warned. This is absolutely untrue: for ten days prior to Aug. 6, U.S. bombers rained thousands of leaflets upon the Japanese mainland spelling out the fearful consequences of continuing the war. The first bomb on Aug. 6 was followed by a three-day waiting period, during which the Japanese High Command had triple the time needed to change its mind; when no reply was forthcoming, the second bomb was unleashed.

I feel we were completely justified. As usual with the liberal media nowadays, Uncle Sam is always at least partially wrong in whatever he does.

Richard F. Oles
Baltimore

I was reminded of the words of Robert E. Lee: "It is good that war is so terrible, lest we grow fond of it."

Edwin Moore
8/31/70 *San Diego*

Nuclear Energy

Now that Ralph Nader and his Raiders have confidently predicted that nuclear plant construction will be stopped in five years, how much longer do they figure it will take to stop this country altogether?

Ernest D. Hosley
Southwick, Mass.

Of course, nuclear energy is not perfectly safe. Is anything? The only way we can judge the desirability of nuclear power is by comparing it with its alternatives. And, so far, no country has been able to offer a better, cleaner, cheaper, safer alternative.

John S. Hendricks
12/29/75 *Los Alamos, N. Mex.*

Selective Killer

Oh joy, a bomb that destroys people without destroying buildings or vehicles!

If we have come this far with modern technology, couldn't we design a bomb that destroys buildings, vehicles and weapons—and not people?

(Mrs.) Kathy Forte
8/22/77 *Providence*

A march for peace in the Soviet Union in 1982

A Bleak Hope

I am one of those young Europeans (18) you described. I think one factor of this alienation mentioned has been forgotten—the atomic threat. While we are the first generation who seems completely alienated, don't forget we are the first generation whose inheritance includes such destructive power. It is very easy to notice in the behavior of the young the permanent impression that they are fighting for a place in a world in which they may not live to see the symbolic year 2000. So, what is surprising in the fact that more and more Europeans join the ecologist movement?

This movement can bring a little hope to many young people who are uncertain, but they know it is a bleak hope.

François Bompart
12/5/77 *Sillé-le-Guillaume, France*

An Atomic Scare

After the Three Mile Island accident [April 9], I intend to vote against any politicians who say "Maybe" to nuclear power, regardless of their opinions on all other matters.

What good is a chicken in every pot if the broth is radioactive?

Charlotte Reese
4/30/79 *Minden, Nev.*

Fateful Pause

If the world is as close to the brink of nuclear war as headlines say, Reagan and Brezhnev are meeting in the wrong place. There's only one spot where the masters of our fate should confer:

Hiroshima. It's ghosts might give them pause.

Larry Foley
12/21/81 *Townsville, Australia*

Europe's Pacifism

Critics of the European disarmament movement [Nov. 30] depict it as a motley collection of trends: nationalism, pacifism and isolationism. What the detractors don't consider is that this group is driven by people who have known the reality of World War II. The way to prevent a nuclear war is to get rid of nuclear weapons.

Joseph E. Peacock
12/28/81 *Alkmaar, The Netherlands*

Uranium Ban

Blocking the export of uranium from Darwin by the Australian Council of Trade Unions [Nov. 30] should not be criticized. It may be the only contribution that Australia can make toward world peace.

John McGee
12/28/81 *Sydney*

Nuclear Freeze

I wish to commend your magazine for the bold, incisive look into the terrible threat of nuclear war, from which it is unlikely a winner can emerge [March 29]. The prospect of a nuclear exchange between the U.S. and the Soviet Union is more than the issue of the '80s. The control and dismantling of these weapons of massive death present the greatest social and environmental challenge in the history of mankind. A fateful juncture in the course of human civilization and in the evolution of life on this planet is now upon us.

David J. Bine
4/19/82 *Silver Spring, Md.*

Nuclear Picnic

If it is true that "the superpowers citizens are expected to pack their cars with picnic gear and take off for the quiet countryside [April 26]. Two weeks later they are supposed to return, begin to rebuild their homes and live happily every after. It is a grotesque scenario that only a depraved Government would try to sell to its citizens.

John M. Kuypers
5/17/82 *New Orleans*

Nuclear Stakes

Your article on nuclear missiles [Jan. 31] brought out both the idealistic and the realistic positions on the issue. However, the Europeans would be wise to be realistic and realize that American defense forces have helped them maintain a free, prosperous life throughout the post-World War II period. If the West cannot remain united on the question of security, Western Europe risks becoming Finlandized.

Peter George Glick
2/21/83 *Washington, D.C.*

Green Growth

I disagree with your contention that West Germany has produced a generation, including many supporters of the Greens, with little or no historical perspective [Feb. 28]. To the contrary, German history is part of the reason why this movement is so strong. Its members know enough about the cold war era not to let it happen again.

Christof Braun
La Jolla, Calif.

By opposing nuclear weapons and showing indifference to NATO, West Germany's Green Party is unrealistic. The collapse of the Atlantic Alliance would leave West Germany vulnerable to Soviet aggression and would destroy the strength that has preserved peace for 35 years.

Richard Melnick
3/28/83 *Carle Place, N.Y.*

TV Armageddon

In your criticism of ABC's movie *The Day After*, you state that "there are no people here, only targets, stick figures on a Midwestern landscape waiting to be wasted" [Oct. 24]. It is this attitude, detached and impersonal, that makes it possible for the superpowers to continue to build their nuclear arsenals, without realizing that the "stick figures" involved are our families, our neighbors and ourselves.

J. Randall Cotton
11/14/83 *Morganton, N.C.*

Celebrities

Hollywood makes more than movies, Broadway more than shows. Fame brings with it the constant gaze of the public eye. Once a performer, athlete or politician has captivated the curiosity of the masses, virtually every move on and off camera is news. TIME has examined the professional and private lives of many celebrities to reveal what is beneath the celluloid image. Groucho Marx, Barbra Streisand and Ronald Reagan are among the well-known people who have expressed a point or two in letters to TIME.

Nina Rosa

As an enthusiastic reader of your magazine of long standing, I would like to call your attention to a gross mistake in the issue of Nov. 3, on p. 51, under the heading of "Mortality," where you state: "The following presentations have opened and closed since October 1: *Luana, Symphony in Two Flats, Nina Rosa,*" etc.

As the composer of *Nina Rosa*, I would like to tell you that *Nina Rosa* is in its 58th performance in New York and selling seats for many weeks in advance, after having played last year in Chicago for a whole season. The show has no intention of closing its New York run, now, or in the near future. . . .

Sigmund Romberg
11/24/30 *New York City*
To Nina Rosa, *its author, company, producers and composer, apology and congratulations that TIME was misinformed.—ED.*

This England

What's this you've been publishing about the Dook of York that our distributors have been fools enough to censor and tear out over here? Please post me (letterpost) the censored article and send me a bill for a year's subscription to TIME. I don't know TIME, I ought to do so.

H. G. Wells
9/16/35 *London*
To Novelist Wells has gone forward by letterpost the "censored article" on the "Dook of Kent" (not York) together with a bill for a year's subscription to TIME.—ED.

Harpo Speaks

I can talk but I hate to interrupt Groucho. I spoke in public last year in Portland when I asked for a raise in salary but I don't think anyone heard me. I make a practice of speaking every time Chico makes a grand slam, so you can look for another speech in 1937. Regret I can't get Zeppo in this wire.

Harpo Marx
9/14/36 *Culver City, Calif.*

Innovator

Pioneer and innovator in many ways of presenting the news, TIME through its first 15 years has shown a degree of originality that has been refreshing and oftentimes delightful. I wish the magazine a long life in serving the public by disseminating accurate information written in a manner to keep the reader from drowsing. . . .
2/28/38 *Franklin D. Roosevelt*

Gentle Demurrer

Many thanks for the flattering reference to my gaudily crowned head in TIME for July 7, but may I file a gentle demurrer to your repeated use of the adjective "dwarfish" in describing my person. Although I actually stand five feet four inches in socks, I have never objected to being ribbed about my size. Your pet word, however, strikes me as inappropriate as it carries a connotation of the monstrous and stunted. Let me suggest that such phrases as "smallish," "minute," "miniature" and even "pocket-size" Billy Rose would be considerable more appetizing. Of course, if your mind is made up, I assure you that I would rather be labelled "dwarfish" than not be mentioned in your splendid magazine at all. Kindest regards.

Billy Rose
8/4/41 *New York City*

Gags & Dollars

In your cinema department of July 7, you omitted, it seems to me, some of the most fascinating facts in the life and career of my friend Bob Hope. You neglected to mention the 20 years he spent in Alcatraz for kicking little children and beating dogs. It's not very often I get mad, but to speak of the "appealing avarice" of Hope, the one man in the business who does not deserve such snide reporting, is fantastic. I'm glad to be interviewed at any time about any of my friends and particularly when it's for your fine magazine, but please, please let me talk to a reporter possessing some sense of humor. Those quotes about his being known as "a hard man with a dollar" are mine. The gag about his quitting placing $2 bets after one of his entries finished out of the money is mine. I kid about Bob Hope in the same way that Hope speaks of Crosby as "the little fat man who sings." And when a TIME correspondent walks up to me at Lakeside Golf Course and wants some remarks about Hope, I expect them to be used in the spirit in which they are given.

Bing Crosby
8/4/41 *Hollywood, Calif.*
Actor Crosby is a loyal friend and Actor Hope has many good qualities. (He has played some 1,000 benefits in the past four years.) But TIME had, besides Crosby's "gags," reliable sources that indicate that a certain amount of friction is present when dollars leave Hope's fingers.—ED.

Correction

In your Letters of this week, Billy Rose says, "I ACTUALLY STAND FIVE FEET FOUR INCHES IN SOCKS . . .

This is true, providing Billy Rose is one of those peculiar individuals who wears his socks over his shoes!

In the spirit of fun.

Arthur Murray
Arthur Murray Dance Studios
8/25/41 *Beverly Hills, Calif.*

Appreciation

I appreciate greatly that not once was the word obscene mentioned in your article. Epithet too easily used which assailed unanimously the appearance of "Interpretation of Dreams" by Freud, psychologic documents which is and always will remain, in spite of all, the most important and sensational of our epoch.

Salvador Dali
1/18/43 *Carmel, Calif.*

Flattered

A couple of years ago [July 7, 1941] one of your reporters did an article on yours truly that burned me no end. It flattered me in reverse as only TIME usually does. After looking at the cover and reading the article of the Sept. 20 issue am convinced that TIME has turned sissy. . . . Thanks.

Bob Hope
10/11/43 *Hollywood*

Lillian to Tallulah

The Dec. 4 TIME misquotes me as saying at a Moscow reception that the actor doesn't make much difference to the play, as 100 guests and the stenographic word will testify. I said that although many actors have made plays successful, no actor has made a good play into a bad play or a bad play into a good play, which is a very different statement, and would quiet the excitable Miss Bankhead who in TIME, Dec. 11, says, "I loathe Lillian . . . she doesn't know what she's talking about. Of course, she's really a wonderful playwright . . . If Lillian had a good play right now, I'd do it — even though I hate her."

Accustomed as I am to yearly public greetings from the well-bred daughter of our plantation south, I think the time has come to say that hate from Miss Bankhead is a small badge of honor, and praise undesirable. Miss Bankhead will never again act in a play of mine, only because I can stand only a certain amount of boredom.

Lillian Hellman
2/5/45 *Moscow*
Stand back, men!—ED.

Reactions to a Review

Please know how grateful I am for your generously gracious remarks about Henry V [April 8] both for myself and for those associated with me in making this film. I personally feel your kind words mean not only much to Henry V but to every producer director both here and in Hollywood who dreams of attempting finer things in films. It has inspired and encouraged me to want to do something new again and I am bold to hope that men like Kanin, Wyler, Capra, Welles and many others in Hollywood will not scorn to share this feeling with me. . . .

Laurence Olivier
4/29/46 *London*

Groucho Clears It Up

I see where numerous relatives of mine have written TIME, frantically yelping that they are cousins of Sam Marx of M-G-M [April 8]. The Marx fortunes have certainly sunk to a low ebb when members of the family find it necessary to rush into print to claim relationship to anyone.

I don't know about the rest of them, but I was born during a volcanic eruption in one of the banana countries in Central America. I don't remember which one—I don't even remember the bananas, I hardly remember the stalk.

At the age of three, an utter stranger apprenticed me to a basket weaver in Guatemala. I soon learned to weave with such dexterousness that, by the time my second teeth arrived, I was known throughout the village as the basket child of Guatemala.

After I was run out of Guatemala, I met two other fellows, named, I believe, Harpo and Chico. After considerable

Grace Kelly

Fred Astaire

Audrey Hepburn

Bing Crosby

bickering, they convinced me that America, softened up by an excess of rationing, could be persuaded to swallow another dose of Casablanca—this one to be called A Night in Casablanca.

Well, we made the picture and that's that. The point is that Harpo and Chico are brothers but they are both strangers to me. And, as for Sam Marx of M-G-M who reluctantly confesses to being their cousin—well, he's slightly mistaken. The fact of the matter is, he happens to be their joint child by a former marriage.

Groucho Marx
5/11/46 *Beverley Hills, Calif.*

"Jewess" Acceptable

I've always considered myself a "Jewess" and always will. This is the first time I've ever head that it's supposed to be a slur. To me and my friends it is a most acceptable word as long as it is not preceded by the word "dirty."

Lilian Roth
9/9/46 *Montreal*

You're the Tops

Love that cover. Those cracks. That magazine. You're the tops. No time on my hands. Too busy rereading TIME.

Hedda Hopper
8/18/47 *Kansas City, Mo.*

Queen for a Day

The "Queen for a Day" program originated from Earl Carroll Theater, Hollywood, not from Broadcasting Studio [March 15]. For once I am right.

Tokyo Rose
4/5/48 *Tokyo, Japan*
Every rose has its day.—ED.

Current Credit

It has come to my attention that in your Current & Choice section, Lauren Bacall has consistently been left out of the cast of Key Largo.

Inasmuch as there are those of us in Hollywood, Miss Bacall among them, who would rather make Current & Choice than win an Academy Award or make Men of Distinction, won't you please include her in the cast of Key Largo in Current & Choice just once, as she is my wife and I have to live with her.

Miss Bacall is extremely tired of being labeled *et al.*

Humphrey Bogart
11/8/48 *Beverly Hills, Calif.*
See Current & Choice.—ED.

Inspirational Credit

. . . Rather than simply winning "a Hollywood Oscar" [Sept. 19], ex-Sergeant Harold Russell, National Commander of the AMVETS, won two at the same time . . . And no one ever deserved them more than did Russ, who is a constant inspiration to all who know him.

Fredric March
10/17/49 *New Milford, Conn.*

It Was Such Fun

I am writing to thank you for providing me with one of the major thrills of my career: your cover and story in TIME. It is hard to say quite what I feel, but I would like you to know my sincere and grateful appreciation. Nothing could be more exciting, and no one could be happier than I.

The members of your staff whom I met for the many interviews were all so charming and very kind that the whole experience was interesting and such fun to do.

Audrey Hepburn
9/28/53 *Hollywood, Calif.*

Amazing Grace

When you speak of my treating my film fans as "a hilarious joke," I'm afraid that it may convey the impression that I thought their support for me was a joke. I was delighted and touched that these girls I had never met were sincerely interested in my career and personal happiness. I was simply amazed that anybody at that time would want to start a fan club for me.

Grace Kelly
2/21/55 *New York City*

A Good Job

Many copies of the article you have published about myself have been sent to me. Your reporter has made a good job of it, and I want to express my gratitude for the successful representation.

C. G. Jung
3/21/55 *Küsnacht, Switzerland*

The Commuter

Twice recently TIME has described me as an "expatriate." The word suggests, according to Webster's, exile, a withdrawal from one's native country, or a renunciation of natural citizenship in favour of another.

That such an impression might apply to me is very upsetting. Like many other Americans, I have had interests on both sides of the Atlantic for many years, and I have always welcomed any opportunity of serving my country's interests wherever and whenever I could. Despite frequent and largely unnoticed "commuting," I have, admittedly, been obliged by recent circumstances to spend more time abroad than at home. This, however, has not precluded me from completing more than 15 years in the U.S.N.R. (in which I was promoted less than a year ago), or from representing both private and public American interests . . .

Douglas Fairbanks Jr.
8/1/55 *London*
TIME congratulates Captain Fairbanks on his latest promotion.—ED.

Mal de Merde

Much as I am flattered by your reference to me as "the high priest" of something, even something called "merde" [Oct. 1], I must put in my two cent worth of protest. The gentleman quoted, Dean Fitch, may have gone to *Cat On A Hot Tin Roof*, but he went to it with a pair of tin ears and came out of it with a tin horn to blow. *Cat* is the most highly, intensely moral

work that I have produced, and that is what gives it power. It is an outcry of fury, from start to finish, against those falsities in life that provide a good fertilizer for corruption. What it says, in essence, through the character of Big Daddy, is this: when your time comes to die, do you want to die in a hotbed of lies or on a cold stone of truth?

Tennessee Williams
10/22/56 *Charlotte Amalie, V.I.*

A Left to the Typewriter

Your Jan. 28 piece on my appearance on the Ralph Edwards' show was most friendly to me, and I am appreciative. But your reporter, or the man who interpreted my appearance, was both unkind and inaccurate. I knew every man who stepped on the stage, and I was genuinely glad to see him. Sure Ralph got some unexpected answers to some of his questions. But I always thought that was what made *This Is Your Life* a great show.

Jack Dempsey
3/18/57 *Hollywood*

Writer's Cramp

Re the Kazan-Schulberg motion picture *A Face in the Crowd:* your review is stupid.

John Steinbeck
6/24/57 *Paris*
Reader Steinbeck's needle seems to be stuck. Wrote he to TIME, Dec. 26, 1955: TIME's a Nov. 28 review of Ten North Frederick *by John O'Hara is stupid."—ED.*

She Was Framed

With your permission, I'd like to give my opinion of the Kokoschka picture of my sister [mentioned in the May 5th Art section]. I think it's a hideous mess. As great an artist as this man may be today, he certainly goofed in 1926. My sister is a very pretty girl.

Fred Astaire
5/26/58 *Beverly Hills*

Encore

Many people were impressed with your pernicious and less than one-dimensional account [May 5] of my rich and overflowing psyche, which is at the disposal of friends and strangers. Unfortunately, strangers are more attracted to me than my friends, for some unaccountable reason.

My alleged addiction to what you so euphemistically call the bottle is a classic in hyperbole. It is true, however, that I have incessantly forayed into the realm of escape. There are times when I awake and discover it is still I—which is as horrible and macabre a reality as anyone has ever had to endure.

Factually, I was ordered to drink by my doctor after my heart attack in 1952, and I did drink, but I discovered alcohol is the dullest form of escape I've ever experienced in my rigid adventures. During this otiose period I was

continually accompanied by a large bottle of Scotch for which I had (and have) the utmost contempt. So with great character I exorcised this minor unsatisfactory pleasure abruptly and have not drunk since 1954. I still carry a big bottle around with me, but I don't drink.

Oscar Levant
5/26/58 *Beverly Hills*

Nice Note from Nancy

I don't mind being criticized, but I do mind being called "acid-tongued." You see, I am trying to be a Christian, and acid tongues don't help you on the way. I enjoy your pages—or I would not trouble to write you.

P.S. All is forgot, forgiven.

Nancy Astor
8/25/58 *London*

Our Man on PP. 39-41

I am puzzled by the reference in your kindly review of *Our Man in Havana* to my "[slipping in a cruel] pointless caricature of a dumb U.S. business-man." I can't remember any such character.

I grow old . . . I grow old . . .

Graham Greene
11/10/58 *New York City*
See pp. 39-41 of Our Man in Havana.
—ED.

Tallulah's Denial

TIME's charge that I tried to maneuver myself into Harry Truman's lap at a Democratic luncheon is false. I greeted Mr. & Mrs. Truman at his request.

Tallulah Bankhead
11/17/58 *New York City*

Old & New Hands

TIME, Dec. 1, has just welcomed to this country a new batch of British correspondents. It is a gallant gesture, but it is unjust that it should, on the rebound, slap so casually the resident "old hands." As the one of these ancients singled out for occasional "capability" and "high subjectivity," may I say that this country would be lucky, in any decade, to be reported with the wide knowledge and objectivity of the *Economist's* correspondents, the good judgment of Bob Cooper of the London *Times*, the accuracy of Alex Faulkner of the *Telegraph*, and the brilliance of the *Observer's* Patrick O'Donovan. If Mr. Iddon writes often about what is "trivial and gaudy," that may be because there is a great deal in the U.S. today that is trivial and gaudy.

A true knowledge of the U.S. is the fruit of much travel, reading and reflection. It is not to be wafted by TIME's wand onto any generation, incoming or outgoing. Skill in reporting the U.S. is available, at all times and in all generations, to him that can get it.

Alistair Cooke
12/22/58 *New York City*

Tallulah Bankhead, stage and movie star

George Sanders, suave British movie star, played crooks and scoundrels

Brendan Behan, controversial Irish playwright

Salvador Dali, surrealist Spanish artist

The Quare Fellow

I enjoyed reading about myself and my wife in TIME [Dec. 8], and indeed it was very generous of you, but the nicest thing of all happened when a foreign citizen turned around from looking at my picture and said, "I did not realize you were Jewish." "I am not," I said, "but Our Blessed Lord is —I hope I've caught a little of the contagion."

Brendon Behan
1/5/59 *Dublin*

No Contact

For your information [Feb. 8], I do not wear contact lenses or glasses or a monocle.

Deborah Kerr
3/7/60 *London*

No Ghost

My lawyer tells me that he received an inquiry from you as to whether my book, *Memoirs of a Professional Cad*, was ghost-written [March 28].

The answer is no, it was not. No one likes sitting on his astral plane more than I do, but I am far too stingy to contemplate being haunted by someone else's cut, and consequently I am neither ghost-ridden nor ghostwritten.

George Sanders
4/11/60 *Lausanne, Switzerland*

Objectivity

TIME, Jan. 2: "Mailer by last week had even learned not to be a cop hater."

Drear lads, I've never been a cop hater. Too small a role. But one is not a cop lover, for that is cancer gulch.

Norman Mailer
1/20/61 *New York City*

No Need

I am glad to see you are still batting 1,000 regarding any information concerning me. As usual your information stinks. I need a house and a nightclub in Palm Beach like you need a tumor.

Frank Sinatra*
2/24/61 *Beverly Hills, Calif.*

*TIME reported: "Word appeared in the columns that Sinatra was about to buy a Palm Beach pad and a nightclub, too, so he could wage war with an established nightclub owner who had refused to offer Frankie $5,000 for a one-shot appearance."

Mr. Hefner Demurs

I very much appreciate the story on *Playboy's* prospering enterprises in TIME, but I'm not really the superficial, sex-oriented guy your story suggests. I like girls as well as the next fellow, but I spend considerably more time

Raquel Welch

Laurence Olivier

Zsa Zsa Gabor

editing and publishing *Playboy* than I do chasing chicks.

Hugh M. Hefner
4/14/61 *Chicago*

Wronged Rhyme

The verse about the Chinese quoted in your Letters column for Dec. 14 was written by me in March 1935 about the Japanese, who were just then beginning to flex their muscles. I am happy to see anything of mine in TIME, though I would have preferred an ecstatic review of my new book *Everyone but Thee and Me.*

Ogden Nash
2/21/62 *New York City*
To the reader
Who misquoted
Nash:
G-nash.—ED.

Actor's Abode

I was surprised to find myself listed as a Swiss resident [Jan. 11] enjoying, if that is the word, U.S. tax exemption by living abroad. While I believe that movie people, like other Americans, are perfectly within their rights to live and work anywhere they please, the fact is I

have never had Swiss residence or any other foreign residence. Only two of my last twelve pictures have had foreign locations, with U.S. taxes duly paid thereon.

Greg Peck
1/18/63 *Universal City, Calif.*

The Snows of Yesteryear

You make a most unfair and incorrect reference to us in your Feb. 21 story on Beverley Hills. First it was not "one slow summer day," but just before Christmas, and we did not provide "sleds and skis for a couple of hundred friends." It was a long, hard, slogging job of several weeks' organization for a Christmas Snow Party to be given on the Beverly Hills Hotel grounds for Mrs. Abe Leah's charity for needy actors.

Every item, including the artificial snow, was donated. On the day of the party a freak storm washed out everything in a few hours. With the assistance of the studios and some good friends, Mrs. Rathbone in a few hours reorganized her party inside the Beverly Hills Hotel and still realized some $10,000 for the charity. The day following the party Mrs. Rathbone, completely

exhausted, went to the hospital with pneumonia.

Basil Rathbone
2/28/64 *New York City*
TIME bows to Actor Rathbone's memory of that exhausting party 24 years ago.—ED.

Good Hex

You had me scared for a moment. I thought you might put the whammy on me by liking my latest novel *The Source* [May 28]. You pooh-poohed *South Pacific* and it became a great hit. You ridiculed *Hawaii* and it was purchased by nearly 4,000,000 readers. You blasted *Caravan* and it stayed near the top of the lists for half a year. Please spell my name right in your Best Seller box in the long months ahead.

James A. Michener
6/4/65 *Madrid*
TIME did not "pooh-pooh" Tales of the South Pacific, did not even review it, but did say that the "fine, simple Tales" were better than Michener's second book, The Fires of Spring [Feb. 14, 1949].

Bing's Girls

In your "People" section [Dec. 21], you made reference to Kathryn's recent appearance in the musical version of *Peter Pan* in San Francisco. I know you want to be corrected when you're in error. You said Jeanne Miller of the San Francisco *Examiner* panned Mrs. Crosby's performance and described the performance of our little daughter Mary Frances as stodgy.

The only thing that could possibly cause umbrage about Mrs. Crosby's performance was that Miss Miller said she was too girlish and too pretty to be

---

BRICKBATS

Rosemary and I are very pleased and flattered that you printed the photograph of our small city-state. However, I would like to mention that this was not our personal Christmas card, but one that we sent out on behalf of the Asthmatic Children Research Institute. Also, our fourth child is named Monsita Teresa, not "Theresa." Please forgive my pedantic insistence on correct Spanish spelling, but I'm proud of my Latin American orgins.

José Ferrer
1/13/61 *Beverly Hills, Calif.*

"Peter Pan"—which is sort of a mixed criticism.

The reference to Mary Frances as being stodgy was made about another performer in the cast. If Mary Frances is stodgy, then Sammy Davis is taciturn, moribund and laconic. For weeks at a time we have to keep her in a strait jacket.

Bing Crosby
Hollywood
2/4/66

Frost in Monaco

I have been deeply hurt by your inaccuracies regarding the meeting in Seville between Mrs. Kennedy and myself at the Red Cross Ball [April 29]. What you call my frostiness and pique was directed at some of the hundreds of photographers who spoiled the evening for many of us, and certainly not at Mrs. Kennedy, for whom I have admiration and respect. And let me add in refute to your snide and unnecessary remarks that I am delighted to be "upstaged" by Mrs. Kennedy at any time.

Grace Kelly Grimaldi
Monaco
5/13/66

For the Record

I would like to set the record straight in one area of your fair and objective article. It makes it appear as if I found the Screen Actors Guild "thoroughly infiltrated by Communists." This is not so. There undoubtedly were Communists in the guild, but because of our use of a secret ballot, they were never a factor. Indeed, it was the guild that was one of the leaders in the successful fight to keep the film industry from falling under the domination of other unions that were Communist dominated. I am proud of my long association with the guild, and would not want any inadvertent misinterpretation to cast any reflection on its long and honorable history.

Ronald Reagan
Beverly Hills
10/21/66

The Name Game

TIME lists me among the supporters of Senator Kennedy [May 31]. I support Senator McCarthy. When political figures seek our support, we have little to lend but our presence, represented by our names.

Barbra Streisand
Los Angeles
6/7/68

Bomb Advice

In TIME's review of my current novel *Airport* [March 22], a criticism was made that a description of how to build a homemade bomb was needlessly specific. I consider this criticism justified. As a result, in later U.S. and overseas editions of the book, I have fuzzed the bomb description, making it impossible to follow by specific steps.

I now suggest that TIME take its own advice and in future black out details of how to buy firearms such as those displayed (address and all) in the reproduced advertisement.

Arthur Hailey
London
6/28/68

A Word from the Duke

I want to thank you for putting "Old Ty" and me out there for everybody to see [Aug. 8]; and my deep gratitude for the thought and research that went into the article.

I say this in spite of your cursory, patronizing attitude concerning the political beliefs I espouse. I might add that the silent majority of the people in our nation are beginning to vote the way I think and to resent the "care from cradle to grave" philosophy which your articulate liberal-left minority are smugly taking for granted as a way to political power in this country.

John Wayne
Hollywood
10/3/69

Double Trouble

Since you mentioned nudity in your review of the movie *John and Mary* [Dec. 19], I thought you might be interested in the following example of current studio thinking.

Before filming began, I informed the producers that I would not consent to any nude scenes, and was reasured that there would be none. As soon as my work was completed, a double was hired without my consent, and several nude scenes were inserted. I argued and pleaded with the producers for a period of five months, pointing out that these scenes were totally unnecessary and had been added evidently for the sole purpose of conformity with the current trend, but since I had no legal recourse, I lost the argument.

Since the same treatment was accorded my friend Candice Bergen on another film, I suggest it might be beneficial for actresses in the future to contractually insure themselves against this kind of misguided thinking.

Mia Farrow
Manhattan
1/5/70

A No-No

Confident that TIME, the "professional" newsmagazine, would not knowingly indulge in "no-no" journalism, I should like to call to your attention the following facts: 1) There were no "false" claims in my income-tax returns [Sept. 7]; 2) I was not "caught," as the returns disclosed the transactions; 3) the figure of $445,000 is grossly exaggerated, as TIME would have found out, had TIME taken the time to read the 86-page legal opinion of the tax court; and 4) finally, as you should know, there were many others in the entertainment world who, like myself, did not attempt to understand complicated business transactions but relied on poor advice from their financial advisers and made the same kind of unfortunate investments. Earlier court decisions contain a roster of others who were similarly taken. I hope this will enable you to set the record straight.

Doris Day
Beverly Hills
10/5/70

For the Little People

Your story about Mr. Frank Sinatra [Sept. 21] has done a grave injustice to a man who over the years has done more for the "little people" of the world than almost anyone else in show business. Sheriff Ralph Lamb, obviously seeking personal publicity, has grievously violated the code of ethics of his

Doris Day

Carol Burnett

office and should be ostracized for his folly. Mr. Sinatra has been a personal friend of my husband and myself for quite some time, and during this time I have had many opportunities to see his sincere concern for the individual. I am sure you will agree that the story of Frank Sinatra's numerous charitable deeds all around the world has been the topic of many conversations. Mr. Sinatra has never asked for recognition of these deeds. In fact, he is embarrassed if they are brought up. Mr. Sinatra, not only for his great talent but also for his civic concern, justly deserves the title the King.

Raquel Welch
10/12/70 *Nicosia, Cyprus*

No Nude Scenes

Concerning your story on the *National Enquirer* [Feb. 21]: sorry—the leopard has only changed half its spots if their story on Howard Hughes (which included me) is any example.

I was never interviewed by these gentlemen, and furthermore much of their little story is a complete lie. There were never any nude scenes shot during or after a day's shooting. I have never at any time posed in the nude above or below the waist.

Like Lucifer, publications of this ilk always tell a little truth and slip the lies in like chopped liver in a sandwich. The gullible don't know they've been had till they get sick to their stomach.

Jane Russell
4/10/72 *Los Angeles*

Untrue Grit?

I've just read your People item [June 18] about my recent return from China and was amazed to find I've turned into John Wayne.

From overwhelmingly positive and enthusiastic comments, you chose to excerpt out of context a quote critical of China. I wish there weren't such eagerness to discredit this extraordinary country.

Candice Bergen
7/9/73 *New York City*

Moral Support for 34 Years

It is not my habit to write to papers after reading reviews of my books. But after coming across the one by Martha Duffy on my novel *The Eye of the Storm* [Jan. 14], in which she refers to me as "living in Sydney with several dogs and a male housekeeper," I feel I must draw your attention to an incorrect, and I should have thought gratuitous, biographical detail. The distinguished and universally respected man who has given me his friendship and moral support over a period of 34 years has never been a housekeeper. *I* am that, and shall continue playing the role at least till I am paralyzed; it keeps me in touch with reality.

Patrick White
3/25/74 *Sydney, Australia*

Ginger Rogers

Mia Farrow

Raquel Welch

The Hustle Embraced

If the Hustle, the dance with partners [Aug. 25], is a sign of things to come, I embrace it. Dancing with a partner is prettier and friendlier than just standing opposite someone thinking your own thoughts, doing your own thing. It is a social grace, nicer than saying hello and it is fun to exchange bons mots while dancing with an old friend or someone you have just met.

Above all there is something joyous about dancing. There is a sense of taking part and a sense of accomplishment as one fits the steps to the music. It is too bad that the name of the new dance is not more romantic, but then I guess the young people would not like it.

Ginger Rogers
Eagle Point, Ore.

I like the idea of the Hustle. It is much nicer dancing with a partner.

Ruby Keeler
9/8/75 *Laguna, Calif.*

Question of Tastes

Your reviewer charges me with bad taste in using Dr. Josef Mengele, late of Auschwitz, as the villain of my novel *The Boys from Brazil* [Feb. 23]. I must concede that what I have done is almost on a par with putting a would-be assassin on the cover of a national magazine or publishing a list of a dead President's rumored mistresses.

Ira Levin
3/15/76 *New York City*

Critic Simon

New York Magazine Critic John Simon [Dec. 26] (with whom I've had no contact, to my knowledge) cannot be a very happy man.

If he must dwell on the physical, he should notice that Liza Minnelli possesses the most beautiful eyes since Elizabeth Taylor first batted her baby violets. She has other very nice attributes, but they're merely happy accidents of nature.

Her talent, however, is no accident. Her ability to reach an audience, and touch the very core of so many people, is a result of hard work and professional dedication. But most of all, she has heart—that indefinable something that separates the ordinary from the extraordinary.

Could Mr. Simon be suffering from a simple case of heart envy?

Carol Burnett
1/16/78 *Beverly Hills, Calif.*

A Warm Probe

I would like to thank you very much for taking the trouble to probe accurately the deeper recesses of whatever the hell I am, and also for the warmth and kindness of your treatment of me.

Peter Sellers
3/24/80 *Paris*

Permissive Society

Appalled readers have chastised TIME for publishing the results of a scientific study and a photo of a President embracing his wife. Events which stimulate moral discussion are important news topics. Should sex education be taught in schools? Is *Catcher in the Rye* an evil book? What do new life-style trends reveal about our society? Reports on subjects from drugs to pornography prompt diverse responses from the audience of TIME.

Obvious Distinction

It used to be a pleasure to put TIME into the hands of the children in my current events class; but now I have to "censor" and cut out an item every now and then, and I am not at all sure that I want to continue taking the trouble of doing this. One alternative would be, of course, cancellation.

I think that a simpler and much better solution would be, however, for you to adopt this rule: "TIME will print no details of anything which, while it may be 'right' or 'moral' in some other country, is not 'right' or 'moral' in our United States."

It is this sort of item which I most often have to "censor" out of TIME. Take, for example, your item about how the Prime Minister of Japan procured an heir* [Aug. 15]. You cannot imagine how impossible it would have been for me to explain to my group of children why that sort of thing is wrong in the United States and yet right in Japan. Their little minds would not grasp the distinction, obvious though it is; and so I appeal to you to strike all such stories out of TIME. Will you? Otherwise I cannot promise to continue using TIME in my class.

(Miss) Mary Fairfax
8/22/27 *Chicago, Ill.*
Let not Teacher Fairfax continue to "censor" from TIME such truthful items as that to which she takes exception, but rather explain with patience the distinction, obvious though it is.—ED.

*From a concubine of his household, since his wife is childless.—ED.

"Damn" & "Hell"

Your paper is a welcome weekly visitor in my home; it contains an excellent summary of the events of the day. But there is one respect in which it might be improved; that is by the elimination of the vulgarity which is so frequently quoted; e.g., in the last issue on p. 14, one article is headed "Damn Big Dam," and on p. 16, the words of Senator Norris are quoted: "Take a bundle of straw and go across the river and start a little hell of his own." Such quotations are the fly in the ointment. They have a bad influence on the minds of the children in a family by a paper which otherwise is an excellent journal for the home.

(Rev.) George M. Cummings
4/6/31 *Washington, D.C.*
TIME doubts that the omission of "damn" and "hell" from its pages, where they never appear wantonly and almost always in quotation, would greatly ameliorate the moral condition of a U.S. child in A.D. 1931. Mr. Cummings' request must be denied in the interest of realistic reporting. But TIME will continue to delete obscenities.—ED.

Nudist

That nudist picture was a hell of a thing to label Medical. . . .
W. C. Bartlett, M.D.
Alma, Neb.

Printable S. O. B.

The other day I was reading the New York *Times*, as is my custom, and came to the story of the trial of ex-Convict Manny Strewl for kidnapping O'Connell, the nephew of the Albany political big-shots [July 24 *et seq.*]. It told how O'Connell identified Strewl in court as one of the kidnappers, and how Strewl jumped up and said (I quote the *Times*, dashes and all): "Why you ——, You're a —— liar. I saved your life and you know it." Of course it was nothing to me, but I couldn't overcome a curiosity as to what a man like Strewl actually calls another man who wants to send him up for 50 years. So I looked in the *Herald Tribune*. It said: "I saved your life, you ——, and you know it." Still not expecting to learn any more, I bought a copy of the tabloid *Daily News*. And did I find it! Listen to this (now I quote the *News*): "With a snarl Strewl leaped to his feet and before he could be silenced, shouted at the witness: 'You damned liar. You dirty son of a bitch—you dirty skunk.* I saved your life and now you are trying to hang me.' "

Wowie!

Did you ever see anything like that in a newspaper before?

Leonard Page
3/26/34 *New York City*
Investigation indicates that Capt. Joseph Medill Patterson's lusty Manhattan tabloid Daily News *was indeed the first modern metropolitan newspaper to spell out "son of a bitch."—ED.*

Outrageous

For many years we have been faithful readers of TIME. The picture of the President and Mrs. Roosevelt embracing one another in the [March 26] issue was, in our estimation, outrageous. TIME has every right to give its readers real news and real pictures, but some discretion should be shown when our popular Chief Executive and his wife are being photographed. The wife of a gangster is usually seen kissing her husband through bars, and various movie actors and actresses are snapped during moments of osculation. The President and First Lady are in too high a position—a world famous position—to be thus shown in any magazine.

Tristan Hearst
Burton Jamieson Jr.
Brown University
4/9/34 *Providence, R.I.*

Cinemaddict v. Boycott

. . . As a movie fan of more than eight years standing, let me enter my protest against the protesters. When the Catholic league condemns a picture such as *Little Man, What Now!* because the heroine unhappily conceives her child before she is fully ready for marriage, although the picture is · a splendid symbol of faith; and condemns *Manhattan Melodrama* because a criminal is not pictured as being rotten all the way to the core, then it has become more than censorship. It is stupidity.

James Whitsett
7/30/34 *Reidsville, N.C.*

Sexeducation

Congratulations on your plain-spoken and strictly TIME-worthy Havelock Ellis article [March 9]. We will stop publishing our sexeducational magazine as useless if you continue along these lines.

Edward L. Keating
Editor, Married Happiness Magazine
3/23/36 *Mount Morris, Ill.*

Syphilis Problem

Please accept my hearty congratulations for the fearless and courageous discussion of syphilis that appeared in the Oct. 26 issue of TIME. Syphilis is undoubtedly the greatest single solvable health problem which confronts the American people today. Solution, however, depends primarily upon shifting public consideration of the disease from social to scientific grounds so that a patient with syphilis will be regarded merely as the victim of a serious communicable disease rather than a social outcast. This achievement in turn, depends much more upon bringing the known facts impressively to popular attention than upon the acquisition of any new knowledge about syphilis. Your feature in the Oct. 26 issue is the most important contribution toward that end which has come to my attention. . . .

Frank J. Jirka, M.D.
Director of Public Health,
Department of Public Health
11/16/36 *Springfield, Ill.*

More About Marijuana

There is no doubt marijuana as a drug should be eliminated from any consideration. There is no justification for its use at any time. It is an addiction drug which by its use causes changes in personality invariably for the worse. . . . Moreover it has no place in rational therapeutics. . . .

J. C. Geiger, M.D.
Director Public Health
San Francisco

. . . I realize that you would not admit even condoning the use of marijuana and that you would stand up for your right to print the truth. . . .

I question the scientific basis of some of your opinions, I object to your implications; and I wonder why you did not give adequate treatment to the case against marijuana.

John Wildenthal Jr.
U.S.N.R.
8/16/43 *Austin, Tex.*
TIME would be shocked to think that its story had attracted anyone to marijuana. The facts of TIME's story were based on recent findings by outstanding authorities. Reports based on earlier studies have sometimes been more sensational than scientific.

TIME's considered advice: if you must smoke cigarettes, stick to the standard brands.—ED.

What's Up?

What on earth is the matter with everyone today? I am only 17, but . . . there is something radically wrong with the English town which "adopted" Norah Carpenter because she became the "proud" mother of illegitimate quadruplets [March 13]; with the hundreds of people who showered her with presents and admiration. . . .

If everyone in the world accepts as a normal and rightful thing the making of a heroine out of any unmarried mother merely because she happens to produce three more than the usual number of illegitimate children—if this is the moral code under which we will operate in the world to come, I, for

Dr. Alfred Kinsey, left, and associates at the Indiana University Institute for Sex Research

one, have no desire to live in that world.

Elizabeth Gellhorn
4/3/44 *Los Angeles*

Help Wanted

Sexual Behavior in the Human Male [Jan. 5]. What about sexual behavior in the human female? If man had a little understanding of their behavior it would help. . . .

Donald Hydock
2/16/48 *Mt. Morris, N.Y.*
Let Reader Hydock bide his time. Professor Kinsey's second volume, Sexual Behavior in the Human Female, *will be published early next year.—ED.*

Breeding Desires

Words can't express how shocked I was to read "Sex in the Schoolroom."

Does the State of Oregon actually believe that a child of 12 or 13 once sexually enlightened will wait until, let's say, the ripe old age of 18 to put into practice what he's learned? I doubt it . . . Talking about sex only breeds desires. . . .

For seniors in high school, my answer is definitely yes. . . . As for the junior high deal—God forgive you, Oregon. . . .

Helen Travis
4/12/48 *Portsmouth, Va.*

The Facts of Life

The emotional seismographs record letter-writer Travis' tremors over teaching sex in the Oregon schoolrooms. Her theory is that knowledge leads to experimentation [April 12]. The truth is exactly the opposite . . . Curiosity is a powerful emotion, and when allied with the sex urge can be-

devil with passionate proficiency. Knowledge satisfies curiosity, thus greatly reducing the emotional pressures.

This is no unsupported claim. Shortly after World War I, Wisconsin began offering frank sex instruction to most of its high-school students. As a result, the venereal disease rate among its drafted [white] men in World War II was the lowest in the nation: 6.3 per 1,000 as against 170 per 1,000 in some other states . . .

The result [of the Oregon program] in 25 years will be colossal . . .

F. Alexander Magoun
Massachusetts Institute of Technology
5/3/48 *Cambridge, Mass.*

Sex Before Marriage?

Your excellent article on "Sex Before Marriage" [Feb. 13] was more than well done . . . It is about time the subject was aired . . . It is because of the lack of understanding given to us earlier that this phase of life, which is more than the basis for a happy marriage, is why we humans suffer from the grotesque bugaboo inflicted on us by our so-called religious instructors.

A. James Mahefkey
Rochester, N.Y.

. . . The statement by Anthropologist Murdock . . . is wholesome advice. It is an indisputable fact that destructive guilt and inferiority complexes very often result from inhibitions built up in the mind of the adolescent by the platitudes of ignorant clergymen and parents. Clergymen should be equally interested in the physical and mental health of the youth under their influence, as well as in their moral health. Sex in itself, like love, is beautiful and not the dirty nasty something many youths are taught to believe. We clergymen ought to be brave enough to face new ideas.

R. S. Caldwell
Pastor, Bedford Presbyterian Church
3/6/50 *Bedford, Pa.*

The Women

. . . Although we do not approve fully of Mr. Kinsey, your Aug. 24 cover is, in short, terrific.

(Miss) Alva Lucero
(Miss) G. Campbell
Omaha

Can't buy our Aug. 24 TIME; our newsstands sold out. All holier-than-thous want to read your report on Kinsey's book. Be prepared for indignant letters to the editor.

Captain & Mrs. C. N. Beecham
Wichita, Kans.

. . . Your article on Dr. Kinsey and his work made me furious. The article treats "sex" as something dirty. This is obvious from the insertion of the smutty cartoon by Peter Arno . . . Decent, healthy people, who can enjoy love, regard Dr. Kinsey's work as a serious, scientific study, and do not try to undermine the effects of this work with sarcasm.

Adolph E. Smith
9/7/53 *New York City*

Professor Kinsey's undertaking reminds me of Mark Twain's story about the dinosaur that was reconstructed from three bones and 20 barrels of cement.

Fritz Stein
Cleveland

Any man who could get that much straight-forward information from one, let alone nearly 6,000 women, should be TIME's Man of the Year.

R. C. Tomlinson
9/14/53 *W. Orange, N.J.*

Glaring Limbs

Re "Paperback Recession" [July 5]: I have heard . . . people say that they will not read a paperback in any public place. Why? The cover! A person with any degree of pride . . . would hesitate to sit in a bus, subway, plane or train with a picture of some naked limbs . . . glaring boldly from the cover . . . I nearly didn't buy [Hemingway's] *To Have and Have Not* simply because of the cover. I knew I'd feel like a damn heel going up to the clerk and paying her for the book. For years publishers of hardbacked books have seen fit to limit their covers to the title and the author's name — a very satisfactory arrangement.

Michael B. McHale
8/2/54 *Whittier, Calif.*

Honest Swedes

. . . The maidenly squeals of the U.S. regarding Sweden's sex habits are most unbecoming. In a land where that national substitute for royalty—The Hollywood Crowd—has made a game of sex and a mockery of marriage; in a land where the vitality, or much of it, which made this country powerful has trickled down two generations to find itself running cloudily through the veins of foolish old men like Tommy Manville and foolish young pimps like Minot Jelke; where 22-year-old boys slip cyanide into their parents' champagne; where middle-aged mothers and grandmothers moon like adolescents over a toothy piano player; in a land where sex has become so naughtyfied that its outflow has been redirected to the channel of physical violence; where nice girls are taught early that it is legal to tease but evil to please . . . it might be more discreet to observe a mum respect for the pragmatic, clearhead and honest Swedes . . .

(Mrs.) Beatrice Sisk
(Irate housewife and mother)
5/14/55 *Hartford, Conn.*

Puritan Hangover

Re "Sin & Criminalty" in the May 30 issue: . . . To make criminal any sexual activity in which husband and wife engage with mutual consent and love is . . . ridiculous. What married people do in bed is no more the business of lawmakers than is the way they cook their eggs when they get up. When a state has sensibly taken the position that adultery is none of its business, it cannot consistently take the view that any sexual activity is its business, provided that such activity does not involve "force," etc.

The general American attitude that conventional sexual intercourse is the only "proper" expression of sexual desire—and, worse, the legislating of that attitude—is a hangover from the Puritan fathers, from whom so few of us descended. The prudery and naiveté of such an attitude must also make us a laughingstock in nations of more wisdom and maturity.

Constance MacMillan
6/27/55 *Buffalo*

Legion of Decency

I have read with interest your article on Avery Dulles [June 11] and have been enlightened in some respects, if not in others. As I understand it, the Legion of Decency is trying not only to protect its own interests, but that of all the American people. Perhaps they would like to have absolute control of business so that our minds may not be poisoned by films, books, or any other medium of communication that is not in sympathy with the Catholic clergy's ideas.

It seems to me that the individual is capable of determining in his own right whether or not something is immoral. I hope that the time will not come when anyone will tell me what I can read, see or think.

Joseph E. LaVoie
7/9/56 *Norfolk, Va.*

Kinsey's Behavior

Dr. Alfred Kinsey [Sept. 3] was a great and wonderful man. I shall never forget the wisdom, patience and deep understanding with which he talked to

227

me once when I was deeply disturbed and asked him for help. I doubt that many people outside of Bloomington know of the social ostracism accorded Dr. Kinsey and his family because of his research into that "nasty" subject, sex. I grew up there, and watched parents forbidding their children to play with the Kinsey children, and the Kinseys being "cut" when they attended social functions. What a price for a dedicated researcher to have to pay for personal courage and intellectual honesty.

Anna E. Richardson
9/17/56 *Indianapolis*

Healthy Sweden

Having subjected myself to the "sinful" way of life here for a year now, I've come to the conclusion that Sweden is a damned sight more natural and healthy in its morals than us Victorian fuddyduddies and frustrated consumers of pornographic sex trash.

William H. Bartsch
5/27/57 *Stockholm*

B.B.'s Bounties

There will undoubtedly be much controversy concerning your revealing photograph of Bardot. The moralists, plus all the many frustrated wives and husbands, will point the finger of outraged disgust at this bountifully endowed young woman. Actually, there lives hardly one normal man who does not secretly wish that his own wife could bring herself to be as provocative to him as Brigitte is.

William H. Tatro
9/8/58 *Bakersfield, Calif.*

Are Nudes Sexy?

I've just read your Aug. 18 item on the seminude show girls in Las Vegas. I don't think a bishop of the Roman Catholic faith has a right to tell nightclub owners to "dress" their performers . In France (nearly 90% Catholic), seminude show girls have been parading in nightclubs for umpteen years; French bishops don't insist on them covering up."

Irene Marshall
9/15/58 *Idyllwild, Calif.*

The Nature of Beauty

Prelate Byrne's threatened denial of the sacraments of communion and confession to a Miss Universe contestant and her Catholic mother [July 20] is just another very good reason for being an American Protestant.

H. William Ohman
Staten Island, N.Y.

Good for the archbishop! He is one of the few remaining individuals who realize that true beauty is enhanced by maidenly modesty and womanly dignity.

He sees through the vulgarity and flesh worship of the public parading of the body.

Mrs. F. Lavelle
8/3/59 *Pittsburgh*

Inflammatory Bathing Suit

Regarding poor little Sue Ingersoll and her inflammatory bathing suit [July 27]: Can anything be more apparent from this episode than that the Roman Catholic hierarchy is using any and every means to control our

public life? Soon we won't be able to do much in a public way without the permission of Archbishop So-and-So.

Kathryn N. Rhodes
Hayward, Calif.

What a furor over a mere bathing suit! One is bound to feel sorry for the poor tormented celibates who find such things as girls-in-bathing-suits lust inciting and damaging to morals.

J. Addison Smith
Seattle

In general, we Lakota (Sioux) are learning to conform to the customs of our white brothers and sisters. There is one custom that we do not intend to conform to—bathing beauty contests. Even the poorest of our Lakota women manage to cover their nakedness. They do not make public display of their bare hide or their bathing habits.

Silas Left Hand Bull
8/17/59 *Pine Ridge, S. Dak.*

Shocking Tennessee

Granted, Tennessee Williams' plays are objectionable and shocking to those critics who have forgotten their college literature. I suggest they reread Dante's *Inferno* or Voltaire's *Candide*. Anyone familiar with these masterpieces could hardly be shocked by anything as mild as *Suddenly, Last Summer*.

Dean Miller
5/2/60 *Boulder, Colo.*

Catcher Explained

Our tenth-grade English class has just finished reading *The Catcher in the Rye*. We were neither impressed

Coming out of the closet and onto the streets, gay Americans on the march

nor corrupted by the language in the book. Nor did we think it a "beautiful and moving" story. Repeating unpleasant language, which most of us have already heard somewhere, was not the point of studying this book. We read it because it is well written, and we learned a lot from discussing Holden Caulfield's problems.

Linda Stretch
Germantown Friends School
Philadelphia

At the instigation of student protest against the stench of its vocabulary, *Catcher* has recently been removed from circulation by our library.

Elva McAllaster
Professor of English
Greenville College
5/30/60 *Greenville, Ill.*

Four-Letter Words

Merriam-Webster should be commended for including the so-called "four-letter words" in the new edition of their dictionary. I have looked up all of the words I searched for in vain during my childhood, and I find they look no more obscene than the words surrounding them on the page.

Jim Rader
10/20/61 *Chicago*

Pornography Pondered

The pornography Essay [April 16] was a welcome oasis in the desert of avant-garde literature that pretends to depict realism.

Obscenity may be difficult to define but not to recognize. The pages of obscene literature are truly a barren wasteland that must be forsaken now by the readers, so that this type of scribbling may soon be abandoned by the writers.

Sarnia Brooks
Detroit

I was amused by your Tolstoyan "phallacy"—a particularly black and lacy Freudian slip but rather appropriate.

Bob Warren
4/30/65 *Berkeley, Calif.*
But hardly a slip.—Ed.

Transistors & Teddy Bears

Our children's childhood is being snatched from them by greedy adults who use a child's normal curiosity for their own warped purposes [March 11]. We have endured the pre-teen-bra era and the pre-teen coketail party. Now we are faced with children aping the current sad folk-singer types. How tragic that the "nubes" wail of lost loves before the age of ten! If we lower the level of disturbance much more, prenatal psychiatrists will be needed.

(Mrs.) Patricia C. Hosmer
Chagrin Falls, Ohio

With the stress on early sophistication, can anyone doubt that some-

Actors in the buff scandalized Broadway in 1969

where an enterprising genius is planning contraceptive bubble gum?

(Mrs.) Elinor C. Lewis
3/25/66 *New York City*

Sex Responsibility

Often the only sex education many of us teen-agers get is from what our pals tell us or from what we read in *The Carpetbaggers*. It's about time parents and teachers woke up to their responsibility.

Christopher A. Bates
6/23/67 *Auckland, N.Z.*

Psychedelic Effects

In your excellent story you failed to note that the new psychedelic, STP, was named after the effects it produces —serenity, tranquility, and peace.

Michael Woods
7/14/67 *Dunkirk, N.Y.*

Learning About Life

I am a ninth-grade student, and I have read Salinger's *The Catcher in the Rye*, Orwell's *1984* and Goldings's *Lord of the Flies*, and these are only a few of the "dirty books" I have read. I found nothing at all wrong with them, except they told me a lot about life, which I eventually would have had to learn anyway.

Deborah Rechnitz
8/23/68 *Denver*

Don't Be Squeamish

I too have seen *Oh! Calcutta!* [June 27]. If your critic found it to be a "rousing celebration of the body beautiful," why did your picture editor use an air brush on the photograph of nudes accompanying the story? And if "quadriliterals beginning with the letters f, c and s" are here considered to be more "festive than aggressive," why not spell out the festive words?

When you open a can of worms, you should not be squeamish.

E. Warren Smith
Manhattan

That play where everyone cavorts around with their clothes off is supposed to "liberate" our minds or something? Most of our critics and intellectuals have been going around with their minds unbuttoned for some time. These naive pundits should take Dr. Freud's advice to Lorelei Lee (*Gentlemen Prefer Blondes*, by Anita Loos). He told her to cultivate a few inhibitions and get some sleep.

David B. Saxton
7/11/69 *Cottage Grove, Ore.*

End of a Gimmick?

Pessimistic over the sex explosion [July 11]? Not me. Perhaps at last people will get so accustomed to the sight of the human body undraped that they will no longer spend their time and money just to see it. Soon movies, magazines, plays, etc., will have to come up with some other gimmick to attain the attention of the public and the dollar. Who knows? Maybe someone will even rediscover the use of thought and talent.

The end of morality, some say. How about the end of a gimmick and the beginning of art?

Robert E. Cannon
Pasadena, Calif.

Your cover story was interesting but inconclusive. You failed to point out the chief casualties of the current smut cycle: style, class and grace, which continue to be indispensable qualities of enduring art. Today's vendors of sexual kitsch have kept the dirty bath water (in some cases literally) and thrown out the baby, and with it their chances of eventual

Changing mores: Hugh Hefner's *Playboy* mansion and, top, the beach at Saint Tropez

general given you your highly prized American culture; if the truth be known, 95% of American culture is the homosexuals' culture.

Perhaps it is finally time we realize that we contribute to a society that despises us. We want our rights now, not 100 years from now. Try to vizual-ize 12 million homosexual men and women marching on Washington.

Yes, edgy indeed.

S. M. Gibson
Williamsport, Pa.

Last September, after three months in the U.S. Navy, I walked into a doctor's office on base. In a tear-filled outburst. I told him I am, had been, and will always be gay. The Navy is now processing my discharge under the case of Fraudulent Enlistment.

A search for patriotism, fatherly favor, and stability prompted me to hide in the epitome of all-maleness, the military vacuum. Anguished realization that I was denying myself a firm part of my whole being forced me to tell the truth. I am grateful for your article, which has given me insight as to the kind of public reception I will receive when I no longer boast, "I am an American sailor," but cry out more proudly, "I am an American hom-sexual."

Anthony G. Lunde, U.S.N.
10/14/69 *Bainbridge, Md.*

Everyman an Addict

Whom are we trying to fool? We don't mind if our kids take drugs [March 16]. We help teach them. We use TV to orient then at an early age to the rigors of American life, tension headaches, nervous stomachs, sleepless-ness, etc. Then we tell them how to cure these ailments: a pill to go to sleep, a pill to wake up, a pill to calm you down, a pill to pep you up. We tell them that a tension headache will de-velop if we hurry to meet a deadline, but no sweat: take a pill. We get up in the morning screaming for a cup of coffee or a cigarette so we can begin the day. Even the vitamin pill fits into our little scheme. Give the kid his daily vitamin requirement in one pill to get his mind off good food that will enhance his physical well-being; soon he won't have much regard for his body.

Let's face it, we are all addicts of some sort, and the only time our apathy is shook is when or if we find out our own kid is hooked.

(Sgt.) Rod Blissett
U.S.A.F.
4/3/70 *Columbus, Ohio*

Let Us Enjoy

Wasn't it Samuel Butler who said, about a century ago, that man is the only animal who doesn't realize that the purpose of life is to enjoy it? Some-where beneath the crush of fears, in-hibitions, traumas and guilt complexes in all of us, there's probably a basic being who knows full well that's why

survival. Boredom will rescue us from their brand of entertainment.

Fred Saidy
7/18/69 *Douglaston, N.Y.*

In the Eyes of the Beholders

John Wayne at 62, fully clothed, fat and half blind, is capable of gener-ating more excitement, sexiness, ten-derness, courage, humor, honesty, understanding, peace and, in the same breath, revolution in every man, women or child who watches him on the screen for one performance than all the nudothespians of *Hair, Che!* and *Oh! Calcutta!* combined could produce on stage if they were to do their thing from now until the year 2010, when they reach the Grand Duke's age. Hell, they can't even compete with the fig leaf on TIME's cover, which has more zip, unzipped, than either of the two characters posing behind it. By the way, which one is the good guy?

Mrs. Laurence Andren
Cody, Wyo.

If God had wanted us to run around in the nude, we would have been born naked.

Annette M. Weidhaas
7/25/69 *St. Louis*

Drug Debate

I commend you on the fine article on pop drugs [Sept. 26]. It was most poignant and struck close to home. I was a grasshopper, but luckily enough I stopped a couple of months ago. I have heard a lot about how you can't get hooked just blowing grass. I've got too many friends disproving that theory. We all started on grass, but they are now dropping acid, popping speed and sniffing glue. Getting high is a great feeling, but it is a greater feeling being free and seeing someone else, and not yourself, ruin his life.

Dawn Wells
10/10/69 *Washington, D.C.*

Homosexual Rights

As a lesbian, I felt that the article was for the most part informative and objective. However, I was vastly amused by one line: our "new militancy is making the heterosexual citizens edgy."

For centuries we have written your music and your literary masterpieces, painted your beautiful pictures, de-signed your clothing, danced and acted in your plays, styled your hair, and in

he's here but doesn't know how to utilize the realization.

Thanks to those in Masters and Johnson's profession [May 25], who dedicate themselves full time to helping make life more pleasurable for humanity. May they rip the puritanical curtain and let the sunshine in. Let us *all* enjoy!

(Mrs.) Liz Schenk
Lake Oswego, Ore.

I find the current preoccupation with sex quite unnecessary. As every psychologist knows, sex is an instinctive drive, like that for taking food when hungry. One would never think of giving courses to improve the desire to take food. But this, precisely, is what your two masters of somatic intimacy are doing with sex.

As every man sooner or later discovers, sex is largely a waste of time. Remember what Lord Chesterfield said about it: the pleasure is momentary, the position ridiculous, and the expense damnable.

Philip Eibel, M.D.
6/15/70 *Montreal*

The Right to Decide

Laws aimed at controlling the adult's consumption of pornography are a waste of public money and police time.

No book ever forced itself on an offended reader. No movie theatre shanghais its audience. Anyone old enough to vote has the right—the duty, in fact—to decide for himself what books he will read, what films he will view, what pictures he will look at.

Must we grown-up Americans depend on Big Brother Government to control our minds and our tastes—at the cost of our own tax dollars? Rather let that money be spent to hire more policemen to patrol our streets, not our bookstores, and to pay the police a salary commensurate with the danger and difficulty of their work. This would do more to prevent sex crimes, not to mention other kinds of crime, than all the censorship laws on the books.

Norma S. Hass
11/2/70 *Dundee, Ill.*

Love Is All

Your review of Dennis Altman's book is an unfair putdown. Your reviewer's statement that "homosexual love is regarded as deviant because no children can be born of it" is pure nonsense. Is sex over 60 deviant? Is sex for a vasectomized man deviant? Is sex for a woman after a hysterectomy deviant?

The important thing is to love, to have the ability to project this strong emotion toward another *human being*. The sex of the person to whom this love is directed is quite as unimportant as the physical means by which it may be expressed

David Moore Jones
3/27/72 *Grand Blanc, Mich.*

Immense Fun

We Pacific Islanders look on with pop-eyed amazement at Western attitudes to sex. Nothing more false, more stultifying, more anxiety-breeding (except your economy) can be imagined.

We believe that God made us and gave us certain varied faculties and functions, and at the proper times, indicated by nature and not by regulations, we use them.

We have immense fun. We believe that sexual things are private to the two people concerned, and we never dicuss them in public. We believe in good manners, in consideration of the feelings of all; and we terribly regret that Western madnesses are spreading over the lovely games of sex.

Moape Vesikula
9/18/72 *Suva, Fiji*

Polluted Society

In an America where intellectuals introduced drugs as the means to a meditative exerience, where honored maga-

zines are polluted with pornography, where ministers have forgotten that Jesus never interfered with Caesar's laws, where free love has unleashed an epidemic of venereal disease, where destructive protest has been honored as righteous dissent, where the killing of unborn babies is thought a small price to pay for the pleasure of sex, where the purpose of law is forgotten and the letter of the law is worshipped like a plastic god, where tradition's moral sense is spat upon—in such an atmosphere, can you truly expect a bone-weary citzenry to become indignant about still another Watergate?

A. J. Venglarcik
11/6/72 *Strathers, Ohio*

Shocked, Titillated and Disgusted

Your cover story on *Last Tango* terrified me. A society that spends so much time thinking about, filming and writing about sex obviously does not have much else it considers important enough to occupy it.

We are now nearly ready for the takeover, from wherever it may come. We have not the mental vigor left to resist, and someone will walk off with the house while we are preoccupied in the bedroom.

Thomas S. Loeber
Coos Bay, Ore.

I was shocked, titillated, disgusted, fascinated, delighted and angered just by reading your story on *Last Tango in Paris*. I can't wait to see the movie!

Lea Ainsworth
2/12/73 *Lubbock, Texas*

The Pornographers' Nightmare

Bravo, bravo, bravo for Mr. Burger [July 2]! It was a pleasant surprise to read that someone has the foresight and courage to take a stiffer stand against pornography.

Anyone who claims that pornography is not harmful has closed his mind to the existence of illegitimate births, rape, adultery, broken marriages and venereal disease.

I hope that the nightmare facing publishers of pornography and makers of obscene films will not only set them back to the Dark Ages but into oblivion, where they can stay until they resolve to use their "creativity" to produce something that will build rather than demoralize and destroy.

Ladean H. Rupp
Tremonton, Utah

Sexual puritanism and oppression are two sides of the same coin, and this is why they do not permit erotic literature in the dictatorships of the left and the right.

What troubles the Justices of the Supreme Court more than anything else seems to be the "prurient interest." Really, what's wrong with prurience? Why should the harmfulness of prurience be axiomatic?

Whether I get hungry or thirsty,

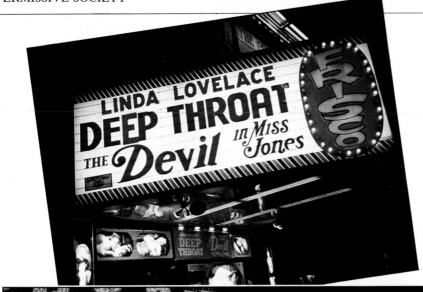

"X-rated theaters" brought pornographic films to the general public

sleepy or prurient is my own private business and need not concern the Chief Justice at all.

What the world needs is less violence and maybe somewhat more prurience.

Heidi Hillgarter
7/30/73 *Fränsta, Sweden*

Every End in Sight

In your article on the current streaking fad [March 18], you say that "no end seems in sight." On the contrary. They are all in sight.

Robert K. Fessler
Pittsburgh

Why is it that all males streak away from the camera while females seem to streak toward the lens?

(Mrs.) Carol Bidwell
4/8/74 *Reston, Va.*

One Thing Proved

The one thing streaking has proved is that all men are not created equal.

Joan N. Beyer
4/29/74 *Point Pleasant, N.J.*

Liberty or Lust?

Fie on the porno peddlers who profit from ignorance and lust [April 5]. Fie on the libertines who raise phony cries of censorship. And fie on the decent folk whose self-righteous apathy has permitted this appalling advanced case of acne to creep across the face of America.

(Mrs.) Jean G. Tuthill
5/3/76 *Denver*

Mechanics of Sex

Miss Hite's unnatural obsession with the clinical mechanics of sex [Oct. 25] leaves me with a grimy feeling and a slightly squeamish stomach.

What this poor misguided woman has yet to discover is that if two people really love each other and have entered into a marriage for life, the rest comes naturally.

Carole Panaro
11/5/76 *Brookfield, Wis.*

Latest Abomination

The Episcopal Church's acceptance of homosexuals to the Holy Sacrament

of Communion [Jan. 24] and now as priests is too much.

The church's apparent desire to "get with it," as evidenced by its other activities in revising the liturgy of the Book of Common Prayer, has caused much dissatisfaction among its members. Yet the hierarchy continues to press on.

This latest abomination is the end. I hereby resign my membership in the Protestant Episcopal Church.

H. Richard Mottram
Huntsville, Ala.

I must admit that this is the first time I've ever heard sin being referred to as "an alternative life-style."

(The Rev.) H. L. Merriweather
2/14/77 *St. Louis*

Religious Garbage?

It was with great dismay and utter disbelief that I learned about the report on human sexuality [June 13]. I find it incredible that some Catholic theologians are giving their approval to extramarital sex and teaching that such relationships can be "creative and integrative for all involved." Who repealed God's commandment: Thou shall not commit adultery?

This is the kind of cheap, do-it-yourself theology that shocks all God-fearing people of whatever religious affiliation. These theologians are not religious leaders offering spiritual food to their followers. They are misleading the faithful and giving them religious garbage to eat.

(The Rev.) S. C. Limanowski
7/4/77 *Boynton Beach, Fla.*

Anita Bryant v. the Gays

Even though I am the mother of two small children, I cannot even begin to understand Anita Bryant's reasoning regarding homosexual rights. She is so worried about homosexuals serving as teachers. Quite frankly, I believe that if my son is not safe in a classroom with a male homosexual teacher, then surely my daughter is not safe with a male heterosexual teacher.

Carol Bellomo
7/4/77 *Flushing, Mich.*

That New Morality

Your article on "The New Morality" [Nov. 21] really hit an alltime conversation peak in my sociology class. Though it might be true that more and more people are sleeping together for love, there is still a very strong belief in having sex for the fun of it. Most people in my class concluded that it wouldn't be so bad to have a mistress or to be one. Just be sure to get the extra fringe benefits without any strings attached.

Marjorie Tananbaum
12/12/77 *Washington, D.C.*

Sin-in-Law

When a friend of mine introduces or refers to the man with whom his daughter is living in an unmarried state he calls him my "sin-in-law."

Lewis H. Goldman
12/18/78 *Washington, D.C.*

Decadence Defined

When a nation parodies its laws, decides its ethics, makes a mockery of its economy and voluntarily abdicates its power, that is called decadence.

Henri René
Pacific Grove, Calif.

I think the word decadence is an excuse used by the self-righteous to impose their morality on other people.

David Rubin
10/1/79 *New York City*

Sex and Children

Those who advocate child-with-child or child-with-adult sex are sick and are seeking to justify what they did, what they are doing, or what they want to do.

Edwin G. Troutman, M.D.
9/28/81 *Fort Worth*

Herpes Message

Although your intentions are laudable, you seem to taunt those individuals who are not stern believers in sexual austerity. The message appears to be that anyone who gets herpes certainly deserves it and that it is a damn good thing this epidemic came along to bring back the good old days.

Joel Ratner
Beachwood, Ohio

I never had a chance to become a sexual hedonist because I was too old for the sexual revolution. Now, thanks to herpes, I can stop regretting having missed it.

Robert Young
Deerfield, Ill.

Perhaps today's sexual liberation is more restrictive than old-fashioned morality ever was!

Frank W. Schnitzler
8/23/82 *Manasquan, N.J.*

Squealing on Sex

Laws like the "squeal rule," requiring federally funded clinics to notify parents when they give contraceptives to minors [Feb. 7], will only widen the existing gap between parent and teenager. Girls who seek professional guidance should not have their privacy violated. It is far wiser to have a girl 16 and counseled than 16 and pregnant.

Patricia A. Hodder
Bellerose, N.Y.

As a teen-ager, I was outraged to hear of the squeal rule. Most of my friends who are on birth-control pills received them through counseling at Government-funded clinics. Without the secrecy promised by the clinics,

my best friends would have been added to the list of tragic stories about unwed mothers.

Kristin D. Merriman
2/28/83 *Boston*

Cocaine Folly

The article on the widespread use of cocaine [April 11] reads like the decline and fall of an empire. The U.S. is a nation that has so much. Yet something is missing when its people must build up their confidence with a false god like cocaine. There is no need to fear Soviet weapons; Americans are doing the job by destroying themselves.

Betty J. Ott
5/2/83 *Linz, Austria*

Success Rate for Sexual Therapy

I was interested to read about sexologists' squabbles over the "cure rate" for the "disorder" of low sexual desire [June 13]. So low sexual desire is a disorder? How about low desire to play tennis? Who is going to cure sexologists of the delusion that it's their

place to tell other people what to want and how much to want it?

Diana F. Ackerman
7/4/83 *St. Andrews, Scotland*

Sex '80s-Style

As a cautious middle-aged man, I have been patiently biding my time until the sexual revolution became so prevalent that I could join without embarrassment to myself or my family [April 9]. Shucks, now it is over. My predicament illustrates how "he who hesitates is lost."

Felix A. Gaudin
New Orleans

So the baby-boomers have rediscovered the traditional values of fidelity, obligation and marriage. In the meantime, those of us who grew up in the '50s are left to deal with the broken marriages and lives that resulted when the commitment of a long-term marriage did not measure up to the promises of the Me generation.

Ruth Litke
7/4/83 *St. Cloud, Minn.*

Playboy and **Penthouse** spawned a host of imitators

The Royals

Eighteenth century Federalists decided not to crown George Washington as monarch, but Americans have never lost their fascination with royalty. The dashing Prince of Wales interested TIME's early audience, particularly when he gave up his throne for the woman he loved. The romance of Charles and Di intrigued millions. Just as the world watched Princess Elizabeth grow up decades ago, it watches her grandson as earnestly in the '80s.

Wales Flayed

I wish to protest and protest strongly against such antics on the part of the Prince of Wales as you describe in your issue of Nov. 2. No decent young man dresses himself up in girl's clothes and appears in a farce called *The Bathroom Door.*

There are enough scatter-brained girls who call themselves "vamps" without the Prince making a "Royal Vamp" of himself. I visited England last year and I want to say that a great many people in London *know him for what he is.* Too many Americans think he is a sweet, baby-faced "innocent," "embarrassed" young man!

That is perfect nonsense, and anyone with half an eye should know it. I only hope this incident will open people's eyes in this country. In England everyone knows the truth.

Mary Elizabeth Robinn
11/16/25 *Boston, Mass.*

Wales Praised

I have just arrived from England and happened to see in your edition of Nov. 16 the letter about the Prince of Wales. Why should Mary Elizabeth Robinn object to the Prince dressing up as a girl in *The Bathroom Door?* Young college men the world over do the same thing and the play is perfectly harmless; so why should anyone object? As for saying that England knows him for what he is—yes, they *do.* They know him as the greatest ambassador England ever had—and the most popular Prince—and don't expect him to be an Angel from Heaven! He works harder than most people suppose; why shouldn't he play sometimes?

I can only think that the English who ran their Prince down to an American were sadly lacking in loyalty. They are probably in the pay of the Reds! I should be grateful for an answer to this question, so that when I return to England I can tell my friends: *Why an American woman should concern herself with the behavior of the heir to the British Throne?*

I feel sure that the one person who would be most amused at Mary Elizabeth Robinn's letter would be the Prince himself! He is such a wonderful *sport* and can afford to laugh!

"A Visitor from England"
11/30/25 *Detroit, Mich.*

Chord

I imagine you have struck a responsive chord in the presentation of "P'incess Lilybet" as the frontispiece of TIME, April 29. Even a 100% American like myself can find a tender spot in my heart for such a winsome British baby—May happy days follow her footsteps.

(Subscriber) Wm. L. Sexton
5/13/29 *New York City*

Four-Fifths Queen

Your lengthy article "MAY QUEEN" in TIME, March 17, is quite a compliment to MAY.

It also corroborates a story about H.R.H. Prince of Wales when inspecting the Canadian soldiers in the trenches.

He came across a picture of the King and Queen in the familiar two ovals, with the words GEORGE FIFTH written under the picture of the King. He said nothing, but wrote under the picture of his mother, "THE OTHER FOUR FIFTHS."

William Yates
4/7/30 *Green River, Wyo.*

Bwthyn Bach to Gwellt

Several months ago there was in the N.Y. *Times* magazine section an article

about a playhouse made and furnished by the peoples of Wales for dear little Princess Elizabeth. My small daughters and I were greatly interested. But now I see in the TIME's Rotogravure section for April 3 pictures of the poor wrecked house gutted by fire, and we wonder how it could have become ignited on its journey to the Princess. Although I recall seeing no mention of any of this in TIME, still I feel it is news that interests mothers and little girls, at least, and I should be greatly obliged if you could give some details of the unfortunate end of such a kindly-meant project. We wonder if the little Princess was disappointed or if she never knew about it.

Harriet B. Woolfenden
5/23/32 *Dearborn, Mich.*
Almost three times taller than her uncle Edward of Wales is six-year-old Princess Elizabeth's Bwthyn Bach to Gwellt or "Little Cottage with the Straw Roof." Built at a cost of $10,000 to advertise the products of 100 Welsh firms, the cottage drew Welsh crowds at Cardiff's Ideal Home & Building Exhibition last autumn. Insured for $6,250, it caught fire while traveling on a truck toward London, has been reconstructed and now contains the original furniture which was on a second truck. Not until Princess Betty is nearly double her present age will she be permitted to play with the real gas stove and other grown-up gadgets in her cottage.—ED.

Jubilee

Congratulations TIME scores again. . . . I have read reviews of the Silver Jubilee and the biography of George V in a number of magazines—but TIME's account tops them all. As a former Canadian, I can say that you truthfully portray His Majesty as neither showman, dictator nor demagog. . . .

Your account shows George V not merely the force for union but the faithful servant of his people. He has endured, along with them, a quarter of a century that was the most crucial test of a nation's and a king's character. . . .

M. M. Lachovitz
5/20/35 *Cleveland, Ohio*

Hours of Bereavement

Any woman who can "charm" a sad King into a cheerful smile deserves praises, instead of criticisms. Mrs. Ernest Simpson is beautiful, young, slim and graceful. She is a socialite and has the good sense to add her husband on all her outings with royalty.* With all the titled women in the realm to entertain him, King Edward VIII shows an artistic appreciation in selecting a young married woman, and a clever American, to entertain him during his long hours of bereavement. He has traveled all over the world and yet only an American woman can "charm" him, socially.

I have met several members of the Royal family, and of several royal and ex-royal families, during my travels in Europe; I have found them very lovable, unassuming, plain mortals. . . .

(Mrs.) K. Russell
10/12/36 *San Francisco, Calif.*

*Husband Ernest Simpson was not aboard the yacht Vahlin for the Balkan cruise, was not in the party at Balmoral Castle [Oct. 5].—ED.

The young Duke of Windsor, in female costume, in the *H.M.S. Pinafore,* 1909

Morals & Monarchs

TIME continues to be my favorite News Magazine for the simple reason that I want the news. Some of the news is unpleasant to take, especially for a Minister of the Gospel, but I can take it. I was born a Britisher, and as blood is thicker than water, I still have a warm place in my heart for the British Isles. For this reason the escapades of King Edward VIII, and especially his relations with Mrs. Simpson, while almost revolting to a strict Churchman, seem to me to have a far deeper significance than that which is generally attributed to them.

The King seems to be a national symbol of the moral decline of the English-speaking people of the world. I lived under the austere reign of Her Majesty Queen Victoria, and while her reign was irksome to those who were immorally inclined, she did in a most decisive way, place her moral stamp upon the English-speaking people of the world, and while in many cases the imposed morality was nothing more than a veneered hypocrisy, on the whole, the standards were high, and the British Empire attained its Golden Age under this noble monarch. I also lived under King Edward VII, and witnessed the expectancy of those who desired a looser morality. King Edward VII, although known as a wild Prince, nevertheless held to the high standards set by his illustrious mother, although he contributed nothing to the high morality of the British Isles. Since then I watched the trend of the English under the easy-going morality of King George V, and noted with interest and sorrow the readiness with which the subjects of King George accepted the new morality which was ushered in with the Jazz Age.

And now, we see upon the British Throne a monarch who seems to sneer at contentions which have long since demonstrated their worth, and . . . is openly revolting against the tried and tested virtues of the English-speaking people of the world. As an interpreter of history who believes there is a vital relationship between peace and morality, between prosperity and decency, between high standards of living and Godliness, I believe the present moral decline of the British monarchy and the English-speaking people is symbolical of their failing influence in the affiars of the world, and unless there is a speedy return to the high standards of the past, the peoples of India and the Orient will not remain subject to the present leadership, but will throw off the shackles of those whom they can no longer respect. . . .

John R. Stevenson
Minister, Grace Presbyterian Church
San Francisco, Calif.

All I've got to say about this report that the King of England may abdicate (resign over here) and tie up with Mrs. Simpson, is that the latter will be cold-decked—drew for a king and caught a jack.

Abe Clawhammer
Beaumont, Tex.

. . . Every wife and mother in every English-speaking country will be harassed by hussies swinging their loose hips like Mrs. Simpson. Public opinion is the only thing that will stop the gals who are borned to prowl and stop the American Mrs. Simpson from breaking the heart of the kind, proud man whom the whole world has come to love, Edward the Eighth of England.

Lois B. Arthur
11/2/36 *Indianapolis, Ind.*

Simpson's Status

Re TIME, Oct. 26, p. 21, and the subsequent TIME items with regard to Mrs. Wallis Warfield Simpson.

1) Should King Edward VIII marry Mrs. Simpson would she become Queen of England, Empress of India, etc.?

2) And should they have children would they be eligible for the throne?

3) Just what constitutes a "commoner"?

4) I understand the King's sister-in-law, the Duchess of York, is a so-called commoner, although I believe her father was a duke or earl, but her daughters are constantly referred to as the next in line for the throne after their father.

5) In this connection, is the claim to the throne of the daughters of the Duchess of York prior to the claims of the sons of Princess Mary, sister of the King and the Duke of York, who I believe is older than the Duke of York? . . .

Westwarren Gwaltney
11/23/36   *Greensboro, N.C.*
1) She would become legally no more and no less than Queen-Empress Mary was during the life-time of George V, namely the Consort of His Majesty the King Emperor.
2) Yes. There is no such thing in British Law as a morganatic marriage.
3) The absence of any superior rank.
4) The Duchess of York was the daughter of a peer and as such enjoyed before her marriage the courtesy title Lady Elizabeth Bowes-Lyon. She was none the less technically a commoner. Upon her marriage she assumed the rank and style of her husband, namely she is a princess of the United Kingdom with the style Royal Highness.
5) Under the British Law the succession is: first, the Duke of York; second, his elder daughter Princess Elizabeth; third, her younger sister Princess Margaret Rose; fourth, the Duke of Glou-
*cester; fifth, the Duke of Kent; sixth, his son Prince Edward; seventh, Princess Mary; eighth, her elder son who enjoys the courtesy title of Viscount Lascelles; ninth, his brother Master Gerald David Lascelles.—*ED.

Time & England

Front-paged in the N.Y. *Sun* is the news that TIME has at last been allowed to appear uncensored and unexpurgated on newsstands in England. This is indeed a strange commentary! How much better it would have been for the British if, instead of devoting so much effort to expurgating TIME and debating the propriety of TIME's news in the House of Commons, they had let the people know the truth twelve months ago. . . .

From the day the King had Mrs. Simpson's name published in his *Court Circular* he apparently threw over all discretion about his romance and Mrs. Simpson became the biggest news since the declaration of War. TIME reported it, not as chit-chat, but soberly—too soberly, I sometimes thought.

So what? So TIME was damned and deleted in Parliament and on the British newsstands. And also—so England is out a darn good King and the world was almost out a darn good Empire.

C. Jackson Holdrun
12/21/36   *Bristol Pa.*
Censored not by Parliament or other officialdom but by news-distributors, who feared England's strict libel laws, were TIME's reports of the Edward-Simpson story, beginning Sept. 24, 1934. Last week Lord Beaverbrook's

London Daily Express, *world's largest daily (circulation: 2,040,599), said: "Perhaps if the newspapers had shown less 'restraint' and told more of things earlier on, events would have been different. The public might have better grasped and understood the issues."—*ED.

Masterpiece

Your report of the British monarch's abdication in your Dec. 21 issue was one of your masterpieces. It was accurate (according to my best information). It was unprejudiced. And I prophesy that history will view the affair with the same perspective you have so ably employed.

Hugh Bullock
1/11/37   *New York City*

Chagrin

Please add my name to the list of those NOT approving your selection for Man of the Year. I was chagrined to find Mrs. Simpson occupying this position of honor.

Could you please explain to those of your readers who were deeply disappointed with your selection the standards or measurements which you used? I had thought that certain ethical qualifications were implied as well as certain positive accomplishments. . . .

Gerold C. Wichmann
1/18/37   *Denver, Colo.*
*No woman on earth ever made more or bigger headlines than Wallis Warfield Simpson. Known to practically no one when 1936 began, to practically everyone when it ended, she fulfilled TIME's prime criterion for the news-character most indelibly identified with the past year. Not with the quality but with the calibre of Mrs. Simpson's achievements is TIME concerned.—*ED.

Sound George VI

In your issue of March 8, you state "George VI is sound in that in which King George V was most sound and King Edward VIII by no means sound —Character—and so is Her Majesty."

Haven't you drawn your conclusions a little early in the game? Time will tell. David Windsor is in the forefront of the battle for human rather than property rights, and for the spirit of marriage as opposed to the Letter of the Law. He stands in a symbolic relation to his age, and will influence it as his brother never will.

Nancy T. Pope
3/29/37   *Denver, Colo.*

God Save the King

Being an Englishman and living in Montreal for the last 20 years, and not speaking French, I am writing to you to inform you that the French-Canadian is patriotic to both King and country.

And, may we further inform you that the King and Queen have not begun a "Royal Torture.",. . . but, in their own words, "we are looking forward to our trip to Canada." May we also inform

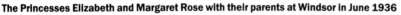

The Princesses Elizabeth and Margaret Rose with their parents at Windsor in June 1936

you that if any of you Americans were presented to the King and Queen of England you would not know whether to stand on your head, shake hands, or bow . . .

And if you wish it we can also send you a letter from Americans who were here to see the King and Queen and who said that we were lucky and indeed fortunate to have such a great King and Queen, and that they hoped that one day they would also be subjects of our King and Queen.

We suggest that you read and learn a little more of what is going on in Canada and thus broaden your stilted views of Canada and its people.

And, as a last word, "God Save Our King and Queen, and God Save the British Empire."

G. Garraway
6/5/39 *Montreal, Que.*
If any U.S. citizens renounced their citizenship in Montreal, they may have trouble getting across the border coming home.—ED.

Royal Visit

Congratulations upon a difficult job performed with a modicum of success. You have managed to introduce a cheap and flippant note even in your account of persons most sacred to Canadians: your story of the Royal Visit to Canada.

Your talk of bullet-proof glass, for instance, is just plain tommyrot. Even though British law has made the gangster's profession a precarious one in this country, still we do know the difference between bullet-proof glass and unshatterable or safety glass, with which latter the Royal car and many others in Canada are equipped. Your insistence upon this entirely fictitious bullet-proof glass is one of the most odious insinuations you could suggest against a loyal people.

Again, your article gives the impression that, because in Quebec and Montreal the crowds failed to yell hysterically and throw vast quantities of ticker tape and toilet paper—as happens in certain cities—their loyalty to Their Majesties was very cool. . . .

Charles J. Bastien
6/19/39 *Montreal, Que.*

Royal Visit (Finis)

When it comes to making fools of themselves, Americans take the cake. I was pleased to find that you had scraped the veneer from the recent Royal Visit [June 19] and had seen it for what it obviously was—an invitation to the next chestnut pulling. Three cheers for TIME.

Frederick B. Hill Jr.
University, Va.

Congratulations to TIME on its clear and complete account of the U.S. Visit of the two rulers of a defaulting debtor nation.

M. H. Wilson
7/10/39 *Seattle, Wash.*

December 1936: King Edward VIII's decision shocks a nation

A Lot More Useful

After donating the largest contribution I could afford to the drive in our city for an ambulance for Britain, after knitting until I could count knit and purl in my sleep for Bundles for Britain, after wrapping bandages until my arms were sore, I sat down to read your magazine of Sept. 2 and what should I come across but an article on the Duchess of Windsor, whom I had admired. She sent for Wayne Forrest, a famous hairdresser, to come to Nassau to do her hair. For this trip he had to fly and bring a permanent-wave dryer, packets of nail polish, rouge, powder, lipstick. All this would cost a large sum of money.

Now wouldn't it be better and a lot more useful and wiser to contribute this money to the war cause and arrange your own hair and manicure your own nails as thousands of us women do. And if Hitler does conquer England, as he seems to be doing, I don't believe it will matter much if Wally has a new permanent or if she wears a new color on her fingertips.

Kate Williams
9/23/40 *North Girard, Pa.*

Record?

TIME's account of the visit of the Windsors [Oct. 6] was one of the cruelest bits of writing ever to appear in your notoriously unkind pages, which must set a record of some sort. Rather a cheap record, however, because the officially snubbed Windsors are quite defenseless; hardly fair game for your newshawk's acid-tipped beak. . . .

To our recent guests, "the slightly moth-eaten Prince Charming, the fading Juliet," one shamed American's apology.

Lela Cole Kitson
10/27/41 *El Paso, Tex.*
TIME cannot undertake to portray the Duke and Duchess of Windsor as shim-

Wallis Simpson was TIME's first "Woman of the Year"

mering dream children in order to spare the feelings of incurable romantics.—ED.

Unemployed Duke?

Your statement [March 26] that the Duke of Windsor is "technologically unemployable, an obsolete man" shocked many of us in the film industry. We take issue with you on your flip and curt dismissal of a man who is one of the colorful figures of our time. As spokesman for a group of actors, writers and directors, I have today cabled the Duke of Windsor offering to form an independent producing company to star him in a picturization of his own life story, or a story of his own choosing, or the post of technical adviser on a film project embodying his own ideas and philosphy. . . . We hold that the Duke of Windsor is a highly employable man and in no sense obsolete.

Chester Morris
4/23/45 *Los Angeles*
Hollywood has seen some strange sights. But TIME is willing to bet a small Balkan kingdom against the head of Actor Morris' press agent that Holywood will never see Britain's ex-King Edward VIII as a cinemactor.—ED.

For King & Country

. . . Re the article on the departure of the Royal Family for South Africa . . . [Feb. 10], I think it's about time America began to grow up in its ideas on the British throne in general, and what it means.

Our love, admiration and respect for it is not just a unique and somewhat endearing form of sentimentality. It is one of the few remaining powerful moral-political forces left in the world today. Americans should be learning to understand that the movements of a man who, by his very existence in the world, puts common ground beneath the feet of diplomats and housewives, financiers and factory hands; laborites, liberals and tories; who commands the absolute loyalty of this island and makes possible the unity of the Commonwealth, are not to be dismissed, nor are those of his family, with ignorant frivolity by you or anyone else. They are much too important.

. . . As for his "tottering Empire," we'll let that go. But very few of us here have any doubts whatever about one thing: that it will almost certainly be called upon to perform again all by itself for a couple of years, the next time the world's bacon needs saving.

Muriel Kurnitz
3/17/47 *London, England*

Cover Girl

Regardless of Princess Elizabeth's awareness of her royalty and approaching responsibilities, she will be more thrilled with your Boris Chaliapin's cover picture [Mar. 31] of her true beauty and charm. That is what every girl desires above all else, if she is totally honest. You have given the world a very realistic picture of a very lovely young woman. It is a delightful illustration and a magnificent reproduction in exquisite coloring and superb composition.

Leslie H. Pearl
4/21/47 *Glyndon, Md.*

Protested Pratfall

In TIME's issue of Dec. 1 . . . you publish: "A Royal Pratfall."

I protest! I protest against the expressions used with regard to our Crown Princess Juliana: "Plump Princess Juliana . . . [danced] the conga. . . . She slipped, and stayed down, while [the Duke of Gloucester] tried to tug her up, . . ."

It seems highly improbable that: 1) our Crown Princess would dance the conga, and 2) that this vulgar dance would be allowed at Buckingham Palace. . . .

But what most goes against the grain . . . is the vulgar and contemptuous way your correspondent expresses himself. . . .

Mrs. M. Bouman-Over
The Hague,
12/21/47 *The Netherlands*
TIME reported the vulgar facts.—ED.

Faith, Hope & Beauty

Amid all the angular, pot-bellied, emaciated, fat, cynical, complacent and evil-browed rulers, politicians, moguls, authors and social climbers which your columns must perforce exhibit, the charming figure of Princess Elizabeth [March 15] stands out like the morn-

ing star of human faith and hope. Alive, intelligent, eager, energetic, she is the quintessence of beauty . . . a blessing to mankind. . . .

A. W. Sinclair
4/5/48 *Madison, Tenn.*

Royal Reading

Your profile of Princess Margaret [June 13] read like a [movie] scenario . . . For the first time in many years of reading TIME, I suspect the veracity of your researchers. How in the world could you dig up such material on a royal personage?

Anyhow, it made good reading . . .
Dolores E. Kelly
7/4/49 *Jackson Heights, N.Y.*
Let Reader Kelly swallow her doubts, remember that the truth often makes better reading than fiction.—ED.

Tribute

. . . Congratulations from the depths of my heart for your soul-stirring eulogy, "The King Is Dead." This masterpiece could profitably be read by every American—man, woman and child . . .

Newton L. Nichols
Captain (ret.), U.S.N.
3/3/52 *Baltimore, Md.*

Woman of the Year

. . . Elizabeth II is undoubtedly a lovely young lady (and Queen) full of "the significance of a fresh young blossom on roots that had weathered many a season of wintry doubt" (oh brother!), BUT—either Dwight Eisenhower, Captain Carlsen, Konrad Adenauer or Eleanor Roosevelt had a more, much more, substantial claim to the title . . .

Frank G. Rivera
Los Angeles

. . . I felt that a deeper significance was lost in your great and sincere sentiment. For there are overtones of sadness in this British idealization of their lovely Queen . . . True enough, the British people have always regarded their rulers as subconscious symbols of their glory. But behind the smiles of courage and the brave, half-filled stomachs, there must be a gnawing despair in many a British heart that the light and glory of empire are growing dim . . .

P. J. Clinton
1/26/53 *New York City*

The Queen's Leisure

In your otherwise charming article on the Queen in your issue of Jan. 5, you say that the Tories took exception to her having dined with Douglas Fairbanks.

The Queen's leisure hours are all too few, and no one of whatever political creed would presume to criticize where she chose to spend them; but what shocked everyone was the ensuing publicity, for it is an unwritten law in Great Britain that when a King or Queen pays an entirely private visit, no mention of it should appear in the press . . .

Juliet Duff
2/2/53 *Wilton, Salisbury, England*

Royal Manners

Your March 16 picture of Queen Elizabeth II removing her own wrap was disgusting . . . You called it "a moment of royal informality"; I call it plain old bad manners. Let's hope the American male doesn't take stock in this incident. They are already prone to be lax . . . As for the Duke of Edinburgh, I'm sure he must know better.

Sally Hawkins
4/6/53 *Los Angeles*

The Greatest Show on Earth

Re the coronation (which TIME, June 8 depicted so graphically): Is Ringling Bros. and Barnum & Bailey really the greatest show on earth?

Albert M. Webb
Barbados, B.W.I.

. . . The British [had] a gay time crowning their Queen. I only hope that the bill will not be sent to this side of the Atlantic . . .

Robert Smith
6/22/53 *Bloomington, Ind.*

Royal Merits

TIME's splendid report of the coronation sums up neatly the merits of royalty in a modern world. American respect goes to a British institution, though many Englishmen may doubt its overall advantages . . .

After the moving words of the Prime Minister and the address of the Queen, I am convinced that they will strive to make this ancient institution an instrument of the general welfare, and that Anglo-Saxon genius in the field of politics will leave nothing unturned to enhance its value and usefulness . . .

Walter Mann
6/22/53 *Philadelphia*

The Coronation

Your excellent coverage of the coronation sets new standards of high-level reporting, with the best of historical and political perspectives added for good measure. We share the happiness of a close neighbor who is throwing a swell shindig . . . We strongly suspect the drinks—and possibly the eats—are on us, so we may be pardoned if we view the proceedings with a jaundiced eye, [but] remembering always that our neighbor has lost much more than money in fighting two wars that were ours as well as his own—even before we got into them. So we doff our hats and raise our voices in enthusiastic salute: "God Save the Queen!"

Arthur T. Grant
6/29/53 *Philadelphia*

Nice Quiet Corroboree

Your Feb. 15 story about Sydney's welcome to the Queen . . . sounded as if it had been written by a jaundiced remittance man who had spent his money from home on an inglorious lost weekend and was suffering . . . Sydney's welcome was admittedly noisy and uninhibited, but the spirit of the welcome was a gay and happy greeting . . . The Queen and the Duke of Edinburgh may have found our welcome tiring but not tiresome, as you pointedly suggest. Doubtless, there were far too many official functions and politicians and too much heat, but we are not quite the unmannered, uncouth colonials your article implies . . . Your

presidential parades and important civic affairs are not conducted with all that much of decorum and *savoir faire.*

Ira Schimke
Sydney, Australia

. . . The surging, yelling hysteria of the Sydney people, which you Americans have attributed to the ignorance of staring hooligans and wild colonials, was only our spontaneous, uninhibited and uncontrollable greeting to the Queen . . . You, who have no monarch, can never understand . . .

Betty Randall
Strathfield, N.S.W.

I was fascinated by TIME's report of Queen Elizabeth's boisterous reception in Australia. The Aussies are a delightfully unpredictable people . . .

Alexander Markey
3/15/54 *Bombay, India*

Helping Lame Dukes

Your paragraph about the hazing of the Duke of Edinburgh at Melbourne University [March 15] missed an amusing point. During his visit to Australia, he received so many presents of walking sticks that he suggested, jokingly, that he should be given a pair of crutches. The Melbourne University students obliged.

Neville Smith
4/12/54 *Melbourne Australia*

In the Ditch

Due to the fact that I did not have TIME, May 31, I missed seeing the piece on Prince Bernhard's auto accident: "Trying to pass a road truck . . . he

Royal sisters

Princess Margaret

zigged when he should have zagged." I now am receiving copies of it from quite a few friends in the U.S. with a certain amount of biting comment, which I would gladly accept if it had been my fault. However, I enclose an eyewitness report (American), and in view of that, I don't think it is fair to write as you did, as it apparently gives me the reputation of a b.f.*

Bernhard
Soestdijk Palace
7/26/54 *The Netherlands*
**i.e.* bloody fool.

The Church & Margaret

The March 21 article on Princess Margaret and Peter Townsend once more focuses our attention on the logical absurdities which Anglicanism gets itself into these days. Elizabeth, as "head of the church," cannot officially approve of Margaret's marriage to a divorced man (presumably because such marriages violate the law of God), although, according to other Anglican authorities, she might approve of it as "big sister" (presumably because such marriages do not violate the law of God). Nor, in this same anomalous situation, can the Archbishop of Canterbury approve the marriage (presumably because such marriages violate the law of God), even though he may "readmit her to Communion after a decent interval" (presumably because such marriages do not violate the law of God) . . . It is certainly to be noted that the English Church of 1533 tended to uphold the laws of God a little more briskly than does the modern English Church . . .

(The Rev.) Robert J. Stowe, S.J.
4/18/55 *Los Gatos, Calif.*

Princess Elizabeth

June 2, 1955: on the balcony of Buckingham Palace after the coronation of Queen Elizabeth II

Margaret's Decision

Meg made the only right decision. What true parent would wish his daughter to marry a divorced father of two children, 16 years her senior?

F. C. Denham
Scotia, N.Y.

The eloquent faces of the two young people placed on the rack by the churchmen of England make one wonder if we are not still living in the Dark Ages . . .

Mrs. E. B. Benson
Vermillion, S. Dak.

As a British subject, I am delighted with Princess Margaret's decision. She has shown us she is a young woman with high principles. In this day and age, when so much glamor is attached to the "Hollywood type," it is refreshing to see this example shown by our Princess, who is mature enough to know the importance of duty to church and family.

June L. Hornby
11/21/55   *Lincoln, Neb.*

This is one of the many congratulations you will receive on the super excellent Nov. 7 article on Princess Margaret. It will enable the English-speaking world to fairly judge everybody involved; to sense the damage already done and what might have been done to the prestige of the monarchy, Britain and the Commonwealth. If royalty is to survive, a princess must act like one or vacate.

H. S. Temple
Victoria, B.C.

Thank you for your touching story. Our hearts go out to Peter Townsend whose conduct was above reproach during the entire proceedings. He was ac-

corded some cruel treatment from almost everyone, including Margaret.

Elinore F. Rucker
11/26/55   *Plainfield, N.J.*

Fine Young Couple

H.M. Queen Elizabeth and the Duke of Edinburgh are two fine people who by their way of life make no mean contribution to the maintenance and consolidation of friendship and good will among the peoples of the West, of Africa and of Asia; yet TIME [Feb. 18] gives space to scurrilous rumors about their private activities.

I. Thomson
Montreal

Why hint that things are wrong when duty takes a man from his home for four months? And why imply that if a couple don't have a baby in five years they are out of love? Where is your balanced judgment? Where is your common sense?

(The Very Rev.) H. C. L. Heywood
Provost of Southwell
Southwell, Nottinghamshire,
3/11/57   *England*

Royal Visit

I found your cover picture of Prince Philip disappointing, disgusting and irritating. I am a Spaniard, and I cannot bear to see pictures of English royalty.

Joaquin A. Barretto
Manila

A deep bow to Prince Philip. To find a place in the sun while standing in the long shadow cast by Queen Elizabeth is a notable achievement indeed.

James McLaughlin
Mt. Pleasant, Mich.

Your cover picture of Prince Philip shows the whole world how stupid we English are for tolerating such a fantastic circus uniform.

Karl John Wilson
Santiago

I am not a monarchist, but in this inelegant 20th century, perhaps England's Queen is as important to America as she is to Britain.

Gladys U. Waters
11/11/57   *Stamford, Conn.*

Philip's Schooling

I was amazed that you left out the fact that Prince Philip received the first three years of his schooling in an American school at Saint Cloud, near Paris. Here he learned about George Washington long before he knew anything about George III and played baseball before he ever heard of cricket. "Those days in the MacJannet Country School," Prince Philip told me, when I saw him at the Louvre reception last April, "were the happiest of my life."

Donald R. MacJannet
11/18/57   *Geneva*

Royal Visit to Sierra Leone

As an American citizen who has spent almost 30 years in this lovely country, I wish to protest your distorted report of the Queen's visit to Sierra Leone [Dec. 15].

I myself had a ringside seat directly behind Her Majesty at the gorgeous spectacle to which your reporter referred in such disparaging terms. There were 51 paramount chiefs, each carried in a hammock, surrounded by drummers, dancers and singers, pantomiming something that was particularaly characteristic of that chiefdom.

The chiefs were carried in hammocks, not because they were intoxicated, as your reporter suggested, but for generations when motor transportation was not available, that was the way chiefs were transported from place to place. A few chiefs at Bo had to be helped up to the dais where the Queen sat because they were feeble with age, not drunk.

Mabel I. Silver, M.D.
The Evangelical United Lutheran
Hospital
3/2/62   *Rotifunk, Sierra Leone*

Moneyed Prince Charlie

My attention has been drawn to your report [Nov. 27] entitled "The Princely Pauper." There is no truth whatever in the story that Prince Charles has sold his autograph at any time. There is also no truth whatever in the story that he sold his composition book to a classmate. In the first place, he is intelligent and old enough to realize how embarrassing this would turn out to be, and second, he is only too conscious of the interest of the press in anything to do with himself and his family. The suggestion that his parents keep him so short of money that he has to find other means to raise it is also a complete invention. Finally, the police would not have attempted to regain the composition book unless they were quite satisfied that it had been obtained illegally.

As to the essays in the book, you may be interested to know that the one about corruption in government, which you quote, was in fact a précis from Lecky's *History of England*.

Richard Colville
Buckingham Palace
12/11/64 *London*
The Royal family's press officer mounts a princely defense in his belated offer to clarify the case.

Enjoyable Retreat

The British monarchy may well be a contemporary "retreat to Camelot" [June 27], but it is a far more enjoyable adventure than that provided by the droll leadership of most Western republics. At least the monarchy, for all of its faults, gives us some relief from the total lack of style of most of today's politicians.

Anthony J. Short, S.J.
Chantilly, France

Political graft, corruption in your judiciary, race riots and arson, the burning of your own country's flag in public, the murder of prominent citizens including your own President, drug addition—you name it and you've got it.

No thanks; we'll keep our Royal Family and all the decadence that goes with it. You keep your Black Panthers and the almighty dollar.

James E. S. Rusbridger
7/11/69 *London*

Like Mother, Like Daughter

Princess Anne's ill humor with our lady reporters [Aug. 3] reminds me of a delightful story about her mother and grandmother. The Queen took Princess Elizabeth and Princess Margaret to a ship launching. When Princess Elizabeth started to enter a "no admittance" area, a guard spoke up and said, "I'm sorry, little lady, but you must not enter." The princess stomped her foot and replied, "I'm *not* a little lady! I am the Princess Elizabeth."

The serene and lovely Queen smiled at the guard and said, "She's right, you know, she is not a little lady. But she will learn."

Harriet B. Moore
8/24/70 *Laguna Hills, Calif.*

Behind Château Walls

After reading the daily newspapers, the Duchess of Windsor finds the world "full of violence and horror" [Nov. 19]. Here is a woman whose advantageous social and financial position could easily exert a positive force. Yet the duchess remains complacent and has chosen to recede into boredom and loneliness. None of us can afford to live behind château walls.

Elizabeth Darrow
Loretta Lloyd Swanson
12/10/73 *Davis, Calif.*

The Brightest and the Best

The observation that Princess Anne's Mark Phillips is not too bright [Nov. 19] is most interesting.

Considering that he got the "best catch" in England, a huge increase in yearly income, very likely a title, became a worldwide celebrity, and will start house keeping in a five-bedroom house says a great deal for his lack of intelligence.

Bruce Stock
Fort Lauderdale, Fla.

It is interesting to find the most sentimental people on earth (the Americans) so strangely vitriolic in reporting the wedding of a young princess (English) to the man she loves. As a Canadian, I come to the conclusion that your tawdry article on Princess Anne's wedding arrangements reflects the constant envy of the time-honored institutions of Canada and Britain that you in the States sigh for. In frustration you create tinsel titles for movie and parade queens and baseball "Kings of Swat." But no matter how you try, Swat is not as sweet as real kings and queens and a thousand years of tradition.

Eileen Learoyd
Victoria, B.C.

TIME's recent commentaries on the British royal family were unwarranted and unusually shallow.

The popularity of Princess Anne and her family was affirmed by the wedding crowds cheering "We want Anne." The princess' unwillingness to suffer fools raises her in the estimation of many.

As out of place as it may seem in a world of rootless mass-think, where unprincipled striving is king, the royal pageantry of Britain reminds us of a democratic evolution the benefits of which all free peoples reap today.

Derrick E. Ward
12/10/73 *West Vancouver, B.C.*

Defending the Princess

As a piece of reporting, your article on the wedding preparations of Princess Anne and Captain Mark Phillips [Nov. 19] could be described as cheap prattle of an antimonarchy gossip columnist. Your correspondent may, of course, have written it with tongue in cheek, but he should remember that had he written such comments during the reign of the first Queen Elizabeth, he would surely have lost his head.

Martin J. Pooley
Redhill, England

It was very bad taste to gibe at Princess Anne on the romantic occasion of her marriage. Do not forget that Princess Anne belongs to a dynasty, whereas the aged Duchess of Windsor, displayed on the next page, is only an American woman who tried her best to gate-crash the royal throne of England—without success, thank God.

Lady Constance Conway
12/17/73 *Stellenbosch, South Africa*

July 29, 1981: a human Union Jack waits for the royal wedding carriage to pass

America Recaptured

The visit of Queen Elizabeth [July 19] marked the first time in our history that the British could have recaptured America without firing a shot.

Russell J. Thomas
8/9/76 *Vicksburg, Miss.*

Older Women's Lib

Right on to Princess Margaret and Roderic Llewellyn [Oct. 10]! As a fiftyish, unmarried woman, I find some younger men attractive and fun to be with, this seems to be mutual.

While an older man may be admired for his choice of a much younger lover or wife, many people seem to think it is disgraceful if the situation is reversed, and the woman is older than the man. Perhaps the Margarets of this world will help to change this.

Ethel E. Johnson
11/14/77 *San Pedro, Calif.*

The Professionals

While Britain operates with a professionally trained management team of Elizabeth, Philip, Charles & Co., we muddle on with cattle ranchers, third-rate lawyers and peanut farmers with no leadership background. You don't suppose they'd lend us Charles, do you?

Richard F. Schafer
Anchorage, Alaska

So Prince Charles "believes it is essential to make a concerted effort to reduce the barriers of prejudice and misunderstanding." Considering the royal family's long-cherished prejudice against Roman Catholics, one hopes that he will some day have the courage to practice what he preaches.

Mary Charles
6/5/78 *Dublin*

Lovely Diana

Ah, for a loaf of bread, a jug of wine and Di [April 20].

Robert T. St. John
New York City

As a young man awash in a sea of hard-boiled, frowzy, careerist "woman," I would like to meet someone with the grace and loveliness of Lady Diana.

James J. McMahon III
Crofton, Md.

Thank goodness for the lovely Diana. At last, a model who can represent for girls what being a lady is all about.

Barbara Anderson
Portland, Ore.

You have reported a cover story about a 19-year-old girl who is to marry a 32-year-old man. Her chief qualification in this matrimonial derby is her virginity, followed closely by her "ability to do the job" and her "child-bearing potential." We have come far, and have far to go.

Cynthia Conley
5/11/81 *New York City*

Darling Diana

Prince Charles could not have done better if he had tried a glass slipper on the foot of every young lady in Britain. Lady Diana [April 20] is truly a rare gem.

Buff Finley
5/18/81 *Knoxville, Tenn.*

Royal Wedding

While it was truly the wedding of the century ["Magic in the Daylight," Aug. 3] it was more than just a ceremony. It was a healthy display of the monarchy, alive and functioning. As an American I still find royalty's mystery captivating and its majesty enchanting.

Theresa L. Thayer
Detroit

It was a good show. Now back to the world of 4 million unemployed, the Northern Ireland debacle and riots in the streets. Solve them. That would be what I would call a really good show.

Philip Schacca
8/24/81 *West Hempstead, N.Y.*

Baby William

Three cheers for little Prince William Arthur Philip Louis [July 5]! It's splendid to see the British lavish all that affection on the royal family and its newest member after fighting a war that leaves a big debt to pay off.

Katy Murphy
St. Louis

The birth of a healthy, wanted baby anywhere in the world is always cause for rejoicing. The maudlin delight that the new royal baby in England is male is sickening. England's greatest decades have been in the reigns of its Queens.

Mary Scott
7/26/82 *Toronto*

Royal Hunt

When I was little, I dreamed of marrying a prince. After reading about how the press pursues the Princess of Wales [Feb. 28], I realize how nice it is that my prince is a pharmacist.

Dalene Vanden Hoek
Grand Rapids

No wonder Diana refused to pose for pictures on her recent skiing holiday with Prince Charles. She is constantly hounded by reporters who will print anything and call her a "spoilt brat" and a "monster." These terms more accurately describe those who refuse to give the Princess a moment's peace.

Kelly Fitzgerald
3/21/83 *McAllen, Texas*

Before a crowd of thousands, Prince Charles kisses his bride on the balcony of Buckingham Palace

Prince William at Kensington Palace

The Last Word

Historians spend centuries measuring the impact of great men and women on civilization, but the earliest reactions to the death of an important figure, the first reviews of a lifetime's accomplishments, are appropriately considered in the weekly newsmagazine. World leaders, scientists, artists, show business stars, kings and queens are among the extraordinary people whose very different legacies fascinate TIME readers.

Florenz Ziegfeld

In your almost adequate account of the picturesque showman, the late Florenz Ziegfeld [Aug. 1], you failed to tell of his first independent production. When he left his first job with Buffalo Bill's show in the West . . . he worked his way through the small western towns with a one man show of "dancing ducks and invisible fish." He would place his half-dozen ducks on an overturned box, under which was a coal oil lamp which heated the box and caused the ducks to move from foot to foot as if dancing. He carried a fish bowl full of water and no fish: hence "invisible fish."

Perhaps Ziegfeld was also responsible for the story of the gentleman who boarded the train with a large box in which were many air holes. Another man . . . asked what was in the box. The gentleman answered, "A mongoose." The traveler asked what a mongoose was. He was told that it was an animal which ate snakes and he was taking it to a friend who had delirium tremens. The second man asked to look in the box and finding it empty he exclaimed. "What kind of mongoose is that?" He was told that it was an imaginary mongoose to eat imaginary snakes."

Charles Edward Thomas
8/28/32 *Indianapolis, Ind.*
Other Ziegfeldiana: He liked buttoned shoes but did not dare wear them. He had scores of guns, was an adept shot. To his elaborate camp at Lake Edward, Que. he shipped hundreds of Louisiana bullfrogs, put them in a fenced bay, fed them crushed biscuit. When he wanted frogs' legs for lunch, which was often, his daughter Patricia would go out and shoot some with her .22.—ED.

Calvin Coolidge

. . . "Death of Coolidge" is the finest thing of the kind I have ever read. I found it dignified, sympathetic and very moving but not at all mawkish or sentimental. . . .

Mildred B. Allen
1/30/33 *Orange, N.J.*

Will Rogers

If one did not see newspapers and relied on TIME, as many do, your article "Death in the Arctic" [Aug. 26] is most unsatisfactory, I felt TIME would be one publication to sense what Rogers meant to the U.S. as its most important private citizen, unique in annals. He certainly represented success in more ways than any other American and at the same time was considered a more ideal American than any other of the 120 million. . . . Modest, humble, truthful, great, he possessed every fine trait of all times combined with every modern interest and appreciation of our age. In my lifetime no individual has been so honestly and deservedly mourned by the people. I suggest TIME do its duty to its readers.

Walter Wanger
9/9/35 *Los Angeles, Calif.*
It is TIME's job to present facts, not to eulogize. But to the extent that its report of the death of Will Rogers and Wiley Post did not fully reflect the enormous public emotion at this tragedy, TIME failed in its purpose. TIME had no better public friend, no more generous booster, no more enthusiastic reader than Will Rogers. Therefore it takes this occasion to salute him posthumously.—ED.

King George V

May I take this means of extending to you my appreciation for the thoughtful and delicate way in which you handled the deathbed scene of the late King George V in your [March of Time] broadcast? . . .

It reaches here at 7:30 p.m. My wife was in the other room, but when your speaker reached that incident of the broadcast, his hushed voice drew Mrs. Hinman to the radio, and I heard a sob. Mrs. Hinman was born in Yorkshire, England. I was born, and, for more than forty years, lived under the British flag, and we felt we had lost a friend.

W. Platt Hinman
2/10/36 *Huntington Park, Calif.*

Franklin Delano Roosevelt

. . . I am a soldier, and I am proud to have lived and fought during an era which produced so great and sincere a leader of this country. The ideals for which he stood and fought will live always if we are intelligent enough to preserve them. At the coming San Francisco parley, may the leaders of the conference remember these ideals. To insure this, I humbly suggest they put another chair at the table — to remain there for Roosevelt.

Richard C. Gelula
Army Air Forces
4/30/45 *New York City*

King George V at the ceremony of the Order of the Bath, 1928

All week I have been waiting impatiently for this week's issue of TIME [April 23], knowing that in its usual clear fashion it would frame into words the thoughts and tears and hopes and fears of all the 137 million Americans who this week bade farewell to our beloved President.

Your simple account of how his death touched the armed forces, the man in the street, the great and near-great, near & far, and your eloquent tribute to him and to his brave wife, said completely what I have sought to convey to my children. It will be reverently put in their diary as the "requiem" in his memory.

Pandit Nehru with Mahatma Gandhi

Franklin Delano Roosevelt

George Bernard Shaw

And it is all the greater because you did not see eye-to-eye with him.

A memorial like this issue of TIME renews my faith in the undying eternal greatness of our beloved country and in that precious term "American." God bless you for portraying it so truly.

Rose K. Herrmann
5/7/45 *Scarsdale, N.Y.*

Out here on the roughest front the 7th Division has yet bumped into in its four major operations, a platoon of doughboys from the 184th listened while I read to them your inspiring write-up on the President's death [April 23].

Thanks for giving my men a vivid picture of what really took place. It was my first issue and reached the front in eight days. . . .

It worked fine and they kept me reading in spite of the cook's calls for chow.

David B. Spessard
Lieutenant, U.S.A.
c/o Postmaster
6/4/45 *San Francisco*

Mahatma Gandhi

The world owes you a debt of gratitude for the wonderful paragraphs on Mahatma Gandhi in TIME, Feb. 9. I have rarely seen such inspired journalism.

Fred Field Goodsell
2/23/48 *Boston, Mass.*

George Bernard Shaw

Coming to "G.B.S.: 1856-1950" [Nov. 13], my eyes widened, my lips parted and became dry as they always do whenever a hot passion of love or justified anger surges through me.

This time it was boundless admiration for a matchless evaluation of G.B.S.'s controversial personality and literary importance . . .

Arthur J. A. Koerner
Waco, Tex.

How G.B.S. would love his obituary!
Lionel B. Moses
12/4/50 *Evanston, Ill.*

King George VI

I must be one of many thousands in these Islands who were deeply moved by the manner in which you carried the sad news of the King's death . . . One section of your article said: "In London's High Court, when the news came, King's Counselor Harold Shepherd had just finished cross-examining a defendant . . ." The title is that of King's Counsel — now, of course, Queen's Counsel . . . Incidentally, the incident that you referred to was a trial of a murder case, and because of its nature . . . the judge adjourned it for ten minutes only. Every other court . . . in London adjourned until the next day.

Godfrey Russell Vick, Kt.Q.C.
London, England

In your old, early days, you at least played devil's advocate to republicanism; now you are the canonizer of monarchy. Not that we on this side of the border do not appreciate your tribute to our late King and your admiration of our monarchical institution. But it is, to us, a droll confirmation of Shaw's statement that America would sue for inclusion in the British Empire.

Thomas Allen
3/10/52 *Peterborough, Ont., Canada*

Joseph Stalin

Stalin's lust for more power, and the praises from the people he had fooled, are meaningless to him now. We read of his mother's tender care for him, her teachings and desires that he should be good for humanity and himself . . . What is there left to say but to quote the Bible: "For what shall it profit a man, if he shall gain the whole world, and lose his own soul? Or what shall a man give in exchange for his soul?"

Mrs. W. A. Edlund
4/6/53 *Denver*

Albert Einstein

What a magnificent tribute to Einstein in your issue of May 2 . . . Amid the welter of myriad, too-definite theories of God abroad today, how serene and reverent were Einstein's beliefs in the awareness of the great Spirit in the universe . . .

Lucretia E. Hemington
Washington, D.C.

. . . Only when a person contemplates the nature of the universe can he arrive at anything approaching truth. Dr. Einstein spent his life doing just that . . .

James H. Farley
5/16/55 *Columbus, Ohio*

James Dean

. . . You have devoted 92 lines of the October 10 Cinema section to a busty English vaudeville actress called Diana Dors, explaining in unnecessary detail the color of her lawnmower and second-hand Rolls-Royce, yet in your Milestones column you give only a scant nine lines to the memory of America's greatest young actor, James Dean, who was killed in an untimely accident . . .

J. Boland
10/31/55
Alton, Ill.

H. L. Mencken

I was saddened by the death of H. L. Mencken and angered that his waning years had to be spent in forced inactivity. How it must have galled him to sit on the sidelines during an era that produced a Harry Truman, a Joe McCarthy, an Arthur Godfrey and, of course, a Liberace, an era in which a man without some kind of fraternal badge in his lapel is regarded as suspect. As for your Feb. 6 tribute to Mencken, I felt that it was excellent. It neither glorified nor damned him but presented him as he was — a true Corinthian, but at the same time a gentleman.

David Gregory Rossie
3/19/56
Windsor, N.Y.

Joseph McCarthy

Your article "The Passing of McCarthy" [May 13] was well written, well documented and objective. His last years must have been like those of Boyle and Joxer Daly, those other two friends of John Barleycorn in *Juno and the Paycock*. They, too, saw "the whole worl's in a state o' chassis."

Claude de Crespigny
Houston

In the passing of Senator Joseph McCarthy, America lost one of her heroes, who was crucified on a stony patch of bigotry and political expediency. God rest his soul.

James A. Boules
3/27/57
Pasadena, Calif.

Pope Pius XII

Pius had many divisions. We of the Free World will sorely miss the comfort and real power of his moral force. (I am a Lutheran.)

William C. Redeen
Captain, U.S.A.F.
11/3/58
Bitburg, West Germany

John Foster Dulles

Mr. Dulles is gone, and all America will miss him. But most of all, he'll be missed by those of us whom I know are many—ex-Marines—who saw in him a man with spine, guts and self-respect. This was an American. This was a man.

Bill Graves
6/15/59
Levittown, Pa.

George C. Marshall

In the millions of words written when General of the Army George C. Marshall crossed "over the river to rest in the shade of the trees," nobody more completely depicted the dignity and

Pope Pius XII

Albert Einstein

Joseph Stalin

humility of that great American than did the TIME writer who marked the passing of that illustrious man [Oct. 26].

John M. Virden
Colonel, U.S.A.F. (ret.)
11/16/59
Chevy Chase, Md.

Ernest Hemingway

You are to be commended for your fine obituary on Ernest Hemingway [July 14]. You have captured his lasting contribution to our language and literature with the objectivity and good sense that Hemingway himself would have admired.

When I first heard of his death, I was reminded of a line from *Death in the Afternoon:* "If two people love each other there can be no happy end to it." In a sense, Ernest Hemingway's love affair was with the tragic world which he created in his novels, and with the tragic characters who rimmed that world.

What happened at Ketchum was, ironically, no happy end.

Alexander Medlicott Jr.
7/28/61
Seattle

Dag Hammarskjold

Dag Hammarskjold was killed in the service of the world and working for world peace. Others will express their sorrow better than I, but I must express myself.

Dag Hammarskjold has been attacked by persons and by some governments of the world. In spite of this, none of his effectiveness was lost by it, and in reality, he came out stronger.

Peace has lost a most tireless worker, and therefore in recognition of his valuable contribution to this cause, I nominate Dag Hammarskjold as TIME's Man of the Year.

Georgia Blanchard
Clarion State College
9/29/61
Clarion, Pa.

Marilyn Monroe

Such venom, such malignity, such vindictiveness, such cold-blooded malevolence must, indeed, have curdled the blood of the author of "The Only Blonde in the World."

Even while this poor butterfly, broken on the wheel, was being laid in her grave, I read the article, and every ounce of decency in me rose up in rebellion against such complete lack of common charity.

Better to have had the understanding of Thomas Hood, when he wrote:
One more Unfortunate
Weary of breath
Rashly importunate,
Gone to her death!
Take her up tenderly,
Lift her with care;
Fashioned so slenderly,
Young, and so fair!

(Mrs.) Ada R. Corder
8/17/62
Salt Lake City

As usual, TIME has expressed the exquisite sentiment to end all in its superb description of the molding of Marilyn Monroe [May 31]. I knew Marilyn well in those days when she looked like "nothing much at all, a glass of milk with some lipstick near the rim." I knew her not as a worshipper but as an aspiring fellow artist who had the rare pleasure of sharing her joys and woes and wistfulness, and who saw beyond the glass of milk, deep into its nourishing contents.

There was nothing accidental about Marilyn, not even her death. It was all ordained. No one ever worked harder, or planned more meticulously to please her worshipers. Why the wailing over her "untimely" departure? She packed a more lasting wallop in her short span as a star than most of us will if we live to be 100. She needed the rest, and God knows she had earned it; let's let her have it.

6/7/63
Hal Gould
New York City

Pope John XXIII

Pope John had become the Pope of the world, not just Christ's Vicar on Earth to us Catholics. This wonderful man in his short reign became a loved figure; his death has cast a gloom over mankind.

6/14/63
Finbarr Slattery
Killarney, Ireland

John Fitzgerald Kennedy

We are stunned into paralysis. We cry our outrage not for revenge but for the massive loss of this man, the President. He made enormous contributions to every human being in the world. He was a singular leader of our lifetime.

11/29/63
L. R. Nicholl
Claremont, Calif.

Douglas MacArthur

Twice I saw him. On the beach at Morotai and in the foothills of Mindanao. There was an aura of greatness about him. He gave the impression of being aloof and austere and was not universally loved, but the devotion he inspired from associates would not have come from a lesser source than greatness [April 10].

Relentless in war, forgiving in peace, he will tower in the annals of our history. One of the truly great Americans has gone to his reward.

4/24/64
Ken Gustafson
Thief River Falls, Minn.

Pandit Nehru

Mr. Nehru's death is undoubtedly a setback to peace. With his policy of nonalignment, Mr. Nehru showed to the world that the friend of the U.S. need not be the enemy of the U.S.S.R., and vice versa. The world may have to wait for a long time before another Nehru or the like of him appears on the world scene.

6/12/64
K. Kumaraswami
Kilpauk, Madras, India

Winston Churchill

As an Englishwoman eight years resident in this country and, incidentally, a subscriber to TIME for most of those years, may I thank you from the bottom of my heart for your delightful tribute to our beloved "Winnie." I spent the years of World War II near London and within the "invasion area" of the south coast of England, and I know to what extent Sir Winston's great example of indomitable courage and faith in the ultimate outcome influenced us all to "carry on."

Edythe F. Marsh
Marion, Conn.

Your tribute to Mr. Churchill was a well-written, accurate and moving memorial to that great man. Surely future generations will know this as the "Age of Churchill," just as we know Greece's finest hour as the Age of Pericles. But how fitting that your cover story in this sad week of remembering should deal with youth and future. We look with gratitude to the past; we look (as one must always) to the future with hope.

2/12/65
(Mrs.) Susan Williams
Manhattan, Kans

Edward R. Murrow

I read of Edward Murrow's death [May 7] with considerable sorrow. In the early days of World War II, I worked in the BBC studio adjacent to one he used. On quite a few occasions, Murrow came into our room to try out his opening lines on a British audience. One of these remains in my mind very clearly: "I have just come in from Piccadilly Circus tube station. There is a heavy raid in progress. But in the station itself, things appear to be quiet with the exception of a small man in a dirty overcoat who is very busy. He has a stick of chalk in his hand and is dutifully inscribing on the wall 'Home Rule for Wales.' That, in its way, conveys the spirit of London in the middle of this bombing raid at 1 o'clock on a September morning." It is perhaps needless to say that our reaction was unanimous and most appreciative.

5/21/65
James Douglas
Geneva

Adlai Stevenson

It was fitting that when Adlai Stevenson met his death [July 23], America was making world history with its Mariner conquest of Mars. It was fitting because Stevenson believed in man; he knew that there was nothing man could not do, from the vilest destruction to

1945: British Prime Minister Winston Churchill in Berlin

Ho Chi Minh   Robert Kennedy   Adlai Stevenson

the most inspiring creativity. But it was his hope that America would be a leader in the latter.

(Rep.) Patrick W. Nee
7/30/65   *Statehouse, Boston*

Martin Luther King

Dr. Martin Luther King was TIME's Man of the Year in 1964. Considering the meaningful humanistic events of the last two decades, he will surely be recognized for his role as a leader of this century. I have no words for those who killed him. But as a father, I bleed for others' sons who may die in the streets, having hopelessly cast aside the idea of nonviolent attainment of the principles of our Constitution. King preached as a man of God, but men of conscience must remember him as a man of the people.

William Stephens
4/12/68   *Arlington, Va.*

Dwight D. Eisenhower

Your excellent cover article on General Eisenhower, the great soldier President [April 4], really touched me and carried my heart to Abilene. How accurately you report that he embodied serene America. Standing on his achievements, Ike may truly be regarded as one of America's, nay, the world's greatest generals. Adlai Stevenson once said: "I venture to suggest that patriotism is not a short and frenzied outburst of emotion but the tranquil and steady dedication of a lifetime." The same can be said of Ike, the hero who despised heroics.

Anurup Banerjee
Calcutta, India

A commentary on the violent age in which we live was reflected in the question of our six-year-old daughter, while watching the funeral of Eisenhower.

She asked: "Mother, who shot him?"
Mrs. Desmond Herbert
4/18/69   *Jackson, Mich.*

Robert F. Kennedy

I was sitting alone in a perimeter observation tower in Viet Nam when I heard of the tragic and violent death of Senator Robert F. Kennedy [June 14]. How and why can death be so prevalent in an advanced civilization such as ours? At that moment, my attention became fixed on the M-60 machine gun which rested, black and suddenly very ugly, in front of me. I wondered when I would have to kill or be killed. I was disgusted with myself, for had I the courage of a Kennedy or a King, I would be fighting this war at home with words, rather than in a perimeter tower with guns. With that thought in mind, I pledged myself to peace — and at the same time felt very hypocritical, for I knew full well that when it came right down to it I would have to do my talking with the M-60.

(A/1C) Richard W. U.S.A.F. Clatworthy
6/21/69   *A.P.O., San Francisco*

Ho Chi Minh

Despite Ho Chi Minh's shortcomings —and they were considerable—I think we would have to agree that he was a man dedicated to his people against Western colonialism.

If Ho is remembered for anything, it will have to be for his undying dedica-

tion to his people, a quality not found too often in our policians today, and they prove it after they're elected.

Philip J. Schacca
9/26/69   *West Hempstead, N.Y.*

Gamel Abdel Nasser

The abrupt demise of President Nasser dealt a resounding blow to further efforts to resolve the Middle East crisis. Amid all the tributes paid to this great man were traces of foreboding among the political leaders of the world. The absence of a powerful representative mouthpiece for the Arab nations can only aggravate the already explosive atmosphere currently in the contiguous region of the Suez. All too often the death of the great statesman produces a plethora of regret not accompanied by equally sincere actions and efforts.

Mason Chen
10/26/70   *Singapore*

J. R. R. Tolkien

I read with sadness that J. R. R. Tolkien had died [Sept. 17]. I was introduced to *The Hobbit* and *The Lord of the Rings* four years ago as a ninth-grader. Something about the trilogy tantalized me as did no other books I had read.

Perhaps it was escape literature, but I think not. Frodo's adventures evoked in me the feeling of love and righteousness for everything. They did not cause me to escape the "cruel world," but to fight harder for a better one.

Frodo lives forever!

Judy Schwartz
10/8/73   *Oswego, N.Y.*

P. G. Wodehouse

I would like to thank you for your sensitive article on P. G. Wodehouse [Feb. 24]. Having first "discovered" him as I was browsing through a bookstore, I have since become addicted to Wodehouse's gentle lunacy. Bertie Wooster, the Oldest Member and Lord Emsworth are now a permanent part of my existence as well as umpteen million other people's. All of us find solace in that slightly askew world where Bertie is saved from the altar rails and the Empress of Blandings is guarded against foul play at the hands of Sir Gregory.

Wodehouse may have passed on, but he has left a legacy that even Creosote would envy.

John Bechtel
3/10/75 *Austin, Texas*

Aristotle Onassis

In ending your article "One of the Last Tycoons" on Aristotle Onassis [March 24], you state that "he left little legacy—no monuments, no great acts of philanthropy, no record of achievement other than a succession of business deals." To you socialists it may indeed seem that he left little legacy, since he did not create mendicants by giving away the wealth he created; rather, as Horatio said of himself, "I have erected a monument more enduring than bronze" in the thousands of jobs he created.

William W. Morgan Jr.
4/14/75 *Uden, The Netherlands*

Chiang Kai-shek

Your article on President Chiang Kai-shek's death [April 14] must have contained truth and insight, but I could not read it. Every TIME in Taiwan had that page torn out. It must have hit home.

John Stewart
5/19/75 *Taipei*

Chou En-lai

Your posthumous praise of Communist Chou En-lai [Jan. 19] was impressive. You should have been as kind to J.F.K.

Jerry Jacobs
Monroeville, Ind.

You would not have praised murderous criminals like Hitler or Stalin. Why do you praise Chou?

Murray I. Franck
2/9/76 *New York City*

Howard Hughes

It is ironic that Billionaire Howard Hughes [April 19] suffered from malnutrition.

It is sadder still that he never really looked at the world in which he lived and made his fortune. The world of nature, of which he owned a great many acres, is a beautiful and fascinating place, which he seems to have overlooked entirely.

He was indeed a poor creature.

(Mrs.) Helen Miller
5/10/76 *Rochester*

Mao Tse-tung

One-quarter of mankind mourns the death of Chairman Mao [Sept. 20].

Although my family escaped from China after the Communists' takeover, I, like the millions of overseas Chinese who repudiate Mao's political philosophy, am saddened by this great man's passing.

Mao was a poet and statesman as well as a politician and educator. He transformed China from a prostrate and humiliated country into a strong and self-sufficient nation. His revolutionary government altered the balance of power in Asia and the strategic thinking of the world. His teachings transformed the Chinese, long known to be loose as sand as a nation, into a unified, well-disciplined people devoted to building a strong country.

Despite their lack of freedom, the 800 million Chinese revere and adulate him, because he drove out the foreigners and restored to China much of its former power and self-respect.

Bernadette P. N. Lee Shih
Rancho Palos Verdes,
10/11/76 *Calif.*

Pablo Picasso

In reading about the 50,000 shots Photographer David Douglas Duncan had taken of the late Picasso's works [Nov. 8], I was reminded of my favorite Picasso story: A man had vowed that he would marry the most beautiful girl in the world. When his friends came around to meet the bride, they saw a cross-eyed woman without much of a forehead, no chin to speak of, a crooked nose and a drooping mouth. In response to their amazed queries, the groom explained, "Well, you either like Picasso or you don't."

E. G. Rothblum
12/13/76 *Vienna*

Groucho Marx

Groucho was the divine king of comedy, and his passing is disheartening to his fans. Your article was far too short to encompass his accomplishments or even to describe the joy he brought to millions. His impact will never be forgotten.

Steven Casper
Baltimore

Is it my imagination, or were you guys a little skimpy with the Groucho Marx obituary.

Woody Allen
9/19/77 *New York City*

Elvis Presley

Elvis Presley.
The King is dead. Long live the King!

Carol Bachelder
12/12/77 *Boise, Idaho*

President Tito

Leonid Brezhnev

Aristotle Onassis

John Lennon

Peter Sellers

Princess Grace

Hubert H. Humphrey

Too often Hubert Humphrey was seen only as the ebullient eternal optimist, a Don Quixote verbally tilting at windmills and dreaming the impossible dream. But his idealism lifted us to share in that dream and, in so doing, his idealism conquered our skepticism.

W. Ray Kohler
2/6/78 *Woodbury, N.J.*

Pope John Paul I

The passing of Pope John Paul I [Oct. 9] was a terrible shock. Many people are going to wonder how God could snatch him away before his time. But in the long run, I believe he did what he was raised up to do and did it well. He showed us what the *esse* of the papal office is and, underneath, has always been: a simple, loving pastor rather than a crowned autocrat. His example was the vital thing.

(The Rev.) John B. Pahls Jr.
10/30/78 *Brewster, N.Y.*

General Franco

One thing you failed to mention is that after Spain's Civil War, Franco rebuilt the country without anybody's help—help that was given in abundance to Germany, Japan, England, Italy and even the U.S.S.R. after World War II.

Jorge Neves B.
1/1/79 *Lima*

President Tito

Each paper and magazine speaking about Tito's death [May 19] mentions him as the final link with the old. What about Hirohito, the Japanese Emperor? He survived all the leaders of World War II, and is still reigning!

Stef Van Den Bos
6/16/80 *Amsterdam*

Peter Sellers

Peter Sellers is dead [Aug. 4], but his unique creations—Dr. Strangelove, Inspector Clouseau, Chance the gardener —will live on. Generations not yet born will hail Sellers as a comic genius in the tradition of Chaplin, Keaton and Lloyd. Sellers made us laugh. What better epitaph can a man have?

Larry Bauer
9/1/80 *Cleveland*

John Lennon

For the first time in my life I feel old. When I was growing up in the '60s, the Beatles represented all the excitement, hopes and dreams of my generation. The future was boundless, it could only get better and better, and no words can recapture the feeling of being alive in that time. Now, with the death of John Lennon [Dec. 22], I feel that the spirit of the '60s is over.

Ron Eckert
1/5/81 *Ardmore Pa.*

Princess Grace

Your article on the death of Princess Grace [Sept. 27] rankled. One sought the tender word to soothe but found instead such derisive phrases as "princess of an amusement park" and "suppressed clucks" in reference to her restrained but motherly defense of her children. And why describe 15,000 carnations as being "dumped" on her bridal yacht from a plane when the word showered would have been more apt?

Grace Falk
10/18/82 *New York City*

Leonid Brezhnev

After I read your obituary on Leonid Brezhnev, my first thoughts were that he was not such a bad guy after all. However, the details about his role in the bloody Afghanistan coup brought me back to reality.

Danny Van Loo
12/13/82 *Nieuwpoort, Belgium*

Yuri Andropov

Soviet leaders, since they are not elected by their citizens, do not represent the will of their people but are just spokesmen for the Communist cause. It will take more than the death of Yuri Andropov [Feb. 20] to reduce U.S.-Soviet tensions.

Thomas C. Corrigan
3/12/84 *Branford, Conn.*

Index

254

Index of Contributors

This is a selected list of those correspondents who are, or were, well known names of the period. Any such lists must, by their nature, be subjective, and as the range of topics and personalities covered in this collection is immense, some readers may consider that certain omissions have occurred in the compilation of this Index. Should this be the case, the publishers would like to assure them that no offense was intended.